Global Economic Co-operation

To Co-operation

Global Economic Co-operation

A Guide to Agreements and Organizations

Bernard Colas, Editor

Preface by Javier Pérez de Cuéllar

Second Edition

Management Books 2000

Kluwer Law & Taxation Publishers
Deventer Boston

United Nations
University Press

First edition published in French in 1990 by La Documentation française

Revised edition published in English in 1994

UK, Commonwealth and South Africa exclusively:
Management Books 2000 Ltd
125a The Broadway, Didcot, Oxfordshire OX11 8AW
Tel: 0235-815544 Fax: 0235-817188

Europe exclusively (excluding UK and Ireland):
Kluwer Law and Taxation Publishers

PO Box 23
7400 GA Deventer/The Netherlands
Tel: +31 5700 47261
Fax: +31 5700 22244
Telex: 49295

675 Massachusetts Avenue
Cambridge MA 02139/USA
Tel: +1 617 354 0140
Fax: +1 617 354 8595

Japan exclusively:
United Nations University Press
The United Nations University
53-70, Jingumae 5-chome
Shibuya-ku, Tokyo 150
Tel: +81 3 3499 2811
Fax: +81 3 3406 7345

The United Nations University is an organ of the United Nations established by the General Assembly in 1972 to be an international community of scholars engaged in research, advanced training, and the dissemination of knowledge related to the pressing global problems of human survival, development and welfare. Its activities focus mainly on peace and conflict resolution, development in a changing world, and science and technology in relation to human welfare. The University operates through a worldwide network of research and postgraduate training centres, with its planning and coordinating headquarters in Tokyo, Japan.

Printed and bound in Great Britain by BPC Wheatons Ltd, Exeter

British Library Cataloguing in Publication Data is available

Management Books 2000: ISBN 1-85252-210-0
Kluwer: ISBN 90-6544-793-1
UNU: ISBN 92-806-0867-2

Contents

Preface

I wish to welcome the publication of the updated English edition of *Global Economic Co-operation: A Guide to Agreements and Organizations*, and to congratulate its editor, Bernard Colas, on the painfully thorough research that he and his international team have had to undertake to produce an exhaustive document valuable not only to students and researchers of law, but also to international experts who seek to update their knowledge in the area of global economic law.

My congratulations are two-fold. As a former Secretary-General of the United Nations, I can but appreciate the major role played by the World Organization and its major specialized agencies in the establishment and the strengthening of a new world order based on the dramatic increase of trade and exchanges between nations and and on a higher awareness of common economic concerns worldwide. Nowadays, as the editor points out, there are some 65 bodies and over 300 international economic agreements, the objective of which is to monitor and to guarantee harmonious economic relations between industrialized and developing countries, between the North and the South, between the rich and the poor, on an equal footing and in fairness to all. And even though this remains a very ambitious goal to achieve, the very adoption and signing of these agreements largely reflect the firm commitment of the international community, including the international legal system, to the establishment of a more orderly mechanism of economic exchanges in the world.

As the present President of the World Commission on Culture and Development, responsible for preparing a World Report on these issues, I can only praise Mr Colas for having brought to the forefront the very pressing issue of common resources and environmental protection. For it is clearly established today that the destruction inflicted by humans on their own environment has reached the alarming point where it can no longer be prevented or even monitored by any single country. No one government is in a position to fight single-handedly the pollution of the oceans that threatens to eradicate entire species and to unbalance our ecological system. No one state is capable of providing unilateral solutions to such problems as safe drinkable water, still unavailable to almost two-thirds of the world's rural poor.

Environmental management today is everybody's problem. It therefore needs universal solutions that only universal legal instruments can codify and guarantee. Mr Colas's reminder is an extremely useful one.

Javier Pérez de Cuéllar

Preface to the First Edition

It is a most enjoyable task to write a few introductory lines to this book *Accords économiques internationaux: répertoire des accords et des institutions.*[1]

Bernard Colas is to be congratulated for conceiving it, for establishing its structure, and for bringing together – with a particular sense of organization – a strong team from various parts of the world. He has directed it within the framework of the International Economic Law Society.

Interest in this book is assured. As well as being a compendium of texts, it also provides a classification of texts with an analysis of their content. It meets a definite need and is a particularly useful working tool for students, researchers, international agents, lawyers, economists and observers of current affairs.

The field of international economic law has existed for some considerable time, although academic opinion has only recently paid it serious attention. Up until the time of the Second World War, it was primarily composed of trade agreements, often called treaties of commerce and navigation.

At the multilateral level, the general provisions seemed irrelevant before 1914. However, international trading relations became important as a result of economic liberalism, increasing financial stability, the free movement of persons and in particular the free movement of capital, which allowed for large investments. The First World War, however, brought restrictions on the movement of capital and goods.

In President Wilson's famous programme of the fourteen points of 1918, he mentioned among the peace objectives, the removal, as far as possible, of all economic barriers and the establishment of an equality of trade conditions among all the nations. Article 23, paragraph (e) of the Pact of the League of Nations provides for equitable treatment for the commerce of all members. However, the economic conferences that were held in Brussels in 1920 and in Genoa in 1922 failed. A third major conference, held in Geneva in 1927, produced a text on customs disarmament but signatures were not followed by ratifications.

Chapter IX of the UN Charter, adopted in 1945, addressed the issue of international economic and social co-operation. A few years later, the Havana Charter attempted to establish an economic system, but its limited number of ratifications did not permit it to enter into force. The GATT system, originally adopted in 1948, has, however, had progressive success in implementing a trading regime.

The originality of this work lies largely in that the texts presented include not only the basic agreements of the main international organizations in the economic field, but also the most important substantive agreements adopted by them, or at their initiative.

The book presents these texts in four sections: (1) organization of trade and production, (2) financial and monetary co-operation, (3) contracts, payments and dispute settlement, and (4) management of common resources and environmental protection.

The presence of this fourth section might at first seem audacious but it is certainly justified. Environmental protection constitutes, to a degree, a restriction on international trade. In theory, industrial and trading activities may be viewed as being unconstrained but the reality is different. This is shown by this section's presentation

(1) Title of the first edition published in 1990 by La Documentation Française and Wilson & Lafleur

of the mechanisms for the protection of fauna and flora, the quantitative limitations on the exploitation of natural resources (for example, in the field of fisheries), and the prohibition of certain actions. International mechanisms which restrict private activities and which organize the international management of resources in Antarctica, on the sea-bed and in outer space are also described. With this fourth section, this book establishes, truly, that international economic relations have a scientific and technical dimension that cannot be ignored.

A final remark is perhaps called for. The work of Bernard Colas and his team is a contribution of great value to the study of the present international economic system. But one must point out the absence of a general economic theory. This observation is neither a criticism nor felt to be a deficiency.

In reality, international economic relations are dominated by pragmatism. The Final Act of the Bretton Woods Conference in July 1944 recommended to the participants that, in addition to implementing the specific monetary and financial measures which were the subject of the Conference, they should seek notably to reduce obstacles to international trade and promote mutually advantageous international commercial relations, and bring about the orderly marketing of staple commodities at prices fair to the producer and consumer alike. These recommendations remain just as relevant today. Clearly international trade and economic relations at the global level do not constitute a planned economic system. Nevertheless, one cannot conclude that an automatic and blind application of the market economy prevails.

For instance, the equitable regulation of commodities that was considered at Bretton Woods was subsequently attempted with various commodity agreements. However, they have not been altogether successful. The principles of absolute equality of partners and non-discrimination – basic tenets of the market economy – are not the only considerations to be taken into account. UNCTAD's principles, adopted in 1964 and at each of its consecutive conferences, are based on the theory of compensatory inequality, which is contrary to economic liberalism. The same can be said of the generalized system of preferences granted by industrialized countries to their trading partners in developing countries. The GATT, too, has for the last quarter of a century adopted a similar approach.

Finally, the texts adopted in 1974 by the UN General Assembly – the Declaration on the New International Economic Order and the Charter on Economic Rights and Duties of States – have not come into force, although there are several fields in which they have been applied.

In summary, then, there is no doctrine or general theory dealing with international economic relations. The whole is heterogeneous and solutions have been expressed in agreements. We therefore welcome in this present text its precise and structured analysis of this complex field.

As francophone jurists – and on behalf of the International Economic Law Society which supported this initiative – we would like to express our satisfaction in the publication by La Documentation Française. This is an important book which responds to a true need.

Claude-Albert Colliard
Professeur émérite at University of Paris I Panthéon-Sorbonne
Member of the International Law Institute

Louis Sabourin
Professor at ENA, University of Quebec
and at University of Paris I Panthéon-Sorbonne
President of International Economic Law Society, Canada

Introduction

International economic relations are governed by a variety of institutions and a complex web of principles, most of which have been established by treaties adopted since the Second World War. This book aims at giving a complete and coherent picture of the global economic, legal and institutional system. It is intended to serve the needs of scholars, international business lawyers, government officials and legislators working in this field, as well as those engaged in the operation of international trade. For the general reader interested in global economic regimes, this book will prove a useful guide.

The agreements selected here – some 300 in total – cover those multilateral treaties which are open to all states, and which regulate trade, money, finance and environmental protection and facilitate the negotiation of international contracts and the enforcement of arbitral awards and judicial decisions. A selection of decisions and recommendations of global international organizations which are important in directing state behaviour in this field has also been included, together with some influential texts of a private nature which facilitate trade transactions. The key role played by international organizations in initiating and promoting such agreements is reflected both in the descriptions in this guide of some 70 relevant organizations and in the analysis of the agreements. Technical data, with selected bibliographies and addresses complete the texts.

The global economic order covered in this book has evolved as a result of the need to liberalize trade and payments after the Second World War, and has developed taking into account the needs of developing countries. More recently, environmental considerations have become a significant issue commanding attention in many fields of economic activity.

Motivated primarily by the desire to liberalize trade and payments, financial and monetary issues were first addressed at the Conference of Bretton Woods in 1944. This led to the setting up of a new international monetary order [section 2]. The International Monetary Fund (IMF) was established, as well as an international credit system for reconstruction purposes and the International Bank for Reconstruction and Development (IBRD). Although the proposal at the same time to establish an International Trade Organization never came to fruition, the IMF and the IBRD have in fact provided favourable conditions for reducing obstacles to international trade.

The pillar of today's international economic trading system is the General Agreement on Tariffs and Trade (GATT) [section 1]. Its basic principles of liberalism, non-discrimination and fair trade have been strongly reinforced by developments in complementary sectors: facilitation of customs procedure, use of food and health regulations, recognition of standardization, improvement of business practices, protection of intellectual property, unification of transport regulations, and interconnection of international communications. The difficulties which may arise from the diversity of domestic legislation have also been dealt with through the unification of substantive commercial laws, rules on conflict of laws, and judicial and arbitration rules [section 3].

These efforts, combined with the effects of technological developments, have strengthened economic ties between countries and have led to an enormous expansion in world trade. In pure economic theory, trade liberalization should have led to a "positive-sum game"; in practice, however, it has not benefited all trading nations equally.

Some countries have succeeded in developing their economies, but drastic differences in economic development and bargaining power between the industrialized parts of the world and the less developed countries have remained. Although technical and financial assistance has been provided to these countries through global international organizations in order to raise the level of food and industrial production, to promote trade, and to limit the balance-of-payments and external debt problems, the situation still needs greater attention.

Some legal solutions to the inequality problem found an expression both in the foundation of UNCTAD in 1964 and in the urgent calls to transform international legal structures into a New International Economic Order (NIEO). Positions of developing countries have been, since the mid-1970s, progressively changing. Many have adopted a more market-oriented approach, notably towards transnational corporations and foreign investments, and have softened their claims in favour of an NIEO.

The North-South debate is now an issue in global environmental negotiations. Many developing countries agree to raise their environmental standards and participate in the global effort to protect the environment in exchange for concessions from industrialized countries on increased financial flows and technological transfer.

Increasingly, the global proportions of environmental damage will make these demands meaningful and will command a genuinely co-operative effort on a world-wide scale. Steps in that direction have already been taken by the international community and were given a new impetus by the Conference on Environment and Development (Rio de Janeiro, 1992). Measures for the management of world resources through the controlled trade of endangered species have been ongoing and transfrontier co-operation has expanded to include the preservation of the natural environment with agreements having been concluded on the prevention and compensation of marine and air pollution. Nuclear and toxic substances are also controlled by international agreements, as are activities in common areas – the high seas, Antarctica, and outer space (see section 4).

In the years to come, the implications of globalization and of growing interdependence will be at the top of the world agenda. A greater need for co-operation will be required not only in macro-economic policy and trade policy, but also in domestic policies which have an impact on the international economy and on environmental issues. Efforts made to manage world interdependence equitably through co-operation and law need support. Global balance based on world-wide regimes could be threatened by the development of regional trade blocks. These could be disruptive to the world economy, particularly if they fail to integrate the less-developed countries.

The preparation of this book was made possible by the participation of a number of specialized authors from around the world who wished to contribute to the understanding of international economic rules and organizations. The transition from the first edition published in French in 1990 by La Documentation Française and Wilson & Lafleur has been facilitated by the work of Michael D. Young. Editing work has been done with the assistance of Catherine Leonard and others to whom I wish to express my sincere appreciation. I am grateful to Mr Javier Pérez de Cuéllar, former Secretary-General of the United Nations, for having written the preface and to Professor Louis Sabourin and the late Dean Claude-Albert Colliard for their support. I would also like to thank the International Economic Law Society (SDIE) under whose auspices this book has been prepared, and all those who have given their help and co-operation.

Bernard Colas
February 1994

Note

If you wish to keep up to date with some of the issues raised in this book, you should write to the International Economic Law Society. It publishes a quarterly bulletin which follows and analyses major international economic events.

The Society, as well as publishing its Bulletin, organizes meetings and seminars, participates as observer in inter-governmental conferences and co-operates with many organizations.

The International Economic Law Society is a non-profit organization which aims at promoting the knowledge, exchange of information and development of international law at both national and international levels. Its membership includes economists, members of the legal profession and individuals interested in international economic relations.

At present, there are two branches of the Society, at the following addresses:

International Economic Law Society (Canada)
445, St-Laurent Blvd. 5th floor
Montreal
Quebec
CANADA H2Y 2T8
Tel. (514) 954-3471
Fax. (514) 954-3451

International Economic Law Society (France)
Société de droit international économique
Maison de l'Europe
35 rue des Francs-Bourgeois
75004, Paris
FRANCE
Tel. (33-1) 44 61 85 85
Fax. (33-1) 42 74 70 44

Authors and main contributors

Louise ALLARD, former Principal Administrator in Tourism to the Organisation for Economic Co-operation and Development (OECD)

Denis AUDET, Administrator, Trade Directorate, Organisation for Economic Co-operation and Development (OECD)

Frédéric BENECH, European Patent Attorney, French Trademark and Patent Counsel

Bernard COLAS, DEA (Paris 1), Lawyer, Quebec Bar, Consultant to the Organisation for Economic Co-operation and Development (OECD), Vice-President of the International Economic Law Society

Hugh J. CHEETHAM, LL.M.(LSE), Member of the Law Society of Upper Canada and of the Quebec Bar, qualified for membership in the Law Society of England

Anne DAGNEAU de RICHECOUR, DESS International Energy Law (Paris 1)

Maguelonne DÉJEANT-PONS, Doctor of Law, Administrator at the Council of Europe

Mary E. FOOTER, Iuris doctor, LL.M., Fellow in Public International Law, British Institute of International and Comparative Law, London

Patricia FORD, student, Middle Temple, London, UK

Ian JOHNSTONE, Program Officer in Collective Security and Peacekeeping, International Peace Academy (New York), former Associate Legal Officer, Office of the Legal Counsel, United Nations

Patricia GEORGET, DESS (Paris 1), Legal Officer, Legal Office, United Nations

Jean-André LASSERRE, DEA(Paris 1), Research Manager, President of the International Economic Law Society (France)

Catherine LEONARD, B.A., P.G. Dip., LL.B. (Otago, New Zealand), admitted as Barrister and Solicitor of the High Court of New Zealand

Alain LEROUX, DESS (Paris 1), Legal Adviser to the Intergovernmental Organization for International Carriage by Rail, Berne

Glenn S. McDONALD, LL.B., B.C.L. (McGill University), Graduate Institute of International Studies (Geneva)

Jean-Louis MAGDELÉNAT, Lawyer, Quebec Bar, Doctor of Law, Doctor of Civil Law (McGill), Diploma de Tecnico de Aviación Comercial, Instituto Iberamerico de Derecho Aereo, del Espacio y de la Aviación Comercial

Gabrielle MARCEAU, LL.M.(LSE), Ph.D. (London), Lawyer, Quebec Bar, Vice-President of the International Economic Law Society

Barthélémy MERCADAL, Professor of Trade Law, Conservatoire national des arts et métiers (CNAM), Scientific Director of Institut de droit international des transports (IDIT) (Rouen)

Ralph OSTERWOLDT, Legal Department, Environmental Affairs, World Bank

Alain PRUJINER, Doctor of Law, Solicitor, Quebec Bar, Professor at Laval University (Quebec)

Susan REYE, B.A. (Queensland), LL.B. (Australian National), Doctor of Law (Paris II), Legal Affairs, OECD Nuclear Energy Agency (NEA), formerly at the Australian Law Reform Commission, the Australian Department of Foreign Affairs and Trade, and the Australian Attorney-General's Department

Maryse ROBERT, Economist, M.Sc. (Applied Economy), HEC (University of Montreal), The Fletcher School of Law and Diplomacy, Tufts University, Medford, MA, USA

Oscar J. RODRIGUEZ-AGUILAR, M.A., Ph.D., London School of Economics and Political Science (LSE)

Joel SALTSMAN, LL.B. (Toronto), LL.M. (LSE), MBA (EAP Paris), International Relations Department, Société Internationale de Télécommunications Aéronautiques (SITA), Geneva

Richard TARASOFSKY, LL.M.(LSE), Barrister and Solicitor Ontario Bar, IUCN – The World Conservation Union, former Member Visiting Lecturer at the Foundation for International Environmental Law and Development, Kings College, London (UK)

Sarah WILLIAMS, International Chamber of Commerce, Paris

Michael D. YOUNG, B.A., M.A. (Johns Hopkins University), Editor of *The Lebanon Report* and Associate Editor of *The Beirut Review*

The editors and contributors wish to thank the following persons for their invaluable assistance in carrying out this project: Eric BOUCHARD and Geneviève de DIVONNE as well as Jean-Paul CHAPDELAINE, Caroline LONDON, Yvonne MULLER, Martin ST-AMANT and Vladimir VASAK.

Opinions expressed in this book are those of their authors.

Acknowledgments

Michel ANDRIEU, OECD
I. ANSAH, Office of Special Adviser to the Director-General, GATT
Hutton ARCHER, Chief, Public Information Service, ICAO
B. ATHANÉ, Director, OIML
Michel AUGÉ, former Assistant Secretary-General, CCC
Ibrahim AYOUB, Chief of Protocol, IFAD
Neil BAKMANN, Head of Marketing Division, Intersputnik
Elias BARRIOS, Ministerio de Relaciones Exteriores, Panama
Christopher BEEBY, New Zealand Ambassador, France
Jaques BERNEY, Deputy Secretary General, CITES
Susan BLACK, Legal Office, ICAO
Céline BLAIS, Department of External Affairs, Canada
Mr BOREL, Direction of Public International Law, Switzerland
Sylvia BROERE-MOORE, Chief, Public Relations and Information, UNIDO
Dennis BROUGHAM, Public Information Officer, IEC
Patrick CARRIÈRE, ILO
Hervé CASSAN, Professor, University of Paris 5
Robert COX, Information Officer, Public Relations and Information Section, UNIDO
Jean-Pierre CRISTEL, IOSCO
R.J. DAWSON, Chief, Joint FAO/WHO Food Standards Programme
Christian DEREPPE, General Services (Documents), CCC
L.-P. DUCOMMUN, Adviser, UPU
Adair DYER, First Secretary, HCOPIL
Ms EMPEY, CCC
Pierre FABIAN, Department of Public Information, UN
Josée FECTEAU, Legal Service, FAO
Norjanah FLAKS, Information Assistant, UNCTAD
Hans-Jorgen FRICK, Chief, Official Relations Branch, ILO
Daniel GERVAIS, Legal Adviser, WIPO
Janice GOERTZ, Senior Public Information Officer, ITC
Marie-Andrée GUYOT, Conservation des traités, Ministère des affaires étrangères, France
Gregor C.M. HEINRICH, Legal Services, BIS
Gerold HERRMANN, Secretary, UNCITRAL
O. JANKOWITSCH, Legal Division, AIEA
P.J.H. JONKMAN, Secretary General, PCA
G. KAKKAR, Legal Officer, ICAO
James KANU, Information Officer, WFC
Jin KUI, Senior Liaison Officer, WMO
Francine LAMBERT, Information Officer, ITU
Guy LAMBERT-DAYNAC
Hans LASSEN, Information Officer, ECE
Sun LIN, Director, Environmental Law and Institutions Programme Activity Centre, UNEP
Geraldine MACKRIELL, P.A. to Executive Secretary, CCAMLR (Aust.)
B.J. MASON, Foreign & Commonwealth Office, UK
David B. MELTZER, Attorney, INTELSAT
Hans-Friedrich MEYER, Division of Public Information, IAEA

Paul MITCHELL, Chief, Public Affairs & Information Branch, WFP
Francis MWANZA, Public Affairs & Information Branch, WFP
M. NAWAZ, Director, Legal Services Division, IFAD
Antonio R. PARRA, Legal Adviser, ICSID (The World Bank)
Anthony PIEL, Legal Counsel, WHO
Mr de PROOST, Head Treaty Section, Belgium
Guiliano PUCCI, Legal Officer, FAO
Juan PUMAREDA, Ministry of Foreign Affairs (Ministerio de Asuntos Exteriores), Spain
Estela SANIDAD, Membership Co-ordinator, World Bank Group
Ricardo SATELER, Assistant Legal Counsel, WIPO
Marina SCHNEIDER, Research Officer, UNIDROIT
W. SCHRAGE, Environment and Human Settlements Division, ECE
Jesper SCHULTZ, Ministry of Foreign Affairs, Denmark
Sami SHUBBER, Senior Legal Officer, WHO
David SMALL, Deputy Legal Counsel, OECD
David STEPHEN, United Nations
Margrete STEVENS, ICSID
W.W. STURMS, Director, Legal Division, IAEA
Genevieve THWAITES
Jesper ULDALL-SCHULTZ, Ministry of Foreign Affairs, Denmark
Anke VARCIN, Head, Promotion and Press Services, ISO
N. VENTOSA, Secretariat, OECD Nuclear Energy Agency
Paul VÉRON, Director of Communications, UIC
John WEST, OECD
Paul H. WHITE, Assistant to the Secretary General, IRU
Norman WILLIAMS, Assistant General Counsel, Intelsat
David WOODS, Information Division, GATT
Marie ZAIDENBANDT, External Relations Office, UNESCO
Jon ZYLMAN, Legal Adviser, United States Department of State

Users' Guide

Every agreement analysed in this volume is supplemented by an "information profile". The profile includes the date and location where the agreement was signed or adopted, the date of its entry into force, the number of parties which have become party to the agreement, a brief commentary describing each agreement, the duration of the accord, the possibility of reservations, the official language(s) in which it was drafted, the depositary of the accord, as well as information on protocols and amendments.

The last heading in the "information profile" gives the reader one or more sources where the entire text of the agreement under discussion may be found.

The following is an explanatory outline of the words and abbreviations used in the "information profiles".

SIGNED: The date (day/month/year) on which the agreement was signed marks the end of the negotiations culminating in the treaty, and formalizes the treaty's text, thus making it definitive.

ADOPTED: This indicates the date (day/month/year) on which the multilateral body or conference formally agreed upon the resolution, decision, or declaration.

IN FORCE (ENTRY INTO FORCE): This indicates the date (day/month/year) from which the agreement entered into force. In cases where the agreement has not yet entered into force, the conditions for implementation are mentioned in the commentary on the agreement. [See Article 24-3 of the Vienna Convention on the Law of Treaties.] In the case of resolutions, the implementation date is indicated only when mentioned in the agreement.

PARTIES: The number of states which are parties to an agreement (as of 14 April 1993) is indicated in the profile. At the end of the book, readers will find a detailed list of states and the agreements they are party to.

The protocol provisions of the agreements discussed include such information as eligibility to become party, or "access", to the agreement, the possibility of reservations, the duration of the agreement, its depositary, and the language(s) in which the agreement was drafted. Since agreements vary regarding these provisions, three-letter explanatory codes referring to each of the above headings indicate the nature of the agreement's provisions. In parentheses following the code, readers will find a reference to the number or article in the treaty defining the specific provision. If necessary, additional explanation is provided in the commentary on the agreement.

ACCESS: Depending on their objectives, agreements can be "open" to all states wishing to adhere to their provisions, or they can be "closed" when they are limited to a specific number of states.

ALS (= All states): The agreement is open to all states. In the present volume, this will mean all those states which are members of the United Nations or one of its specialized agencies.

ASO (= All states & organizations): The agreement is open to the participation of all states as defined above as well as, under certain conditions, intergovernmental organizations.

CON (= Conditional): Access to the agreement is dependent on the meeting of certain conditions defined by the article in the parentheses. These conditions may be adherence to another treaty, membership in a particular organization, the achievement of a specified level of production, etc. Since the present volume deals solely with agreements having global membership, we have excluded reference to conditions where access requires membership in a given region.

ENT (= Enterprises): Indicates that an agreement is between enterprises, including state enterprises. These types of agreements have important repercussions on international economic law, and therefore had to be included.

RESERVATIONS: Although there are wide differences in the practical application of reservations, two types of agreements exist: those which allow for reservations, and those which do not. According to Article 2-1 of the Convention on the Law of Treaties (Vienna, 1969) "reservation" means a unilateral statement, however phrased or named, made by a state, when signing, ratifying, accepting, approving or acceding to a treaty, whereby it purports to exclude or to modify the legal effect of certain provisions of the treaty in their application to that state.

PRO (= Prohibited): Reservations are prohibited by the agreement's provisions.

PAU (= Partial authorization): Indicates that the agreement provides that specified reservations may be made.

USP (= Unspecified): When the agreement in question does not mention the issue of reservations, Article 19 of the Vienna Convention on the Law of Treaties provides that a state may formulate a reservation unless the reservation is incompatible with the object and purpose of the agreement. (See also Article 20 of the Vienna Convention.)

DURATION: Most of the economic agreements analysed in this volume are not limited in their duration, except in the case of agreements covering commodities, which in general are limited to five years.

USP (= Unspecified): The agreement contains no provision regarding its duration.

ULT (= Unlimited): The agreement provides that the duration is unlimited.

DET (= Of determined duration): The lifetime of the agreement is dependent on the occurrence of certain events or actions foreseen by the parties, after which the agreement terminates. In some cases, the duration of an agreement may be dependent on another agreement.

REN (= Renewable): Although the duration of the agreement is dependent on the occurrence of certain events, principally the passage of a specific period of time, it can be renewed by the tacit agreement of the parties, or otherwise. The number that follows indicates the number of years after which the agreement can be renewed.

MIN (= Minimum): Indicates that the agreement will cease to have effect if the number of states party to the agreement falls below a certain minimum number.

DEPOSITARY: The depositary is designated by the negotiating states to an agreement. The depositary's role is to maintain the treaty records and function as a central point of communication for the notifications required. It receives notifications and informs the parties and the states entitled to become party to the treaty of acts, notifications and communications relating to the treaty. The depositary is also responsible for registering the treaty with the Secretariat of the United Nations in accordance with Article 102 of the UN Charter (Arts. 76 to 80 of the Vienna Convention).

The name of the depositary is indicated here by the organization's acronym (i.e. "UN" equals the Secretary General of the United Nations). When the depositary is another state, it can be indicated by the acronyms established by the International Standards Organization (ISO) (i.e. BE for Belgium, CA for Canada, FR for France, GB for the United Kingdom, IT for Italy, MX for Mexico, NL for the Netherlands, RU for Russia, US for the United States, etc.).

LANGUAGES: Indicates the official language or languages in which the agreement is drafted. This also indicates the languages which can be invoked if a dispute arises around the interpretation of the agreement. The languages are identified by their first three letters, and in parentheses are listed the "authorized" but unofficial translations of the agreement. The abbreviation "etc." indicates that an assembly or an organization may, in pursuance of the agreement, make additional translations.

In general, conventions and resolutions adopted by the United Nations are drafted in the six working languages of the Organization: Arabic, Chinese, English, French, Russian and Spanish.

AMENDMENTS: Indicates whether an agreement has been modified by protocols, amendments, or revisions. It also gives the name of the city where the conference adopting the modification took place, as well as the date (day/month/year) of the conclusion or the adoption of the modification and, between parentheses, its date of entry into force. A line between parentheses (-) indicates that conditions have not been met for it to enter into force. [see Part IV of the Vienna Convention on the Law of Treaties.]

SOURCES: Indicates the sources for the texts of the accords and their amendments. Sources are identified by an abbreviation indicating the collection in which the texts may be found, followed by the year and other information permitting the reader to find the appropriate agreement.

BISD	*Basic Instruments and Selected Documents*, GATT
DJI	*Documents Juridiques Internationaux*
Can TS	*Canadian Treaty Series*
HCOPIL Col.	*Collection of Conventions*, Hague Conference on Private International Law, 1988
ILM	*International Legal Material*
JDI	*Journal du Droit International (Clunet)*
JORF	*Journal Officiel de la République Française*
LNTS	*League of Nations Treaty Series*
RGDIP	*Revue Générale de Droit International Public*
RTAF	*Recueil des Traités et Accords de la France*
UKTS	*United Kingdom Treaty Series*
ULB	*Uniform Law Review, published by* UNIDROIT
UN Doc.	*Documents from the United Nations*

UNTS	*United Nations Treaty Series*
UST	*US Treaties and Other International Agreements*

Texts of agreements are also reproduced in:

Cheng, Ch.J., *Basic Documents on International Trade Law, 2nd ed.*, Dordrecht: Martinus Nijhoff Publishers, 1990.
Kunig, Ph., N. Lau and W. Meng, *International Economic Law, Basic Documents*, Berlin: W. de Gruyter, 1989.
Osmanczyk, Edmund Jan, *The Encyclopedia of the United Nations and International Agreements, 2nd ed.*, New York: Taylor and Francis, 1990
Schermers, H.G. (ed.), *International Organization and Integration: Annotated Basic Documents and Descriptive Directory of International Organization and Arrangements, 2nd ed.*, The Hague: A.W. Sijthoff, 1982.
Sohn, L.B., *International Organization and Integration*, Dordrecht: Martinus Nijhoff Publishers, 1984.
Zamora, Stephen and Ronald A. Brand, *Basic Documents of International Economic Law*, two volumes, Chicago: CCH International, 1990.

For information on the status of treaties, one should consult:

Bowman, M.J. and D.J. Harris, *Multilateral Treaties: Index and Current Status*, London: Butterworths, 1984 (with cumulative supplements).
United Nations, *Multilateral Treaties Deposited with the Secretary General*, New York: United Nations Publication (annual).

Basic books of international economic law include:

Bernhardt, R. (ed.), *Encyclopedia of Public International Law*, published by the Max Planck Institute of Comparative Public Law and International Law, Amsterdam: North-Holland Publishing Company, 12 volumes, 1981-1990.
Carreau, D., Th. Flory and P. Juillard, *Droit International Economique*, 3rd ed., Paris: LGDJ, 1990.
Goldman, B. (ed.), *Jurisclasseur de Droit International*, Paris; Editions Techniques, 10 volumes, 1966-.
Jackson, John H. and William J. Davey, *Legal Problems of International Economic Relations: Cases, Materials and Text, 2nd ed.*, American Casebook Series, St. Paul, Minn.: West Publishing Co., 1986.
Seidl-Hohenveldern, Ignaz, *International Economic Law*, Dordrecht: Martinus Nijhoff Publishers, 1989.
Verloren van Themaat, P., *The Changing Structure of International Economic Law: a Contribution of Legal History of Comparative Law and of General Legal Theory to the Debate on a New International Economic Order*, The Hague: Martinus Nijhoff Publishers, 1981.

Acronyms

ANRPC	Association of Natural Rubber Producing Countries
APEF	Association of Iron Ore Exporting Countries
BIPM	Bureau international des poids et mesures [International Bureau of Weights and Measures]
BIS	Bank for International Settlements
CAC	Joint FAO/WHO Codex Alimentarius Commission
CCC	Customs Co-operation Council
CIPEC	Intergovernmental Council of Copper Exporting Countries
CMI	International Maritime Committee
CPA	Cocoa Producers' Alliance
ECE	United Nations Economic Commission for Europe
FAO	Food and Agriculture Organization of the United Nations
GATT	General Agreement on Tariffs and Trade
HCOPIL	The Hague Conference on Private International Law
IAEA	International Atomic Energy Agency
IATA	International Air Transport Association
IBA	International Bauxite Association
IBRD	International Bank for Reconstruction and Development
ICAO	International Civil Aviation Organization
ICC	International Chamber of Commerce
ICC-CA	The ICC International Court of Arbitration
ICJ	International Court of Justice
ICSG	International Copper Study Groups
ICSID	International Centre for Settlement of Investment Disputes
ICTB	International Customs Tariffs Bureau
IDA	International Development Association
IEC	International Electrotechnical Commission
IFAD	International Fund for Agricultural Development
IFC	International Finance Corporation
ILO	International Labour Organisation
IMF	International Monetary Fund
IMO	International Maritime Organization
INMARSAT	International Maritime Satellite Organization
INSG	International Nickel Study Group
INTELSAT	International Telecommunications Satellite Organization
INTERSPUTNIK	International Organization of Space Telecommunications
IOSCO	International Organization of Securities Commissions
IRF	International Road Federation
IRU	International Road Transport Union
ISO	International Organization for Standardization
ITC	International Trade Centre UNCTAD/GATT
ITSG	International Tin Study Group
ITU	International Telecommunication Union
MIGA	Multilateral Investment Guarantee Agency
OECD	Organisation for Economic Co-operation and Development
OIML	Organisation Internationale de Métrologie Légale [International Organization of Legal Metrology]
OPEC	Organization of the Petroleum Exporting Countries

OTIF	Intergovernmental Organization for International Carriage by Rail
PCA	Permanent Court of Arbitration
UIC	International Union of Railways
UN	United Nations
UNCITRAL	United Nations Commission on International Trade Law
UNCTAD	United Nations Conference on Trade and Development
UNDP	United Nations Development Programme
UNEP	United Nations Environment Programme
UNESCO	United Nations Educational, Scientific and Cultural Organization
UNIDO	United Nations Industrial Development Organization
UNIDROIT	International Institute for the Unification of Private Law
UPEB	Union of Banana Exporting Countries
UPU	Universal Postal Union
UT	International Conference for Railway Technical Unity
WFC	World Food Council
WFP	World Food Programme
WHO	World Health Organization
WIPO	World Intellectual Property Organization
WMO	World Meteorological Organization
WTO	World Tourism Organization

Detailed Contents

0.0.1 GLOBAL CO-OPERATION

001 A – **United Nations** (UN)
001 B – International **Court of Justice** (ICJ)
001.01 – United Nations Charter (San Francisco, 26.06.1945)
001.02 – Statute of the International Court of Justice (San Francisco, 26.06.1945)
001.03 – Declaration on the Establishment of a **New International Economic Order** (UNGA Res.3201(S-VI), 01.05.1974)
001.04 – Programme of Action on the Establishment of a New International Economic Order (UNGA Res.3202(S-VI), 01.05.1974)
001.05 – Charter on **Economic Rights and Duties** of States (UNGA Res.3281(XXIX), 12.12.1974)
001.06 – Declaration on **International Economic Cooperation**, in Particular the Revitalizing of Economic Growth and Development of the Developing Countries (UNGA Res.S-18/3, 01.05.1990)

1. ORGANIZATION OF TRADE AND PRODUCTION

1.1 Trade and Customs Co-operation

1.1.1 Trade

111 A – **General Agreement** on Tariffs and Trade (GATT)
111 B – **United Nations Conference** on Trade and Development (UNCTAD)
111 C – **International Trade Centre** UNCTAD/GATT (ITC)
111.01 – General Agreement on Tariffs and Trade (Geneva, 30.10.1947)
111.02 – **Havana Charter** Establishing an International Trade Organization (Havana, 24.03.1948)
111.03 – Constitution of the United Nations Conference on Trade and Development (UNGA Res.1995(XIX), 30.12.1964)
111.04 – International Trade Centre CNUCED/GATT (UNGA Res.2297(XXII), 12.12.1967)
111.05 – Generalized **System of Preferences** (Dec.75 (S-IV), 13.10.1970)
111.06 – Arrangement Regarding International Trade in Textiles, and Protocol ("**Multifibre Agreement**") (Geneva, 20.12.1973)
111.07 – Agreement on **Technical Barriers** to Trade (Geneva, 12.04.1979)
111.08 – Agreement on **Government Procurement** (Geneva, 12.04.1979)
111.09 – Agreement on Interpretation and Application of Articles VI, XVI and XXIII ("**Subsidies Code**") (Geneva, 12.04.1979)
111.10 – Agreement on **Import Licensing** Procedures (Geneva, 12.04.1979)
111.11 – Agreement on Implementation of Article VI ("**Antidumping Code**") (Geneva, 12.04.1979)
111.12 – Arrangement Regarding **Bovine Meat** (Geneva, 12.04.1979)
111.13 – International **Dairy Agreement** (Geneva, 12.04.1979)

111.14 – Agreement on Trade in **Civil Aircraft** (Geneva, 12.04.1979)
111.15 – Differential and more Favourable Treatment, Reciprocal, and more Complete Participation of Developing Countries ("**Enabling Clause**") (Dec.L-4903, 28.11.1979)
111.16 – Trade Measures Taken for **Balance of Payments** (Dec.L-4907, 28.11.1979)
111.17 – Safeguard Action for **Development Purposes** (Dec.L/4.897, 28.11.1979)
111.18 – Understanding Regarding Notification, Consultation, **Dispute Settlement** and Surveillance (Dec.L-4907, 28.11.1979)
111.19 – Ministerial Declaration on The **Uruguay Round** (Punta del Este, 20.09.1986)
111.20 – Agreement on the **Global System of Trade Preferences** (GSTP) Among Developing Countries (Belgrade, 13.04.1988)
111.21 – Final Act Embodying the **Results of the Uruguay Round** of Multilateral Trade Negotiations (15.12.1993)

1.1.2 Customs Co-operation

112 A – **Customs Co-operation** Council (CCC)
112 B – International **Customs Tariffs** Bureau (ICTB)
112.01 – International Convention Relating to the Simplification of **Customs Formalities** (Geneva, 03.11.1923)
112.02 – Convention Establishing a Customs Co-operation Council (Brussels, 15.12.1950)
112.03 – Convention on **Nomenclature** for the Classification of Goods in Customs Tariffs (Brussels, 15.12.1950)
112.04 – Convention on the **Valuation of Goods** for Customs Purposes (Brussels, 15.12.1950)
112.05 – International Convention to Facilitate the Importation of **Commercial Samples** and Advertising Material (Geneva, 07.11.1952)
112.06 – Customs Convention Regarding **ECS Carnets** for Commercial Samples ("ECS Convention") (Brussels, 01.03.1956)
112.07 – Customs Convention on **Containers** (Geneva, 18.05.1956)
112.08 – Customs Convention on the Temporary Importation of **Commercial Road Vehicles** (Geneva, 18.05.1956)
112.09 – Customs Convention on the International Transport of Goods Under Cover of **TIR Carnets** (Geneva, 15.01.1959)
112.10 – Customs Convention on the Temporary Importation of **Packings** (Brussels, 06.10.1960)
112.11 – Customs Convention Concerning Facilities for the Importation of Goods for Display or Use at Exhibitions, Fairs, Meetings or Similar Events ("**Fairs Convention**") (Brussels, 08.06.1961)
112.12 – Customs Convention on the Temporary Importation of **Professional Equipment** ("Professional Equipment Convention") (Brussels, 08.06.1961)
112.13 – Customs Convention on the **A.T.A. Carnet** for the Temporary Admission of Goods ("ATA Convention") (Brussels, 06.12.1961)
112.14 – Customs Convention concerning **Welfare Material** for Seafarers (Brussels, 01.12.1964)
112.15 – Customs Convention on the Temporary Importation of **Scientific Equipment** ("Scientific Equipment Convention") (Brussels, 11.06.1968)
112.16 – Customs Convention on the Temporary Importation of **Pedagogic Material** ("Pedagogic Material Convention") (Brussels, 08.06.1970)
112.17 – Customs Convention on the International **Transit of Goods** ("ITI Convention") (Vienna, 07.06.1971)
112.18 – Customs Convention on **Containers** (Geneva, 02.12.1972)

1.2 Commodities

1.2.1 Economic Agreements

1.2.2 Commercial Agreements

1.2.3 Intergovernmental Transparency Groups

1.2.4 Producers' Organizations

124.01 – Agreement Establishing the Organization of **Petroleum** Exporting Countries (Bagdad, 14.09.1960)
124.02 – Agreement Establishing the **Cocoa** Producers' Alliance (Abidjan, 20.01.1962)
124.03 – Convention of the Intergovernmental Council of **Copper** Exporting Countries (Lusaka, 08.06.1967)
124.04 – Association of **Natural Rubber** Producing Countries (ANRPC) (London, 21.05.1968)
124.05 – Agreement Establishing the International **Bauxite** Association (Conakry, 08.03.1974)
124.06 – Agreement Establishing the Union of **Banana** Exporting Countries (Panama, 17.09.1974)
124.07 – Agreement Establishing the Association of **Iron Ore** Exporting Countries (Geneva, 03.04.1975)
124.08 – Agreement Establishing the International **Tea** Promotion Association (Geneva, 31.03.1977)
124.09 – Agreement Establishing the Association of **Tin** Producing Countries (London, 29.03.1983)

1.3 Food and Health

1.3.1 Food

131 A – **Food and Agriculture** Organization of the United Nations (FAO)
131 B – World **Food Programme** (WFP)
131 C – World **Food Council** (WFC)
131 D – International Fund for **Agricultural Development** (IFAD)
131.01 – Constituent Act of the United Nations Food and Agriculture Organization (Quebec, 16.10.1945)
131.02 – Establishment of the World Food Programme (UNGA Res.1714(XVI), 19.12.1961)
131.03 – Establishment of the World Food Council (UNGA Res.3348(XXIX), 17.12.1974)
131.04 – Agreement Establishing the International Fund for Agricultural Development (Rome, 13.06.1976)

1.3.2 Health

132 A – World **Health** Organization (WHO)
132 B – Joint FAO/WHO **Codex Alimentarius** Commission (CAC)
132.01 – Constitution of the World Health Organization (New York, 22.07.1946)
132.02 – Statutes of the Joint FAO/WHO Codex Alimentarius Commission (WHA Res. 16.42, 20.27, 1962)
132.03 – International **Health** Regulations (WHA Res. 22.46, 25.07.1969)
132.04 – International Code of Marketing of **Breast-Milk** Substitutes (Geneva, 21.05.1981)

152.03 – Constitution of the International Organization for Standardization (London, 14.10.1946)
152.04 – Agreement Establishing an International Organization of Legal Metrology (Paris, 12.10.1955)

1.6 Intellectual Property

160 A – World **Intellectual Property** Organization (WIPO)
160.01 – Convention Establishing the World Intellectual Property Organization (Stockholm, 14.07.1967)

1.6.1 Industrial Property

161.01 – Convention for the Protection of **Industrial Property** (Paris, 20.03.1883)
161.02 – Madrid Agreement for the Prevention of False or Deceptive **Indications of Origin** on Goods, as Revised (Madrid, 14.04.1891)
161.03 – Madrid Agreement Concerning the International Registration of **Marks** (Madrid, 14.04.1891)
161.04 – The Hague Agreement Concerning the International Deposit of **Industrial Designs** (The Hague, 06.11.1925)
161.05 – Nice Agreement Concerning the International Classification of Goods and Services for the Purposes of Registration of **Marks** (Nice, 15.06.1957)
161.06 – Lisbon Agreement for the Protection of **Appellations of Origin** and their International Registration, as Revised (Lisbon, 31.10.1958)
161.07 – International Convention for the Protection of New Varieties of **Plants** (Paris, 02.12.1961)
161.08 – Locarno Agreement Establishing an International Classification for **Industrial Designs** (Locarno, 08.10.1968)
161.09 – **Patent** Co-operation Treaty (Washington, 19.06.1970)
161.10 – Agreement Concerning the International **Patent** Classification (Strasbourg, 24.03.1971)
161.11 – **Trademark** Registration Treaty (Vienna, 12.06.1973)
161.12 – Agreement establishing an International Classification of the Figurative Elements of **Marks** (Vienna, 12.06.1973)
161.13 – Budapest Treaty on the International Recognition of the Deposit of **Micro-organisms** for the Purposes of **Patent** Procedure (Budapest, 28.04.1977)
161.14 – Geneva Treaty on the International Recording of **Scientific Discoveries** (Geneva, 03.03.1978)
161.15 – Treaty on the Protection of Intellectual Property in Respect of **Integrated Circuits** (Washington, 26.05.1989)

1.6.2 Copyright

162.01 – Berne Convention for the Protection of **Literary and Artistic Works**, as revised (Berne, 09.09.1886)
162.02 – Universal **Copyright** Convention (Geneva, 06.09.1952)
162.03 – International Convention for the Protection of Performers, Producers of **Phonograms** and Broadcasting Organizations (Rome, 26.10.1961)
162.04 – Convention for the Protection of Producers of **Phonograms** Against

1.8 Transport

1.8.0 Multimodal Transport

180.01 – Convention on International **Multimodal** Transport of Goods (Geneva, 24.05.1980)
180.02 – United Nations Convention on the Liability of **Operators of Transport Terminals** in International Trade (Vienna, 19.04.1991)

1.8.1 Road Transport

181 A – United Nations **Economic Commission** for Europe (ECE)
181 B – International **Road Transport** Union (IRU)
181 C – International **Road** Federation (IRF)
181.01 – Constitution of the International Road Transport Union (Geneva, 23.03.1948)
181.02 – Convention on the Contract for the International **Carriage of Goods** by Road (Geneva, 19.05.1956)
181.03 – Convention on the Taxation of **Road Vehicles** Engaged in International Goods Transport (Geneva, 14.12.1956)
181.04 – Agreement Concerning the Adoption of Uniform Conditions of Approval and Reciprocal Recognition of Approval for **Motor Vehicle Equipment** and Parts (Geneva, 20.03.1958)
181.05 – Statutes of the International Road Federation (IRF Res., 02.12.1964)
181.06 – Convention on the **Contract** for the International Carriage of Passengers and Luggage by Road (Geneva, 01.03.1973)
181.07 – Convention on Civil Liability for Damage Caused During Carriage of **Dangerous Goods** by Road, Rail and Inland Navigation Vessels (CRTD) (Geneva, 10.10.1989)

1.8.2 Rail Transport

182 A – International Conference for **Railway Technical Unity** (UT)
182 B – Intergovernmental Organization for International **Carriage by Rail** (OTIF)
182 C – International Union of **Railways** (UIC)
182.01 – International Agreement on Railway Technical Unity (Berne, 21.10.1882)
182.02 – Statutes of the International Union of Railways (Paris, 20.10.1922)
182.03 – International Convention to Facilitate the Crossing of Frontiers for **Goods** Carried by Rail (Geneva, 10.01.1952)
182.04 – International Convention to Facilitate the Crossing of Frontiers for **Passengers and Baggage** Carried by Rail (Geneva, 10.01.1952)
182.05 – Convention Concerning International **Carriage** By Rail (Berne, 09.05.1980)

1.8.3 Maritime Transport

183 A – International **Maritime** Organization (IMO)
183 B – International **Maritime** Committee (CMI)
183.01 – International Convention for the Unification of Certain Rules of Law Relating to **Bills of Lading** (Brussels, 25.08.1924)
183.02 – International Convention for the Unification of Certain Rules Relating to the Limitation of **Liability of Owners** of Sea-Going Vessels (Brussels, 25.08.1924)

1.8.4 Air Transport

184.06 – Convention Supplementary to the 1929 Warsaw Convention for the Unification of Certain Rules Relating to International **Carriage** by Air Performed by a Person Other than Contracting Carrier (Guadalajara, 18.09.1961)

1.8.5 Space Transport

185.01 – Agreement on the Rescue of **Astronauts**, the Return of Astronauts, and the Return of Objects Launched into Outer Space (London, Moscow, Washington, 22.04.1968)
185.02 – Convention on the International **Liability** for Damage Caused by Space Objects (London, Moscow, Washington, 29.03.1972)
185.03 – Convention on **Registration** of Objects Launched into Outer Space (New York, 12.11.1974)

1.9 Communications

1.9.1 Postal Communication

191 A – Universal **Postal** Union (UPU)
191.01 – **Constitution** of the Universal Postal Union (Vienna, 10.07.1964)
191.02 – Universal Postal **Convention** (Washington, 14.12.1989)
191.03 – **Postal Parcels** Agreement (Washington, 14.12.1989)
191.04 – **Money Orders** Agreement (Washington, 14.12.1989)
191.05 – **Giro** Agreement (Washington, 14.12.1989)
191.06 – **Cash-on-Delivery** Agreement (Washington, 14.12.1989)

1.9.2 Telecommunication

192 A – International **Telecommunication** Union (ITU)
192.01 – **Radio** Regulations (Geneva, 06.12.1979)
192.02 – International Telecommunication **Convention** (Nairobi, 06.11.1982)
192.03 – International Telecommunication **Regulations** (Melbourne, 09.12.1988)
192.04 – **Constitution** of the International Telecommunication Union (Nice, 30.06.1989)
192.05 – International Telecommunication **Convention** (Nice, 30.06.1989)
192.06 – **Constitution** of the International Telecommunication Union (Geneva, 22.12.1992)
192.07 – **Convention** of the International Telecommunication Union (Geneva, 22.12.1992)

1.9.3 Satellites

193 A – International **Telecommunications Satellite** Organization (INTELSAT)
193 B – International Organization of **Space Telecommunications** (INTER-SPUTNIK)
193 C – International **Maritime Satellite** Organization (INMARSAT)
193.01 – Agreement Relating to the International Telecommunications Satellite Organization "INTELSAT" (Washington, 20.08.1971)

2. MONETARY CO-OPERATION, FINANCIAL ASSISTANCE AND ECONOMIC FORUMS

2.1 International Monetary System

2.1.1 Monetary Co-operation

2.1.2 Central Bank and Securities Supervisors Co-operation

2.2 Financial Assistance

2.2.1 World Bank Group

2.2.2 United Nations Development Programme

2.3 International Forums

2.3.1 Industrialized Countries

231 A – Group of **Five**
231 B – Group of **Seven**

2.3.2 Monetary Forums

232 A – Group of **Ten**
232 B – Group of **Twenty-Four**

2.3.3 Developing Countries

233 A – Group of **Seventy-Seven**

3. CONTRACTS, PAYMENTS AND DISPUTE SETTLEMENT

3.0 Institutions

300 A – The Hague Conference on **Private International Law** (HCOPIL)
300 B – International Institute for the Unification of **Private Law** (UNIDROIT)
300 C – United Nations Commission on International **Trade Law** (UNCITRAL)
300 D – International **Chamber of Commerce** (ICC)
300.01 – Statutes of the International Chamber of Commerce (ICC Res., 24.06.1920)
300.02 – Statute of the International Institute for the Unification of Private Law (Rome, 15.03.1940)
300.03 – Statute of the Hague Conference on Private International Law (The Hague, 31.10.1955)
300.04 – Establishment of the United Nations Commission on International Trade Law (UNGA Res.2205(XXI), 17.12.1966)

3.1 Private International Obligations

3.1.1 Unification of Laws

311.01 – Convention relating to a Uniform Law on the International **Sale of Goods** (The Hague, 01.07.1964)
311.02 – Convention relating to a Uniform Law on the **Formation of Contracts** for the International Sale of Goods (The Hague, 01.07.1964)
311.03 – Convention on the **Limitation Period** in the International Sale of Goods (New York, 14.06.1974)
311.04 – United Nations Convention on **Contracts** for the International Sale of Goods ("Vienna Convention") (Vienna, 11.04.1980)
311.05 – Convention on **Agency** in the International Sale of Goods (Geneva, 15.02.1983)
311.06 – UNIDROIT Convention on International **Factoring** (Ottawa, 28.05.1988)
311.07 – UNIDROIT Convention on International **Financial Leasing** (Ottawa, 28.05.1988)

3.1.2 Conflict of Laws

312.01 – Convention on the Law Applicable to International **Sales of Goods** (The Hague, 15.06.1955)
312.02 – Convention Concerning Recognition of the **Legal Personality** of Foreign Companies, Associations and Foundations (The Hague, 01.06.1956)
312.03 – Convention on the Law Applicable to **Transfer of Property** in case of International Sales of Goods (The Hague, 15.04.1958)
312.04 – Convention on the Law Applicable to **Products Liability** (The Hague, 02.10.1973)
312.05 – Convention on the Law Applicable to **Agency** (The Hague, 14.03.1978)
312.06 – Convention on the Law Applicable to **Trusts** and on their Recognition (The Hague, 01.07.1985)
312.07 – Convention on the Law Applicable to **Contracts** for the International Sale of Goods (The Hague, 22.12.1986)

3.1.3 Standard Provisions

313.01 – **Incoterms** (International Rules for the Interpretation of Trade Terms) (ICC Res., 26.06.1936)
313.02 – International **Marketing** Codes (ICC Res., 1937)
313.03 – Uniform Customs for **Contract Guarantees** (ICC Res., 1978)
313.04 – Provisions Concerning a **Unit of Account** (UNGA Res.107(XXXVII), 16.12.1982)
313.05 – Uniform Rules on Contract Clauses for an Agreed Sum due upon **Failure of Performance** (UNGA Res.135(XXXVIII), 19.12.1983)
313.06 – Uniform Rules of Conduct for **Interchange of Trade Data** by Teletransmission (ICC Res., 22.09.1987)

3.2 Payment Mechanisms

3.2.1 Bills of Exchange, Promissory Notes and Cheques

321.01 – Convention Providing a **Uniform Law** for **Bills of Exchange** and Promissory Notes, and Protocol (Geneva, 07.06.1930)
321.02 – Convention for the Settlement of Certain **Conflicts of Laws** in Connection with Bills of Exchange and Promissory Notes, and Protocol (Geneva, 07.06.1930)
321.03 – Convention on the **Stamp Laws** in Connection With Bills of Exchange and Promissory Notes, and Protocol (Geneva, 07.06.1930)
321.04 – Convention Providing a **Uniform Law** for **Cheques** (Geneva, 19.03.1931)
321.05 – Convention for the Settlement of Certain **Conflicts of Laws** in Connection with Cheques, and Protocol (Geneva, 19.03.1931)
321.06 – Convention on the **Stamp Laws** in Connection with Cheques (Geneva, 19.03.1931)
321.07 – United Nations Convention on International **Bills of Exchange** and International Promissory Notes (UNGA Res.43/165, 09.12.1988)
321.08 – UNCITRAL Model Law on International **Credit Transfers** (UNCITRAL Dec., 15.05.1992)

3.2.2 Documentary Credits and Guarantees

322.01 – Uniform Custom and Practice for **Documentary Credits** (ICC Res., 03.06.1933)
322.02 – Uniform Customs for **Collections** (ICC Res., 1956)
322.03 – Uniform Rules for **Demand Guarantees** (ICC, 03.12.1991)

3.3 Judicial Proceedings

3.3.1 Judicial Competence

331.01 – Convention on the Jurisdiction of the **Selected Forum** in the Case of International Sales of Goods (The Hague, 15.04.1958)
331.02 – Convention on the **Choice of Court** (The Hague, 25.11.1965)

3.3.2 Judicial Co-operation

332.01 – Convention Relating to **Civil Procedure** (The Hague, 01.03.1954)
332.02 – Convention on the **Service** Abroad of Judicial and Extrajudicial Documents in Civil or Commercial Matters (The Hague, 15.11.1965)
332.03 – Convention on the Taking of **Evidence** Abroad in Civil or Commercial Matters (The Hague, 18.03.1970)
332.04 – Convention on International **Access** to Justice (The Hague, 25.10.1980)

3.3.3 Recognition and Enforcement of Judgments

333.01 – Convention on the Recognition and Enforcement of **Foreign Judgments** in Civil and Commercial Matters (The Hague, 01.02.1971)

3.4 Arbitration

3.4.1 Arbitration Conventions

341.01 – Protocol on **Arbitration Clauses** (Geneva, 24.09.1923)
341.02 – Convention on the **Execution** of Foreign Arbitral Awards (Geneva, 26.09.1927)
341.03 – Convention on the **Recognition and Enforcement** of Foreign Arbitral Awards (New York, 10.06.1958)
341.04 – European Convention on International **Commercial Arbitration** (Geneva, 21.04.1961)
341.05 – Arrangement Relating to Application of the European Convention on International Commercial Arbitration (Paris, 17.12.1962)
341.06 – UNCITRAL Model Law on International **Commercial Arbitration** (UNGA Res.40/72, 11.12.1985)

3.4.2 Institutions and Rules

342 A – **Permanent Court** of Arbitration (PCA)
342 B – The **ICC International Court** of Arbitration (ICC-CA)
342 C – International Centre for Settlement of **Investment Disputes** (ICSID)
342.01 – Convention for the Pacific Settlement of International Disputes (The Hague, 29.07.1899)
342.02 – Statute of the Permanent Court of Arbitration: Convention for the Pacific Settlement of Disputes (The Hague, 18.10.1907)
342.03 – **ICC Rules** of Conciliation and Arbitration (ICC Res., 01.07.1921)
342.04 – **Rules of Arbitration** and Conciliation for Settlement of International Disputes between Two Parties of Which Only One is a State (PCA Res., 1962)
342.05 – Convention on the Settlement of Disputes Between States and Nationals of other States (Washington, 18.03.1965)
342.06 – **Arbitration Rules** (ICSID Res., 01.01.1968)
342.07 – UNCITRAL **Arbitration Rules** (UNGA Res.98(XXXI), 15.12.1976)
342.08 – UNCITRAL **Conciliation Rules** (UNGA Res.52(XXXV), 04.12.1980)

4. MANAGEMENT OF COMMON RESOURCES AND ENVIRONMENTAL PROTECTION

4.1 Conservation of Natural Resources

4.1.0 Environmental Co-ordination

410 A – United Nations **Environment** Programme (UNEP)
410.01 – Declaration of the United Nations Conference on the **Human Environment** (Stockholm, 16.06.1972)
410.02 – The Rio Declaration on **Environment and Development** (Rio de Janeiro, 14.06.1992)

4.1.1 Protection of Wild Flora and Fauna

411.01 – Convention for the Preservation of **Fauna and Flora** in their Natural State (London, 08.11.1933)
411.02 – International Convention for the Regulation of **Whaling** (Washington, 02.12.1946)
411.03 – International Convention for the Protection of **Birds** (Paris, 18.10.1950)
411.04 – International **Plant** Protection Convention (Rome, 06.12.1951)
411.05 – Convention on **Wetlands** of International Importance especially as Waterfowl Habitat (Ramsar, 02.02.1971)
411.06 – Convention on International Trade in **Endangered Species** of Wild Fauna and Flora (CITES) (Washington, 03.03.1973)
411.07 – Convention on the Conservation of **Migratory Species** of Wild Animals (CMS) (Bonn, 23.06.1979)
411.08 – Convention on **Biological Diversity** (Rio de Janeiro, 05.06.1992)

4.1.2 Marine Pollution

412.01 – International Convention for the Prevention of Pollution of the Sea by **Oil** (London, 12.05.1954)
412.02 – Tanker Owners Voluntary Agreement Concerning Liability for Oil Pollution **(TOVALOP)** (London, 07.01.1969)
412.03 – International Convention Relating to **Intervention** on the **High Seas** in Cases of Oil Pollution Casualties (Brussels, 29.11.1969)
412.04 – International Convention on **Civil Liability** for Oil Pollution Damage (CLC) (Brussels, 29.11.1969)
412.05 – Contract Regarding a Supplement to Tanker Liability for Oil Pollution **(CRISTAL)** (London, 14.01.1971)
412.06 – International Convention on the Establishment of an International Fund for **Compensation** for Oil Pollution Damage (FUND) (Brussels, 18.12.1971)
412.07 – Convention on the Prevention of Marine Pollution by **Dumping of Wastes** and other Matter (London, Mexico, Moscow, Washington, 29.12.1972)
412.08 – Protocol Relating to **Intervention** on the **High Seas** in Cases of Pollution by Substances other than Oil (London, 02.11.1973)
412.09 – International Convention for the Prevention of Pollution from Ships, and 1978 Protocol **(MARPOL 73/78)** (London, 02.11.1973)
412.10 – Protocol Relating to the International Convention for the Prevention of Pollution from Ships, 1973 (London, 17.02.1978)
412.11 – International Convention on **Oil Pollution** Preparedness, Response and Co-operation (OPRC) (London, 30.11.1990)

4.1.3 Air Pollution

413.01 – Convention on Long-Range Transboundary **Air Pollution** (LRTAP) (Geneva, 13.11.1979)
413.02 – Convention for the Protection of the **Ozone Layer** (Vienna, 22.03.1985)
413.03 – Protocol to the 1979 Convention on Long-Range Transboundary Air Pollution on the Reduction of **Sulphur Emissions** or their Transboundary Fluxes by at least 30 per cent (Helsinki, 08.07.1985)
413.04 – Protocol Relating to Substances Affecting the **Ozone Layer** (Montreal, 16.09.1987)
413.05 – Protocol to the 1979 Convention on Long-Range Transboundary Air Pollution concerning the Control of Emissions of **Nitrogen Oxides** or their Transboundary Fluxes (Sofia, 31.10.1988)
413.06 – Protocol to the 1979 Convention on Long-Range Transboundary Air Pollution concerning the Control of Emissions of **Volatile Organic Compounds** or their Transboundary Fluxes (Geneva, 18.11.1991)
413.07 – Framework Convention on **Climate Change** (New York, 09.05.1992)

4.1.4 Transboundary Environmental Impact

414.01 – Convention on **Environmental Impact Assessment** in a Transboundary Context (Espoo, 25.02.1991)
414.02 – Convention on the Transboundary Effects of **Industrial Accidents** (Helsinki, 17.03.1992)
414.03 – Convention on the Protection and Use of Transboundary **Water Courses** and International Lakes (Helsinki, 17.03.1992)

4.3.2 *The Law of the Sea*

432.01 – Convention on the **High Seas** (Geneva, 29.04.1958)
432.02 – Convention on the **Continental Shelf** (Geneva, 29.04.1958)
432.03 – Convention on the **Territorial Sea** and the Contiguous Zone (Geneva, 29.04.1958)
432.04 – Convention on Fishing and Conservation of the Living Resources of the **High Seas** (Geneva, 29.04.1958)
432.05 – Optional Protocol of Signature concerning the Compulsory Settlement of Disputes (Geneva, 29.04.1958)
432.06 – Convention for the International Council for the **Exploration** of the Sea (Copenhagen, 12.09.1964)
432.07 – United Nations Convention on the **Law of the Sea** (Montego Bay, 10.12.1982)

4.3.3 *Antarctica*

433.01 – **Antarctic** Treaty (Washington, 01.12.1959)
433.02 – Convention on the Conservation of Antarctic **Marine Living** Resources (Canberra, 20.05.1980)
433.03 – Convention on the Regulation of Antarctic **Mineral** Resource Activities (Wellington, 02.06.1988)
433.04 – Protocol on the **Environmental Protection** to the Antarctic Treaty (Madrid, 04.10.1991)

4.3.4 *Use of Outer Space*

434.01 – Treaty on Principles Governing the Activities of States in the Exploration and **Use of Outer Space**, Including the Moon and other Celestial Bodies (London, Moscow, Washington, 27.01.1967)
434.02 – Agreement Governing the **Activities of States** on the Moon and Other Celestial Bodies (New York, 05.12.1979)

0.0.1 Global Co-operation

This section examines the system of world-wide economic co-operation through the work of the principal organs of the United Nations. It includes a description of the organization, focusing on the economic role of the General Assembly and the Economic and Social Council. It describes, at some length, International Court of Justice decisions on economic matters. An outline of the key economic provisions of the United Nations Charter, as well as the most important economic declarations and resolutions of the General Assembly, is provided. Information on the many specialized agencies and sub-organs that make up the United Nations "family" can be found in their specific sections – for example, the World Bank [see 221 A], the IMF [see 211 A], the GATT [see 111 A], etc.

Ian Johnstone

SELECTED BIBLIOGRAPHY

The academic literature on the United Nations is extensive. For a general description of the work of the organization, a useful text is:

UN, *Basic Facts about the United Nations,* New York: United Nations Publications, 1989.

The annual reports of the Secretary-General on the work of the organization are also a good source:

Pérez de Cuéllar, J., *Anarchy or Order: Annual Reports 1982-1991,* New York: United Nations, 1991.

The work of the International Court of Justice is reviewed in:

Rosenne, S., *The World Court: What it is and How it Works, 4th rev. ed.,* Dordrecht: Martinus Nijhoff Publishers, 1989.

Fitzmaurice, Sir G., *The Law and Procedure of the International Court of Justice,* Cambridge: Grotius Publications, 1986.

The legislative history of and practice under the United Nations Charter are dealt with comprehensively in:

Cot, J.P. and A. Pellet, *La Charte des Nations Unies. 2nd ed.,* Paris: Economica, 1991.

Goodrich, L.M., E. Hambro and A.P. Simons, *United Nations Charter: Commentary and Documents. 3rd ed.,* New York: Columbia University Press, 1969.

Bowett, D.S., *The Law of International Institutions. 4th ed.,* London: Stevens & Sons, 1982.

001 A – UNITED NATIONS (UN)

The United Nations emerged from the United Nations Conference on International Organization in San Francisco, attended by representatives of 50 states. It officially came into existence on 24 October 1945, when the Charter of the United Nations was ratified by a majority of signatories including the five permanent members of the

Security Council: China, France, the former Soviet Union, the United Kingdom and the United States. As of 10 May 1993, the organization has 181 member states.

While the United Nations is known primarily for its role in the maintenance of international peace and security, most of its work, measured in terms of money and personnel, is directed towards economic and social programmes. Its purposes, as set out in Article 1 of the Charter, include the achievement of international co-operation in economic, social, cultural or humanitarian matters, and the harmonization of state actions in the attainment of the common ends of the organization.

STRUCTURE

There are six principal organs of the UN: the General Assembly, the Security Council, the Economic and Social Council (ECOSOC), the Trusteeship Council, the International Court of Justice and the Secretariat. The surrounding "UN system" comprises various subsidiary organs: 16 specialized agencies and two other autonomous bodies (namely, the IAEA and the GATT).

The **General Assembly** is composed of all member states of the organization. Each member has one vote; decisions on important questions are made by a two-thirds majority while other questions are decided by a simple majority. It holds regular annual sessions from September to December, in New York, and it may meet in special sessions within 24 hours of a request by the Security Council, by a majority of the UN members or by one member if the majority concurs.

The Assembly serves, among other things, as a forum for harmonizing international action in the economic, social and related fields. It can make recommendations on any matter within the scope of the Charter or relating to the powers and functions of a UN organ. Most questions before the Assembly are referred to one of the seven Main Committees: First Committee (Political and Security); Special Political Committee (Political questions not discussed by the First Committee); Second Committee (Economic and Financial); Third Committee (Social, Humanitarian and Cultural); Fourth Committee (Trusteeship); Fifth Committee (Administrative and Budgetary); and Sixth Committee (Legal). The Assembly has also established various procedural committees, subsidiary organs, and *ad hoc* bodies, and it reviews the activities of various UN programmes and institutions, including the United Nations Development Programme and the United Nations Children's Fund.

The Second Committee (Economic and Financial) is the central UN debating forum on international economic issues. It is the body that takes global economic initiatives, or approves those submitted by other bodies, such as strategies for UN Development Decades and the promulgation of a Charter of Economic Rights and Duties of States [see 001.05].

As a deliberative organ, the Assembly cannot adopt binding decisions, except on matters relating to the internal workings of the organization. Nevertheless, its resolutions and declarations have influenced the development of international law in various ways. Declarations are regularly adopted that purport to interpret Charter provisions, for example. The authoritative weight these constructions carry depends on the circumstances surrounding their adoption as well as on the subsequent practice of states concerned. Resolutions that purport to declare legal principles independent of a treaty provision cannot create direct obligations but again, depending on the circumstances of their adoption, they may be regarded as vehicles for the evolution of state practice and evidence of customary international law. At a minimum, decisions and declarations of the Assembly express the will of a majority of members and are, to that extent, a reflection of world opinion. In addition, the Assembly occasionally formulates treaties open for accession by members, thereby being instrumental in creating legal obligations.

The **Security Council** is composed of 15 members: China, France, the Russian Federation, the United Kingdom, and the United States on a permanent basis, plus ten other states elected by the General Assembly for two-year terms. The Russian Federation, declaring itself the continuing international legal personality of the former Soviet Union, took over its seat in December 1991. Decisions on substantive matters require nine votes including the concurring votes of all five permanent members, giving each permanent member a veto power.

The Security Council has primary responsibility for the maintenance of international peace and security. Under Article 25 of the Charter, members agree to accept and carry out the decisions of the Security Council and under Article 48 they are bound to carry out mandatory decisions taken under Chapter VII, including the imposition of economic sanctions pursuant to Article 41.

The **Economic and Social Council** (ECOSOC) has the main responsibility, under the authority of the General Assembly, for the discharge of the economic and social functions of the United Nations. Since 1973, 54 states have been members. Previously it held two sessions per year but in 1992 it began holding just one unified substantive session. Decisions are taken by a simple majority. The day-to-day work of ECOSOC is carried out in its subsidiary bodies: five regional commissions, six functional commissions, six standing committees and a number of expert governmental bodies.

While ECOSOC's terms of reference are wide, its powers are limited. It makes or initiates studies on international economic, social, cultural, educational, health and related matters. It makes recommendations to the General Assembly, members of the UN and relevant specialized agencies. It prepares draft conventions for submission to the General Assembly and organizes major conferences on matters within its competence. ECOSOC also consults with non-governmental organizations involved in matters with which the Council deals.

Since much of the work of the UN system in the economic and social fields falls directly within the competence of the specialized agencies, the substantive work of the Council tends to focus on those areas in which no agency operates. A more important function of ECOSOC, at least as conceived by the architects of the UN, is to co-ordinate the economic and social activities of the UN system as a whole. It performs this function by entering into agreements with agencies meeting the criteria of Article 57 of the Charter – that is, intergovernmental organizations having wide international responsibilities in the economic and social fields [see 001.01 on the co-ordinating role of ECOSOC].

The **Trusteeship Council** is, in principle, composed in equal numbers of UN members administering trust territories and those not, with the permanent five enjoying an automatic right to membership. As the number of administering states has decreased, however, the only current members are the permanent five, with the United States being the only administering state. The Council meets in annual sessions and fulfils its task of supervising the administration of the Trust Territories by examining reports from the Administering Authority, accepting petitions from the Territory and undertaking missions.

The **International Court of Justice** is the subject of a separate commentary [see 001B].

The **Secretariat** comprises the Secretary-General and such staff as the organization may require. The Secretary-General is appointed by the General Assembly upon the recommendation of the Security Council, for a period of five years. He is the chief administrative officer of the organization. In addition, he may bring to the attention of the Security Council any matter which, in his opinion, threatens international peace and security and may use his good offices to resolve international disputes. The present Secretary-General is Boutros Boutros-Ghali (Egypt, installed 1 January 1992). The staff of the Secretariat currently numbers some 25,000 people from around the world.

As part of a restructuring programme which became effective on 1 March 1992, the economic offices of the Secretariat were consolidated in the new Department of Economic Development. Prior to this, responsibilities for economic activities were spread among the Office of the Director-General for Development and International Economic Co-operation, the Department of International Economic and Social Affairs, the Department of Technical Co-operation for Development, the United Nations Centre on Transnational Corporations, and the Centre for Science and Technology for Development.

FUNDING

The main source of funding for the regular programme budget of the UN comes from the contributions of member states. They are based primarily on the ability to pay calculated in terms of national income, with adjustments to take into account per capita income. The General Assembly has fixed a maximum rate of 25 per cent of the total budget for any one contributor, which so far applies only to the United States, and a minimum rate of 0.01 per cent of the total budget. Member states are assessed on a similar scale for the costs of peace-keeping operations. Activities outside the regular and peace-keeping programmes are financed mainly by voluntary contributions.

In his 1992 Report on the Work of the Organization, the Secretary-General referred to the on-going financial crisis faced by the United Nations and noted that at the time of writing the Report, only 52 member states had fully paid their annual contributions. As of the end of September 1992, the level of outstanding contributions to the regular budget was over US$908 million and unpaid peace-keeping assessments amounted to US$844 million.

CONCLUSIONS

Generally, the United Nations has not been a significant force in world economic management. The problems of the organization in the economic sector are well-known and there has been no shortage of proposals for reform, both from organs and groups within the UN system and those outside. With respect to the Secretariat, a first step was taken on 1 March 1992, when 14 Under-Secretary-General and Assistant-Secretary-General posts were eliminated, concentrating the decision-making process within seven departments, including the newly created Department of Economic Development. ECOSOC is another often-discussed target for reform, due to the overlap between its work and that of the Second and Third Committees of the General Assembly. Furthermore, the Secretary-General has proposed an early warning function for ECOSOC, encompassing threats to security and well-being from energy crises, the debt burden, risk of famine, the spread of disease, and so on.

It is unlikely that the UN will displace the Bretton Woods institutions [see section 2] and the GATT [see 001 A] in the area of economic policy in the near future, but it could assume greater leadership in policy-making on issues such as narcotics and human rights, including economic and social rights.

The prospects for strengthening the co-ordinating role of the UN are improved by the relative consensus among governments on international economic management reflected in the 1990 Declaration on International Economic Co-operation [see 001.06]. This consensus may be reinforced by the increasing awareness of the need to tackle environmental issues globally. Conceivably, the aftermath of the United Nations Conference on Environment and Development (UNCED) [see 410.02] will lead to significant institutional reform of the UN in the economic and social sectors generally.

PUBLICATIONS

The numerous United Nations publications include the *Yearbook of the United Nations*, the *United Nations Juridical Yearbook*, the *International Law Commission Yearbook*, *Repertory of Practice of the United Nations Organs*, and the *United Nations Chronicle*.

Ian Johnstone

ADDRESS

United Nations Building, New York, N.Y. 10017, United States
T. (212) 963-1234, Fx. (212) 963 4879

001 B – INTERNATIONAL COURT OF JUSTICE (ICJ)

The International Court of Justice, principal judicial organ of the United Nations, operates on an equal and complementary footing with the other organs. The Statute of the ICJ is an integral part of the UN Charter. The Court is composed of 15 independent judges elected by the General Assembly and by the Security Council, each acting separately. The judges are elected without regard to their nationality, although in practice one judge from each of the five permanent members of the Security Council has usually sat on the Court. No two judges may be nationals of the same state and, as stipulated in the Statute of the Court, the electors are to bear in mind that the main forms of civilization and the principal legal systems of the world should be represented in the body as a whole.

In keeping with the principle of independence, judges of the nationality of the parties in a dispute may sit in a case before the Court, though they must disqualify themselves if they have a personal interest in the affair or if, for any reason, they consider they should not take part. Article 31 of the Statute, however, provides that if the Court includes upon the bench a judge of the nationality of one of the parties, the other party may choose a judge *ad hoc*. In principle, this arrangement ensures that the viewpoint of each of the parties receives the full attention, consideration and understanding of the Court; in practice, it tends to provide a counterbalancing vote.

The Statute of the International Court of Justice allows for the possibility of a case being heard by a Chamber, the number of judges to be determined by the Court with the approval of the parties. These judges are elected by the Court but, in practice, the parties control the choice by retaining the option of abandoning the proceedings or submitting the case to arbitration if the Chamber is not composed to their satisfaction.

Only states may be parties in a case before the Court. The Court has jurisdiction over all matters that the parties refer to it and over matters provided for in the UN Charter or in treaties and conventions. States may submit in advance to the compulsory jurisdiction of the Court by making a declaration to that effect either with or without conditions attached. Additionally, the Court may give an advisory opinion on any legal question at the request of authorized bodies, such as the Security Council, the General Assembly or a specialized agency. Unlike decisions of the Court in contentious cases, advisory opinions are not binding.

ECONOMICALLY-RELATED DISPUTES

Among the most important cases in which the Court specifically addressed economic issues are two relating to fisheries. The *Anglo-Norwegian Fisheries* case (1951) involved a dispute over the method adopted by Norway in 1935 of measuring the scope of its territorial waters. In a decision that affected the subsequent development of the law of the sea, the Court held in favour of Norway, partly because of its historical title consolidated by "constant and sufficiently long practice". In one of the more controversial aspects of the ruling, the Court took account of the vital economic needs of Norwegian fishing villages in deciding the legitimacy of the claim.

In the fisheries jurisdiction cases (*United Kingdom v. Iceland* and *Federal Republic of Germany v. Iceland*, 1974), the ICJ dealt with the proposed extension by Iceland of the limits of its exclusive fisheries zone from a distance of 12 to 50 nautical miles. The Court decided in two separate but substantively identical opinions that, while Iceland's special dependence on its fisheries gave it preferential rights in the 50-mile zone, it had failed to give reasonable regard to the interests of other states in contravention of the principle enshrined in Article 2 of the 1958 Geneva Convention on the High Seas [see 432.01]. Accordingly, the Court imposed an obligation on all parties to undertake negotiations to find an equitable solution, based on the applicable law.

Two cases decided by the Court involving commercial matters are *Barcelona Traction, Light and Power Co.* (Belgium v. Spain, 1970) and *Electtronica Sicula S.P.A. (ELSI)* (United States v. Italy, 1989). In the first, the Court declined to grant Belgium standing to exercise diplomatic protection over Belgian shareholders in a Canadian company which had suffered damage at the hands of Spanish authorities. Rather than "lift the corporate veil", the Court applied the general rule of diplomatic protection, which grants that right to the state under the laws of which the company was incorporated.

The *ELSI* case, decided by a Chamber of the Court, involved the requisition by the Mayor of Palermo of the plant of a wholly-owned subsidiary of a US company. The Chamber rejected the US claim that the requisition order violated three provisions of the Treaty of Friendship, Commerce and Navigation of 1948 between Italy and the United States.

The Chamber jurisdiction of the Court provides a useful alternative to arbitration for states that would rather not submit disputes to the full Court. It can be particularly useful for economic disputes, which are often suited to decision by a few judges with special knowledge of the relevant practice. The procedure and relevant law is the same and judgments of the Chamber are as binding as those of the full Court. Furthermore, because the wishes of the parties regarding the composition of the Chamber are taken into account, the parties can be relied on to co-operate with the Court, thereby mitigating the problem of non-appearance as happened several times in the 1970s and 1980s.

The power of the Court to enforce its own judgments is limited. By Article 94 of the Charter, all United Nations members undertake to comply with the decisions of the Court. If any party fails to comply, the other party may refer the matter to the Security Council and the Council may take action to enforce the judgment. There have been occasions when losing states have refused to comply with an order of the Court and several have been referred to the Security Council but, for varying reasons, enforcement measures have never yet been adopted.

PUBLICATIONS

The publications of the Court include three annual series: *Reports of Judgments, Advisory Opinions and Orders*, *Bibliography* of works and documents relating to the Court, and a *Yearbook*. The Court also publishes *Pleadings* from cases it hears.

I.J.

ADDRESS

Peace Palace, Carnegie Plein 2, 2517 KJ The Hague, The Netherlands
T. (31 70) 392 4441, Fx. (31 70) 364 9928

001.01 – UNITED NATIONS CHARTER (UN)

Concluded : 26.06.1945, San Francisco
In force : 24.10.1945
Parties : 181

The Charter of the United Nations, adopted in 1945, sets out rights and duties of signatory states in the domains of international peace and security, economic and social development and the protection of human rights. It is both a multilateral treaty and a constitutional instrument, whose broad language requires interpretation in light of the changing conditions of international life.

Amendments to the Charter enter into force only when adopted by a two-thirds majority of the General Assembly and ratified by two-thirds of the members of the Organization, among whom must be the five permanent members of the Security Council. The first amendment came in 1965 when the membership of the Security Council was increased from 11 to 15 (Art. 23) and the number of affirmative votes required to adopt a measure was increased from seven to nine, five of which must come from the permanent five on substantive matters (Art. 27). In that same year, ECOSOC was expanded from 16 to 27 members and then, in 1973, to 54 (Art. 61). In 1968, the number of affirmative votes required in the Security Council to convene a General Conference to review the Charter was increased from seven to nine (Art. 109).

ECONOMIC AND SOCIAL PROVISIONS

Chapters IX and X of the Charter reflect the desire at San Francisco to give the United Nations a substantial role in the economic and social fields. Chapter IX relates to international economic and social co-operation generally, while Chapter X sets out the functions and powers of the Economic and Social Council (ECOSOC).

These provisions mark a significant advance from the Covenant of the League of Nations, where little reference was made to international economic and social activities. Despite this inattention in the Covenant, considerable economic co-operation did occur throughout the League years. More specialized agencies were created and the theory of functionalism, which holds that co-operation among states in various functional fields can contribute to the cause of peace, gained currency. The framers of the Charter were inspired by this history of co-operation and they recognized the need to design a functionally decentralized but co-ordinated system.

Article 55, the key Charter provision on economic and social activities, stipulates that the United Nations is to promote, *inter alia*, higher standards of living, full employment, conditions of economic development and solutions to international economic problems. Under Article 56, members pledge to take joint and separate action, in co-operation with the Organization, for the achievement of those purposes.

While the range of UN economic activities is extensive, the Organization is empowered only to make recommendations in this field (Art. 58). Efforts to promote the various goals of Article 55 have led to the proclamation of Four Development Decades (beginning in 1961 and lasting until the year 2000); the establishment of a programme for technical assistance, which became the United Nations Development

Programme [see 222 A]; the creation of new subsidiary bodies such as the United Nations Industrial Development Organization [see 151 A]; the convening and institutionalizing of the United Nations Conference on Trade and Development (UNCTAD) [see 111 B]; the call for a New International Economic Order [see 001.03]; and the adoption of the Charter of Economic Rights and Duties of States [see 001.05].

CO-ORDINATION PROVISIONS

Article 57 of the Charter reflects the principle that the objectives of the Organization in the economic and social fields should be pursued in conjunction with the autonomous specialized agencies. Article 58 calls upon the UN to co-ordinate the activities of the specialized agencies, which has proved to be a difficult task. The primary mechanism for co-ordination is the agreements entered into between the UN and specialized agencies pursuant to Article 63. These Agreements contain various common features such as reciprocal rights to propose agenda items and the right of ECOSOC to make recommendations to the given specialized agency, as well as provisions relating to consultation and reporting.

Co-ordination is also undertaken by the Administrative Committee on Co-ordination, comprising the Secretary-General and the administrative heads of the specialized agencies, and the General Assembly's Advisory Committee on Administrative and Budgetary Questions (ACABQ), which considers the budgets of the agencies. The Committee on Programme and Co-ordination is a 36-member intergovernmental body charged with programme co-ordination throughout the United Nations system.

The difficulties of co-ordination are due in part to the limited powers granted to ECOSOC. Article 60 assigns ECOSOC, under the authority of the General Assembly, primary responsibility for the discharge of the economic and social functions of the organization. Its specific powers, enumerated in Article 64, include the power to make arrangements to obtain reports from the specialized agencies on steps taken to implement General Assembly and ECOSOC recommendations. However, the specialized agencies, like member states, are under no obligation to comply with ECOSOC recommendations nor even to submit reports. To compound the problem, the agreements with the Bretton Woods institutions – the International Monetary Fund (IMF) [see 211 A], the International Bank for Reconstruction and Development (IBRD) [see 221 A] , and the International Finance Corporation (IFC) [see 221 C] – stress the independent character of these organizations. The considerable autonomy with which they operate has been jealously guarded by these institutions and by governments that resist the "one state, one vote" principle in the United Nations.

I.J.

Access : CON (Art. 3, 4)
Reserves : USP
Duration : USP
Deposit. : US, UN (Art. 111)
Language : Chi, Eng, Fre, Rus, Spa (Art. 111)

Modific. :Res.1991 A et B (XVIII) 17.12.63 (31.08.65); Res.2101(XX) 20.12.65 (12.06.68); Res.2847 (XXVI) 20.12.71 (24.09.73)

Reference :1, 557, 638 UNTS – Can TS 1945/7, 1973/4 – RTAF 1966/8, 1967/85, 1976/3 – JDI 1966, 1968, 1976 – UKTS 1946/67, 1966/2, 1969/5, 1973/130 – 1 Paeslee – JORF 13 Jan 46, 21 Jan 66, 22 Nov 67, 11 Feb 76

001.02 – STATUTE OF THE INTERNATIONAL COURT OF JUSTICE – ICJ

Concluded : 26.06.1945, San Francisco
In force : 24.10.1945
Parties : 57

For a description of the ICJ, see 001 B.

Access : ALS (Art. 93 Chart.,35)
Reserves : AUT (Art. 36-3)
Duration : USP
Deposit. : UN
Language : Chi, Eng, Fre, Rus, Spa

Reference : Can TS 1945/7 – UKTS 1946/67 – 1 Paeslee – JORF 13 Jan 46

001.03 – DECLARATION ON THE ESTABLISHMENT OF A NEW INTERNATIONAL ECONOMIC ORDER – UN

Adopted : 01.05.1974, UNGA Res.3201(S-VI)

On 1 May 1974, at a special session on development, members of the General Assembly proclaimed, in the Declaration on the Establishment of a New International Economic Order (NIEO), their determination "to work urgently for the establishment of a new international economic order based on equity, sovereignty, interdependence, common interest and co-operation among states, irrespective of their social systems". The stated goals were to correct inequalities, redress existing injustices, eliminate the widening gap between the developed and developing countries and ensure steadily accelerating development. The Declaration sets out various principles on which the new international economic order should be founded and calls upon all states to exert maximum effort with a view to its implementation.

I.J.

Reference : ILM 13:744

001.04 – PROGRAMME OF ACTION ON THE ESTABLISHMENT OF A NEW INTERNATIONAL ECONOMIC ORDER – UN

Adopted : 01.05.1974, UNGA Res.3202(S-VI)

The Progamme of Action deals in greater detail with the problems and objectives proclaimed in the Declaration [see 001.03], but it does not impose legally binding obligations on states in the expectation that these would come in later negotiations. It contains chapters on, *inter alia*, raw materials, the international monetary system, industrialization, technology transfer and sovereignty over natural resources. It aims at a gradual shift in the terms of trade between developed and developing countries, and in the greater participation by developing countries in international financial markets and institutions.

Subsequent efforts to bring about a new international economic order have met with little success. In particular, the call in 1979 by the Assembly for the launching of a round of global negotiations on international co-operation for development failed.

Moreover, the latest economic plan adopted by the United Nations, the Declaration on International Economic Co-operation [see 001.06], does not refer to the NIEO.

I.J.

Reference : ILM 13:744

001.05 – CHARTER ON ECONOMIC RIGHTS AND DUTIES OF STATES – UN

Adopted : 12.12.1974, UNGA Res.3281(XXIX)

The General Assembly adopted, in December 1974, the Charter of Economic Rights and Duties of States. The Charter provides that each state shall exercise permanent sovereignty over its wealth, natural resources and economic activities, and grants the right to nationalize, expropriate or transfer ownership of private property with appropriate compensation. It sets out the right of every state to engage in international trade and to associate in organizations of primary commodity producers. It calls upon all states to co-operate in promoting the expansion and liberalization of world trade and it contains a prohibition against the use of economic, political or other coercion in order to obtain from another state the subordination of its sovereign rights.

In the Article on expropriation, it is stipulated that "appropriate" compensation is to be determined by reference to the "relevant laws and regulations and all circumstances that the state (adopting such measures) considers pertinent". It is not clear whether this provision purports to reject the principle that matters of compensation are subject to international law or whether it formulates a different conception of the applicable international law. This uncertainty was sufficient to cause a significant minority of states to vote against or abstain from voting for the resolution. The vote was 120 in favour and six against (Belgium, Denmark, the Federal Republic of Germany, Luxembourg, the United States and the United Kingdom), with ten abstentions (Austria, Canada, France, Ireland, Israel, Italy, Japan, Norway, the Netherlands and Spain).

I.J.

Reference : ILM 14:263

001.06 – DECLARATION ON INTERNATIONAL ECONOMIC CO-OPERATION, IN PARTICULAR THE REVITALIZING OF ECONOMIC GROWTH AND DEVELOPMENT OF THE DEVELOPING COUNTRIES – UN

Adopted : 01.05.1990, UNGA Res.S-18/3

The 1990 Special Session of the General Assembly on International Economic Co-operation for Development provided a new opportunity to assess the world economic situation and the needs of developing countries. The Declaration is a reflection of the consensus made possible by the end of the Cold War, at least in regard to general policy directions. It includes a strong call for the revitalization of economic growth and social development in the developing countries, with special attention to be given to the needs of the least developed. It recognizes that the 1980s were viewed as a lost decade for many countries. The restoration of a long-term approach to development, rather than short-term adjustment strategies, is called for. It refers to the debt problem and the need for environmentally sound development. The benefits to development that can accrue from the protection of human rights and the "peace dividend" are referred to. It also refers to the important role of the United Nations system in revitalizing development, with special mention being made of the specialized agencies.

The Declaration does not, however, contain any substantive concessions from developed countries beyond a vague undertaking to implement the agreed international target of devoting 0.7 per cent of GNP to official development assistance.

I.J.

1. Organization of Trade and Production

The reduction of both natural and artificial barriers to trade has substantially increased the volume of world trade since the end of the Second World War. The international trade in manufactured goods, for example, increased 12-fold between 1947 and 1991. As a result, the interdependence between all countries has also increased. This chapter deals with the legal framework, largely developed since 1945, within which international trade in commodities, industrial goods and services occurs.

The General Agreement on Tariffs and Trade (GATT) has been the major force behind the reduction of tariff barriers to trade in industrial goods and in removing non-tariff barriers to trade [see 1.1.1]. Its contribution has been complemented by other agreements such as those aimed at simplifying and harmonizing customs regulations and procedures [see 1.1.2].

Developing countries, many of which are major exporters of commodities, have seen a continuing deterioration in their terms of trade. Some have, under the framework provided by the United Nations Conference on Trade and Development (UNCTAD), called for international commodity agreements in order to stabilize international export prices of commodities. Market intervention mechanisms provided by some agreements have had limited success [see 1.2.1]; other forms of co-operation have taken place between both exporters and importers of specific commodities [see 1.2.2 and 1.2.3] as well as among producing countries [see 1.2.4].

Some mechanisms have been established in order to increase agricultural production and to facilitate trade in food products [see 1.3.1]. Standards have been set and assistance provided in order to improve health [see 1.3.2] and social and working conditions [see 1.4.1]. Codes of conduct have been adopted by international organizations to recommend to transnational corporations good practices on working conditions and in regard to national economies [see 1.4.2].

With industrialization and the increasingly rapid pace of technological progress [see 1.5.1], standardization [see 1.5.2] and intellectual property rights [see 1.6] have become important features of international economic competition in goods and services.

The development of fast and effective transportation and communication systems has dramatically contributed to increased levels of international trade. Agreements have been adopted which facilitate frontier crossing by travellers [see 1.7.2] and the circulation of goods and passengers. Although there have been efforts to regulate multimodal transport, each means of transport (road, rail, maritime, air and space) has its own legal regime which deals primarily with issues of traffic, contract of carriage and carriers' liability [see 1.8]. International co-operation in postal services [see 1.9.1] and telecommunications [see 1.9.2] has provided the basis for the development of a global communication infrastructure: a key factor in strengthening the global economy.

Bernard Colas

1.1 Trade and Customs Co-operation

1.1.1 Trade

Today's multilateral trading system originated in the negotiations, initiated during the Second World War between the the United States and Britain, on the shape of the post-war international economy. The need was discussed for international institutions for trade comparable to what were to become the International Monetary Fund (IMF) [see 211 A] and the Bank for International Reconstruction and Development (IBRD, often called the "World Bank") [see 221 A]. The form and function of a third pillar to the new international economic system was formalized when the US presented proposals for an International Trade Organization (ITO) to a conference in London in 1946. These proposals were reviewed at subsequent conferences in New York, Geneva and Havana. The final version, completed in Havana in March 1948, became known as the Havana Charter [see 111.02]. The General Agreement on Tariffs and Trade (GATT) came into being as part of the negotiations at a conference in Geneva in 1947 [see 111 A]. Ultimately the US refused to ratify the Charter, but the GATT has remained in force.

Today, the main agreement regulating international trade is still the GATT [see 111.01]. It was first amended in March 1955 and Part IV, which provided special treatment for developing countries, was added in February 1964. As the growth in membership made further amendments difficult, the parties turned to the adoption of various GATT codes during the Tokyo Round of negotiation (concluded in 1979). Some of these codes have expanded the coverage of GATT; others have provided details of application. The most recent round of multilateral negotiations under GATT began in September 1986 at Punta del Este, Uruguay. The Uruguay Round, the most ambitious to date, is attempting to move the GATT into new substantive areas of trade such as services, intellectual property and trade-related investment while, at the same time, reforming existing areas.[1]

This section also deals with UNCTAD [see 111 B] and the ITC [see 111 C], which directly address issues of the developing countries. GATT and UNCTAD agreements covering trade activities world-wide are summarized.

Regional agreements, which are outside the scope of this book – such as those of the European Communities (EC) and the North American Free Trade Agreement (NAFTA), as well as provisions of some organizations such as the recommendations and decisions of the Organisation for Economic Co-operation and Development (OECD) which is limited to its 24 member countries – have also had a significant global impact on international trade.

Gabrielle Marceau and Hugh J. Cheetham

SELECTED BIBLIOGRAPHY

Dam, Kenneth, *The GATT: Law and the International Economic Organization*, Chicago: Midway Reprint: University of Chicago, 1977.

Gelpin, R., *The Political Economy of International Relations*, Princeton: Princeton University Press, 1987.

(1) The GATT Trade Negotiations Committe on 15 December 1993 adopted the Final Act Embodying the Results of the Uruguay Round of Multilateral Trade Negotiations. Just prior to publication, an additional commentary has been added to this section which covers this development [see 111.21].

Hudec, R.E., *The GATT Legal System and World Trade Diplomacy*, 2nd ed. Salom, NH: Butterworth Legal Publishers, 1990.
Jackson, J.H., *World Trade and the law of GATT: A Legal Analysis of the General Agreement on Tariffs and Trade*, Indianapolis: Bobbs-Merrill, 1969.
– – –, *The World Trading System: The Law and Policy of International Economic Relations*, Cambridge, Mass.: MIT Press, 1989.
– – –, and W.J. Davey, *Legal Problems of International Economic Relations*, 2nd ed. St Paul: West, 1986.
Long, Oliver, *The Law and its Limitations in the GATT Multilateral Trade System*, London: Graham and Trotman, 1987.
McGovern, E., *International Trade Regulations*, Exeter: Globefield Press, 1982.
Petersmann, E.-U. and M. Hilf, *The New GATT Round of Multilateral Trade Regulations: Legal and Economic Problems*, Deventer: Kluwer Law and Taxation, 1988.
Simmonds, K.R. and B.H.W. Hill, *Law and Practice under the GATT*, Dobbs Ferry, N.Y.: Oceana Publications, 1988 (Looseleaf).
Zammit Cutajar, M., *UNCTAD and the South-North Dialogue: the First Twenty Years*, Oxford; New York; Toronto: Pergamon Press, 1985.
Zheng, H., *The Legal Structure of International Textile Trade*, New York: Quorum Books, 1988.

111 A – GENERAL AGREEMENT ON TARIFFS AND TRADE (GATT)

ORIGIN OF THE GATT

The GATT was never intended to be an organization and still is not, in the legal sense. It came into being as a result of a first round of tariff negotiations at the Geneva conference of 1947 on the proposed International Trade Organization (ITO). Subsequent tariff negotiations were to be conducted under the auspices of the ITO once it was established. In order to ensure that the agreed concessions at the Geneva conference would not be undercut by other trade measures, the GATT incorporated many of the commercial policy provisions of the ITO draft charter (as reflected in Chapter IV of the Havana Charter) [see 111.02].

The General Agreement was initially brought into effect by a "Protocol of Provisional Application" (effective 1 January 1948). This allowed prospective signatories to avoid having to present the GATT for domestic approval should this be necessary.

By the time the final ITO draft charter – the Havana Charter – was completed in 1948, a new US Congress had been elected. It was opposed to most trade policies of the administration and was particularly hostile to the Havana Charter's social welfare agenda (Chaps. II and III). Support from the American business community had also decreased as a result of the detrimental impact of the new tariff levels under the GATT and the fact that the UK could not be persuaded to give up its system of Commonwealth Preferences. In December 1950, the US administration quietly issued a press release which stated that it would not be re-submitting the Charter to Congress for approval. This effectively destroyed the ITO as it seemed futile to establish such an organization without the support of the world's leading economic power. The demise of the ITO did not, however, signal the end of multilateral trade as evidenced by the growth of the GATT.

The GATT gained *de facto* status as a specialized agency of the United Nations in 1952, through an exchange of letters between the Secretary-General and the Executive-Secretary of the GATT.

THE GENERAL AGREEEMENT ON TARIFFS AND TRADE

The primary goal of the GATT is international trade liberalization. Its text is composed of articles which provide for the reciprocal reduction of tariffs, and those which set out obligations on trade practices which can act to counter the effect of agreed tariff concessions [see 111.01 for a fuller description].

The General Agreement has evolved through periodic rounds of multilateral negotiations on substantive aspects of the Agreement: the Geneva Round (1947), the Annecy Round (1949), the Torquay Round (1950-1951), the Geneva Round (1955-1956), the Dillon Round (1961-1962), the Kennedy Round (1963-1967), the Tokyo Round (1973-1979), and the Uruguay Round (1986-) [see 111.19].

Prior to the Kennedy Round, these negotiations dealt primarily with reducing tariffs, as efforts to expand policy areas had met with resistance. However, by the end of the Tokyo Round in 1979, the need to confront the increasing use of non-tariff barriers, particularly by developed countries, led to the adoption of a number of codes dealing with specific practices [see 111.07 to 111.14].

Notwithstanding the principle of non-discrimination found in Article 1 of the GATT, the GATT Codes bind only those contracting parties (CPs) which have ratified them. Generally speaking, these Codes have not been ratified by developing countries and have tended to fragment the GATT system, creating different obligations for developed and developing countries. The negotiations of the Uruguay Round are attempting to correct this fragmentation by assimilating the Tokyo Codes into the main body of the General Agreement.

Given the limited scope of the GATT, concerned states have agreed in other forums to co-ordinate other aspects of trade having extraterritorial economic impact. The operations of transnational enterprises have also encouraged co-ordination of policy between states independently of the GATT. Some of these measures are reflected in the resolutions and recommendations of institutions such as UNCTAD [see 111 B] and the OECD.

The Uruguay Round seeks to broaden the scope of the GATT and reintroduces the idea of a comprehensive international trade organization to co-ordinate international economic activities, as was envisaged in the Havana Charter.

STRUCTURE

Having come into being as a provisional trade agreement, the GATT did not provide for a formal institutional structure to implement and administer its provisions. The only body envisaged in the General Agreement was the contracting parties meeting in conference and acting together on a consensual basis: "the CONTRACTING PARTIES" (expressed in capitals when designated in their collective capacity). Although the Agreement contains no authority for the creation of other bodies, the CPs have, in fact, developed other institutional mechanisms: the Council of Representatives; Committees, Working Parties and Panels; the Consultative Group of Eighteen; and the position of Director-General.

(i) The CONTRACTING PARTIES

The CONTRACTING PARTIES is the only body in the GATT system with the power to legislate and give definitive interpretations of the Agreement. It is the body in which disputes are determined and in which the conformity of CPs' trade policies with the GATT is decided. The CONTRACTING PARTIES also have the authority to grant waivers from GATT obligations to CPs under Article XXV-5. Decisions are taken by consensus and parties involved in a dispute always maintain the right to oppose any decision.

(ii) The Council of Representatives

The Council, established by a decision of the CONTRACTING PARTIES of 4 June 1960, acts as the executive body of the GATT. Its legal status is that of the CONTRACTING PARTIES's inter-sessional assembly. Membership is open to all CPs and two-thirds are represented in the Council. Its chairman is elected on a yearly basis by the CONTRACTING PARTIES.

The Council prepares the sessions of the CONTRACTING PARTIES, sets the agenda, and also oversees the work of subsidiary bodies, such as panels and committees (defined hereafter), and makes recommendations about their reports to the CONTRACTING PARTIES. It appoints panel members and sets out the terms of reference of panels. The Council plays a pivotal role in the final determination of a dispute in that only panel reports adopted by Council are presented to the CONTRACTING PARTIES, and are thus eligible to be given effect. Decisions of the Council are taken by consensus and parties involved in a dispute maintain the right to vote opposing a decision. While the principle of consensus has slowed down the implementation process of many panel decisions, it does seem necessary to ensure that economically powerful nations agree to a regime of dispute settlements.

(iii) Committees/Working Parties/Panels

It is in the committees, working parties and panels that the actions and activities of the GATT take shape.

(a) Committees. Committees are established to deal with fundamental issues on a continuing basis. Some of these committees reflect traditional concerns of the CPs – for example, the Committee on Balance of Payments Restrictions and Tariff Concessions. The Committee on Trade and Development, established under Part IV of the Agreement, is evidence of the growing place of developing countries in the GATT system. Committees are also set up to direct multilateral trade negotiations, and various committees exist under the 1979 codes negotiated at the Tokyo Round.

Membership on any of these committees is open to all CPs. The chairpersons of most of these committees are appointed by the Council. The chairperson of the Committee on Trade and Development is by custom from a developing country and the chairperson of the multilateral negotiation committee is the Director-General.

(b) Working Parties. Working parties are established by the Council on an *ad hoc* basis to deal with specific issues delegated by it. These working parties report back to the Council, which may adopt their recommendations. Membership is open to any CP wishing to be included.

(c) Panels. Panels are established by the Council when parties to a dispute have been unable to settle their differences under the consultation procedure [see 111.18]. Members of panels act in their individual capacities as trade experts and not as representatives of their governments. Panel reports must be adopted by the Council before being presented to the CONTRACTING PARTIES.

(iv) The Consultative Group of Eighteen

The Group is a consultative body, established to provide advice to the Council on key trade policy issues. Originally created in 1965, the Group was permanently established by a decision of the CONTRACTING PARTIES in 1979. By advising CPs on new developments in international trade, the Group facilitates the way CPs carry out their GATT obligations.

The Group's membership is restricted to 18, one of which is the EC and a majority of which (ten) are developing countries. Given the balanced nature of its composition and the fact that the chairperson of the Group is the Director-General, the Group's recommendations have great influence in the Council.

(v) The Director-General

The Director-General is the chief administrative officer of the GATT. The position reflects the evolution of the original position of Executive Secretary. While the Director-General may play a major part in attempting to mediate trade disputes or differences over policy issues in the Council or among CPs, his or her main function lies in being the chairperson of the multilateral negotiations. A recent example of this has been the focal role Arthur Dunkel has played in maintaining the momentum of the Uruguay Round.

The Director-General also oversees the GATT **Secretariat** which provides administrative and research services to the various bodies of the GATT.

CO-OPERATION

The GATT co-operates with the IMF [see 211 A] for the application of the Tokyo decisions in favour of developing countries [see 111.15, 111.16 and 111.17], and for the application of Article XII (Restrictions to Safeguard the Balance of Payments) and Art. XVIII (Governmental Assistance to Economic Development). The CONTRACTING PARTIES are obliged to consult with the IMF in cases dealing with monetary reserves, balance of payments or foreign exchange arrangements (Art. XV). In practice, since the breakdown of the par-value system [see 2.1], the IMF can no longer adequately perform its advisory function regarding the level of import restrictions required in such cases.

The GATT also co-operates with UNCTAD through the International Trade Centre [see 111 C] and, informally, with the OECD.

In the present Uruguay negotiations, the GATT has collaborated with the World Intellectual Property Organization (WIPO) [see 160 A] for the negotiation of TRIP issues (Trade Related Intellectual Property). If the Multilateral Trade Organization (MTO)[1] envisaged by the Uruguay Round proposals comes into being [see 111.19], it would offer a continuous forum to develop co-operation with other international organizations, and thereby could extend the links between trade and the environment [see section 4], trade and labour standards [see 1.4], and other areas.

G.M. and H.J.C.

ADDRESS

William Rappard Centre, 154, rue de Lausanne, CH-1211 Geneva 21, Switzerland
T. (41 22) 739 5111, Fx. (41 22) 731 4206

111 B – UNITED NATIONS CONFERENCE ON TRADE AND DEVELOPMENT (UNCTAD)

UNCTAD is the principal organ of the General Assembly in the field of trade and development. It is a permanent body, created by Resolution 1995(XIX) on 30 December 1964, and its budget forms part of the normal UN budget [see 001 A]. It is composed of representatives of 185 member states who meet in a Conference every four years. Many intergovernmental and non-governmental organizations participate in its work as observers.

UNCTAD was formed as a result of pressure from developing countries, following the beginning of the GATT round of negotiations of 1960. Most European

(1) The name of this proposed organization has now been changed to World Trade Organization [see 111.21].

countries had by then resolved their balance of payment problems following the Second World War but the gap between rich and poor countries was increasing.

From its inception, UNCTAD sought to be an alternative forum to the GATT where developing countries could express their views. UNCTAD's objective is to encourage the development of international trade by promoting the specific interests of the developing countries. It engages in deliberations, policy analysis, negotiations, implementation follow-up and technical co-operation. One of its most important functions is to review and facilitate the co-ordination of activities of other bodies within the UN system in the field of international trade and related problems of economic development. It also liaises with the General Assembly and commissions, bodies and working groups of ECOSOC [see 001 A].

UNCTAD has been very active in providing an institutional setting for the negotiation and adoption of multilateral agreements in areas such as commodities, trade and shipping. Since 1964, UNCTAD has been recognized as having special responsibilities within the UN system for the negotiation of new international commodity agreements and for the renegotiation of existing ones. It approved in 1976 an Integrated Programme for Commodities [see 121.02] which was followed by the conclusion in 1980 of the Common Fund for Commodities [see 121 B] and other international commodity agreements [see 1.2.1 and 1.2.2]. It has also served as a forum for the negotiation of terms of reference for autonomous international study groups on particular commodities [see 1.2.3].

UNCTAD drafted the set of principles for the control of restrictive business practices [see 111.05] and laid down the basis for the establishment of the well-known target of 0.7 per cent of gross national product for official development assistance accorded by developed countries. The Generalized System of Preferences (GSP) [see 111.05] was established under UNCTAD's auspices in 1970. More recently UNCTAD has assisted developing countries in the negotiation on the Global System of Trade Preferences Among Developing Countries (GSTP) [see 111.20].

With regard to maritime issues, UNCTAD has reached agreements on international conventions on liner conferences [see 183.15], on multimodal transport [see 180.01] and on the registration of ships [see 183.21].

Against the background of the changing nature of the North-South debate and of the evolution in the global political and economic environment, the eighth Conference of UNCTAD took place in Cartagena de Indias, Colombia in February 1992. Member states decided to establish a new partnership for development by focusing on the analysis of national experiences so as to enable them to draw appropriate lessons for the formulation and implementation of policies at the national and international levels and for international economic co-operation. Another salient element is the recognition of common interests of countries in different regions and of different levels of development.

On that basis, the Cartagena Commitment formulates policies and measures at the national and international levels in the interconnected fields of finance, trade, commodities, technology and services with a view to accelerating the development process. It further sets out policy recommendations on relatively novel concepts in the development dialogue, particularly "good management" at both the national and the international levels, the role of the market, the importance for development of democratic systems based on popular consent and public accountability, and the observance of human rights both as a moral imperative and as an important factor for development. A particularly important feature is the priority attached to the elimination of poverty and the mandate given to UNCTAD to focus its attention on poverty alleviation, thereby examining issues closely related to human development. The Commitment also provides guidelines for expanding work in UNCTAD on sustainable development.

STRUCTURE

Traditionally, member states have been divided into four geographic groupings: (A) the Afro-Asian group, (B) primarily OECD countries, (C) Latin American countries, and (D) Eastern Europe. In practical terms, however, another geopolitical alignment has replaced this formal division: on one side are the OECD countries and on the other are the Group of 77 [see 233 A] (currently 129 members) together with the countries of central and eastern Europe (D). China and Israel are considered independently. Since the Cartagena Conference, the group system role in substantive discussions has greatly diminished.

The UNCTAD **Conference** usually meets every four years at ministerial level to formulate major policy guidelines and decide on a programme of work. UNCTAD has a permanent **Secretariat** in Geneva headed by a Secretary-General who is nominated by the UN Secretary-General and approved by the General Assembly. Following Cartagena, the executive body of UNCTAD will remain the **Trade and Development Board** which will continue to meet biannually, and in addition in "Executive Session", and report to the General Assembly through the Economic and Social Council (ECOSOC) [see 001 A].

However, the Board has established new subsidiary machinery to implement the programme of work agreed to at UNCTAD VIII (Cartagena, 1992). Topics of a general nature will be taken up by standing committees, while questions of a more technical character will be examined in *ad hoc* working groups.

Standing Committees:
- Commodities;
- Poverty Alleviation;
- Economic Co-operation among Developing Countries; and
- Developing Services Sectors: Fostering Competitive Services Sectors in Developing Countries.

Ad Hoc Working Groups:
- Investment and Financial Flows; Non-debt-creating Finance for Development; New Mechanisms for Increasing Investment and Financial Flows;
- Trade Efficiency;
- Comparative Experiences with Privatization;
- Expansion of Trading Opportunities for Developing Countries; and
- Interrelationship between Investment and Technology Transfer.

Other Main Bodies:
- Special Committee on Preferences; and
- Intergovernmental Group of Experts on Restrictive Business Practices.

All UNCTAD member states are eligible to participate in the work of these bodies. In light of the provisions of the Cartagena Commitment, external bodies – such as enterprises, trade unions, the academic community and non-governmental organizations – will be more closely associated with UNCTAD's work.

CO-OPERATION

UNCTAD consults with intergovernmental, regional and non-governmental bodies. UNCTAD also maintains close liaison with many commissions and working groups of the UN (such as the UNCTC) and the GATT [see 111 A]. In the near future, the secretariat of the United Nations Commission on Transnational Corporation (UNCTC) will be transferred to Geneva and will work under UNCTAD supervision.

PUBLICATIONS

UNCTAD produces a good *Handbook of International Trade and Development Statistics.* There are the annual *Trade and Development Report*, the *Least-Developed Countries Report* and the *UNCTAD Commodity Yearbook*. The *UNCTAD Bulletin* is published six times a year. There are occasional publications as well. Conference resolutions are found in *Report of the Conference on Trade and Development at its # Session*. Resolutions and decisions of the Trade and Development Board are found in *Trade and Development Board, Official Records, Supplement #.*

G.M.

ADDRESS

Palais des Nations, CH-1211 Geneva 10, Switzerland
T. (41 22) 917 12 34, Fx. (41 22) 907 0042

111 C – INTERNATIONAL TRADE CENTRE UNCTAD/GATT (ITC)

ITC was established by the CONTRACTING PARTIES of the GATT [see 111 A] on 19 March 1964 as part of the GATT's efforts to expand the trade of developing countries. ITC was then a division of the GATT secretariat, responsible for helping developing countries promote their exports by providing trade information, advice on export marketing, marketing techniques and training.

In 1967 UNCTAD [see 111 B] and the GATT recommended that ITC be jointly operated by the two organizations. This new status was approved by the GATT, the UN General Assembly and UNCTAD, and took effect on 1 January 1968 under a similar mandate. In 1974, ITC was officially recognized as a "joint subsidiary organ" of the GATT and the United Nations, the latter acting through UNCTAD. Its regular budget is financed by the GATT and the United Nations. Its technical co-operation budget is financed by the United Nations Development Programme (UNDP) [see 222 A] and by voluntary contributions from individual governments.

ITC is headed by an Executive Director. Appointment and promotion of professional staff is subject to the approval of the GATT and UNCTAD. ITC does not have a membership of its own but contracting parties of the GATT and members of UNCTAD are *de facto* members of ITC. Representatives of these governments meet annually at ITC's intergovernmental Joint Advisory Group (JAG).

The work of ITC involves technical co-operation in four main areas: institutional infrastructure, including business organizations, for trade promotion and export development; product and market research, development and promotion; import operations and techniques; and human resource development for trade promotion.

ADDRESS

Palais des Nations , CH-1211 Geneva 10, Switzerland
T. (41 22) 730 01 11 , Fx. (41 22) 733 44 39

SELECTED BIBLIOGRAPHY

Glover, Frederick J., *1964-1984: An Historical Account of Twenty Years of Service to Developing Countries and Annex: Principle Documentary Sources*, Geneva, Switzerland: ITC UNCTAD/GATT, 1984.

G.M.

111.01 – GENERAL AGREEMENT ON TARIFFS AND TRADE – GATT

Concluded : 30.10.1947, Geneva
In force : 01.01.1948
Parties : 110

The General Agreement is divided into four parts. Part I consists of the first two articles, which concern the most-favoured-nation obligation and bindings. Part II (Arts. III to XXIII) contains the substantive commercial policy provisions and Part III includes most of the procedural provisions and certain miscellaneous substantive provisions such as customs unions and free-trade areas (Art. XXIV). Part IV, added to the original agreement in 1964, deals with trade issues in regard to developing countries (Arts. XXXVI to XXXVIII).

GUIDING PRINCIPLES

The GATT system attempts to achieve its primary goal of international trade liberalization through various principles, the most important of which are:

- the non-discrimination principle expressed in most-favoured-nation treatment (MFN) and national treatment (NT);
- the exception to the non-discrimination principle in favour of regional preferences;
- the use of tariffs as the only acceptable form of protection and the reduction of tariffs through reciprocal concessions;
- the prohibition against quantitative restrictions (QRs);
- the possibility of safeguard, antidumping and antisubsidy measures; and
- the promotion of the trade of developing countries.

1. The Non-discrimination Principle
The most-favoured-nation (MFN) (Art. I) and national treatment (NT) (Art. III) principles together comprise the general non-discrimination principle formally introduced into international trade relations by the GATT.

The MFN standard requires that any "advantage, favour, privilege, or immunity" granted by one contracting party (CP) to a product of another country, in relation to imports or exports, will be accorded "immediately and unconditionally" to like products from all CPs. This provision has magnified the effect of tariff reductions as any tariff concession made by a CP is automatically made available to all other CPs. The clause applies not just to tariffs but also to the wide range of measures which can regulate goods through the complete process of bringing a product to market and selling it.

The National Treatment (NT) obligation (Art. III) requires that once goods from other CPs have entered a member state they must be treated, in regard to internal taxation and regulation, in the same manner as goods produced in that member state. Like the MFN clause, the scope of the NT clause is extremely wide and covers all laws, regulations and requirements affecting the sale, purchase, transportation, distribution and use of products in a domestic market.

General Exceptions: There are a number of exceptions to the MFN principle which allow for the preferential treatment of goods from certain CPs. These exceptions include preferential regional trading arrangements (e.g. customs unions and free trade areas) and discriminatory treatment in favour of developing countries (Part IV).

Other exceptions allow CPs to avoid specific GATT obligations. Thus, the CONTRACTING PARTIES may grant waivers from GATT obligations under Article XXV-5. Exceptions to protect national security are authorized under Article XXI. The possibility exists to impose antidumping duties against one trading partner only (as opposed to safeguard measures, which must be imposed in a non-discriminatory way – Art. XIX). Article XX provides for general exceptions to protect health, public morals and, significantly, the environment. This last exception is the source of increased debate as more trade-restrictive measures are implemented to protect the environment.

2. Regional Groupings

Although mentioned as an exception to the MFN principle, the right to form a regional economic grouping is a fundamental characteristic of the present international trading system. Regional arrangements are neither good nor bad for international trade and most economists would agree that only the practice of a regional arrangement can reveal its actual impact. While regional economic integration has never been prohibited by the GATT, Article XXIV attempts to impose conditions to ensure that regional groupings inside the GATT are "trade creative" generally. Probably because of the consensus principle, none of the notified regional groupings has ever been opposed by the Council.

The trend towards bilateral and regional preferential arrangements may, however, threaten the goal of multilateral trade liberalization in the long term. While the European Communities and the North American Free Trade Agreement, for instance, have increased, or are likely to increase, trade between their member states, they can also decrease trade between the region in question and other CPs. The conflict between the US and the EC on subsidies as well as the bilateral negotiations between the US and Japan on the "Structural Impediment Initiative" are evidence of some polarization between CPs.

3. Reciprocity of Tariff Concessions

Tariffs are taxes on the value, weight or volume of goods. They are the form of protection that the GATT authorizes as they are the most transparent and thus the most easily regulated. Tariff concessions in the GATT are made on a reciprocal basis.

The GATT's focus has primarily been on tariff reduction. This has been extremely effective, as reflected in the lowering of the average industrial tariff in developed countries from over 50 per cent in 1947 to approximately 5 per cent in 1990.

Prior to the Kennedy Round (1963-1967), tariff bindings were negotiated item by item with no particular binding being final until an agreement on all items being negotiated was reached. In the Kennedy Round, tariff bindings of industrialized countries moved to a linear approach whereby a country would offer to reduce its bindings by a set amount on an across the board basis. In the Tokyo Round (1973-1979), the linear approach was modified to allow for a larger proportion of higher tariff rates to be included in the Agreement than lower tariff rates. The use of this modified linear approach is estimated to have reduced the average tariff on durable industrial products by approximately 35 per cent.

4. Elimination of Quantitative Restrictions

Quantitative restrictions or quotas are restrictions on the number, volume, value or origin of imported goods. They are prohibited by Article XI primarily because they stifle competition and because their administration is less transparent than tariffs.

There are, however, many exceptions to the general prohibition. The main ones include permitting the use of quotas on imports of agricultural and fish products where quotas are necessary to implement government measures designed to stabilize national markets in the affected product (Article XI-2). Thus, Japan can use this provision to restrict its rice market, and Canada and other countries can use it to operate their supply management systems through marketing boards.

As well, Article XII permits the use of quotas on a temporary basis during a balance of payments crisis and Article XVIII allows quotas to be used by developing countries to assist in the establishment of a particular industry for the purpose of furthering national economic development.

Voluntary Export Agreements (VEAs) – that is, agreements between a state and a firm or a group of firms limiting the number of exports from one country – and Voluntary Export Restraints (VERs), alleged to be voluntary restrictions on exports from one state to another, bypass the GATT prohibition on quota restrictions. Under the Uruguay Round proposals, VERs and similar arrangements would be prohibited. However, antidumping and antisubsidy actions would still be outside GATT control and could be used in place of VERs by CPs to restrict import levels.

5. Safeguard Measures, Antidumping and Antisubsidy Actions

Article XIX allows a CP to take temporary protective measures in the face of a sudden increase in fairly traded imports which are causing or threaten to cause serious injury to a domestic industry. In such circumstances the affected CP is to take action only to the extent necessary, on a temporary basis. The GATT's safeguard clause is a form of the usual "safety-valve" provision found in most trade agreements. Safeguard measures must be imposed on a non-discriminatory basis after notification to the GATT secretariat and compensation must be offered to CPs.

In practice, this clause has proved to a certain extent ineffective. CPs often bypass GATT control by using VERs or VEAs (grey area measures outside the scope of the GATT) or by resorting to antidumping and antisubsidy actions.

6. The GATT and the Developing Countries

From its very beginning the GATT has struggled with the role and place of developing countries within the GATT system. At the centre of this struggle has been the extent to which developing countries should be subject to the full discipline of the GATT principles and standards. The GATT's history shows that the result of this struggle has been continual movement towards lessening the extent of these obligations. Such action is becoming even more imperative now for many reasons, including the fact that today developing countries make up the vast majority of CPs and countries associated with the GATT. Five of the major steps in this evolution within the GATT are as follows:

Amendment of Article XVIII – Governmental Assistance to Economic Development (1955): These were the first major amendments to the GATT to deal with the specific circumstances of developing countries. They allowed the governments of these countries to take actions inconsistent with GATT principles in order to protect infant industries and deal with balance of payment problems.

Adoption of Part IV – Trade and Development (1964): Part IV was added to the General Agreement to clarify the position of developing countries within the GATT system. Developing countries would not be required to make the same concessions as developed countries on tariffs or on the removal of non-tariff barriers (note particularly Article XXXVI-8). Part IV does not, however, provide a specific legal basis for preferential arrangements with or between developing countries.

The Creation of the ITC (1964): As part of the effort to help developing countries expand trade, on 19 March 1964, in parallel to the adoption of Part IV of the GATT, the CONTRACTING PARTIES created the International Trade Centre [see 111 C]. Today this Centre is a semi-autonomous institution under the joint sponsorship of GATT and UNCTAD.

The General System of Preferences (1971): Pursuant to waiver granted under Article XXV-5, developed countries were authorized to grant, for a period of ten years, preferential treatment (i.e. lower tariffs) to developing countries on a wide range of goods [see 111.05]. Although labelled preferential, it has been argued that the GSP has had the dubious effect of forming patterns of trade for developing countries which are determined by developed countries.

The Tokyo Round Decisions (1979): Three decisions were made at the end of the Tokyo Round which affected the differential treatment granted to developing countries under the GATT. The first and most important of these was "Differential and More Favourable Treatment Reciprocity and Fuller Participation of Developing Countries" (L/4903), more commonly referred to as the "Enabling Clause" [see 111.15]. Its primary purpose was to institutionalize the right of developing countries to grant preferential treatment to developing countries, instead of its being reliant on a waiver. The Enabling Clause also provided for the extension of the General System of Preferences established in 1971 [see 111.05].

The other two decisions dealt with trade measures which developing countries could take when there was a balance of payments crisis [see 111.16] and to safeguard infant industries [see 111.17].

Gabrielle Marceau and Hugh J. Cheetham

Access : CON (Art. XXXIII)
Reserves : PAU (Art. XXXI, XXXV)
Duration : USP
Deposit. : GATT, UN (Art. XXVI)
Language : Eng, Fre (Art. XXVI)

Modific. :Protocol (Dillon Round) 1962 (15.08.62); Supplementary Protocol 1963 (07.07.63); Protocol (Kennedy Round) 1967 (01.01.68); Supplementary Protocol 1967 (-); Protocol 1971 (11.02.73); Protocol (Tokyo Round) 1979 (01.01.80); Supplementary Protocol 1979 (01.01.80)

Reference :BISD 1969 – 55, 440, 441, 501, 620-629, 858 UNTS – Can TS 1947/27, 1948/12, 1948/30, 1948/31, 1951/6, 1968/19, 1981/20, 1981/41 – 1 Paeslee – UST 31/2

111.02 – HAVANA CHARTER ESTABLISHING AN INTERNATIONAL TRADE ORGANIZATION – UN

Concluded : 24.03.1948, Havana

The Havana Charter was intended to establish, within the UN system, a multilateral trade organization, the International Trade Organization (ITO), to administer and co-ordinate economic activities of states and enterprises affecting international trade. Through promoting international co-operation in the fields of trade and employment, the ITO was to contribute towards the United Nations' goal of global "stability and well-being which are necessary for peaceful and friendly relations among nations" (Art. 1).

The Charter was divided into nine chapters. The first laid down the Charter's purposes and objectives, and the remaining chapters dealt with the following subjects: fair labour standards and employment (Chapter II); specific needs of European reconstruction and the special rights of developing countries (Chapter III); a wide range of commercial policies that affect the flow of trade, namely, tariffs, preferences, internal taxation, regulation, quotas, subsidies, dumping and safeguarding measures (Chapter IV); standards relating to restrictive business practices used by firms (Chapter V); intergovernmental commodity agreements (Chapter VI); the structure and function of the ITO (Chapter VII); the settlement of disputes (Chapter VIII); and general provisions such as trading relations with non-members and security exceptions (Chapter IX). Disputes under the provisions could be referred to the International Court of Justice [see 001 B] or to arbitration.

In light of the current debate taking place in the Uruguay Round over the need to address domestic regulation, trade in services, barriers to investments, and all trade-related areas including intellectual property rights, the Havana Charter prophetically reflects the present negotiators' desires to co-ordinate all aspects of commercial policies in international trade. The idea of the ITO also has many parallels with the Uruguay Round's proposed Multilateral Trade Organization. Moreover, the emphasis put on the relationship between domestic employment and international trade (Chapter I) is also indicative of the Uruguay Round negotiators' conviction that international stability and well-being can only be achieved by relating and integrating domestic and external economic policies.

G.M. and H.J.C.

Reference : UN Doc. E/CONF.2/78 – Can TS 1948/32

111.03 – CONSTITUTION OF THE UNITED NATIONS CONFERENCE ON TRADE AND DEVELOPMENT – UNCTAD

Adopted : 30.12.1964, UNGA Res.1995(XIX)

The aspirations of developing countries were somewhat dampened after the GATT negotiations of 1960-1961 as they believed their interests had not been properly taken into account. In the meeting of ministers of the CONTRACTING PARTIES of the GATT in 1961, the need for some concessions in favour of developing countries was raised. Also in 1961, the UN General Assembly expressly recognized the need for special treatment for underdeveloped countries [Res. 1707(XVI) 1961].

In 1962 the UN General Assembly recommended that ECOSOC [see 001 A] convene the UN Conference on Trade and Development. Between 1962 and 1964, UNCTAD was formed and its purpose was to claim preferential treatment for developing countries along similar lines to Article 15 of the Havana Charter [see 111.02].

On 30 December 1964, the UN General Assembly, under Article 22 of the UN Charter, formally recognized UNCTAD as one of its permanent bodies, and its Charter was adopted by Resolution 1995(XIX). One of the fundamental aspects of the Charter is expressed in General Principle VIII, which advocates an exception to the GATT most-favoured-nation principle in favour of developing countries.

The formation of UNCTAD paved the way towards the adoption of Part IV of the GATT and led to the adoption of the Generalized System of Preferences [see 111.05] and the Global System of Trade Preferences [see 111.20].

G.M.

Modific. :UNGA Res.2904(XXVII) (26.09.72); Res.31/2 A (29.09.76); 31/2 B (21.12.76); Res.34/3 (04.10.79)

111.04 – INTERNATIONAL TRADE CENTRE CNUCED/GATT – ITC

Adopted : 12.12.1967, UNGA Res.2297(XXII)
In force : 01.01.1968

The International Trade Centre was established by the CONTRACTING PARTIES of the GATT on 19 March 1964. In 1968 the United Nations, through UNCTAD, joined the GATT as a co-sponsor of ITC. The resolution approving this joint sponsorship was adopted by the UN General Assembly on 12 December 1967 (Res. 2297(XXII) and took effect on 1 January 1968 [see 111 C].

111.05 – GENERALIZED SYSTEM OF PREFERENCES – UNCTAD

Adopted : 13.10.1970, Dec.75 (S-IV)

The UN General Assembly launched the idea of preferential treatment and tariff preferences for developing countries in 1961. UNCTAD [see 111 B], established between 1962 and 1964, continued to promote the idea of preferential treatment to developing countries, and in 1965 the OECD set up a Special Group on Preferences which acknowledged the need for tariff preferences in favour of developing countries. In 1968 UNCTAD reached a unanimous agreement on the proposed Generalized System of Preferences (GSP). A Special Committee on Preferences was established as a subsidiary organ of UNCTAD's Trade and Development Board. Developed countries participated in the negotiations through the OECD.

On 12 October 1970, the Special Committee on Preferences adopted a text entitled "Agreed Conclusions" which defines the modalities of the system. In October 1970, the Trade and Development Board, in its Decision 75(S-IV), adopted the report of the Special Committee on Preferences, which is legally recognized as an informal international agreement. This decision of the Trade and Development Board is called the Generalized System of Preferences (GSP).

The GSP is essentially a tariff policy for developing countries. It was to be a system through which developed countries could give preferential tariff treatment to manufactured or semi-finished exports from developing countries for a minimum period of ten years. It was to be a generalized system of non-reciprocal and non-discriminatory preferences on manufactured goods in favour of the developing countries.

The developed countries, known as "donors" (members of the OECD and formerly of COMECON), may make arrangements for non-reciprocal and non-discriminatory preferences for manufactured and semi-finished exports from both the developing countries and the countries of Central and Eastern Europe, the "beneficiaries". This may be by way of offers or individual schemes of preferences.

The individual national schemes of preferences resulting from the Generalized System of Preferences were extended beyond their initial period of ten years.

The GSP, as an exception to the MFN principle of the GATT [see 111.01], needed to be authorized by the CONTRACTING PARTIES. In 1971, the CONTRACTING PARTIES granted a waiver for a renewable period of ten years under GATT Article XXV-5 to countries covered by Part IV of the GATT. The limited procedure of a waiver was used in order to avoid Part IV being given a broader interpretation of including preferences. During the Tokyo Round the so-called enabling clause gave full and permanent legitimacy to this system of preferences.

While the GSP is preferential and non-reciprocal, it is not in fact general or non-discriminatory. The GSP, as well as the Enabling Clause, is essentially an authorization for developed countries to grant preferences to the developing countries of their choice. The granting state can select the receiving state and establish conditions. Developed countries have never agreed on a common and generalized policy through the GSP.

G.M.

111.06 – ARRANGEMENT REGARDING INTERNATIONAL TRADE IN TEXTILES, AND PROTOCOL ("MULTIFIBRE AGREEMENT") – GATT

Concluded : 20.12.1973, Geneva
In force : 01.01.1974
Parties : 37

Although negotiated under the auspices of the GATT, the Multifibre Agreement (MFA) has its own institutional framework and sets out the rules and regulations for trade in textiles between the major importing and exporting countries. There were some 37 parties to the 1986 Protocol Extending the Arrangement Regarding International Trade in Textiles (Protocol of Extension) to the current MFA, including major trading partners like the US, Japan and the EC.

The initial response to quantitative restraints on trade in cotton textiles during the 1950s led to the adoption of the Short-Term Arrangement (STA) from 1961-1962 and the Long-Term Arrangement (LTA) from 1962-1974, as extended. The advent of man-made, chemical fibres like polyester and nylon made the LTA obsolete and a new multilateral agreement, the MFA, was adopted in 1974 to replace the outdated LTA.

Originally approved for a period of four years, it has since been extended on three separate occasions, in 1977, 1981 and 1986. The MFA, as extended under the 1986 Protocol, includes not only cotton, wool and man-made fibres but also silk blends and certain textiles made from vegetable fibres (Para 24 of Protocol of Extension).

The objectives of the MFA are on the one hand to progressively liberalize the world trade in textiles products, to promote developing countries' exports and to encourage adjustment by the developed countries in their textile industries. On the other hand, it seeks to ensure the orderly and equitable development of the textiles market, to avoid market disruption and to ensure the "orderly" growth in the textile trade (Art. 1).

OPERATION

There are two key components to the operation of the MFA. First, the agreement allows for the importing countries to safeguard domestic production and supply by introducing restraints, in the form of quotas, based on quantity. Safeguards can usually be imposed under one or two procedures. As a normal procedure under Article 3, a participating country must first determine that its market is being "disrupted" by imports of particular textiles products, as defined in Annex A to the Agreement. The importing country is then under a duty to consult with the participating country (or countries) exporting the particular product (temporary restraints are provided for in Art. 3-6). The two sides can then agree to restrict trade in that product but only within the parameters of Annex B to the Agreement.

Should parties fail to reach agreement within 60 days, the importing country may proceed with unilateral restraints but at a level not less than provided in Annex B (Art. 3-5). Unilateral restraints may not exceed one year although they can be extended by agreement subject to the terms of Annex B (Art. 3-8). Likewise, an importing country can also initiate a new Article 3 procedure once the original restraints expire.

Second, the Agreement operates a well-known loop-hole, by allowing participating importing countries to negotiate separate bilateral agreements with exporting countries, thereby opening the way to bilaterally-managed trade in textiles within the framework of a multilateral agreement. Thus, under the MFA, restraints can be implemented under Article 4 to eliminate "real risks of market disruption" while allowing for the orderly and equitable growth of trade even though the term "real risks" remains undefined (Art. 4-2). A determination of "market disruption" according to Annex A "shall be based on the existence of serious damage to domestic producers or actual threat thereof". The Annex then proceeds to list the factors to be considered in determining "serious damage" (Annex A, Paragraph II).

Article 4-3 limits the MFA safeguard mechanism by specifying that these bilateral agreements shall "on overall terms, including base levels and growth rates, be more liberal than" Article 3 measures. The base level for imported goods, the growth rate of the base level and standards of flexibility are set out in Annex B. Some importing countries have argued that some of the provisions of this Article may be less liberal than Annex B otherwise requires but that this is acceptable if the agreement is more liberal "overall". However, many of these bilateral arrangements establish procedures for imposing additional restraints on products not specifically regulated at the outset.

The MFA encourages participating countries to grant more favourable terms with regard to restrictions on the exports of developing countries (Art. 6-1) although in practice it has remained largely ineffectual since the majority of MFA restraints have been aimed at developing country exports. This same article also urges special treatment for new entrants, small suppliers and cotton producers and for products sent abroad for processing and subsequent re-importation (Art. 6-6).

Under Article 8-1, parties to the MFA agree not to circumvent the Agreement through "trans-shipment, re-routing or action by non-participants" and to co-operate administratively in avoiding circumvention (Art. 8-2). Likewise, Article 8-3 provides measures designed to assure that participating countries' exports against which measures are taken, under Articles 3 and 4, shall not be restrained more severely than exports of similar goods from non-participants.

STRUCTURE

Another important feature of the MFA is its institution of a supervisory mechanism and dispute settlement procedures. Article 10 establishes the **Textiles Committee** (TC) which, as required by the GATT, consists of representatives of all participating countries. It reports to the GATT Council at least annually on the operation of the MFA and conducts studies on the textile trade (Arts. 10-2 and 10-4). The TC may also, upon request, give its opinion on any dispute involving "divergence of view between the participating countries as to the interpretation or application" of the MFA (Art. 10-3).

Article 11 establishes a **Textiles Surveillance Body** (TSB) to supervise the implementation of the MFA and to settle disputes among participants. It consists of a Chairman and ten members (increased from eight members in 1989), drawn equally from the importing and exporting textile countries. The TSB is a standing body and meets as necessary "to supervise the implementation" of the MFA (Arts. 11-1 and 11-2). It also reviews all restrictions on the trade in textiles annually, as well as a wide variety of actions notified to it under Articles 3 and 4 (Arts. 11-11 and 11-12).

The TSB acts as a conciliator of bilateral negotiations and disputes (Arts. 3-5(ii), 9-3, 11-4 and 11-5). In the case of Article 3 "restraints" procedures, the TSB is authorized to determine "whether the agreement is justified" in accordance with the terms of the MFA (Art. 3-4). However, in most other cases, it is authorized only to make recommendations to the parties concerned (e.g. Arts. 3-5(iii) and 4-4). Participating countries are required only to "endeavour to accept in full" such recommendations although if they do not follow them they must give reasons for not doing so (Art. 11-8).

The TSB can impose no sanctions although it may refer matters to the TC or the GATT Council (e.g. Art. 3-5(iii)) and its observations and recommendations are to be "taken into account" during proceedings before the GATT CONTRACTING PARTIES (Art. 11-9 and 11-10).

MODIFICATIONS

The 1986 Protocol of Extension (the "Protocol") extended the Agreement until 31 July 1991, whereupon it was further extended until 31 December 1992 and latterly by a further year until 31 December 1993. Like the predecessor Protocols of Extension, it has two parts: a brief formal Protocol and a set of "Conclusions of the Textiles Committee" which details agreed changes to the functioning of the Arrangement. The Conclusions are expressly incorporated as "an integral part" of the Protocol (Para. 1).

The Protocol continues the managed trade in textiles, by extending product coverage from cotton and original MFA fibres through to essentially all textile fibres (Para. 24). Paragraph 3 of the Protocol stipulates that the participants have "agreed that the final objective is the application of GATT rules to trade in textiles". Paragraph 8 deals with import "surges" that sometimes occur after expiration of unilateral Article 3 restraints. Originally limited to one year's duration under MFA III, the 1986 Protocol allows that a restraint previously applied may be extended for one further period of 12 months.

Paragraph 10 of the Protocol includes special consideration for "predominant" textile-exporting countries on reaching mutually satisfactory agreements with importing countries on growth rates although at the same time the latter shall limit their demands for re-negotiation of restraint agreements. Paragraph 11 authorizes exporting and importing countries to agree upon reductions in established restraint levels to deal with import "surges" within previously under-utilized MFA quotas ("anti-surge mechanisms"), with compensation payable by importing countries where appropriate.

Paragraph 13 of the Protocol expands upon Article 6 of the MFA with respect to special treatment for developing countries, extended to include "least developed countries", as well as special recognition for cotton producers and other particularly vulnerable groups. Paragraph 18 requires participating countries to avoid, as far as possible, changes in rules of origin, product classification schemes (including the introduction of the harmonized system of tariff nomenclature) and other rules and procedures likely to adversely affect participants.

The 1986 Protocol further strengthens the supervisory mechanism of the MFA (Paras. 19 to 23); in particular the TSB has been given a new power to interpret MFA provisions (Para. 22). Finally, for the first time, Paragraph 27 introduces a completely new subject into the MFA – the infringement of registered trademarks and designs in the trade in textiles and clothing, favouring national regulation as the means to deal with the associated problems.

Despite the improvements introduced into the 1986 Protocol, it remains hard to justify the continued existence of an agreement which is clearly in breach of the main aims of the GATT and there have been repeated calls to subject the MFA to the rules and discipline of the GATT. Whilst there has been general agreement that the MFA should be phased out, there is plenty of disagreement as to the exact mode and the time-frame in which this should be done. Worse still, it has been left to the present, protracted round of Multilateral Trade Negotiations, the Uruguay Round, to try to resolve this by seeking to secure the eventual integration of the textiles and clothing sector into the GATT on the basis of strengthened GATT rules and disciplines.

The proposed means of achieving this is to phase out restraints, in a three-stage procedure, over a ten-year period, initially intended to commence on 1 January 1993, which would culminate in the integration of all products by 1 January 2003. For products remaining under restraint, at whatever stage, the Uruguay Round agreement on textiles lays down a formula for increasing existing growth rates.

Whilst the Agreement focuses largely on the phasing out of MFA restrictions, it also recognizes that members can maintain non-MFA restrictions, not justified under any GATT provision, subject to their being brought into conformity with the GATT within one year of entry into force of a Uruguay Round agreement, or their progressive phasing out.

The new Agreement also provides for possible anti-circumvention commitments including trans-shipment, re-routing, false declaration as to country of origin and falsification of official documents; a specific transitional safeguard mechanism for products not yet integrated into the GATT at any stage; all MFA members should seek to abide by GATT rules and disciplines so as to improve market access and to ensure the application of policies relating to fair and equitable trading conditions, and they should avoid discriminating for general trade policy reasons against textile imports. A new institution, the **Textiles Monitoring Body** (TMB), would be established to oversee the implementation of commitments and to conduct a major review prior to the end of each stage.

Mary E. Footer

SELECTED BIBLIOGRAPHY

Blokker, J., *International Regulation of World Trade in Textiles*, Deventer; Boston: Kluwer Law and Taxation, 1989.

Access : CON (Art. 13)
Reserves : USP
Duration : REN (Art. 16)
Deposit. : GATT (Art. 13-1)
Language : Eng, Fre, Spa

Modific. :Protocols extending the Arrangement 14.12.77 (01.01.78); 29.12.81 (01.01.82); 31.07.86 (01.08.86); 31.07.91 (01.12.91); 09.12.92 (01.01.93)

Reference : BISD 21, 24, S28/3, S33/7 – Can TS 1978/28 – UST 25/1

111.07 – AGREEMENT ON TECHNICAL BARRIERS TO TRADE – GATT

Concluded : 12.04.1979, Geneva
In force : 01.01.1980
Parties : 35

The Standards Code expands the provisions of the GATT on product standards (GATT, Art. X). It seeks to ensure that unnecessary obstacles to international trade are not created by technical regulations and standards – including packaging, marketing and labelling requirements – nor by methods for certifying conformity with those regulations and standards (the Preamble and Art. 2-1). The national treatment obligation is reinforced. Signatories may adapt technical regulations and standards which are appropriate to their needs, provided these do not create unnecessary obstacles to trade. Signatories are also encouraged to use international standards as much as possible.

As well as these substantive rules, the Code outlines procedural rules on the development of product standards by signatories and on transparency in their application. It requires adequate notice and opportunity to comply with new standards prior to their implementation and, during the formulation stage, the rule-making process allows for input by signatories.

The Code does not apply to services, technical specifications included in government procurement contracts or standards established by companies for their own use. A Committee on Technical Barriers to Trade supervises the Agreement and deals with consultation and dispute settlement processes provided for under the Agreement.

Notwithstanding the introduction of this Agreement, signatories still face the problem of contracting parties' not recognizing product testing conducted in the exporting state prior to importation.

Gabrielle Marceau and Hugh J. Cheetham

Access : CON (Art. 15)
Reserves : CST (Art. 15)
Duration : USP
Deposit. : GATT (Art. 15)
Language : Eng, Fre, Spa

Reference : BISD 26 – Can TS 1980/41 – UST 31/1 – ILM 18:1079

111.08 – AGREEMENT ON GOVERNMENT PROCUREMENT – GATT

Concluded : 12.04.1979, Geneva
In force : 01.01.1981
Parties : 12

Article III-8 of the GATT sets out possibly the most important exception to the national treatment obligation: procurement by government agencies for government purposes. The problems associated with this exception became evident by the 1970s with the increased size and role of governments in national economies. Discrimination in favour of domestic producers was widespread as a result of this exception being used by governments as a means of stimulating national economic growth. This situation led to the negotiation of the present Agreement.

Scope: The Agreement provides that non-discriminatory national treatment rules are to apply to purchases of goods made by government bodies. It originally set out a threshold contract value of SDR 150,000. This threshold amount was recently reduced to SDR 130,000 (BISD 33 Supp. 19 [1987]). The scope of the Agreement is, however, limited to those agencies listed in Annex 1 of the Agreement. Certain sectors – for example, transport, farming, defence, postal services and others – are specifically excluded. The Agreement does not apply to contracts for services unless these are incidental to a sale of goods (e.g. financing and insurance).

Notwithstanding these significant restrictions which narrow the application of the Agreement, it does provide a first step and a basis for future negotiations to expand both the list of agencies subject to it and the scope of its application. The lowering of the threshold amount in 1987 is encouraging in this regard.

DETAILS OF THE AGREEMENT

The Agreement sets out a procedure for the bidding process and establishes rules for such matters as public announcements of tenders, qualification of bidders, time limits and tender documents, and so on. It also contains a dispute settlement procedure which is initiated through bilateral consultations between the governments of the supplier and buyer. If these consultations are not successful, the parties move to a multilateral conciliation procedure.

However, this obligation, as with any other obligation undertaken by contracting parties, binds only the federal jurisdiction of a federal state (such as the US or Australia), not the provinces or the states. Since state and provincial governments are often very important actors in the economic activities of any country, this Code has limited impact. Article XXIV-12, which will be maintained under the Uruguay Round proposals, fortunately has been interpreted as limiting the rights of federal states to be exempted from non-compliance for purchases made by regional and local governments and authorities within their territory. This remains an issue of some debate between the EC and the US.

G.M. and H.J.C.

Access : CON (Art. IX-1)
Reserves : PRO (Art. IX-2)
Duration : USP
Deposit. : GATT (Art. IX-12)
Language : Eng, Fre, Spa

Modific. : Protocol 02.02.87 (14.02.88)

Reference : BISD 26, 33/19 S34/12 – Can TS 1981/39 – ILM 18:1052

111.09 – AGREEMENT ON INTERPRETATION AND APPLICATION OF ARTICLES VI, XVI AND XXIII ("SUBSIDIES CODE") – GATT

Concluded : 12.04.1979, Geneva
In force : 01.01.1980
Parties : 28

The fundamental principle of the GATT is one of free competition for trade whereby the most efficient firm of any nationality should win the favours of customers world-wide. This trade race should therefore not be distorted by governmental intervention. Hence, Article VI provides that countervailing duties (taxes) may be imposed by a contracting party (CP) to offset trade-distorting government subsidies in aid of the production and exportation of goods elsewhere. In addition to this fundamental rule, the Agreement attempts to regulate subsidies through three other provisions: (i) a loose requirement to report and notify subsidies (Article XVI-1); (ii) the restraint of export subsidies (Article XVI-3 and 4); and (iii) the creation of rights in respect of new production subsidies (Art. XXIII).

The Subsidies Code attempts to step up the regulation of subsidies by first giving direction as to the manner in which subsidy complaint investigations are to be carried out by domestic agencies. In particular, these provisions of the Code increase the threshold for a finding of material injury. The Code also seeks to provide more guidance as to the meaning of a subsidy. This is done primarily through a list of illustrative examples set out in an Annex to the Code (the list is based on a list prepared by a 1960 Working Party). The list is not, however, definitive and this has been the principal reason for the Code's failure to restrain the application of countervailing duties.

Subsidies are at the heart of conflicts in international trade. However, the identification and exact calculation of subsidies is a difficult issue. Direct and indirect taxation and other financial burdens have to be considered in addition to direct financial support. In the aerospace industry, for instance, Germany has argued that the real level of US government support for its civil aviation industry is far greater than in Europe. Some have also argued that the US has always strongly supported its military aviation and authorized the civil aviation industry to benefit from research and other developments brought about by military programmes.

G.M.

Access : CON (Art. 19-2)
Reserves : CST (Art. 19-3)
Duration : USP
Deposit. : GATT (Art. 19-12)
Language : Eng, Fre, Spa

Reference : BISD 26 – Can TS 1980/42 – UST 31/1 – ILM 18:579

111.10 – AGREEMENT ON IMPORT LICENSING PROCEDURES – GATT

Concluded : 12.04.1979, Geneva
In force : 01.01.1980
Parties : 27

Quotas are one of the main barriers to trade. This form of discretionary protectionism is administered primarily through the use of import licensing. Under a licensing system, the importing country only allows imports to be brought in by a licensed importer and then only up to the volume or amount that the importer's licence provides. Article XI-1 of the GATT addresses import licensing in its general prohibition against quotas but does not directly consider its use.

The Tokyo Round Agreement attempted to rectify this by focusing on the procedures used in administering the licensing process. The abuse of these procedures has been considered as a source of significant delay and corruption in the issuing of licences. The Agreement is designed to simplify procedures and ensure fairness in administration.

Articles II and III of the Agreement oblige signatories to avoid using licensing procedures in a manner which restricts trade. Thus, signatories are required to publish information about quotas, to provide that any restrictions apply equally to all applicants, and to ensure that licences remain in force for reasonable periods of time.

Notwithstanding these attempts to inject some transparency into the import licence-issuing procedure, the Agreement has not attracted a large number of signatories, reflecting the desire of many countries to retain as much discretionary control as possible over the impact of trade policy on their economies.

Gabrielle Marceau and Hugh J. Cheetham

Access : CON (Art. 5-1)
Reserves : CST (Art. 5-2)
Duration : USP
Deposit. : GATT (Art. 5-10)
Language : Eng, Fre, Spa

Reference : BISD 26 – Can TS 1980/40 – UST 32/2

111.11 – AGREEMENT ON IMPLEMENTATION OF ARTICLE VI ("ANTIDUMPING CODE") – GATT

Concluded : 12.04.1979, Geneva
In force : 01.01.1980
Parties : 25

For economists, dumping refers to the practice of selling goods in a foreign market at a lower price than the price of similar goods in the exporter's home market. Article VI of the GATT was enacted in order to restrain actions of contracting parties against dumping by foreign firms. It authorizes member states to impose antidumping duties against dumped goods in their territory equal to the margin of dumping – that is, the difference in prices.

By the 1960s, antidumping actions had increased. An attempt to address this trend was made during the Kennedy Round (1963-1967) and resulted in the adoption of an Antidumping Code. This Code intended to clarify the broad definitions found in Article VI, to provide procedural requirements in antidumping investigations and to bring all signatories into conformity with the GATT.

Dissatisfaction with the 1967 Code (brought about primarily because the US did not ratify it) led to further negotiations on a revised Code during the Tokyo Round (1973-1979) in conformity with the Subsidies Code which had just been negotiated. The principal changes from the 1967 Code were the elimination of the requirement that dumping be the "principal" cause of injury, the inclusion of a procedure for accepting exporters' undertakings, the prohibition on retroactive assessment, the limitation of provisional duties and new arrangements for the resolution of disputes.

An important element of the 1979 Antidumping Code was to sanction the US practice since 1974 of considering sales below full costs of production in the home market of the exporter outside the "ordinary course of trade" and therefore excluding them from the price comparison. This extension of the concept "in the ordinary course of trade" has legitimized a second definition of dumping: it is now accepted that national antidumping laws require that prices of imports cover their full cost of production.

One of the main problems of antidumping determination is that prices used for the comparison, as well as the costs of production, are often constructed unilaterally by national antidumping authorities according to the "best available information". Determination of injury caused to the domestic industry has transformed antidumping laws into very strategic trade instruments. Unfortunately the Uruguay Round proposals would not change in any important way the definition of dumping nor clarify the level of injury required for the imposition of antidumping duties.

G.M.

Access : CON (Art. 16-2)
Reserves : CST (Art. 16-3)
Duration : USP
Deposit. : GATT (Art. 16-12)
Language : Eng, Fre, Spa

Reference : BISD 26 – Can TS 1980/43 – ILM 18:621

111.12 – ARRANGEMENT REGARDING BOVINE MEAT – GATT

Concluded : 12.04.1979, Geneva
In force : 01.01.1980
Parties : 26

Since its inception agricultural products have been *de facto* excluded from the discipline of the GATT. Although the Tokyo Round was not able to produce any comprehensive agreement on agriculture, it was able however to complete more narrow negotiations on two agricultural products: bovine meat and dairy products.

The bovine meat agreement covers live bovine animals, meat and edible offal of bovine animals, fresh, chilled, frozen, salted, in brine, dried or smoked as well as other prepared or preserved meat or offal of bovine animals. Any other product may be added by the International Meat Council (IMC).

The IMC is also the body designated to hear disputes between parties to the agreement and it may make recommendations on the dispute on a consensual basis.

G.M. and H.J.C.

Access : ALS (Art. VI-1-a)
Reserves : PAU (Art. VI-1 b)
Duration : REN 3 (Art. VI-4)
Deposit. : GATT (Art. VI-1-c)
Language : Eng, Fre, Spa (Art. VI-1-c)

Reference : BISD 26 – Can TS 1980/38 – UST 32/2

111.13 – INTERNATIONAL DAIRY AGREEMENT – GATT

Concluded : 12.04.1979, Geneva
In force : 01.01.1980
Parties : 16

The International Dairy Agreement was adopted during the Tokyo Round and follows the same pattern as the Arrangement Regarding Bovine Meat. Dairy products covered under the dairy products agreement include milk and cream, concentrated or not, sweetened or not, butter, cheese and curd, and casein as well as any other product that the International Dairy Products Council (IDPC) may decide to add.

This Agreement establishes specific committees to deal with certain milk powders, milk fat and certain cheeses and fixes minimum export prices for each of these products.

The Agreement includes a commitment to co-operate with the Food and Agricultural Organization (FAO) [see 131 A] in food aid. Disputes under the Agreement are heard by the IDPC on a consensual basis.

G.M. and H.J.C.

Access : ALS (Art. VIII-1-a)
Reserves : CST (Art. VIII-1-b)
Duration : REN 3 (Art. VIII-4)
Deposit. : GATT (Art. VIII-1-c)
Language : Eng, Fre, Spa (Art. VIII-1-c)

Reference : BISD 26 – UST 31/1

111.14 – AGREEMENT ON TRADE IN CIVIL AIRCRAFT – GATT

Concluded : 12.04.1979, Geneva
In force : 01.01.1980
Parties : 22

The security exception of Article XXI of the GATT has always allowed states to exclude military machinery from the scope of the General Agreement, including aircraft. This Agreement seeks to ensure that civil aircraft is covered under a separate agreement. It provides for the duty-free treatment of civil aircraft and engines and all their parts, components and sub-assemblies, as well as all ground flight simulators. The Agreement also calls for purchasers of civil aircraft to have the freedom to select suppliers and repair services on the basis of commercial and technological factors. Quotas and import-licensing requirements imposed in a manner inconsistent with the GATT are expressly prohibited. These provisions were designed to reduce pressure on government-owned airlines to buy domestically-produced aircraft.

Importantly, the Agreement imposes obligations relating to subsidies on signatories trading in civil aircraft, as provided in the Agreement on Interpretation and Application of Articles VI, XVI and XXIII [see 111.09] and in the Agreement on Technical Barriers to Trade [see 111.07]. Special procedures for surveillance, review, consultation and settlement of disputes are administered by the Committee on Trade in Civil Aircraft.

An annex contains a list of goods covered by the Agreement, and products are often added to this list at annual reviews. Military airplanes and related products are expressly excluded.

G.M. and H.J.C.

Access : CON (Art. 9-1)
Reserves : CST (Art. 9-2)
Duration : USP
Deposit. : GATT (Art. 9-10)
Language : Eng, Fre

Modific. : 17.01.83 (17.01.83); 27.01.84 (27.01.84); 01.01.85 (01.01.85); Protocol 02.12.86 (01.01.88)

Reference : BISD 26, S30/4, S31/4, S31/5, S34/24 – Can TS 1980/39 – UST 31/1

111.15 – DIFFERENTIAL AND MORE FAVOURABLE TREATMENT, RECIPROCAL, AND MORE COMPLETE PARTICIPATION OF DEVELOPING COUNTRIES ("ENABLING CLAUSE") – GATT

Adopted : 28.11.1979, Dec.L-4903

This decision was made at the Tokyo Round in 1979. More commonly referred to as the "Enabling Clause", the decision provided for the extension of the General System of Preferences (GSP), originally established in 1971 [see 111.05]. It provides a permanent legal framework, within the multilateral system, for different and more favourable treatment of developing countries.

G.M. and H.J.C.

Reference : BISD 26

111.16 – TRADE MEASURES TAKEN FOR BALANCE OF PAYMENTS – GATT

Adopted : 28.11.1979, Dec.L-4907

This decision, also taken at the Tokyo Round, imposes additional conditions to those in the GATT regarding the use of restrictive import measures taken for balance of payment purposes. It provides a basis, primarily for developing countries, for the use of measures other than quotas (e.g. tariff surcharges) in the face of balance of payment difficulties. This view is reflected in the changes to Article XVIII incorporated in the decision.

G.M. and H.J.C.

Reference : BISD 26

111.17 – SAFEGUARD ACTION FOR DEVELOPMENT PURPOSES – GATT

Adopted : 28.11.1979, Dec.L/4.897

This decision interprets Sections A and C of Article XVIII with less rigidity. It allows the use of balance of payment measures by developing countries in regard to the development, modification or extension of production structures (i.e. infant industries).

G.M. and H.J.C.

Reference : BISD 26

111.18 – UNDERSTANDING REGARDING NOTIFICATION, CONSULTATION, DISPUTE SETTLEMENT AND SURVEILLANCE – GATT

Adopted : 28.11.1979, Dec.L-4907

This Understanding reinforced the new rule-oriented approach to which the contracting parties had returned in the seventies. It codified the practice of creating "advisory" panels – although panels are not formally mentioned in Article XXIII-2

(GATT). An "Agreed description of the customary practice of the GATT in the field of dispute settlement", initially adopted in 1966, was attached to maintain past practice.

The Understanding set out the composition of panels and their terms of reference, to be determined within 30 days of a request for a panel. The task of panels was to "assist the Parties to deal with the matter", including an objective assessment of the facts of the case and the applicability of and conformity with the General Agreement. Their power of enquiry was clarified and provisional reports to the parties were institutionalized.

During the Tokyo Round (1973-1979), specific dispute procedures were adopted in most of the codes established during that Round. Generally, these codes have more stringent time limits and procedures, and sometimes provide for compulsory conciliation as, for example, in the Subsidies Code.

Subsequent Developments: On 12 April 1989, on a provisional basis, the GATT Council adopted the ministerial decision on dispute settlement of the Montreal mid-term review of the Uruguay Round. These new procedures are more specific and time limits have been tightened as follows: consultations (ten days to reply, 30 days to begin consultation or otherwise an automatic right to a panel), the establishment and composition of panels (60 days after the beginning of a panel), a panel's maximum duration (six months), and the possibility of voluntary expeditious arbitration.

The mid-term decision also institutionalized procedures for multiple complainants, for the intervention of third contracting parties, for emergency cases and for special advice for developing countries.

Delays for the adoption of panel reports are to be avoided and the total period from initiating consultations to decisions by the Council after a panel report cannot exceed 15 months. The implementation of the recommendations from such a report must be considered by the Council no longer than six months after its adoption.

G.M. and H.J.C.

Reference : BISD 26

111.19 – MINISTERIAL DECLARATION ON THE URUGUAY ROUND – GATT

Adopted : 20.09.1986, Punta del Este

The most recent round of multilateral negotiations began in September 1986 at Punta del Este, Uruguay[1]. The Round, the most ambitious yet, is attempting both to move the GATT into new substantive areas of trade and to reform, in a comprehensive way, the existing areas of coverage. The negotiations have been divided into 15 negotiation groups, ranging from such traditional subjects as tariff reduction, textiles and clothing, and matters covered in the existing codes, as well as new subjects such as services, intellectual property and trade-related investment.

The contracting parties are currently reviewing a comprehensive text prepared by the Director-General, which represents the basis for a possible agreement for the Round. If adopted, the Dunkel Text, as it is known, will move the GATT and international trade into a new era.

This Text contains institutional provisions which provide for the establishment of a formal multilateral trade organization (MTO), thereby calling for the formalization of the GATT's *de facto* position as an international organization. The MTO would

(1) The GATT Trade Negotiations Committee on 15 December 1993 adopted the Final Act Embodying the Results of the Uruguay Round of Multilateral Trade Negotiations. Just prior to publication, an additional commentary has been added to this section which covers the development [see 111.21].

offer a continuous negotiating forum to develop further the interaction between trade and related matters like trade and competition issues.

The institutional provisions will also provide for reform of the dispute settlement mechanism, thereby continuing the trend towards a rule-oriented system. More specifically, these provisions include shorter periods for the various stages in the dispute settlement process and an appeal procedure of panel decisions. The traditional consensus rule of the Council would be abolished so that the states concerned in a dispute will not be able to block the adoption of a panel decision which disfavours them.

In addition, the Dunkel Text provides for the replacement of all the 1979 codes with new codes. These will update and improve the previous codes, and new ones will be added on matters such as safeguards, intellectual property, trade-related investment measures and agriculture.

G.M. and H.J.C.

Reference : GATT Press no. 1396

111.20 – AGREEMENT ON THE GLOBAL SYSTEM OF TRADE PREFERENCES (GSTP) AMONG DEVELOPING COUNTRIES – UNCTAD

Concluded : 13.04.1988, Belgrade
In force : 19.04.1989
Parties : 40

The initiative of a mini-GATT between developing countries began in 1971 with the 1971 Protocol Relating to Trade Negotiations among Developing Countries. The 1971 Protocol provided a legal framework for tariff concessions along the lines of the GATT. It never gained any impetus from the Enabling Clause of the Tokyo Round and never had more than 20 parties.

UNCTAD reacted more enthusiastically to the 1979 Enabling Clause [see 111.15] which made further collaboration and integration among developing countries legally possible. In 1982 the Ministers of the Group of 77 [see 233 A], meeting in New York, formally decided to open negotiations to conclude a Global System of Trade Preferences (GSTP). In 1987, the UNCTAD secretariat produced a draft for a GSTP which is an illustration of what national trade policies would look like if they respected the principles of the New International Economic Order.

At the 1989 UNCTAD session, the GSTP Charter was adopted. It expressly states that "economic co-operation among developing countries is a key element in the strategy of collective self-reliance and an essential instrument to promote structural changes" and that the "GSTP would constitute a major instrument for the promotion of trade among developing countries members of the group of 77".

DETAILS OF THE AGREEMENT

The GSTP is exclusively for the participation of the members of the Group of 77. Contrary to the GSP, it is generalized, which means it covers all products, it is non-discriminatory and so benefits equally all participants, and it is mutual – that is, it prescribes a MFN treatment among members of the GSTP with, however, possible derogations.

The GSTP envisages the possibilities of safeguard measures and more preferential treatment for the less developed countries among them. Finally, the GSTP does not replace existing regional and sub-regional arrangements.

A committee of participants has been established with the main functions of reviewing the possibility of promoting further negotiations for the enlargement of the schedules of concessions and for enhancement of trade among participants through other measures. It may at any time initiate negotiations.

G.M.

Access : CDN (Art. 1-a, 25)
Reserves : PAU (Art. 31)
Duration : USP
Deposit. : YU
Language : Ara, Eng, Fre, Spa

Reference : ILM 27:1208

111.21 – FINAL ACT EMBODYING THE RESULTS OF THE URUGUAY ROUND OF MULTILATERAL TRADE NEGOTIATIONS - GATT

Adopted : 15.12.1993

On 15 December 1993, the Final Act Embodying the Results of the Uruguay Round of Multilateral Trade Negotiations (the so-called "GATT 1994") was agreed by the Trade Negotiations Committee representing the 114 contracting parties of the GATT. On the same day, GATT 1994 was notified to the US Congress. It constitutes the most comprehensive trade package since the Havana Charter but enjoys much more international support than the never-born post-war agreement.

The Final Act covers all of the negotiating areas set out in the Punta del Este Declaration (September 1986) with two exceptions. First, the results of the "market access negotiations", in which individual countries have made binding commitments to reduce or eliminate specific tariffs and non-tariff barriers to merchandise trade, are subsequently to be recorded in national schedules which will form an integral part of the Final Act. Second, the "initial commitments" on the liberalization of trade in services are also subsequently to be recorded in national schedules.

The GATT 1994 generally follows the structure of the Draft Final Act introduced in December 1991 by the former Director-General, Mr Dunkel, to reinvigorate negotiations.

In addition to the texts of the agreements, the Final Act also contains text of Ministerial Decisions and Declarations, which further clarify certain provisions of agreements relating to the least-developed countries, the World Trade Organization, notification procedure, customs valuation, technical barriers to trade, net food-importing developing countries, trade in services, regional arrangements, government procurement, dispute settlement, dumping and subsidies.

One of the most important elements of the GATT 1994 is the establishment of a permanent international organization, the World Trade Organization (WTO), which will supervise and co-ordinate activities under GATT 1994 and integrate all agreements and arrangements concluded under the auspices of the GATT, including an integrated dispute settlement procedure.

New provisions on trade-related aspects of intellectual property, services, trade-related investment, preshipment inspection, sanitary and phytosanitary measures, and rules of origin have broadened the scope of multilateral disciplines and reduced the scope of unilateral trade actions. Existing codes on technical barriers to trade [see 111.07], customs valuation [see 112.22], dumping [see 111.11], and import licensing procedures [see 111.10] have been clarified and the disciplines resulting therefrom tightened.

A reinforced Agreement on Subsidies and Countervailing Measures contains a definition of subsidies and it distinguishes subsidies considered as prohibited, actionable and non-actionable. The Agreement also introduces the concept of a "specific" subsidy. Only specific subsidies are to be subject to the disciplines set out in the Agreement, while actionable subsidies are to be countervailable if they cause "serious prejudice".

The Final Act includes the Agreement on Agriculture which provides a framework for the long-term reform of agricultural trade and domestic policies. The agricultural package provides for specific commitments in the area of market access, domestic support and export competition. Such commitments are to be reflected in the GATT schedules of legal commitments relating to each country member. Tariffs on agricultural products are to be reduced by an average 36 per cent in the case of developed countries, with a minimum reduction of 15 per cent per tariff line, and 24 per cent in the case of developing countries, over six and ten years respectively, while least-developed countries are not required to reduce their tariffs. Domestic support measures benefiting agricultural producers that have, at most, a minimal impact on trade distorting effects or effects on production are excluded from reduction commitments. Members are required to reduce the value of mainly direct export subsidies to a level 36 per cent below the 1986-90 base period level over the six-year implementation period, and the quantity of subsidized exports by 21 per cent over the same period. The package is conceived as part of a continuing process, with the long-term objective of securing substantial and progressive reductions in support and protection.

A new agreement on safeguard measures has introduced the requirement that "adjustment programmes" be put into place in the case of safeguard measures lasting more than one year. The Agreement also sets a "sunset clause", i.e. safeguard measures can last for a maximum period of four to eight years. "Grey Measures", such as voluntary export restraints and orderly marketing arrangements, are now prohibited and existing measures are to be phased out within 180 days from the entry into force of the WTO and, in all cases, before 31 December 1999.

The Agreement on Textiles and Clothing provides for the gradual integration of this sector into the GATT over the period ending 1 January 2005. It also contains a specific transitional safeguard mechanism.

The General Agreement on Services rests on three pillars. The first is a Framework Agreement containing basic obligations which apply to all member countries, including a relative MFN obligation, transparency requirements, the reasonable, objective and impartial administration of domestic regulation and the National Treatment. The second concerns national schedules of commitments containing specific further national commitments which will be subject to a continuing process of liberalization. The third is a number of annexes addressing the special situations of individual service sectors. There are general and security exceptions, institutional provisions including consultation, dispute settlement, and the establishment of a Council of Services.

In addition to the changes brought by the Mid-Term Review Ministerial Meeting [see 111.18], the Understanding on Rules and Procedures Governing the Settlement of Disputes will establish an integrated system permitting WTO members to base their claim on any of the multilateral trade agreements. For this purpose, a Dispute Settlement Body (DSB) will exercise the authority of the General Council, and that of the councils and committees of the relevant agreements.

Under the integrated dispute settlement procedure, panel reports are to be adopted within 60 days of their issuance, unless the DSB decides by consensus not to adopt the report, or one of the parties notifies the DSB of its intention to appeal on issues of law. Appellate proceedings are not to exceed 60 days from the date the appeal is lodged. The outcome is to be adopted within 30 days following its issuance, unless the DSB decides by consensus against its adoption. An important feature of GATT 1994 is that parties to a panel review process will not have the right to veto such a report.

The Decision on Achieving Greater Coherence in Global Economic Policy-Making sets out concepts and proposals with respect to achieving greater coherence in global economic policy-making, including exchange rate. It recognizes that, while difficulties whose origins lie outside the trade field cannot be redressed through measures taken in the trade field alone, there are nevertheless interlinkages between the different aspects of economic policy. This decision brings closer together the IMF [see 211 A], the World Bank [see 221 A] and the WTO by reinvigorating the initial objectives of the Bretton Woods' fathers in 1945.

GATT 1994 is scheduled to be signed by the members in April 1994 and its provisions to enter into force on 1 January 1995 or after the date of the entry into force of the WTO. After all member states ratify the Final Act of the Uruguay Round, obligations under the old GATT will *de facto* be phased out. In the meantime, and in the eventuality that some contracting parties do not ratify the GATT 1994, obligations under the old GATT would still bind the contracting parties. This could lead to a complex situation with different treatments between trading partners depending on what agreements they have signed and is contrary to the main goal of the negotiations of the Uruguay Round. At the time of the publication of this book, analysts are, however, optimistic that all 114 states will fairly quickly ratify the Final Act.

Gabrielle Marceau

Language : Eng, Fre, Spa

Reference : Gatt Doc. MTM/FA

1.1.2 Customs Co-operation

This section describes the various international agreements and organizations which, through their promotion of simplified and harmonized customs regulations and procedures, have helped facilitate the movement of goods, services and people across national frontiers.

The key agreements in the customs co-operation field are introduced in the section describing the main organization in the area – the Customs Co-operation Council [see 112 A].

Agreements which are regional are outside the scope of this book (e.g. the Customs Convention concerning Spare Parts Used for Repairing Europ Wagons, to which only European countries are parties). Some agreements which have relevance to this section are presented elsewhere – for example in the sections on tourism [see 1.7.2] and transport [see 1.8].

The author, *Glenn S. McDonald*, is grateful to Maureen Irish of the University of Windsor Law Faculty for her assistance on the Harmonized System summary [see 112.24] and to Michel Augé, former Assistant Secretary-General of the CCC, for his guidance.

SELECTED BIBLIOGRAPHY

McGovern, Edmond, "Chapters 3 and 4", *International Trade Regulation: GATT, The United States and the European Community*, Exeter: Globefield Press, 1986.

Sherman, Saul L. and Hinrich Glashoff, *Customs Valuation: Commentary on the GATT Customs Valuation Code*, Deventer; Boston: Kluwer Law and Taxation, 1988.

Sturm, R., *Customs Law and Administration*, 3rd ed., Dobbs Ferry, N.Y.: Oceana Publications, (Looseleaf).

De Pagter, Henk and Richard van Raan, *The Valuation of Goods for Customs Purposes*, Deventer: Kluwer Law and Taxation, 1981.

112 A – CUSTOMS CO-OPERATION COUNCIL (CCC)

The Customs Co-operation Council (CCC) was established on 15 December 1950 by 13 European countries [see 112.02]. The CCC was to administer the Nomenclature Convention [see 112.03] and the Convention on the Valuation of Goods for Customs Purposes [see 112.04], concluded at the same time. Its broader mandate was to secure the highest possible degree of harmony and uniformity in the customs systems of its member states and, in that context, to study the problems inherent in the development and improvement of customs technique and customs legislation [see 112.02, Preamble].

The activities of the CCC fall under five main headings:

- **Nomenclature and Classification:** The CCC administers and assures the continuing development of the Harmonized System of classification [see 112.24], now governing more than 90 per cent of world trade.
- **Customs Valuation:** The CCC administers the two international conventions which now apply in this area: the Convention on the Valuation of Goods for Customs Purposes [see 112.04], for which it has sole responsibility, and the GATT Customs Valuation Code [see 112.22] for which it has responsibility at the technical level.
- **Customs Procedures:** The CCC continues to initiate and administer a variety of international conventions concerning customs procedures, the most important of which are the Kyoto and Istanbul Conventions [see 112.19 and 112.25].
- **Customs Enforcement and Control:** The Nairobi Convention [see 112.21] is the key instrument in this area. As part of its effort to combat customs fraud, the CCC works closely with other international organizations, in particular INTERPOL (the International Criminal Police Organization) and those UN agencies involved in the suppression of drug trafficking.
- **Training and Technical Assistance:** The CCC's long-standing programme of training and technical assistance in favour of developing countries was extended in 1991 to the countries of Eastern Europe.

MEMBERSHIP AND FUNDING

The CCC has 126 members and two official languages, English and French. Its budget for 1991-92 was 406 million Belgian Francs.

STRUCTURE

The CCC's **Secretariat**, based in Brussels, employs just over 100 people. Technical and administrative staff are recruited from the customs administrations of member countries. The **Council,** which normally comprises the heads of these customs administrations, meets once a year. It is assisted by an **Executive Committee** of 17 members (the Policy Commission) and numerous technical committees which meet from September to July.

The CCC's priorities for the 1990s are: to promote the CCC's instruments as international customs standards and ensure their uniform application; to develop standardized and simplified import/export procedures; to develop practical control and enforcement measures against all forms of smuggling and customs fraud; to help members develop training facilities; and to promote systems for electronic data interchange between Customs and other parties. The Washington Declaration, adopted by the CCC in July 1989, defines the role to be played by the organization regarding the harmonization and computerization of customs procedures.

CO-OPERATION

The CCC works with the Transport Division of the ECE [see 181 A] on matters involving cross-border transport. It works with the Trade Division of the ECE, along with UNCTAD [see 111 B] and ISO [see 152 C], in the increasingly important area of standardization and computerization of customs procedures. The CCC also collaborates closely with the GATT. To cite one example, administration of the GATT Customs Valuation Code [see 112.22] is shared between the two organizations, with the CCC ensuring the uniform interpretation and application of the Code at the technical level and the GATT dealing with broader questions of commercial policy. Other organizations with whom the CCC co-operates closely include the UPU [see 191 A], UNESCO [see 171 A], ICAO [see 184 A], ILO [see 141 A], IATA [see 184 B] and the ICC [see 300 D].

PUBLICATIONS

These include the *CCC Annual Report, Introducing the Harmonized System, Harmonized Commodity Description and Coding System* (bilingual edition), *GATT Agreement on Customs Valuation, Customs Technique Compendium,* and the *Kyoto Convention Handbook.*

Glenn S. McDonald

ADDRESS

26-38 rue de l'Industrie, B-1040 Brussels, Belgium
T. (32 2) 508 42 11, Fx. (32 2) 508 4240

112 B – INTERNATIONAL CUSTOMS TARIFFS BUREAU (ICTB)

The International Customs Tariffs Bureau (ICTB) was established by the Convention Concerning the Creation of an International Union for the Publication of Customs Tariffs (Brussels, 5 July 1890) (modified by the Protocol of 16 December 1949). The organization translates and publishes in five languages (English, French, German, Italian and Spanish) the customs tariffs of all the countries of the world. *The International Customs Journal*, consisting of updated customs tariffs or supplements of these tariffs, is periodically distributed to the ICTB's 71 member states. It is the responsibility of the latter to ensure that copies of the journal are made available to interested parties within their territories.

ADDRESS

38, rue de l'Association, B-1000 Brussels, Belgium
T. (32 2) 516 8774, Fx. (32 2) 218 3025

112.01 – INTERNATIONAL CONVENTION RELATING TO THE SIMPLIFICATION OF CUSTOMS FORMALITIES – LN

Concluded : 03.11.1923, Geneva
In force : 27.11.1924
Parties : 42

In order to give effect to the principle of the equitable treatment of commerce (Art. 23 of the Covenant of the League of Nations), the contracting states undertake not to hinder their commercial relations through excessive, unnecessary or arbitrary customs regulations and related formalities. The latter are to be simplified and adapted to the needs of foreign trade, with no hindrance caused to such trade except that absolutely necessary to safeguard the essential interests of the state (Art. 1).

Specifically, the contracting states undertake to observe the principle of equitable treatment in respect of all matters dealt with in the Convention (Art. 2), to reduce import and export prohibitions and restrictions to a minimum (Art. 3), to publish promptly all customs regulations and related formalities and refrain from enforcing the same prior to such publication (Art. 4), to provide appropriate legal or administrative remedies to those prejudiced by the arbitrary or unjust application of customs regulations (Art. 7), and to reduce as far as possible the number of cases in which certificates of origin are required (Art. 11).

Article 10 provides for the temporary admission, free of import duties, of samples and specimens which are imported into the territory by manufacturers or traders of another contracting state. Temporary importation and exportation in general are dealt with in the form of guidelines in Article 16 and its associated Annex. Another set of guidelines, found in the Annex to Article 14, is designed to simplify and render more uniform and reasonable customs regulations governing the rapid passage of goods through customs, the examination of travellers' luggage, the treatment of goods in bond, warehousing charges and related matters. The Convention is accompanied by a Protocol, concluded on the same date.

G.S.M.

Access : CON (Art. 25)
Reserves : USP
Duration : USP
Deposit. : LN/UN
Language : Eng, Fre (Art. 23)

Reference : 30 LNTS – UKTS 1925/16 – JORF 11 Dec 1926

112.02 – CONVENTION ESTABLISHING A CUSTOMS CO-OPERATION COUNCIL – CCC

Concluded : 15.12.1950, Brussels
In force : 04.11.1952
Parties : 126

The Convention established the Customs Co-operation Council (CCC), with its headquarters at Brussels (Arts. I and VII). Under the Convention, the CCC enjoys such legal capacity in the territory of each of its member states as may be necessary for the exercise of its functions (Art. XIII, Art. II of the Annex). The Convention was signed at the same time as the Convention on Nomenclature for the Classification of Goods in Customs Tariffs [see 112.03] and the Convention on the Valuation of Goods for Customs Purposes [see 112.04]. For a description of the work of the CCC, see 112 A.

G.S.M.

Access : ALS (Art. XVIII)
Reserves : USP
Duration : ULT (Art. XIX)
Deposit. : BE
Language : Eng, Fre

Reference : 157 UNTS – Can TS 1971/38 – UST 22/1 – UKTS 1954/50 – 1 Paeslee

112.03 – CONVENTION ON NOMENCLATURE FOR THE CLASSIFICATION OF GOODS IN CUSTOMS TARIFFS – CCC

Concluded : 15.12.1950, Brussels
In force : 11.09.1959
Parties : 16

The first initiatives for the development of an international customs nomenclature were launched in the latter half of the nineteenth century. Work done in the 1930s and 1940s led to the development of the Customs Co-operation Council Nomenclature (CCCN) (until 1974 called the "Brussels Tariff Nomenclature"). The Convention incorporating the CCCN came into force, together with its 1955 Protocol of Amendment, on 11 September 1959.

In adopting a standard customs nomenclature, the contracting parties to the Convention sought to simplify international tariff negotiations, to eliminate biases inherent in national nomenclatures, to facilitate the comparison of trade statistics, and to simplify the import/export process for those involved in it.

Under Article II of the Convention, the contracting parties undertake to compile their customs tariffs in conformity with the CCCN (Para. a). They agree to adopt the CCCN headings integrally, without omission or addition or departure from the given numbering (Para. b), although they may create subdivisions of these headings (Para. c). The contracting parties assume no obligations in respect of rates of customs duties (Art. VII).

The CCCN, annexed to the Convention, comprises General Rules for the Interpretation of the Nomenclature, Section and Chapter Notes, and the CCCN headings themselves. The headings are identified by a four-digit code, in contrast to the Harmonized System which uses six digits. Correlation with the United Nations Standard International Trade Classification (SITC) has been achieved via the creation of special subdivisions of CCCN headings, which contracting parties are encouraged to incorporate into their customs tariffs. The Customs Co-operation Council (CCC) [see 112 A] administers the Convention with a view to securing uniformity in its interpretation and application (Art. III). To this end, a Nomenclature Committee, operating under the authority of the CCC, prepares Explanatory Notes and Classification Opinions (Arts. III and IV).

The CCCN gained world-wide acceptance in the 1960s. All major industrial nations adopted the system with the exception of the US and Canada. The CCCN has undergone several modifications, the most recent taking effect on 1 January 1988 when the CCCN headings were made to correspond with their Harmonized System counterparts at the four-digit level. The new Harmonized System of classification has now effectively replaced the CCCN [see 112.24]. Although 15 countries are still parties to the Nomenclature Convention, seven of these have ratified the Harmonized System Convention. The Nomenclature Committee is no longer active.

G.S.M.

Access : CON (Art. X, XI, XIII)
Reserves : USP
Duration : ULT (Art. XIV)
Deposit. : BE
Language : Eng, Fre

Modific. :Protocol (amending Annex) 01.07.55 (11.09.59); Amendements to Annex 16.06.60, 08.12.60, 09.06.61 (01.01.65); Amendment to Article XVI 16.06.60 (01.01.65); Amendment to Annex 09.06.70 (01.01.72); Amendment to Annex 18.06.76 (01.01.78); Amendment to Article XIV 13.06.78 (01.07.79); Amendment to Article XVI 13.06.78 (01.01.79); Amendment to Annex 14.06.83 (01.01.88)

Reference : 347 UNTS – UKTS 1960/29

112.04 – CONVENTION ON THE VALUATION OF GOODS FOR CUSTOMS PURPOSES – CCC

Concluded : 15.12.1950, Brussels
In force : 28.07.1953
Parties : 12

The Convention grew out of a perceived need for greater uniformity in customs valuation as a means of simplifying tariff negotiations, preventing the manipulation of national valuation standards for protectionist purposes, and enabling importers and exporters to predict accurately the amount of customs duties to be paid.

The contracting parties to the Convention undertake to incorporate into their domestic law the Brussels Definition of Value (BDV), contained in Annex I, and to apply it in conformity with the provisions of the Interpretative Notes set out in Annex II (Arts. II and III).

The Customs Co-operation Council (CCC) [see 112 A] administers the Convention with a view to securing uniformity in its interpretation and application (Art. V). To this end, a Valuation Committee, operating under the authority of the CCC, prepares Explanatory Notes as a guide to the application of the BDV and issues Valuation Opinions in order to resolve specific problems submitted by members (Arts. V and VI).

The BDV uses a notional standard for customs valuation. The "normal price" is the price which given goods would fetch in an open market sale under competitive conditions (Annex I, Art. I-1). This price includes all costs incurred in delivering the goods to the buyer at the place of importation into the country (a c.i.f. calculation). It excludes any duties or taxes the buyer must pay upon importation (Annex I, Art. I-2). The type of market transaction the BDV envisages is defined in greater detail in Article II of the Definition. The Interpretative Notes complete the Definition. Most importantly, they provide for the use of the price actually paid or payable in an open market sale as a basis for valuation (Note 5 to Art. I).

Until 1979, the BDV was the only international standard for customs valuation. A second system was introduced with the conclusion of the GATT Customs Valuation Code [see 112.22] in 1979. The two systems now co-exist although the GATT system has won much wider acceptance. None of the major industrial nations are now contracting parties to the BDV Convention. The CCC is encouraging its members who are not parties to either of the valuation agreements to adopt the GATT Code.

G.S.M.

Access : CON (Art. XII, XIII, XV)
Reserves : USP
Duration : ULT (Art. XVI)
Deposit. : BE
Language : Eng, Fre

Modific. : Amendment to Annexes 1 and 2 07.06.67 (18.04.72)

Reference : 171 UNTS – UKTS 1954/49 – RTAF 1974/29

112.05 – INTERNATIONAL CONVENTION TO FACILITATE THE IMPORTATION OF COMMERCIAL SAMPLES AND ADVERTISING MATERIAL – ECE/GATT

Concluded : 07.11.1952, Geneva
In force : 20.11.1955
Parties : 57

The Convention, drawn up by the contracting parties to the GATT in November 1952, establishes uniform regulations for the importation of commercial samples and advertising material with a view to the further expansion of international trade (Preamble).

The contracting parties undertake to grant duty-free admission to samples imported into their territories which are of negligible value and used only for soliciting orders for goods of the kind represented by the samples (Art. II). Certain written advertising materials are also accorded, in limited quantities, the same exemption (Art. IV). Samples not covered by Article II are to be admitted duty-free into the territory for a period of at least six months, subject to the deposit of import duties or the furnishing of other security (Art. III). Advertising films are also granted temporary, duty-free admission under the same conditions (Art. V).

Article VI prohibits the application of import prohibitions and restrictions other than import duties to goods qualifying for duty-free entry or temporary admission under Articles II to V, except in furtherance of defined public policy objectives. States may make reservations in respect of specific provisions of the Convention, subject to acceptance of the same by all other contracting parties (Art. XIV).

Annex B.3. of the 1990 Istanbul Convention [see 112.25] terminates and replaces, as between the contracting parties having accepted that Annex, the provisions of the present Convention concerning temporary admission – namely, Articles III, V, VI-1-b and VI-2 (Annex B.3., Art. 9).

G.S.M.

Access : ALS (Art. IX, X)
Reserves : CST (Art. XIV)
Duration : USP
Deposit. : UN
Language : Eng, Fre

Reference :221 UNTS – Can TS 1974/23 – UKTS 1955/81 – UST 8/2 – JORF 3 Jul 1964 – RTAF 1964/44

112.06 – CUSTOMS CONVENTION REGARDING ECS CARNETS FOR COMMERCIAL SAMPLES ("ECS CONVENTION") – CCC

Concluded : 01.03.1956, Brussels
Party : 1

The ECS Convention establishes a standard document, the ECS carnet, which contracting parties to the Convention undertake to accept as due security for the temporary duty-free admission onto their territories of commercial samples, including certain types of advertising films (Arts. II and XVII). Samples imported under cover of ECS carnets are to be re-exported within the period of validity of the carnet (maximum one year) and within the period determined by the customs authorities of the country of importation (Arts. V and VII).

In connection with the issue of the carnet, a "guaranteeing association" undertakes to pay any import duties or other charges which may be imposed where the conditions governing temporary admission, in particular re-exportation, are not complied with (Art. II). A model ECS carnet is set out in the Annex to the Convention. The Convention is also accompanied by a Protocol of Signature, concluded on the same date.

The ECS Convention was intended to complement the Commercial Samples Convention of 1952 [see 112.05]. In June 1976, the Customs Co-operation Council recommended that the contracting parties to the ECS Convention denounce it, since the ATA Convention of 1961 [see 112.13] had come to duplicate its functions. Only Haiti has not done so.

G.S.M.

Access : CON (Art. XIX, XXII)
Reserves : PRO (Art. XXVI)
Duration : ULT (Art. XXIII)
Deposit. : BE
Language : Eng, Fre

Reference : 343 UNTS – UKTS 1959/29 – UST 20/1

112.07 – CUSTOMS CONVENTION ON CONTAINERS – ECE

Concluded : 18.05.1956, Geneva
In force : 04.08.1959
Parties : 39

The Convention is designed to develop and facilitate the use of containers in international traffic (Preamble). Contracting parties agree to grant temporary admission free of import duties, import taxes and other restrictions to containers (including their normal accessories) which are re-exported within three months of their date of importation (Arts. 1 to 3).

Those contracting parties using a system of container transport under customs seal undertake to accept for such transport containers complying with the provisions of Annex 1 and to apply the approval procedures set out in Annex 2 (Art. 7). The provisions of the Convention do not apply to containers imported into a country and subsequently used for the carriage of goods within the frontiers of that same country (Art. 11).

The Convention contains two annexes and is accompanied by a Protocol of Signature.

Since its entry into force on 6 December 1975, the 1972 Containers Convention [see 112.18] has terminated and replaced, as between its contracting parties, this 1956 Containers Convention (Art. 20 of the 1972 Convention).

G.S.M.

Access : CON (Art. 12)
Reserves : PAU (Art. 18)
Duration : MIN (Art. 15)
Deposit. : UN (Art. 23)
Language : Eng, Fre

Reference : 338 UNTS – UKTS 1959/80 – UST 20/1 – JORF 26 Jan 1960

112.08 – CUSTOMS CONVENTION ON THE TEMPORARY IMPORTATION OF COMMERCIAL ROAD VEHICLES – ECE

Concluded : 18.05.1956, Geneva
In force : 08.04.1959
Parties : 30

The Convention has as its goal the facilitation of international road traffic (Preamble). Under Article 2, contracting parties undertake to grant temporary admission free of import duties, import taxes and other restrictions, to vehicles registered in the territory of another contracting party and imported for commercial use in international road traffic by undertakings operating from that other territory (Art. 2, Para. 1).

The vehicles are to be covered by temporary importation papers, issued by authorized associations for the purpose of guaranteeing payment of import duties and taxes where the vehicle is not re-exported within the period of validity of the papers (Arts. 2, 7 and 13).

Contracting parties are not obliged to grant temporary admission pursuant to the Convention to vehicles used for the transportation of passengers or the carriage of goods entirely within the importing state (Art. 13).

The five annexes to the Convention set out models and formal specifications for the various documents to be used in its implementation. The Convention is accompanied by a Protocol of Signature, concluded on the same date. The Convention replaced the Draft International Customs Convention on Commercial Road Vehicles of 1949 (45 UNTS) (terminated in 1966).

Annex C of the 1990 Istanbul Convention [see 112.25] terminates and replaces, as between those contracting parties having accepted that Annex, the present Convention (Annex C, Art. 11).

G.S.M.

Access : CON (Art. 33)
Reserves : PAU (Art. 39)
Duration : MIN (Art. 36)
Deposit. : UN (Art. 45)
Language : Eng, Fre

Modific. : Addition of new Article 25 bis (26.05.83)

Reference : 327 UNTS – UKTS 1960/1 – JORF 26 Jan 1960 – RTAF 1960/9

112.09 – CUSTOMS CONVENTION ON THE INTERNATIONAL TRANSPORT OF GOODS UNDER COVER OF TIR CARNETS – ECE

Concluded : 15.01.1959, Geneva
In force : 07.01.1960
Parties : 37

The Convention is designed to facilitate the international transport of goods by road vehicle (Preamble). It applies where goods are transported, without intermediate reloading, across one or more frontiers between a customs office of departure of one contracting party and a customs office of destination of another or of the same contracting party, in road vehicles or in containers carried on such vehicles. These vehicles may be carried on another means of transport during part of the TIR operation (Art. 2).

The Convention establishes two regimes. Chapter III (Arts. 4 to 18) governs transport in sealed road vehicles or containers, while Chapter IV (Arts. 19 to 28) governs the transport of "heavy or bulky goods" (defined in Art. 1-h). Transport under both regimes is to be performed under cover of "TIR carnet", a document issued by authorized associations which guarantee the payment of any customs duties or other charges incurred as a result of irregularities in the TIR operation (Arts. 3-b, 5, and 6). The carnet must conform to the model found in Annex 1 of the Convention (Art. 7).

Goods carried pursuant to Chapter III (sealed transport) are not subject to the payment or deposit of customs duties and taxes at customs offices *en route* to their destination nor, as a general rule, are they subject to examination at these offices (Art. 4). Road vehicles and containers used in sealed transport must meet the technical requirements set out in Annexes 3 and 6 respectively. The approval procedure for road vehicles and containers is laid down in Annexes 4 and 7, while certificates of approval must conform to the specimens reproduced in Annexes 5 and 8 (Art. 17).

Goods carried pursuant to Chapter IV (transport of heavy or bulky goods) are similarly exempt from the payment or deposit of customs duties and taxes at Customs offices *en route* to their destination (Art. 20). On the issue of examination, Article 27 states that "as far as possible" Customs authorities shall respect the identification marks and seals affixed by the Customs authorities of other contracting parties. Note that, in adhering to the Convention, states may elect not to apply the provisions of Chapter IV. The Convention allows only one other reservation – that in relation to the dispute settlement provisions of Article 44 (Art. 45).

The Convention's nine annexes, together with its Protocol of Signature, form an integral part of it. The Convention replaced the Draft International Customs Convention on the International Transport of Goods by Road of 1949 (45 UNTS) (terminated in 1965). However, the TIR Convention of 1975 [see 112.20], as of its entry into force on 20 March 1978, terminated and replaced, as between its contracting parties, the present 1959 Convention (Art. 56-1 of the 1975 Convention). Among the contracting parties to the 1959 Convention, only Japan has not ratified the 1975 Convention.

G.S.M.

Access : CON (Art. 39)
Reserves : PAU (Art. 45)
Duration : MIN (Art. 42)
Deposit. : UN (Art. 51)
Language : Eng, Fre

Modific. : Amendment to Annex 3 (19.11.63); Amendment to Annexes 3 and 6 (01.07.66)

Reference : 348 UNTS – UKTS 1960/18 – UST 20/1 – JORF 22 Jan 1960 – RTAF 1960/8

112.10 – CUSTOMS CONVENTION ON THE TEMPORARY IMPORTATION OF PACKINGS – CCC

Concluded : 06.10.1960, Brussels
In force : 15.03.1962
Parties : 35

Contracting parties to the Convention undertake to grant temporary admission to packings. These are to be admitted into the territory free of import duties and import prohibitions and restrictions, subject to their re-exportation within three months where the packings are imported empty, or six months, where they are imported filled (Arts. 1, 2 and 5). Packings granted temporary admission are not to be used within the country of importation except for the purpose of exportation of goods (Art. 7). National legislation regarding the assessment of import duties on packed goods is not affected by this Convention (Art. 3).

Annex B.3. of the 1990 Istanbul Convention [see 112.25] terminates and replaces, as between those contracting parties having accepted that Annex, the present Convention (Annex B.3., Art. 9). Under Annex B.3., the period for re-exportation of packings is fixed at six months or more, with no distinction made as to whether the packings are imported empty or filled (Art. 6). Note also that contracting parties accepting Annex B.3. agree to grant temporary admission to packings without requiring a customs document or security, although they may require a written undertaking to re-export (Art. 5). Under the 1960 Convention, contracting parties merely agree to dispense with the requirement of security "wherever ... possible" (Art. 4).

G.S.M.

Access : ALS (Art. 15)
Reserves : PAU (Art. 20)
Duration : ULT (Art. 17)
Deposit. : CCC (Art. 22)
Language : Eng, Fre (Art. 22)

Reference : 473 UNTS – UKTS 1978/77 – JORF 15 Apr 62 – RTAF 1962/15

112.11 – CUSTOMS CONVENTION CONCERNING FACILITIES FOR THE IMPORTATION OF GOODS FOR DISPLAY OR USE AT EXHIBITIONS, FAIRS, MEETINGS OR SIMILAR EVENTS ("FAIRS CONVENTION") – CCC/ECE/UNESCO

Concluded : 08.06.1961, Brussels
In force : 13.07.1962
Parties : 53

Under the Fairs Convention, goods intended for display or use at exhibitions, fairs, meetings or similar events are granted "temporary admission" – that is, they can be imported free of import duties, import prohibitions and other restrictions, provided they are subsequently re-exported within six months (Arts. 1, 2 and 4). The Convention also provides for a waiver of import duties, import prohibitions and restrictions in respect of certain goods used, used up or consumed in connection with the above events. There is no requirement of re-exportation in this case (Arts. 6 and 7).

The definition of "event" under the Convention is wide and includes events which have purely local or national participation (Art. 1). In this respect the Convention goes much further than pre-existing international agreements, such as the Convention on International Exhibitions (Paris, 1928) or the 1958 Recommendations of the ECE concerning international sample fairs and specialized international displays, which were either limited in their scope or not binding.

Annex B.1. of the 1990 Istanbul Convention [see 112.25] terminates and replaces, as between those contracting parties having accepted that Annex, the Fairs Convention (Annex B.1., Art. 9). The basic provisions of the latter are reproduced, almost integrally, within the framework of the wider 1990 Convention wherein the acceptance of standard temporary admission papers (ATA carnets) will be obligatory. Contracting parties to the Fairs Convention are only bound to accept the ATA carnet if they are also contracting parties to the 1961 ATA Convention [see 112.13].

G.S.M.

Access : ALS (Art. 18)
Reserves : PAU (Art. 23)
Duration : ULT (Art. 20)
Deposit. : CCC
Language : Eng, Fre

Reference : 473 UNTS – UKTS 1963/61 – JORF 3 Nov 1964 – RTAF 1964/60

112.12 – CUSTOMS CONVENTION ON THE TEMPORARY IMPORTATION OF PROFESSIONAL EQUIPMENT ("PROFESSIONAL EQUIPMENT CONVENTION") – CCC

Concluded : 08.06.1961, Brussels
In force : 01.07.1962
Parties : 49

With a view to facilitating the international exchange of specialized skills and techniques (Preamble), contracting parties to the Convention agree to admit professional equipment into their territories free of import duties and import prohibitions and other restrictions for a period not normally exceeding six months (Arts. 2 and 4).

The special conditions applying to the grant of temporary admission and the types of equipment eligible for such treatment are specified in each of the Convention's three annexes. On adhering to the Convention, contracting parties must accept at least one annex. They may subsequently accept one or more further annexes (Arts. 15 and 17). The annexes accepted by a party, together with the body of the Convention, form a single legal instrument (Art. 8). Contracting parties are bound only *vis-à-vis* those other contracting parties who have accepted the same annex(es).

Annex A covers equipment for the press or for sound or television broadcasting, Annex B cinematographic equipment and Annex C other professional equipment. Illustrative lists of the kinds of equipment covered accompany each annex. The Convention also applies to vehicles designed or specially adapted for the purposes specified in the annexes.

Annex B.2. of the 1990 Istanbul Convention [see 112.25] terminates and replaces, as between those contracting parties having accepted that Annex, the Professional Equipment Convention (Annex B.2., Art. 8). States accepting Annex B.2. are required to apply its provisions in respect of all three categories of equipment mentioned above. This constitutes a significant change in the letter, though not in the application, of the 1961 Convention since the parties to the latter have, almost without exception, accepted all three of its annexes.

Under Annex B.2., the minimum period for re-exportation has been increased to 12 months, except for vehicles, where customs officials retain the discretion to decide on an appropriate period (Art. 5). Contracting parties to the 1990 Convention are also bound to accept ATA and CPD carnets (for goods and means of transport respectively) for all temporary admission procedures conducted thereunder. Contracting parties to the Professional Equipment Convention are bound to accept the ATA carnet only where they are also parties to the 1961 ATA Convention [see 112.13].

G.S.M.

Access : ALS (Art. 15)
Reserves : PRO (Art. 20)
Duration : ULT (Art. 17)
Deposit. : CCC
Language : Eng, Fre

Reference :473 UNTS – UKTS 1963/62 – UST 20/1 – JORF 3 Jul 1962 – RTAF 1962/24

112.13 – CUSTOMS CONVENTION ON THE A.T.A. CARNET FOR THE TEMPORARY ADMISSION OF GOODS ("ATA CONVENTION") – CCC

Concluded : 06.12.1961, Brussels
In force : 30.07.1963
Parties : 53

The Convention is designed to facilitate the importation of goods granted temporary duty-free admission within the territories of contracting parties. It prescribes a standard document, the ATA carnet, which is backed by the security normally required by customs authorities for temporary admission.

Contracting parties to the ATA Convention agree to accept the ATA carnet for goods temporarily admitted under the 1961 Fairs Convention [see 112.11] and the 1961 Professional Equipment Convention [see 112.12] where they are parties to those conventions. They may also accept the carnet for goods temporarily imported under other international temporary importation conventions or for temporary admission procedures under their national laws and regulations (Art. 3).

The Customs Co-operation Council (CCC) [see 112 A] drew up the Convention in response to a recommendation received from the International Chamber of Commerce (ICC) [see 300 D] in 1958. The CCC, in close co-operation with the ICC, has promoted the acceptance of the ATA Convention over the years. The model of the ATA carnet, contained in the Annex to the Convention, was modified in 1989.

Annex A of the 1990 Istanbul Convention [see 112.25] terminates and replaces, as between the contracting parties to that Convention, the ATA Convention (Annex A, Art. 19). Note that Annex A provides for the use of a special document, the "CPD carnet", in respect of the temporary admission of "means of transport". An "ATA carnet" continues to be used for the temporary admission of goods (Arts. 1 to 3 of Annex A).

G.S.M.

Access : ALS (Art. 20)
Reserves : PAU (Art. 26)
Duration : ULT (Art. 22)
Deposit. : CCC
Language : Eng, Fre

Reference : 473 UNTS – Can TS 1972/31 – UKTS 1964/10 – UST 20/1 – JORF 23 Nov 1963 – RTAF 1963/80

112.14 – CUSTOMS CONVENTION CONCERNING WELFARE MATERIAL FOR SEAFARERS – CCC

Concluded : 01.12.1964, Brussels
In force : 11.12.1965
Parties : 40

The Convention, drawn up by the Customs Co-operation Council [see 112 A] in close collaboration with the ILO [see 141 A], is designed to facilitate the transfer to and utilization of welfare material by seafarers through the adoption of uniform customs provisions (Preamble). "Welfare material" is defined as material for the pursuit of cultural, educational, recreational, religious or sporting activities (Art. 1). An illustrative list of such material is set out in the Annex to the Convention.

Under Article 3 of the Convention, contracting parties agree to grant to welfare material, subject to its re-exportation, relief from import duties and taxes and all prohibitions or restrictions of an economic character. Attendant formalities and delays are to be kept to a minimum. Welfare material used on board ship, as well as that used in onshore hostels, clubs or recreational centres for seafarers, qualifies for temporary admission under the Convention (Arts. 4 and 5). The latter establishments must be managed by official or non-profit organizations and any welfare material imported for use there must be re-exported within six months (Arts. 1 and 5).

Annex B.5. of the 1990 Istanbul Convention [see 112.25] terminates and replaces, as between those contracting parties having accepted that Annex, the present Convention (Annex B.5., Art. 8). Under Annex B.5., the period for the re-exportation of welfare material has been increased to a minimum of 12 months (Art. 5). The Annex also stipulates that temporary admission of welfare material shall be granted without a customs document or security being required (Art. 4). The present 1964 Convention imposes no obligation in this respect.

G.S.M.

Access : ALS (Art. 12)
Reserves : PAU (Art. 17)
Duration : ULT (Art. 14)
Deposit. : CCC
Language : Eng, Fre

Reference : 550 UNTS – UKTS 1966/58 – JORF 20 May 1967 – RTAF 1967/38

112.15 – CUSTOMS CONVENTION ON THE TEMPORARY IMPORTATION OF SCIENTIFIC EQUIPMENT ("SCIENTIFIC EQUIPMENT CONVENTION") – CCC

Concluded : 11.06.1968, Brussels
In force : 05.09.1969
Parties : 54

The present Convention was designed to remedy certain shortcomings which became apparent in the 1950 UNESCO-sponsored Agreement on the Importation of Educational, Scientific and Cultural Materials [see 171.03] as a result of increasingly strong international scientific co-operation.

Contracting parties to the Convention undertake to grant temporary admission to scientific equipment, including spare parts and tools, which is to be used within their territories solely for purposes of scientific research or education (Art. 2). Temporary admission involves the waiver of all import duties and taxes, and import prohibitions and restrictions of an economic character, subject to the re-exportation of the equipment within six months of its date of importation (Arts. 1 and 6).

Temporary admission, at the option of a contracting party, may be made subject to one or more of the conditions set out in Article 3. Under Article 4, a contracting party may suspend its undertakings under the Convention where goods of equivalent scientific value to those whose temporary admission is sought are produced and available in the country of importation.

Annex B.5. of the 1990 Istanbul Convention [see 112.25] terminates and replaces, as between those contracting parties having accepted that Annex, the present Convention (Annex B.5., Art. 8). Under Annex B.5., the period for re-exportation of covered equipment is increased to a minimum of 12 months (Art. 5). Most of the conditions which may be imposed on temporary admission pursuant to Article 3 of the Scientific Equipment Convention are automatically imposed, in a somewhat modified form, by Article 3 of Annex B.5. The provision made under Article 4 of the Scientific Equipment Convention for the suspension of undertakings is not reproduced in Annex B.5. Note finally that neither customs documents nor security may be required by a contracting party before granting temporary admission under the Annex B.5., although reservations are allowed in respect of this provision. In any case, a party may request an inventory and written undertaking to re-export (Arts. 4 and 6). Under the 1968 Convention, contracting parties merely agree not to require security "wherever ... possible" (Art. 5).

G.S.M.

Access : ALS (Art. 19)
Reserves : PRO (Art. 24)
Duration : ULT (Art. 21)
Deposit. : CCC
Language : Eng, Fre

Reference :690 UNTS – Can TS 1974/34 – UKTS 1969/127 – JORF 12-13 Jan 1970 – RTAF 1970/2

112.16 – CUSTOMS CONVENTION ON THE TEMPORARY IMPORTATION OF PEDAGOGIC MATERIAL ("PEDAGOGIC MATERIAL CONVENTION") – CCC

Concluded : 08.06.1970, Brussels
In force : 10.09.1971
Parties : 38

The present Convention was designed to complement the agreements drawn up earlier by the CCC [see 112 A], in collaboration with UNESCO [see 171 A] and the ILO [see 141 A], to facilitate the temporary importation of educational, scientific and cultural materials [see 112.11, 112.12, 112.14, 112.15].

The Pedagogic Material Convention closely follows the Scientific Equipment Convention of 1968 [see 112.15] in its structure. Under Article 2 of the present Convention, contracting parties undertake to grant temporary admission to pedagogic material, including spare parts and tools, which is to be used within their territory solely for purposes of education or vocational training. Temporary admission is defined exactly as in the earlier Convention. Re-exportation must also occur within six months (Arts. 1 and 6). A non-limitative list of pedagogic material is set out in an Annex to the Convention.

The same optional conditions and the same possibility for the suspension of obligations found in the Scientific Equipment Convention are also provided for in the present Convention (Arts. 3 and 4).

Annex B.5. of the 1990 Istanbul Convention [see 112.25] terminates and replaces, as between those contracting parties having accepted that Annex, the present Convention (Annex B.5., Art. 8). The comments made concerning the differences between that Annex and the Scientific Equipment Convention apply equally here [see 112.15].

G.S.M.

Access : ALS (Art. 17)
Reserves : PRO (Art. 20)
Duration : ULT (Art. 21)

Deposit. : CCC
Language : Eng, Fre

Reference : 817 UNTS – JORF 13 Sep 1973 – RTAF 1973/37

112.17 – CUSTOMS CONVENTION ON THE INTERNATIONAL TRANSIT OF GOODS ("ITI CONVENTION") – CCC

Concluded : 07.06.1971, Vienna
Parties : 3

The ITI Convention has as its goal the facilitation of the "through" transport of goods contained in "transport-units" (including containers) via land, sea and/or air across one or more frontiers. To this end, it sets out a series of procedures designed so that customs authorities *en route* to the final destination of a shipment can normally limit their controls to an examination of documents and a confirmation that security measures previously taken (customs seals and fastenings or identification marks) have not been disturbed. Standard guarantee cards issued by approved associations provide the required guarantees.

The contracting parties to the Convention also undertake to provide administrative assistance to one another where the rules of the Convention are breached or other irregularities arise in connection with the ITI operation (Arts. 33 and 34). The Convention sets out a framework for the creation, through bilateral or multilateral agreement among interested parties, of "ITI areas" for the purpose of further simplifying the ITI procedure (Arts. 26 to 32).

The four annexes to the Convention set out models for the various documents to be used in the procedure (Annexes 1, 3 and 4) as well as the minimum technical requirements to be met by customs seals and fastenings (Annex 2). The annexes form an integral part of the Convention (Art. 60).

Five states must ratify or accede to the Convention before it enters into force – three months after the fifth ratification or accession (Art. 51).

G.S.M.

Access : ALS (Art. 50)
Reserves : PAU (Art. 53)
Duration : ULT (Art. 54)
Deposit. : CCC
Language : Eng, Fre

112.18 – CUSTOMS CONVENTION ON CONTAINERS – CCC/UN/IMO

Concluded : 02.12.1972, Geneva
In force : 06.12.1975
Parties : 23

The Convention is designed to develop and facilitate international carriage by container (Preamble). Contracting parties undertake to grant temporary admission free of import duties, import taxes and other restrictions to containers (including their normal accessories) which are re-exported within three months of their date of importation (Arts. 1, 3 and 4).

In contrast to the 1956 Containers Convention [see 112.07], contracting parties to the 1972 Convention agree to allow containers granted temporary admission to be used for the carriage of goods in internal traffic, although they may subject such use to one or more of the conditions laid out in Annex 3 (Art. 9).

Annex 1 specifies the manner in which containers must be marked in order to benefit from the provisions of the Convention (Art. 2). Annex 6 contains a set of Explanatory Notes for the interpretation of various provisions of the Convention and its annexes. Containers used in the transport of goods under customs seal must meet the technical requirements set out in Annex 4. Approval for this purpose is to be granted under one of the procedures laid down in Annex 5 (Art. 12). The Convention contains seven annexes and is accompanied by a Protocol of Signature.

Pursuant to Article 20, the present Convention, since its entry into force on 6 December 1975, has terminated and replaced, as between its contracting parties, the 1956 Containers Convention [see 112.07]. Further, Annex B.3. of the 1990 Istanbul Convention [see 112.25] terminates and replaces, as between those contracting parties having accepted that Annex, Articles 2 to 11 and Annexes 1 (Paras. 1 and 2) to 3 of the present Convention – that is, all substantive provisions not involving transport under customs seal (Annex B.3., Art. 9). Note that under Annex B.3., the period for the re-exportation of containers is increased to a minimum of six months (Art. 6).

G.S.M.

Access : ALS (Art. 18)
Reserves : PAU (Art. 26)
Duration : MIN (Art. 24)
Deposit. : UN (Art. 28)
Language : Chi, Eng, Fre, Rus, Spa (Art. 28)

Modific. : Amendments to: Annexes 4 and 6 11-13.05.81 (08.03.83); Annexes 1, 5, 6 and 7 13-15.02.84 (18.09.85); Annex 6 06-08.05.85 (01.01.88); Art. 1-c and Annex 6 25-27.05.87 (01.03.90)

Reference : 988 UNTS – Can TS 1976/49

112.19 – INTERNATIONAL CONVENTION ON THE SIMPLIFICATION AND HARMONIZATION OF CUSTOMS PROCEDURES ("KYOTO CONVENTION") – CCC

Concluded : 18.05.1973, Kyoto
In force : 25.09.1974
Parties : 54

The Kyoto Convention is one of the key instruments in the series of international conventions elaborated by the Customs Co-operation Council (CCC) [see 112 A] for the purpose of simplifying and harmonizing customs procedures and, ultimately, promoting international trade and other international exchanges. The Convention is designed to facilitate this process by offering states the possibility of selective and progressive application of its substantive rules (Preamble).

The body of the Convention sets out a number of general provisions essential for the implementation of the instrument, such as those concerning administration, accession, and amendment. The substantive rules are contained in the annexes, each of which deals with a particular sphere of customs activity.

On adhering to the Convention, states must ratify at least one annex and may subsequently accept one or more further annexes (Art. 11). Each of the annexes accepted by a contracting party, together with the body of the Convention, form a single legal instrument (Art. 8). In accepting an annex, a contracting party undertakes to abide by all Standards and Recommended Practices (substantive rules) contained therein, subject to any reservations it makes in respect of these (Arts. 2 and 5).

The CCC supervises the administration and development of the Convention. Most of this work, including the preparation and proposal of new annexes, is carried out by the Permanent Technical Committee, operating under the authority of the CCC (Art. 6). An annex enters into force three months after it has been accepted by five contracting parties (Art. 12). As of 31 May 1993, 26 of the Convention's 31 annexes had entered into force. The annexes cover the entire range of customs procedures, including importation, exportation, duty-free admission, temporary admission, inward and outward processing, transit, free zones, warehousing, and right of appeal.

G.S.M.

Access : ASO (Art. 11)
Reserves : PAU (Art. 2, 5, 9)
Duration : ULT (Art. 14)
Deposit. : CCC
Language : Eng, Fre

Reference : 950 UNTS – UKTS 1975/36 – JORF 5 Jan 1975 – RTAF 1975/2

112.20 – CUSTOMS CONVENTION ON THE INTERNATIONAL TRANSPORT OF GOODS UNDER COVER OF TIR CARNETS – ECE

Concluded : 14.11.1975, Geneva
In force : 20.03.1978
Parties : 45

The 1975 TIR Convention was adopted by a revising conference convened in accordance with Article 46 of the 1959 TIR Convention [see 112.09].

The Convention applies where goods are transported, without intermediate reloading, across one or more frontiers between a customs office of departure of one contracting party and a customs office of destination of another or of the same contracting party, in road vehicles, combinations of vehicles or containers. The 1975 TIR Convention, in contrast to that of 1959, allows for the multimodal transport (rail, sea, air) of containers, provided part of the journey between the beginning and end of the TIR operation is made by road (Art. 2).

The transport operations are performed under cover of TIR carnet, issued by authorized associations who undertake to pay any customs duties and other charges incurred as a result of irregularities in the TIR operation (Arts. 3-b, 6 and 8). The TIR carnet is to conform to the model reproduced in Annex 1 (Art. 3-b). Goods carried under the TIR procedure are exempt from payment or deposit of customs duties and taxes at customs offices *en route* to their destination (Art. 4). Where these goods are carried in sealed road vehicles, combinations of vehicles or containers, they are not, as a general rule, subject to examination *en route* (Art. 5).

Chapter III(a) (Arts. 12 to 14) specifies the conditions of approval for vehicles and containers engaged in TIR operations under customs seal. Road vehicles must comply with the technical conditions laid down in Annex 2 of the Convention and must be approved according to the procedure specified in Annex 3. The certificate of approval is to conform to the specimen reproduced in Annex 4 (Art. 12). Containers must meet the technical requirements laid down in Part I of Annex 7 and must be approved according to the procedure set out in Part II of the same Annex. Containers approved for the transport of goods under customs seal in accordance with the 1956 and 1972 container conventions [see 112.07 and 112.18] are accepted for transport under the TIR procedure without further approval (Art. 13).

The transport of "heavy or bulky goods" (defined in Art. 1-k) is subject to the provisions of Chapter III(c) of the Convention (Arts. 29 to 35). These goods may be carried in non-sealed vehicles or containers. No certificate of approval is required for road vehicles or containers transporting heavy or bulky goods, yet customs officials are to ensure that the conditions of Paragraph 3 of Article 29 are met (Art. 29, Explanatory Note 0.29).

The procedure for transport under cover of TIR carnet is governed by Chapter III(b) (Arts. 15 to 28). Article 26 provides for that situation where the TIR operation is partly conducted in the territory of a non-state party to the Convention.

The Convention's eight annexes form an integral part of it (Art. 51). Explanatory notes, interpreting various provisions of the Convention and setting out certain recommended practices, are found in Annex 6 and Part III of Annex 7. The absence of explanatory notes in the 1959 TIR Convention is one indication of the relatively greater precision of the more recent Convention. Also in contrast to the 1959 Convention, states adhering to the 1975 Convention cannot preclude the application of the provisions governing the transport of heavy or bulky goods. The only permitted reservation is that in respect of the dispute settlement procedures of Article 57 (Art. 58).

Since its entry into force on 20 March 1978, the Convention has terminated and replaced, as between its contracting parties, the 1959 TIR Convention (Art. 56).

G.S.M.

Access : ASO (Art. 52)
Reserves : PAU (Art. 58)
Duration : MIN (Art. 55)
Deposit. : UN (Art. 64)
Language : Eng, Fre, Rus

Modific. : Amendments to: Annexes 2 and 6 20.10.78 (01.08.79); Annexes 1 and 6 18.10.79 (01.10.80); Annex 6 03.07.80 (01.10.81); Annex 6 23.10.81 (01.10.82); Annex 6 27-28.10.83 (01.08.84); Annex 6 10-12.10.84 (01.08.85); Annexes 1, 2 and 6 9-11.10.85 (01.08.86); Annexes 1, 6 and 7 8-10.10.86 (01.08.87); Annex 2 18-20.11.87 (01.08.88); Art. 18 and Annex 1 18-20.11.87 (23.05.89); Annexes 2 and 7 24-25.11.88 (01.08.89); Annexes 2, 6 and 7 13-14.09.89 (01.08.90); Annex 6 01-02.11.90 (01.08.1991)

Reference : 1079, 1142 UNTS – UKTS 1983/56 – JORF 5 Dec 1979 – RTAF 1979/55

112.21 – INTERNATIONAL CONVENTION ON MUTUAL ADMINISTRATIVE ASSISTANCE FOR THE PREVENTION, INVESTIGATION AND REPRESSION OF CUSTOMS OFFENCES ("NAIROBI CONVENTION") – CCC

Concluded : 09.06.1977, Nairobi
In force : 21.05.1980
Parties : 30

The Nairobi Convention is the most important in the series of initiatives undertaken by the Customs Co-operation Council (CCC) [see 112 A] to combat customs fraud, increasingly international in its scope. The Convention, designed to replace existing CCC recommendations on customs enforcement, establishes a system of information exchange between its contracting parties.

The body of the Convention contains a series of provisions dealing with general assistance procedures and the overall functioning of the Nairobi instrument. The Convention has 11 annexes, each dealing with a particular sphere of co-operation between states. Any annex which a contracting party accepts, together with the body of the Convention, constitute a single legal instrument (Art. 10).

Under Article 2 of the Convention, contracting parties undertake that their customs administrations afford each other mutual assistance with a view to preventing, investigating and repressing customs offences. The principle of reciprocity underlies this provision, as it underlies the Convention as a whole; however, a contracting party is bound to assist another only in so far as both have accepted the same annex. The Convention also seeks to avoid any overlap of jurisdiction. Customs administrations request assistance *vis-à-vis* other customs administrations who provide such assistance only within the limits of their competence. Paragraph 3 of Article 2 specifies that the obligation to provide assistance does not extend to requests for the arrests of persons or the recovery of duties, taxes, charges, fines or any other monies on behalf of another contracting party.

Article 3, a general escape clause, allows a contracting party to refuse to give assistance, or to give it subject to certain conditions or requirements, where this would otherwise infringe upon its sovereignty, security or other substantial national interests or prejudice the legitimate commercial interests of any public or private enterprise. The Convention does not allow reservations (Art. 18).

Upon adhering to the Convention, a state must accept at least one annex. It may subsequently accept one or more additional annexes (Art. 15). An annex enters into force three months after two states have accepted it (Art. 16).

The 11 annexes of the Convention, all of which are now in force, cover the entire range of goods which might be the subject of a customs offence. Annex X concerns assistance against the smuggling of narcotic drugs and psychotropic substances. It complements the existing UN conventions in this area. Annex XI concerns assistance against the smuggling of works of art, antiques and other cultural property. Annexes I through IX apply in respect of all other goods. They deal with:

- assistance by a customs administration on its own initiative (Annex I);
- assistance, on request, in the assessment of import or export duties and taxes (Annex II);
- assistance, on request, relating to controls (Annex III);
- assistance, on request, relating to surveillance (Annex IV);
- enquiries and notifications, on request, on behalf of another contracting party (Annex V);
- appearance by customs officials before a court or tribunal abroad (Annex VI);
- presence of customs officials of one contracting party in the territory of another contracting party (Annex VII);
- participation in investigations abroad (Annex VIII); and
- pooling of information (Annex IX).

The CCC is responsible for the administration of the Convention under Article 12. In June 1983, it set up an **Enforcement Committee** to assume various functions related to the Convention and to customs enforcement in general. In promoting the aims of the Convention, the CCC works closely with numerous other international organizations, among them INTERPOL and the UN bodies involved in the suppression of customs fraud.

G.S.M.

Access : ASO (Art. 15)
Reserves : PRO (Art. 18)
Duration : ULT (Art. 19)
Deposit. : CCC
Language : Eng, Fre

Modific. : Amendment to Article 15 (27.07.89)

Reference : 1226 UNTS – Can TS 1990/41 – UKTS 1984/10

112.22 – AGREEMENT ON IMPLEMENTATION OF ARTICLE VII AND PROTOCOL ("CUSTOMS VALUATION CODE") – GATT

Concluded : 12.04.1979, Geneva
In force : 01.01.1981
Parties : 31

The Customs Valuation Code was concluded within the framework of the GATT Tokyo Round of negotiations [see 111.01]. In keeping with the aim of the Round to bring non-tariff measures under more effective international discipline, the Code rules were designed to translate the general principles contained in GATT Article VII into more precise form. There was widespread dissatisfaction with the first international customs valuation standard, the Brussels Definition of Value (BDV), due to its inherent vagueness [see 112.04]. United States valuation rules, not based on the BDV, were also widely criticized as protectionist. The GATT Code was thus conceived as a fair, uniform and neutral system for the valuation of goods which would preclude the use of arbitrary or fictitious customs values (Preamble).

The primary basis for customs value under the Code is the transaction value of the goods – that is, the price actually paid or payable for the goods when sold for export to the country of importation, adjusted if necessary to include specified other costs (Arts. 1 and 8). The transaction value will not apply under certain, defined circumstances, notably where a close relationship between the buyer and seller has influenced the price (Art. 1).

Articles 2 to 7 set out alternative methods of valuation which apply whenever the transaction value method does not. Subject to an exception listed in Article 4, they are to be applied in the order in which they are listed in the Code (Interpretative Notes, General Note). These methods yield: the transaction value of identical goods (Art. 2); the transaction value of similar goods (Art. 3); the deductive value (Art. 5); and the computed value (Art. 6). Where none of these valuation methods can be used, Article 7 offers a fall-back method – any "reasonable means" consistent with the provisions of the Code and available data.

The parties to the Code undertake to incorporate the provisions of the Code into their domestic laws, regulations and administrative procedures (Art. 25-1). They also agree to provide in their legislation a right of appeal to judicial authority in respect of customs valuation disputes (Art. 11). All laws, regulations, judicial decisions and administrative rulings of general application giving effect to the Code are to be published (Art. 12).

The annexes to the Code form an integral part of it. The articles of the Code are to be read and applied in accordance with the Interpretative Notes found in Annex I (Art. 14).

A **Committee on Customs Valuation**, operating under the GATT's auspices, administers the Code at a general, policy-oriented level. A **Technical Committee on Customs Valuation** works under the auspices of the Customs Co-operation Council [see 112 A] to ensure the uniform interpretation and application of the Code at the technical level (Art. 18 and Annex II).

Developing countries are allowed to delay the application of the Code and to apply some of its provisions with greater flexibility pursuant to Article 21 and the Protocol to the Agreement.

In contrast to the BDV, which uses a "notional" standard of customs valuation [see 112.04], the GATT Code opts for a "positive" standard, reflected in its choice of the actual price paid (transaction value) as the primary basis for customs valuation. The GATT standard is now far more widely used than the BDV. All major industrial countries, including the US and Canada, are parties to the Code. The GATT Secretariat estimates that 73 per cent of world trade was governed by it in 1990.

G.S.M.

Access : CON (Art. 22)
Reserves : CST (Art. 23)
Duration : USP
Deposit. : GATT (Art. 30)
Language : Eng, Fre, Spa

Modific. : Protocol 01.11.79 (01.01.81)

Reference : 1235 UNTS – BISD 26 Supp. – Can TS 1981/37/38 – UST 34/1

112.23 – INTERNATIONAL CONVENTION ON THE HARMONIZATION OF FRONTIER CONTROLS OF GOODS – ECE

Concluded : 21.10.1982, Geneva
In force : 15.10.1985
Parties : 26

The aim of the Convention is to facilitate the international movement of goods through the harmonization of frontier controls (Preamble). To this end, formalities are to be eased and the number and duration of controls reduced, in particular by national and international co-ordination of control procedures and of their methods of application (Art. 2).

The Convention applies to all goods imported, exported or in transit, when moved across one or more maritime, air or inland frontiers. It applies to all control services of the contracting parties (Art. 3).

The contracting parties undertake to achieve the aims of the Convention by co-ordinating their customs and other control services (Art. 4), by co-operating with each other and with competent international bodies (Art. 6), by co-ordinating their frontier controls with those of adjacent countries (Art. 7), by increasing their use of documents aligned on the United Nations Layout Key (Art. 9), and by providing wherever possible simple and speedy treatment for goods in transit (Art. 10).

The contracting parties retain the right to impose restrictions and prohibitions relating to importation, exportation or transit for reasons of public policy, but these are to be applied, to the extent possible, in conformity with the provisions of the Convention (Art. 11). Emergency measures are to be proportionate to the emergency and limited to its actual duration (Art. 12).

The Convention is complemented by seven annexes which form an integral part of it (Art. 13):

- Annex 1: harmonization of customs controls and other controls;
- Annex 2: medico-sanitary inspection;
- Annex 3: veterinary inspection;
- Annex 4: phytosanitary inspection;
- Annex 5: control of compliance with technical standards;
- Annex 6: quality control; and
- Annex 7: rules of procedure of the Administrative Committee referred to in Article 22 of the Convention.

G.S.M.

Access : ASO (Art. 16)
Reserves : PAU (Art. 21)
Duration : MIN (Art. 19)
Deposit. : UN (Art. 16)
Language : Eng, Fre, Rus, Spa

Reference : UKTS 1988/40 – JORF 1 Oct 1988 – RTAF 1988/50

112.24 – INTERNATIONAL CONVENTION ON THE HARMONIZED COMMODITY DESCRIPTION AND CODING SYSTEM – CCC

Concluded : 14.06.1983, Brussels
In force : 01.01.1988
Parties : 69

The Convention establishes a combined tariff/statistical nomenclature for the description, classification and codification of goods moving in international trade in order to facilitate international trade, international trade negotiations and the collection, comparison and analysis of international trade statistics (Preamble).

The Harmonized System (HS), contained in the Annex to the Convention, is a more detailed, modern nomenclature than the Customs Co-operation Council Nomenclature (CCCN) on which it is based and which it replaces [see 112.03]. The HS comprises 5,019 product groups identified by six-digit codes arranged under 1,241 headings, 96 chapters, and 21 sections. In order to ensure the uniform application of the System, the HS includes General Rules for its interpretation and Section, Chapter and Subheading Notes, all of which are binding. Nonbinding Explanatory Notes and Classification Opinions are prepared by the Harmonized System Committee to the same end.

Under Article 3 of the Convention, contracting parties undertake to bring their customs tariff and statistical nomenclatures into conformity with the HS. They may create additional product subdivisions for their own purposes, but only at a level beyond that of the six-digit code. Contracting parties assume no obligation in relation to rates of customs duty (Art. 9). The HS is intended to serve as a multipurpose nomenclature. Thus, contracting parties agree to publish their import and export trade statistics in HS form, except where exceptional considerations, such as commercial confidentiality or national security, dictate otherwise (Art. 3). Note that under the CCCN Convention, the use of statistical digits was optional.

The Convention allows developing countries to apply the HS partially, to the four-digit level only (Art. 4), although only one country (Malawi) has so far done so. Developing countries are also entitled to special technical assistance under Article 5 of the Convention.

Sections I to IV of the HS cover agricultural products broadly speaking, Section V mineral products, Section VI chemical and parachemical products, Section VII plastics, rubber and articles thereof, Sections VIII to X certain products of animal or vegetable origin, Section XI textiles and textile articles, Section XII articles generally worn or carried, Section XIII products obtained from mineral materials, Section XIV precious stones and metals, Section XV base metals and articles of base metal, Section XVI machinery, mechanical appliances and electrical equipment, Section XVII vehicles and transportation equipment, Section XVIII precision instruments, Section XIX arms and ammunition, Section XX miscellaneous manufactured articles, and Section XXI works of art, collectors' pieces and antiques.

In response to the work on the HS, a new version of the UN's Standard International Trade Classification, SITC Rev.3, was implemented in 1988. Correlation with the HS has been maintained for all goods except refined petroleum products which the SITC describes in more detail. A high degree of correlation also exists between the HS and the latest version of the International Standard Industrial Classification of All Economic Activities, ISIC Rev.3, the recommended UN system for national economic and social statistics, and the Provisional Central Product Classification, the new UN classification for goods and services.

The HS Convention is administered by the **HS Committee**, composed of representatives of each of the parties to the Convention (Art. 6). Under the authority of the Customs Co-operation Council (CCC) [see 112 A], the Committee prepares Explanatory Notes and Classification Opinions to assist in the interpretation of the HS. It proposes amendments to the Convention in response to the needs of users and changes in technology or patterns of international trade (Arts. 7 and 8). The Committee may be assisted in its work by subcommittees or working parties which it establishes (Art. 6).

Classification questions are first examined by the CCC Secretariat, which then refers them to the HS Committee for appropriate action. The Committee also has primary responsibility for the settlement of disputes between contracting parties (Art. 10).

In order to promote the uniform application of the HS and to help countries transpose their customs tariffs to the new system, a programme for the exchange of national classification rulings has been set up. A Review Sub-Committee has also been established to review the entire Nomenclature on an ongoing basis. The latter has been amended once, with effect 1 January 1992. The Protocol of Amendment of 24 June 1986 was designed solely to bring the HS Convention into force on 1 January 1988.

The CCC estimates that the HS now governs more than 90 per cent of world trade and is applied by more than 80 countries (not all of whom have acceded to the Convention). The GATT now conducts its tariff negotiations on the basis of the HS. Use of the HS by non-governmental bodies has been modest to date although there is considerable potential for the private use of the System.

Glenn S. McDonald & Maureen Irish

Access	: CON (Art. 11)
Reserves	: PRO (Art. 18)
Duration	: ULT (Art. 15)
Deposit.	: CCC
Language	: Eng, Fre
Modific.	: Protocol 24.06.86 (01.01.88); Amendment to Annex 05.07.89 (01.01.92)
Reference	: Can TS 1988/38 – UKTS 1989/15 – JORF 15 Mar 1988 – RTAF 1988/11

112.25 – CONVENTION ON TEMPORARY ADMISSION ("ISTANBUL CONVENTION") – CCC

Concluded : 26.06.1990, Istanbul
Parties : 2

For the purpose of facilitating access to internationally regulated temporary admission facilities, the Istanbul Convention gathers together in a single instrument the existing legal instruments dealing with temporary admission. It also introduces, at the international level, certain facilities which until now have been granted unilaterally by some CCC members. The Convention simplifies and harmonizes the formalities relating to temporary admission and offers a framework for the introduction of temporary admission facilities in respect of new categories of goods.

Under the temporary admission procedure, goods and/or means of transport, imported for a specific purpose and intended for re-exportation in the same condition within a specified period of time, can be brought into the customs territory without payment of import duties and taxes and without application of import prohibitions or restrictions of an economic character (Art. 1).

Contracting parties to the Convention undertake to grant temporary admission to the goods and/or means of transport covered by the annexes which they have accepted (Art. 2). Unless otherwise provided for in an annex, they retain the right to make temporary admission subject to the production of a customs document and provision of security (Art. 4). For these purposes they are to accept temporary admission papers – "ATA carnets" for goods, "CPD carnets" for means of transport – issued and used in accordance with the conditions laid down in Annex A of the Convention (Art. 5; Annex A, Art. 2).

Goods and means of transport granted temporary admission must be re-exported within the period set out in the relevant annex and within the period of validity of the temporary admission papers (maximum one year) (Art. 7; Annex A, Arts. 5 and 7). Temporary admission normally terminates upon the re-exportation of the goods and/or means of transport (Art. 9). Other cases of termination, including accidents and force majeure, are enumerated in Articles 12 to 14.

The Convention establishes an **Administrative Committee**, composed of the contracting parties to the Convention. This Committee supervises the implementation of the Convention, considers amendments to it and decides upon the incorporation of new annexes (Arts. 22 and 23).

The annexes which a contracting party accepts, together with the body of the Convention, constitute a single legal instrument (Art. 28). In acceding to the Convention, states must accept Annex A, concerning temporary admission papers, and at least one other annex. They may subsequently accept one or more further annexes (Art. 24).

Several of the annexes are intended to replace earlier Conventions concluded in respect of the same subject matter [see the list below]. Thus, Annex A terminates and replaces, as between the contracting parties to the present Convention, the 1961 ATA Convention [see 112.13].

The Convention has 12 other annexes besides Annex A. Each contains special provisions applicable to a particular type or class of goods:

- goods for display or use at exhibitions, fairs, meetings or similar events (Annex B.1.) [intended to replace Treaty 112.11];
- professional equipment (Annex B.2.) [intended to replace Treaty 112.12];
- containers, pallets, packings, samples and other goods imported in connection with a commercial operation (Annex B.3.)[intended to replace: Arts. 3, 5 and 6 (1-b and 2) of Treaty 112.05; 112.10; European Convention on Customs

Treatment of Pallets Used in International Transport, (Geneva, 1960); and Arts. 2-11 and Annexes 1 (Paras. 1 and 2) to 3 of Treaty 112.18];
- goods imported in connection with a manufacturing operation (Annex B.4.);
- goods imported for educational, scientific or cultural purposes (Annex B.5.) [intended to replace Treaties 112.14, 112.15 and 112.16];
- travellers' personal effects and goods imported for sports purposes (Annex B.6.) [intended to replace Arts. 2 and 5 of the Convention concerning Customs Facilities for Touring (New York, 1954)] [see 172.01];
- tourist publicity material (Annex B.7.) (intended to replace the Additional Protocol to the Convention concerning Customs Facilities for Touring, Relating to the Importation of Tourist Publicity Documents and Material (New York, 1954) [see 172.02]);
- goods imported as frontier traffic (Annex B.8.);
- goods imported for humanitarian purposes (Annex B.9.);
- means of transport (Annex C) [intended to replace the customs conventions on the temporary importation of private road vehicles [see 172.03], of commercial road vehicles [see 112.08] and of aircraft and pleasure boats] [see 172.05];
- animals (Annex D); and
- goods imported with partial relief from import duties and taxes (Annex E).

The Convention will enter into force three months after five states have ratified or acceded to it (Art. 26).

G.S.M.

Access : ASO (Art. 24)
Reserves : PAU (Art. 29; Annex A, Art. 18)
Duration : ULT (Art. 31)
Deposit. : CCC (Art. 25)
Language : Eng, Fre, (Ara, Chi, Rus, Spa)

1.2 Commodities

International agreements on commodities have existed in one form or another since the mid-nineteenth century and are still important instruments of international economic co-operation. In general, the aim of such agreements is to reduce price fluctuations, to improve long-term producer earnings and to provide a steady, adequate and reasonably priced supply of a particular commodity to the consumer. The agreements can be divided into various categories according to their antecedents, the range of participation, regulatory mechanisms and form. They may be negotiated within the United Nations framework, drawing on recognized principles within the UN system, or alternatively outside it.

Broadly speaking, commodity agreements fall into three main categories: international commodity agreements concluded between exporter and importer states; single interest and other intergovernmental producers' associations, or producers' alliances; and non-governmental cartels. Some agreements have regulatory mechanisms, often called economic provisions, and can include an export control system (quotas) and/or an international stock system (buffer stock). Other agreements are operated under a multilateral contract system and several simply provide a co-ordinative and informative function. Likewise, the agreements may exist in the form of treaties or as informal arrangements within an intergovernmental forum – for example, the Food and Agricultural Organization (FAO) [see 131 A].

More specifically, international commodity agreements share four common characteristics which distinguish them from producers' alliances and non-governmental cartels. First, the agreement is a multilateral treaty, negotiated in pursuance of the internationally recognized principles of the Havana Charter [see 111.02] and now that of UNCTAD [see 111 B]. Second, the interests of both exporting and importing parties are represented. Third, the agreement contains regulatory or co-ordinative machinery in order to achieve its objectives, principally the stabilization of prices and supply. Finally, the agreements establish an international commodity organization, with international legal personality, capable of pursuing a number of functions assigned to it.

Mary E. Footer

SELECTED BIBLIOGRAPHY

Khan, K.R., *The Law and Organisation of International Commodity Agreements*, Dordrecht: Martinus Nijhoff Publishers, 1982.

1.2.1 Economic Agreements

Legally binding agreements concluded between producing and consuming states, which contain market intervention mechanisms, are often called "international commodity control agreements". These agreements contain detailed economic clauses aimed at stabilizing prices. In consequence, they provide for intervention in the relevant commodity market by means of the assignment of production and export quotas and the buying and selling of buffer stocks. They are distinguishable from those commodity mechanisms which lack market regulatory powers and which are listed under commercial agreements [see 1.2.2].

Only two of the original five international commodity control agreements with specific price-stabilization mechanisms are still operational (cocoa and natural rubber); the one on coffee has been extended for a limited period with the suspension of its economic clauses. Following the collapse of tin some of the tin-producing countries have introduced supply management mechanisms into their producers' alliances, as for example with the Association of Tin Producing Countries [see 124.09]. In the case of sugar, the renegotiated agreement has been deprived of economic clauses altogether.

Despite earlier expectations, the negotiation of new commodity agreements and the renegotiation of existing ones under the evolving Integrated Programme for Commodities [see 121.01], have been disappointing, resulting in only one such agreement which incorporates economic clauses, that of the Natural Rubber Agreement of 1979, renewed in 1987 [see 121.06].

Mary E. Footer and Oscar J. Rodríguez-Aguilar

121.01 – INTEGRATED PROGRAMME FOR COMMODITIES – UNCTAD

Adopted : 30.05.1976, Res.93 (IV)

On 30 May 1976, at its Fourth Session in Nairobi, UNCTAD adopted "without dissent" a resolution approving the Integrated Programme for Commodities (IPC). The Resolution signified the acceptance by the international community of a new policy approach on commodities, thereby emphasizing the importance of commodity trade for developing countries. Unlike the former Havana principles on commodity trade regulation [see 111.02] which dealt with product-specific problems arising out of temporary market imbalances, the IPC supported the longer-term objective of an improvement in the terms of trade of developing countries. This was to be achieved by the stablization of market conditions and prices in primary commodity trade. Henceforth, the focus was to be shifted to an overall integrated programme for "a comprehensive range of commodities of export interest to developing countries", thereby placing all commodity agreements under a single programme.

The 18 commodities initially selected for inclusion in the IPC encompass food commodities, agricultural raw materials and minerals. Other commodities may be added. In order to achieve its goals, the Resolution embraces a comprehensive range of permissible international measures. These include the setting up of international commodity stocking arrangements; the harmonization of stocking policies and co-ordination of national stocks; the establishment of pricing arrangements and internationally agreed supply management measures; compensatory facilities for the stablization of export earnings; the improvement of market access for the primary and processed products of developing countries and so on.

The crucial part of the Resolution is its operative paragraphs which launch a parallel process of discussion and negotiation within UNCTAD. They call both for the convening of a negotiating conference on a common fund for commodities no later than March 1977 [see 121.02], and for preparatory meetings, complete with procedures and timetables, for international negotiations on individual products.

Mary E. Footer

Reference : UN Doc. TD/217, 12 July 1976, pp. 2-8

SELECTED BIBLIOGRAPHY

Corea, Gamani, *Taming Commodity Markets: The Integrated Programme and the Common Fund in UNCTAD*, Manchester; New York: Manchester University Press; St Martin's Press, 1992.

121.02 – AGREEMENT ESTABLISHING A COMMON FUND FOR COMMODITIES – UNCTAD

Concluded : 27.06.1980, Geneva
In force : 19.06.1989
Parties : 106

The Common Fund Agreement, concluded in 1980, marked the end of a series of protracted negotiations, under the direction of the UNCTAD Secretariat, aimed at fulfilling the objectives embodied in Resolution 93 (IV) of UNCTAD [see 121.01]. The Fund is intended to serve as the key instrument of the Integrated Programme for Commodities (IPC) and to facilitate the conclusion and functioning of International Commodity Agreements (ICAs), particularly in commodities of special interest to developing countries (Art. 2). The Agreement came into force in June 1989 and the Governing Council held its first meeting in July. The Common Fund commenced operations on 15 September 1989. It is headquartered in Amsterdam, the Netherlands.

DETAILS OF THE AGREEMENT

Through a First Account, the Fund is to contribute "to the financing of international buffer stocks and internationally co-ordinated national stocks all within the framework of ICAs". Through a Second Account, the Fund is "to finance measures in the field of commodities other than stocking" that are jointly sponsored by producers and consumers within the framework of international commodity bodies. The Fund also exists "to promote co-ordination and consultation through its Second Account with regard to measures in the field of commodities other than stocking, and their financing, with a view to providing a commodity focus" (Art. 3). These measures include research and development, productivity improvement, marketing and marketing promotion. Under the Agreement, the Common Fund and the ICAs are to respect each other's autonomy thereby obviating any idea of the Fund being authorized to make policy recommodations – albeit of a non-binding nature – to associated International Commodity Organizations (ICOs) (Art. 7-4). It is envisaged, however, that ICOs which have been established in order to implement the provisions of the relevant ICA, which provide either for international buffer stocks or internationally co-ordinated national stocks, should avail themselves of the Fund's First Account provided that an Association Agreement has been concluded with the Fund.

The financial resources and capital structure of the Common Fund consist of obligatory contributions by all members amounting to US$470 million ("Directly Contributed Capital"), divided into 37,000 paid-in shares and 10,000 payable shares (Art. 9). Each state party to the Agreement must make a basic contribution by subscribing to 100 paid-in shares of US$10,000 each, with the remainder being drawn from recognized groups of member states, according to their ability to pay (Art. 10).

Of the total of direct contributions, US$400 million is attributed to the First Account, although members may allocate a part of their subscription (aggregate volume of US$70 million) to the Second Account (Art. 10-3). The Second Account is constituted mainly of voluntary contributions, with the exception of the aforementioned US$70 million, to which each member may contribute from its obligatory subscription (Art. 18). A target volume for the initial voluntary contribution was fixed at US$280 million. A third source of Fund capital is from the ICOs, or members of such organizations which are associated with the Common Fund. Upon association with the Fund, an ICO is required to deposit in cash one-third of its maximum financial requirement (MFR) (Art. 14). In the event that an associated ICO has exhausted its financial resources through stock purchases, it may alternatively pledge the Common Fund Stock of equivalent value (Art. 14-2). Additionally, member states of the relevant ICO shall provide guarantee capital to the Common Fund in an amount of two-thirds of the Maximum Financial Requirement (MFR) of that ICO (Art. 14-4).

The Common Fund is also authorized to borrow capital from its members and international financial institutions; in respect of First Account operations, it may also borrow in the capital markets (Art. 16-5).

Under the framework of the First Account, associated ICOs have the right to withdraw their cash deposits in order to meet stocking costs and for that same purpose the Common Fund may also grant loans at rates as low as financially bearable (Art. 17-10).

As to Second Account operations, any International Commodity Body (ICB) can qualify as a recipient of loans provided that it operates on a world-wide basis and comprises both producers and consumers. Thus, producers' alliances are excluded [see 1.2.4] (Art. 18-3 and Schedule C].

STRUCTURE

The Fund has a Governing Council, an Executive Board, a Managing Director and a staff (Art. 19). The plenary organ is the **Governing Council** in which all powers of the Common Fund are vested and on which all members are represented by one Governor and one alternate (Art. 20). The Governing Council is empowered to delegate any implementing functions to the **Executive Board**, made up of 28 Executive Directors, and responsible, under the terms of the Agreement, for the operation of the Common Fund (Art. 22). The Managing Director, assisted by the appropriate staff, is entrusted with the everyday administration of the Fund (Art. 24).

Voting in the Governing Council and on the Executive Board, whose voting pattern reflects that of the Governing Council, is by means of a combination of voting based upon the equality principle, whereby each member state holds 150 basic votes, topped up by a system of weighted voting. Under the latter system an additional number of votes is distributed in proportion to the size of a member state's stake in the directly contributed capital, with one vote being granted for each US$50,000 of guarantee capital provided by a member state to the Common Fund in respect of its membership in all ICOs associated with the Fund (Arts. 21 and 23 and Schedule D).

The Agreement specifies that wherever possible decisions should be taken without a vote and otherwise by a simple majority (Arts. 21 and 23); for some more important decisions qualified majority voting is required (Art. 35 or Art. 51).

Any question of interpretation or application of any of the Agreement's provisions must be submitted to the Executive Board. Its decision can be referred for review by any member of the Fund to the Governing Council, whose decision is final. In the event that the Governing Council cannot reach a decision, it may refer the matter to arbitration (Art. 52). Likewise any dispute arising between the Fund and a withdrawing member, or arising from the termination of the Fund's operations, may be submitted to arbitration under the terms of Article 53-2 unless an alternative arbitral procedure exists in an Association Agreement between the Fund and an associated ICO.

M.E.F.

Access : ASO (Art. 4, 56)
Reserves : PAU (Art. 53, 58)
Duration : USP
Deposit. : UN (Art. 55)
Language : Ara, Chi, Eng, Fre, Rus, Spa (Art. 58)

Reference : UN Doc. TD/IPC/CF/CONF.25 (1980) – ILM 19:896

SELECTED BIBLIOGRAPHY

Corea, Gamani, *Taming Commodity Markets: The Integrated Programme and the Common Fund in UNCTAD*, Manchester; New York: Manchester University Press; St Martin's Press, 1992.

121.03 – SIXTH INTERNATIONAL TIN AGREEMENT – ITC

Concluded : 26.06.1981, Geneva
In force : 01.07.1982, provisionally
Parties : 25

On 24 October 1985 the Buffer Stock Manager of the **International Tin Council** (ITC) announced to the London Metal Exchange that he had insufficient funds to honour his contracts and was forced to discontinue market support operations. The refusal of the producing and consuming members of the Sixth International Tin Agreement to meet the outstanding debts of the ITC means that it is now in the process of being wound up. Despite the collapse of the Sixth Tin Agreement, the producing countries' alliance, the Association of Tin Producing Countries [see 124.09], is still in existence.

The objectives of the Sixth Tin Agreement, one of the world's oldest international commodity agreements, were designed primarily to regulate world production and consumption of tin, to prevent excessive fluctuations in the price of tin and to secure an adequate supply of tin at prices deemed fair to consumers and remunerative to producers.

DETAILS OF THE AGREEMENT

There were two main operational mechanisms in the Sixth Agreement: the use of a buffer stock and the application of export controls, when necessary, to reinforce the buffer stock operations under specified circumstances, so as to adjust supply and demand. Under previous Agreements, the buffer stock was financed by producers only but, in the present Agreement, contributions were assessed equally from producers and consumers alike.

The ITC, established under previous international tin agreements, headquartered in London, UK, and composed of all the members, was charged with the administration of the Sixth Tin Agreement. It was responsible for appointing an independent Executive Chairman to administer and operate the Agreement, a Buffer Stock Manager and a Secretary of the Council.

SUBSEQUENT DEVELOPMENTS

The failure of the Sixth Tin Agreement is due to a number of long- and short-term factors. These include a fall in world consumption of tin, the absence from the Agreement of a major producer (Bolivia) and a major consumer (the US), increased production and sales of tin by non-member states, tin smuggling in order to avoid high royalties, taxes and fees of some governments, authorized forward trading by the Buffer Stock Manager with insufficient safeguards, an earlier decision to switch to Malaysian dollars for buffer stock price ranges which exposed Tin Agreement tin to widespread currency fluctuations, and the refusal of the six exporting members to fulfil their promise made in September 1985 to contribute an additional 60 million pounds sterling in cash to the ITC.

The ensuing "tin crisis" has had a strong impact on other negotiations for internationally traded primary commodities. Since the collapse of tin, seven international commodity agreements have been renegotiated, or are in the process of renegotiation. They include wheat, cocoa, olive oil, natural rubber, sugar, jute and, latterly, coffee and, once again, cocoa. Of those seven, only the International Agreement on Natural Rubber of 1987 [see 121.06] includes a market stabilization mechanism whilst the agreements on cocoa and coffee presently in the process of renegotiation contain similar "economic clauses", although the export quota system under the International Coffee Agreement of 1983 has been suspended [see 121.04].

M.E.F.

Access : CON (Art. 54)
Reserves : PRO (Art. 61)
Duration : DET 5 (Art. 59)
Deposit. : UN (Art. 50)
Language : Ara, Chi, Eng, Fre, Rus, Spa

Reference : UN Doc. TD/TIN.6/14/Rev.1 – UNTS 1282/205

SELECTED BIBLIOGRAPHY

McFadden, E.J., "The Collapse of Tin: Restructuring a Failed Commodity Agreement", *AJIL* 80 (1986): 811.

121.04 – INTERNATIONAL COFFEE AGREEMENT – ICO

Adopted : 16.09.1982, London
In force : 11.09.1985
Parties : 75

The International Coffee Agreement (ICA) of 1983 was approved by the International Coffee Council (ICC) in its Resolution No. 320, adopted on 16 September 1982 at the third plenary meeting of its 38th session held in London from 6 to 16 September 1982. It entered into force provisionally on 1 October 1983. The Agreement was then extended for two years until 30 September 1991, with modifications, under ICC Resolution No. 347 of 3 July 1989. ICC Resolution No. 352 further extended the ICA of 1983 until 30 September 1992. ICC Resolution No. 355 added a further extension to the extended ICA of 1983 until 30 September 1993. However, its economic provisions are currently inoperable following suspension by the ICC of the export quota system under that 3 July 1989 Resolution. The ICC called for the negotiation of the new ICA by 31 March 1993 but this has so far proved impossible.

This international commodity agreement also raises questions of uniformity of the commodity as well as of the homogeneity of producing countries' interests. For example, the African countries, relative newcomers to the world market, are beneficiaries of preferential trading with the EC through the Lomé Convention.

The Agreement has as its main objectives the achievement of fair and remunerative prices for both producers and consumers through a reasonable balance between world supply and demand for coffee (Art. 1). It is administered by the International Coffee Organization (ICO), created under the first International Coffee Agreement of 1962, with headquarters in London, UK.

STRUCTURE

The ICO exercises its powers through three main organs. First is the **International Coffee Council** (ICC), which is the highest authority of the Organization. It consists of all the ICO members, and meets annually. Decisions are taken by a distributed two-thirds majority vote (Arts. 9 and 10). Second, the **Executive Board**, made up of eight exporting and eight importing members, is elected for each coffee year. It is responsible to and works under the general direction of the ICC in ensuring the continuity of the Agreement (Art. 16). Finally, an **Executive Director**, assisted by a staff, is the chief administrative officer of the ICO (Art. 21).

Under normal circumstances, the Agreement is designed to operate through a complex system of export quotas in order to control the supply side. A target price range is set by the ICC, with different price ranges for the principal groups of coffee and a composite price range (Art. 38).

National basic quotas, or basic export tonnages, determined on the basis of the volume of average exports in a number of preceding years, form the starting point for the operation of the system. At the beginning of each coffee year, the ICC draws up a comprehensive estimate as to prospective world demand and distributes the global quantity thus calculated among the members in proportion to their basic quotas (Art. 35-1 and 35-2). Quarterly quotas are also fixed in order to avoid seasonal fluctuations (Art. 36). If market conditions so require, the annual and quarterly quotas may be adjusted by the ICC (Arts. 37 and 39).

In order to maximize the benefits of the export quotas regime and to prevent their sole effect being the accrual of benefits to non-member producing countries, certain so-called standard clauses are included in the Agreement. Thus, importing countries are required to limit from non-members the entry of a quantity of coffee higher than the annual average imported during a number of preceding years (Art. 45-1). However, exporting countries must refrain from selling coffee to non-members on terms more favourable than those offered to importing members (Art. 2-3). They must also adopt production policy measures to ensure adequate compliance with established quotas and undertake to provide adequate stocking facilities (Art. 42).

In order to verify compliance with the quota system, certificates of origin must be produced to cover coffee exports from exporting members (Art. 43). One of the central features of the ongoing negotiations for a new agreement focuses on a demand from some importing members for stricter controls on coffee exports by the exporting members themselves as the certificate of origin system has been variously abused throughout its history. In fact, the July 1992 talks broke down because of the refusal of some of the consumer nations to impose restrictions on coffee imports which were not certified according to the country of origin. Following this deadlock in negotiations, most producers now want to restrict production in the hope of buttressing world prices.

The issue of controls in producing countries has been a cause of concern to consuming countries. The latter feel insufficient restrictions at origin will lead to the re-emergence of a two-tier market and they have therefore pushed for a producer-policed, market-orientated new agreement. They also agreed to a selective system of quota adjustments and a new agreement which would remain uninterrupted for three years to ensure market stability, except where otherwise justified by exceptional circumstances. These were to include a significant drop in either demand or supply, a major change in membership of the ICO, technical elements such as market weightings, growth in composition of group indicators, a period for moving to average prices and a reference to the number of days which would trigger quota allocation. The producers' response was to call for a review on the well-functioning of the system after 18 months' operation and to include among the exceptional circumstances, issues related to the low-level of prices which interfere with the objectives of the Agreement, to the technical elements and to the selective adjustment of quotas. They also wished to know the established volume of coffee for quota adjustments, the number of adjustments by group of coffee and by year, as well as the number of adjustments by quarter.

Despite the fact that both consumers and producers had jointly agreed to a selective quota system to go into operation on the first day after the new agreement was due to commence, a quota allocation on a quarterly basis and consideration for producers to export at increased percentage levels during successive quarters, the most recent round of negotiations broke down completely on 31 March 1993. Failure to reach agreement on a new ICA has been met by a decision by representatives of 40 coffee producing countries in September 1993 to set up the Association of Coffee Producing Nations to be headquartered in Brasilia, in order to promote the co-ordination of coffee policies among its members, to promote consumption in both producing and consuming countries, to establish a balance between global supply and demand based on fair and remunerative prices, to promote quality improvements in the product and to contribute to the development of the producing states. The new Association will operate a retention scheme, effective 1 October 1993, in respect of 20 per cent of each country's coffee exports until the price of coffee reaches 75 US cents per pound; 10 per cent of coffee exports until the price hits 80 US cents per pound and above that level there will be no further retention. The retention programmes of individual countries will be monitored by the Association, with the assistance of an independent auditor.

Since the export quota system has currently been suspended pending the outcome of protracted negotiations over a new agreement, the ICA remains in force solely as a source of statistical data and to fulfil certain administrative functions.

Under the dispute settlement mechanism of the Agreement, members are encouraged to enter into consultations on any matter arising out of the Agreement although either party can, with the consent of the other, request the Executive Director to establish an independent panel to act as conciliator between the parties (Art. 57). Failing this, "any dispute concerning the interpretation or application" of the Agreement may be referred to the ICC for decision under the formal dispute settlement procedure of Article 58.

Where a dispute has been referred, the ICC may be required to seek the opinion of an advisory panel before delivering its decision (see the *Selective Quota* case (1965) and the *Distribution of Coffee Shortfalls* case (1985)). Enforcement measures include the suspension of a party's voting rights in the ICC and on the Executive Board (Arts. 45 and 58). The ICC can decide to exclude any member by a two-thirds majority vote if the member is found to be in breach of its obligations, provided that such breach significantly impairs the operation of the Agreement (Articles 58 and 66). As with the International Cocoa Agreement (Art. 54) [see 121.05], the ICA provides for separate measures related to processed coffee (Art. 46). However, the earlier practice of submitting this type of dispute to outside arbitration has been abandoned in the light of experience gained from the *Solubles Coffee* case of 1969. Instead Article 46 refers to the same conciliation and dispute settlement mechanism of Article 57 and 58 in such cases.

There was also a Promotion Fund, conducted through the **Promotion Committee,** comprising all the exporting members, which met twice a year. Due to a dramatic fall in prices and, in turn, income, it constituted one of the major budget cuts in the ICO's recent past. It appointed a **Board of Management**, composed of six representatives. Working groups and committees were also appointed to examine specific matters. It was instrumental in setting up the "Organisation africaine et malgache du Café" (African and Malagasy Coffee Organization) (OAMCAF) which benefits from a global quota and which votes on behalf of its members in the ICC. In its time, the Promotion Fund has financed the establishment of "Centre du Café", Paris, "Nordic Coffee Centre", Oslo, and "Coffee Development Group", Washington, DC, to act as regional centres for coffee promotion.

A separate discussion of OAMCAF and other similar initiatives are excluded here as they represent regional commodity groupings and promotional activities rather than true international commodity arrangements.

Oscar J. Rodríguez-Aguilar

Access : CON (Art. 62)
Reserves : PRO (Art. 63)
Duration : DET 6 (Art. 68)
Deposit. : UN (Art. 71)
Language : Eng, Fre, Por, Spa (Art. 71)

Modific. :ICO Dec. 26.08.83; 26.09.83; 29.09.83; 07.12.83; 13.04.84; 21.09.84; 30.09.84; 19.09.85; 19.09.86; 30.09.87; 23.09.88; 27.09.91; Extension of the Agreement: 03.07.89 (01.10.89); 28.09.90 (01.10.91); 27.09.91 (25.09.92)

Reference :ICO Doc. EB-2142/82, EB-2142/82/Add.1/Rev.1 and EB-2142/82/Add.2; OJ L308, 1983, p. 4 and Res. No. 347 (E) of 3 July 1989 – UKTS 1986/27

121.05 – INTERNATIONAL COCOA AGREEMENT – ICCO

Concluded : 25.07.1986, Geneva
In force : 20.01.1987
Parties : 40

The fifth successive international agreement on cocoa, adopted on 16 July 1993, will replace the present International Cocoa Agreement (ICCA) which was adopted at Geneva by the UN Conference on Cocoa, 1986. The 1986 ICCA failed to prevent mounting stockpiles and a disastrous collapse of prices – production has grown more rapidly than consumption over the last 20 years. The 1993 ICCA negotiated under the auspices of UNCTAD in Geneva is not expected to come into effect until February, 1994, pending enabling legislation in various signatory countries.

Besides seeking "to promote the development and strengthening of international co-operation in all sectors of the world cocoa economy", one of the key aims of the 1986 Agreement, which expires on 30 September 1993, is "to contribute towards stabilization of the world cocoa market" through a variety of measures, chief of which is the interventionist role of the Buffer Stock as a means of stabilizing prices (Art. 1).

STRUCTURE

The **International Cocoa Organization** (ICCO), originally established under the Agreement of 1972, continues to administer the Agreement and is headquartered in London, UK. It functions chiefly through its highest authority, the **International Cocoa Council** (Art. 2). A part of the organization's responsibilities is also delegated to an **Executive Committee**, composed of equal numbers of members from both exporting and importing countries, elected for each cocoa year by countries in each of those categories, votes being based upon a quota system (Art. 15). The Executive Committee's chief task is to "keep the market under continuous review" and recommend "such measures as it may consider available" to the Council (Art. 17-2). Administrative duties are undertaken by the Executive Director whilst the Buffer Stock Manager is responsible for operating the Buffer Stock (Art. 20).

CURRENT STATUS

Buffer Stock operations, intended to stabilize prices, were suspended in 1988, after cocoa purchases reached the maximum allowed by the Agreement. The Buffer Stock reached its capacity of 250,000 tonnes. Since economic clauses were suspended, the Buffer Stock only sells defective cocoa to pay for operating costs. It is presently held at 232,000 tonnes, of which 100,000 tonnes held under the previous Agreement of 1980 form part (Art. 30). A further 100,000 tonnes can be added provided the Agreement is extended beyond the third cocoa year, after its entry into force. For the first time the International Cocoa Agreement of 1972 required consuming countries to participate in financing a buffer stock by contributions. This has been carried through in subsequent agreements through a levy system. It now constitutes a major bone of contention in current negotiations because there are arrears on levy payments.

Consumers contend that outstanding arrears of US$137.6 million by producers should be cleared. They argue that the amount would be enough to finance a withholding scheme of cocoa and the new agreement. Producers want the financial burden to be shared equally (by 50 per cent of each group on whatever basis, levy or otherwise). An export quota system, although not discussed, is still technically on the negotiating table but consumers find this totally unacceptable. Both parties have agreed on a production policy to get supply and demand more in balance. Efforts to negotiate a new agreement with economic clauses, based on a withholding scheme and including a buffer stock rather than a quota system, have now been abandoned in favour of an agreement based on voluntary production control, promotion of consumption and running down of the organization's 232,000 tonnes of Buffer Stocks.

The present Buffer Stock is financed from a levy on trade of 2 US cents per pound, payable by exporting members on all cocoa exports other than fine or flavour cocoa, and by importing members on imports of cocoa from non-member countries (Art. 32). (Currently the levies are not collected, due to the suspension of the ICCA's economic clauses, and the Buffer Stock is financed through the sale of its contents.)

Producer and consumer countries have agreed the orderly disposal of the Buffer Stock which will be released onto the market over a maximum of four and a half years, starting in 1993-1994, at a rate of 51,000 tonnes per annum, in equal monthly instalments, subject to possible ICCO Council revision at the end of the first year. This will enable those producer countries in arrears to pay off their debts.

The centrepiece of the new 1993 ICCA will be a production management plan, drawn up by the producer countries. Producers and consumers will be brought together in a Production Management Committee to establish the parameters for and to secure compliance with the supply targets under the plan. The Agreement also calls for the establishment of a Consumption Committee which calls on cocoa importers to remove or substantially reduce domestic taxes and import tariffs.

The following features of the 1986 Agreement, despite their suspension in anticipation of the new ICCA coming into force, are nevertheless recited here in full. All references to borrowing are deleted. Price levels are denominated in special drawing rights (SDRs) to lessen the impact of exchange rate fluctuations on price levels, denominated in a single currency, under a regime of floating exchange rates.

The Agreement further establishes a range of prices within which the Buffer Stock Manager can intervene in order to finance Buffer Stock operations. A bracket of prices has been established for the needs of the Buffer Stock operations, around a "free zone" of 30 US cents in which the Buffer Stock cannot intervene. The price structure sets upper and lower intervention prices of SDR 2,270 per tonne and SDR 1,600 per tonne respectively, as the range within which cocoa prices are to be defended (Art. 27). However, where the 1986 Agreement innovates is by the introduction of a "may sell" price of SDR 2,215 per tonne and a "may buy" price of SDR 55 per tonne. Whereas the Buffer Stock Manager must intervene when the indicator price of cocoa beans is at, above or below the upper or lower intervention prices, when the price is at or above the "may sell" price or at or below the "may buy" price he is empowered to intervene, or not, at his own discretion (Arts. 36 and 37). Under the third round of negotiations in 1992, consumers wanted a price range of SDR 840 per tonne to SDR 1,260 per tonne. (This amounts to raising their price offer by just SDR 50 to a medium price of SDR 1,050.) Producers would like to see price ranges between SDR 1,180 and SDR 1,770 per tonne. This represents a median price of SDR 1,475, down from SDR 1,820 at the beginning of the negotiations. (Whilst discussions have been in progress, cocoa prices have languished close to a 17-year low.)

There is provision for withholding cocoa in order to supplement the Buffer Stock, which remains the main supply regulatory mechanism to achieve the principal aim of the Agreement. Under the scheme, an additional 120,000 tonnes of cocoa may be withheld from the market. Such withholdings, subject to the fulfilment of certain preconditions, are activated in order to defend lower intervention prices in tranches of 30,000 tonnes (Art. 40). During the fourth round of negotiations, producers and consumers have recently accepted to withdraw 350,000 tonnes from the market.

A further innovation is the inclusion of rules and procedures for the automatic revision of price levels both at an annual review and at a special buffer-stock-related review, in case the Council is unable to reach agreement on the question of revision. The maximum adjustment, either at an annual or at a special review, of each of the prices set in the Agreement is limited to SDR 115 per tonne (Art. 27, Sections B and C).

Dispute Settlement Procedures: Finally, the Agreement provides dispute settlement procedures which include consultations on the "interpretation and application of the Agreement". This can lead to the establishment of a conciliation procedure (Art. 61). Under the restrictive structure of the Agreement, a "disputes" procedure can only be referred to the Council should consultations fail. The Council may be required to seek the opinion of an *ad hoc* advisory panel before deciding the dispute (Art. 62).

Enforcement measures include the suspension of a party's voting rights in the Council and on the Executive Committee as well as any additional rights enjoyed by that member without prejudice to that member's continuing liability, financial or otherwise, under the Agreement (Art. 63).

Article 54 provides for a special express consultative procedure with regard to processed cocoa which aims to avoid serious injury to the cocoa economy of the respective importing and exporting countries, failing which the affected member can call upon the Council's good offices to intervene in the matter.

O.J.R.-A.

Access : CON (Art. 65, 68)
Reserves : PRO (Art. 71)
Duration : FXD 3 (Art. 75)
Deposit. : UN (Art. 66)
Language : Ara, Eng, Fre, Rus, Spa

Modific. : ICC Dec. 1992

Reference : UN Doc. TD/COCOA.7/22/Rev. 1 – UNTS 1/15033 – RGDIP 1987/2

121.06 – INTERNATIONAL NATURAL RUBBER AGREEMENT – INRO

Concluded : 20.03.1987, Geneva
In force : 03.04.1989
Parties : 27

This Agreement is the successor to the International Natural Rubber Agreement of 1979, the first new international commodity agreement concluded under the IPC [see 121.01]. It was adopted on 20 March 1987 by the UN Conference on Natural Rubber which met at Geneva from 9 to 20 March 1987, under the auspices of UNCTAD [see 111 B] and it expires at the end of 1993, with a possible extension for a further year. Its main objectives are to "achieve a balanced growth between the supply of and demand for natural rubber", "to help stabilize the export earnings from natural rubber of exporting members, and to increase their earnings based on expanding natural rubber export volumes ..." and "to seek to ensure adequate supplies of natural rubber to meet the requirements of importing members ..." (Art. 1).

Its continued operation is undertaken by the **International Natural Rubber Organization** (INRO), created under the 1979 Agreement, and headquartered in Kuala Lumpur, Malaysia. The Organization functions through its highest authority, the **International Natural Rubber Council**, on which one delegate from each of INRO's members serves (Art. 6). The Council meets twice a year, normally in May/June and October/November and is entrusted with the application of the Agreement. It may, by special vote, delegate the exercise of any, or all, of its powers to one or more of the "technical Committees" named in Article 18. These include a Committee on Administration and a Committee on Buffer Stock Operations, each committee comprising a maximum of 12 members divided equally between exporting and importing members. It is also responsible for nominating an Executive Director to administer the Agreement and a Buffer Stock Manager.

The Council's voting procedures are as follows. Exporting members collectively have 1,000 votes and importing members collectively have 1,000 votes. They are distributed among each of the two groups, calculated as nearly as possible in proportion to the volume of their respective net exports of natural rubber or net imports of natural rubber over a five-year period. Council decisions are carried by a simple majority (Art. 14).

As with the 1979 Agreement, the international natural rubber Buffer Stock is to be "the sole instrument of market intervention for price stabilization". It thereby marks a departure from other international commodity agreements with international, or quasi-international stocks, which are complemented with regular, or contingent, regulation of exports.

The Buffer Stock consists of 550,000 tonnes, divided into a normal Buffer Stock of 400,000 tonnes and a contingency Buffer Stock of 150,000 tonnes (Art. 26). The total capacity of the Buffer Stock under the 1987 Agreement includes the total stocks still held under the previous Agreement. As with the 1979 Agreement, both the normal and contingency stocks are to be financed equally by the importing and exporting members, with initial financing set at 70 million Malaysian ringgits and apportioned among all members according to their share of votes in Council or, exceptionally, their share in trade (Art. 27).

The total costs of the normal and contingency stock are to be paid in cash (Art. 28). Unlike the 1979 Agreement, the 1987 Agreement does not provide for borrowing to finance purchases for the contingency Buffer Stock although the 1987 Agreement envisages the Council's taking full advantage of financing facilities of the Common Fund for Commodities [see 121.02].

The basic structure of the price range in the 1979 Agreement has been maintained, with a reference price of 201.66 Malaysian/Singapore cents per kilo, whilst the upper and lower indicative prices remain unchanged at 270 and 150 Malaysian/Singapore cents per kilo respectively (Art. 29). Around the reference price are the upper and lower intervention prices at plus and minus 15 per cent of the reference price. At these levels, the Buffer Stock Manager may intervene in the market but is not obliged to do so.

At plus and minus 20 per cent of the reference price are the upper and lower trigger action prices, set at levels at which the Buffer Stock Manager must intervene in order to stabilize prices. Finally, around these levels, although not specifically related to the reference price, are the upper and lower indicative prices, which are limits that cannot be breached by the trigger action prices when the reference price (and consequently the intervention and trigger action prices) is revised up or down (Art. 30).

The 1987 Agreement, like its predecessor, makes provision for semi-automatic revisions of the reference price, based on market trends and/or net changes in the Buffer Stock's size, with two modifications (Art. 31). First, the periodicity of reviews of the reference price is now every 15 months instead of every 18 months, as was the case in the 1979 Agreement. (The periodicity of the indicative price review remains at 30 months.) Second, whereas the 1979 Agreement provided that, at the time of the regular price review, the reference price would automatically be revised 5 per cent up or down, the 1987 Agreement, while maintaining this provision allows for Council, by special vote, to decide on a greater percentage adjustment.

As in the 1979 Agreement, when purchases or sales for the Buffer Stock reach the 400,000 tonne level, the Council shall meet and decide, by special vote, the price at which the contingency Buffer Stock should be brought into action to defend the lower or upper indicative prices (Art. 31).

The 1987 Agreement includes provisions dealing with complaints and disputes. Complaints are dealt with under Article 54 which, upon referral to the Council, sets in train a consultation procedure. Should the Council decide as a result of the complaint that a member is in breach of its obligations under the Agreement, it may vote to suspend that member's voting rights or exceptionally to exclude the member signalling withdrawal under Article 54.

Disputes which concern the interpretation or application of the Agreement may be settled by Council which may seek the opinion of an advisory panel (Art. 55).

Mary E. Footer

Access : CON (Art. 61)
Reserves : PRO (Art. 67)
Duration : DET 5 (Art. 66)
Deposit. : UN (Art. 56)
Language : Ara, Chi, Eng, Fre, Rus, Spa

Reference : UN Doc. TD/RUBBER.2/16/Rev.1

1.2.2 Commercial Agreements

Commercial agreements are multilateral agreements between exporting and importing countries which establish a legal regime to govern the international trade in a particular commodity and which involve the mutual exchange of rights and obligations between parties to those agreements. This is sometimes referred to as the "multilateral contract system" because these international commodity agreements support pure contractual arrangements designed to promote the long-term development of a particular commodity but are bereft of any price-stabilization devices like the export quota system or buffer stock mechanism found in international commodity control agreements [see 1.2.1].

Within the framework of the multilateral contract system there exists a wide range of possibilities. They vary, on the one hand, from agreements with a simple consultation process and mutual agreement on likely national sales and purchases, to, on the other hand, agreements embodying a complete commitment on the part of exporting and importing countries to a set of legally binding contracts for the sale and purchase of a given commodity under certain stated conditions. The latter may even be reinforced by a judicial system and penalties for non-fulfilment.

Like the international commodity control agreements, the pure commercial agreement type of commodity arrangement also provides for the establishment of an international organization to administer the agreement. The type of international commodity agreement which falls into this category includes the International Tropical Timber Agreement [see 122.01], the International Agreement on Olive Oil and Table Olives [see 122.02] and the International Agreement on Jute and Jute Products [see 122.04]. Reference may also be had to the International Wheat Convention [see 122.03] and the International Sugar Agreement (ISA) [see 122.05]. Under its 1977 Agreement, the ISA did include economic clauses in the form of a type of buffer stock, known as "Special Stocks", in addition to export quotas. Both interventionist techniques were abandoned in later agreements.

Mary E. Footer and Oscar J. Rodríguez-Aguilar

122.01 – INTERNATIONAL TROPICAL TIMBER AGREEMENT – ITTO

Concluded : 18.11.1983, Geneva
In force : 01.04.1985
Parties : 51

The International Tropical Timber Agreement (ITTA) was adopted within the framework of the UN Conference on Tropical Timber held at Geneva from 14 to 31 March and 7 to 18 November 1983.

Its aims are to provide an effective framework for co-operation and consultation between tropical timber producing and consuming members with regard to all relevant aspects of the tropical timber economy. Additionally, it aims to promote the expansion and diversification of the international trade in tropical timber and the improvement of structural conditions in the tropical timber market, to promote and support research and development with a view to improving forest management and wood utilization, to improve market intelligence, to encourage increased and further processing of tropical timber in producing member countries, to encourage members to support and develop industrial tropical timber reforestation and forest management activities, to improve marketing and distribution of tropical timber exports of producing countries, to encourage the development of national policies aimed at sustainable utilization and conservation of tropical forests and their genetic resources and at maintaining the ecological balance in the regions concerned (Art. 1).

The ITTA is administered by the **International Tropical Timber Organization** (ITTO), which functions through the International Tropical Timber Council (ITTC), the highest authority of the organization (Art. 6), three permanent Committees – the Committee on Economic Information and Market Intelligence, the Committee on Reforestation and Forest Management and the Committee on Forest Industry (Art. 24) – and an Executive Director and staff (Art. 16).

The ITTC meets at least once a year, at which it elects a Chairman and a Vice-Chairman (each for one year), one from among the producing countries and the other from among the consuming countries with these offices alternating between the two categories of members on an annual basis (Art. 8). Each member is represented on the ITTC by one representative and such alternates and advisers as may be required (Art. 6). Decisions are taken by consensus, failing which a simple distributed majority vote is sufficient, except where the Agreement provides otherwise (Art. 12).

The ITTO is financed through two accounts: the Administrative Account to be met by a variety of contributions from its members (Art. 19) and the Special Account which can draw on the Second Account of the Common Fund for Commodities [see 121.02], regional and international financial institutions and voluntary contributions and is primarily concerned with financing specified approved projects (Art. 20).

The operational activities of the ITTC and the permanent Committees fall into two basic categories. The first consists of arranging for the formulation and implementation of projects in the fields of research and development, market intelligence, further and increased processing, reforestation, and forest management. The second is involved *inter alia* with continuously monitoring the trade and ongoing activities in the tropical timber economy, regularly reviewing the future needs of the trade and the support and assistance being provided at various levels for tropical timber production, identifying and considering problems and possible solutions to them, conducting relevant studies and encouraging increased transfer of know-how and technical assistance (Art. 23).

Should a member fail to fulfil its obligations under the ITTA, or should a dispute arise as to its interpretation or application, the matter shall be referred to the ITTC, whose decision shall be final (Art. 29).

Mary E. Footer

Access : CON (Art. 34, 35)
Reserves : PRO (Art. 43)
Duration : DET 5 (Art. 42)
Deposit. : UN (Art. 33)
Language : Ara, Eng, Fre, Rus, Spa

Reference : UN Doc. TD/TIMBER/11/Rev.1

122.02 – INTERNATIONAL AGREEMENT ON OLIVE OIL AND TABLE OLIVES – IOOC

Concluded : 01.07.1986, Geneva
In force : 01.12.1988
Parties : 9

The International Agreement on Olive Oil and Table Olives (IOOA) is the successor to three similar agreements of 1956, 1963 and 1979. The present Agreement was adopted on 1 July 1986 by the UN Conference on Olive Oil, called by the Secretary-General of UNCTAD [see 111 B], which met in Geneva from 18 June to 2 July 1986.

The IOOA has four broad objectives: (1) within the framework of international co-operation and concerted action, to foster the co-ordination of production, industrialization and marketing policies for olive oil and olive oil products; (2) with respect to the modernization of olive cultivation and olive-oil extraction, to encourage research and development to modernize, improve and reduce the costs of the industry; (3) with respect to the expansion of international trade in olive products, to apply measures to extend the production and consumption of, and the international trade in, olive products; and (4) with respect to the standardization of international trade in olive products, to facilitate the study and application of measures balancing production and consumption and to lessen the drawbacks of fluctuating market supplies (Art. 1).

STRUCTURE

The institutional structure of the Agreement provides for an **International Olive Oil Council** (IOOC), headquartered in Madrid, Spain, and composed of members' representatives, or their alternates, from mainly producing countries and mainly consuming countries (Arts. 3 and 4). It elects a Chairman and Vice-Chairman, each for a term of one year (1 November to 31 October) and meets twice a year, in Spring and Autumn (Arts. 8 and 9). Council decisions are taken by consensus or, alternatively, by an exchange of correspondence without calling a session, provided no member objects (Art. 11).

There is also an **Executive Secretariat**, comprising an Executive Director, senior officials and staff, appointed by the Council, to administer the IOOA (Art. 16). A number of committees are also involved in carrying out the functions of the Agreement, notably a Financial Committee for the Administrative Budget, a Publicity Fund and an Economic Committee (Arts. 24 and 35).

The IOOA contains provisions for an Administrative Budget (Art. 17) with contributions from all members, based on their share of participation in the organization, calculated according to an arithmetical formula (Art. 10). There are also detailed provisions for the financing of technical co-operation programmes in olive cultivation, olive-oil extraction and table olive processing (Art. 18) and for the Publicity Fund to be financed by mainly producing members (Arts. 19 to 23).

The operational activities and programmes of the IOOA are directed at resolving problems in different branches of the industry through close co-operation with several specialized institutes, encompassing scientific research into the biological value of olive oil and table olives as well as the improvement of olive-oil extraction and table olive processing techniques and studies on olive oil chemistry, designed to draw up international standards and unify methods of analysis.

There are several dispute settlement clauses in the IOOA which deal variously with source and appellations of origin of olive oils (Art. 30) and with the interpretation of designations and definitions of table olives (Art. 34). In both cases should direct negotiation fail, the matter may be reconciled by the IOOC after seeking an advisory opinion in accordance with Article 50-1 and various other specialized international institutions.

Any other dispute concerning the interpretation or application of the IOOA, other than the two aforementioned ones, and not settled by negotiation, may be referred to the IOOC. Again the Council shall decide the dispute after receiving a substantiated opinion from an advisory panel (Art. 50-2). Should a member be found in breach of the Agreement, the IOOC may impose sanctions ranging from a simple warning to the suspension of that member's voting rights or even exclusion in accordance with Article 58 (Art. 50-5).

The statutes of the IOOA allow any member or observer member of the UN, subject to the consent of the IOOC, to attend Council sessions as observers (Art. 14). Currently the governments of 33 countries are observers.

M.E.F.

Access : CON (Art. 53)
Reserves : PRO (Art. 61)
Duration : DET 5 (Art. 60)
Deposit. : UN (Art. 51)
Language : Ara, Eng, Fre, Ita, Spa

Reference : UN Doc. TD/OLIVE OIL.8/7 – UNTS 1219/135

122.03 – INTERNATIONAL WHEAT CONVENTION – IWC

Concluded : 14.03.1986, London
In force : 01.07.1986
Parties : 46

The original International Wheat Agreement (IWA) has been extended eight times, the last extension being in 1983 whereupon a revised Agreement was negotiated and finalized in 1986. This Agreement ran until 30 June 1991, whereupon it has been twice extended, the most recent extension being until 30 June 1995. The Agreement, like its predecessors, constitutes two binding international agreements, linked with one another by a joint preamble:

(i) Wheat Trade Convention, 1986 (WTC) (concluded 14.03.1986, London; in force 01.07.1986; no. of parties 46).

(ii) Food Aid Convention, 1986 (FAC) (concluded 13.03.1986, London; in force 01.07.1986; no. of parties 24).

WHEAT TRADE CONVENTION (WTC)

The key objectives of the WTC are to further international co-operation in all aspects of the trade in wheat and other grains, to promote the expansion of the international trade in grains, to contribute to the stability of international grain markets and to enhance world food security, to provide a forum for the exchange of information and discussion among members regarding the trade in grains, and to provide a framework for the possible negotiation of a future agreement with economic provisions (Art. 1).

Structure: Of the main institutions, the **International Wheat Council** (IWC), established under the provisions of the IWA of 1949, is the supreme authority and is charged with the administration of the WTC (Art. 9). Membership of the IWC consists of both exporting and importing members, each of which together holds a total of 1,000 votes (Art. 12-3). Of that total, no single exporting member may hold more than 333 votes and no single importing member may hold more than 333 votes (Art. 12-6).

The IWC meets at least twice in each crop year (Art. 13-2). It is assisted by a **Secretariat**. There is also an **Executive Committee**, comprising six exporting and eight importing members, which meets as required (Art. 15). The **Sub-Committee on**

Market Conditions, made up of technical representatives from six exporting and six importing members, provides a forum for debate. It usually holds nine meetings a year (Art. 16).

The WTC is an instrument of international co-operation designed primarily to contribute to the transparency of the market in grains. This is done by collecting and disseminating information and by acting as a forum for discussion and exchange of information on the development of the wheat market between exporting and importing countries (Art. 3). No attempt is made to influence the market through interventionist techniques although the possibility of introducing economic clauses continues to be explored (Art. 22). The new Agreement does provide for the convening of special consultations if developments in the international grain market seriously threaten to affect members' interests (Art. 4).

Although still called a Wheat Trade Convention, the 1986 WTC has broadened its scope to include other grains such as barley, maize (corn), sorghum and rice.

FOOD AID CONVENTION (FAC)

The **Food Aid Committee** was established on 1 July 1986 to administer the FAC which, together with the WTC, forms the IWA of 1986. Its aims are to secure, through a joint effort by the international community, the achievement in physical terms of the World Food Conference target of at least 10 million tonnes annually of grain suitable for human consumption as food aid to developing countries (Art. I). Additionally, it aims to review operations under the FAC and the food situation in developing countries.

The obligations of member countries are basically quantitative, ensuring that the volume of aid to developing countries is maintained in times of falling grain supplies and rising grain prices. Aid is mostly bilateral and is supplied as far as possible on a voluntary basis, either through contributions in grain or in cash to purchase grain (Art. III). Members are encouraged to bear the cost of transporting their aid, especially to low-income countries. Should the latter countries in a particular region experience a substantial production shortfall in food grain, the Food Aid Committee may recommend that its members increase aid to cover such emergency needs (Art. VIII).

The Food Aid Committee meets at least twice in each grain year (July-June) (Art. XI). It is supported in its administrative functions by the Secretariat of the IWC.

PUBLICATIONS

IWC: *Market Reports; Shipments of Wheat and Flour, World Wheat Statistics.*
FAC: *Report on shipments by members of the Convention.*

M.E.F.

Access	: ALS (Art. 27)
Reserves	: USP
Duration	: FXD (Art. 33)
Deposit.	: UN (Art. 23)
Language	: Eng, Fre, Rus, Spa
Modific.	:IWC Dec. 30.06-03.07.86; 09-11.12.86; 08-10.07.87; 15.09.87; 06-07.07.88; 10-12.07.89; 10-11.07.90; 25-26.06.91
Reference	: IWO Doc. IWA (86)1 – UST 32/5 – RGDIP 1987/1 – JORF 15 Jul 87

122.04 – INTERNATIONAL AGREEMENT ON JUTE AND JUTE PRODUCTS – IJO

Concluded : 03.11.1989, Geneva
In force : 12.04.1991, provisionally
Parties : 27

The International Agreement on Jute and Jute Products of 1989 is a successor agreement to that of 1982, which was the second new international commodity agreement to be negotiated under the UNCTAD Integrated Programme for Commodities [see 121.01]. It was negotiated at the United Nations Conference on Jute and Jute Products, held at Geneva from 30 October to 3 November 1989.

The 1989 Agreement maintains many of the features of the earlier agreements, including the basic aims, the most important of which are: "to enhance the competitiveness of jute and jute products"; "to maintain and enlarge existing markets as well as to develop new markets for jute and jute products"; "to develop end-uses of jute, including new jute products ..."; and "to promote the expansion and diversification of international trade in jute and jute products"; it also maintains the objectives relating to the improvement of yields and quality in jute agriculture and the improvement of quality of jute products and reduction in the cost of their production (Art. 1).

Like the predecessor Agreement, and reminiscent of the International Tropical Timber Agreement [see 122.01], the objectives of the 1989 Agreement are to be achieved by means of projects on research and development, market promotion and cost reduction which may include human resources development (an element not specifically mentioned in the 1982 Agreement); they are also to be achieved by the collation and dissemination of information relating to jute and jute products, and by the study of cyclical trends in the world jute economy. There are, however, as with the predecessor Agreement, no economic provisions in the form of price stabilization mechanisms although further consideration is to be given to this subject as well as other important issues concerning jute and jute products.

Structure: The basic institutional framework of the 1982 Agreement is carried forward with the retention of the **International Jute Organization** (IJO), headquartered in Dhaka, Bangladesh, in order to administer and supervise the operation of the Agreement. It functions through the **International Jute Council** and the **Committee on Projects** with the assistance of an Executive Director and staff (Art. 3).

Membership of the IJO is open to both exporting and importing countries and may include the EC and any other intergovernmental organization (Arts. 4 and 5). The **International Jute Council** (IJC) is the highest authority of the Organization and consists of all members of the IJO, each represented by its delegate, or alternate (Art. 6). It elects a chairman and vice-chairman for each jute year (1 July to 30 June inclusive), one from among the representatives of exporting members and the other among the representatives from the importing member, which offices alternate between the two categories of members each year (Art. 8).

The IJC meets in regular session at least once in every half year and at other times in special session upon the request of the Executive Director, in agreement with the Chairman of the IJC, or upon request of a majority of one of the categories of members or members holding at least 500 votes (Art. 9). Votes are distributed equally among the exporting and importing members, each category holding a total of 1,000 votes, with votes beyond 150 for each member distributed within each group pro rata according to annual average volume of net exports or net imports (Art. 10). Council decisions and recommendations are taken by consensus, failing which matters are decided by a simple distributed majority unless otherwise provided for in the Agreement (Art. 12).

The IJO is assisted by an Executive Director, appointed by special vote of the

Council who, as chief administrative officer, is responsible to the IJC for the administration and operation of the Agreement. He is assisted in this work by a staff (Art. 16).

The operational activities of the IJO are concentrated on identifying and selecting projects in the fields of research and development, market promotion and cost reduction and arranging for their preparation, implementation and monitoring (Arts. 24 to 27 *in extenso*). As with the previous Agreement, the 1989 Agreement sets out a list of criteria for the approval of projects but is slightly broader in its extent such that the selection of projects may potentially benefit importing members, both those producing jute and those not involved in jute production, as well as exporting members (Art. 28). A Committee on Projects is responsible to, and works under the general direction of, the Council in considering and technically appraising and evaluating project proposals (Art. 29).

Financing of such projects is either through another financing and executive agency as provided for in Article 14 or through the Organization's "Special Account" and carried out either by an executing agency or, where appropriate, the IJO itself (Art. 22). Possible sources of finance for the Special Account include the Second Account of the Common Fund for Commodities [see 121.02], international and regional financial institutions, and voluntary contributions from governments or other sources.

Any complaint or dispute brought under the new Agreement shall be referred to the Council whose decision in the matter is binding (Art. 33).

M.E.F.

Access : CON (Art. 37)
Reserves : PRO (Art. 47)
Duration : DET 5 (Art. 46-1)
Deposit. : UN (Art. 38)
Language : Ara, Chi, Eng, Fre, Rus, Spa

Reference : UN Doc. TD/JUTE.2/6/Rev.1 and Add.1

122.05 – INTERNATIONAL SUGAR AGREEMENT – ISO

Concluded : 20.03.1992, Geneva
In force : 20.01.1993, provisionally
Parties : 11

The international regulation of sugar dates back to the last century and the Paris Sugar Convention of 1864. The current International Sugar Agreement (ISA) of 1992 is the tenth of such agreements and succeeds the 1987 Agreement. It was adopted on 20 January 1993 by the UN Sugar Conference at a special conference held in Geneva. The new ISA of 20 January 1993 does not have any economic clauses; it is valid for three years, whereupon it is renewable on an annual basis. It is similar to the previous one and is essentially an administrative agreement which concentrates on two aspects. First, it provides a forum for international co-operation in sugar matters by providing a meeting place and, second, it gathers statistics and provides market and economic analyses.

The prime purpose of the ISA is to "further international co-operation in connection with world sugar matters and related issues" and to "provide an appropriate framework for preparation of a possible new international sugar agreement with economic provisions". Other objectives are "to encourage the consumption of sugar" and "to facilitate the trade in sugar by collecting and providing information on the world sugar market and other sweeteners".

Structure: The **International Sugar Organization** (ISO), headquartered in London, UK, is charged with the administration of the ISA and its operation. It functions through the **International Sugar Council** (ISC), an **Administrative Committee** and its Executive Director and staff.

The ISC is the highest authority of the Organization and consists of all the ISO members. Each member has one representative in the Council, with one or more alternates. The ISC meets at least once a year. Its chief purpose is to administer the Agreement and to pursue the liquidation of the Stock Financing Fund, established under Article 49 of the International Sugar Agreement, 1977. The exporting members hold a total of 1,000 votes and the importing members hold a total of 1,000 votes, with members' shares in the total vote apportioned over the members within each of those two groups. Council decisions and all recommendations are taken by simple distributed majority.

The ISC is assisted by an **Executive Committee** consisting of ten exporting members and ten importing members, elected annually, to which it may delegate certain powers. An Executive Director, assisted by a staff, is appointed by the ISC to act as the chief administative officer of the Organization.

The ISO acts as "a centre for the collection and publication of statistical information and studies on world production, prices, exports and imports, consumption and stocks of sugar (including both raw and refined sugar as appropriate) and other sweeteners as well as taxes on sugars and other sweeteners". The current International Sugar Agreement, like its predecessors, remains deprived of any price stablization mechanisms although it remains a declared objective to reintroduce economic provisions.

The 1987 Agreement introduced, as an exceptional measure, a special distribution of votes between the two categories of members for the purposes of contributions to the administrative budget of the ISO: these are no longer calculated on the basis of the number of votes held by the members for the purposes of decision-making. Second, a new element was introduced with the establishment of the **Single Committee on Sugar Market Evaluation, Consumption and Statistics**, which is composed of both exporting members and importing members, under the chairmanship of the Executive Director. This Committee aims to keep under continuous review matters relating to the world economy of sugar and other sweeteners. Its focus is on market behaviour and factors affecting it with special reference to the participation of developing countries in world trade, the effects of the use of sugar substitutes, the relative tax treatment of sugar and other sweeteners, the effect on the consumption of sugar in different countries, means of promoting consumption, research into new uses of sugar and so on.

Any dispute concerning the interpretation or application of the ISA and not settled among the members involved, may at the request of any member party to the dispute be referred to the ISC. A majority of members, holding not less than one-third of the total votes, may require the Council to seek the opinion of an advisory panel, whereupon it shall decide the dispute by special vote. Should a member be found in breach of the Agreement, the ISC may take specific measures, including the suspension of that member's voting rights, or even exclusion.

Oscar J. Rodríguez-Aguilar

Access : CON
Reserves : USP
Duration : DET 5
Deposit. : UN

Language : Ara, Chi, Eng, Fre, Rus, Spa

Reference : UN Doc. TD/SUGAR/11/5/Rev.1

1.2.3 Intergovernmental Transparency Groups

Intergovernmental approaches to commodity issues shifted considerably from a commodity price stabilization approach in the mid-1970s to a market transparency approach in the late 1980s. Following the first oil shock, the prevailing view was that market interventions were necessary to stabilize commodity prices in order to minimize commodity price volatility. In this context, the Common Fund for Commodities was negotiated which aimed, *inter alia*, at facilitating the financing of commodity agreements designed to stabilize commodity prices. In practice, however, the price stabilization objective of the Common Fund has never been activated and, in the meantime, the collapse of the International Tin Agreement (ITA) in 1986, which sought to stabilize tin prices, destroyed most of the support for similar objectives. The recent negotiation of intergovernmental transparency groups for nickel, copper and tin [see 123.02, 123.03, 123.04] reflects this trend away from market stabilization agreements to the low-profile but more effective transparency agreements.

Denis Audet

123.01 – TERMS OF REFERENCE ON THE INTERNATIONAL LEAD AND ZINC STUDY GROUP – ILZSG

Concluded : May 1959, New York
In force : January 1960
Parties : 30

The ILZSG was formed in 1959 to provide opportunities for regular intergovernmental consultations on lead and zinc matters. Particular attention is given to providing regular and frequent information on lead and zinc supply and demand. In this connection, the Group carries out a one-year forecast of mine and metal production, and metal consumption for both commodities. The Group also makes studies and prepares documents on relevant issues as requested by country members. For example, environmental issues are dealt with by the Subcommittee on Environment and Regulations.

This Group has been active for over 30 years and it had 30 country members in early 1993, accounting for about 90 per cent of the western world's lead and zinc production. The general annual session of the Group is attended by industry representives as advisers in national delegations. An Industrial Advisory Panel has been established to provide an opportunity for industry representatives to submit their views to the Group on relevant issues. The statistics of the Group are highly praised and the overall functioning of the Group is generally regarded as a model for intergovernmental co-operation on commodities. The recently negotiated terms of reference for copper, nickel and tin study groups (see below) have largely been guided by the experience and functioning of the ILZSG.

Headquartered in London, UK, the Group has no market intervention power. Through the dissemination of reliable statistics, the Group is improving market transparency. As a result, each country member and, in turn, respective metals producers and consumers, can by themselves modify their production and consumption plans accordingly. By gathering both producing and consuming countries into one organization, the Group cannot pursue objectives that would be associated with those of a producer organization (cartel) or a consumer organization.

Denis Audet

Access : ALS (Art. 1)
Reserves : NSP
Duration : NSP
Deposit. : ILZSG
Language : Eng, Fre

123.02 – TERMS OF REFERENCE OF THE INTERNATIONAL NICKEL STUDY GROUP – INSG

Concluded : 02.05.1986, Geneva
In force : 23.05.1990
Parties : 13

The INSG was inaugurated in June 1990 when the 12 countries and the European Economic Community which had completed the ratification process decided to bring the terms of reference of the Group into force. The terms of reference provide for the creation of an intergovernmental organization to bring together nickel producing and consuming countries which collect and disseminate statistical information on the international nickel economy, and to provide a forum for discussions of issues of concern to the nickel industry. The INSG's headquarters is in The Hague, Netherlands and, in April 1993, the Group had 13 countries and the EC as members. The Group is working actively on the preparation of a comprehensive statistical bulletin and on setting up subcommittees to discuss a wide range of nickel-related issues. Having comparable objectives and a similar institutional set-up to the ILZSG (described above), the Group pursues market transparency objectives and has no market intervention power.

The negotiation of the terms of reference and the coming into force of the INSG have been adversely affected by the various concerns that arose following the collapse of the International Tin Council (ITC) [see 121.03]. While the purpose of the INSG was clearly different from the price stabilization objective of the ITC, many participant countries were particularly sensitive to the issues of potential financial liabilities associated with membership, the legal personality of the Group, and the level of adequate membership of such a Group. These same issues have been raised during the negotiation of the copper and tin study groups which were also negotiated in the late 1980s.

D.A.

Access : ALS (Art. 19-3)
Reserves : USP
Duration : NSP
Deposit. : UN
Language : Eng, Fre, Rus, Spa

Reference : UN Doc. TD/NICKEL/12

123.03 – TERMS OF REFERENCE OF THE INTERNATIONAL COPPER STUDY GROUP – ICSG

Concluded : 24.02.1989, Geneva
In force : 23.01.1992
Parties : 15

The ICSG was inaugurated in November 1992 when some 18 participating countries representing about 68 per cent of the western world's copper metal production agreed to bring the terms of reference of the Group into force. The Group collects and disseminates copper statistics and provides a forum for discussing copper-related issues. The terms of reference also provide for the preparation of a short-term forecast of mine and metal production, and metal consumption, as well as the establishment of an Industry Advisory Panel. The Group has recently decided to establish its headquarters in Lisbon, Portugal.

For a description of the Convention of the Intergovernmental Council of Copper Exporting Countries, see 124.03.

D.A.

Access : ASO
Reserves : PRO (Art. 25)
Duration : NSP
Deposit. : UN
Language : Ara, Chi, Eng, Fre, Rus, Spa

Modific. : Amendment to para. 13 and 14 (15.08.92)

Reference : UN Doc. TD/COPPER/14

123.04 – TERMS OF REFERENCE OF THE INTERNATIONAL TIN STUDY GROUP – ITSG

Concluded : 07.04.1989, Geneva
Parties : 12

Concluded in April 1989, the terms of reference of the ITSG provide for the collection and dissemination of tin statistics and a forum for discussing tin-related issues. The Group will come into force when countries representing at least 70 per cent of world trade in tin have notified their acceptance to join the Group. The terms of reference also provide for an early entry into force, after 31 December 1989, if the countries which have ratified decide to bring the terms of reference into force among themselves.

D.A.

Access : ASO (Art. 5)
Reserves : PRO (Art. 24)
Duration : NSP
Deposit. : UN
Language : Ara, Chi, Eng, Fre, Rus, Spa

Reference : UN Doc. TD/TIN 7/13

1.2.4 Producers' Organizations

Producers' organizations, alliances or associations are autonomous, self-regulating, intergovernmental economic institutions operating within the structure of international commodity trade with the intention of improving the terms of trade of developing producer countries *vis-à-vis* the developed consumer countries. They differ from international commodity agreements because the latter comprise both producers and consumers of the relevant commodity and are essentially aimed at stabilizing prices at levels deemed fair to consumers and remunerative to producers, whilst producers' organizations, although also concerned with price stabilization, seek primarily to secure economic and social benefits for their members from the production, processing and marketing of a commodity.

The majority of producers' organizations display two characteristics: they are exclusively associations of states and they invariably have a conventional basis – that is, the constituent documents form an agreement between states, or other subjects of international law; they are usually governed by international law.

The institutional arrangements in individual producers' organizations display structural differences with respect to number and composition of the principal constituent bodies. Some organizations provide for three main bodies, consisting of a supreme policy-making organ, or assembly, an executive one and a secretariat, as in the case of the Organization of Petroleum Exporting Countries (OPEC) [see 124.01] or the Cocoa Producers' Alliance (CPA) [see 124.02], whilst others simply have two principal bodies, one a policy-making organ and the other a secretariat, as in the case of the International Tea Promotion Association (ITPA) [see 124.08].

Mary E. Footer and Oscar J. Rodríguez-Aguilar

SELECTED BIBLIOGRAPHY

Pollard, D.E., *Law and Policy of Producers' Associations*, 1984.

124.01 – AGREEMENT ESTABLISHING THE ORGANIZATION OF PETROLEUM EXPORTING COUNTRIES – OPEC

Concluded : 14.09.1960, Baghdad
In force : 01.10.1960
Parties : 12

OPEC was established under the terms of the Baghdad Agreement, signed on 14 September 1960 by the five principal exporters of petroleum (Saudi Arabia, Iran, Iraq, Kuwait and Venezuela). The Statutes of the Organization were adopted at the Caracas Conference, 15 to 21 January 1961, and have been amended several times since, most recently in June 1980.

Formally speaking, there are 12 member states: Algeria (1969), Gabon (1975), Indonesia (1962), Iran (1960), Iraq (1960), Kuwait (1960), Libya (1962), Nigeria (1971), Qatar (1961), Saudi Arabia (1960), United Arab Emirates (Abu Dhabi [1967], Dubai [1973], Sharjah [1974]), Venezuela (1960). In fact, the geographical extension of OPEC is larger because its decisions bind those member states of the Organization of Arab Petroleum Exporting Countries (OAPEC) which are not members of OPEC. Since OAPEC is a regional organization, rather than a universal organization, it is not included in this survey.

The principal objective of OPEC is to co-ordinate and unify the petroleum policies of the member states and to determine the best means of safeguarding their interests on both individual and collective levels (Art. 2A). In order to attain its goal, the Organization takes measures designed to stabilize the price of petroleum in the international oil markets in order to eliminate all harmful and unnecessary fluctuations, with due regard being given to the interests of producer states and to the necessity of securing a steady income for them (Art. 2B). Other aims include ensuring an efficient, economic and regular supply of petroleum to consuming states and a fair return on their capital to those investing in the petroleum industry (Art. 2C).

In June 1968, OPEC members adopted a Declaratory Statement of Petroleum Policy, calling on member states to: (1) undertake direct exploration for and development of hydrocarbon resources; (2) seek participation in the equity of existing concessions and the progressive and accelerated relinquishment of acreage of present contract areas; (3) establish conservation rules to be followed by operating oil companies; and (4) determine posted or tax reference prices. A further Declaration of March 1975, adopted by the Conferences of the Sovereigns and Heads of State of the OPEC member countries, added new policy guidelines and indicated that the Organization should seek, in consultation and co-operation with other countries of the world, the establishment of a new economic order based on justice, mutual understanding and a genuine concern for the well-being of all peoples.

STRUCTURE

OPEC functions through its **Conference,** which meets at least twice a year and consists of representatives of each of the member states, normally headed by the ministers responsible for oil, mines and energy (Arts. 11 and 12). It formulates general policy, appoints a Secretary-General and Deputy Secretary-General for a term of three years each and elects a Chairman to the **Board of Governors** (Arts. 14 and 21). The Board of Governors meets at least twice a year and consists of one Governor nominated by each member country for a two-year term (Arts. 18 and 19). There is a permanent **Secretariat** comprising the Office of the Secretary-General, a Research Division (Energy Studies, Economics and Finance, and Data Services), a personnel section, a public information department, the OPEC News Agency (established 1980), a legal office and the OPEC Economic Commission (established 1964)) (Arts. 25 to 35).

Meetings of OPEC finance ministers are held on a regular basis (at least twice yearly) to co-ordinate policies on financial and monetary matters of common interest and to act as a Ministerial Council for the OPEC Fund. The OPEC Secretariat is responsible for organizing meetings of the Conference of OPEC Oil Ministers.

ACTIVITIES

The Organization's main activities include conducting a continuous programme of research, with particular emphasis on energy and related matters, monitoring, forecasting and analysing developments in the energy and petrochemical industries and the evaluating hydrocarbons and products and their non-energy uses, analysing economic and financial issues and maintaining data services. It also gives attention to training, the transfer of technology to developing countries, the exchange of information and the development and management of tanker fleets.

Since 1987, the Fund has developed seven action programmes and granted 419 loans amounting to US$2,207 million which is distributed in the following way: 241 loans for the financing development programmes (9) and development projects (232) and 178 for financing balance of payments support.

The Fund's resources are derived from member states' contributions (Art. 4). Initially, amounting to US$800 million, the Fund's resources reached US$3,435 million in 1986, of which effectively US$2,621 has been paid in by member states.

OPEC Fund: The OPEC Fund for International Development (OPEC Fund), in its revised form of 27 May 1980, is the successor to the "OPEC Special Fund" which was established on 28 January 1976 [19 I.L.M.(1980)879]. The OPEC Fund is a "multilateral agency for financial co-operation and assistance established by OPEC Member Countries" (Art. 1.01). It is actively involved in the financing of development projects (particularly energy projects) as well as in extending loans and grants and making contributions and/or providing loans to international agencies which benefit developing countries (Art. 2).

The Fund has three main bodies: a **Ministerial Council**, a **Governing Board** and a **Director-General**, assisted by a staff (Art. 5). The Ministerial Council is the supreme organ of the OPEC Fund and provides an agency function in co-ordinating the views and policies of its members and at times representing them, as per Art. 2.03, in negotiations related to aid issues described in Art. 5.02 v). The Governing Board has original broad powers in policy as well as operational issues (Art. 5.05 and 5.06) whilst the Centre for OPEC Studies secures the organization, promotion and diffusion of research and information programmes about OPEC and about the historical socio-economic and cultural realities of OPEC member states.

Mary E. Footer

Access : CON (Art. 7)
Reserves : USP
Duration : USP
Deposit. : Iraq (Art. 3)
Language : Eng

Reference : 443 UNTS – 2 Paeslee

124.02 – AGREEMENT ESTABLISHING THE COCOA PRODUCERS' ALLIANCE – CPA

Concluded : 20.01.1962, Abidjan
In force : May 1962
Parties : 13

The Cocoa Producers' Alliance (CPA) was established under the terms of the Abidjan Charter of 20 January 1962, signed by five producing countries. It has since been re-grouped with 13 members, providing more than 87 per cent of world cocoa production: the five founding members – Brazil, Cameroon, Ghana, Côte d'Ivoire and Nigeria – have been joined by the Dominican Republic, Ecuador, Gabon, Malaysia, Mexico, São Tomé and Príncipe, Togo, and Trinidad and Tobago.

Its aims are to exchange technical and scientific information, to discuss problems of mutual concern, to promote economic and social relations between the producing countries, to ensure the proper supply of the market at remunerative prices and to promote cocoa consumption.

STRUCTURE

The Organization has three principal organs: the **Council of Ministers,** which is the supreme authority and meets ordinarily once a year in September/October; the **General Assembly;** and the **Secretariat,** which is responsible for the application of decisions taken by intergovernmental organs. All decisions are taken by a simple majority vote other than those concerning the budget, distribution of and differences or questions arising from contributions, amendments, decisions about headquarters, winding up of the Alliance, interpretation of its Charter, measures related to ensuring an adequate stocking of the market at remunerative prices and the expansion of consumption and fundamental questions related to the International Cocoa Agreement [see 121.05], where a qualified majority of three-quarters of the members, present and voting, is required.

The CPA serves primarily as a discussion forum amongst cocoa-producing countries with a view to adopting a common position during the course of large international negotiations. Likewise, it intends to involve itself in international regulatory mechanisms should existing ones fail.

Oscar J. Rodríguez-Aguilar

Access : CON (Art. 3)
Reserves : USP
Duration : USP
Deposit. : Côte d'Ivoire
Language : Eng, Fre (Art. 20)

Reference : CPA-AC 293/REV.2

124.03 – CONVENTION OF THE INTERGOVERNMENTAL COUNCIL OF COPPER EXPORTING COUNTRIES – CIPEC

Concluded : 08.06.1967, Lusaka
In force : 07.08.1967
Parties : 4

The "Conseil intergouvernemental des pays exportateurs de cuivre" (CIPEC) was founded by the Convention of Lusaka, adopted at the Intergovernmental Conference on Copper (1 to 8 June 1967). Its original signatories were Chile, Peru, Zaire and Zambia. Peru has now withdrawn. However, Portugal was admitted as an observer member in 1991, during the Mining Ministers' Conference in Vina del Mar, Chile.

CIPEC attempted to operate as a cartel but failed, primarily because – unlike oil – there exist close substitutes for copper. The organization's intentions of manipulating the copper market were, therefore, unrealistic. CIPEC operated thereafter as a copper information-gathering institution with headquarters located in Paris until its demise in June 1992. One reason for dissolution was Chile's opening up of its economy to the free market. Another, was the distinct inability of its African associates to meet their financial commitments.

CIPEC's documentation has now been sent to Santiago, Chile, where it is presently in a dormant state. Under the auspices of the Chilean Mining Ministry, efforts are being made to re-establish links with its African partners, who have not, in fact, announced their withdrawal from the organization. CIPEC's remaining affairs are being administered by personnel from the Chilean Copper Commission, keeping manpower at a minimum and magazine subscriptions alive. Nevertheless, Zambia and Zaire have been given a deadline to comply with payment of arrears to the organization.

Whilst CIPEC's financial affairs await resolution, Chile has taken the initiative in advancing participation in the newly-established Grupo Internacional de Estudio del Cobre (GIEC), or International Copper Study Group [see 123.03]. GIEC's mandate began in Geneva in January 1992. Already consolidating membership of 18 copper producing and consuming countries, GIEC's objectives will be – excluding its operation as a cartel – presumably very similar to CIPEC's. For this reason an outline of the dormant organization's *raison d'être* is given below.

CIPEC's original objectives were to co-ordinate measures designed to foster, through the expansion of the industry, dynamic and continuous growth of real earnings from copper exports and to ensure a real forecast of such earnings. It also aimed to promote and harmonize decisions and policies of member states relating to the production and marketing of copper for member states; and to increase resources derived from copper exports in order to benefit the economic and social development of the producer states, bearing in mind the interests of the consumers.

STRUCTURE

The organization had three main organs: the **Conference of Ministers,** which was the supreme authority and met annually, at which a new Chairman was elected by ordinary session; the **Executive Committee**, constituted by representatives of all member states and associate members (meetings were held four times a year); and the **Secretariat**, with a Secretary-General, whose appointment was for two years, subject to renewal. His role was basically an informative one. There was also a Committee on Marketing Policy.

CIPEC did not intervene directly in such futures markets as COMEX or the LME to maintain prices. Its strategy was to follow the market, to take note of market mechanisms and to use them in order to stabilize prices. Although production of the original CIPEC member states accounted for some 52 per cent of total world copper production, it had limited powers of intervention due to its lack of homogeneity and an absence of major copper producers, including the US and the former Soviet Union. Instead, it played the role of initiator or indicator of trends, as in the period 1974-1975 following a programme of reduction in CIPEC exports.

Its main activities were concentrated in organizing committees and working parties as well as providing an information and advisory service for its members through the Copper Information Bureau. The latter presented reports on the demand and supply of copper, marketing, government agreements and regulations, technical advances in mining, transformation and utilization of copper, labour, transport and other factors which affected the copper industry and all other problems relating to the marketing and sale of copper and its by-products.

O.J.R.-A.

Access : CON (Art. 2)
Reserves : USP
Duration : ULT (Art. 30)
Deposit. : CIPEC
Language : Eng, Fre, Spa (Art. 33)

Modific. : Res. (21.06.77); (07.12.77); (31.12.86)

Reference : CIPEC Doc. CM/102/77 Fin

124.04 – ASSOCIATION OF NATURAL RUBBER PRODUCING COUNTRIES (ANRPC) – ANRPC

Concluded : 21.05.1968, London
In force : 08.04.1970
Parties : 7

The Association of Natural Rubber Producing Countries (ANRPC) was founded on 21 May 1968 at London. The Association's Statutes were amended by the six natural rubber-producing countries on 16 October 1970 at Kuala Lumpur, Malaysia. The ANRPC subsequently regrouped with eight member states as follows: India (1975), Indonesia (1970), Malaysia (1970), Papua New Guinea (1975), Singapore (1970), Sri Lanka (1968), Thailand (1970) and Vietnam (1970). However, Vietnam's membership in the ANRPC terminated with effect from 1 January 1977, as its subscription was in arrears.

Its objectives are, *inter alia*, to bring about co-ordination in the production and marketing of natural rubber, to promote technical co-operation among its members, which together produce around 89 per cent of the world's natural rubber supply, and to bring about fair and stable prices for natural rubber.

STRUCTURE

The ANRPC has two main bodies. The first is the **Assembly**, at which representatives from each of the member states meet annually. All decisions are taken by a simple majority vote provided that at least half of the annual production of the Association is represented. Second is the **Executive Committee**, which meets in between annual Assembly sessions and which also supervises the general work of the Committee of Experts. In addition, the organization has a Secretary-General and a **Secretariat**.

Since its foundation, the ANRPC has concentrated its efforts on the creation of a mechanism for stabilizing the price of natural rubber. Notably, it was responsible for developing the project for the first International Agreement on Natural Rubber of 1982 [see 121.06].

The ANRPC also organizes seminars, workshops and meetings connected with: (i) the progress and development of rubber smallholders; (ii) the Technical Committee on South American Leaf Blight; (iii) the improvement of natural rubber statistics in member countries; (iv) rubber contact and marketing; and (v) matters connected with the International Natural Rubber Organization (INRO) [see 121.06].

Mary E. Footer

Access : CON (Art. 2, 21)
Reserves : USP
Duration : USP
Deposit. : Malaysia (Art. 22)
Language : Eng

Modific. : Amended 16.10.1970 (24.01.1971)

Reference : 1045 UNTS

124.05 – AGREEMENT ESTABLISHING THE INTERNATIONAL BAUXITE ASSOCIATION – IBA

Concluded : 08.03.1974, Conakry
In force : 29.07.1975
Parties : 11

The International Bauxite Association (IBA) was established on 29 July 1975 when the last of the seven founding member states deposited its instrument of ratification to the Conakry Agreement of 8 March 1974. The IBA now has 11 members (the founding members are shown in italics), spread over three geographical areas: Africa (Ghana, *Guinea, Sierra Leone*), the Caribbean (*Guyana, Jamaica,* Dominican Republic, *Suriname*), Europe, Asia and the Pacific (*Australia,* India, Indonesia and the former *Yugoslavia*).

This producers' organization was originally concerned with releasing supplementary revenues in order to compensate for the high petroleum prices of 1973. Its more recent aims are to promote the orderly and rational development of the bauxite industry, and to secure fair and reasonable returns for member countries from the exploitation, processing and marketing of bauxite and its products, bearing in mind the interests of consumers.

STRUCTURE

The structure of the organization is as follows. There is a **Council of Ministers** which is the supreme organ and meets once a year to develop the Association's general policy. The IBA also has an **Executive Board**, composed of two representatives from each member state, which meets three times a year and is responsible to the Council of Ministers for the execution of the policy which is decided upon. Finally, there is the **Secretariat** which is responsible for carrying out the administrative functions of the IBA and whose two main departments are Administration and Finance, and Economic and Technical Information.

ACTIVITIES

The organization's main activities are to provide an exchange of information concerning all aspects of exploitation, processing, marketing and the use of bauxite and its derivatives. It studies the elaboration of a pricing policy for bauxite and alumina and extends to member states, upon request, technical assistance in negotiations with transnationals engaged in the exploitation and processing of bauxite.

The IBA's influence, while not comparable to that of OPEC's [see 124.01], is not negligible. The IBA has influenced the control of the exploitation and processing of bauxite whilst co-ordinating the action of its member states. Equally, it has influenced the adoption, in 1976, of a minimum sale price of bauxite destined for use as aluminium base. In the indexation of prices, the minimum price of aluminium is calculated according to the mean price of bauxite and aluminium, based on the average price of 99.5 per cent of primary aluminium ingot.

It should be noted, however, that member states are not bound to respect a maximum price. In this regard, they are entirely at liberty to proceed with necessary adjustments. The IBA nevertheless monitors whether prices reflect real market conditions. In fact, the Association only recommends "prices that the market can bear".

M.E.F.

Access : CON (Art. II)
Reserves : USP
Duration : ULT (Art. XXVII)
Deposit. : Jamaica (Art. XXVIII)
Language : Eng, Fre (Art. XVIII, XIII)

Modific. : Amendment 1977 (-)

Reference : 1021 UNTS – ILM 13:1245

124.06 – AGREEMENT ESTABLISHING THE UNION OF BANANA EXPORTING COUNTRIES – UPEB

Concluded : 17.09.1974, Panama
In force : 10.02.1976
Parties : 8

The Unión de Países Exportadores de Banano (UPEB) was established by the Agreement of 17 September 1974, which extended the Panama Agreement of 8 March 1974 and brought to an end what had come to be known as the "banana war". It has eight members: Colombia, Costa Rica, Dominican Republic, Guatemala, Honduras, Nicaragua, Panama and Venezuela.

The UPEB's objectives are *inter alia*: to secure and defend remunerative prices for bananas grown and exported by member states, to promote the adoption of common policies with a view to rationalizing output, exports, transportation and marketing and pricing policies, to explore new markets, to harmonize export availabilities and export demand, to develop technical assistance programmes, with respect to cultivation, processing, marketing and transportation of bananas, to ensure a greater participation of member states in the world banana economy and to promote diversification programmes.

STRUCTURE

The UPEB's structure is concentrated around three principal organs. The **Conference of Ministers** is the supreme organ. It is made up of economic or agricultural ministers of the member states and it meets periodically to examine problems of general interest. Its directives are transmitted to the **Council of Representatives**, or **Permanent Council**, of the governments which implement them. Voting in both the organs is by majority vote (1,000 in total): 25 per cent (250 votes) are distributed equally among the member states and 75 per cent (750 votes) according to the most recent exports during a period, fixed by the Conference. However, the voting system has not been used so far because all the decisions have been taken by consensus. The **Office of the Executive Director** is a permanent institution which fulfils the administrative and technical functions of the organization.

COMUNBANA (Comercializadora Multinacional de Banano/Multinational Bureau for Banana Marketing), a technical bureau, set up by UPEB in 1977 but operated exclusively by transnational corporations to allow member states to participate in the management of the marketing process, failed in practice and no longer exists.

ACTIVITIES

The UPEB's activities include the development of statistical information and a system of economic analysis for the study of the global and regional banana situation, the development and formulation of a co-ordinated scientific and technological research programme, the study of projects such as a global banana agreement so as to stabilize international prices and to co-ordinate the national positions of member states, the development of increased and more direct participation by member states in banana marketing through the opening up and expansion of non-traditional markets, the establishment of the banana-exporting countries' own marketing organizations and the development of a bibliographic database specialized in bananas and plantains. UPEB is today the largest and most complete documentation and information centre on banana and plantain in the world.

Oscar J. Rodríguez-Aguilar

Access : CON
Reserves : PRO (Art. 41)
Duration : DET 10 (Art. 35)
Deposit. : Panama
Language : Spa

Reference : UNTS 1/21294

124.07 – AGREEMENT ESTABLISHING THE ASSOCIATION OF IRON ORE EXPORTING COUNTRIES – AIOEC

Concluded : 03.04.1975, Geneva
In force : 12.10.1975
Parties : 9

Subsequent to the creation of an informal group on iron ore at UNCTAD II, in New Delhi in 1968, the ratification of the Agreement of April 1975 by seven countries (Art. 36) and the first meeting of ministers in Geneva in November 1974, the Association of Iron Ore Exporting Countries (AIOEC) was founded on 12 October 1975. Nine countries are currently members of AIOEC: Algeria, Australia, India, Liberia, Mauritania, Peru, Sierra Leone, Sweden and Venezuela.

Its aims are to promote close co-operation among member countries in order to safeguard their interests in relation to the iron export industry, to ensure the orderly and healthy growth of export trade in iron ore, to secure fair and remunerative returns from the exploitation, processing and marketing of iron ore with a view to improving their export earnings and terms of trade, to contribute to the economic and social development of member countries and to encourage the processing of iron ore in member countries, including into iron and steel, and lastly to provide a forum for the exchange of informal and effective and meaningful consultations on problems relating to the iron export industry (Art. 5).

The organization is funded by equal annual contributions from member countries (Art. 32).

STRUCTURE

The supreme authority of AIOEC is the **Conference of Ministers** which meets bi-annually (Arts. 7 and 8). Decisions are taken by unanimous consent of the representatives of member countries present (Art. 9). The organization also has a **Board** which meets twice a year, with the same voting requirements as the Conference of Ministers (Art. 11). It is responsible for the direct management of AIOEC's affairs, including the annual budget of the association and providing for suitable arrangements in the field of consultation and co-operation with other organizations (Arts. 12 and 13). It is also responsible for the supervision and evaluation of the technical, consultative and executive functions of the **Secretariat** and can appoint a technical committee to assist it in its work (Arts. 15 and 16).

The Secretariat acts upon the instructions of the Conference of Ministers and the Board (Art. 17) and is involved primarily in requesting, collecting and processing information relevant to the iron ore industry. It also provides this information to member countries and gives advice on request. In addition, it undertakes regular reviews of market conditions and technical studies on, for example, the supply and demand of iron ore, trends in prices, scrap availability, marketing and transportation, and the impact of technological advances on consumption and processing of iron ore. The Secretariat consists of a Secretary-General, appointed on a rotating basis for four years at a time, assisted by a staff (Arts. 20 and 21).

The main activities of AIOEC are purely restricted to a consultative role without powers for concerted government action to intervene in the iron ore market and influence prices. It remains mainly a forum for the exchange of information and shared experience of the iron ore industry.

Mary E. Footer

Access : CON (Art. 2, 35)
Reserves : USP
Duration : ULT (Art. 41)
Deposit. : India (Art. 42)
Language : Eng, Fre, Spa (Art. 42)

Reference : ILM 14:1139

124.08 – AGREEMENT ESTABLISHING THE INTERNATIONAL TEA PROMOTION ASSOCIATION – ITPA

Concluded : 31.03.1977, Geneva
In force : 23.02.1979
Parties : 8

The International Tea Promotion Association (ITPA) was established on 23 February 1979, subsequent to an agreement by states which participated in the "Intergovernmental Conference of Tea Producing Countries", 7 to 17 September 1976 at Geneva. (The Conferences had been convened by the International Trade Centre, a combined UNCTAD/GATT initiative.) Of the original ten members, the organization now only has eight – Bangladesh, Indonesia, Kenya, Malawi, Mauritius, Mozambique, United Republic of Tanzania, and Uganda. The two traditional and major tea producers, Sri Lanka and India, withdrew from the ITPA on 29 September 1982 and 25 July 1984, respectively, due to the inability of the tea-producing countries to agree on a scheme of export quotas for tea. Opposition to a scheme of shared export restrictions came largely from the new African producers, such as Kenya.

By a resolution of 21 November 1984, adopted by the Governing Board of ITPA, it was decided to suspend Article 1-2 (but only with respect to the phrase "and to formulate programmes to achieve this objective"), Article 1-3 and Articles 11 to 13 for an initial period of two years.

Its aims are to promote the co-ordination of policies and actions of its members to maintain and increase the demand for and the consumption of tea in present and potential markets by formulating appropriate programmes and collecting and allocating national and international resources for this purpose. It also aims to foster the removal of tariff and non-tariff barriers in tea (technical barriers to trade, in particular); to establish relations with governments, representatives of the tea trade and related interests; where appropriate, to import promotion bodies in tea-consuming countries; and to collect, analyse and disseminate market information.

STRUCTURE

The ITPA consists of a **Governing Board** which meets twice a year and is made up of one or more representatives of all members; it elects a Chairman and two Vice-Chairmen from among its members. The Governing Board is assisted by an Executive Director and his staff, appointed by the former.

Funds for the Association come from member governments' contributions. Its main focus is on the study of the development of the international trade in tea in all its aspects.

M.E.F.

Access : CON
Duration : USP
Deposit. : UN
Language : Eng

Reference : 1128 UNTS

124.09 – AGREEMENT ESTABLISHING THE ASSOCIATION OF TIN PRODUCING COUNTRIES – ATPC

Concluded : 29.03.1983, London
In force : 01.10.1983
Parties : 7

This producers' organization is also known as the International Tin Producers' Association ("Association des pays producteurs d'étain") and comprises seven members: Australia, a developed producer country, and Nigeria, Zaire, Bolivia, Indonesia, Malaysia and Thailand. Two non-members, Brazil and Chile, have participated in the past in meetings as observers and have joined members in applying the export quota system, described below.

Its key aims are to undertake research and development on tin and to reduce the involvement of third parties in the marketing of tin. Since the collapse of the Sixth International Tin Agreement [see 121.03], the ATPC has been actively promoting a supply management scheme among its producing countries, the so-called "supply rationalization scheme" (SRS) which aims at regulating the supply of tin to world markets through the application of a system of export quotas. This supply restriction scheme, among producing countries, has enjoyed a considerable degree of initial success and has led to a recovery in world tin prices.

Between March 1987 and mid-1989, world tin stocks have been reduced from

73,000 tonnes to 3,000 tonnes. However, by June 1990, and largely as the result of reduced discipline among the member countries, tin stocks once again rose to over 45,000 tonnes. This was matched by a subsequent fall in tin prices to US$5,707 per tonne in September 1990 and led to criticism from those participating in the scheme. In October 1990, they decided to further strengthen their system of export controls and to significantly reduce their total export quotas.

M.E.F.

Access : CON
Reserves : USP
Duration : USP
Deposit. : Malaysia
Language : Eng

1.3 Food and Health

1.3.1 Food

Many international organizations take part in providing food aid to developing countries in crisis, and in helping these countries to develop their agricultural production. Four such organizations play a major role: two specialized agencies of the UN, the Food and Agriculture Organization (FAO) and the International Fund for Agricultural Development (IFAD), and two UN subsidiary bodies, the World Food Council (WFC) and the World Food Programme (WFP).

The mission of these organizations is at once humanitarian and economic. The WFP manages a system for distributing excess food production to the less developed world, and operates programmes with the aim of increasing agricultural productivity and rural living standards in these countries [see 131 B]. The IFAD provides low-cost financing for individuals and businesses to increase agricultural production in developing countries [see 131 D]. The FAO analyses and distributes information, and supports programmes on nutrition, agriculture and the environmental effects of agricultural activity. It also promotes education and research, and provides expert advice to governments [see 131 A]. To co-ordinate UN activity within this field, and to develop systematic long-term policies in regard to the world food problem, the WFC was established in 1974 [see 131 C].

Joel Saltsman

SELECTED BIBLIOGRAPHY

Marchiso, S. and A. di Blase, *The Food and Agriculture Organization (FAO)*, Dordrecht: Martinus Nijhoff Publishers, 1991.

Talbot, Ross B., *The Four World Food Agencies in Rome: FAO, WFP, WFC, IFAD*, Iowa State University Press, 1990.

131 A – FOOD AND AGRICULTURE ORGANIZATION OF THE UNITED NATIONS (FAO)

The Food and Agricultural Organization (FAO) is one of the specialized agencies of the United Nations. Its objectives are as follows:

- to raise the levels of nutrition and the standards of living of people;
- to secure improvements in the efficiency of the production and distribution of all foods and agricultural products;
- to better the condition of rural populations;
- to contribute toward an expanding world economy; and
- to ensure humanity's freedom from hunger.

Given these aims, FAO's functions are to collect, analyse, interpret and disseminate information relating to nutrition, food and agriculture, including fisheries, marine products, forestry and primary forestry products. It also promotes and recommends national and international action with respect to research, education and administration relating to nutrition, food and agriculture, the conservation of natural resources, the improvement of the production, processing, marketing and distribution of agricultural products, the adoption of policies to ensure adequate agricultural credit, and the adoption of international policies with respect to agricultural commodity arrangements. FAO also provides technical assistance to governments in its fields of competence.

STRUCTURE

A **Conference** meets every two years in regular session, in which each member nation has only one vote. Since 1991, it is also open to certain regional economic integration organizations. It determines the Organization's policy, elects members to the Council, elects a Director-General, approves the budget and the contributions of member states (Art. IV of the FAO Constitution). It can also, by a two-thirds majority of votes, make recommendations relating to food and agriculture.

A **Council** meets between sessions of the Conference and acts as the managing body of the Organization. It is composed of representatives from 49 countries who are elected on a rotating basis for a period of three years. It holds at least three sessions between the regular sessions of the Conference, and appoints commissions, committees and working parties to assist it in its work. Among the more important committees assisting the Council are the Programme Committee, which deals with questions of economic development, and the committees on finance, constitutional and legal matters, commodity problems, fisheries, forestry, agriculture, and world food security (Art. V-6).

A Director-General is elected by the Conference, and heads the **Secretariat**. He has full power and authority to direct the work of the organization, subject to the general supervision of the Conference and the Council (Art. VII-4).

CO-OPERATION

The Conference, the Council, and the Director-General have used the powers conferred on them by the FAO constitution to establish Subsidiary Bodies. These may be groups composed of experts (e.g. the Panel of Experts on Improved Weed Management, and the Panel of Experts on Agricultural Mechanization), or of representatives of member states (e.g. the Joint FAO/WHO/OAU Regional Food and Nutrition Commission for Africa). One of the significant achievements of the FAO has been the establishment of the so-called Codex Alimentarius Commission, which is responsible for carrying out the joint FAO/WHO programme on food standards [see 132 B]. A significant number of specialized committees have been established under the CAC to elaborate specific food-related standards.

Of the 16 UN specialized agencies (Arts. 57 and 63 of the UN Charter) [see 001 A], the FAO is the one which employs the greatest number of people. The majority work in the field, world-wide, on projects co-ordinated by the FAO's headquarters in Rome, regional offices, and liaison offices.

FUNDING

The organization's budget is paid by the member states (US$744,668,000 for the period 1992-1993) and contributions of the members are calculated on the basis of

GNP. However, other sources of financing also exist. For example, the UNDP [see 222 A] finances projects and there is also a system of trust funds. These funds consist of voluntary contributions from various governments for specified projects. Given the nature of a trust fund, the contributor(s) exercises direct control over the project it is funding.

PUBLICATIONS

The FAO publishes monographs, technical publications, and Yearbooks, including *Trade Yearbook, FAO Commodity Review and Outlook, Food and Agricultural Legislation, Yearbook of Fishery Statistics.* With the WHO and the OIE (International Epizooty Office), it also publishes *Animal Health Yearbook.*

Jean-Paul Chapdelaine and FAO

ADDRESS

Via delle Terme di Caracalla , 00100 Rome, Italy
T. (39 6) 57971, Fx. (39 6) 5797 3152

131 B – WORLD FOOD PROGRAMME (WFP)

The World Food Programme was created on an experimental basis by the UN General Assembly in 1961, following a resolution taken at the FAO Conference of the same year. Its initial purpose was to establish a system which would redistribute agricultural surpluses. In December 1965, the WFP became a permanent institution.

WFP provides food aid, primarily to people in low-income, food-deficit countries, to assist in the implementation of economic and social development projects, and to provide relief for victims of natural and man-made disasters. Food is supplied, for example, as an incentive in development self-help schemes or as part wages in labour-intensive projects. Since 1963, WFP has undertaken 1,615 development and quick action projects in 116 countries, 1,122 emergency operations in 108 countries, and 55 long-term refugee and displaced persons operations in 21 countries.

Projects assisted by the Programme cover a wide range of activities designed to promote rural development and to help increase agricultural food production. Activities include the settlement and resettlement of groups and communities, land reclamation and improvement, irrigation, forestry, road building, hospital training and community development, and human resources development such as the feeding of expectant or nursing mothers and school children, and support to education and training, and to health programmes.

Projects to assist agricultural and rural development accounted for 65 per cent of development projects in 1991, with a total value of US$292 million. At the end of 1991, WFP was assisting 96 human resource development projects with an aggregate value of US$1,129 million, mainly projects for mothers and pre-school and primary school-children.

Some of WFP projects are specificially intended to alleviate the effects of structural adjustment programmes (particularly programmes which involve reductions in public expenditure and in subsidies for basic foods).

WFP is the only multilateral organization with a mandate to use food aid as an investment resource. It is the second largest source, in terms of actual transfer of resources in the United Nations, after the World Bank group and the largest source of grant aid in the UN system. In 1990, WFP's share in total grant assistance for development amounted to 25.3 per cent. WFP handles more than one-quarter of the world's food aid.

WFP headquarters are in Rome, with three-quarters of its staff of more than 1,500 assigned to country offices in 82 countries, with projects in 92 developing countries.

Other services provided by the Programme include purchasing, transporting and monitoring bilateral food aid donations.

STRUCTURE

The **Committee on Food Aid Policies and Programmes** (CFA), which meets twice a year, is the governing body of the WFP. The CFA exercises full intergovernmental supervision and direction for all activities of the Programme, including food aid policy, administration, operations, funds and finances. It comprises 42 members, of which 21 are elected by the Economic and Social Council of the United Nations (ECOSOC) [see 001 A], and 21 by the Food and Agriculture Organization (FAO) Council [see 131 A]. The members, 27 from developing countries and 15 from economically more developed countries, serve three-year terms and are eligible for re-election. It provides a forum for intergovernmental consultation on national food aid programme and policies; reviews trends in food aid requirements and availabilities; formulates proposals for effective co-ordination of multilateral food aid; and examines and approves projects submitted to it by the Executive Director. It also examines and approves the administrative and project budgets of the Programme.

The Executive Director is responsible for the management and administration of the Programme. Jointly appointed by the Secretary-General of the UN and the Director-General of the FAO, in consultation with the CFA, the Executive Director is accountable to the CFA for all aspects of the Programme.

CO-OPERATION

WFP has contacts with about 300 local and international non-governmental organizations involved in relief and development activities. These include the Catholic Relief Services (CRS), the Cooperative for American Relief Everywhere (CARE), Caritas International, Save the Children Fund (SCF), Oxfam, World Vision International (WVI), International Committee for the Red Cross (ICRS), International Council of Voluntary Agencies, Médecins sans Frontières International and Africare.

RESOURCES AND FUNDING

The Programme is funded through voluntary contributions from donor countries and intergovernmental bodies such as the European Community. Contributions are made in commodities, cash and services, with the aim that cash and services pledged should together amount to at least one-third of the total. The 26th FAO Conference and the 46th session of the Assembly set a pledging target of US$1.5 billion for the biennum 1993-94. During the pledging conference, contributions are also made to the International Emergency Food Reserve (IEFR) which was established by the United Nations in 1975 and is administered by the WFP, with a target of 500,000 tonnes of cereals. The Programme also provides services to bilateral donors in the field of food aid and administers various subtrust funds financed through extra-budgetary contributions.

In 1991, WFP received a total of US$1,437 million – including outstanding obligations – from regular and extra-budgetary resources against an expenditure of US$1,422 million.

PUBLICATIONS

The WFP publishes the *WFP Journal* (quarterly) and the *World Food Programme Food Aid Review* (annually). It also produces videos on emergency relief operations and development projects carried out by the Programme.

WFP

ADDRESS

426, Via Cristoforo Colombo, 00145 Rome, Italy
T. (39 6) 57 971, Fx. (39 6) 512 7400

131 C – WORLD FOOD COUNCIL (WFC)

The World Food Council is an organ of the United Nations and was established in December 1974 by UN General Assembly Resolution 3348 (XXIX) on the recommendation that same year of the World Food Conference (Res. XXII of 16 November 1974). It began its activities on 17 December 1974.

According to Resolution XXII, the World Food Council is defined as "an organ of the United Nations reporting to the General Assembly through the Economic and Social Council, to serve as a co-ordinating mechanism to provide overall, integrated and continuing attention for the successful co-ordination and follow-up of policies concerning food production, nutrition, food security, food trade and food aid, as well as other related matters, by all agencies of the United Nations system".

In essence, the objective of the Council is to define an international food policy which can promote food security and improve international co-operation. One of the tangible results of its efforts is the establishment of the International Fund for Agricultural Development (IFAD) [see 131 D].

The WFC has numerous responsibilities despite its status as a subsidiary organ of the UN. For example, it receives periodic and special reports from the Committee on World Food Security (Para. 5, Res. XXII) and the Governing Board of the IFAD (Para. 7, Res. XXII); it oversees the implementation of resolutions of the World Food Council and the UN General Assembly; it identifies countries urgently needing food assistance; and it works jointly with the FAO to promote food production and to set goals for establishing reserves of certain foodstuffs such as grain.

STRUCTURE

The World Food Council is made up of 36 members, elected by the UN General Assembly on a three-year rotating basis after nomination by ECOSOC, with one-third of the members retiring every year to be replaced through elections by the General Assembly, on the basis of nominations by the Economic and Social Council [see 001 A]. Retiring members are eligible for re-election. The Council elects its President, establishes a programme of action, and makes recommendations aimed at stimulating governments and the international community to adopt appropriate policies and programmes in the fight against hunger and poverty.

The Council informs the UN General Assembly of its activities through ECOSOC (Para. 7, Res. 3348 XXIX).

Jean-Paul Chapdelaine and WFC

ADDRESS

c/o FAO, Via delle Terme di Caracalla, 00100 Rome, Italy
T. (39 6) 57 971, Fx. (39 6) 5797 3152

131 D – INTERNATIONAL FUND FOR AGRICULTURAL DEVELOPMENT (IFAD)

The International Fund for Agricultural Development is one of the specialized agencies of the United Nations. The Agreement Establishing IFAD ("the Agreement") was adopted by the UN Conference on the Establishment of an International Fund for Agricultural Development on 13 June 1976.

In the wake of the 1974 world food crisis, the call for urgent and co-ordinated measures for future food production resulted in the establishment of IFAD. The objectives of IFAD are "to provide financing for projects and programmes, specifically designed to introduce, expand, or improve food production systems and to strengthen related policies and institutions within the framework of national priorities and strategies, taking into consideration the following: the need to increase food production in the poorest food deficit countries; the potential for increasing food production in other developing countries; and the importance of improving the nutritional level of the poorest populations in developing countries and the conditions of their lives" (Art. 2).

To carry out its mandate, IFAD provides grants and loans to its developing member countries. The proportion of the grants is normally not required to exceed one-eighth of the resources committed in any financial year (Art. 7-2-b). Loans are the major form for financing projects for which IFAD has three levels of lending based on the per capita income of the country, determined on the basis of 1976 US$ prices. The countries with a per capita income of US$300 per annum or less receive loans, preferably on highly concessional terms. These are interest-free loans which carry 1 per cent service charge and are repayable over a period of 50 years, including a grace period of ten years. Those with a per capita income above US$300 and not more than US$500 can, generally, receive loans on intermediate terms. They carry an interest rate of 4 per cent and are repayable over 20 years, including a grace period of five years. All other developing member countries of the organization are eligible to receive loans on ordinary terms only, with an interest rate of 8 per cent and a maturity period of 15 to 18 years, including a grace period of three years (Lending Policies and Criteria, Para. 31).

Projects may be co-financed with IBRD [see 221 A], regional development banks, other international organizations and bilateral aid agencies. IFAD has its own regulations which the recipients of its loans are required to follow for the procurement of goods to be financed from the proceeds of IFAD loans. As a general rule, these regulations conform to the principles of international competitive bidding and give appropriate preference to supplies from developing member countries of IFAD. When a project is co-financed with an international financial institution (e.g. IBRD, the African Development Bank, etc.) which also supervises the implementation of the project, including the components financed by IFAD, the co-financing institution applies its own regulations for the procurement of goods. This is so irrespective of

IFAD's regulations, except in the case of projects which are co-financed on a parallel basis – that is, indentifiable components financed exclusively by one co-financer only. In such a case, IFAD's regulations are applicable for the procurement of goods financed solely by IFAD.

For consultant services under an IFAD project, the recipient of the loan is required to follow the procedures of the international institution which is entrusted by IFAD with the responsibility of supervising its financed projects, whether exclusively financed or co-financed by IFAD. In the case of the former, all member countries of IFAD are eligible to participate in the competition to provide services and appropriate preference is to be given to services from developing member countries of the organization.

MEMBERSHIP

Membership of IFAD is open to any state which is a member of the United Nations or of any of its specialized agencies, or of the International Atomic Energy Agency (IAEA). Membership is classified into three categories. As of May 1993, the organization had 149 members, divided into Category I, comprising 22 OECD countries, Category II, consisting of 12 OPEC members and the rest of the 115 developing countries are classified in Category III.

The original members of IFAD are the countries which are listed in the Membership Schedule to the Agreement, and which joined the organization within one year from 30 November 1977, the date on which the Agreement entered into force and effect. Those countries which joined the organization after that period are the non-original members. Each of the members is classified in one of the three categories of membership. The classification is determined with the concurrence of the prospective member, at the time of the approval of its membership (Art. 3-3-a). This classification may be altered, with the concurrence of the member concerned, by a two-thirds majority of the total number of votes of the Governing Council.

The classification of membership at the first instance was necessary as each original member of Category I and Category II had the obligation, under the Agreement, to contribute to the initial resources of IFAD (Art. 4-2-a). In addition, the system of classification of members is important as it determines the voting power of each in the governing bodies of IFAD.

STRUCTURE

The structure of IFAD is made up of a Governing Council, an Executive Board, and the President and such staff as may be necessary (Art. 6). The organization has a total of 1,800 votes and each of the membership categories has 600 votes. These 600 votes are divided within the members of the category in accordance with the formula laid down in the Agreement. In Category I, for example, 82 per cent of the votes are distributed according to each member's paid contribution to the resources of the Fund, the remaining 17.5 per cent of the votes of the Category being equally divided among the members of the Category. In Category II, 75 per cent of the votes are distributed according to the paid contribution of each member to the resources of the Fund and the remaining 25 per cent of the votes are divided equally amongst its members. In the case of Category III, its 600 votes are equally divided amongst its members, regardless of any contribution paid by any of its members. As of January 1993, each member in Category III had 5.31 votes. In view of the principle to seek a decision in any of the governing bodies initially through consensus in lieu of voting, it is rare that the organization resorts to voting. In its 15 years of existence, the vote was taken in the Governing Council only on two occasions.

The **Governing Council**, where each member is represented by its Governor, is the supreme governing body of the organization and, except for the powers assigned by the Agreement to the Executive Board, all the remaining powers of the Fund are vested in the Council. It meets once a year in an annual session, normally in the month of January, and can be summoned to a special session if the need arises. A decision in the Governing Council may require a majority of two-thirds, three-quarters, four-fifths, or a simple majority of the total number of votes, depending on the nature of the proposal to be voted upon. For instance, approval of the administrative budget, appointment of the President and adoption of broad policies, criteria and regulations governing the functioning of the organization would require a two-thirds majority in the Council. Amendment of the Agreement can only be adopted by four-fifths of the majority of the total number of votes.

The **Executive Board** consists of 18 members and 17 alternate members. It is responsible for the conduct of the general operations of the Fund and for this it exercises the powers assigned to it by the Agreement and those delegated to it by the Governing Council (Art. 6-5-c). Each of the three categories of members in the Governing Council elects or appoints six members and six alternate members (except Category I, which appoints five alternates) of the Executive Board from within its own category (Art. 6-5-a). The members and alternate members serve for a period of three years. For operational purposes, the Executive Board is the body that determines the proportion of the Fund's resources to be committed in any financial year for projects and programmes (Art. 7-2-a) and it approves the financing for projects (Art. 7-2-c). All operational decisions are required to be taken by the Board by a majority of three-fifths of the votes cast, provided that such majority consists of more than 900 votes (Art. 6-6-b). In the Board, the Chairman tries to obtain decisions through consensus in lieu of votes. So far, the Board has not resorted to voting for decision-making on any proposal.

The President of the organization is appointed by the Governing Council by a majority of no less than 1,200 votes. The term of office of the President is four years and any one person can hold the office for a maximum of two terms (Art. 6-8-1). The President chairs the meetings of the Executive Board without the right to vote, heads the **Secretariat**, and is the legal representative of the Fund.

FUNDING

The resources of the Fund consist of initial contributions made by the member states, which was mandatory for Category I and II members, and voluntary for Category III members on joining IFAD. Additional contributions were to be obtained in the following ways: through replenishments decided by the Governing Council, approximately for a period of three years, on the basis of negotiations between Categories I and II, with the participation of the representation of Category III; through increases in the states' contributions authorized by the Governing Council; and by special contributions. The special contributions do not count either in calculating weighted voting rights, or towards determining the ratio of burden sharing between Category I and II member states.

The initial resources amounted to US$1,019 million (56 per cent for Category I, 43 per cent for Category II and 1 per cent for Category III), and the First Replenishment to US$1,093 million, with the share of each Category being 57 per cent, 41 per cent, and 2 per cent, respectively. The Second Replenishment was of the level of US$479 million and the share of each category in the total, came to 58 per cent for Category I, 38 per cent for Category II, and 4 per cent for Category III. The total of the Third Replenishment was US$567 million, Category I contributing US$187,600 million in core contributions and US$192 million in supplementary contributions. The latter related to US$3 for each US$1 contributed by Category III in freely convertible currency. In the Third Replenishment, Category II contributed US$124 million and Category III, US$65 million.

In addition, IFAD administers Special Resources for Sub-Saharan Africa. These funds have been used by the organization since 1985 to undertake operations to rehabilitate agriculture and rural development in those Sub-Saharan African countries which have been affected by drought and desertification.

CO-OPERATION

IFAD, unlike other international financial organizations, does not supervise its own projects. In the Agreement, it is mandatory for the organization to entrust the responsibility for the administration of its loans for the purpose of the supervision of the execution of the project and disbursement of the proceeds of the loan, to other competent international institutions (Art. 7-2-g). The major international institutions, *inter alia*, which carry out loan administration responsibilities for IFAD are the IBRD [see 221 A] and the regional developing banks. With each of these institutions, IFAD has concluded a Co-operation Agreement, which lays down the policies and principles which they follow and adhere to in carrying out their responsibilities on behalf of IFAD. The services of these institutions are also used for the appraisal of projects which IFAD may have initiated.

PUBLICATIONS

IFAD publishes an Annual Report. Since 1979, it has published various studies relating to agricultural development and alleviation of rural poverty, notably, *The State of World Poverty* (published in 1992).

IFAD

ADDRESS

Via del Serafico 107, I-00142 Rome, Italy
T. (39 6) 54591, Fx. (39 6) 504 3463

131.01 – CONSTITUENT ACT OF THE UNITED NATIONS FOOD AND AGRICULTURE ORGANIZATION – FAO

Concluded : 16.10.1945, Quebec
In force : 16.10.1945
Parties : 160

FAO replaced the International Institute of Agriculture (founded in Rome in 1905 and dissolved in 1944) which sought to improve the situation of farmers through intergovernmental co-operation. The FAO Constitution was adopted at the Quebec Conference of October 1945, making the Organization a specialized agency of the United Nations.

The FAO Constitution sets down the structures of the Organization and outlines its principal objectives. It can be amended by a two-thirds majority of the vote during

Conference sessions; this majority, however, must be greater than half the number of total members of the Organization. An amendment not involving new obligations for member nations or associate members shall take effect immediately, unless the resolution by which it was adopted provides otherwise. Amendments involving new obligations shall take effect for each member nation and associate member accepting the amendment on acceptance by two-thirds of the member nations of the Organization.

On 16 October 1945, even before the United Nations became operational as an organization, 34 states had signed the FAO Constitution thereby allowing it to go into effect.

Jean-Paul Chapdelaine

Access : CON (Art. II,XXI)
Reserves : USP
Duration : USP
Deposit. : FAO (Art. XXI)
Language : Ara, Chi, Eng, Fre, Spa (Art. XXII)

Modific. :Amendments 1946 (1946); 1947 (1947); 1949 (1949); 1950 (1950); 1951 (1951); 1953 (1953); 1955 (1955); 1957 (1957); 1963 (1963); 1965 (1965); 1967 (1967); 1969 (1969); 1971 (1971); 1973 (1973); 1975 (1975); 1977 (1977); 1979 (1979); 1991 (1991)

Reference :Can TS 1945/32 – UKTS 1946/47, 1972/96, 1974/48, 1976/46, 1979/55, 1983/82 – 2 Paeslee – UST 12/1, 13/3, 14/2, 17/1, 18/3, 21/2, 23/1, 25/1, 27/3, 29/3

131.02 – ESTABLISHMENT OF THE WORLD FOOD PROGRAMME – WFP

Adopted : 19.12.1961, UNGA Res.1714(XVI)

WFP was established jointly by the Food and Agriculture Conference Resolution 1/61 of 24 November 1961, and by the United Nations General Assembly Resolution 1714 (XVI) of 19 December 1961, on an experimental basis for three years. Operations commenced in January 1963. The Programme was extended by the UN General Assembly Resolution 2095 (XX) of 20 December 1965 on a continuing basis.

On 28 November 1975, the UN/FAO Intergovernmental Committee of the World Food Programme was transformed into a Committee on Food Aid Policies and Programmes (CFA) by UN General Assembly Resolution 3404(XXX).

J.-P.C.

Modific. :Renewed UNGA Res.2095(XX) 20.12.65 (20.12.65); UNGA Res.3404(XXX) 28.11.75 (28.11.75); Res.46/22 05.12.91 (05.12.91)

Reference : ILM 14:285

131.03 – ESTABLISHMENT OF THE WORLD FOOD COUNCIL – WFC

Adopted : 17.12.1974, UNGA Res.3348(XXIX)

The World Food Conference, held in Rome from 5 to 16 November 1974, recommended the establishment of a World Food Council (Res. XXII), as well as an International Fund for Agricultural Development. The Conference had other effects as well:

- it highlighted the problems of malnutrition;
- it favoured the increase in food production, the improvement in consumption and distribution of food, and the creation of a world food security system;
- it called for the establishment of a global information and early-warning system to deal with problems of food and agriculture; and
- it recommended assistance from donor countries in supplying at least ten million tonnes of grain in food aid per year.

General Assembly Resolution 3348(XXIX) established the WFC according to the objectives and guidelines set out in Resolution XXII adopted by the World Food Conference on 16 November 1974.

J.-P.C.

Modific. : Res.31/120 16.12.76 (16.12.76)

131.04 – AGREEMENT ESTABLISHING THE INTERNATIONAL FUND FOR AGRICULTURAL DEVELOPMENT – IFAD

Concluded : 13.06.1976, Rome
In force : 30.11.1977
Parties : 149

The Agreement was adopted by the UN Conference, on the creation of an International Fund for Agricultural Development, held at the FAO and WFC headquarters from 10 to 13 June 1976.

The establishment of IFAD had been recommended by the World Food Conference, held in Rome from 5 to 16 November 1974 [see 131.03].

Access : CON (Art. 13-1)
Reserves : PAU (Art. 13-4)
Duration : USP
Deposit. : UN (Art. 13-2)
Language : Ara, Eng, Fre, Spa (Art. 13-5)

Modific. : Governing Council Res.44/X 11.12.86 (11.03.87)

Reference : 1059 UNTS – RTAF 1978/13 – Can TS 1977/44 – ILM 15:916 – UKTS 1978/41 – UST 28/7 – JORF 11 Dec 77

1.3.2 Health

In the first years following the Second World War, the urgent priorities for international health organizations were to combat epidemic diseases and to rebuild health care systems in war-ravaged areas. These had been the traditional aims of predecessor bodies to the World Health Organization (WHO) [132 A]. With the passage of time, however, WHO came to pay increasing attention to the broader mandate expressed in its Constitution. The underlying principle of this instrument is that lasting improvements in health and living conditions depend on social and economic reforms.

Today, therefore, WHO concerns itself with issues going beyond the important core activity of fighting and preventing disease. These include education and technical training, research and development programmes, standards work, environmental protection, and advice and technical assistance to governments on subjects such as improving sanitation and containing health system costs.

With the expansion of WHO's mandate, its activities have brought it into closer contact with the FAO [see 131 A], particularly as regards hygiene standards and food quality. Since 1960, the work of standard-setting for food products has been undertaken jointly by these two organizations through the Codex Alimentarius Commission (CAC) [132 B].

Joel Saltsman

132 A – WORLD HEALTH ORGANIZATION (WHO)

The WHO is one of the United Nations' family of specialized agencies created in the aftermath of the Second World War. The founding of WHO in 1946 at the International Health Conference in New York followed half a century of intergovernmental efforts for the prevention and control of diseases such as cholera, plague, smallpox and typhus.

While the immediate priorities of WHO were to rebuild health care systems and combat epidemic diseases, its main objective was far broader: "the attainment by all peoples of the highest possible level of health". Under the WHO constitution, "health" means "a state of complete physical, mental and social well-being and not merely the absence of disease or infirmity". Responsibility for improving the world's health thus involves WHO in a broad range of social and economic development activities.

The WHO has the following constitutional responsibilities:

- providing technical assistance to governments by strengthening their health systems, including support for training;
- undertaking actions to prevent and control major communicable diseases, such as malaria, poliomyelitis and AIDS, as well as non-communicable diseases such as cancer, diabetes and heart disease;
- promoting improved nutrition, housing, sanitation, environmental and working conditions;
- proposing international agreements;
- promoting scientific and professional co-operation;
- conducting research and operating technical services;
- developing international standards for food and pharmaceutical products; and
- providing public information, education and advocacy on health matters.

The importance of the Organization's mission, the scale on which it works (5,500 specialists in over 100 countries) and its impact on individuals as well as on communities and governments, makes the WHO one of the pillars of the United Nations' system of multilateral co-operation.

An example of a WHO initiative is the Global Strategy for Health for All by the Year 2000 adopted by the World Health Assembly (see below) in 1981. The Strategy gave detailed expression to the Assembly's 1977 decision that the main policy target of governments and of WHO should be the attainment by all the people of the world by the year 2000 of a level of health that will permit them to lead a socially and economically productive life. The Strategy centres on the development of a health system infrastructure, beginning with primary health care, that delivers countrywide programmes to the whole population. It emphasizes the need for a high degree of community involvement, and for selecting technology appropriate for the country concerned. The UN General Assembly has endorsed the Strategy and has urged other international organizations to collaborate with WHO. During the 1990s, profound changes in political, economic and social conditions in many parts of the world have required adjustment of the means of implementation of the strategy, particularly to ensure the affordability of, sustainability of, and equitable access to primary health care.

MEMBERS

In addition to its member states (currently numbering 184), WHO also admits as associate members territories which are not responsible for the conduct of their international relations.

STRUCTURE

The work of the Organization is carried out by three bodies. The **World Health Assembly** is the supreme decision-making body of WHO. Composed of representatives of each member state, the Assembly meets annually, usually in Geneva, to decide on major policy matters and to approve the biennial programme budget.

The **Executive Board,** which meets twice yearly, gives effect to the decisions and policies of the Assembly, prepares Assembly agendas and submits advice and proposals to it, including plans for the Organization's work programme. Every three years the Assembly elects, on a regionally balanced basis, 31 member states to designate one Board member each. The Board members are health experts who act in their personal capacity rather than as spokespersons for their countries. The **Secretariat** is headed by a Director-General appointed by the Assembly on the nomination of the Executive Board.

An important characteristic of WHO is its decentralization in six regional organizations, each composed of a Regional Committee and a Regional Office. Each regional organization is an integral part of WHO created by the Assembly with the consent of the members from each region. The six regions are: Africa, the Americas, South-East Asia, Europe, the Eastern Mediterranean, and the Western Pacific.

The Regional Committees, on which both members and associate members are represented, formulate policies for matters of an exclusively regional character and supervise the work of their administrative organs, the regional offices. Seventy per cent of WHO staff work outside WHO headquarters, either in field programmes or in the regional offices.

Some of the regional organizations trace their roots to bodies in existence before the WHO was founded. For example, the regional organization for the Eastern Mediterranean has antecedents dating back to 1843 in Alexandria, Egypt. In 1949, the Second World Health Assembly approved an agreement to integrate the Washington-based Pan American Sanitary Organization (founded in 1902 and later renamed the Pan American Health Organization) with WHO. By virtue of the Agreement, the Pan American Sanitary Conference and The Pan American Sanitary Bureau serve as the Regional Committee and Regional Office of the WHO for the Western Hemisphere while retaining their respective names.

CO-OPERATION

The WHO Constitution requires it to work closely with other organizations of the United Nations system. Historically, its closest partner has been UNICEF. The International Code of Marketing of Breast-milk Substitutes [see 132.04], for example, was initiated through a joint WHO/UNICEF meeting and the two organizations continue to co-operate in the promotion and implementation of that Code. The WHO also operates joint programmes, for example, in the field of nutrition with FAO [see 131 A], in teacher training with UNESCO [see 171 A], and in occupational health with the ILO [see 141 A]. Outside the UN framework, the WHO collaborates officially with about 160 professional, charitable and other non-governmental organizations.

PUBLICATIONS

WHO communicates health information and research results through an active publishing programme consisting of seven periodicals and about 80 new books each year. The works range from laboratory and training manuals to policy guides and expert reports on technical health problems.

Joel Saltsman

ADDRESS

20 avenue Appia, CH-1211 Geneva 27, Switzerland
T. (41 22) 791 21 11, Fx. (41 22) 791 07 46

132 B – JOINT FAO/WHO CODEX ALIMENTARIUS COMMISSION (CAC)

The purpose of the Joint WHO/FAO Codex Alimentarius Commission (CAC) is to ensure the safety of food products moving in trade, to promote fair practices in food trade, and to establish guidelines for national systems of food regulation. The Commission is an important part of WHO food safety activity, which aims to reduce the incidence of disease by improving the monitoring and control of food-borne hazards.

The Commission is the main feature of the Joint FAO/WHO Food Standards Programme, created in 1962 by resolutions of the FAO Conference [see 131 A] and the Executive Board of the WHO [see 132 A]. The Programme was set up at a time of increasing world-wide interest in reducing non-tariff barriers to international food trade, and in safeguarding the health of the consumer. The Programme works to improve the adequacy of commercial practices involved in the food products trade by promoting and co-ordinating international work on food standards. Membership of the Commission, which is open to member states of the FAO or the WHO, stands at 144 in 1993. Its budget is administered on behalf of both organizations by FAO, which provides 83 per cent of the annual funding, the remaining 17 per cent coming from WHO.

The Codex Alimentarius, published by FAO and WHO in Rome, is a collection of internationally adopted food standards presented in a uniform manner. In addition to approximately 230 individual commodity standards, it includes 37 codes of hygienic and technological practice and approximately 2,400 Maximum Residue Limits for pesticides. Codex standards for raw and processed food commodities moving in international trade, cover aspects such as uniform labelling requirements, the use of food additives, the presence of contaminants or residues of pesticides or veterinary drugs,

sanitary (or hygiene) requirements, nutritional quality, and composition and analysis.
Among the most important products of the Commission's work are:

- the General Principles of Food Hygiene (1969, revised 1985);
- the Code of Ethics for International Trade in Food (1979, revised 1985);
- the Agreement on Technical Barriers to Trade (1979) [see 111.07];
- a world-wide standard for irradiated foods (1983);
- the International Code of Marketing of Breast-Milk Substitutes (1981) [see 132.04];
- the General Standards for the Labelling of pre-packed foods (1985, revised 1991); and
- the Guideline Levels for Radionuclides in Foods Following Accidental Nuclear Contamination for Use in International Trade (1989).

J.S.

ADDRESS

c/o CAC Secretariat, FAO, Via delle Terme di Caracalla, I-00100 Rome, Italy
T. (39 6) 57971, Fx. (39 6) 5797 3152

132.01 – CONSTITUTION OF THE WORLD HEALTH ORGANIZATION – WHO

Concluded : 22.07.1946, New York
In force : 07.04.1948
Parties : 184

The Constitution was prepared and adopted during the International Health Conference held in New York from 19 June to 22 July 1946. Signed on 22 July 1946 by the representatives of 61 states, the Constitution entered into force on 7 April 1948. (Pursuant to Article 80, the Constitution comes into force when 26 states have become parties to it.) The same Conference adopted the Final Act, the Arrangement for the Establishment of the WHO Interim Commission, and the Protocol Regarding the International Office of Public Hygiene. The latter text is reproduced in 9 UNTS.
For a description of the Organization, see 132 A.

Joel Saltsman

Access : ALS (Art. 3)
Reserves : USP
Duration : USP
Deposit. : UN (Art. 82)
Language : Chi, Eng, Fre, Rus, Spa (Art. 82)

Modific. : WHA Res. 12.43 28.05.59 (25.10.60); WHA Res. 18.48 20.05.65 (-); WHA Res. 20.36 23.05.67 (21.05.1975); WHA Res. 26.37 22.05.73 (03.02.77); WHA Res. 29.38 17.05.76 (20.01.84); WHA Res. 31.18 18.05.78 (-); WHA Res. 39.6 12.05.86 (-)

Reference : 14, 377, 970, 1035 UNTS – Can TS 1946/32 – UKTS 1948/43, 1961/24, 1975/109, 1977/50, 1984/41 – 3/4 Paeslee – UST 11/1/2, 26/1, 28/2 – RTAF 1964/70, 1975/62, 1977/97

132.02 – STATUTES OF THE JOINT FAO/WHO CODEX ALIMENTARIUS COMMISSION – CCA

Adopted : 1962, WHA Res. 16.42, 20.27
Parties : 144

The Statutes of the Commission were prepared by the Conference of the FAO in 1961 (11th Conference Report, Res. 12/61), and confirmed in 1966 by the 47th meeting of the FAO Council. In 1962 the World Health Assembly confirmed the 1961 enactment of the Statutes by the FAO.

For a description of the Organization, see 132 B.

J.S.

132.03 – INTERNATIONAL HEALTH REGULATIONS – WHO

Adopted : 25.07.1969, WHA Res. 22.46
In force : 01.01.1971
Parties : 184

The International Health Regulations adopted by the 22nd World Health Assembly (WHA Res. 22.46) result from the revision and amalgamation of the International Sanitary Regulations of 1951 with the additional regulations of 1955, 1956, 1960, 1963 and 1965.

They replace the provisions of the International Sanitary Conventions of 1892, 1903, 1912 and 1926 (as amended in 1938 and 1944), the "Arrangements" of the same nature (1934), the International Sanitary Convention for Aerial Navigation (1933, modified in 1944 and extended in 1946), as well as the Pan-American Sanitary Convention (1905). In addition, they amend some of the terms of the Pan-American Sanitary Code (1924).

The Regulations aim to ensure the greatest possible security against the spread of diseases from one country to another, while erecting the fewest possible obstacles to international movement. Recognizing the growing importance of epidemiological surveillance as a means of detecting and eradicating communicable diseases, the new Regulations were designed to strengthen the international application of epidemiological principles, to improve the identification, reduction or elimination of sources of infection, to improve hygiene in ports, airports and neighbouring areas, to anticipate the spread of vectors and, in general, to encourage epidemiological projects at the national level that minimize the risk of infections entering its borders.

In 1973, the 26th World Health Assembly amended the 1969 Health Regulations, particularly the provisions regarding cholera. In 1981, following the world-wide eradication of smallpox, the 34th Assembly further amended the Regulations to remove smallpox from the list of diseases subject to their terms.

States which are parties to the Regulations are entitled to put forward reservations, but they have force only if agreed to by the World Health Assembly.

J.S.

Access : CON (Art. 90,91)
Reserves : PAU (Art. 88,89)
Duration : USP
Deposit. : WHO (Art. 94)

Language : Eng, Fre (Art. 94)

Modific. : 1973 (01.01.74); 1981 (01.01.82)

Reference : 764 UNTS – UKTS 1971/18, 1982/19 – UST 21/3, 25/1 – JORF 5 Oct 74

132.04 – INTERNATIONAL CODE OF MARKETING OF BREAST-MILK SUBSTITUTES – WHO

Adopted : 21.05.1981, Geneva

In 1981 the World Health Assembly adopted, by resolution, the International Code of Marketing of Breast-milk Substitutes. The Code was adopted as a recommendation in a resolution which urged all member states to support and implement its provisions.

This Code aims "to contribute to the provision of safe and adequate nutrition for infants, by the protection and promotion of breast-feeding, and by ensuring the proper use of breast-milk substitutes, when these are necessary, on the basis of adequate information and through appropriate marketing and distribution". The main focus of the Code is to ensure that breast-milk substitutes are not marketed or distributed in ways that may interfere with the protection and promotion of breast-feeding. The Code states that its purpose is not to ban or interfere with sales of breast-milk substitutes but rather to deal with certain marketing practices relating to these products which include infant formula, bottles and teats.

The Code bans all advertising and promotion of these products and specifies various banned practices such as point of sale advertising, discount coupons, tie-in sales, the giving of samples, the use of health care systems for promotional purposes, and financial and material inducements to marketing employees.

The Code recognizes the need for breast-milk substitutes when mothers do not breast-feed, or only do so partially, and provides a degree of consumer protection covering both the quality and labelling of products. Products are to meet the "applicable standards" recommended by the Codex Alimentarius Commission [see 132 B] and also the Codex Code of Hygienic Practice for Foods for Infants and Children.

While only 12 countries have implemented the Code in the form of legislation which provides sanctions (including Guatemala, India, Brazil, Nigeria, the Philippines, Mexico, and Tunisia), over 100 countries have implemented it in part. For example, in the UK and Scandinavia there are voluntary agreements between companies to abide by the Code.

Catherine Leonard

1.4 Labour and Transnational Corporations

1.4.1 Labour

Three central themes of international relations – the maintenance of peace, the promotion of economic development and the protection of human rights – all find their expression in the work of the International Labour Organisation (ILO) [see 141 A]. Although in highly developed countries the ILO's aims are being achieved, in most of the world the injustices that preoccupied the ILO's founders continue to flourish: poverty, lack of education, child labour, high unemployment, hazardous working and living conditions, inadequate health care, and denial of collective bargaining rights. In response, the scale and scope of international action in the labour field have continued to expand since the founding of the ILO in 1919.

Since the early 1970s, the ILO and UNCTAD [see 111 B] have been paying close attention to the impact of transnational corporations on national economies and working conditions. Declarations and codes of conduct have been issued setting out principles relating to employment, training, trade unions and the transfer of technology. The aims, among others, of these codes are to discourage restrictive business practices and promote the access of developing countries to technology [see 1.4.2].

Joel Saltsman

141 A – INTERNATIONAL LABOUR ORGANISATION (ILO)

The International Labour Organisation was created in June 1919, by the Treaty of Versailles (Part XIII), as an autonomous part of the League of Nations. At the end of the Second World War, it became the first specialized agency of the United Nations, under the terms of the Liaison Agreement dated 14 December 1946.

The founders of the ILO started from the premise that future wars would only be avoided and lasting peace maintained if social reforms were undertaken to remove the most flagrant injustices and hardships that affected vast numbers of people throughout the world. ILO founding principles also stress that the pursuit of economic progress is inseparable from the struggle for social justice. In particular, the 1944 Philadelphia Declaration reaffirmed the principles that:

- labour is not a commodity;
- freedom of expression and association are essential to progress;
- poverty anywhere threatens prosperity everywhere;
- the war against poverty should be carried on through a free and democratic process in which representatives of workers and employers enjoy equal status with those of governments; and
- the central aim of national and international policy must be to attain conditions whereby all human beings can pursue both their material well-being and their spiritual development in conditions of freedom and dignity, of economic security and equal opportunity.

The specific objectives of the ILO, defined in its Constitution and restated in the Philadelphia Declaration, are to further national programmes that will achieve:

- full and satisfying employment and higher living standards;
- facilities for the training and mobility of workers;
- a just sharing of the fruits of progress through adequate wages and proper working conditions;
- the effective recognition of the right of collective bargaining, and the promotion of.co-operation between workers and employers;
- universal social security programmes to provide basic income and medical care;
- adequate protection of workers' lives and health; and
- social protection in other areas, notably child welfare, maternity, nutrition, housing and education.

STRUCTURE

A unique feature of the ILO among intergovernmental organizations is its tripartite structure. The principle that representatives of workers, employers and governments have an equal voice applies to the deliberations of all ILO bodies. Three main bodies direct the work of the ILO: the International Labour Conference, the Governing Body and the International Labour Office.

The **International Labour Conference** is the annual general assembly of all ILO member states. Each member state is represented by two government delegates, an employer delegate and a worker delegate. Each June in Geneva, the Conference adopts international labour standards in the form of Conventions and Recommendations, and passes resolutions to guide overall ILO policies. Every two years, the Conference approves the ILO work programme and budget, and every three years it elects a new Governing Body.

The **Governing Body** is the executive council of the ILO which meets three times a year. It establishes the agenda for the Conference and other meetings, forecasts the consequences of Conference decisions, and directs the activities of the International Labour Office. The 56 members include 14 worker representatives, 14 employer representatives, and 28 government seats, of which ten are permanently held by large industrial countries (Brazil, China, France, Germany, India, Italy, Japan, the UK, the USA, and Russia). A 1986 amendment to the Constitution (not yet in force at the end of 1993) would increase the membership to 112 and eliminate the permanent seats.

The **International Labour Office** in Geneva is the permanent secretariat of the ILO. At its head is a Director-General appointed by the Governing Body. The Office serves not only as the administrative agency of the Organisation, but also as a research, documentation and action centre. Among its other activities, it recruits and guides the ILO's technical co-operation experts throughout the world; operates an extensive publishing programme; and works closely with labour and social affairs ministries, trade union bodies and employers' organizations. It operates through over 40 field offices and several regional offices (in Bangkok, Lima, Addis Ababa, Beirut and Geneva).

In addition to the above bodies, the ILO organizes periodic regional conferences and maintains permanent advisory committees to deal with issues of specific interest to a region or an economic sector. These include industrial committees, a Joint Maritime Commission, a Joint Committee on Postal and Telecommunications Services, and interorganizational committees involving other international organizations such as UNESCO [see 171 A] and WHO [see 132 A].

The ILO has established two organizations for advanced training: The International Institute for Labour Studies (Geneva) and the International Centre for Advanced Technical and Vocational Training (Turin).

FUNDING

The ILO budget consists of contributions from member states in proportion to their national product. For the period 1992-1993, the total annual budget was US$404.7 million.

PUBLICATIONS

Every year, the ILO issues a wide range of publications, including the *International Labour Review*, a scholarly journal covering economic and social subjects of international interest (every two months), the *Official Bulletin* (quarterly), the *Legislation Series*, reproducing the texts of major labour and social security laws, and data on labour statistics in the form of a *Yearbook* and a *Bulletin of Labour Statistics*. In addition, the ILO publishes a number of books, including codes, research monographs and textbooks on management.

Joel Saltsman

ADDRESS

International Labour Office, 4 route des Morillons, CH-1211 Geneva , Switzerland
T. (41 22) 799 61 11, Fx. (41 22) 798 8685

SELECTED BIBLIOGRAPHY

Ghébali, V.-Y., *The International Labour Organisation: A Case Study on the Evolution of UN Specialised Agencies*, Dordrecht: Martinus Nijhoff Publishers, 1988.

141.01 – CONSTITUTION OF THE INTERNATIONAL LABOUR ORGANISATION – ILO

Concluded : 28.06.1919, Versailles
In force : 10.01.1920
Parties : 162

This Constitution is the basic agreement of the ILO. For a description of the Organization, see 141 A.

J.S.

Access : ALS (Art. 1)
Reserves : USP
Duration : USP
Deposit. : ILO (Art. 1)
Language : Eng, Fre

Modific. : Amendments 14.06.23 (04.06.34); 07.11.45 (26.09.46); 09.10.46 (20.04.48); 25.06.53 (20.05.54); 22.06.62 (22.05.63); 22.06.72 (01.11.74); 1986 (-)

Reference : 2 UNTS – Can TS 1946/28/48, 1954/5 – UKTS 1948/47 – 1 Paeslee – UST 5/1, 7/1, 14/1, 25/3 – JORF 11 Jan & 24 Feb 20

141.02 – INTERNATIONAL LABOUR CODE – ILO

Since 1919, the Conference has adopted 172 conventions and 179 recommendations. Collectively they constitute the **International Labour Code**. The Code defines minimum standards in areas of ILO concern. These areas include fundamental freedoms of workers, promotion of full employment, vocational training, the protection of health, social security and collective bargaining. They may apply to all workers (e.g. the Convention Concerning Workplace Air Pollution, Noise and Vibration [see 141.08]), or to certain categories such as women, migrant workers or young people (e.g. the Convention Concerning Night Work by Women [see 141.04]). Given the large number of international conventions relating to the working environment, several only have been included in this text in order to provide examples.

Conventions and recommendations alike must be adopted by a two-thirds majority vote of the Conference. As with treaties, conventions become binding on member states which ratify them and subject those states to international supervision regarding compliance. Specifically, governments ratifying a convention are expected to make regular reports to the ILO on its application. Each member state is required to submit conventions and recommendations to the competent national authority within a period of one year or, at most, 18 months (Art. 19-5, 19-6).

Unlike conventions, recommendations do not require ratification and have no binding effect on member states. They either amplify the conventions or deal with questions which do not involve formal obligations by way of guidelines for national policy in given fields.

The ILO exerts its influence in several ways to encourage governments to apply ILO standards. The reports referred to above are examined by a committee of independent experts and a tripartite committee of the Conference. Although these committees have no formal powers to impose their views or administer sanctions, they exert considerable moral pressure on member states through their observations, findings and recommendations.

Second, even where conventions have not been ratified, the ILO may require governments to present reports detailing the extent to which their legislation and national practice meets the standards. These requests, often the result of representations from professional bodies or other member states, can also involve the creation of a commission of inquiry.

Third, special procedures exist to examine complaints concerning the alleged violation of trade union rights. Complaints are first examined by the Committee on Freedom of Association, and may then in some cases be submitted to a Commission for further investigation and conciliation.

Finally, the ILO also monitors compliance with conventions adopted outside the ILO framework but in areas of ILO concern, such as the International Convention on Economic, Social and Cultural Rights (UN, 1966).

J.S.

Access : CON
Deposit. : ILO
Language : Eng, Fre

141.03 – CONVENTION CONCERNING THE USE OF WHITE LEAD IN PAINTING – ILO

Concluded : 25.10.1921, Geneva
In force : 31.08.1923
Parties : 56

The objective of the Convention is to protect workers from exposure to white lead and sulphate of lead, as well as from products containing these pigments. The parties undertake "to prohibit...the use of white lead and sulphate of lead and of all products containing these pigments, in the internal painting of buildings, except where the use of white lead or sulphate of lead or products containing these pigments is considered necessary for railway stations or industrial establishments by the competent authority after consultation with the employers' and workers' organizations concerned" (Art. 1). It is, however, permissible to use white pigments containing a maximum of 2 per cent of lead. These provisions do not apply to artistic painting or fine lining. The governments define the limits of such forms of painting, and regulate the use of white lead, sulphate of lead, and all products containing these pigments.

"The employment of males under eighteen years of age and of all females shall be prohibited in any painting work of an industrial character involving the use of white lead or sulphate of lead or other products containing these pigments" (Art. 3). However, the competent authorities have the power, after consulting the employers' and workers' organizations concerned, to permit the employment of painters' apprentices in the work prohibited for the purpose of furthering their education in the trade.

The parties undertake to regulate the use of white lead, lead sulphate, and other products containing these pigments, in operations for which their use is not prohibited according to the principles stipulated in the Convention.

After consultation with the employers' and workers' organizations concerned, the competent authority in each contracting state shall take the steps it considers necessary to ensure the observance of the Convention's regulations. Statistics with regard to lead poisoning among painters are being gathered to determine morbidity and mortality.

Maguelonne Déjeant-Pons

Access : ALS (Art. 9)
Reserves : PRO
Duration : USP
Deposit. : ILO
Language : Eng, Fre

Reference : 38 UNTS

141.04 – CONVENTION CONCERNING NIGHT WORK BY WOMEN (REVISED) – ILO

Concluded : 09.07.1948, Geneva
In force : 27.02.1951
Parties : 47

The history of this Convention illustrates the potential for conflict between international economic agreements and regional legislation.

Concluded in 1948, the Convention is based on a previous version first adopted in 1919. It prohibits the employment of women at night in industrial undertakings (mining, manufacturing and construction). Exceptions are made for family businesses, *force majeure*, vital national interests, women in technical or management positions, and women in the health professions not performing manual work.

In a decision dated 25 July 1991, the Court of Justice of the European Communities ruled invalid the provisions of the French *Code de Travail* which prohibited the employment of women for night work. The court held that such legislation by any member state was incompatible with the provisions of the Treaty of Rome, and with EC Directive 76/207 (06.02.76) concerning the principle of equality of treatment between men and women.

Some EC countries, such as the UK, were not affected as they had never ratified the Convention. But for others – France, Belgium, Italy, Spain, Portugal and Greece – the decision presented them with a contradiction between international obligations. By the end of February 1992, all these states had resolved the conflict by denouncing the present Convention, and no EC country now adheres to it.

In an effort to strike an acceptable balance between policies of special protection for female workers and equality of opportunity, the ILO adopted a series of new measures:

(a) Convention No. 171 of 1990, which aims at improving the working conditions of all night workers, paying special attention to the protection of health and the employment rights of pregnant women and mothers of newborns;
(b) Recommendation No. 178 of 1991, which supplemented Convention No. 171 by providing more detailed guidelines on working hours, rates of pay and social services;
(c) a 1990 Protocol, partially revising Convention No. 89, provides that signatory states may, under certain strictly defined conditions and procedures, authorize night work for women.

For its part, the EC Commission put forward in 1991 a draft Directive dealing with standards for working hours, with emphasis on night work, to ensure that minimum rules for worker protection would be respected throughout the European Community.

Joel Saltsman

Access : ILO (Art. 14)
Reserves : PRO
Duration : NSP
Deposit. : ILO
Language : Eng, Fre

141.05 – CONVENTION CONCERNING THE PROTECTION OF WORKERS AGAINST IONIZING RADIATIONS – ILO

Concluded : 22.06.1960, Geneva
In force : 17.06.1962
Parties : 40

The objective of the Convention is to protect workers against ionizing radiations. The parties undertake to give effect to the Convention by means of laws or regulations, codes of practice or other appropriate means.

Scope: The Convention applies to all activities involving exposure of workers to ionizing radiations in the course of their work. It does not apply, however, to radioactive substances, whether sealed or unsealed, nor to apparatuses generating ionizing radiations from which only limited doses can be received.

DETAILS OF THE CONVENTION

Article 3 states "in the light of knowledge available at the time, all appropriate steps shall be taken to ensure effective protection of workers, as regards their health and safety, against ionizing radiations". To this end, appropriate rules and measures should be adopted, and data essential for effective protection must be made available by the member states.

Every effort must be made to restrict the exposure of workers to ionizing radiations to the lowest practicable level, and any unnecessary exposure is to be avoided (Art. 5). Maximum permissible doses of ionizing radiations that may be received from sources external or internal to the body, and maximum permissible amounts of radioactive substances, are fixed for various categories of workers (Art. 6). Such maximum permissible doses and amounts must be kept under constant review in the light of current knowledge.

Appropriate warning systems must be used to indicate the presence of hazards from ionizing radiations, and any information necessary in this connection must be supplied to the workers. Appropriate monitoring of workers and places of work must be carried out in order to measure the exposure of workers to ionizing radiations and radioactive substances, with a view to ascertaining whether the applicable levels are respected. The parties undertake either to provide appropriate inspection services for the purpose of supervising the application of the Convention's provisions or to satisfy themselves that appropriate inspection is being carried out. They also report regularly on the implementation of the Convention.

Maguelonne Déjeant-Pons

Access : ALS (Art. 17)
Reserves : PRO
Duration : USP
Deposit. : ILO
Language : Eng, Frc

Reference : 431 UNTS – UKTS 1963/41 – RTAF 1972/46 – JORF27 Aug 72

141.06 – CONVENTION CONCERNING PROTECTION AGAINST HAZARDS OF POISONING ARISING FROM BENZENE – ILO

Concluded : 23.06.1971, Geneva
In force : 27.07.1973
Parties : 29

The Convention seeks to protect workers against the hazards of poisoning arising from benzene.

Scope: It applies to all activities involving exposure of workers to aromatic hydrocarbon benzene, as well as to products where the benzene content exceeds 1 per cent by volume. The Convention does not apply, however, to the production of benzene, to the use of benzene for chemical synthesis or in motor fuel, or to analytical or research work carried out in laboratories.

DETAILS OF THE CONVENTION

The parties undertake to use harmless or less harmful substitute products rather than benzene whenever they are available (Art. 2). The use of benzene and of products containing benzene is to be prohibited in certain work processes to be specified by national laws or regulations (Art. 4).

Occupational hygiene and technical measures are to be taken to ensure effective protection of workers exposed to benzene or to products containing benzene. Where workers are exposed to benzene or products containing benzene, the employer shall ensure that the concentration of benzene in the air of the places of employment does not exceed a maximum which shall be fixed by the competent authority of each contracting state at a level not exceeding a ceiling value of 25 parts per million (80 mg/m^3).

Workers who may have skin contact with liquid benzene or liquid products containing benzene must be provided with adequate means of personal protection against the risk of absorbing benzene through the skin. Workers who are to be employed in work processes involving exposure to benzene or products containing benzene must undergo a thorough pre-employment medical examination for fitness, which includes a blood test, and periodic re-examinations which must include biological tests (Art. 9).

The word "benzene" and the necessary danger symbols must be clearly visible on any container holding benzene or products containing benzene (Art. 12). The parties agree to take appropriate steps to provide that any worker exposed to benzene, or products containing benzene, receives appropriate instructions on measures to safeguard health and to prevent accidents, as well as on the appropriate action to be taken if there is any evidence of poisoning.

M.D.-P.

Access : ALS (Art. 16)
Reserves : PRO
Duration : USP
Deposit. : ILO
Language : Eng, Fre

Reference : 885 UNTS – JORF 16 Nov 73 – RTAF 1973/41

141.07 – CONVENTION CONCERNING PREVENTION AND CONTROL OF OCCUPATIONAL HAZARDS CAUSED BY CARCINOGENIC SUBSTANCES AND AGENTS – ILO

Concluded : 24.06.1974, Geneva
In force : 10.06.1976
Parties : 25

The Convention seeks to protect workers against hazards caused by carcinogenic substances and agents in the workplace.

The parties periodically determine the carcinogenic substances and agents to which occupational exposure shall be prohibited or made subject to authorization or control. This control is carried out by the appropriate inspection services of each contracting state. Exemptions from prohibition may only be granted by the issuing of a certificate specifying in each case the conditions to be met. In making the determinations as to which substances are prohibited, consideration shall be given to the latest information contained in the codes of practice or guides which may be established by the International Labour Office, as well as information from other competent bodies.

DETAILS OF THE CONVENTION

The parties must make every effort to have carcinogenic substances and agents to which workers may be exposed in the course of their work replaced by non-carcinogenic substances or agents or by less harmful substances or agents. The number of workers exposed to carcinogenic substances or agents, and the duration and degree of such exposure, must be reduced to the minimum compatible with safety.

The parties shall prescribe the measures to be taken to protect workers against the risks of exposure to carcinogenic substances or agents and must ensure the establishment of an appropriate system of records. They also must take steps so that workers who have been, are, or are likely to be exposed to carcinogenic substances or agents are provided with all the available information on the dangers involved and on the measures to be taken. The parties also agree to take measures to ensure that workers are provided with such medical examinations, or biological or other tests or investigations, during the period of employment and thereafter, as are necessary to evaluate their exposure and supervise their state of health in relation to the occupational hazards.

The parties must, by laws or regulations or any other method consistent with national practice and conditions, and in consultation with the most representative organizations of employers and workers concerned, take such steps as may be necessary to give effect to the provisions of the Convention. They must also specify the persons or bodies on whom the obligation of compliance with the provisions of the Convention rests.

M.D.-P.

Access : ALS (Art. 8)
Reserves : USP
Duration : USP
Deposit. : ILO (Art. 7)
Language : Eng, Fre (Art. 14)

Reference : 1129 UNTS 5 – IEL 974:48/1

141.08 – CONVENTION CONCERNING THE PROTECTION OF WORKERS AGAINST OCCUPATIONAL HAZARDS IN THE WORKING ENVIRONMENT DUE TO AIR POLLUTION, NOISE AND VIBRATION – ILO

Concluded : 20.06.1977, Geneva
In force : 11.07.1979
Parties : 28

This Convention aims to protect workers against occupational hazards in the working environment.

Scope: The Convention applies to all branches of economic activity. However, a member state may, after consultation with the representative organizations of employers and workers concerned, exclude from its application particular branches of economic activity in respect of which special problems of a substantial nature arise.

A member may accept the obligations of this Convention separately in respect of air pollution, noise and vibration.

DETAILS OF THE CONVENTION

The Convention provides that national laws shall prescribe that measures be taken for the protection and control of, and protection against, occupational hazards in the working environment due to air pollution, noise and vibration.

The competent authority of each member state shall establish criteria for determining the hazards of exposure to air pollution, noise and vibration in the working environment and, where appropriate, shall specify exposure limits on the basis of these criteria.

M.D.-P.

Access : ALS (Art. 18)
Reserves : USP
Duration : USP
Deposit. : ILO
Language : Eng, Fre

141.09 – CONVENTION CONCERNING OCCUPATIONAL SAFETY AND HEALTH AND THE WORKING ENVIRONMENT – ILO

Concluded : 22.06.1981, Geneva
In force : 11.08.1983
Parties : 16

The objective of the Convention is to prevent accidents or damage to health by minimizing occupational hazards.

The parties must, in the light of national conditions and practice, and in consultation with the most representative organizations or employers and workers, formulate, implement and periodically review a coherent national policy on occupational safety, occupational health and the working environment (Art. 4). The aim of the policy shall be to prevent accidents and injury to health arising out of, linked with, or occurring during the course of work, by minimizing, as far as is reasonably practicable, the causes of hazards inherent in the working environment. The formulation of the policy shall indicate the respective functions and responsibilities of public authorities, employers, workers and others, taking into account both the complementary character of such responsibilities and the national conditions and practice.

The situation regarding occupational safety and health and the working environment must be reviewed at appropriate intervals, either overall or in respect of particular areas, with a view to identifying major problems and evolving effective methods for dealing with them, establishing priorities of action, and evaluating results.

The parties must, by laws or regulations or any other method consistent with national conditions and practice and in consultation with the representative organizations or employers and workers concerned, take such steps as may be necessary to implement the national policy outlined in Article 4.

The enforcement of laws and regulations concerning occupational safety and health and the working environment must be secured by an adequate and appropriate system of inspection, and must be enforced by adequate penalties for violations of the laws and regulations.

Responsibility of Employers. Employers are required to ensure that, so far as is reasonably practicable, the workplace, machinery, equipment and processes under their control are safe and without risk to health. They must also ensure that, so far as is reasonably practicable, the chemical, physical and biological substances and agents under their control are without risk to health when the appropriate measures of protection are taken. They must provide, where necessary, adequate protective clothing and protective equipment to prevent, so far as is reasonably practicable, risks of accidents or of adverse effects on health. And finally, employers are required to provide, where necessary, measures to deal with emergencies and accidents, including adequate first aid arrangements.

M.D.-P.

Access : ALS (Art. 24)
Reserves : PRO
Duration : USP
Deposit. : ILO
Language : Eng, Fre

1.4.2 Transnational Corporations

It has long been recognized that firms and especially transnational corporations can defeat the attempts of states to regulate trade. At the multilateral level, the first attempt to control restrictive business practices having global effects took place during the Economic Conference at the League of Nations in 1927. The International Labour Organisation (ILO) [see 141 A] also made proposals in 1944 for the regulation of what they called "industrial arrangements". This concern for ethics and for the general behaviour of private enterprises is today embodied in the tripartite declarations of the ILO [see 142.01].

During the Second World War, the link between trade and security became very apparent. International trade was seen to be crucial for long-term peace and it was felt that the practices of enterprises should not be allowed to threaten this fundamental objective.

Thus, the Havana Charter [see 111.02], recognizing that distortions to trade could result directly from the actions of enterprises and/or from their tolerance by states, included a complete chapter on the control of restrictive business practices. It also contained provisions on labour standards. The Havana Charter was never adopted and it is said that one of the main objections of the US Congress to the Charter was the chapter on labour standards.

Other bodies, such as ECOSOC [see 001 A] and the Council of Europe, have also unsuccessfully attempted to draft codes of ethics for firms, or at least codes of competition to regulate private enterprises. The draft Code on Transfer of Technology, prepared within the framework of UNCTAD, and a Draft Code of Conduct on Transnational Corporations, sponsored by the United Nations Commission on Transnational Corporations (UNCTC), have now fallen by the wayside and most work of the secretariat of UNCTC is now being transferred to UNCTAD in Geneva [see 111 B]. The need to address behaviour and ethics of firms remains.

The codes which have been adopted by global organizations are the ILO Tripartite Declaration [142.01] and the UNCTAD Code on Restrictive Business Practices [142.02]. They contain innovative sections which are addressed directly to enterprises, as does the 1976 OECD Guidelines for Multinational Enterprises.

Bernard Colas and Gabrielle Marceau

SELECTED BIBLIOGRAPHY

Grosse, Robert, "Codes of Conduct for Multinational Enterprises", *JWTL* 16/5: 414-433.

Raymond, Vernon, *Storm over the Multinationals*, Cambridge, Mass.: Harvard University Press, 1977.

Horn, Norbert (ed.), *Legal Problems in Codes of Conduct for Multinational Enterprises*, Deventer: Kluwer Law and Taxation, 1980.

142.01 – TRIPARTITE DECLARATION OF PRINCIPLES CONCERNING MULTINATIONAL ENTERPRISES AND SOCIAL POLICY – ILO

Adopted : 16.11.1977, Geneva

In the 1970s, the ILO became concerned with the social aspects of the activities of multinational enterprises in host countries. In 1977, after extensive work within the ILO, its Governing Body adopted this Declaration which represents a consensus among representatives from national governments, multinational enterprises and labour unions on issues such as employment, vocational training, conditions of work and life, and industrial relations.

This Declaration aims to encourage the positive contribution which multinational enterprises can make to economic and social progress, and to minimize and resolve the difficulties which their various operations may cause.

The Declaration, based on the respect of the sovereign rights of states, sets out principles which governments, employers' and workers' organizations and multinational enterprises are recommended to observe on a voluntary basis. Where applicable, it makes reference to relevant conventions and recommendations of the ILO.

Major principles in the Code include statements that multinational enterprises should: (1) take fully into account established general policy objectives of the countries in which they operate; (2) give priority to local personnel in employment and training; (3) use technologies which generate employment, both directly and indirectly; and (4) provide workers with information about the firm to allow meaningful negotiations. The Code also states that governments should promote good labour and employment practices.

In order to increase its effectiveness, the Governing Body of the ILO set out a follow-up procedure in March 1978. Governments are invited to report on the application of the Declaration and a tripartite commission is mandated to examine and evaluate their reports.

B.C. and G.M.

Reference : ILM 17:422

142.02 – SET OF MULTILATERALLY AGREED EQUITABLE PRINCIPLES AND RULES FOR THE CONTROL OF RESTRICTIVE BUSINESS PRACTICES – UNCTAD

Adopted : 05.12.1980, UNGA Res.35/63

The so-called UNCTAD Code on RBPs was inspired by the EC and US competitive systems, the 1973 Guidelines of the International Chamber of Commerce, and the various OECD recommendations and decisions in the area of restrictive business practices especially the OECD's 1976 Guidelines for Multinational Enterprises.

This Code of Conduct was approved on 22 April 1980, by a special conference convened under the auspices of UNCTAD [see 111 B]. On 5 December 1980, the UN General Assembly unanimously adopted the Code as Resolution 35/63.

In recalling the need for the liberalization of international trade, the Code promotes free competition in the international trade of goods and services, particularly in the developing world. To this end, the Code seeks to prevent abuse of the dominant position held by multinational corporations in a market. Corporations are also called on to respect national legislation on this issue and to conform to the injunctions of the competent state authorities. Conferences responsible for examining the implementation of the Code met in 1985 and 1990, and will continue to do so periodically.

B.C. and G.M.

Reference : ILM 19:813

1.5 Industrial Development and Standardization

1.5.1 Industrial Co-operation

Increased awareness that industrialization is a dynamic instrument of growth essential to economic and social development has progressively enhanced UNIDO's role. This body has been assisting developing countries, since its creation in 1966, to promote and accelerate their industrialization and to co-operate with industrialized countries' private and public sectors.

However, the developing countries' share in total manufacturing output is still very low. Efforts to increase it may only be successful if accompanied by industrialized countries' granting generous market access to developing countries' production.

151 A – UNITED NATIONS INDUSTRIAL DEVELOPMENT ORGANIZATION (UNIDO)

The United Nations Industrial Development Organization (UNIDO) was established on 21 June 1985 when the Constitution of UNIDO entered into effect after having been ratified by 80 states. UNIDO became a specialized agency of the United Nations on 17 December 1985 when the UN General Assembly approved the Agreement between the UN and UNIDO as foreseen in Article 57 of the Charter of the UN [see 001.01] and Article 18 of the Constitution of UNIDO [see 151.01].

The Organization established in 1985 took over the activities, assets, obligations and staff of the autonomous UNIDO established by UN General Assembly Resolution 2152(XXI) of 17 November 1966 and the autonomous Organization ceased to exist on 31 December 1985.

Under its Constitution, the primary objective of UNIDO is the promotion and acceleration of industrial development in the developing countries with a view to assisting the establishment of a new international economic order. UNIDO has the mandate to promote industrial development and co-operation on global, regional and national, as well as sectoral, levels. Its functions include the initiation, co-ordination and follow-up of industrial development activities within the UN system with a view to enabling UNIDO to play the central co-ordinating role.

STRUCTURE

The **General Conference** consists of representatives of all member states of UNIDO. It is the plenary organ and holds a regular session every two years, unless it decides otherwise. Special sessions may also be convened.

The **Industrial Development Board** consists of 53 member states elected by the General Conference: 33 from Asia, Africa, Latin America or the Caribbean; 15 from countries in Western Europe and North America, as well as Japan, Australia and New Zealand; and five from countries in Eastern Europe. The Board holds at least one regular session each year in addition to any special sessions.

The **Secretariat** is headed by the Director-General, who is appointed by the General Conference upon the recommendation of the Board. The Director-General is appointed for a period of four years and may be reappointed for only one additional four-year term. He or she is the chief administrative officer of the Organization and appoints the staff of the Secretariat. The Secretariat also comprises such Deputy Directors-General as are required. Their appointments are subject to approval by the Board.

The main subsidiary organ is the **Program and Budget Committee** whose function it is to assist the Board in financial matters such as the review of the programme of work and the regular and operational budgets of UNIDO.

As of 15 May 1993, UNIDO had 162 member states.

ACTIVITIES

UNIDO's main activities include:

- encouraging and extending assistance to developing countries for the development, expansion and modernization of their industries;
- assisting developing countries in the establishment and operation of industries in order to achieve full utilization of locally available natural and human resources and to contribute to self-reliance;
- providing a forum and acting as an instrument to serve the developing and industrialized countries in their contacts, consultations and negotiations;
- developing special measures designed to promote co-operation among developing countries and between developed and developing countries; and
- co-ordinating all activities of the UN system relating to industrial development.

CO-OPERATION

UNIDO's Constitution calls on the Organization to assist in the formulation of development, scientific and technological programmes and plans for industrialization in the public, co-operative and private sectors.

Through its special trust-fund schemes, UNIDO gives industrial partners from both the public and private sectors the opportunity to co-operate through projects arranged, supervised and carried out by the Organization. This has resulted in close working relationships with a number of internationally well-known corporations. UNIDO also works with regional and interregional organizations for the planning and promoting of industrial development.

UNIDO maintains Investment Promotion Services in Athens, Cologne, Paris, Seoul, Tokyo, Vienna, Warsaw, Washington, and Zurich as well as two industrial co-operation centres, based in Moscow and Beijing. It also has UNIDO Country Directors in the field in developing countries who work there in conjunction with United Nations Development Programme (UNDP) representatives [see 222 A].

FUNDING

UNIDO is financed by contributions from member states under a system of assessment. Other funding sources include technical assistance costs paid by UNDP [see 222 A], voluntary contributions, special assistance funds, contributions from intergovernmental and non-governmental organizations, trust funds, self-financing arrangements and private contributions. The Industrial Development Fund was created in 1976 as an additional source of voluntary contributions.

In 1992 UNIDO implemented projects having a value of US$945 million. The Industrial Development Fund financed some US$154 million worth of projects.

PUBLICATIONS

These include UNIDO's *Annual Report, Country Industrial Reviews, Development and Transfer of Technology Series, Handbook of Industrial Statistics* (biennial), *Industry Africa* (annual), *Industry and Development: Global Report, UNIDO Newsletter* (monthly), and *UNIDO Update* (quarterly).

UNIDO and Martin St-Amant

ADDRESS

Vienna International Centre, Wagramerstrasse 5, PO.Box: 300, 1400 Vienna, Austria
T. (43 1) 211310, Fx. (43 1) 232156

151.01 - CONSTITUTION OF THE UNITED NATIONS INDUSTRIAL DEVELOPMENT ORGANIZATION - UNIDO

Concluded : 08.04.1979, Vienna
In force : 21.06.1985
Parties : 162

This Constitution is the basic agreement of UNIDO. For a description of the Organization, see 151 A.

Access : ALS (Art. 3-a)
Reserves : PRO (Art. 27)
Duration : USP
Deposit. : UN (Art. 28)
Language : Ara, Chi, Eng, Fre, Rus, Spa (Art. 29)

Reference : UN Doc. A/CONF.90/19 – JDI 1986 – ILM 18:681

1.5.2 Standardization

The economic benefits of standardization for a single country are well-known. It favours growth in many sectors by fostering lower production costs through economies of scale resulting from fewer product lines. Standards promote competition linked to quality by providing objective measurements and methods against which products can be judged. They also serve as tools for quality management. The impact of such benefits is multiplied many times when standard-setting occurs on a world-wide basis.

At the international level, however, standardization is a double-edged sword. At its best, international consensus on standards for products and services both represents a guarantee to producers that products conforming to standards will be marketable throughout the world, and provides a greater assurance to consumers that what they buy meets objective levels of quality and functionality. Conformity to international standards facilitates access to foreign markets and stimulates international trade.

At the same time, standards can also act as barriers to trade or in other ways serve as weapons of international competition. By influencing the content of a standard, for example, a country or interest group can obtain a significant advantage by directing an industry's technological development in a way most favourable to that country or group's competitive strengths.

International standards work is of great importance to developing countries as well as to developed ones. In the absence of international standards, countries are thrown back on their own resources. Either they must organize and finance their own national standards bodies, or align themselves with the standards of a more powerful trading partner. If standards which are effective, up-to-date and accessible are available internationally, countries avoid having to duplicate work, and may even gain a greater degree of commercial independence through access to a wider range of foreign markets.

The increasingly rapid pace of technological progress is placing heavy demands on the international standards system. Standards making is a voluntary activity which is based on a search for consensus, a process that is necessarily time-consuming. While standards organizations struggle to adapt traditionally slow working methods and structures to this increasing speed of change, their activities are sometimes outpaced by *de facto* standardization implemented by corporations for whom standards are a key element in corporate strategy.

Joel Saltsman

152 A – BUREAU INTERNATIONAL DES POIDS ET MESURES [INTERNATIONAL BUREAU OF WEIGHTS AND MEASURES] (BIPM)

Trade and scientific co-operation between nations has long depended on the existence of mutually acceptable structures within which reliable measurements of all kinds can be made and verified. In recent years, the dramatic growth in trade in high technology products, telecommunication and navigation networks, and international scientific projects, both pure and applied, implicitly demands an ever-increasing degree of uniformity and precision in measurement. This is the objective of the Bureau International des Poids et Mesures (BIPM), founded by the Convention du Mètre signed in Paris in 1875.

The BIPM's mandate is to establish and co-ordinate the basis for a single, coherent system of physical measurements throughout the world. It goes about its task in various ways, from direct dissemination of the unit (as in the case of mass) to co-ordination through international comparisons of national representations of units.

STRUCTURE

Under the terms of the Convention du Mètre, the BIPM operates under the direction of the *Comité International des Poids et Mesures* (CIPM). The body which governs the CIPM is the **Conférence Générale des Poids et Mesures** (CGPM). The CGPM elects the 18 members of the CIPM and brings together every four years the representatives of the Convention's 47 member nations. In addition to its other duties, the CIPM prepares proposals for the CGPM and oversees the work of eight *Comités consultatifs*.

Each *Comité consultatif* brings together international experts in a particular field to serve as advisers on scientific and technical matters. The *Comités* examine advances in physics that directly influence metrology (the field of knowledge concerned with measurements), initiate international comparisons, prepare recommendations for discussion by the CIPM, and advise the CIPM on the scientific work of the BIPM laboratories. Currently this work, carried out in collaboration with national laboratories, falls within the following main areas:

- mass and related quantities;
- frequency and time scales;
- length, including stabilized lasers;
- electricity;
- photometry and radiometry;
- ionizing radiations;
- temperature; and
- units.

CO-OPERATION

The CIPM and the BIPM co-operate closely with other international organizations concerned with metrology. In addition to its links with the International Organization for Legal Metrology (OIML) [see 152 D], ISO [see 152 C] and the IEC [see 152 B], the BIPM maintains a complex web of agreements and working relationships with a world-wide network of specialized measurement organizations. Examples include the International Union of Pure and Applied Chemistry and the International Radio Consultative Committee of the International Telecommunication Union [see 192 A].

PUBLICATIONS

The BIPM publishes a range of monographs, reports and conference proceedings, as well as the journal *Metrologia*. One of its most widely used publications is *Le Système International d'Unités* (SI) 6th edition, 1991.

Joel Saltsman

ADDRESS

Pavillon de Breteuil, 92312 Sèvres Cedex, France
T. (33 1) 45 07 70 70, Fx. (33 1) 45 34 20 21

152 B – INTERNATIONAL ELECTROTECHNICAL COMMISSION (IEC)

Founded in 1906, the IEC provides global standards for the electrical and electronic industries, whose products account for more than 25 per cent of international trade. IEC standards make it possible for electrical and electronic equipment, systems, sub-systems and components to work together no matter where they are designed, manufactured, assembled or used. More than 100 countries base their national standards on those of the IEC, which are also frequently used unchanged in international trade.

The members of the IEC are the 44 national committees, one for each country. Together these countries represent over 80 per cent of the world's population and produce more than 95 per cent of the world's electrical energy. Each national committee must be as representative as possible of all electrical interests in its country: manufacturers, users, governmental authorities, teaching and professional bodies. Its members are drawn from organizations in these fields, and its work is usually recognized and supported by its government.

The scope of the IEC's activities is vast and is growing increasingly complex with the rapid development of electronics technologies. Each year the IEC publishes about 9,000 pages of standards on subjects ranging from test methods and appliance switches to reactor instrumentation, integrated circuits, fibre optics and superconductivity. Since 1930, the IEC has developed the system of units of measurement for electrical quantities which forms the basis of the International System in use today throughout the world.

STRUCTURE

The IEC is governed by a **Council** consisting of the IEC President, national committee presidents, and several non-voting members. The Council is assisted by a **Committee of Action** composed of the IEC President and 12 members designated by national committees and elected by the Council for six-year terms. This Committee is responsible for ensuring the smooth functioning of the IEC.

The technical work of developing international standards in each specific area of electrotechnology is carried out by over 80 technical committees, 120 subcommittees, and 700 working groups of the IEC, all supervised by the national committees. The IEC employs procedures similar to those of ISO for adopting its standards.

Engineers working in private industry frequently contribute by writing standards for the IEC on a voluntary basis. They are often encouraged by their companies to do so as private industry has an obvious interest in keeping abreast of the activities of the international standardization world. Some of these engineers may also write standards for ISO [see 152 C], thereby taking part in the activities of both organizations.

CO-OPERATION

The IEC co-operates closely with ISO. They often share information for purposes of efficiency. One of their most important joint efforts has been the establishment of the Joint Technical Committee No. 1 which deals with information technology.

In addition, the IEC works in close connection with other organizations concerned with standards, notably the BIPM [see 152 A], OIML [see 152 D], ITU [see 192 A], the ILO [see 141 A] and WHO [see 132 A]. It also conducts joint activities with the IAEA [see 421 A], the GATT [see 111 A], the CCITT [see 192 A], UNESCO [see 171 A], UPU [see 191 A], WIPO [see 160 A] and the ECE [see 181 A]. Non-governmental organizations with which the IEC works include the International Union of Producers and Distributors of Electrical Energy (UNIPEDE) and the International Conference on Large High Tension Electric Systems (CIGRE).

To date, IEC has published nearly 3,000 items, including 2,000 international electrotechnical standards. Other publications include its *Bulletin* (every two months), an annual *Yearbook* and a multilingual dictionary (12,000 terms).

J.S.

ADDRESS

Central Bureau, 3 rue de Varembé, 1211 Geneva 20, Switzerland
T. (41 22) 734 01 50, Fx. (41 22) 733 3843

152 C – INTERNATIONAL ORGANIZATION FOR STANDARDIZATION (ISO)

ISO is a world-wide federation of national standards bodies. Founded in 1947, the object of ISO is to promote the development of standardization and related activities throughout the world with a view to facilitating international exchange of goods and services, and to developing co-operation in the spheres of intellectual, scientific, technological and economic activity. The results of ISO's technical work are published as International Standards.

The aim of international standardization is to facilitate trade, exchange and technology transfer through enhanced:

- product quality and reliability at reasonable prices;
- user safety, environmental protection, and reduction of waste;
- compatibility and interoperability of goods and services;
- simplification for improved usability;
- reduction in the number of models, extension of production series, and thus reduction in costs; and,
- distribution efficiency and ease of maintenance.

Necessarily associated with standardization, the verification of conformity to standards, such as in suppliers' declarations and third-party certifications, enhances user confidence in qualified products and services.

By the end of 1992, ISO had published 8,651 International Standards, covering everything from colour fastness of textiles to the interfacing of computer systems. The scope of ISO's work covers the entire field of standardization with the exception of standards for the electrical and electronic industries. These are the responsibility of the International Electrotechnical Commission (IEC) [see 152 B]. Together, ISO and the IEC form a specialized system for world-wide standardization.

MEMBERS

ISO's members, totalling 92 in January 1993, fall into two categories: member bodies and correspondent members. Each of the 71 member bodies is the national body "most respresentative of standardization in its country". Only one such body for each country may be a member. Most of the 21 correspondent members are organizations in developing countries which do not yet have their own national standards bodies. Correspondent members do not take an active part in the technical work, but are entitled to be kept informed about the work of interest to them.

ISO has also recently established a third category, subscriber membership, for countries with very small economies. Subscriber members will pay reduced membership fees that nevertheless allow them to maintain contact with international standardization.

STRUCTURE

The administrative structure of ISO consists of the **General Assembly** (meeting once every three years), a **Council** consisting of a President, a Vice-President and 18 elected member bodies, and a **Central Secretariat** headed by the Secretary-General. Beyond this small central core, ISO operates in a decentralized way with most of its work being carried out through **technical committees**.

At January 1993, there were 179 technical committees, each dealing with a separate subject. These, together with their subcommittees (624 in total) and working groups (1,885), operate in 34 countries with the support of technical secretariats. Detailed rules of procedure for technical committee work are set out in the ISO/IEC Directives.

The decision to establish a technical committee is taken by the ISO Council, and its scope is approved by the ISO Technical Board on behalf of the Council.

The Central Secretariat in Geneva co-ordinates ISO operations, administers voting and approval procedures, and publishes the *International Standards.*

In addition to technical committees, the Council has established a series of **advisory committees**. One of the most important of these is the ISO Committee on Consumer Policy, whose mandate is to promote consumer protection by expanding consumer participation in national and international standardization work.

ADOPTION OF STANDARDS

The development of an International Standard is a voluntary process which requires that a consensus be reached among the various interests participating in committees' deliberations: producers, users (including consumers), governments, and the scientific community. This procedure is designed to encourage the adoption of the International Standard by as many countries as possible. The process begins with the preparation of a new work item (NWI) which is sent for study to the competent technical committee. Once the committee members have agreed on the terms of a committee draft (CD), the CD is sent to the Central Secretariat which registers it as a Draft International Standard (DIS). If the DIS is approved by 75 per cent of ISO member bodies entitled to vote, it is published as an International Standard.

Resulting as they do from a voluntary standard-writing process, ISO International Standards have no binding force on member bodies.

CO-OPERATION

One of the best examples of co-operation is the ISO/IEC Joint Technical Committee on information technology – an overlapping field – (known as JTC-1). It has some 25 sub-committees and more than 60 active working groups, making the JTC-1 one of the main forums for voluntary, industry-wide standardization in the IT field. In the field of computer communications, JTC-1 develops International Standards (known collectively as the standards for Open Systems Interconnection (OSI)) in close co-operation with the International Telegraph and Telephone Consultative Committee (CCITT) of the International Telecommunication Union (ITU) [see 192 A].

ISO technical committees and sub-committees liaise with some 450 other international organizations. These organizations may be granted liaison status which comprises two categories: "A" (effective contribution to the work) and "B" (wish to be kept informed only). Liaison status confers the right to submit papers, attend meetings, and participate in discussions.

ISO co-operates, and has consultative status, with most of the specialized agencies of the United Nations, including the UN Economic and Social Council (ECOSOC) [see 001 A]. Organizations it liaises with include the GATT [see 111 A], CCC [see 112 A], IEC [see 152 B], ITU [see 192 A], OIML [see 152 D], IATA [see 184 B] and IBWM.

PUBLICATIONS

ISO International Standards, ISO Standards Handbook, Press Service (weekly), *ISO 9000 News* (every two months), *ISO Catalogue* (annual), *Memento* (annual), and the *ISO Bulletin* (weekly).

J.S.

152 D – ORGANISATION INTERNATIONALE DE METROLOGIE LEGALE [INTERNATIONAL ORGANIZATION OF LEGAL METROLOGY] (OIML)

Created by a convention signed in Paris in 1955, the International Organization of Legal Metrology (OIML) works to harmonize and co-ordinate internationally the administrative and technical regulations on measurements and measuring instruments authorized in various countries. Its mandate covers the portion of metrology (i.e. the field of knowledge concerned with measurements) known as "legal metrology". Legal metrology is concerned with all applied metrology subjected to regulation by law or governmental decree. In most countries, legal metrology regulates measurements with a view to protecting the health and financial dealings of individuals, the environment, and public safety. By controlling aspects of the quality of products and services, legal metrology also plays a role in developing a country's economic competitiveness.

In addition to its main objective, the OIML actively promotes the development of legal metrology within its 51 member states and 34 corresponding members, paying special attention to developing countries.

STRUCTURE

The *Bureau International de Métrologie Légale* (BIML) in Paris co-ordinates the administrative work of the OIML and of its 170 technical secretariats located in and financed by various host countries. As the general secretariat of the OIML, the BIML also acts as a documentation centre for its members and edits the OIML's trimestrial periodical, the *Bulletin de l'Organisation Internationale de Métrologie Légale.*

The work plans of the technical secretariats are authorized by a steering committee named the *Comité International de Métrologie Légale*, composed of official representatives from member states. The main lines of OIML policy, including financial policy, are in the hands of the **Conférence Internationale de Métrologie Légale**, which meets every four years.

CO-OPERATION

The OIML co-operates closely with the BIPM [see 152 A], ISO [see 152 C], IEC [see 152 B] and other international and regional (European) institutions, and has formal agreements with various United Nations agencies such as UNESCO [see 171 A] and UNIDO [see 151 A].

PUBLICATIONS

In addition to its periodical, the OIML issues model regulations (International Recommendations made by the Conference) recognized by the GATT as international standards, and recommended for voluntary adoption by member states. It also publishes a *Bulletin of OIML* (quarterly), *Vocabulary of Legal Metrology*, and a collection of *International Documents.*

J.S.

ADDRESS

11, rue Turgot, 75009 Paris, France
T. (33 1) 48 78 12 82, Fx. (33 1) 42 82 17 27

152.01 – METRIC CONVENTION – BIPM

Concluded : 20.05.1875, Paris
In force : 01.01.1876
Parties : 47

This Convention is the basic agreement of the BIPM. For a description of the organization, see 152 A.

Access : ALS (Art. 11)
Reserves : USP
Duration : USP
Deposit. : FR (Art. 11)
Language : Fre

Modific. : Sèvres 06.10.21 (01.07.28)

Reference : UKTS 1923/24 – 3/4 Paeslee – JORF 24 Dec 1875, 6 Sep 28

152.02 – STATUTES OF THE INTERNATIONAL ELECTROTECHNICAL COMMISSION – IEC

Adopted : 1908, London

These Statutes form the basic agreement of the IEC. For a description of the organization, see 152 B.

Access : ENT
Language : Eng, Fre, Rus (Art. 16)

Modific. : (1949); (1963); (1974); (1986)

152.03 – CONSTITUTION OF THE INTERNATIONAL ORGANIZATION FOR STANDARDIZATION – ISO

Adopted : 14.10.1946, London
In force : 23.02.1947

This Constitution is the basic agreement of the ISO. For a description of the organization, see 152 C.

Access : ENT
Language : Eng, Fre, Rus (Art. 19)

152.04 – AGREEMENT ESTABLISHING AN INTERNATIONAL ORGANIZATION OF LEGAL METROLOGY – OIML

Concluded : 12.10.1955, Paris
In force : 28.05.1958
Parties : 51

This Agreement is the basic act of the OIML. For a description of the organization, see 152 D.

Access : ALS (Art. XXXII)
Reserves : USP
Duration : REN 12 (Art. XXXVI)
Deposit. : FR (Art. XL)
Language : Fre (Art. XL)

Modific. : Amendments 12.11.63 (18.01.68)

Reference : 560 UNTS – Can TS 1982/33 – RTAF 1958/25, 1970/100 – UKTS 1962/60, 1968/36 – UST 23/4 – 3/4 Paeslee – JORF 20 Jul 58

1.6 Intellectual Property

Intellectual property comprises two main branches: industrial property, which is primarily concerned with inventions, trademarks and industrial designs [see section 1.6.1], and copyright, which deals most notably with literary, musical, artistic, photographic and audiovisual works [see section 1.6.2].

The World Intellectual Property Organization (WIPO) is the most significant intergovernmental organization in this field, having world-wide membership. It promotes the conclusion of new international treaties and the modernization of national legislation. The United Nations Educational, Scientific and Cultural Organization (UNESCO) [see 171 A] and the International Labour Organisation (ILO) [see 141 A] have also been involved in the adoption of conventions. If the Uruguay Round is concluded, the General Agreement on Tariffs and Trade (GATT) too will attain competence in the field [see 111.19].

Bernard Colas

SELECTED BIBLIOGRAPHY

WIPO, *Background Reading Material on Intellectual Property*, Geneva, 1988.

160 A – WORLD INTELLECTUAL PROPERTY ORGANIZATION (WIPO)

WIPO was established by the Stockholm Convention of 14 July 1967. The origins of WIPO can be found in the United International Bureaux for the Protection of Intellectual Property, established after the 1893 meeting between the secretariats responsible for administering the Paris and Berne Conventions on industrial property and the protection of literary and artistic works, respectively.

Since 17 December 1974, WIPO has been a specialized agency of the UN. Its objective is to promote the protection of intellectual property throughout the world through co-operation among states, and to ensure administrative co-operation among the intellectual property unions, which are comprised of groups of states bound by a multilateral treaty.

One of the most important achievements of WIPO has been in norm-setting and international registration. At present, there are 29 multilateral treaties for which WIPO is responsible. It is currently working on a proposed Patent Law Treaty, the preparations of a possible Protocol to the Berne Convention for the Protection of Literary and Artistic Works [see 162.01], a proposed treaty for the settlement of intellectual property disputes between states, a proposed treaty on the simplification of trademark procedures and a proposed model law on the protection of performing artists and producers of sound recordings.

WIPO is also active with regard to patent information and documentation, and provides assistance to developing countries and to countries in transition from a centrally planned to a market economy system.

STRUCTURE

WIPO is composed of four organs: a General Assembly, a Conference, a Co-ordination

Committee, and an International Bureau.

The **General Assembly** is WIPO's supreme organ and includes all states which are parties to the 1967 WIPO Convention and which are members of the Paris and/or the Berne Unions. Each state has one vote. It appoints a Director-General nominated by the Co-ordination Committee, reviews and approves the reports and activities of the Co-ordination Committee and gives it instructions, and adopts the biennial budget of expenses common to the unions.

The **Conference** is composed of member states of WIPO whether or not they are members of any of the unions. It meets biennially in ordinary session, during the same period and at the same place as the General Assembly. It discusses matters in the field of intellectual property, adopts the budget of the Conference and within the limits of the budget establishes legal-technical assistance for the developing countries, and adopts amendments to the 1967 WIPO Convention.

The **Co-ordination Committee** meets annually and is composed of states party to the WIPO Convention who are members of the Executive Committee of the Paris Union, the Berne Union, or both. It gives advice to the organs of WIPO and the unions and prepares the draft agenda, the draft programme and the budget for the General Assembly and the Conference.

The **International Bureau** is the secretariat of WIPO and of some 20 treaties or unions, including the Paris and Berne Unions. It is directed by a Director-General who is assisted by three Deputy Directors-General, and follows the instructions of the General Assembly.

The role played by the International Bureau is of particular importance. It organizes meetings, acts as the depositary of the treaties administered by WIPO, directs the patent registration service, administers the service for the International Deposit of Industrial Designs (since 1928), is responsible for the service for the International Registration of Appellations of Origin (since 1966) and administers the Patent Co-operation Treaty, the Film Register Treaty, and so on.

Nine of the Unions administered by WIPO have their own intergovernmental bodies which adopt their own programmes of action and budgets.

FUNDING

The funds of WIPO come from contributions of the member states and taxes and sums received for services rendered. The annual budget is estimated at some 30 million Swiss francs.

CO-OPERATION

WIPO co-operates with most UN bodies as well as with the GATT [see 111 A], UNIDROIT [see 300 B], regional patent and trademark bodies, and regional economic integration organizations.

PUBLICATIONS

WIPO publishes numerous books, guides, laws, treaties and magazines, including: *Industrial Property* (monthly), *Copyright* (monthly), *Les Marques Internationales* (French, monthly), *International Designs Bulletin* (monthly), *Les Appelations d'Origine* (French, irregular), and *PCT Gazette* (fortnightly).

Bernard Colas

ADDRESS

34 chemin des Colombettes, PO.Box: 18, CH-1211 Geneva 20, Switzerland
T. (41 22) 730 9111, Fx. (41 22) 733 5428

SELECTED BIBLIOGRAPHY

Bogsch, Arpad, *Brief History of the First 25 Years of the World Intellectual Property Organization*, Geneva: WIPO, 1992.
International Bureau of Intellectual Property, *The First 25 Years of the WIPO from 1967 to 1992*, Geneva: WIPO, 1992.

160.01 – CONVENTION ESTABLISHING THE WORLD INTELLECTUAL PROPERTY ORGANIZATION – WIPO

Concluded : 14.07.1967, Stockholm
In Force : 26.04.1970
Parties : 134

The Convention sets the objectives and the institutional framework of WIPO [see 160 A], while respecting the autonomy of the Paris Union which was established by the 1883 Convention for the Protection of Industrial Property, and the 1886 Berne Convention for the Protection of Literary and Artistic Works.

Access : ALS (Art. 5, 14)
Reserves : PRO (Art. 16)
Duration : USP
Deposit. : SE, WIPO (Art. 20)
Language : Eng, Fre, Rus, Spa, (Ger, Ita, Por, etc)

Modific. : 02.10.79 (01.06.84)

Reference : 828 UNTS – UST 21/2 – ILM 6:782 – UKTS 197 – 3/4 Paeslee – Ind. Prop. juil 84, déc 84 – RTAF 1974/67 – JORF 27 Nov 74

1.6.1 Industrial Property

The possession of technology has become a crucial factor in a country's ability to develop and prosper. It gives its possessor a substantial competitive edge on the world market. Considerable investment, however, is required to develop technology and, since the beginning of the nineteenth century, economic actors have increasingly relied on patents, trademarks and industrial design property rights to secure that investment.

The conventions described in this section protect industrial property rights internationally. The basic multilateral convention in the field is the Paris Convention of 1883 [see 161.01] which has been supplemented and developed by later agreements. The global regime for the protection of industrial property is completed by regional agreements such as the European Patent Convention.

Frédéric Benech

SELECTED BIBLIOGRAPHY

Adams, John, *Merchandising Intellectual Property*, London: Butterworths, 1987.

Baxter, J.W. and John P. Sinnott, *World Patent Law and Practice*, New York: Matthew Bender, 1985.

Beier, Friedrich-Karl, *German Industrial Property, Copyright and Anti-trust Laws*, IIC Studies 6, Weinheim et al.: Verlagsgesellschaft, 1989.

Callmann, Rudolf and Louis Altman, *Callmann on Unfair Competition, Trademarks and Monopolies*, 6 Vols, 4th ed., Deerfield: Callaghan and Co., 1981-.

Chisum, Donald S. and Michael A. Jacobs, *World Intellectual Property Guidebook: United States*, New York: Matthew Bender, 1992.

Cornish, William R., *Intellectual Property: Patents, Copyright, Trade Marks and Allied Rights*, London: Sweet & Maxwell, 1991.

Chromecek, Milan and Stuart C. McCormack, *World Intellectual Property Guidebook: Canada*, New York: Matthew Bender, 1991.

Horwitz, E., *World Trademark Law and Practice*, New York, 1982.

Hughes, Roger T. and John J. Woodley, *Hughes and Woodley on Patents*, Ontario: Butterworths, 1984-.

Hughes, Roger T., *Hughes on Trade Marks*, Ontario: Butterworths, 1984-.

Ruester, Bernd (ed.), *World Intellectual Property Guidebook: Federal Republic of Germany, Austria, Switzerland*, New York: Matthew Bender, 1991.

Sinnott, John P., *World Patent Law and Practice: Patent Statutes Regulations and Treaties*, 13 Vols, New York: Matthew Bender, 1974-.

Straus, Joseph and Rainer Moufang, Antony Rich (transl.), *Deposit and release of Biological Material for the Purposes of Patent Procedure: Industrial and Tangible Property Issues*, Baden-Baden: Nomos, 1990.

WIPO, *Industrial Property Laws and Treaties*, Geneva, 1976-.

– – –, *Symposium on Industrial Property and Economic and Technological Development*, Geneva, 1988.

161.01 – CONVENTION FOR THE PROTECTION OF INDUSTRIAL PROPERTY – WIPO

Concluded : 20.03.1883, Paris
In Force : 06.07.1884
Parties : 107

The 1883 Paris Convention, generally known as the "Union Convention", established certain obligatory principles of international law in regard to the protection of industrial property. "The protection of industrial property has as its object patents, utility models, industrial designs, trademarks, service marks, trade names, indications of source or appellations of origin, and the repression of unfair competition" (Art. 1-2).

The principles established by the Convention are particularly important in relation to patents, marks, and industrial designs and models.

A "patent" is defined as a document, issued by a government office, which describes the invention and creates a legal situation in which the patented invention can normally only be worked (i.e. made, used, sold, imported) with the authorization of the patentee. This protection of the invention is limited in time (generally 15 to 20 years). In order to be protected by a patent, an invention must have general novelty, an inventive step, and industrial application.

Trademarks or service marks are generally defined as a distinctive sign which serves to differentiate an enterprise's goods and/or services from those of its competitors. An industrial design or model is a title to an industrial property which aims to protect the shape and the external or particular ornamental aspect of a useful article.

DETAILS OF THE CONVENTION

The main rules instituted by the Convention concern equality of protection, the right of priority and independence of title.

Under the provisions on national treatment, the Convention provides that, as regards the protection of industrial property, each contracting state must grant the same protection to nationals of other contracting states as it grants to its own nationals. Nationals of countries outside the Union, who are domiciled or have a real and effective industrial or commercial establishment in one of the countries of the Union, are treated as nationals of the countries of the Union.

A right of priority is established. Thus, on the basis of a regular first application filed in one of the contracting states, the applicant may, within a certain period of time (12 months for patents and utility models; six months for industrial designs and trademarks) apply for protection in any other contracting state. These later applications will then be regarded as if they had been filed on the same day as the first application.

The Convention provides for the independence of titles whereby the granting of a title (patents, trademarks, models) in one contracting state does not oblige the other contracting states to grant a title. Moreover, a title cannot be refused, annulled or terminated in any contracting state on the grounds that it has been refused or annulled or has terminated in any other contracting state.

Since 1967, the Union Convention has been administered by WIPO (Stockholm Act, 1967).

SUBSEQUENT DEVELOPMENTS

As the Convention was drafted to the advantage of the technology-exporting countries, it has gradually became a source of contention as more developing countries have signed it. Indeed, since 1958 more than 50 countries, the majority of which are importers of technology, have signed the Convention. This has effectively reversed the balance of voting power within the Union from technology exporters to technology importers.

The technology importers sought to revise the Convention, in particular the crucial Article 5-a which, if amended, would have allowed developing countries to work patents free of charge in the areas of security and health (areas of public interest), or in areas relating to the vital interests of the country. These efforts to amend the Convention, the latest of which took place at the beginning of the 1980s, were unsuccessful as they were rejected by certain industrialized countries.

Given the limited collective power of the developing countries within the GATT, the industrialized countries are looking increasingly towards that forum as a framework in which to deal with the issues of industrial property [see 111.19].

Frédéric Benech

Access : ALS (Art. 21)
Reserves : PAU (Art. 19, 20, 21)
Duration : USP (Art. 26)
Deposit. : WIPO (Art. 29)
Language : Eng, Fre, Ita, Spa, (Ger, Por, Rus) (Art. 29)

Modific. : Brussels 14.12.1900 (14.09.02); Washington 02.06.11 (01.05.13); The Hague 06.11.25 (01.06.28); London 02.06.34 (30.07.38); Lisbon 31.10.58 (04.01.62); Stockholm 14.07.67 (26.04.70 art.13-30 and 19.05.70 art.1-12); modified 02.10.79 (03.06.84)

Reference : 828 UNTS – Can TS 1928/3, 1951/10 – UKTS 1970/61 – UST 21/2, 24/2 – 3/4 Paeslee – RTAF 1962/3, 1975/53 – JORF 17 Aug 75 – JDI 1962 – RCDIP 1962/1

161.02 – MADRID AGREEMENT FOR THE PREVENTION OF FALSE OR DECEPTIVE INDICATIONS OF ORIGIN ON GOODS, AS REVISED – WIPO

Concluded : 14.04.1891, Madrid
In Force : 15.07.1892
Parties : 31

The Madrid Agreement establishes a system of seizure of "all goods bearing a false or deceptive indication by which one of the countries to which this Agreement applies, or a place situated therein, is directly or indirectly indicated as being the country or place of origin" (Art. 1-1).

Seizure shall also take place "in the country where the false or deceptive indication of source has been applied, or into which the goods bearing the false or deceptive indication have been imported" (Art. 1-2). According to Article 2, "seizure shall take place at the instance of the customs authorities, who shall immediately inform the interested party ... if he so desires, [to] take appropriate steps in connection with the seizure effected as a conservatory measure". In this sense, then, the scope of the Agreement is limited.

The countries to which the Agreement applies undertake to prohibit the use of all indications capable of deceiving the public as to the source of goods (Art. 3 bis).

The subsequent Stockholm Act of 1967 transfers the administration of the Agreement to WIPO.

The Agreement is open to member states of the Paris Union [see 161.01].

F.B.

Access : CON (Art. 5)
Reserves : USP
Duration : USP
Deposit. : SE, WIPO
Language : Fre (Art. 6)

Modific. : Revised Washington 02.06.11 (01.05.13); The Hague 06.11.25 (01.06.28); London 02.06.34 (01.07.38); Lisbon 31.10.58 (01.06.63); Supplemented by the Additional Act Stockholm 14.07.67 (12.08.75)

Reference : 828 UNTS – UKTS 1892/13 – RTAF 1968/32 – JDI 1968 – JORF 3 Aug 1892, 9 Oct 30, 2 Aug 39, 6 Apr 68

161.03 – MADRID AGREEMENT CONCERNING THE INTERNATIONAL REGISTRATION OF MARKS – WIPO

Concluded : 14.04.1891, Madrid
In Force : 15.07.1892
Parties : 33

This Agreement is a procedural instrument to simplify the international registration of marks. As such, it does not fundamentally affect the foundation of the law.

The internationally registered mark is transmitted to the national trademark office of each designated country. There are, therefore, as many national registrations as there are member states designated in the registration application.

Every application for international registration must be preceded by an initial registration of the mark in its country of origin. The international registration of a mark must be filed with the World Intellectual Property Organization (WIPO) [see 160 A], and presented by the administration of the country of origin. At that point, the protection of the mark in each of the contracting countries is the same as if the mark had been filed there directly (Art. 4); the international mark is then dealt with in line with the national legislation of the contracting country.

Thus, the impact of the Agreement is that the registration of an international mark with WIPO in Geneva means a mark does not have to be registered separately in each country in order to have international protection.

The international registration of a mark benefits from unionist priority. The registration of a mark is effective for 20 years and can be renewed indefinitely. It is also possible to voluntarily limit the number of countries in which a mark is registered.

The Agreement is open to all countries which are members of the Paris Convention for the Protection of Industrial Property [see 161.01].

SUBSEQUENT MODIFICATIONS

The most important modifications of the Agreement are those of 1957 and 1989. The Nice Act of 1957 introduced a system of international registration whereby a mark becomes independent of its national registration after a period of five years. Previously, international registration was dependent on the national registration for the entire period of registration. In other words, if the national registration was withdrawn or annulled, the international registration also ceased to be effective. This benefited third parties wishing to annul the registration of a mark as they merely had to proceed with their actions at the national level of registration.

The 1957 Nice Act also allowed for the registration of goods and services by class according to the International Classification of Goods and Services [see 165.05].

A number of countries, however, including the Anglo-Saxon countries, did not accept the Madrid Agreement because they considered it to be incompatible with their legal traditions. After the Stockholm Conference in 1967, WIPO addressed this situation by adding a supplementary treaty which became the Vienna Convention [see 161.11]. However, that Convention is now considered obsolete following conclusion of the 1989 Madrid Protocol, which intends to make it possible for the UK and three other countries of the EC, not members of the Madrid Union, as well as the US, to become parties to the Madrid system of international trademark registration.

The 1989 Protocol to the Madrid Agreement introduces the following main changes:

- the applicant may base his application for international registration not only on the registration of his mark in the national office of the country of origin, but also on an application for national registration filed with that office;
- each contracting party in which the applicant seeks protection may, within 18 months (instead of one year), and an even longer period in the case of opposition, declare that protection cannot be granted to the mark in its territory;
- the office of each contracting party may receive higher fees than under the Madrid Agreement; and
- an international registration which is cancelled may be transformed into national applications benefiting from its filing date and, where applicable, priority date (a possibility which does not exist under the Madrid Agreement).

Furthermore, the Protocol establishes links with the future trademark system of the European Communities. Once that system is in force and the European Communities are party to the Protocol, it will be possible for an application for international registration under the Protocol to be based on a Community application or registration; and it will be possible to obtain the effects of a Community registration through an international registration effected under the Protocol.

Regulations of 21 June 1974 specify the modalities for the Madrid Agreement.

F.B.

Access : CON (Art. 14)
Reserves : USP
Duration : ULT (Art. 15)
Deposit. : SE, WIPO (Art. 17)
Language : Fre, (etc) (Art. 17)

Modific. : Revised Brussels 14.12.1900 (14.09.02); Washington 02.06.11 (01.05.13); The Hague 06.11.25 (01.06.28); London 02.06.34 (13.06.39); Nice 15.06.57 (15.12.66); Stockholm 14.07.67 (12.08.75); amended 02.10.79 (23.10.83); Protocol Madrid 27.06.89 (-); and Regulations (21.06.74); amended (29.09.75); (24.11.81); (15.12.83)

Reference : 583, 828 UNTS – Ind. Prop. 1988/12 – RTAF 1960/27, 1975/53 – JORF 3 Aug 1892, 14 May 1960, 17 Aug 75

161.04 – THE HAGUE AGREEMENT CONCERNING THE INTERNATIONAL DEPOSIT OF INDUSTRIAL DESIGNS – WIPO

Concluded : 06.11.1925, The Hague
In Force : 13.06.1939
Parties : 21

The Hague Agreement set up an international system for the registration of industrial designs and models to ensure their protection in the signatory states by means of a single registration with WIPO.

In contrast with the Madrid Agreement of 1891 on the registration of marks [see 161.03], it is not necessary under the present Agreement for an industrial design or model to be registered first in the country of origin.

The international registration allows the creator of the design or model to forgo the registration of his creation in each of the individual states which are party to the Agreement. The international registration is merely declaratory; as a registration, it produces in each of the contracting countries the same effects as if the designs or models had been registered directly in those countries. In other words, the Hague Agreement prescribes only a certain number of common principles which allow for the significant simplification of administrative procedures as relates to registration, the duration of protection, and so on.

The Agreement respects the fundamental principle of the Paris Convention – namely, the protection of national treatment. The Agreement does not act as a limitation on national laws; each of the contracting countries may determine or qualify, according to its national legislation, what it considers a design or model.

Together the countries signing the Hague Agreement make up the "Hague Union". This Union is made up of three groups of states: those states which have signed both the 1934 Act and the 1960 Act, those which have signed the 1934 Act only, and those which have signed the 1960 Act only. The goal of the 1960 Act was, principally, to allow for a larger membership by relaxing certain requirements and allowing the contracting parties greater freedom. However, it was only partially successful.

F.B.

Access : CON
Reserves : USP
Duration : USP
Deposit. : WIPO
Language : Eng, Fre, (etc)

Modific. : Revised London 02.06.34 (25.06.39); The Hague 28.11.60 (01.08.84); Additional Act Monaco 18.11.61 (01.12.62); Stockholm 14.07.67 (27.09.75); Protocol Geneva 29.08.75 (01.04.79); Amended (02.10.79)

Reference : 74 LNTS – Ind.Prop. 1978/7-8, 1981/6 – JORF 2 Aug 39, 8 Oct 75 – RTAF 1962/46, 1975/67, 1980/55

161.05 – NICE AGREEMENT CONCERNING THE INTERNATIONAL CLASSIFICATION OF GOODS AND SERVICES FOR THE PURPOSES OF REGISTRATION OF MARKS – WIPO

Concluded : 15.06.1957, Nice
In Force : 08.04.1961
Parties : 36

The objective of the Nice Agreement is to establish "a common classification of goods and services for the purposes of the registration of marks" [see Madrid Agreement of 1891: 161.03]. The classification applies to the international registration of marks and national registration in the territories of the contracting states, which reserve the right to use the classification either as a principal or as a subsidiary system.

Article 2 stipulates that the international classification shall not bind the contracting countries in respect of either the evaluation of the extent of the protection afforded to any given mark or the recognition of service marks. The value of the classification therefore is administrative rather than legal. The classification includes a list of 42 classes (34 for goods and eight for services).

The Agreement is open to states which are members of the Paris Union.

F. B.

Access : CON (Art. 9)
Reserves : USP
Duration : FXD (Art. 10)
Deposit. : WIPO
Language : Eng, Fre, Rus, Spa, (Ara, Ita, Por, Ger) (Art. 14)

Modific. : Stockholm 14.07.67 (18.03.70); Geneva 13.05.77 (06.02.79); Amended 02.10.79 (06.09.82)

Reference : 550, 828 UNTS – Ind.Prop. 1977/6, 1979/1,10 – UKTS 1963/23, 1970/71 – UST 23/2 – JORF 14 May 60, 17 Aug 75, 1 Aug 80 – RTAF 1960/27, 1975/53, 1980/41

161.06 – LISBON AGREEMENT FOR THE PROTECTION OF APPELLATIONS OF ORIGIN AND THEIR INTERNATIONAL REGISTRATION, AS REVISED – WIPO

Concluded : 31.10.1958, Lisbon
In Force : 25.09.1966
Parties : 17

The Agreement was conceived of within the framework of the Paris Convention for the Protection of Industrial Property [see 161.01]. Its objective is to protect appellations of origin and their international recording.

Appellation of origin means "the geographical name of a country, region, or locality, which serves to designate a product originating therein, the quality and characteristics of which are due exclusively or essentially to the geographical environment, including natural and human factors" (Art. 2) ("Champagne" is an example).

The parties to the Agreement undertake to ensure protection of appellations of origin against any usurpation or imitation (Art. 3), even if the true origin of the product is indicated or if the appellation is used in translated form or accompanied by terms such as "kind", "type", "make", "imitation", or the like. Appellations of origin can be registered with WIPO, but the practical effects of this registration are limited due to the small number of signatory states.

The Agreement is open to members of the Paris Union [see 161.01].

F.B.

Access : CON (Art. 14)
Reserves : USP
Duration : MIN (Art. 15)
Deposit. : SE, WIPO
Language : Fre, (etc) (Art. 17)

Modific. : Revised Stockholm 14.07.67 (31.10.73); Amended 02.10.79 (05.11.83)

Reference : Ind.Prop. 1980/7-8 – RTAF 1968/33, 1975/53 – JDI 1968/3 – JORF 6 Apr 68, 17 Aug 75

161.07 – INTERNATIONAL CONVENTION FOR THE PROTECTION OF NEW VARIETIES OF PLANTS – WIPO

Concluded : 02.12.1961, Paris
In Force : 10.08.1968
Parties : 23

This Convention seeks to protect new varieties of plants whose importance for the development of agriculture is established. It applies to all botanical genera and species (Art. 4), and the states that are party to the Convention constitute the International Union for the Protection of New Varieties of Plants, known as UPOV (the acronym for the French name).

To come within the protection of the Convention, the new variety must fulfil a certain number of conditions (Art. 6): the variety must be clearly distinguishable from any other variety whose existence is a matter of common knowledge; it must not have been previously offered for sale or marketed in the territory of the state where protection is sought and, since the 1978 amendment, in the territory of any other state; the variety must be sufficiently homogeneous, having regard to the particular features of its sexual reproduction or vegetative propogation; the variety must be stable in its essential characteristics; and the variety must be given a denomination destined to be its generic designation.

The breeder's prior authorization is required for the production (for purposes of commercial marketing), the offering for sale, and the marketing of the reproductive or vegetative propagating material as such of the variety. Vegetative propagating material is deemed to include whole plants.

SUBSEQUENT MODIFICATIONS

The UPOV Convention was amended in March 1991, notably to take into account the growing importance of patents in the field of biotechnology. When the Protocol comes into force, the Convention will no longer specifically exclude simultaneous protection of new varieties of plants by means of a patent and a special title of protection, as is provided in the present Convention. In addition, a special title of protection could then be dependent on another title. In other words, it could be necessary to have a licence for a previous title in order to use a depending variety.

F.B.

Access : CON (Art. 31)
Reserves : PRO (Art. 40)
Duration : ULT (Art. 41)
Deposit. : UPOV
Language : Fre, (etc) (Art. 42)

Modific. : Revised Geneva 10.11.72 (11.02.77); 00.03.91 (-)

Reference : 815 UNTS – Prop.Ind. 1979/2 – UKTS 1969/74, 1980/79, 1984/11 – RTAF 1972/7, 1977/21, 1983/21 – JDI 1983 – JORF 13 Jan 72, 5 Apr 77

161.08 – LOCARNO AGREEMENT ESTABLISHING AN INTERNATIONAL CLASSIFICATION FOR INDUSTRIAL DESIGNS – WIPO

Concluded : 08.10.1968, Locarno
In Force : 27.04.1971
Parties : 19

The Agreement establishes an international classification for industrial design which facilitates, for example, the research of prior art. The countries to which the Agreement applies constitute a Special Union. The offices of the Special Union, being the national industrial property office of each contracting state, must indicate in the official documents reflecting the deposit or registration of industrial designs the applicable symbol of the International Classification. It must do the same in any publication such office issues in respect of the deposit or registration.

A Committee of Experts established by the Agreement is responsible for amending the Agreement.

The classification consists of 32 classes and 223 subclasses. It also includes an alphabetical list of goods with explanatory notes as to their class and subclass. Some 6,250 such notes on various types of products are on the list.

The Agreement is open to states which are party to the Paris Convention [see 161.01].

F.B.

Access : CON (Art. 9-1)
Reserves : USP
Duration : FXD (Art. 10)
Deposit. : CH, WIPO (Art. 14)
Language : Eng, Fre, (etc) (Art. 14)

Modific. : 02.10.79 (23.11.81)

Reference : ILM 8:1 – Ind. Prop. Oct 83 – UST 23/2 – JORF 2 Oct 75 – RTAF 1975/63

161.09 – PATENT CO-OPERATION TREATY – WIPO

Concluded : 19.06.1970, Washington
In Force : 24.01.1978
Parties : 56

The Patent Co-operation Treaty chiefly concerns the filing of international applications for patents by nationals or residents of a contracting state to this convention.

The application should be filed with the national patent office of the applicant, or with the patent office where the applicant has his residence, or with another receiving office if the contracting state of the applicant (on a national or residence basis) has concluded an agreement with the organization whereby the receiving office can act as such. This receiving office can be a state office of a contracting state or an office such as the US Patent and Trademark Office or the European Patent Office.

This application has the same effect as a national patent application. It leads to an international search which is carried out by an International Searching Authority such as the European Patent Office (research department of The Hague) or the US Patent and Trademark Office. This results in a documentary search report on prior art for inventions which are the subject of the application. Once this is completed, the necessary procedures to obtain a national patent begin within each of the designated states, and they follow their normal course until the patent is granted.

There is also an optional preliminary examination phase in which an applicant may request a preliminary examination report to determine whether the claimed invention appears to be novel, to involve an inventive step, and to be industrially applicable. The report determines by simple yes or no whether the invention may be patented. Only those states which have adopted Chapter II of the present Treaty may request a preliminary examination report.

The Treaty is open to all the state parties of the Paris Convention [see 161.01] and has become increasingly successful in recent years.

F.B.

Access : CON (Art. 62)
Reserves : PAU (Art. 64)
Duration : USP
Deposit. : WIPO (Art. 68)
Language : Eng, Fre, (Ger, Jap, Por, Rus, Spa) (Art. 67)

Modific. : (29.03.78 Chap.II); Amended 02.10.79 (03.05.84); Modified 03.02.84 (01.01.85)

Reference : Ind.Prop. 1980/11, 1984/11,12, 1985/12 – UST 28/7 – ILM 9:991, 10:452 – RTAF 1978/26

161.10 – AGREEMENT CONCERNING THE INTERNATIONAL PATENT CLASSIFICATION – WIPO

Concluded : 24.03.1971, Strasbourg
In Force : 07.10.1975
Parties : 27

The International Patent Classification was established in order to set up a uniform system of classification of patents, inventors' certificates, utility models and utility cetificates.

The classification, in English and French (Art. 3), is solely of an administrative character (Art. 4), and is established and amended by a Committee of Experts (Art. 5).

The Agreement is open to states which are party to the Paris Convention [see 161.01].

F.B.

Access : CON (Art. 12)
Reserves : USP
Duration : FXD (Art. 14)
Deposit. : WIPO (Art. 16)
Language : Eng, Fre, (Ger, Jap, Por, Rus, Spa, etc) (Art. 16)

Modific. : Amended 02.10.79 (25.02.82)

Reference : UKTS 1975/113, 1983/82 – UST 26/2

161.11 – TRADEMARK REGISTRATION TREATY – WIPO

Concluded : 12.06.1973, Vienna
In Force : 07.08.1980
Parties : 5

A treaty which would reform the Madrid Agreement Concerning the International Registration of Marks (1891) [see 161.03] was initially proposed. However, as the Madrid Agreement was generally agreeable to its parties, WIPO decided on a new treaty – the present one – which would coexist alongside the Madrid Agreement. Subsequently, the Madrid Agreement was in fact modified (in 1989) and, in 1991, the five member countries of the present Treaty decided to suspend its application in anticipation of the Treaty's being replaced by the Protocol of 1989.

The Trademark Registration Treaty (TRT) institutes an international registration of trademarks within a larger, if more complicated, framework than that of the Madrid Agreement. It is an agreement which deals only with procedural matters.

DETAILS OF THE TREATY

The initial term of any international registration is ten years, and this may be renewed for further terms of ten years on payment of a fee. It is not necessary to register a trademark in one's own state. The TRT trademark, like that of the Madrid Agreement, becomes a series of national trademarks in the states where protection has been requested.

The Treaty is open to states which are parties to the Paris Convention [see 161.01].

F.B.

Access : CON (Art. 39)
Reserves : PAU (Art. 42)
Duration : USP
Deposit. : WIPO (Art. 45)
Language : Eng, Fre, (Ger, Ita, Jap, Por, Rus, Spa, etc) (Art. 44)

Modific. : Modified 1980 (03.06.84)

161.12 – AGREEMENT ESTABLISHING AN INTERNATIONAL CLASSIFICATION OF THE FIGURATIVE ELEMENTS OF MARKS – WIPO

Concluded : 12.06.1973, Vienna
In Force : 09.08.1985
Parties : 5

The Agreement establishes an international classification system of the figurative elements of marks. The competent offices in the contracting countries must include the appropriate international classification symbols in the official documents and publications relating to registrations and renewals of marks.

The Agreement establishes a Committee of Experts to periodically amend and add to the international classification.

The classification is comprised of 29 categories, 144 divisions and 1,563 sections in which the figurative elements of marks must be placed.

The Agreement is open to states which are parties to the Paris Convention [see 161.01].

F.B.

Access : CON
Reserves : PAU (Art. 4, 16)
Duration : FXD
Deposit. : WIPO
Language : Eng, Fre

161.13 – BUDAPEST TREATY ON THE INTERNATIONAL RECOGNITION OF THE DEPOSIT OF MICRO-ORGANISMS FOR THE PURPOSES OF PATENT PROCEDURE – WIPO

Concluded : 28.04.1977, Budapest
In Force : 19.08.1980
Parties : 24

In the Treaty, the contracting states which allow or require the deposit of micro-organisms for the purposes of patent procedure shall recognize, for such purposes, the deposit of a micro-organism with any international depositary authority, whether this authority is on their territory or not.

The international depositary authority is defined by the Treaty as a scientific institution capable of preserving micro-organisms. To acquire the status of an international depositary authority, a depositary institution must benefit from assurances furnished by that contracting state to the Director General of WIPO to the effect that the institution complies and will continue to comply with the requirements of the Treaty.

On 1 January 1992, there were 22 international depositary authorities established along guidelines found in Article 7 of the Treaty: seven in the UK, three in the Soviet Union (situation until 24.12.91), two each in Germany, the Republic of Korea and the USA, and one each in Australia, Bulgaria, France, Hungary, Japan and the Netherlands.

A depositor who had previously been obliged to apply for a patent in more than one contracting state, from now on need only transmit the micro-organism to a single international depositary authority, and make reference to this when he applies for a patent in any of the contracting states.

The Treaty is open to states which are parties to the Paris Convention [see 161.01]. It is supplemented by a series of regulations.

F.B.

Access : CON (Art. 15)
Reserves : USP
Duration : USP
Deposit. : WIPO (Art. 19)
Language : Ara, Eng, Fre, Ger, Ita, Jap, Por, etc (Art. 18)

Modific. : Modified 1980 (24.05.84); Regulations 1981 (31.01.81)

Reference : Ind.Prop. 1977/5, 1981/4 – ILM 17:285 – UST 32/2 – RTAF 1980/56

161.14 – GENEVA TREATY ON THE INTERNATIONAL RECORDING OF SCIENTIFIC DISCOVERIES – WIPO

Concluded : 03.03.1978, Geneva
Parties : 2

A "scientific discovery" is the recognition of phenomena, properties or laws of the material universe not hitherto recognized and capable of verification. Any discoverer of a scientific discovery who is a national of one of the contracting states may request international recording of that discovery.

This Treaty will enter into force three months after the deposit of the tenth instrument of ratification or accession. However, with the collapse of the Soviet Union, which was its main promoter, it is most probable that it will never come into force.

F.B.

Access : CON (Art. 16)
Reserves : PRO (Art. 18)
Duration : USP

Deposit. : WIPO (Art. 21)
Language : Ara, Eng, Fre, Ger, Ita, Por, Rus, Spa (Art. 20)

Reference : Ind.Prop. 1978/4

161.15 – TREATY ON THE PROTECTION OF INTELLECTUAL PROPERTY IN RESPECT OF INTEGRATED CIRCUITS – WIPO

Concluded : 26.05.1989, Washington
Party : 1

The objective of the Treaty is to protect for a minimum period of eight years (Art. 8) original layout-designs of integrated circuits, whether or not the integrated circuit concerned is incorporated in an article (Art. 3).

Protection is accorded in the territory of each of the contracting parties to natural persons who are nationals of, or are domiciled in the territory of, any of the other contracting parties; and legal entities and natural persons who, in the territory of any of the other contracting parties, have a real and effective establishment for the creation of layout-designs (topographies) or the production of integrated circuits (national treatment) (Art. 5).

The contracting parties undertake, as a minimum, to consider unlawful the partial or entire reproduction of layout-designs, their importation, sale or distribution for commercial purposes of the layout-design or an integrated circuit in which the layout-design is incorporated, without the authorization of the holder of the right (Art. 6).

Nevertheless, the contracting parties do not consider the reproduction of layout-designs without the authorization of the holder illegal, where the act is performed by a third party for the private or sole purposes of evaluation, analysis, research or teaching (Art. 6). The sale or distribution of unauthorized integrated circuits may be considered lawful when acquired innocently, as is the marketing of unauthorized integrated circuits put on the market by, or with the consent of, the holder of the right (exhaustion of rights).

The Treaty also allows any contracting party to provide for the possibility of its executive or judicial authority granting a non-voluntary licence, subject to equitable remuneration and to judicial review, if a third party has made unsuccessful efforts to obtain the authorization of the author where that grant is found to be necessary to safeguard a national purpose deemed to be vital by that authority. Similarly, any contracting state may apply measures, including the granting of a non-voluntary licence in application of its laws in order to secure free competition or prevent abuses by the holder of the right (Art. 6).

Any contracting party is free not to protect a layout-design until it has been ordinarily commercially exploited, separately or as incorporated in an integrated circuit, somewhere in the world, or until it has been the subject of an application for registration filed with the competent public authority (Art. 7).

The contracting parties are free to implement their obligations under the Treaty through a special law on layout-designs or its law on copyright, patents, utility models, industrial designs, unfair competition or any other law or a combination of any of those laws (Art. 4).

Finally, the Treaty makes provision for a mechanism to settle disputes arising from its interpretation or implementation (Art. 14). A contracting party may request to enter into consultation with another contracting party, or it may resort to any other means to bring about an amicable settlement to the dispute arising between the parties. In case of failure, and at the request of either of the parties, the Assembly must convene a panel of three members to examine the matter. The panel prepares a written report on the basis of which the Assembly, by consensus, makes recommendations to the parties.

The Treaty shall enter into force after the deposit of the fifth instrument of ratification or accession (Art. 16). However, with Japan and the US, the most important producers of integrated circuits, not at present wishing to ratify the Treaty, other countries may be discouraged from becoming parties to the Treaty.

Bernard Colas

Access : ASO (Art. 15)
Reserves : PRO (Art. 13)
Duration : USP
Deposit. : WIPO (Art. 19)
Language : Ara, Chi, Eng, Fre, Rus, Spa, (etc) (Art. 18)

Reference : WIPO. Doc. IPIC/DC/46 – ILM 28:1484

1.6.2 Copyright

England, in 1709, was the first country to introduce copyright. The so-called Queen Anne's Statute included provisions which responded to the growth of the printed word by granting authors copyright over their printed works for a specific period of time. Continental European countries have subsequently adopted laws on "authors' rights" which afford not only protection of the exploitation rights of the author but also his moral rights.

As problems of international editorial and literary piracy in the nineteenth century had not been solved through domestic legislation, nor through bilateral agreements, the First International Conference on Copyright in Berne in 1886 drafted the first multilateral Convention for the Protection of Literary and Artistic Works [see 162.01]. It sets out two basic principles which have remained, namely, the principle of equality of protection of foreign and domestic works (the so-called principle of national treatment of foreign works), and the determination of specially granted rights (so-called minimum rights) which would be available in every case to works protected by the Convention in member states.

The development of technology led to new ways of exploiting and copying original creations in the fields of literature and the arts. In response to this, copyright laws and treaties have progressively widened their scope of application regarding the persons and types of works to be protected, and the rights to be recognized.

Bernard Colas

SELECTED BIBLIOGRAPHY

Hughes, Roger T., *Hughes on Copyright and Industrial Design*, Ontario: Butterworths, 1984-.

Nimmer, Melville B. and David Nimmer, *Nimmer on Copyright: a Treaties on the Law of Literary, Musical and Artistic Property, and the Protection of Ideas*, New York: Matthew Bender, 1978-.

Nimmer, Melville B. and P. Geller, *International Copyright Law and Practice*, New York, 1988.

Stewart, Stephen M., *International Copyright and Neighbouring Rights*, London: Butterworths, 1989.
WIPO, *Copyright and Neighbouring Rights Laws and Treaties*, Geneva, 1987-.

162.01 – BERNE CONVENTION FOR THE PROTECTION OF LITERARY AND ARTISTIC WORKS, AS REVISED – WIPO

Concluded : 09.09.1886, Berne
In Force : 05.12.1887
Parties : 95

The Berne Convention of 1886 which, since its first revision in Berlin in 1908, has more generally been known as the "revised Berne Convention", protects the rights of authors *jure conventionis* in their literary and artistic works against certain unauthorized uses of such works including reproduction, broadcasting, communication to the public, adaptation and translation. It also guarantees national treatment to authors who are nationals of one of the Berne Union countries and offers certain minimum standards in the field of enforcement of rights, such as presumptions of ownership of rights and rights to seize illicit copies of protected works.

Since its inception, the Convention has been regularly revised. The 1908 Berlin Conference dispensed with any formality in the protection accorded by the Convention. Moreover, the enjoyment and exercise of the rights granted under the Convention were made independent of the existence of protection in the country of origin of the work. Various possibilities of making reservations, however, were maintained.

The Rome Revision of 1928 reduced these possibilities significantly. It also established the *droit moral* of the author – that is, the right to claim authorship and to object to certain modifications to works, or other similar derogatory actions (Art. 6bis), as well as the right to prevent unauthorized broadcasting (Art. 11bis).

The Brussels Conference of 1948 instituted a minimum term of protection: the life of the author and 50 years after his death (Art. 7). It also added works of applied arts to the list of works protected by the Convention (Art. 2-1), and recognized the author's exclusive right of authorizing the public recitation of his or her works (Art. 11ter).

The 1967 Stockholm Conference had the merit of adding to the Convention the authors' right to authorize the reproduction (Art. 9) and any communication to the public of their works (Art. 11ter). While it was never implemented, Articles 1 to 20 from the Stockholm text were re-adopted at the Paris Revision Conference of 1971, which also added an Appendix to Article 21 containing special provisions allowing developing countries, under certain stated conditions, to issue compulsory licences for translation and reproduction of foreign works. To date, eight countries have made use of this possibility.

WIPO has recently undertaken the preparation of a Protocol to the Berne Convention which, according to the preparatory documents submitted by the International Bureau of WIPO to the Committee of governmental experts studying this proposed Protocol, could clarify the existing, or establish new, international norms where under the present text of the Berne Convention doubts may exist as to the extent to which the Convention applies. Among the rights considered are the right to authorize or prohibit the rental or lending of certain categories of works, the right of importation, the right of public display, and certain aspects of the collective administration of rights.

Bernard Colas

Access : ALS (Art. 29)
Reserves : PAU (Art. 28-1, 28-b, 30, 32-2)
Duration : ULT (Art. 29)
Deposit. : WIPO, SE (Art. 26)
Language : Eng, Fre, (Ara, Ger, Ita, Por, Spa) (Art. 37)

Modific. : Completed Paris 04.05.1896 (09.12.1897); Revised Berlin 13.11.08 (09.09.10); Completed Berne 20.03.14 (20.04.15); Revised Rome 02.06.28 (01.08.31); Brussels 26.06.48 (01.08.51); Stockholm 14.07.67 (-); Paris 24.07.71 (10.10.74); Amended 1979 (In force)

Reference : 828 UNTS – UKTS 1990/63 – Can TS 1948/22 – 3/4 Paeslee – RTAF 1974/51 – JDI 1987 – JORF 28 Aug 74

162.02 – UNIVERSAL COPYRIGHT CONVENTION – UNESCO

Concluded : 06.09.1952, Geneva
In Force : 16.09.1955
Parties : 89

This Convention (known as the UCC) resulted initially in efforts made to draw legal ties between states parties to the Berne Union and states parties to inter-American copyright conventions, both of which have different legal traditions. Its adoption allowed states which may not have been able to join the Berne Union to become members of an international convention. With the United States' joining the Berne Convention in 1989, the UCC became less significant. The Convention was revised in Paris in 1971 during the same diplomatic conference which led to the revising of the Berne Convention [see 162.01].

As with the Berne Convention, the UCC rests on a few basic principles and contains a series of provisions determining the minimum protection to be granted, and special provisions for developing countries. Some basic principles of the UCC are the following:

- the principle of national treatment where works of nationals of any contracting state and work first published in that state enjoy in each other's contracting state the same protection as that other state awards to works of its nationals first published in its own territory (Art. II);
- the principle of the "independence" of protection where such protection is independent of the existence of protection in the country of origin of the work (if, however, a contracting state provides for a longer term than the minimum prescribed by the Convention and the work ceases to be protected in the country of origin, protection may be denied once protection in the country of origin ceases); and
- the compliance with formalities as a condition of copyright where contracting states may under their domestic law have such requirements.

In the last case, these requirements shall be satisfied with regard to all works protected in accordance with the Convention and first published outside its territory and where the author of which is not one of its nationals if, from the time of the first publication, all the copies of the work published with the authority of the author or other copyright proprietor bears the symbol ©, accompanied by the name of the copyright proprietor and the year of first publication. In contrast, the Berne Convention provides that protection cannot be conditional upon compliance with any formality.

The minimum standards of protection relate to the works and rights to be protected, and the duration of the protection. The works covered are literary, scientific and artistic works, including writings, musical, domestic and cinematographic works, and paintings, engravings and sculpture. Subject to certain permitted exceptions, the rights referred to in the Convention include the basic rights ensuring the author's economic interests, including the exclusive right to authorize reproduction by any means, public performance and broadcasting, and the exclusive right of the author to make, publish and authorize the making and publication of translation of works (Art. V). Regarding the duration of protection, the general rule is that protection must not be less than the life of the author and 25 years after his death (Art. IV).

Finally, the Convention institutes two systems of compulsory licensing: a system for all contracting states to translate works after the expiration of certain periods of time and after compliance with certain formalities, and a system for developing countries to reproduce, under certain conditions, works for use in connection with systematic instructional activities and to translate works for the purpose of teaching, scolarship or research.

B.C.

Access : ALS (Art. VIII, IX)
Reserves : PRO (Art. XX)
Duration : USP
Deposit. : UNESCO (Art. XXI)
Language : Ara, Eng, Fre, Ger, Ita, Por, Spa, etc (Art. XVI)

Modific. : Revised Paris 24.07.71 (10.07.74, Protocol 11.09.72)

Reference : 216 UNTS – Can TS 1962/13 – RTAF 1974/61 – UKTS 1957/66 – UST 6/3, 25/2 – JDI 1975 – JORF 30 Nov 55, 10 Oct 74

162.03 – INTERNATIONAL CONVENTION FOR THE PROTECTION OF PERFORMERS, PRODUCERS OF PHONOGRAMS AND BROADCASTING ORGANIZATIONS – WIPO/UNESCO/ILO

Concluded : 26.10.1961, Rome
In Force : 18.05.1964
Parties : 38

The objective of the Rome Convention is to establish international protection (20 years minimum) of the rights of performers, producers of phonograms and broadcasting organizations, based on the principle of national treatment.

The Convention provides performers with the possibility of preventing certain acts they have not consented to, such as the broadcasting and the communication to the public of their performance and the fixation of their unfixed performance (Art. 7). Producers of phonograms enjoy the right to authorize or prohibit the direct or indirect reproduction of their phonograms (Art. 10); and broadcasting organizations enjoy the right to authorize or prohibit certain acts, namely the rebroadcasting of their broadcasts, the fixation of their broadcasts, the reproduction of such fixations, and the communication to the public of their television broadcast if such communication is made in places accessible to the public against payment of an entrance fee (Art. 13).

When a phonogram published for commercial purposes is used directly for broadcasting or for any communication to the public, a single equitable remuneration must be paid by the users to the performers, the producer of the phonograms, or to both (Art. 12).

The Convention allows for a number of possibilities for making reservations in order to allow for its adaptation to various national legal contexts. It is open to states that are party to the Berne Convention for the Protection of Literary and Artistic Works [see 162.01] or the Universal Copyright Convention (Geneva, 1952) [see 162.02].

B.C.

Access : CON (Art. 23)
Reserves : PAU (Art. 16)
Duration : USP
Deposit. : UN (Art. 34)
Language : Eng, Fre, Ger, Ita, Por, Spa (Art. 33)

Reference : 496 UNTS – UKTS 1964/38 – ULR 1962 – JORF 9 Mar 88

162.04 – CONVENTION FOR THE PROTECTION OF PRODUCERS OF PHONOGRAMS AGAINST UNAUTHORIZED DUPLICATION OF THEIR PHONOGRAMS – WIPO/UNESCO

Concluded : 29.10.1971, Geneva
In Force : 18.04.1973
Parties : 43

Faced with a tremendous increase in the unauthorized reproduction of phonograms, which was causing serious prejudice to authors, performers and producers of phonograms, WIPO [see 160 A] in co-operation with UNESCO [see 171 A] and ILO [see 141 A], convened a Diplomatic Conference which adopted this Convention in 1971.

Under Articles 2 and 3, each contracting state agrees to protect the producers of phonograms who are nationals of other contracting states against the making of duplicates without the consent of the producer and against the importation of such duplicates, where the making or importation is for the purposes of distribution to the public. The Convention provides a term of protection of no less than 20 years from the first fixation or the first publication of the phonogram (Art. 4).

The Convention also stipulates that where compliance with certain formalities is required under national law, these are considered as fulfilled if all authorized copies bear a notice consisting of the symbol (P) in a circle, accompanied by the year of the first publication. The producer must also be sufficiently identified (Art. 5).

Contracting states may also provide for compulsory reproduction licences for the purpose of teaching or scientific research provided such licences give rise to an equitable remuneration, are only for the territory of the state in question, and do not extend to the export of copies (Art. 6).

The protection may be provided as a matter of copyright law, neighbouring rights law, unfair competition law or penal law.

B.C.

Access : ALS (Art. 9)
Reserves : PAU (Art. 10, 7-4)
Duration : USP
Deposit. : UN (Art. 9)

Language : Eng, Fre, Rus, Spa, (Ara, Dut, Ger, Ita, Por) (Art. 13)

Reference : 866 UNTS – UKTS 1973/41 – UST 25/1 – RTAF 1973/32 – JORF 26 Jul 73

162.05 – CONVENTION RELATING TO THE DISTRIBUTION OF PROGRAMME-CARRYING SIGNALS TRANSMITTED BY SATELLITE – WIPO/UNESCO

Concluded : 21.05.1974, Brussels
In Force : 25.08.1979
Parties : 15

This Convention provides for the obligation of each contracting state to take adequate measures to prevent the unauthorized distribution on or from its territory of any programme-carrying signal transmitted by satellite. The distribution is unauthorized if it has not been authorized by the organization – typically a broadcasting organization – which has decided what the performance consists of. The obligation exists in respect of organizations which are "nationals" of a contracting state (Art. 2-1).

SUBSEQUENT DEVELOPMENTS

The provisions of this Convention are not applicable, however, where the distribution of signals is made from a direct broadcast satellite (Art. 3).

In order to facilitate the implementation of this Convention, a Committee of Governmental Experts in 1979 drew up two sets of model provisions: one affording the broadcasting organizations a right to authorize the distribution of programme-carrying signals with a view to the implementation of the Convention, and the other prohibiting unauthorized distribution.

B.C.

Access : ALS (Art. 9)
Reserves : PAU (Art. 8)
Duration : USP
Deposit. : UN (Art. 9)
Language : Eng, Fre, Rus, Spa (Art. 12)

Reference : 1144 UNTS – ILM 13:1447

162.06 – MADRID MULTILATERAL CONVENTION FOR THE AVOIDANCE OF DOUBLE TAXATION OF COPYRIGHT ROYALTIES – WIPO

Concluded : 13.12.1979, Madrid
Parties : 4

The purpose of this Convention, negotiated under the auspices of WIPO, is to avoid taxation of copyright royalties in two countries, *inter alia* by providing a model bilateral agreement to that effect.

An author residing in state A who receives copyright royalties in states A and B, may be taxed twice on these royalties unless states A and B succeed in co-ordinating their fiscal policies.

The Convention defines copyright royalties as "payments of any kind made on the basis of the domestic copyright laws of the Contracting State in which these royalties are originally due, for the use of, or the right to use, a copyright in a literary, artistic or scientific work, as defined in the multilateral copyright conventions, including such payments made in respect of legal or compulsory licences or in respect of the *droit de suite*" (Art. 1). The Convention does not cover royalties due in respect of the exploitation of cinematographic works.

The Convention is supplemented by an independent Protocol which extends the scope of the Convention to royalties paid to performers, producers of phonograms and broadcasting organizations "in respect of rights related to copyright or 'neighbouring' rights, in so far as the latter royalties arise in a State party to this Protocol and their beneficiaries are residents of another State party to this Protocol".

The Convention will enter into force after the deposit of the tenth instrument of ratification, acceptance or accession.

B.C.

Access : ALS (Art. 11)
Reserves : PAU (Art. 12)
Duration : USP
Deposit. : UN (Art. 11)
Language : Ara, Eng, Fre, Rus, Spa, (Ger, Ita, Por) (Art. 16)

162.07 – TREATY ON THE INTERNATIONAL REGISTRATION OF AUDIOVISUAL WORKS – WIPO

Concluded : 20.04.1989, Geneva
In Force : 27.02.1991
Parties : 7

This convention aims at increasing the legal security in transactions relating to audiovisual works and contributing to the fight against piracy of these works. It establishes an International Register of Audiovisual Works for the purpose of the registration of statements concerning audiovisual works and rights in such works. This International Register is kept by the International Registry of Audiovisual Works, which is an administrative unit of the International Bureau of WIPO located in Klosterneuburg, near Vienna, Austria (Art. 3). The International Registry performs administrative tasks, prepares and provides the secretariat of revision conferences (Art. 6) and receives its direction from the Assembly of the Union established under Articles 1, 5 and 6 of the convention.

Any persons or legal entities from a contracting state who have an interest in an audiovisual work may, in accordance with the procedure provided in the Regulations and Administrative Instructions, apply for registration of such work (Art. 3). Audiovisual work is defined as "a series of fixed related images, with or without accompanying sound, susceptible of being made visible and, where accompanied by sound, susceptible of being made audible" (Art. 2).

Contracting states have undertaken to recognize that a statement recorded in the International Register is considered true until the contrary is proved, except where the statement cannot be valid under the copyright law of that state, or where the statement is contradicted by another statement recorded in the International Register (Art. 4).

The Treaty entered into force on 27 February 1991 after the accession of the fifth contracting state. The first five states to adhere were, in alphabetical order: Austria,

Burkina Faso, Czechoslovakia, France and Mexico. Since then, Argentina has also adhered to the Treaty.

B.C.

Access : ALS (Art. 11)
Reserves : PAU (Art. 13)
Duration : USP
Deposit. : WIPO (Art. 16)
Language : Eng, Fre, (Ara, Ger, Ita, Jap, Por, Rus, Spa) (Art. 15)

Reference : WIPO Doc. 299(E)

1.7 Culture and Tourism

1.7.1 Culture

With the development of international economic relations, governments have contributed to improving the means of communication between peoples and to encouraging a better understanding between nations.

The needs arising from reconstruction after the Second World War, together with certain technical considerations, led to the development of specialized agencies. Among these, the United Nations Educational, Scientific and Cultural Organization (UNESCO) – the main intergovernmental organization operating in the cultural field – can be counted as one of the "Big Four", alongside the International Labour Organisation (ILO) [see 141 A], the Food and Agriculture Organization (FAO) [see 131 A] and the World Health Organization (WHO) [see 132 A]. In fact, during that time, UNESCO could be regarded as having had its own reconstruction role – that of reconstructing the minds of people after the ravages of fascism and militarism. As a spiritual body of the United Nations system, UNESCO was constituted on the assumption that "a peace based exclusively upon the political and economic arrangements of governments would not be a peace which could secure the unanimous, lasting and sincere support of the peoples of the world, and that the peace must therefore be founded, if it is not to fail, upon the intellectual and moral solidarity of mankind". Over time, UNESCO's mission has evolved to include meeting the needs of the developing countries – as is the case for most of the specialized agencies – and promoting the idea of the common heritage of humanity.

The General UNESCO Conference has adopted three main categories of international agreements: the first being two agreements and a protocol which constitute effective instruments in lowering customs barriers and reducing other economic restrictions which impede the exchange of ideas and knowledge through different kinds of materials [see 171.02 and 171.03]; the second category being two conventions which aim to protect the cultural and natural property of its member states [see 171.04 and 171.05]; and the third category being conventions on intellectual property [see 1.6.2]

Patricia Georget

SELECTED BIBLIOGRAPHY

Ayish, Muhammad, I., "International Communication in the 1990s: Implications for the Third World", *International Affairs* (July 1992): 487-510.

Giffard, C. Anthony, *Unesco and the media*, New York: Longman, 1989.

Jones, Philipp W., *International Policies for Third World Education: Unesco, Literacy and Development*, London, New York: Routledge, 1988.

Mayor Zaragoza, Federico, "The Role of Unesco in the Construction of Peace", *Medicine and war* (Jan/Mar 1992): 18-24.

– – –, "A New Design for Unesco", *Science and public policy* (Dec. 1988): 426-430.

– – –, "Organisation des Nations Unies pour l'Education, la Science et la Culture", *Revue des Sciences Morales et Politiques* 144 (2) (1989): 277-293.

Valderrama, Fernando, *Historia de la Unesco*, Paris: Unesco, 1991.

171 A – UNITED NATIONS EDUCATIONAL, SCIENTIFIC AND CULTURAL ORGANIZATION (UNESCO)

The United Nations Educational, Scientific and Cultural Organization is a specialized agency of the United Nations which reports annually to the Economic and Social Council (ECOSOC). It came into being in 1946.

The purpose of UNESCO is to contribute to peace and security by promoting co-operation among nations through education, science, culture and communication. To achieve this purpose, the Organization co-ordinates different types of activities. It promotes education – its major activity – by drawing up plans for literacy programmes, by helping to train teachers, educational planners and administrators and by encouraging the local construction of and equipment for schools. It assists in the establishment of scientific and technological foundations to promote a better use of natural resources (UNESCO's programmes in natural sciences include: Man and the Biosphere, the programme of the Intergovernmental Oceanographic Commission, and the International Hydrological and International Geological Correlation Programmes). It encourages national cultural values and the preservation of cultural heritage by stimulating artistic creativity and supporting the conservation of books, works of art and monuments [see 171.04 and 171.05], as well as the preservation of cultural identities and oral traditions. It collaborates in advancing knowledge and understanding of peoples by developing and supporting all means of communication, notably through its International Programme of Communication [see also 171.02 and 171.03]. Finally, it promotes the social sciences as instruments for the attainment of human rights, justice and peace.

STRUCTURE

The **General Conference** is composed of representatives of 173 member states, each member state having one vote. It meets biennially to determine the policies and main lines of work of the Organization, to make decisions on programmes drawn up by the Executive Board (e.g. the creation of special and technical committees and such other subordinate bodies as may be necessary for its purposes), and to approve the budget of the Organization. It also convenes international conferences in the fields of competence of the Organization and adopts proposals of international conferences and recommendations for submission to the member states.

The **Executive Board** consists of 51 members elected by the General Conference from among delegates appointed by the member states to exercise the powers delegated to them on behalf of the Conference as a whole and not as representatives of their respective governments. It prepares the programme of work of the Organization and corresponding budget estimates, and is responsible for supervising the execution of the programme as adopted by the General Conference. It also recommends to the General Conference the admission of new members to the Organization when they are not already members of the United Nations.

The **Secretariat** consists of a Director-General, nominated by the Executive Board and appointed by the General Conference (the present Director-General is Federico Mayor Zaragoza, from Spain, appointed in November 1987 for a term of six years renewed in 1993), and staff appointed by him to ensure technical and administrative support for all bodies of the Organization.

FUNDING

UNESCO's resources come primarily from three sources: (1) financial contributions from member states as apportioned by the General Conference; (2) subventions obtained from the United Nations Development Programme [see 222 A] (itself financed by the voluntary contributions it receives from the member states of the UN); and (3) various "Funds in Trust" or special funds negotiated from various donors, both multilateral (e.g. the International Bank for Reconstruction and Development [see 221 A]) and bilateral, or funds which (like the United Nations Population Fund (UNFPA)) have been established to finance special programmes or activities and to which member governments contribute voluntarily.

With the approval of the Executive Board, the Director-General is entitled to receive gifts, bequests and subventions directly from governments, public and private institutions, associations and private persons. For the biennium 1992-1993, the net budget as approved by the 26th Session of the General Conference was US$444,704,000.

CO-OPERATION

UNESCO co-operates with both intergovernmental and non-governmental organizations whose interests and activities are related to its purposes.

PUBLICATIONS

UNESCO publishes a large variety of books and periodicals in its fields of activity, including articles, scientific studies, statistics, reports, atlases and maps. Among these are the biannual *Copyright Bulletin*, the monthly illustrated *UNESCO Courier*, and the quarterlies, *Prospects, Impact of Science on Society, Nature and Resources, International Social Science Journal,* and *Museum*. See also the bibliograph of publications issued by UNESCO or under its auspices: *The First Twenty-Five Years, 1946 to 1971*, Paris: UNESCO, 1973, and the Report of the Director-General issued every two years.

Patricia Georget

ADDRESS

7 Place de Fontenoy, 75007 Paris, France
T. (33 1) 45 68 10 00, Fx. (33 1) 45 67 16 90

171.01 – AGREEMENT ESTABLISHING THE UNITED NATIONS EDUCATIONAL, SCIENTIFIC AND CULTURAL ORGANIZATION – UNESCO

Concluded: 16.11.1945, London
In Force : 04.11.1946
Parties : 173

The Constitution of the United Nations Educational, Scientific and Cultural Organization was prepared by a conference convened in London from 1 to 16 November 1945. It came into force on 4 November 1946, after 20 of its signatories had deposited their instruments of acceptance with the Government of the United Kingdom in accordance with Article XV, and it became a specialized agency of the United Nations Organization on 14 December 1946. It reports annually to ECOSOC.

As provided in Article II, "membership of the United Nations Organization shall carry with it the right to membership of the United Nations Educational, Scientific and Cultural Organization", while "states which are not members of the United Nations Organization may be admitted to membership of the Organization upon recommendation of the Executive Board, by a two-thirds majority vote of the General Conference".

The Constitution establishes the structure of the Organization and defines its aims and the responsibilities of the member states.

RESPONSIBILITIES OF THE MEMBER STATES

Each member state is responsible for establishing links between its principal bodies interested in educational, scientific and cultural matters and the Organization (Art. VII). Member states are obliged to report periodically to the Organization on their laws, regulations and statistics relating to educational, scientific and cultural life and institutions, and on the action taken by them upon the recommendations and conventions adopted by the General Conference (Art. VIII).

MODIFICATIONS

The text of the Constitution may be modified by amendments to be accepted by two-thirds of the member states before coming into force for those which involve fundamental alterations in the aims of the Organization or new obligations for the member states; any other amendment will become effective upon receiving the approval of the General Conference by a two-thirds majority, as provided in Article XIII.

P. G.

Access : ALS (Art. II)
Reserves : USP
Duration : USP
Deposit. : GB (Art. XV)
Language : Eng, Fre (Art. XIV)

Modific. : Modified by the 2nd, 3rd, 4th, 5th, 6th, 7th, 8th, 9th, 10th, 12th, 15th, 17th, 19th, 20th, 21st and 24th General Conference

Reference : 4 UNTS – Can TS 1945/18 – UKTS 1946/50 – 3/4 Paeslee – UST 8/2, 10/1, 22/2, 29/3 – JORF 10 Jul 46

171.02 – AGREEMENT FOR FACILITATING THE INTERNATIONAL CIRCULATION OF VISUAL AND AUDITORY MATERIALS OF AN EDUCATIONAL, SCIENTIFIC AND CULTURAL CHARACTER ("BEIRUT AGREEMENT") – UNESCO

Concluded : 15.07.1949, New York
In Force : 12.08.1954
Parties : 31

Having been assigned the task of recommending "such international agreements as may be necessary to promote the free flow of ideas by word and image", UNESCO adopted the so-called "Beirut Agreement" on 10 December 1948 (at the third General UNESCO Conference held in Beirut from 17 November to 11 December 1948). This Agreement replaced a convention for facilitating the international circulation of films of an educational character adopted under the auspices of the League of Nations on 11 October 1933, and suspended in 1939.

The Agreement's purpose is to facilitate the dispatch of visual and auditory material, deemed to be of an educational, scientific, and cultural character, from one country to another. In effect, it allows for a reduction in customs duties and other economic restrictions which may impede the dispatch of this material.

Scope: As defined in Article II of the Agreement, the relevant visual and auditory materials are the following:

- films, filmstrips, and microfilms;
- sound recordings of all types and forms; and
- glass slides; models, static and moving; wall charts, maps, and posters.

The Agreement is also applicable to new audiovisual techniques as they are perfected (e.g. teleprinters, videotape, microfiches, etc.).

DETAILS OF THE AGREEMENT

The materials will be deemed to be of an educational, scientific and cultural character:

(a) when their primary purpose or effect is to instruct or inform through the development of a subject or aspect of a subject, or when their content is such as to maintain, increase or diffuse knowledge, and augment international understanding and goodwill; and
(b) when the materials are representative, authentic, and accurate; and
(c) when the technical quality is such that it does not interfere with the use made of material.

Upon presentation of a certificate, issued either by the exporting country or by UNESCO testifying that the material is of an educational, scientific or cultural nature, any institution or an individual is entitled to import the relevant material, benefiting from the following preferential rights:

- exemption from all customs duties;
- exemption from all quantitative restrictions;
- waiver of import licences;
- exemption from all internal fees or other charges except to the extent that these are imposed on like products of the importing country;
- treatment no less favourable than that accorded to similar products of the importing country, in respect of regulations and practices affecting sale, transportation and distribution, as well as processing and exhibition (Art. III).

The contracting states also undertake to consider ways of reducing to a minimum the restrictions not removed by the Agreement which might interfere with the international circulation of material covered under it. This does not affect the right of the contracting parties to censor material in accordance with their own laws or to adopt measures to prohibit or limit the importation of material for reasons of public security or order.

P.G.

Access : ALS (Art. XI)
Reserves : PAU (Art. XIV)
Duration : USP
Deposit. : UN (Art. X)
Language : Eng, Fre (Art. XVI)

Reference : 197 UNTS – Can TS 1954/4 – UST 17/2

171.03 – AGREEMENT ON THE IMPORTATION OF EDUCATIONAL, SCIENTIFIC AND CULTURAL MATERIALS ("FLORENCE AGREEMENT") – UNESCO

Concluded : 22.11.1950, New York
In Force : 21.05.1952
Parties : 82

The Florence Agreement was unanimously adopted on 17 June 1950 at the fifth General UNESCO Conference held in Florence from 22 May to 17 June 1950. The Agreement is in line with one of UNESCO's major objectives, as stipulated in its Constitution – namely, "initiating methods of international co-operation calculated to give the people of all countries access to the printed and published materials produced by any of them".

As with the Beirut Agreement for visual and auditory material, this Agreement's purpose is to facilitate the importation of educational, scientific, and cultural printed and published material by reducing such obstacles as tariffs, taxes and currency exchange restrictions which restrict their free dissemination. It also extends the definition of visual and auditory material by allowing material to be imported if it is being sent to an authorized institution or organization.

Scope: The Florence Agreement applies to the following products which originate from another contracting state, subject to the conditions laid down in the relevant annexes:

- books, publications, and documents as listed in Annex A; and
- educational, scientific and cultural materials as listed in Annexes B, C, D, and E (i.e. works of art and collectors' pieces having an educational, scientific, or cultural character; visual and auditory materials of an educational, scientific and cultural character; scientific instruments and apparatus; and articles for the blind).

DETAILS OF THE AGREEMENT

The contracting states undertake to give every possible facility to the importation of educational, scientific and cultural materials which are imported exclusively for showing at a public exhibition under certain conditions (Art. III); and to promote the free circulation of educational, scientific or cultural materials, to simplify the administrative procedure governing such importation, and to facilitate the expeditious and safe customs clearance of that material (Art. IV).

MODIFICATIONS

In order to take into consideration "the technical progress which has changed the ways and means of transmitting information and knowledge, and to consider the needs and concerns of the developing countries which became independent, with a view to giving them easier and less costly access to educational, technical and cultural material", UNESCO adopted a Protocol to the Agreement on 26 November 1976, known as the "Nairobi Protocol".

This Protocol extends the customs duty exemptions granted by the Florence Agreement to a wide variety of new material listed in nine annexes:

- books, publications and documents (Annex A);
- works of art and collectors' pieces having an educational, scientific or cultural character (Annex B);
- audiovisual material (Annex C1);
- visual and auditory materials of an educational, scientific or cultural character (Annex C2);
- scientific instruments and apparatuses (Annex D);
- articles for the blind and other handicapped persons (Annex E);
- sports equipment (Annex F);
- musical instruments and other musical equipment (Annex G); and
- materials and machines used for the production of books, publications, and documents (Annex H).

This Protocol is open only to those states which are parties to the Florence Agreement, and to economic and customs unions, on condition that their member states are parties to the Protocol.

P.G.

Access : ALS (Art. IX)
Reserves : USP
Duration : USP
Deposit. : UN (Art. IX)
Language : Eng, Fre (Art. IX)

Modific. : Protocol Nairobi 26.11.76 (02.01.82)

Reference : UKTS 1954/42 – UST 17/2 – JDI 1987 – JORF 30 Oct 53

171.04 – CONVENTION ON THE MEANS OF PROHIBITING AND PREVENTING THE ILLICIT IMPORT, EXPORT AND TRANSFER OF OWNERSHIP OF CULTURAL PROPERTY – UNESCO

Concluded : 14.11.1970, Paris
In Force : 24.04.1972
Parties : 78

This Convention, adopted at the 16th General UNESCO Conference held in Paris from 12 October to 14 November 1970, aims at protecting the cultural property existing within the territory of member states against theft, clandestine excavation, and illicit importation or expropriation.

The Convention defines "cultural property" as "property which, on religious or secular grounds, is specifically designated by each State as being of importance for archaeology, prehistory, history, literature, art or science". It also lists the categories to which the property may belong (Art. 1) and establishes the categories constituting the "cultural heritage" to be protected (Art. 4).

DETAILS OF THE CONVENTION

Member states recognize "that the illicit import, export and transfer of ownership of cultural property is one of the main causes of the impoverishment of the cultural heritage of the countries of origin of such property and that international co-operation constitutes one of the most efficient means of protecting each country's cultural property against all the dangers resulting therefrom" (Art. 2). They undertake to adopt the measures stipulated by the Convention to ensure effective protection of cultural property – for example:

- to set up within their territories one or more national services, where such services do not already exist, for the protection of the cultural heritage, and be responsible for carrying out certain functions (Art. 5);
- to control the circulation of any cultural property (Art. 6) and restrict movement of property illegally removed from any state party (Art. 10); and
- to prevent museums and similar institutions within their territories from acquiring any illegally exported cultural property and to take appropriate steps to recover and return any such property at the request of the state party of origin (Art. 7).

The Convention is open to ratification or acceptance by member states of UNESCO and all non-members invited to accede to it by the Executive Board of the Organization (Arts. 19 and 20). It is subject to revision by the General Conference provided that such revision shall bind only the states which shall become parties to the revised Convention (Art. 25).

P.G.

Access : ALS (Art. 19, 20)
Reserves : USP
Duration : USP
Deposit. : UNESCO (Art. 19)
Language : Eng, Fre, Rus, Spa (Art. 18)

Reference : 823 UNTS – ILM 10:289

171.05 – CONVENTION FOR THE PROTECTION OF THE WORLD CULTURAL AND NATURAL HERITAGE – UNESCO

Concluded : 16.11.1972, Paris
In Force : 17.12.1975
Parties : 134

The aim of the Convention is to establish an effective system, organized on a permanent basis and in accordance with modern scientific methods, for the collective protection of the cultural and natural heritage of outstanding universal value.

DETAILS OF THE CONVENTION

The parties recognize that the duty of ensuring the identification, protection, conservation, presentation and transmission to future generations of any particular cultural and natural heritage, belongs primarily to the state in which it is situated. The contracting states undertake to fulfil these responsibilities through their own efforts and, where appropriate, with international assistance and co-operation. While fully respecting therefore the sovereignty of the states on whose territory the cultural and natural heritage is situated, the parties do at the same time also "recognize that such heritage constitutes a world heritage for whose protection it is the duty of the international community as a whole to co-operate" (Art. 9-1).

Each state party undertakes the following: to adopt a general policy which aims to protect the cultural and natural heritage by developing comprehensive planning programmes; to set up services for the protection of this heritage; to develop scientific and technical studies to counteract the dangers to the cultural and natural heritage; to take appropriate legal, scientific, technical, administrative and financial measures to protect, conserve, and rehabilitate this heritage; and to foster the establishment of national or regional centres for training in the protection, conservation, and presentation of the heritage.

An Intergovernmental Committee for the Protection of the Cultural and Natural Heritage of Outstanding Universal Value (the so-called "World Heritage Committee"), created by the Convention, is composed of 15 states parties; an equitable representation of the different regions and cultures of the world is ensured in the election of the members of the Committee. It is established within UNESCO.

On the basis of inventories submitted by states, the Committee establishes, updates and publishes a World Heritage List and a List of World Heritage in Danger, the latter being a list of the property appearing in the World Heritage List for which major conservation operations are necessary. The Committee then decides on the action to be taken with regard to requests for international assistance from the parties to preserve the cultural and natural heritage included or potentially suitable for inclusion in the Lists.

The Convention also establishes a Fund for the Protection of the World Cultural and Natural Heritage of Outstanding Universal Value (the so-called "the World Heritage Fund"). The resources of the Fund come from compulsory and voluntary contributions made by the the states parties to the Convention, as well as contributions, gifts and bequests from other sources.

Any state which is a party to the Convention may request international assistance in regard to property forming part of the cultural and natural heritage of outstanding universal value situated within its territory. This assistance may take the form of studies by experts, training of staff and specialists, loans, or subsidies.

The parties undertake to submit reports to UNESCO providing information on the legislative and administrative provisions which they have adopted and other action which they have taken in applying the Convention. In 1993, there were 378 properties appearing in the World Heritage List.

The conditions of accession and revision of this Convention are the same as for the Convention on the Means of Prohibiting and Preventing the Illicit Import, Export and Transfer of Ownership of Cultural Property (Paris, 1970) [see 171.04].

Maguelonne Déjeant-Pons

Access	: ALS (Art. 31, 32)
Reserves	: USP
Duration	: USP
Deposit.	: UNESCO (Art. 31)
Language	: Ara, Eng, Fre, Rus, Spa (Art. 30)

Reference	: 1037 UNTS – Can TS 1976/45 – ILM 11:1367 – UST 27/1 – JDI 1976 – JORF 18 Feb 76 – RTAF 1976/8

1.7.2 Tourism

Tourism is a prominent economic activity in international trade. It is one of the reasons which has prompted governments to develop multilateral agreements that facilitate border crossings by travellers and the free circulation of associated goods and services. This was undertaken initially through UN conventions adopted after the Second World War and subsequently through instruments prepared by other international bodies concerned with tourism, namely the World Tourism Organization (WTO) [172 A], the International Institute for the Unification of Private Law (UNIDROIT) [see 300 B] and the International Labour Organisation (ILO) [see 141 A].

These agreements cover facilities in fields essential to international tourism and concern, *inter alia*, goods transported by tourists, promotion abroad by official bodies, transportation, travel contracts, and working conditions in hotels and restaurants. They are described in this section.

Regional intergovernmental organizations not mentioned in this section have also adopted instruments designed to enhance the development of international tourism. Examples include the 1985 OECD Decision-Recommendation of the Council on International Tourism Policy.

Louise Allard

172 A – WORLD TOURISM ORGANIZATION (WTO)

WTO is an international organization of intergovernmental character, created in Mexico on 27 September 1970 with the transformation of the International Union of Official Travel Organizations (IUOTO). IUOTO was an international organization of non-governmental character established under private law in The Hague (Netherlands) in 1925 and subsequently based in Geneva.

The fundamental aim of WTO is the promotion and development of tourism with a view to contributing to economic development, international understanding, peace, prosperity, and universal respect for and observation of human rights and fundamental freedoms (Art. 3).

WTO pays particular attention to the interests of developing countries in the field of tourism. As such, it received special recognition for its role at the international level by the General Assembly of the United Nations on 22 November 1977.

MEMBERSHIP

Membership of the Organization is open to (Arts. 4 to 7):

- sovereign states: *full members* with one vote each;
- territories or groups of territories not responsible for their external relations: *associated members* with no voting rights; and
- international bodies, both governmental and non-governmental, concerned with specialized interests in tourism and commercial bodies or associations whose activities are related to the aims of the Organization or fall within its competence: *affiliate members* with no voting rights.

STRUCTURE

The **General Assembly** (Arts. 9 to 12), the supreme organ of the Organization, is composed of delegates representing full members. It meets every two years.

The **Executive Council** (Arts. 14 to 20) consists of full members elected by the Assembly. It meets at least twice a year. The Council may also include one associate member selected by the associate members of the Organization and a representative of the Committee of Affiliate Members. The Council is primarily responsible for the implementation of the decisions and recommendations of the Assembly and for the preparation of the Organization's accounts and budget estimates. The Council is assisted by six **Regional Commissions** and a **Secretariat** (Arts. 21 to 24).

ACHIEVEMENTS

For a number of years, WTO has been working on a draft convention designed to facilitate international travel and tourist stays. At its 44th meeting in November 1992, the Executive Council adopted a decision requesting the Facilitation Committee to move ahead with this work. The proposed convention would be open to ratification by countries which are members or non-members of the Organization which would be invited to ratify any of the following Annexes:

- Annex I. Passport and visa formalities and facilities applicable to tourist travel, visits and stays;
- Annex II. Health formalities and facilities and facilitation of travel and tourist stays for the disabled;
- Annex III. Currency formalities and taxes, fees, duties and related charges applicable to travel and tourist stays; and
- Annex IV. Tourism representations abroad.

CO-OPERATION

WTO has concluded co-operation agreements with UN agencies (UNEP [see 410 A], ECA and ESCAP) and UN specialized institutions (IMO [see 183 A], ICAO [see 184 A], WHO [see 132 A], UNESCO [see 171 A], FAO [see 131 A] and WMO [see 431 A]). WTO is an executing agency of UNDP [see 222 A].

WTO is currently working with UNCTAD [see 111 B] and the GATT [see 111 A] on the drafting of a brochure and a handbook designed to provide governments with information on the GATS (General Agreement on Trade in Services) [see 111.19] and its relevance to tourism in the areas of investment, transportation, and so on.

PUBLICATIONS

WTO publishes periodical documents, including *WTO News* (six/year), a *Statistical Yearbook* (annual), and a *Compendium of Tourism Statistics* (annual). It also publishes a variety of documents on tourism issues, for example: statistics; promotion and marketing; environment and development; education and training; health, safety and security; faciliation and liberalization; and tourist transportation.

Louise Allard

ADDRESS

Calle Capitän Haya, 42, Madrid 28020, Spain
T. (34 1) 571 0628, Fx. (34 1) 571 3733

SELECTED BIBLIOGRAPHY

Lanquar, Robert, *The Organizational Development of the World Tourism Organization: A Case Study*, Aix-en-Provence, France: Etudes et Mémoires, volume 54, Centre des Hautes Etudes touristiques, 1983.

172.01 – CONVENTION CONCERNING CUSTOMS FACILITIES FOR TOURING – UN

Concluded : 04.06.1954, New York
In Force : 11.09.1957
Parties : 75

This Convention is designed to facilitate international tourism through benefits granted to tourists (described in Art. 1-b).

The Convention covers the temporary importation of personal effects free of import duties and import taxes, as long as they are intended for re-exportation at the end of the trip and are not imported for commercial purposes.

A non-exhaustive list of "personal effects" is provided and includes, among a number of articles imported for personal use, certain quantities of tobacco, alcohol, toilet water or perfume, and travel souvenirs with a ceiling value fixed in US dollars. Note that some of these provisions were revised in the context of the Convention on the Simplification and Harmonization of Customs Procedures (Kyoto, 1973) [see 112.19] and by Annex B.6. of the Convention on Temporary Admission (Istanbul, 1990) [see 112.25].

L.A.

Access : ALS (Art. 14, 15)
Reserves : PAU (Art. 20)
Duration : MIN (Art. 18)
Deposit. : UN (Art. 25)
Language : Chi, Eng, Fre, Rus, Spa

Modific. : Amendment (06.06.67)

Reference : 276, 596 UNTS – Can TS 1957/25 – UKTS 1957/70 – UST 8/1, 19/4 – JORF 27 Jan 60 – RTAF 1960/10

172.02 – ADDITIONAL PROTOCOL TO THE 1954 CONVENTION CONCERNING CUSTOMS FACILITIES FOR TOURING RELATING TO THE IMPORTATION OF TOURIST PUBLICITY DOCUMENTS AND MATERIAL – UN

Concluded : 04.06.1954, New York
In Force : 28.06.1956
Parties : 69

The Protocol aims to facilitate the activity of governments, carried out abroad, of the promotion of their countries as a tourist destination. The Protocol intends to ease the circulation of certain documents and material necessary to this activity, provided it is carried out under the control of official tourist agencies or national tourist publicity agencies affiliated therewith (Art. 4). The following facilities are provided for:

- the importation of certain documents free of import duties and import taxes (Art. 2); and
- the temporary admission of certain materials free of import duties and import taxes (Art. 3) for a period of 12 months maximum. (Note that this will be replaced by Annex B.7 of the Convention on Temporary Admission (Istanbul, 1990) [see 112.25].)

Articles 2 and 3 provide a list of the documents and material covered by the Convention whilst Article 4 describes the conditions under which such facilities are granted.

The contracting states are not bound by the Convention when there are reasons to fear abuse (Art. 2) or when they have to impose prohibitions based on public morality, public security, public health or hygiene (Art. 7). The Annex to the Convention contains a "Model Declaration" for the temporary free admission of tourist publicity material.

The final Act of the UN Conference which led to the adoption of the Protocol mentions two previous agreements covering similar issues:

- the Agreement on the Importation of Educational, Scientific, and Cultural Materials (New York, 1950) [see 171.03]; and
- the International Convention to Facilitate the Importation of Commerical Samples and Advertising Material (Geneva, 1952) [see 112.05].

L.A.

Access : ALS (Art. 8, 9)
Reserves : PAU (Art. 14)
Duration : MIN (Art. 11, 12)
Deposit. : UN (Art. 19)
Language : Eng, Fre, Spa

Reference : 276 UNTS – UKTS 1957/70 – JORF 27 Jan 60 – RTAF 1960/10

172.03 – CUSTOMS CONVENTION ON THE TEMPORARY IMPORTATION OF PRIVATE ROAD VEHICLES – UN

Concluded : 04.06.1954, New York
In Force : 15.12.1957
Parties : 70

The Convention deals with a number of facilities granted to the residents of the contracting states travelling within the territory of other contracting states. More specifically, it covers the conditions under which vehicles owned or rented by non-residents for private use can be admitted into the country of importation without payment of import duties and import taxes.

The main body of the Convention contains seven Chapters as follows:

I. Definitions;
II. Importation without payment of import duties and taxes and free of import prohibitions and restrictions;
III. Issue of temporary importation papers;
IV. Particulars on temporary importation papers;
V. Conditions of temporary importation;
VI. Extension of validity and renewal of temporary importation papers; and
VII. Regularization of temporary importation papers.

The five Annexes cover:

- Annex 1: "Carnet de passages en douane";
- Annex 2: Triptych;
- Annex 3: Diptych;
- Annex 4: Extension of validity of "Carnet de passages en douane"; and
- Annex 5: Model Certificate for the adjustment of undischarged, destroyed, lost or stolen temporary importation papers.

For the contracting states, the entry into force of the Convention automatically terminated the Agreement Providing for the Provisional Application of the Draft International Customs Conventions on Touring, on Commercial Road Vehicles and on the International Transport of Goods by Road (Geneva, 1949).

L.A.

Access : ALS (Art. 33, 34)
Reserves : PAU (Art. 39)
Duration : MIN (Art. 37)
Deposit. : UN (Art. 44)
Language : Eng, Fre, Spa

Modific. : Protocol (23.04.85)

Reference : 282 UNTS – Can TS 1957/34 – UKTS 1959/1 – JORF 27 Jan 60 – RTAF 1960/10

172.04 – CONVENTION ON THE TAXATION OF ROAD VEHICLES FOR PRIVATE USE IN INTERNATIONAL TRAFFIC – ECE

Concluded : 18.05.1956, Geneva
In Force : 18.08.1959
Parties : 18

The Convention is designed to introduce a more liberal fiscal procedure than that of the Convention on the Taxation of Foreign Motor Vehicles (Geneva, 1931).

The Convention applies to vehicles registered in the territory of a contracting state and temporarily imported for private use into the territory of another contracting state. It primarily exempts those vehicles from the obligation to be registered in the other contracting state, as well as from the obligation to pay taxes and charges levied on the possession or circulation of vehicles in the territory of the contracting state (Art. 2) for a period limited to 365 consecutive days (Art. 3).

L.A.

Access : CON (Art. 5)
Reserves : PAU (Art. 11)
Duration : MIN (Art. 8)
Deposit. : UN (Art. 16)
Language : Eng, Fre

Reference : 339 UNTS – UKTS 1963/32 – JORF 26 Jan 60 – RTAF 1960/9

172.05 – CUSTOMS CONVENTION ON THE TEMPORARY IMPORTATION FOR PRIVATE USE OF AIRCRAFT AND PLEASURE BOATS – ECE

Concluded : 18.05.1956, Geneva
In Force : 01.01.1959
Parties : 24

The Convention contains a number of provisions designed to facilitate travel by residents of a contracting state in another contracting state. In this respect, it provides a complement to the Customs Convention on the Temporary Importation of Private Road Vehicles (New York, 1954) [see 172.03].

The Convention covers the conditions under which aircraft or pleasure boats owned or rented by non-residents for private use can be admitted temporarily into the country of importation without payment of import duties and import taxes.

The main elements of the Convention are:

Chapter I: Definitions;
Chapter II: Temporary importation without payment of import duties and import taxes and free of import prohibitions and restrictions;
Chapter III: Issue of temporary importation papers;
Chapter IV: Particulars on temporary importation papers;
Chapter V: Conditions of temporary importation;
Chapter VI: Extension of validity and renewal of the temporary importation papers; and
Chapter VII: Regularization of temporary importation papers.

The Annexes provide samples of the following: "Carnet de passages en douane" for an aircraft and pleasure boats (Annexes 2 and 3 respectively), "Triptych" for pleasure boats (Annex 3), and "Model Certificate for the clearance of temporary importation papers undischarged, destroyed, lost or stolen" (Annex 5). Annex 4 contains both the conditions for the granting of an extension of validity of the "Carnet de passages en douane", and a model for it.

The Protocol of Signature, presented in the Annex, contains a number of declarations. The purpose of these declarations is mainly to recall that the Convention sets out minimum facilities and that contracting states are invited to be more liberal. The Protocol has the same force, effect and duration as the Convention itself of which it is considered to be an integral part.

L.A.

Access : CON (Art. 33)
Reserves : PAU (Art. 39)
Duration : MIN (Art. 36)
Deposit. : UN (Art. 45)
Language : Eng, Fre (Art. 45)

Reference : 319 UNTS – UKTS 1959/16 – UST 8/2 – JORF 26 Jan 60 – RTAF 1960/9

172.06 – CONVENTION ON THE TAXATION OF ROAD VEHICLES ENGAGED IN INTERNATIONAL PASSENGER TRANSPORT – ECE

Concluded : 14.12.1956, Geneva
In Force : 29.08.1962
Parties : 14

This Convention is designed to facilitate the transport of passengers and their baggage across frontiers (Art. 1-b). It explicitly excludes cabotage – that is, transport between two points when those are both situated within the same territory (Art. 3). The vehicles covered (Art. 1-a) are totally exempted from the taxes and charges levied on the circulation or possession of vehicles in the territory of the contracting parties to the Convention.

Because of the nature of the vehicles coming within the scope of the Convention – namely, vehicles involved in road transportation – this Convention potentially applies only to those countries which are members of the Economic Commission for Europe [see 181 A].

L.A.

Access : CON (Art. 4)
Reserves : PAU (Art. 10)
Duration : MIN (Art. 7)
Deposit. : UN (Art. 14)
Language : Eng, Fre

Reference : 436 UNTS – UKTS 1963/43

172.07 – STATUTES OF THE WORLD TOURISM ORGANIZATION – WTO

Concluded : 27.09.1970, Mexico
In Force : 02.01.1975
Parties : 111

The Statutes define the aims, structure and functioning of the WTO [see 172 A]. Switzerland, originally designated as the depositary, was later replaced by Spain.

The Statutes are complemented by an Annex on the Financing Rules.

L.A.

Access : ALS (Art. 5, 6, 7, 41)
Reserves : USP
Duration : USP
Deposit. : ES (Art. 37)
Language : Eng, Fre, Rus, Spa (Art. 39)

Reference : 985 UNTS – UST 27/2 – RTAF 1976/4

172.08 – INTERNATIONAL CONVENTION ON TRAVEL CONTRACTS – UNIDROIT

Concluded : 23.04.1970, Brussels
In Force : 24.02.1976
Parties : 7

The Convention concerns the conditions under which a contract is concluded, for an inclusive price, for a combination of services between a traveller and a travel organizer or intermediary.

The Convention defines the responsibilities of the parties to such contracts, the particulars to be included in the contract, the consequences of a breach of contract by any of the parties, the conditions under which the price may be increased, and the liability of the travel organizer or intermediary for any loss or damage caused to the traveller as a result of non-performance.

L.A.

Access : ALS (Art. 33)
Reserves : PAU (Art. 40)
Duration : USP
Deposit. : BG (Art. 43)
Language : Eng, Fre (Art. 43)

Reference : ILM 9:706

172.09 – CONVENTION CONCERNING WORKING CONDITIONS IN HOTELS, RESTAURANTS AND SIMILAR ESTABLISHMENTS – ILO

Concluded : 25.06.1991, Geneva
Parties : 0

The Convention lays down the principles for improving working conditions in hotels, restaurants and similar establishments. It includes a definition of the categories of establishments covered by the Convention (Art. 1) as well as a definition of the workers concerned (Art. 2). General principles and definitions are provided on hours worked (Art. 4), rest periods (Art. 4), annual leave with pay (Art. 5), and tipping (Art. 6).

A Recommendation, adopted at the same time as the Convention (i.e. during the 78th Session of the ILO General Conference in June 1991), contains general provisions for the working conditions in other related establishments which provide tourist services (Part I). It covers hours of work and rest periods (Part II) and training (Part III).

L.A.

Access : ILO (Art. 10)
Reserves : USP
Duration : USP
Deposit. : ILO (Art. 9)
Language : Eng, Fre (Art. 16)

1.8 Transport

1.8.0 Multimodal Transport

The development of transport and its associated economic activity has led to increased traffic and to increased crossings of national borders. This has called for international co-operation in many fields such as customs law, transport law and standardization [see also 1.1.2 and 1.5.2]. International transport regulations have been successively and independently developed for each mode of transport (road, rail, maritime, air and space transport) and according to specific geographical, economic and technical requirements. With modern transport techniques, there has been an even greater need to regulate multimodal transport.

180.01 – CONVENTION ON INTERNATIONAL MULTIMODAL TRANSPORT OF GOODS – UNCTAD

Concluded : 24.05.1980, Geneva
Parties : 6

Continual growth in international trade throughout the mid-twentieth century saw the increasing use of a combination of vessels and vehicles in the carriage of goods. Whilst specific conventions dealt with carriage by a particular mode of transport, little had been done to address the concerns voiced not only where goods were tran-shipped from one vessel to another but, more importantly, where it was envisaged that the carriage of goods would involve transport not only by sea but also by other means.

The frequent use of multimodal or combined transport of goods was subject to two principal problems. First, where goods are carried by a combination of modes of transport, does the shipper contract with one carrier or with each carrier responsible for their particular leg of the carriage? If with several, which liability regime is to govern disputes concerning loss of or damage to goods? This problem is rendered even more acute where the goods are shipped in containers.

Second, it soon became apparent that even if the contract was to be viewed as being merely between the shipper and one carrier who was responsible for arranging the other legs of the carriage, doubts still existed as to whether the same legal regime prevailed throughout the carriage of the goods.

It was out of a desire to determine certain rules relating to the carriage of goods by international multimodal transport contracts, including equitable provisions concerning the liability of multimodal transport operators, that UNCTAD adopted the Convention on International Multimodal Transport of Goods in 1980.

Scope: The Convention governs "international multimodal transport", which is defined as "the carriage of goods by a least two different modes of transport on the basis of a multimodal transport contract from a place in one country at which the goods are taken in charge by the multimodal transport operator, to a place designated for delivery in a different country" (Art. 1-1). However, it is a requirement that the place for the "taking in charge" or the "delivery" of the goods is located in a contracting state (Art. 2).

DETAILS OF THE AGREEMENT

The responsibility of the multimodal transport operator runs from the time he takes the goods in his charge to the time of their delivery (Art. 14). Once he has taken charge of the goods, the multimodal transport operator is required to issue a multimodal transport document which, at the option of the consignor, may be in a negotiable or non-negotiable form (Art. 5).

The Convention, which was inspired *inter alia* by the Hamburg Rules [see 183.20], places the liability for damage on the multimodal transport operator. Article 16 stipulates: "the multimodal transport operator shall be liable for loss resulting from loss of or damage to the goods, as well as from delay in delivery, if the ... goods were in this charge" – that is, from the moment the operator took them in charge to the moment of delivery. However, this is not the case if "the multimodal transport operator proves that he, his servants or agents or any other person ... took all measures that could reasonably be required to avoid the occurrence and its consequences".

Where liability under Article 16 is established, the multimodal transport operator is entitled to limit his liability "to an amount not exceeding 920 units of account per package or other shipping unit or 2.75 units of account per kilogramme of gross weight of the goods lost or damaged, whichever is the higher" (Art. 18). However, the right to limitation will be lost where it is "proved that the loss, damage or delay in delivery resulted from an act or omission of the multimodal transport operator done with intent to cause such loss, damage or delay or recklessly and with knowledge that such loss, damage or delay would probably result" (Art. 21).

It is to be noted that any stipulation in the multimodal transport contract or multimodal transport document "shall be null and void to the extent that it derogates, directly or indirectly, from the provisions of this Convention" (Art. 28).

RECENT DEVELOPMENTS

The Convention has not been without its critics since its adoption in May 1980, particularly in view of its incorporation of provisions enabling states to regulate and control both multimodal transport operations and operators (e.g. Art. 4), which it was felt effectively stymied the freedom of entrepreneurs.

As a consequence it was, hitherto, thought doubtful whether the Convention would ever enter into force; at present it has been ratified by only six out of a required 30 states. However, with the Hamburg Rules' entering into force on 20 November 1992, with which this Convention is closely aligned, the possibility of this Convention's entering into force has increased.

The commercial consequence of the Convention's entry into force will serve merely to endorse many of the commercial practices currently in operation; for example, the combined transport bills of lading developed by shipowners, the Multimodal Transport Operator Contract (MTO) proposed by the French transport commission, and the International Transport Operator Contract (ITO) developed by the Institute of International Transport Law (IDIT) in Rouen.

In 1991, under the auspices of the International Chamber of Commerce [see 300 D] and UNCTAD [see 111 B], new regulations were developed for multimodal transport; they will be called UNCTAD/ICC Rules Relating to Multimodal Transport Documents. It is proposed that these Rules will steadily replace the ICC Rules of 1975 relating to combined transport documents, the latter having since proved inadequate following recent developments in the carriage of goods.

Patricia Ford and IDIT, Barthélémy Mercadal

Access : ASO (Art. 34)
Reserves : PRO (Art. 35)
Duration : USP
Deposit. : UN (Art. 33)
Language : Ara, Chi, Eng, Fre, Rus, Spa

Reference : UN Doc. TD/MT/CONF/16 – ULR 1980/2 – ILM 19:938

180.02 – UNITED NATIONS CONVENTION ON THE LIABILITY OF OPERATORS OF TRANSPORT TERMINALS IN INTERNATIONAL TRADE – UNCITRAL

Concluded : 19.04.1991, Vienna
Parties : 0

The Convention establishes uniform rules concerning liability for the loss of, damage to, or delay in handing over goods while they are in the charge of operators of transport terminals and are not covered by the laws of carriage arising out of conventions applicable to the various modes of transport.

Scope: The Convention applies to transport-related services performed in relation to goods which are involved in international carriage when the transport-related services are performed by an operator whose place of business is located in a state party, or when the transport-related services are performed in a state party, or when according to the rules of private international law the transport-related services are governed by the law of a state party (Art. 2).

DETAILS OF THE CONVENTION

The operator is liable for loss if the occurrence which caused the loss, damage, or delay took place during the time he has taken the goods in charge until the time he has handed them over to, or has placed them at the disposal of, the person entitled to take delivery of them (Art. 3). He may avoid being liable if he proves that he or his agents took all measures that could reasonably be required to avoid the occurrence and its consequences (Art. 5).

His liability resulting from loss of or damage to goods may be financially limited to an amount not exceeding SDR 8.33 per kilogram of gross weight of the goods lost or damaged (Art. 6), or SDR 2.75 in the case of goods handed over after carriage by sea or by inland waters. These limits of liability may be extended if the operator agrees to it (Art. 6-4). The operator may lose the benefit of the limitation of liability if it is proved that the loss, damage or delay resulted from an act or omission of the operator with the intent to cause such loss, damage or delay, or recklessly and with knowledge that such loss, damage or delay would probably result (Art. 8).

The Convention sets time limits for the notification of loss or damages (Art. 11) and actions are time-barred unless brought within two years (Art. 12).

Article 15 provides that the "... Convention does not modify any rights or duties which may arise under an international convention relating to the international carriage of goods which is binding on a State which is a Party to this Convention or under any law of such State giving effect to a convention relating to the international carriage of goods". This Article covers for instance the Hague Rules and the Hamburg Rules [see 183.01 and 183.20].

The Convention will enter into force after the deposit of the fifth instrument of acceptance.

IDIT, Barthélémy Mercadal

Access : ALS (Art. 18)
Reserves : PRO (Art. 21)
Duration : USP
Deposit. : UN (Art. 17)
Language : Ara, Chi, Eng, Fre, Rus, Spa

Reference : ILM 30:1503

1.8.1 Road Transport

After the Second World War many barriers prevented countries from carrying goods, thereby impeding the development of international trade. The need to improve road infrastructure, to standardize the conditions governing the contract of carriage and to eliminate regulatory barriers to trade were well-recognized.

This situation led to the establishment of intergovernmental bodies which initiated multilateral agreements (notably, the Inland Transport Committee of the United Nations Economic Commission for Europe (ECE) [see 181 A]) and non-governmental organizations (mainly the International Road Transport Union (IRU) [see 181 B] and the International Road Federation (IRF) [see 181 C]). The European Conference of Ministers of Transport (ECMT) has also played an important role within Europe and has developed principles which were incorporated into world-wide agreements.

Article 5 of the General Agreement on Tariffs and Trade (GATT) [see 111.01] provided for the freedom of transit for goods (including baggage), vessels and other means of transport, with the exception of aircraft. Some conventions have been adopted to facilitate transit [see 1.1.2] and the IRU assists in their implementation. The GATT agreement does not apply to the transport of passengers. The facilitation of the crossing of borders by travellers has largely been dealt with in the conventions on touring [see 1.7.2].

Similar to the legal regimes applicable to other means of transport, the law for the contract of carriage of goods by road and for the carriage of passengers and luggage by road has been unified through multilateral conventions. These conventions are primarily concerned with certain aspects of private law [see also section 3] and with procedures such as the making of the contract of carriage, the transport document, the carrier's liability for loss of or damage to the goods and their delay in delivery, the right to sue and to be sued, and jurisdiction. These conventions also provide for the carrier's strict liability, limited by a ceiling on the amount.

Specific provisions regulate the transport of dangerous goods (e.g. the European Agreement Concerning the International Carriage of Dangerous Goods by Road (ADR) of 1967, which follows the UN Recommendations for the Transport of Dangerous Goods).

Bernard Colas

SELECTED BIBLIOGRAPHY

Clarke, M.A., *International Carriage of Goods by Road: CMR*, 2nd ed., London: Sweet and Maxwell, 1991.
Hill, D.J. and A.D. Messent, *CMR: Contracts for the International Carriage of Goods by Road*, London: Lloyd's of London Press, 1984.
Theunis, Jan, *International Carriage of Goods by Road*, London: Lloyd's of London Press, 1987.

181 A – UNITED NATIONS ECONOMIC COMMISSION FOR EUROPE (ECE)

The United Nations Economic Commission for Europe (ECE) is one of the five regional commissions of the United Nations. The ECE region comprises 44 member countries covering the whole of Europe, North America and Israel – highly industrialized countries with a long tradition of market economy and including countries which only recently abandoned central planning and are now attempting their integration into the world economy. The fundamental changes evolving in countries of Central and Eastern Europe provide an important role for the ECE in facilitating the transition of their economies; its role is based upon its experience in promoting dialogue and co-operation between countries of different levels of economic development. This experience makes the ECE also a valuable partner for other regions of the world.

Established in 1947 by the Economic and Social Council of the United Nations (ECOSOC) [see 001 A], the Commission's primary objective in its initial phase was to provide assistance in the reconstruction of war-devastated Europe. Since then, the ECE has become a dynamic and indispensable instrument touching on virtually all areas of economic activity, creating a climate of dialogue and co-operation between its member countries.

As an integral part of the UN, the ECE has contributed to the strengthening of economic relations elsewhere in the world through co-operation with its four sister commissions in other regions, with other UN agencies and with non-governmental organizations, and by participating in global projects aimed at solving the global problems of sustainable development.

ACTIVITIES

In 1990, the Commission laid down two guiding principles to be applied for all ECE activities: the assistance to countries of central and eastern Europe in transition from centrally planned to market economies, and sustainable development.

With a view to adapting its work programme to the changing conditions in Europe, five priorities were designated by the Commission in 1990: the environment, trade facilitation, transport, statistics and economic analysis. Apart from these main areas of co-operation, ECE's activities cover a wide spectrum, ranging from general economic policy issues to areas of practical significance directly influencing aspects of everyday life such as energy, industry, technology, human settlements, agriculture and forestry.

A large number of legally binding multilateral instruments have been elaborated within the framework of the ECE in the areas of trade facilitation, customs, transport, and protection of the environment, as well as non-legally binding recommendations such as regional strategy policy recommendations, codes of conduct and documents containing recommendations for international application.

The work of the ECE is closely linked to the process created by the Conference on Security and Co-operation in Europe (CSCE). The Commission takes up the pertinent provisions and recommendations contained in "Basket Two" of the Helsinki Final Act and the subsequent CSCE documents up to the Charter of Paris for a New Europe (1990). The ECE serves as the key implementing instrument for CSCE in the fields of economics, statistics, science and technology, and the environment.

STRUCTURE

The ECE has its headquarters at the Palais des Nations in Geneva. Its staff, which forms part of the UN Secretariat, comprises about 200 and is headed by an **Executive Secretary** with the rank of Under-Secretary-General of the UN.

The Commission meets anually to review its activities of the previous year, to provide policy guidance and to chart the future of its work. The overall policies and work programmes formulated by the Commission are carried out by a network of 15 specialized **Subsidiary Bodies** which meet periodically throughout the year (viz. the committees on: Agricultural Problems; the Chemical Industry; Coal; Electrical Power; Gas; Housing, Building, and Planning; Inland Transport; Steel; Timber; the Development of Trade; and Water; and the Conference of European Statisticians (which works jointly with the Statistical Commission of ECOSOC); the Senior Advisers to ECE Governments on Science and Technology; the Senior Advisers to ECE Governments on Environmental Problems; and Senior Economic Advisers to ECE Governments).

The activities of the Inland Transport Committee and the Committee on the Development of Trade are particularly relevant in the present context. The latter helped promote East-West trade during the Cold War by establishing a multilateral system of payments, and by drawing up standard contracts and general conditions of sale for such products and services as the sale of mechanical and electrical equipment, timber, solid combustibles, dried fruits, potatoes, and the transfer of know-how.

The Inland Transport Committee establishes common standards for motor vehicles and spare parts, road signs and signals, railway equipment, inland water transport, national registration certificates and insurance documents, customs documents, and so on. The committee's standardization efforts are the result of agreement by the parties to over 40 conventions since 1947.

CO-OPERATION

The ECE collaborates with various other UN bodies (e.g. the FAO [see 131 A], ILO [see 141 A], UNEP [see 410 A] and the Statistical Commission of ECOSOC [see 001 A]), intergovernmental organizations (e.g. OCTI, ECMT, EC, OECD), and non-governmental organizations with status as consultative bodies of ECOSOC (e.g. IRF, IRU).

PUBLICATIONS

The ECE publishes numerous statistical and economic surveys and periodicals related to Europe, including the ECE annual report to ECOSOC; the *ECE Highlights* (quarterly); the *Economic Survey of Europe* (annual); the *Economic Bulletin for Europe* (quarterly); and the Annual Bulletin on Trade in Chemical Products.

Bernard Colas

ADDRESS

Palais des Nations, CH-1211 Geneva 10, Switzerland
T. (41 22) 917 1234, Fx. (41 22) 917 0039

SELECTED BIBLIOGRAPHY

ECE, *Four Decades of the Economic Commission for Europe*, Geneva: United Nations, 1987.

181 B – INTERNATIONAL ROAD TRANSPORT UNION (IRU)

The International Road Transport Union is an international federation of national road transport associations. It represents the commercial operators of road vehicles for hire or reward (i.e. hauliers); for own account (i.e. freight transport carried out as an ancillary function to manufacturing or trading activities); and, for collective passenger transport (e.g. buses, coaches and taxis). Based in Switzerland, the Union is governed by the Swiss law.

The IRU's objective is to contribute to the promotion and prosperity, in all countries, of domestic and international road transport. More specifically, the IRU works for the unification and simplification of regulations and practices relating to road traffic, customs formalities, transport contracts, and road safety. As part of this work, it manages the TIR customs system [see 112.09 and 112.20]. Under this system, lorries sealed by customs officials can cross a number of borders without being required to unload goods at each border for inspection and to pay a large sum as a customs guarantee.

STRUCTURE

The organs of the IRU are: The **Council of Direction** (General Assembly), which acts as the supreme authority of the IRU, and three **Sections** which are in turn responsible for Passenger Transport, Professional Goods Transport (i.e. transport for hire or reward), and Own Account Transport. The Sections decide upon the action required to achieve the aims pursued by the IRU. The executive organ of the Council of Direction is the **Presidential Executive** (Board of Directors) composed of nine members (three members from each Section). Its membership comprises the IRU President, the three Section Presidents who are *ex officio* Vice-Presidents of the IRU, and five other members. They are assisted by study commissions and working groups.

FUNDING

The financial resources of the IRU come from members' annual subscriptions and other revenues.

CO-OPERATION

The IRU has consultative status with ECOSOC and with the Council of Europe. It has liaison committees and a permanent delegation to the European Communities in Brussels. It also co-operates with many IGOs such as the ILO [141 A] (with regard to social matters and professional training), UNCTAD [see 111 B], ISO [see 152 C], UNIDROIT [see 300 B], the CCC [see 112 A], WTO [see 172 A], the World Bank [see 221 A], the OECD, and ECMT (European Conference of Ministers of Transport). It liaises closely with professional international organizations in the transport field in order to encourage a common approach to problems of mutual interest at all levels.

These organizations include: the International Chamber of Commerce (ICC) [see 300 D], the International Road Federation (IRF) [see 181 C], the International Air Transport Association (IATA) [see 184 B], the Universal Federation of Travel Agents Associations (UFTAA).

The IRU is in constant dialogue with national member organizations as well as with the commercial vehicle manufacturers. Most of these manufacturers are associate members of the IRU: the latter may be invited to sit on various commissions without voting rights but with consultative status (e.g. the Technical Commission). The IRU also advises individual governments on problems of transport policy.

PUBLICATIONS

Publications of the IRU include the *Handbook of International Road Transport*.

B.C.

ADDRESS

Centre International, 3 rue de Varembé, PO.Box: 44, CH-1211 Geneva 20, Switzerland
T. (41 22) 734 1330, Fx. (41 22) 733 0660

181 C – INTERNATIONAL ROAD FEDERATION (IRF)

The International Road Federation is a non-governmental, non-profit-making association for the promotion of road infrastructure and road transport, both nationally and internationally.

The IRF was founded in Washington, DC, London, and Paris soon after the Second World War (between 1948 and 1952). These three offices divided their responsibilities regionally: the Washington, DC office being responsible for North and South America, and the Pacific rim; the London office for the Commonwealth; and the Paris office for the French-speaking countries, particularly in Africa, and for continental Europe and the Middle East.

In 1964, the London and Paris offices were consolidated and transferred to Geneva in the form of an association governed by Swiss law. The IRF is currently organized into two offices, in Washington, DC and Geneva, both of which collaborate closely under the supervision of a single international executive committee, the **World Executive Committee**.

The IRF's objectives are the following: to promote the image of road transport infrastructure among the general public and international officials; to promote the planning, construction and maintenance of urban and rural roads; and to promote the development and exchange of information and ideas relating to the economics of road transport, and its technical, sociological and environmental aspects.

To do this, the IRF relies on national road federations, which it helps to set up and which it federates. It relies primarily on international businesses and companies which adhere to its statutes (consulting firms, construction companies, companies running and operating transport infrastructures, fuel, equipment, etc.). Finally, the IRF relies on national administrations with which it is in constant contact.

STRUCTURE

The IRF is composed of active members (national federations and associations, as well as businesses and companies subscribing to the organization), affiliated members who do not have voting rights, and honorary members.

Its bodies are: the **General Assembly** of active members, a **Board of Directors** composed of 36 members, an **Executive Committee** which supervises the workings of the **General Secretariat**, and various Special Committees for the purpose of studying specific problems – for example, the construction and maintenance of roads and the planning and execution of the Single European Act of 1986.

FUNDING

Full members of the IRF pay annual dues, the level of which is determined individually on the basis of each member's turnover. Minimum annual dues are presently set at 3,500 Swiss francs.

CO-OPERATION

The IRF has been granted consultative status to the UN (Cat. B) and various regional commissions including: the Economic Commissions for Europe and Africa, and the Economic and Social Commission for West Asia. It has also been granted consultative status (Cat. B) by the Council of Europe and its supplementary bodies, including the Parliamentary Conference, and the Commission for Territorial Settlement and Local Government.

In addition, the IRF is in permanent contact with the European Conference of Ministers of Transport (ECMT). It is also consulted regularly by the Commission of the European Communities, and more specifically by its Directorate-General for Transport (DGT or DG VII).

The IRF collaborates with the World Bank [see 221 A], as well as with the African Development Bank, the European Investment Bank, and the European Development Fund.

The IRF promotes road transport through a variety of means. It organizes conferences and conventions, including a world convention every four years and regional conventions and symposiums on diverse subjects at regular intervals.

PUBLICATIONS

These include the annual publication of *World Road Statistics*, the bi-monthly *World Highways*, and brochures on economic and technical matters (e.g. *Road Maintenance in Developing Countries*).

B.C.

ADDRESS

63 rue de Lausanne, CH-1202 Geneva, Switzerland
T. (41 22) 731 7150, Fx. (41 22) 731 7158

181.01 – CONSTITUTION OF THE INTERNATIONAL ROAD TRANSPORT UNION – IRU

Adopted : 23.03.1948, Geneva

The IRU Constitution was adopted by the General Assembly in 1948. Representatives from the United Nations Economic Commission for Europe, the International Committee on Refugees (now the International Refugees Organization), the Swiss Government, the General Committee of the AIT/FIA, the International Chamber of Commerce, and the International Institute for the Unification of Private Law, were invited to attend this session of the General Assembly. The result was a reorganization of the BITAC (International Bureau of Motor Coach and Lorry Operators) into a confederation of national road transport federations, associations, and organizations and undertakings.

The organization's first members were from Belgium, Denmark, France, the Netherlands, Norway, and the United Kingdom.

B.C.

Access : ENT
Language : Eng, Fre

181.02 – CONVENTION ON THE CONTRACT FOR THE INTERNATIONAL CARRIAGE OF GOODS BY ROAD – ECE

Concluded : 19.05.1956, Geneva
In Force : 02.07.1961
Parties : 25

The objective of this Convention signed in Geneva is to standardize the conditions governing the contract for the international carriage of goods by road. It completes the transport law standardization efforts begun in 1890 by the Berne Convention on the international transport of goods by rail, followed by the adoption of the Brussels Convention of 1924 governing the maritime transport of goods under bills of lading [see 183.01], and the Warsaw Convention of 1929 on air transport [see 184.01].

Scope: The Geneva Convention of 1956, known usually by its acronym "CMR", applies "to every contract for the carriage of goods by road in vehicles for reward, when the place of taking over of the goods and the place designated for delivery, as specified in the contract, are situated in two different countries, of which at least one is a contracting country" (Art. 1-1). The Convention defines "vehicles" as motor vehicles, articulated vehicles, trailers and semi-trailers as defined in Article 4 of the Convention on Road Traffic of 19 September 1949 (Art. 1-2).

The Convention does not apply to carriage performed under the terms of any international postal convention, funeral consignments, or furniture removal (Art. 1-4).

The Convention applies "irrespective of the place of residence and the nationality of the parties" (Art. 1-1) and irrespective of whether carriage is carried out by states or by governmental institutions or organizations (Art 1-3).

Taking into account the development of combined transport, the CMR also governs:

- all transport where "the vehicle containing the goods is carried over part of the journey by sea, rail, inland waterways or air ... where the goods are not unloaded from the vehicle" (Art. 2) and;
- all transport carried out by successive road carriers governed by a single contract.

DETAILS OF THE CONVENTION

Evidence of the Contract of Carriage. "The contract of carriage shall be confirmed by the making out of a consignment note," (Art. 4) which "shall be *prima facie* evidence of the making of the contract of carriage, the conditions of the contract and the receipt of the goods by carrier" (Art. 9-1). Nevertheless, the Geneva Convention did not make this a condition for implementation of the contract of carriage, and "the absence, irregularity or loss of the consignment note shall not affect the existence or the validity of the contract of carriage which shall remain subject to the provisions of the Convention."

Liability. Following, sometimes word for word, the international convention for the transport of goods by rail (CIM) (Berne, 1890) [see 182.05], the CMR places the onus of liability on the carrier who "shall be liable for the total or partial loss of the goods and for damage thereto occurring between the time when he takes over the goods and the time of delivery, as well as for any delay in delivery" (Art. 17-1).

Nevertheless, the carrier will be relieved of liability if, on the one hand, "the loss, damage or delay was caused by the wrongful act or neglect of the claimant, by the instructions of the claimant given otherwise than as the result of a wrongful act or neglect on the part of the carrier, by inherent vice of the goods or through circumstances which the carrier could not avoid and the consequences of which he was unable to prevent" (Art. 17-2); or on the other hand, if the carrier "establishes that the circumstances of the case, the loss or damage, could be attributed to one or more of the special risks referred to in Article 17-4 of the Convention" (Art. 18-2).

The Convention, however, adds "the carrier shall not be entitled to avail himself of the provisions of this chapter which exclude or limit his liability or which shift the burden of proof if the damage was caused by his wilful misconduct or by such default on his part as, in accordance with the law of the court or tribunal seized of the case, is considered as equivalent to wilful misconduct" (Art. 29-1).

Compensation for Damage. Except in the cases of a declaration of value of goods (Art. 24) or the declaration of a special interest in delivery by the sender (Art. 26), compensation in respect of total or partial loss of goods is calculated according to the commodity exchange price, or if there is no such price, according to the current market price, at the place and time at which they were accepted for carriage (Art. 23). Compensation shall not, however, exceed 25 francs (gold franc weighing 10/31 of a gram, of millesimal fineness 900) per kilogram of gross weight short (Art. 23-3). In the case of delay, compensation should not exceed the carriage charges (Art. 23-5). All further damages are excluded (Art. 23-4).

The 1978 amending Protocol substituted the Special Drawing Right for the Gold franc (Art. 23-3 of the modified CMR).

IDIT, Barthélémy Mercadal

Access	: CON (Art. 42)
Reserves	: INP (Art. 48, 46)
Duration	: MIN (Art. 45)
Deposit.	: UN (Art. 51)
Language	: Eng, Fre

Modific. : Geneva 05.07.78 (28.12.80)

Reference : 399 UNTS – ULR 1978/1 – UKTS 1967/90 – JORF 12 Jul 61 – RTAF 1961/27

181.03 – CONVENTION ON THE TAXATION OF ROAD VEHICLES ENGAGED IN INTERNATIONAL GOODS TRANSPORT – ECE

Concluded : 14.12.1956, Geneva
In Force : 29.08.1962
Parties : 14

This Convention, which aims to facilitate the international transport of goods by road, establishes a special tax system for vehicles used to this end.

Article 2 of the Convention exempts vehicles registered in the territory of one of the contracting parties and temporarily imported in the course of international goods transport into the territory of another contracting party, from paying taxes and charges levied on the circulation or possession of vehicles in the territory of that contracting party. The conditions of this exemption are specified in Article 3:

- the exemption will be granted as long as the conditions laid down in the customs regulations and the regulations in force for the authorization of the transport concerned in the country of admission are fulfilled (Art. 3-1); and
- each contracting party may exclude from the benefit of this exemption any vehicle when the points of departure and of destination are both situated within its territory (Art. 3-2).

Bernard Colas

Access : CON (Art. 4)
Reserves : PAU (Art. 10)
Duration : MIN (Art. 7)
Deposit. : UN (Art. 14)
Language : Eng, Fre

Reference : 436 UNTS – UKTS 1969/112

181.04 – AGREEMENT CONCERNING THE ADOPTION OF UNIFORM CONDITIONS OF APPROVAL AND RECIPROCAL RECOGNITION OF APPROVAL FOR MOTOR VEHICLE EQUIPMENT AND PARTS – ECE

Concluded : 20.03.1958, Geneva
In Force : 20.06.1959
Parties : 20

Concluded under the auspices of the Inland Transport Committee of the ECE, the Agreement sets legal guidelines to establish uniform conditions for the approval of motor vehicle equipment and parts and for approval markings, and it requires the parties to recognize one another's approvals granted in accordance with those conditions.

Experience has shown that the Agreement has contributed to the removal of trade barriers, improvement of safety and the reduction of harmful effects of motor vehicles on the environment.

Regulations are annexed to the Agreement and make up a body of international requirements governing the approval of motor vehicles equipment and parts. They are adopted according to the following procedure. If the competent authorities of at least two of the contracting parties agree to uniform conditions of approval for motor vehicle equipment and parts, they draw up a draft Regulation for this equipment and these parts and communicate it to the UN Secretary-General indicating the date on which they propose it should enter into force as a Regulation annexed to the Agreement. The UN Secretary-General communicates to the other contracting parties the said draft, which then enters into force for all contracting parties which have informed the Secretary-General of their acceptance.

These Regulations may be amended under proposals from a contracting party applying a regulation. The text of any such proposed amendment shall be transmitted to the UN Secretary-General who shall transmit it to the other contracting parties. The amendment shall be deemed to have been accepted unless, within a period of three months following this notification, a contracting party applying the Regulation has expressed an objection. If the amendment is deemed to have been accepted, it enters into force at the end of a further period of two months.

B.C.

Access : CON (Art. 6)
Reserves : PAU (Art. 11)
Duration : USP
Deposit. : UN (Art. 15)
Language : Eng, Fre

Modific. : Regulations no. 1 to 90 from 1960 to 1993

Reference : 335, 609 UNTS – RTAF 1960/10

181.05 – STATUTES OF THE INTERNATIONAL ROAD FEDERATION – IRF

Adopted : 02.12.1964, IRF Res.

These Statutes were approved by the statutory meeting of 2 December 1964, and were modified in 1971.

Access : ENT
Language : Eng, Fre, Ger

Modific. : GA Dec. 02.04.71 (02.04.71);

181.06 – CONVENTION ON THE CONTRACT FOR THE INTERNATIONAL CARRIAGE OF PASSENGERS AND LUGGAGE BY ROAD – ECE

Concluded : 01.03.1973, Geneva
Parties : 2

The Convention was drafted by the Road Transport Working Group of the Inland Transport Committee of the ECE at its 45th, 48th, 49th, and 52nd special sessions, and was approved by the ECE's Inland Transport Committee [see 181 A]. The Convention will begin its implementation 90 days after five states have ratified it (Art. 25).

The objective of the Convention is to standardize the conditions governing the contract for the international carriage of passengers and luggage by road.

Scope: The Convention applies "to every contract for the carriage of passengers and, where appropriate, of their luggage in vehicles by road when the contract provides that the carriage shall take place in the territory of more than one State and that the place of departure or the place of destination, or both of these places, shall be situated on the territory of a Contracting State, irrespective of the place of residence and the nationality of the parties" (Art. 1-1).

DETAILS OF THE CONVENTION

Where passengers are carried, the carrier shall issue an individual or a collective ticket, on which the name and address of the carrier must appear, as well as a statement that the contract is subject to the Convention (Art. 5). The carrier may, and at the request of the passenger shall, issue a luggage registration voucher indicating the number and nature of the pieces of luggage handed over to him (Art. 8).

The carrier is liable for loss or damage or bodily or mental injury to passengers or their luggage, unless the accident was unavoidable or the fault of the passenger. He is not, however, liable to pay damages exceeding SDR 83,333 for each victim (1978 Protocol), or SDR 166.67 for each piece of luggage, nor SDR 666.67 for each passenger (1978 Protocol). This limit is not applicable in the case of wilful misconduct or gross negligence by the carrier and those for whom the carrier is responsible.

Any stipulation which directly or indirectly derogates from the provisions of the Convention are null and void. The period of limitation for actions arising out of the death, wounding, or other bodily or mental injury to a passenger is three years; in all other cases, the period of limitation is one year. Such legal proceedings can take place where the defendant has his principal place of business, is habitually resident or has the place of business through which the contract of carriage was made; or the place where the loss or damage occurred; or the place of departure or of destination of the carriage.

B.C.

Access : CON (Art. 24)
Reserves : PAU (Art. 33)
Duration : MIN (Art. 27)
Deposit. : UN (Art. 36)
Language : Eng, Fre, Rus

Modific. : Protocol 05.07.78 (-)

Reference : UN Doc. ECE/TRANS/2, ECE/TRANS/35 – ULR 1978/1

181.07 – CONVENTION ON CIVIL LIABILITY FOR DAMAGE CAUSED DURING CARRIAGE OF DANGEROUS GOODS BY ROAD, RAIL AND INLAND NAVIGATION VESSELS (CRTD) – ECE

Concluded : 10.10.1989, Geneva
Parties : 0

Although there has been increasing adherence to international technical standards aimed at the safety of dangerous goods during their carriage, accidents could not be ruled out. The potential damage that could ensue following an incident was a major concern particularly in view of the steady increase in the carriage of such goods by road, rail and/or inland navigation vessels. As a remedial measure, the Convention establishes a uniform set of rules aiming to provide adequate and speedy compensation for damage caused during the carriage of dangerous goods by road, rail and inland navigation vessels.

The Convention was adopted at the conclusion of the 51st (extraordinary) session of the Inland Transport Committee of the Economic Commission for Europe of the UN [see 181 A]. A draft text prepared by a UNIDROIT committee [see 300 B] of governmental experts formed the basis of their deliberations.

The Convention applies specifically to claims arising from damage caused during the carriage of dangerous goods by road, rail or inland navigation, save where the claim arises out of any contract for the carriage of goods or passengers (Art. 3). However, it is a requirement that the damage is sustained in the territory of a state party or is caused by an incident occurring in that state party, or, arises as a consequence of preventive measures, wherever taken, to prevent or minimize such damage (Art. 2).

"Dangerous goods" is defined as "any substance or article which is either listed in the classes, or covered by the collective heading of the classes of the European Agreement concerning the International Carriage of Dangerous Goods by Road (ADR) or is subject to the provisions of that Agreement" (Art. 1). "Damage" may *inter alia* be in respect of loss of life or personal injury on board or outside the vehicle carrying the dangerous goods where the goods caused the loss of life or personal injury, or loss of or damage to property (Art. 1).

DETAILS OF THE CONVENTION

Save where the damage arises *inter alia* as a result of an act of war, or was wholly caused by the act or omission of a third party with intent to cause such damage, the carrier at the time of the incident is to be liable for the damage caused by any dangerous goods during their carriage by road, rail or inland navigation (Art. 5). Where the dangerous goods have been loaded or unloaded from the vehicle under the sole responsibility of a person other than the carrier, his servants or agents, and the carrier is able to disclose the identity of that other person, that other person is to be liable for damage caused by such goods during that period of loading or unloading (Art. 6). It is to be noted that carriers may be jointly or severally liable where more than one carrier is involved in an incident.

A carrier will not be entitled to limit his liability where it is proved that the damage resulted from his personal act or omission or an act or omission of his servants or agents committed with the intention of causing such damage or recklessly and with knowledge that such damage would probably result (Art. 10). With respect to the servants or agents, a claimant will need to prove that the servants and/or agents were acting within the scope of their employment.

Where a carrier is entitled to limit his liability, he may do so as follows:

(i) for a road or rail carrier:
  (a) with respect to claims for loss of life or personal injury: 18 million units of account;
  (b) with respect to any other claim: 12 million units of account;

(ii) for a carrier by inland navigation:
  (a) with respect to claims for loss of life or personal injury: 8 million units of account;
  (b) with respect to any other claims: 7 million units of account (Art. 9).

The "unit of account" referred to is the Special Drawing Right as defined by the International Monetary Fund [see 211 A] (Art. 12). Article 11 specifies that a carrier may constitute a limitation fund in the amounts applicable to him, together with interest thereon from the date of the incident until the date of the constitution of the fund. The fund is to be available only for the payment of claims in respect of which limitation of liability may be involved under the CRTD Convention.

A claim for compensation must be brought within three years from the date the person suffering the damage knew or ought reasonably to have known of the damage and of the identity of the carrier (Art. 18-1). In no case, however, will it be possible to bring an action ten years from the date of the incident which caused the damage. Article 19 stipulates the place where such an action for compensation may be commenced.

Patricia Ford

Access : ALS (Art. 22)
Reserves : CON (Art. 24, 25)
Duration : USP
Deposit. : UN (Art. 31)
Language : Eng, Fre, Rus

Reference : UN Doc. ECE/TRANS/79

1.8.2 Rail Transport

The invention of the steam engine had a revolutionary effect in the field of inland transport. The barrier of distance was greatly reduced by this new source of propulsion, and this contributed significantly to the growth in trade. With the consequent linkage of railway tracks between countries, it became important to establish international regulations. The regulations which have developed deal mainly with the contract of carriage, the standardization of railway equipment and the facilitation of border crossings.

The contract of carriage is today covered by two basic agreements: the CIM and the CIV [see 182.05]. The first CIM entered into force in 1893. Like the CIV, signed in 1928, the CIM are uniform rules for the making and execution of the contract for international carriage. In a multilateral framework, both conventions provide rail enterprises and users with the legal security which is necessary to their international relations by allowing direct international transport, with the help of a unique contract of carriage, under a uniform legal regime. In response to changing needs, the International Organization for International Carriage by Rail (OTIF) [see 182 B] periodically ensures the updating of provisions of the CIV and the CIM. It is in that context that it created specific regulations for the international rail transport of dangerous goods.

To run these international transport systems, it was important to standardize technical specifications of railway equipment such as rolling stock, track and structures, and motive power. Competence in the area of standardization lies with both the International Conference for Railway Technical Unity (UT) [see 182 A] and the International Union of Railways (UIC) [see 182 C].

The facilitation of the crossing of frontiers with regard for instance to customs formalities is included in this section [see also 1.1.2 and 1.7.2].

Alain Leroux

182 A – INTERNATIONAL CONFERENCE FOR RAILWAY TECHNICAL UNITY (UT)

At the end of the nineteenth century the Swiss, who were on the verge of becoming a transit hub for European railway transportation, raised at the international level a problem which had previously been dealt with by individual railway companies – namely, that of eliminating technical disparities between Europe's different railway networks.

This initiative, headed by the Swiss Federal Council, led to the establishment of the Railway Technical Unity Convention (UT) (Berne, 1882). It is the oldest intergovernmental agreement on the management of the international transit of railway equipment. The Agreement was revised twice, in 1935 and in 1938, then replaced, in 1968/1970, by a *de facto* arrangement laid out in a working document: the International Agreement on Railway Technical Unity [see 182.01]. In order to facilitate international transit and to develop commercial relations between nations, the Agreement on Railway Technical Unity established technical standards for all equipment to be used for international railway traffic.

In 1982, the members of the UT met in Berne to celebrate the centenary of the Agreement. There they adopted a resolution recognizing the importance of continued international collaboration at the intergovernmental level, and the necessity of maintaining the Agreement on Railway Technical Unity, while adapting it to the continuing evolution in railway technology.

MEMBERSHIP AND STRUCTURE

Nineteen European nations (at May 1993) are members of the UT and these members together make up the International Union of Railway Technical Unity. Its organs are conferences, committees, and the **Managing Secretariat**. As the UT has no permanent institutional structure, the Swiss Federal Transportation Office has taken over the tasks of Managing Secretariat. Under the mandate granted to it, the Federal Transportation Office manages the daily affairs of the UT, collects information of importance to the Union, and disseminates it to the member states.

Alain Leroux

ADDRESS

Office Fédéral Suisse des Transports, Bundeshaus Nord, CH-3001 Berne, Switzerland
T. (41 31) 615 736, Fx. (41 31) 615 595

182 B – INTERGOVERNMENTAL ORGANIZATION FOR INTERNATIONAL CARRIAGE BY RAIL (OTIF)

The OTIF was formally created in 1985. Since then, the Central Bureau for International Transportation (OCTI), which had previously been the secretariat of an International Union, has become the permanent secretariat of the OTIF. At the first General Assembly of the OTIF, the Organization noted that it had inherited control over the Union's property, assets, duties and liabilities which came from the Conventions CIM-CIV (International Convention Concerning the Carriage of Goods by Rail (CIM) and International Convention Concerning the Carriage of Passengers and Luggage by Rail (CIV)).

The Union had come into existence in Berne on 14 October 1890, in the wake of the efforts conducted within the first International Conference for the Transportation of Goods by Railway. The Union's responsibilities were increased with the conclusion of the International Convention on Railway Transportation of Passengers and Baggage (CIV) on 23 October 1924.

After being revised in Berne, a new CIM-CIV Convention was implemented on 1 January 1975. An additional CIV Convention, relating to railway responsibility in the event of death or injury to passengers, became effective on 1 January 1973.

On 9 May 1980, the Eighth Revision Conference of the CIM-CIV ended with the signature of a new Convention on International Railway Transportation (COTIF), to which a protocol on privileges and immunities was added. On 1 May 1985, implementation of the new COTIF Convention began, replacing the CIM-CIV Convention as well as the additional CIV Convention. This was intended as a fundamental revision, designed to separate within the COTIF institutional functions from those relating to transport law. These are set out in the annexes of the COTIF: Annex A deals with the uniform regulations of the CIV, while Annex B deals with the uniform regulations of the CIM. They were last modified with the 1990 Protocol [see 182.05].

STRUCTURE

The **General Assembly** is comprised of the 36 member states (each state having one vote) which ordinarily convenes every five years at the request of the Central Office. The Assembly essentially continues in the role of a Review Conference, as well as other diplomatic conferences.

The **Administrative Committee** is a smaller body, composed of 12 member states elected every five years by the General Assembly on the basis of equitable geographic distribution and according to the amount of the annual contribution. This Committee convenes behind closed doors twice a year. It is entrusted in particular with making regulations to govern the organization and functioning of the Central Office and approving the Organization's programme of work, budget, annual report and annual accounts. Switzerland holds a special juridical position beyond its role as the headquarters and depositary of the Agreement: it has the right to a permanent seat on the Committee, the right to present candidates for the positions of Director-General and Vice-Director-General of the Central Office for International Carriage by Rail (OCTI), and, finally, the Swiss finance federal department supervises the OCTI's accounts.

The **Central Office for International Carriage by Rail** (OCTI) acts as the permanent secretariat of the OTIF. It carries out the decisions of the COTIF and oversees their development by adapting international railway law to current economic and technical realities. It also establishes regulations for the transportation of hazardous materials, compiles and updates a listing of railway lines adhering to CIM-CIV standards regulations, gives legal opinions on the interpretation and application of the Convention, intervenes with a view to facilitating financial relations among railways, acts when needed as a secretariat to the Court of Arbitration set up by the OCTI, and organizes training courses for nationals from the member states. The OCTI's working languages are French and German.

The OTIF also includes two committees made up of representatives from all member states: the **COTIF Revision Committee** and the **Committee of Experts on the Transport of Dangerous Goods**.

FINANCING

Member states pay an annual fee to the OTIF, in proportion to the size, in kilometers, of their railway lines subject to the CIV-CIM Convention. The Organization's annual budget is an estimated 3 million Swiss francs.

CO-OPERATION

The OTIF liaises with the Inland Transport Division of the UN Economic Commission for Europe (ECE) [see 181 A] and other intergovernmental organizations involved in railway transportation (ECOSOC [see 001 A], UNCTAD [see 111 B], UNCITRAL [see 300 C], IAEA [see 421 A], ICAO [see 184 A], IMO [see 183 A], WTO [see 172 A], EC, UNIDROIT [see 300 B], CCC [see 112 A], UT [see 182 A] ...). At present, OTIF and the ECE are working on FACILRAIL, measures aimed at facilitating the crossing of frontiers by international rail traffic.

PUBLICATIONS

The OTIF publishes the quarterly *Bulletin des transports internationaux par chemins de fer*, in French and German; the proceedings of its conferences; the texts of COTIF and its annexes and the lists of railway lines subject to the Convention; and the statutes of the Organization.

A.L.

ADDRESS

Gryphenhübeliweg 30, CH-3006 Berne, Switzerland
T. (41 31) 43 17 62, Fx. (41 31) 43 11 64

182 C – INTERNATIONAL UNION OF RAILWAYS (UIC)

The UIC is primarily a non-profit-making professional association governed by the French law of 1901. Its objective is to promote international co-operation in the field of railway transportation, principally in Europe. The UIC also works to preserve the role of railway transportation against alternative transportation methods by lobbying governments, international bodies, and the mass media on behalf of the railways.

MEMBERSHIP

The UIC includes 92 railway networks belonging to 63 countries and spread over five continents. There are three types of members of the UIC:

- Active Members: this includes all European railway networks and networks attached to them – they are the core of the UIC and comprise networks in Europe, North Africa and the Middle East;
- Associate Members: this includes railways throughout the world;
- Affiliated Members: this includes affiliated or related transportation organizations and bodies, such as metropolitan rail systems, and certain maritime lines.

ACTIVITIES

The UIC's activities include the achievement of technical, operational, commercial and computer unification and standardization, research, and information and data exchange.

STRUCTURE

The **General Assembly** is the highest body of the UIC. It is made up of all the member railways or organizations and, under the presidency of the biennially elected President, it exercises periodical supervision over the organization. The UIC President is elected by the Directors-General of the individual railways.

The **Board of Management** is comprised of 28 member networks selected every two years by the General Assembly. It is responsible for the administrative and financial management of the UIC and it determines the organization's working programme and supervises its execution.

The **Executive Committee** (ExCo), made up of the UIC President and 12 railways, considers and establishes broad policy orientation for the organization. It is responsible for preparing the decisions of the Board of Management.

The **General Secretariat**, based in Paris with a staff of 120, is responsible for implementing the tasks assigned to it by the UIC's various organs. It also disseminates the organization's decisions and publications, and represents the UIC externally. The working languages of the Secretariat are French, English and German.

The **Working Bodies:**

(a) Specialist Committees
The UIC has nine specialist committees, each of which is chaired by a member railway. These constitute a forum for gatherings of railway executives from the main disciplines – namely, passengers, freight, finance, operations, strategic planning, traction and rolling stock (mechanical engineering), way and works (civil engineering), information technology and research.

(b) Ad hoc Groups
The UIC has set up a number of specific project groups:

- the High-Speed Task Force which reports to the Strategic Planning Committee and is concerned with the development of the European high-speed rail network;
- the HIPPS Project Group (Hermes International Planning and Production System) whose aim it is to establish a system of scheduling and monitoring international rail movements.

(c) Permanent Structures
The **European Rail Research Institute** (ERRI), based in Utrecht, manages international research and development programmes; organizes exchanges of information on technical matters; and works in the field of standardization of railway rolling stock and in the development of technical harmonization.

The **Brussels Central Clearing House** (BCC), in Brussels, settles international financial payments between some 20 railways. Reciprocal debts and credits are offset, leaving the resulting balances to be transferred.

The **Vehicle Fleet Bureau**, which manages vehicle fleets in conjunction with the RIC/RIV international agreements, is part of the UIC in Paris.

THE UIC CODE

The UIC Code is a compilation of more than 600 technical leaflets, updated on a regular basis, of either a mandatory or recommendatory nature. They are used as the basis for drafting railway regulations and in preparing specifications for industry. As well as dealing with the technical aspects of railways, the Code also deals with data processing, and with economic and commercial considerations such as costs, management of stock, and prices.

CO-OPERATION

The fact that the organization is both international and specialized has allowed it to obtain observer status on railway matters at the United Nations. The UIC is recognized as a specialized organization operating particularly in areas dealt with by ECOSOC [see 001 A]. It maintains links with organizations such as the EC, ECMT, OCTI [see 182 A], ICAO [see 184 A], IATA [see 184 B], and IRU [see 181 B].

PUBLICATIONS

The UIC publishes studies, reports, research papers, periodicals (*Rail International* and *UIC News*), agreements, standards and procedures, as well as the *General Dictionary of Railway Terms* (11,000 words).

A.L.

ADDRESS

16, rue Jean Rey, 75015 Paris, France
T. (33 1) 44 49 20 20, Fx. (33 1) 44 49 20 29

182.01 – INTERNATIONAL AGREEMENT ON RAILWAY TECHNICAL UNITY – UT

Concluded : 21.10.1882, Berne
In Force : 21.10.1882
Parties : 19

The objective of the International Agreement on Railway Technical Unity (UT) is to facilitate international rail transit, and to guarantee the continuation of international railway operations. By ensuring the compatibility and security of rail techniques, the UT also contributes to the development of commercial ties between countries.

To achieve its objectives, this Agreement sets technical standards to which international railway equipment must conform. These notably involve:

- the gauge of the railway lines;
- the construction and exchange of the rolling stock;
- wagon cargo;
- the height of buffers; and,
- the creation of a standard "Berne" key to lock the wagons.

Work is still in progress to prepare the fourth revision to the Agreement which should take into consideration the advent of highly rapid rail transport. It has become necessary to widen the scope of the Agreement, especially with regard to the compatibility of railway systems in Europe. One can, however, regret the preference that some countries show in raising this issue on a bilateral basis, rather than within the multilateral framework of the UT, thereby weakening this Agreement.

A.L.

Access : ALS
Reserves : USP
Duration : USP
Deposit. : CH
Language : Fre, Ger

Modific. : Revised 1935 ; 1938 ; Replaced de facto by a Working Document 1968 (1970)

182.02 – STATUTES OF THE INTERNATIONAL UNION OF RAILWAYS – UIC

Adopted : 20.10.1922, Paris

In the wake of the First World War, an international conference was convened in Portorosa, Italy, on 23 November 1921 to revive international traffic and exchanges. The question of international railway transportation was pre-eminent in the discussions, in particular the *interpénétration* of rolling stock. From this conference, the idea of creating a European rail association emerged.

A few months later, in May 1922, a follow-up conference was held in Genoa. With the overall objective of promoting international railway traffic, the parties agreed to form a permanent conference of national railway administrations to work towards the standardization and improved conditions of rail systems. The name of the new organization was decided at its first meeting in Paris in October 1922: the International Union of Railways (UIC).

At the same meeting, on 20 October 1922, the Statutes of the UIC were approved. At that time the new organization included 51 networks from 29 countries. In 1992, the UIC, which is officially a non-profit-making organization governed by the French law of 1901, included 92 railway networks belonging to 63 countries, spreading over five continents.

A.L.

Access : ENT
Language : Eng, Fre, Ger

Modific. : Last Version 1984

182.03 – INTERNATIONAL CONVENTION TO FACILITATE THE CROSSING OF FRONTIERS FOR GOODS CARRIED BY RAIL – ECE

Concluded : 10.01.1952, Geneva
In Force : 01.04.1953
Parties : 11

In order to facilitate the crossing of frontiers for goods carried by rail, this Convention sets basic principles for the establishment and operation of stations by two adjoining countries. These principles are intended to be completed by bilateral agreements.

Thus, Article 1 states that "on every railway line carrying a considerable volume of international goods traffic, which crosses the frontier between two adjoining countries, the competent authorities of those countries shall jointly examine the possibility of designating by agreement a station close to the frontier, at which the examinations required under the legislation of the two countries in respect of the entry and exit of all or part of the goods traffic might be effectively carried out ...".

Whenever a station is designated, a zone is set up within which officials and agents of the competent administrations of the country adjoining the territory on which the station is established are entitled to examine goods crossing the frontier in either direction (Art. 2).

The contracting parties have also agreed that their customs administrations do everything in their power to reduce to a minimum the time required for the customs and other examinations (Art. 6), that they would recognize the customs seals of the other contracting parties and would adopt the Standard International Customs Declaration Form annexed to the Convention (Art. 7).

This Convention is analogous to another convention concluded on the same day to facilitate the crossing of frontiers by passengers and baggage carried by rail [see 182.04].

A.L.

Access : CON (Art. 12)
Reserves : USP
Duration : MIN (Art. 14)
Deposit. : UN (Art. 17)
Language : Eng, Fre

Reference : 163 UNTS – JORF 7 May 53

182.04 – INTERNATIONAL CONVENTION TO FACILITATE THE CROSSING OF FRONTIERS FOR PASSENGERS AND BAGGAGE CARRIED BY RAIL – ECE

Concluded : 10.01.1952, Geneva
In Force : 01.04.1953
Parties : 10

In order to facilitate the crossing of frontiers by passengers and baggage carried by rail, the Convention makes provision in its Title I for adjoining contracting states to agree to create a joint border crossing station in order to centralize all customs activities.

Articles 2 and 8 make provision for a range of measures to simplify customs inspection in one station.

To maintain the fluidity and efficiency of traffic, joint customs and police inspections may be organized on the train as it continues *en route* (Title II). Provision is made, therefore, through bilateral agreements for inspection officials to board international trains and to continue their inspection even on the territory of the other state (Art. 9-2).

Finally, in its Title III, the Convention attempts to avoid baggage control in the case of ordinary transit by recommending that member states use *inter alia* the

Standard International Customs Declaration Form annexed to the Convention, and that they recognize customs seals of other contracting states.

A.L.

Access : CON (Art. 12)
Reserves : USP
Duration : MIN (Art. 14)
Deposit. : UN (Art. 17)
Language : Eng, Fre

Reference : 163, 328 UNTS – JORF 7 May 53

182.05 – CONVENTION CONCERNING INTERNATIONAL CARRIAGE BY RAIL – OTIF

Concluded : 09.05.1980, Berne
In Force : 01.05.1985
Parties : 35

The origins of the COTIF (the Convention Concerning International Carriage by Rail) are to be found in the first international convention for the carriage of goods by rail (CIM) signed in Berne on 14 October 1890 (implemented 1 January 1893), which was itself revised numerous times: in Paris in 1896, in Berne in 1905 and 1923, in Rome in 1933, and then in Berne again in 1952, 1961, 1970, 1980, and 1990.

In its fundamental clauses, the COTIF defines the role and functions of the OTIF as well as those of its organs, including the Central Office for International Carriage by Rail, which acts as the permanent secretariat of the Organization.

In Annexes A and B of the Convention, the standard rules for both the contract of international carriage of passengers and baggage by rail (CIV) and the contract of international carriage of goods by rail (CIM) can be found. In these Annexes, the Convention regulates the conclusion and execution of the contract of carriage, liabilities, claims and suits, assertion of rights, as well as the relationship between different railway networks. In other words, the Convention places itself above individual national rights to allow for the direct transportation of goods, passengers, and baggage, with one single transport document and on the basis of a standard transportation law.

In case of death of, or personal injury to, passengers, the Convention provides that the railway is liable for such damage caused by an accident arising out of the operation of the railway and happening while the passenger is in, entering or alighting from railway vehicles (Art. 26 CIV). The railway which is liable is the one which operates the line on which the accident has occurred.

By contrast, the Convention establishes a system of collective responsibility of railways for international carriage of goods whereby each railway involved in the carriage (by the very act of taking over the goods with the consignment note) becomes a party to the contract of carriage and assumes the obligations arising therefrom (Art. 35 CIM). Therefore, any of these railways may be held liable for loss or damage resulting from the total or partial loss of, or damage to the goods between the time of acceptance for carriage and the time of delivery and for the loss or damage resulting from the transit period being exceeded. This system of collective responsibility has been adopted in order to facilitate the conclusion of the contract of carriage, to avoid verification at each border crossing, and to spare the person entitled the difficult search for the railway which was in fact responsible.

The railway may release itself from the liability only if it claims general or special grounds for exemption. Among the general grounds for exemption, the railway has to prove that the loss, the damage or the exceeding of the transit period was caused by a fault on the part of the person entitled, by the inherent vice of the goods (e.g. decay, wastage, etc.) or by circumstances which the railway could not avoid and the consequences of which it was unable to prevent. The special grounds for exemption include carriage in open wagon, absence or inadequacy of packing, defective loading by the consignor, and carriage of live animals.

Where there is wilful misconduct on the part of the railway, compensation is limited to a maximum amount. In a case of gross negligence, the compensation cannot exceed twice that maximum amount. The 1990 Protocol increased the ceiling of this amount and adopted a new definition of wilful misconduct which is the same as that in Article 25 of the Convention for the Unification of Certain Rules Relating to International Carriage by Air (Warsaw, 1929) [see 184.01].

In rail-sea traffic subject to the Convention, the liability rules are either those of the CIM in general or, with a few exceptions, those of maritime law if damage occurs in the course of the sea journey. It falls to the states concerned to agree on a system of responsibility applicable to the particular sea journey.

The Convention is applicable only to those international railway lines which the member states, by common agreement, decide to place within the scope of its provisions. The OCTI is responsible for the preparation, the updating, and the publication of the lists of railway lines which have been submitted to the CIV-CIM. The 1990 Protocol extends the scope of application to other internal carriage performed under the responsibility of the railway and complementary to the carriage by rail.

The Convention is in force over a distance of approximately 250,000 km of railway lines, including several thousand kilometers of roadway and maritime lines completed by railway passage.

The COTIF is followed by a protocol on the privileges and immunities of the Intergovernmental Organization for the International Carriage by Rail (OTIF).

A.L.

Access	: CON (Art. 23)
Reserves	: PAU (Art. 12-3, 27, App.A 3-1)
Duration	: USP
Deposit.	: CH (Art. 22)
Language	: Fre, (Ara, Eng, Ger, Ita) (Art. 28)
Modific.	: 20.12.90 (-)
Reference	: Misc 1982/11 – JORF 25 Aug 87

1.8.3 Maritime Transport

A substantial part of the law relating to maritime transport centres on attempts to harmonize competing interests in relationships, for example, between shipowners and charterers, or carriers and shippers. The economic interests of individual groups has always been one of the determining factors in deciding the extent and degree to which risks, rights and obligations with regard to liability would be attached to any one group. Furthermore, in the pursuit of any concerted international effort, whether in terms of combating marine pollution or in ensuring the safety of life at sea, the financial implications often become of paramount concern.

The conventions noted in this section cover three specific areas of maritime treaty law: those dealing with the setting up of organizations charged with the responsibility of developing and controlling the use of the sea; those specifying limits of liability attaching in the particular circumstance of the convention and ancillary conventions facilitating enforcement of liability; and those dealing with safety. Other conventions are listed as an adjunct to the subject under discussion [see also 4.1.2].

Patricia Ford

SELECTED BIBLIOGRAPHY

Arroyo, Ignacio, *International Maritime Conventions*, Deventer; Boston: Kluwer Law and Taxation, 1991.

Carver, T.G., *Carriage by Sea*, 13th ed., 2 Vol., London: Sweet & Maxwell, 1982.

Henry, Cleopatra Elmira, *The Carriage of Dangerous Goods by Sea: the Role of the International Maritime Organization in International Legislation*, London: St Martin's Press, 1985.

Institute of Maritime Law, *Limitation of Shipowner's Liability: the 1976 Convention*, London: Sweet & Maxwell, 1986.

Mankabady, S., *The International Maritime Organisation: International Shipping Rules*, 2nd ed., London: Sweet & Maxwell, 1987 .

Singh, Nagendra, *International Maritime Law Conventions*, 4 Vol., London: Sweet & Maxwell, 1983.

183 A – INTERNATIONAL MARITIME ORGANIZATION (IMO)

Having realized that measures to improve maritime safety would be more effective if they were implemented on an international scale, a large number of states decided that it was necessary to establish a permanent body to co-ordinate and promote all such action. As a result, between 19 February and 6 March 1948, a maritime conference called by the United Nations in Geneva adopted a Convention establishing the Intergovernmental Maritime Consultative Organization (IMCO) [see 183.05].

The Convention went into effect on 17 March 1958, after 20 states signed it, seven of which possessed an individual total tonnage of at least one million tons. On 22 May 1982, the name of the organization became the International Maritime Organization (IMO).

Originally the IMO was concerned predominantly with technical considerations. Thus, over the past 20 years it has fostered the adoption of some 35 conventions and protocols, and has adopted over 500 codes and recommendations, among them the well-known International Maritime Dangerous Goods Code (IMDG) affecting maritime safety and the prevention of pollution.

STRUCTURE

The IMO's directing organ is the **Assembly** of 140 member states and two associate members, which meets every two years. It elects a **Council** of 32 members serving a two-year term to act as a governing body during the biennium.

The functions of the IMO are carried out by a number of committees in which all member states can participate equally. The oldest committee is the Maritime Safety Committee (MSC), which is assisted by a number of specialized subcommittees:

- safety of navigation;
- radio communications;
- lifesaving appliances;
- standards of training and watchkeeping;
- carriage of dangerous goods;
- ship design and equipment;
- fire protection;
- stability, load lines, and fishing vessel safety;
- cargoes and containers; and
- bulk chemicals.

There are also the Marine Environment Protection Committee, the Legal Committee, the Technical Co-operation Committee and the Facilitation Committee.

A **Secretariat** is responsible for co-ordination and liaison between the Assembly, the Council and the committees and subcommittees. It is directed by a Secretary-General, who is assisted by a staff of some 300 international civil servants. The Secretary-General is appointed by the Council with the consent of the Assembly.

The IMO has concluded official agreements with 32 intergovernmental organizations and has granted advisory status to 44 international non-governmental organizations, which can participate without voting rights in the meetings of the IMO's various organs.

ACTIVITIES

While the IMO at the outset primarily drafted conventions and international regulations, its principal and stated objective today, as stipulated in Assembly Resolution A 500, is to supervise the implementation of these instruments by the member states.

The success of the IMO has led it to extend its original brief, which focused on technical issues and issues of maritime safety and pollution, into matters that were the domain of the International Maritime Committee of 1897 [see 183 B]. As a result, since 1976, the IMO has been responsible for the adoption under its aegis of a number of conventions on maritime commerce.

CO-OPERATION

Following an appraisal of the work undertaken by the IMO in its first 30 years and with an eye to the future, the IMO at the start of the 1990s developed a strategy for the protection of the marine environment and a global programme to assist its implementation. Part of that strategy consists of co-operating fully with other organizations within the United Nations family and relevant international, regional and non-governmental groups to ensure a co-ordinated approach to the protection of the marine environment from pollution from ships and related activities, and to ensure the avoidance of duplication of efforts.

To date, the IMO has co-operated, *inter alia,* with the International Petroleum Industry Environmental Conservation Association (IPIECA) in the provision of a seminar designed to help governments to respond to major oil spills. In addition, following the adoption of a new chapter to SOLAS 1974, the IMO in conjunction with the International Labour Organisation (ILO) [see 141 A] has established a group of experts to examine and draw up procedures for investigating marine accidents with a view to establishing the part played in them by fatigue. The World Health Organization (WHO) [see 132 A] were to be invited to join the group.

PUBLICATIONS

The IMO publishes works on technical maritime matters relating to maritime safety and prevention and control of marine pollution. It also publishes *IMO News* (quarterly).

Patricia Ford and IDIT, Barthélémy Mercadal

ADDRESS

4 Albert Embankment, London SE1 7SR, United Kingdom
T. (44 71) 735 7611, Fx. (44 71) 587 3210

183 B – INTERNATIONAL MARITIME COMMITTEE (CMI)

The CMI is a non-governmental organization whose aim is to contribute by all appropriate means and activities to the unification of maritime and commercial law, maritime customs, usages and practices (Art. 1 of the 1990 statutes).

Prior to the CMI, the International Law Association and the Institute of International Law, both founded in 1873, also sought to unify maritime law. However, two problems existed: first, the fact that the scope of their activities went beyond maritime law meant that there were too many issues to be dealt with at once; and, second, as private bodies whose functions were merely preparatory and advisory, their actions, lacking any real power, did not lead to the adoption of mandatory international standards.

Thus in May 1886, with the support of the International Law Association, a group of maritime law specialists proposed a new system for promoting the unification of maritime law. National associations were to be created in the so-called trading countries and their activities were to be co-ordinated by a central committee. It was agreed that the national associations would include jurists, shipowners, underwriters and all others directly affected by the unification of maritime law. The central committee was named the International Maritime Committee, and it held its inaugural session in Brussels on 6 June 1897, with the full support of the maritime powers.

At the initiative of and according to its usual practice, the Belgian Government convenes diplomatic conferences where the documents prepared by the CMI at its international conferences are negotiated. As a result, 18 Brussels Conventions were adopted in this manner between 1910 and 1971.

Although it has been praised for its tremendous achievements, the CMI has fallen victim since the 1960s to the desire by states to initiate international conventions on their own within the framework provided by the UN system.

MEMBERSHIP

The CMI is composed of 50 national member associations representing 49 nations (Australia and New Zealand comprising one association) (1993 figures), and some 277 individual titular members not having voting rights (Art. 3 of the 1990 Statutes).

STRUCTURE

The CMI **Assembly** includes all members (Art. 5 of the 1990 Statutes) and meets annually in March (Art. 6). The Assembly approves the CMI's annual budget and accounts and elects the officers to the CMI and members to the Executive Council (Art. 8 of the 1990 Statutes).

The **Executive Council** is responsible for maintaining the contact between the CMI and the national associations. It also prepares documents, organizes and supervises commissions and working groups, publishes periodicals and reports to the Assembly on what has been accomplished and on the initiatives which have been adopted (Art. 12 of the 1990 Statutes).

The Assembly, the Executive Council and the international conferences are presided over by the President of the CMI (Art. 10 of the 1990 Statutes). At least every four years, at the initiative of the Assembly, the CMI convenes an international conference (Art. 15 of the 1990 Statutes); more than 30 conferences have been held to date.

CO-OPERATION

Before the IMO – a specialized UN agency – began to take on the responsibility for drafting many maritime law conventions, this function had been carried out by the CMI. Today the CMI's function is that of a valued adviser, preparing draft texts of conventions and contributing to the discussions and development of both public and private international maritime law. The CMI has co-operated with the IMO and other UN agencies on numerous occasions, two recent examples being in the drafting of texts for a new Salvage Convention and a Convention on the Liability of Operators of Transport Terminals in International Trade.

PUBLICATIONS

CMI publishes the *CMI Yearbook* and the *CMI Newsletter* (quarterly).

P.F. and IDIT, B.M.

ADDRESS

Mechelse Steenweg 203, bus 6, B-2018 Antwerp, Belgium
T. (32 3) 218 4887, Fx. (32 3) 218 6721

183.01 – INTERNATIONAL CONVENTION FOR THE UNIFICATION OF CERTAIN RULES OF LAW RELATING TO BILLS OF LADING – CMI

Concluded : 25.08.1924, Brussels
In Force : 02.06.1931
Parties : 40

In 1921 at its Hague Conference, the International Law Association prepared an agreement known as the Hague Rules which aimed at drawing up a framework for the transportation of goods by sea. The intention of the ILA had been that the Rules would be adopted voluntarily by carriers in their bills of lading. However, the carriers were reluctant to comply for fear and distrust of their competitors which, in turn, reinforced the distrust of the shipping interests which had pressed for legislation. Following the failure of the Rules, it became clear that any reform had to be instituted at an international level if it was to be binding. It was in pursuit of these aims that the Rules as formulated formed the basis for the Convention which came to be adopted at Brussels on 25 August 1924, and thus explains why it is "mistakenly" referred to as the "Hague Rules".

Scope: The Hague Rules apply to all "goods" defined as "goods, wares, merchandise and articles of every kind whatsoever except live animals and cargo ... carried on deck" (Art. 1-c). It applies to contracts of carriage covered by bills of lading rather than those under charter-party (Art. 1-b), when the bills of lading are issued in one of the contracting states (Art. 10).

The apparent opposition between Article 3, which is favourable to the shipper, and Article 4, which protects the rights of carrier, reflects the conflicting interests which the Convention endeavours to accommodate.

DETAILS OF THE CONVENTION

Article 3 defines the mandatory duties and obligations of the carrier: he is "bound before and at the beginning of the voyage to exercise due diligence to make the ship seaworthy [and] properly man, equip and supply the ship" (Art. 3-1). He shall then "properly and carefully load, handle, stow, carry, keep, care for, and discharge the goods carried" (Art. 3-2). The bill of lading "shall be *prima facie* evidence of the receipt by the carrier of the goods as therein described" (Art. 3-4).

In contrast, Article 4 stipulates that the carrier is not liable for loss or damage arising or resulting from unseaworthiness (Art 4-1), resulting from any one of the 17 conditions listed in Paragraph two of the same Article, or resulting from reasonable deviation (Art. 4-4).

Neither the carrier nor the ship shall in any event be or become liable for any loss or damage to or in connection with goods in an amount exceeding 100 pounds sterling per package of unit, or the equivalent of that sum in other currency unless the nature and value of such goods have been declared by the shipper before shipment and inserted in the bill of lading (Art 4-5).

MODIFICATIONS

From a practical point of view, the Convention of 25 August 1924 is undoubtedly the most important of the Brussels conventions. It remained unchanged for nearly 40 years but in view of practices which had evolved in the interim, and because of various shortcomings, its amendment proved desirable. Following a conference at Visby in Sweden, the Hague Rules were amended by the Brussels Protocol of 1968 and are now known as the "Hague-Visby Rules" or the "Amended Rules".

According to Article 10 on the scope of application of the 1924 Convention, and amended by the 1968 Protocol, "the provisions of [the] Convention shall apply to every bill of lading relating to the carriage of goods between ports in two different states if: a) the bill of lading is issued in a Contracting State, or b) the carriage is from a Contracting State, or c) the Contract contained in or evidenced by the bill of lading provides that the rules of [the] Convention or legislation of any State giving effect to them are to govern the contract" (Art. 10 of the modified Convention).

The modified Convention replaces the gold franc for the pound sterling (GBP), and makes a number of other substantive changes, including a complex system in which the ceiling for reparations is fixed at "10,000 gold francs per package or unit or 30 gold francs per kilo of gross weight of the goods lost or damaged, whichever is the higher" (Art. 4-5 of the modified Convention).

Unlike the 1924 Convention, the Hague-Visby Rules exclude the carrier or his agents from the benefit of the limitation of liability "if it is proved that the damage resulted from an act or omission of the carrier done with intent to cause damage, or recklessly and with knowledge that damage would probably result" (Art. 4-5 and Art. 4 bis-4).

The difficulty of calculating the value of the gold franc led to the adoption in Brussels on 21 December 1979 of a protocol which replaced the gold franc with Special Drawing Rights (SDRs).

RECENT DEVELOPMENTS

Because of pressure from developing countries, UNCTAD [see 111 B] began a significant reform of the Convention, the result of which was the signature of a new international convention signed on 31 March 1978 and known as the Hamburg Rules [see 183.20]. This Convention, which seeks to co-ordinate maritime law with other transport laws, has now been ratified by the 20 states required under Article 28 for its implementation, and came into force on 1 November 1992.

P.F. and IDIT, B.M.

Access : ALS (Art. 12)
Reserves : PAU (Art. Prot.de sign.,13)
Duration : USP
Deposit. : BE (Art. 11)
Language : Eng, Fre

Modific. : Brussels 23.02.68 (23.06.77); Brussels 21.12.79 (14.02.84); Revised Hamburg 31.03.78 (01.11.92)

Reference : 120 LNTS – UKTS 1931/17, 1977/83, 1984/28 – RTAF 1977/49 – JORF 8 Apr 37, 3 Apr 87 – JDI 1987 – ULR 1967, 1979/2 – RGDIP 1987/2

183.02 – INTERNATIONAL CONVENTION FOR THE UNIFICATION OF CERTAIN RULES RELATING TO THE LIMITATION OF LIABILITY OF OWNERS OF SEA-GOING VESSELS – CMI

Concluded : 25.08.1924, Brussels
In Force : 02.06.1931
Parties : 9

The Convention was agreed during the Brussels Diplomatic Conference of 1922, and was signed in Brussels on 25 August 1924. Its objective was to unify legislation which recognized the principle of limitation of the liability of owners of sea-going vessels, but which differed on the method of this limitation. During 25 years of preparatory talks for the Convention two opposing arguments were voiced. The first, favoured by the British, advocated a lump sum limitation of liability based on the tonnage of the vessel, and the second, favoured by the French, defended the older practice whereby an owner could limit his liability, when it resulted from the actions of a captain, by "abandoning" or ceding his ship and the cargo the ship was carrying on the particular voyage, to his creditors.

DETAILS OF THE CONVENTION

At the expense of unification, agreement was reached and a system adopted giving the shipowner the option of limiting his liability on a lump sum basis based on the tonnage or fixing the limit of liability according to the value of the vessel, its freight and its accessories (Art. 1).

SUBSEQUENT DEVELOPMENTS

Great Britain was dissatisfied with this arrangement and placed the issue on the agenda of the International Maritime Committee's Madrid Conference of 1955. The resulting draft convention, signed in Brussels on 10 October 1957, became the new International Convention Relating to the Limitation of the Liability of Owners of Sea-Going Ships [see 183.07].

The new Brussels Convention adopted the British position, and lists in Article 1 cases in which a shipowner can limit his liability, including cases where liability arises by reason of his ownership, possession, custody or control of the ship. In all the cases, the limitation of the liability of the shipowner varies according to whether there was injury or loss of life, or whether there was only material damage (Art. 3).

The Convention on Limitation of Liability for Maritime Claims (London, 1976) [see 183.18] upgraded the limits of liability set by the 1957 Brussels Convention, and is essentially organized along the same lines. However, it extends the limitation on liability of shipowners, managers, operators and charterers to insurers and salvors (Art. 1) and establishes particular limitations for this category and for passenger carriers (Art. 7). It also replaces the concept of "actual fault or privity" of the shipowner with the "personal act or omission" of the shipowner, as a condition for inapplicability of the limitation of liability.

The Brussels Convention of 1924 is still applicable between states which ratified it without denouncing it and which subsequently did not adhere to the Brussels Convention of 1957 and/or the London Convention of 1976.

P.F. and IDIT, B.M.

Access : ALS (Art. 17)
Reserves : PAU (Art. 18, Prot. I and II)
Duration : USP
Deposit. : BE (Art. 16)
Language : Eng, Fre

Reference : 120 LNTS

183.03 – INTERNATIONAL CONVENTION FOR THE UNIFICATION OF CERTAIN RULES RELATING TO MARITIME LIENS AND MORTGAGES – CMI

Concluded : 10.04.1926, Brussels
In Force : 02.06.1931
Parties : 24

Because differences in national legislation placed obstacles in the way of obtaining credit from vessels, notably through maritime mortgages, the International Maritime Committee proposed in 1902, that the Hamburg Diplomatic Conference unify certain rules relating to maritime liens and mortgages. It took three conferences (Venice 1907, and Brussels 1922 and 1926) and the failure of the first Brussels Convention of 25 August 1924, before agreement was finally to be reached at the Conference of 10 April 1926.

DETAILS OF THE CONVENTION

The 1926 Convention is unambiguous: it is necessary that the number of maritime liens are reduced to a minimum so as to enhance the value of the mortgage or *hypothèque*. To achieve this, the 1926 Convention establishes two categories of liens which become part of the legislation of the contracting states (Art. 3): primary and secondary liens.

Primary liens, also called international liens, are listed in Article 2: mortgages, hypothecations and other similar charges on vessels which, "duly effected in accordance with the law of the Contracting State to which the vessel belongs, and registered in a public register ... shall be regarded as valid and respected in all the other Contracting Countries" (Art. 1). Article 2 makes provision for five primary liens:

- legal costs due to the state, and expenses incurred in the common interest of the creditors in order to preserve the vessel;
- claims arising out of the contract of engagement of the master, crew and other persons hired on board;
- renumeration for assistance and salvage, and the contribution of the vessel in general average;
- indemnities for collisions or other accident of navigation; and
- claims resulting from contracts entered into or acts done by the master.

Secondary liens, which rank immediately after mortgages, may be granted freely through legislation by the contracting parties (Art. 3-2).

The Convention does not apply to "vessels of war, nor to government vessels appropriated exclusively to the public service" (Art. 15), and it adds that the contracting states may choose "not to apply the provisions of this Convention in favour of the nationals of a non-contracting State" (Art. 14).

Because the new International Convention for the Unification of Certain Rules Relating to Maritime Liens and Mortgages (Brussels, 1967) [see 183.13] has not been ratified by a sufficient number of parties, the 1926 Convention remains the only one in force. However, the IMO [see 183 A] and UNCTAD [see 111 B] are presently undertaking a project of reform in this area.

P.F. and IDIT, B.M.

Access : ALS (Art. 18)
Reserves : PAU (Art. 19, Prot. 1 and 2)
Duration : USP
Deposit. : BE (Art. 17)
Language : Fre

Reference : 120 LNTS – JORF 18 Dec 35

183.04 – INTERNATIONAL CONVENTION FOR THE UNIFICATION OF CERTAIN RULES RELATING TO THE IMMUNITY OF STATE-OWNED VESSELS – CMI

Concluded : 10.04.1926, Brussels
In Force : 02.06.1931
Parties : 29

Whereas the provisions of this Convention are applicable in each contracting state, they do not require contracting states to extend the benefits of those provisions to non-contracting states (Art. 6). The effect of the Convention is to subject sea-going ships owned or operated by states, cargoes owned by them, and cargoes and passengers carried on state-owned ships to the same rules of liability and the same obligations as those applicable in the case of privately-owned ships, cargoes and equipment (Art. 1). In reality, however, only ships conducting commercial activity are subject to this. Indeed, Article 3-1 states that the following ships shall not be subject to seizure, arrest or detention by any legal process, or any proceedings *in rem*:

- ships of war, state-owned yachts, patrol vessels, hospital ships, fleet auxiliaries, supply ships and other vessels owned or operated by a state and employed exclusively at the time when the cause of action arises on government and non-commercial service; and
- state-owned cargoes carried on any of the above-mentioned ships, and state-owned cargoes on board merchant ships for government and non-commerical purposes.

Nevertheless, states cannot plead state immunity and thereby claim immunity from prosecution in all cases. Thus, claims in respect of collisions and nautical accidents, claims in respect of salvage or in the nature of salvage and in respect of general average, as well as in respect of contracts relating to such cargoes, may be brought before courts with jurisdiction over the matter.

Patricia Ford

Access : ALS (Art. 10)
Reserves : USP
Duration : USP
Deposit. : BE (Art. 15)
Language : Fre (Art. 14)

Modific. : Additional Protocol Brussels 24.05.34 (23.02.36)

Reference : 176 LNTS – RGDIP 1955/3 – JORF 5 Oct 55

183.05 – CONVENTION ESTABLISHING THE INTERNATIONAL MARITIME ORGANIZATION – IMO

Concluded : 06.03.1948, Geneva
In Force : 17.03.1958
Parties : 140

This Convention lays down the objectives, structures and functions of the different organs of the International Maritime Organization [see 183 A]. In its original version adopted by the UN Maritime Conference in Geneva on 6 March 1948, the Convention was called the Convention on the Inter-Governmental Maritime Consultative Organization.

Access : ALS (Art. 4ss,71)
Reserves : USP
Duration : USP
Deposit. : UN (Art. 76)

Language : Eng, Fre, Spa (Art. 76)

Modific. : Ass.Res.A.69(ES.11) 15.09.64 (06.10.67); A.70(IV) 28.09.65 (03.11.68); A.315(ES.V) 17.10.74 (01.04.78); A.358(IX) of 14.11.75 and A.371(X) of 09.11.77 (22.05.82); A.400(X) 17.11.77 (10.11.84); A.450(XI) 15.11.79 (10.11.84)

Reference : 289 UNTS – UKTS 1958/54, 1967/92, 1968/105, 1978/69, 1982/34, 1986/8/26 – RTAF 1978/40, 1982/34

183.06 – INTERNATIONAL CONVENTION FOR THE UNIFICATION OF CERTAIN RULES RELATING TO THE ARREST OF SEA-GOING SHIPS – CMI

Concluded : 10.05.1952, Brussels
In Force : 24.02.1956
Parties : 37

At the Paris Conference of 1937, the International Maritime Committee sought to institutionalize at an international level the concept of arrest of sea-going vessels. Their deliberations in due course resulted in the adoption of the 1952 Arrest Convention.

DETAILS OF THE CONVENTION

The Convention is concerned with arrest both as a provisional remedy and as a jurisdictional ground. In Article 1, it specifies the maritime claims in regard to which a ship may be arrested and, in Article 2, states that a ship flying the flag of one of the contracting states may be arrested in the jurisdiction of any of the contracting states in respect of any maritime claim. Where a ship is flying the flag of a non-contracting state, that ship may be arrested in the jurisdiction of a contracting state if the arrest is in respect of any of the claims specified in Article 1 or in respect of any other claim permitted by the domestic law of the contracting state (Art. 8).

The arrest must be authorized by the appropriate court of the state in which the arrest takes place (Art. 4), which also "shall permit the release of the ship upon sufficient bail or other security being furnished" (Art. 5).

RECENT DEVELOPMENTS

The 33rd Conference of the International Maritime Committee [see 183 B], held in Lisbon from 19 to 25 May 1985, adopted a draft reform of the 1952 Arrest Convention. It has been forwarded to the executive bodies of the IMO [see 183 A] and UNCTAD [see 111 B] for consideration. However, at the present time, a joint intergovernmental IMO/UNCTAD group of experts is undertaking work on the question of maritime liens and mortgages pursuant to a resolution made in 1985 by the UNCTAD Working Group on International Shipping Legislation. As a consequence, and given the link between the legal questions arising from maritime liens and mortgages and arrest, the working group decided it was preferable to wait for the adoption of a new convention on maritime liens and mortgages before examining the International Maritime Committee's draft reform on arrest.

Patricia Ford and IDIT, Barthélémy Mercadal

Access : ALS (Art. 15)
Reserves : PAU (Art. 10)
Duration : USP
Deposit. : BE (Art. 13)
Language : Eng, Fre

Reference : 439 UNTS – UKTS 1960/47 – JORF 14 Jan 58 – RTAF 1958/3

183.07 – INTERNATIONAL CONVENTION RELATING TO THE LIMITATION OF THE LIABILITY OF OWNERS OF SEA-GOING SHIPS – CMI

Concluded : 10.10.1957, Brussels
In Force : 31.05.1968
Parties : 21

Because of the failure of the convention on the limitation of liability of owners of sea-going ships (Brussels, 1924) [see 183.02], the International Maritime Committee [see 183 B] presented a draft convention to the Madrid Conference of 1955 based entirely on the British principle of a lump sum limitation. Thus, the Convention signed in Brussels on 10 October 1957 put a definitive end to the traditional system of *l'abandon en nature* (i.e. the abandonment of both the ship, and the cargo the ship was carrying on the particular voyage, to the creditor).

DETAILS OF THE CONVENTION

The new Convention is advantageous to the owner, manager, operator and charterer of a ship as well as their servants (Art. 6) in that it limits their liability for the claims listed in Article 1, even in cases where liability arises by reason of ownership, possession, custody or control of the ship (Art. 1-3).

Article 3 of the Convention makes provision for the amount to which an owner of a ship may limit his liability:

- 1,000 gold francs for each ton of the ship's tonnage where the occurrence has only given rise to property claim;
- 3,100 gold francs for each ton of the ship's tonnage where the occurrence has only given rise to personal claims;
- 3,100 gold francs for each ton of the ship's tonnage where the occurrence has given rise both to personal claims and property claims, of which a first portion of 2,100 gold francs for each ton of the ship's tonnage shall be exclusively appropriated for the payment of personal claims and of which a second portion of 1,000 gold francs for each ton of the ship's tonnage shall be appropriated for the payment of property claims; provided, however, that in cases where the first portion is insufficient to pay the personal claims in full, the unpaid balance shall rank rateably with the property claims for payment against the second portion of the fund.

MODIFICATIONS

A protocol signed in Brussels on 21 December 1979, which entered into force on 6 October 1984, modified the 1957 Convention in that it replaced the gold franc with the Special Drawing Right (SDR). The 1979 Protocol also confirms the reference made to SDR in Article 8 of the Convention on Limitation of Liability for Maritime Claims (London, 1976) [see 183.18].

For the states which have ratified, accepted, approved or acceded to the Convention on Limitation of Liability for Maritime Claims (London, 1976) [see 183.18] that Convention replaces and abrogates, as of its entry into force on 1 December 1986, the Brussels Conventions of 25 August 1924 and 10 October 1957, relating to the limitation of the liability of owners of sea-going ships (Art. 17-4).

The London Convention does the following:

- it extends the limitation of the liability of ship-owners to salvors (Art. 1);
- it excludes from limitation of liability certain claims for damage caused by oil or nuclear material, which are regulated by other international agreements arrived at since 10 October 1957 (Art. 3);
- it distinguishes between three types of limitations: a general limitation composed of two limits depending on whether the claim is a property claim or a personal claim; and two specific limitations relating to salvors and passenger carriers (Art. 6); and
- it substitutes the "personal act or omission" of the ship-owner for the "actual fault or privity" of the owner found in the Brussels Conventions of 1924 and 1957, so as to exclude application of limitation of liability (Art. 4).

P.F. and IDIT, B.M.

Access : ALS (Art. 12)
Reserves : PAU (Art. du Prot. de 1979)
Duration : USP
Deposit. : BE (Art. 10)
Language : Eng, Fre

Modific. : Protocol Brussels 21.12.79 (06.10.84)

Reference : UKTS 1968/52 – ULR 1979/2 – RTAF 1959/46 – JORF 6 Dec 59

183.08 – INTERNATIONAL CONVENTION FOR THE UNIFICATION OF CERTAIN RULES RELATING TO THE CARRIAGE OF PASSENGERS BY SEA – CMI

Concluded : 29.04.1961, Brussels
In Force : 04.06.1965
Parties : 10

The aim of the Convention is to establish certain uniform rules relating to the carriage of passengers by sea, and to regulate the liability of ship-owners, charterers or operators.

Scope: The Convention applies "to any international carriage if either the ship flies the flag of a Contracting State or if, according to the contract of carriage, either the place of departure or the place of destination is in a Contracting State" (Art. 2). The term "international carriage" is defined in a similar way to the definition given in the 1929 Warsaw Convention on international carriage by air [see 184.01], and means "any carriage in which according to the contract of carriage the place of departure and the place of destination are situated either in a single State if there is an intermediate port of call in another State, or in two different States" (Art. 1-f).

DETAILS OF THE CONVENTION

The carrier is liable for damage suffered as a result of the death of or personal injury to a passenger if the incident which causes the damage occurs in the course of carriage and is due to the fault or neglect of the carrier or of his servants or agents acting within the scope of their employment. The fault or neglect of the carrier, his servants and agents will be presumed, unless the contrary is proved, if the death or personal injury is the result of shipwreck, collision, stranding, explosion or fire. The liability of the carrier shall not exceed 250,000 gold francs per passenger, unless it is proved that the damage resulted from an act or omission of the carrier done with intent to cause damage or recklessly and with knowledge that damage would probably result (Art. 7).

Any contractual provision concluded before the occurrence which caused the damage shall be held to be null and void if it purports to relieve the carrier of his liability towards the passenger; or prescribes a lower limit to that fixed in the Convention; or shifts the burden of proof which rests on the carrier; or requires disputes to be submitted to any particular jurisdiction or to arbitration.

The Convention does not modify the rights and duties of the carrier provided for in international conventions relating to the limitation of liability of owners of sea-going ships or any national law relating to such limitation (Art. 8); nor does the Convention affect the provisions of any international convention or national law which covers liability for nuclear damage [see 4.2.1].

The Athens Convention Relating to the Carriage of Passengers and their Luggage by Sea (Athens, 1974) [see 183.17] seeks to harmonize and consolidate the present Convention with that of the subsequent Brussels Convention of 1967 [see 183.11].

P.F. and IDIT, B.M.

Access : ALS (Art. 18)
Reserves : PAU
Duration : USP
Deposit. : BE
Language : Eng, Fre

Reference : RCDIP 1965/3 – JDI 1965 – RTAF 1965/64

183.09 – INTERNATIONAL CONVENTION ON LOAD LINES (LL) – IMO

Concluded : 05.04.1966, London
In Force : 21.07.1968
Parties : 127

It had long been recognized that minimum freeboards – the draft to which a ship may be loaded – constituted the most important contribution to the safety of life and property at sea. The aim of the Convention is to specify the limits that will attach to particular vessels.

DETAILS OF THE CONVENTION

Annex I of the Convention contains regulations for determining Load Lines and the conditions for their assignment. Once assigned, Load Lines must be marked amidship on each side of the ship, together with the deck line. Special requirements apply for ships assigned timber freeboards. Provisions are made determining the freeboard of tankers by subdivision and damage stability calculations.

As Load Lines will necessarily vary depending on whether the ship sails in freshwater or saltwater, the region in which she sails and the time of year, Annex II specifies the adjustments necessary depending on the zone, area and/or seasonal period. The Rules specify that owners must provide the ship's master with information relating to the loading and ballasting of the ship.

MODIFICATIONS

The Convention has been subject to various amendments which have sought, *inter alia*, to make certain improvements to the text and to the chart of zones and seasonal areas. None of these amendments has yet entered into force. In 1988, a Protocol was adopted (though not yet entered in force) which is to serve as a means of harmonizing the Convention's survey and certification requirements with those contained in SOLAS 1974 [see 183.16] and MARPOL 73/78 [see 412.09].

Patricia Ford

Access : ALS
Reserves : PAU
Duration : USP
Deposit. : IMO (Art. 33)
Language : Eng, Fre, Rus, Spa (Art. 34)

Modific. : Amendments 12.10.71 (-); Amendment 12.11.75 (-); Amendment 15.11.79 (-); 17.11.83 (-); Protocol 11.11.88 (-)

Reference : 640 UNTS – UST 18 – UKTS 1968/58 – JORF 30 jan 69 – RTAF 1969/9

183.10 – CONVENTION ON FACILITATION OF INTERNATIONAL MARITIME TRAFFIC (FAL) – IMO

Concluded : 09.04.1965, London
In Force : 05.03.1967
Parties : 68

The aim of the Convention is to adopt international standards to facilitate and expedite maritime traffic and to prevent unnecessary delays to ships and to persons and property on board.

DETAILS OF THE CONVENTION

The contracting governments undertake to prevent unnecessary delays to ships (Art. 1), and to co-operate in the formulation of measures for the facilitation of the arrival, stay and departure of ships (Art. 2). They also undertake to co-operate in securing "the highest practicable degree of uniformity" in matters relating to formalities, documentary requirements and procedures (Art. 4); the instrument of this co-operation is to be the International Maritime Organization.

However, Article 6 distinguishes between "standards", whose uniform application is "necessary and practicable" in order to facilitate maritime traffic, and "recommended practices", whose application is "desirable" in order to facilitate maritime traffic. Governments may decide not to conform to the recommended practices on the condition that they notify the Secretary-General of the Organization. This distinction between "standards" and "recommended practices" was applied in the Annex adopted jointly with the Convention, and lists those standards and recommended practices which should be applied. The Annex also contains a reaffirmation by governments of their desire to co-operate in simplifying and reducing formalities, documentary requirements and procedures so as to prevent unnecessary delays to ships and to persons or property on board.

MODIFICATIONS

On 1 May 1992, a resolution was adopted by the FAL Committee at its 21st Session proposing various amendments aimed at restructuring the Annex and upgrading some of the recommended practices. These amendments entered into force on 1 September 1993.

P.F.

Access : ALS (Art. 10)
Reserves : USP
Duration : USP
Deposit. : IMO
Language : Eng, Fre

Modific. : Amendments 28.11.69 (12.08.71); Amendments 00.11.73 (02.06.84); Amendments 00.11.77 (31.07.78); Amendments 00.03.86 (01.10.86); Amendments 00.09.87 (01.01.89); Amendments 00.05.90 (01.09.91); Amendments 01.05.92 (01.09.93)

Reference : 591 UNTS – Can TS 1967/25, 1971/30 – UKTS 1967/46, 1972/63, 1978/63, 1984/67, 1987/10 – ILM 4:502 – JORF 2 Mar 68, 16 Dec 71, 29 Aug 78, 6 Feb 87 – JDI 1968/4 – RTAF 1968/17, 1971/100, 1978/55

183.11 – INTERNATIONAL CONVENTION FOR THE UNIFICATION OF CERTAIN RULES RELATING TO THE CARRIAGE OF PASSENGER LUGGAGE BY SEA – CMI

Concluded : 27.05.1967, Brussels
Parties : 2

This Convention establishes the liability of the carrier of passenger luggage by sea. By and large, it follows the 1961 Convention on carriage of passengers [see 183.08] but, by introducing different wording, creates certain problems.

Scope: Although the definitions of international carriage are identical, the applications differ in that Article 2 of the 1967 Convention requires that there be a connection with a contracting state. This Convention stipulates that it is applicable to any international carriage if the ship is (a) registered in a contracting state, or (b) if the contract of carriage has been made in a contracting state, or (c) if the place of departure according to the contract of carriage is in a contracting state (Art. 2).

DETAILS OF THE CONVENTION

The carrier is liable for loss of or damage to luggage if the incident which causes the loss or damage occurs in the course of carriage and is due to the fault or neglect of the carrier or his servants or agents acting within the scope of their employment (Art. 4). The carrier is not liable, however, for loss or damage to valuables unless agreed expressly and in writing.

The carrier's liability is limited to 10,000 gold francs per passenger for the loss of or damage to cabin luggage; 30,000 gold francs per vehicle for loss of or damage to vehicles including all luggage carried in or the vehicle; and 16,000 gold francs per passenger for the loss or damage to all other articles (Art. 6). The carrier does not benefit from this limitation of liability if it is proved that the damage resulted from an act or omission of the carrier done with the intent to cause damage or recklessly and with knowledge that the damage would probably result (Art. 7).

Passengers have a very short time to give written notice of action for damages, and the actions are time-barred after a period of two or three years (Art. 10).

The Convention is identical to the 1961 Convention in that any claim for damages, however founded, may only be made subject to the conditions and the limits set out in the Convention (Art. 9). Moreover, it also prohibits any contrary contractual provisions, except those which seek to increase the carriers limit of liability.

The Convention includes provisions on jurisdiction (Art. 13) and does not affect the provisions of any international convention or national law which governs liability for nuclear damage (Art. 15). Nor does the Convention modify the rights or duties of the carrier provided for in international conventions relating to the limitation of liability of owners of sea-going ships or in any national law relating to such limitation (Art. 8)

The Convention will come into force three months after its ratification by five states (Art. 21). The Athens Convention Relating to the Carriage of Passengers and their Luggage by Sea (Athens, 1974) [see 183.17] seeks to harmonize and consolidate the present Convention with that of the Brussels Convention of 1961 [see 183.08].

P.F.

Access : ALS (Art. 22)
Reserves : PAU (Art. 18)
Duration : USP
Deposit. : BE (Art. 20)
Language : Eng, Fre

Reference : ULR 1967

183.12 – INTERNATIONAL CONVENTION RELATING TO REGISTRATION OF RIGHTS IN RESPECT OF VESSELS UNDER CONSTRUCTION – CMI

Concluded : 27.05.1967, Brussels
Parties : 5

The objective of the Convention is to give sea-going vessels under construction an official and public status so that they can be mortgaged. The contracting states undertake that their national law shall contain provisions permitting the registration in an official register of the titles to, mortgages, and hypothèques on vessels which are to be or are being constructed within their territories (Arts. 1 and 5).

The effects of the registration of the rights shall be determined by the law of the state where the vessel is to be or is being constructed; however, without prejudice to the provisions of the Convention, all matters relating to the procedure of enforcement shall be regulated by the law of the state where the enforcement takes place (Art. 6).

No contracting state shall allow, except in the case of forced sale, the deregistration of these rights without the written consent of the holders of such rights. In addition, a vessel which is being or has been constructed in a contracting state shall not be eligible for registration in another contracting state unless a certificate has been issued by the former state to the effect that the rights have been deregistered or that such rights will be deregistered on the day when the vessel is registered (Art. 10).

The Convention will enter into force three months after the date of the deposit of the fifth instrument of ratification by a signatory state (Art. 15).

P.F.

Access : ALS (Art. 16)
Reserves : PAU (Art. 12)
Duration : USP
Deposit. : BE (Art. 14)
Language : Eng, Fre

Reference : ULR 1967

183.13 – INTERNATIONAL CONVENTION FOR THE UNIFICATION OF CERTAIN RULES RELATING TO MARITIME LIENS AND MORTGAGES – CMI

Concluded : 27.05.1967, Brussels
Parties : 5

The international convention of the same title, which was signed in Brussels on 10 April 1926 [see 183.03], had only been ratified by a few states. The United States and Great Britain, who were among those who had not ratified that Convention, were responsible in 1967 for the adoption of this new Brussels Convention. It is to take effect three months after the deposit of the fifth instrument of ratification (Art. 19).

DETAILS OF THE CONVENTION

The Convention reduces the number of primary liens on mortgages, in order to encourage mortgage lending, which is necessary for the acquisition and operation of modern ships.

Article 4 of the Convention specifies the claims which are to be secured by way of a maritime lien on the vessel. In contrast to Article 2-5 of the Convention of 1926, it does not include claims of interested parties on lost or damaged goods where that interest arose by virtue of a contract, nor does it include claims of suppliers, repairers and other contractors away from the vessel's home port.

The ranking of the liens, their extinction and priority are stipulated in Articles 5, 7 and 8. Nevertheless, the Convention has no provisions on the scope and tax base of the liens, and simply states that the mortgage is governed by the law of the state in which the ship is registered.

RECENT DEVELOPMENTS

Due in large part to the fact that the method of enforcement was left to the domestic law of contracting states, and that in themselves the provisions tended to give rise to different national legislation on the matter, this Convention was signed by very few states. A draft reform of the 1926 and 1967 Conventions was sent to the IMO [see 183 A] and UNCTAD [see 111 B] following a decision taken by the International Maritime Committee at its Lisbon Conference in May 1985.

In June 1990, the UNCTAD Committee on Shipping recommended to the General Assembly that it convene an international conference to examine and adopt the draft Convention, which aims to further reduce the claims attracting a primary lien and seeks a modification of their ranking. No longer would claims for salvage, wreck removal and contribution in general average be considered primary liens.

Claims for wages, however, and other sums due to the master, officers and other members of the vessel's crew would rank at the head of primary liens, and would include costs of repatriation as well as subscriptions to social security. These claims would be followed by:

- claims in respect of loss of or damage to property occurring, whether on land or on water, in direct connection with the operation of the vessel;
- claims for salvage;
- claims in respect of port, canal or waterway dues and pilotage dues;
- claims based on tort and not capable of being based on contract, for loss of or damage to property, other than cargo, containers or personal effects of passengers travelling on a vessel, occurring in direct connection with the operation of the vessel.

As in the 27 May 1967 Convention, the draft Convention stipulates that all contracting states may grant rights of retention on a ship in the possession of a shipbuilder or ship-repairer to secure claims. The right of retention is to be postponed as against all maritime liens but is to be preferred to registered mortgages or *hypothèques*.

Finally, the draft Convention, like the 1967 Convention, does not stipulate what the tax base of the liens will be.

Patricia Ford and IDIT, Barthélémy Mercadal

Access : ALS (Art. 17, 20)
Reserves : PAU (Art. 14, 16)
Duration : USP
Deposit. : BE (Art. 18)
Language : Eng, Fre

Reference : ULR 1967

183.14 – INTERNATIONAL CONVENTION FOR SAFE CONTAINERS (CSC) – IMO/ECE

Concluded : 02.12.1972, Geneva
In Force : 06.09.1977
Parties : 56

Following the rapid increase in the use of freight containers for the consignment of goods by sea and the development of specialized container ships, the IMO [see 183

A] in 1967 undertook a study of the safety of containerization in maritime transport. In co-operation with the Economic Commission for Europe [see 181 A], the IMO prepared a draft convention which was subsequently considered and adopted at an international conference convened by the United Nations and the IMO in 1972.

The aim of the Convention is two-fold: first, to maintain a high level of safety of human life in the transport and handling of containers; and, second, to facilitate the international transport of containers by providing uniform international safety regulations which would also be applicable to all modes of surface transport.

Scope: The Convention applies to the vast majority of freight containers used internationally, but does not apply to those containers specifically designed for carriage by air.

DETAILS OF THE CONVENTION

Governments of contracting states ("the Administration") or their authorized representatives are required to approve the safety of containers. The Administration (or its authorized representative) will authorize the manufacturer to affix to approved containers a safety approval plate containing the relevant technical data specified by the Convention. In line with the objective of uniformity, a safety approval plate granted by one contracting state is to be recognized by other contracting states, thereby obviating the need for lengthy safety control formalities.

The Convention has been subject to three amendments, the latest being in 1991.

Patricia Ford

Access : ALS
Reserves : PAU
Duration : USP
Deposit. : IMO
Language : Ara, Chi, Eng, Fre, Rus, Spa

Modific. : Amendment 00.04.81 (01.12.81); Amendment 00.06.83 (01.01.84); Amendment 17.05.91 (01.01.93)

Reference : UKTS 1979/40 – 29 UST 3709 – JORF 18 sep 77 – RTAF 1977/64

183.15 – CONVENTION OF A CODE OF CONDUCT FOR LINER CONFERENCES – UNCTAD

Concluded : 06.04.1974, Geneva
In Force : 06.10.1983
Parties : 74

In 1875, as a result of too much competition on the Great Britain/Calcutta line, seven British shipowners decided to amalgamate their cargo-carrying capacity and instituted a system of fixed leaving dates and a common rate to be charged for the carriage of cargo. This was the birth of the private associations of shipowners, called liner conferences, which shaped and regulated the international maritime order until 1971.

In 1971, the developing countries, who depend on liner conferences for the transport of their products, used their power in the UN [see 001 A] to ask for a convention which would provide for an equitable distribution of the transport of goods between states involved in maritime transport. Hitherto, much of the freight and traffic generated by a particular trade would not necessarily have benefited the state using the liner conference, but would have been more likely to benefit the state providing the service; more often than not these shipping lines were usually owned and operated by third countries from within the developed world.

DETAILS OF THE CODE

The Code recognizes that "any national shipping line shall have the right to be a full member of a conference which serves the foreign trade of its country" (Art 1-1), as long as it "shall furnish evidence of its ability and intention ... to operate a regular, adequate and efficient service on a long-term basis ..." (Art. 1-2). "The group of national shipping lines of each of two countries the foreign trade between which is carried by the conference shall have equal rights to participate in the freight and volume of traffic generated by their mutual foreign trade and carried by the conference" (Art. 2-4-a); and "third-country shipping lines, if any, shall have the right to acquire a significant part, such as 20 per cent, in the freight and volume of traffic generated by that trade" (Art. 2-4-b). This distribution scheme is more generally known as the 40/40/20 Rule.

Otherwise, the Code of Conduct deals in its Chapter III with the relations between shipper's organizations and shippers, and recognizes the right of the latter to be consulted on matters of common interest (Art. 11). A mechanism for the settlement of disputes relating to the application or operation of the Code and a binding conciliation procedure are provided for in Chapter VI.

SUBSEQUENT DEVELOPMENTS

It is worth noting that Regulation No. 954/79 of the Council of European Communities of 15 May 1979 allowed for the ratification of the Code of Conduct by member states. Nevertheless, a more limited version of the Code was adopted, since the 40/40/20 Rule was excluded in liner conference traffic between member states, and between member states and other states of the OECD who are parties to the Code, while at the same time granting developing countries the full benefit of the Code.

Following the spectacular breakthrough of outsiders since 1974 and the subsequent decrease of conference traffic, the Group of 77 [see 233 A] called for a modification of the Convention so that the Code of Conduct could apply to the totality of maritime traffic, whether that traffic was controlled by conferences or by outsiders. Indeed, the developing countries are generally of the opinion that the uncontrolled growth of outsiders undermined the original objectives of the Convention, particularly those relating to the protection of the right of national companies in the distribution of cargo.

During the two conferences called to revise the Convention in 1988 and 1991 and held under the auspices of UNCTAD [see 111 B], the Group of 77 defended the application of the 40/40/20 Rule to bulk traffic on the one hand, and to all multimodal transport on the other.

These proposals met with resistance from the countries of "Group B" (the industrialized countries) which argued that the title and the provisions of the Convention left no doubt as to the intentions of its framers, particularly on the question of limiting the scope of application of the 40/40/20 Rule to conference traffic.

Patricia Ford and IDIT, Barthélémy Mercadal

Access : ALS (Art. 48)
Reserves : USP
Duration : USP
Deposit. : UN
Language : Chi, Eng, Fre, Rus, Spa (Art. 54)

Reference : UN Doc. TD/Code 11/Rev.1, Corr 1 – ILM 13:932 – JORF 1 Sep 87, 21 Oct 87

183.16 – INTERNATIONAL CONVENTION FOR THE SAFETY OF LIFE AT SEA (SOLAS) – IMO

Concluded : 01.11.1974, London
In Force : 25.05.1980
Parties : 120

The nineteenth and early twentieth centuries represented the golden age of passenger travel by sea. Emigration from Europe to the Americas and other parts of the world took place on a massive scale and, at this time, before aircraft was in use, sea travel was the only means of travelling to these countries. When accidents occurred, therefore, they frequently led to heavy casualties: the average annual loss of life from British ships alone was 700 to 800 during this period. It was the sinking of the passenger ship *Titanic* in 1912, however, which became the catalyst for international action.

As a result of this disaster, in which over 1,500 passengers and crew died, the British Government called for an international conference on the standards of maritime safety and, on 20 January 1914, the first International Convention for the Safety of Life at Sea (SOLAS) was adopted.

The Convention, whose implementation was delayed because of the First World War, introduced new international provisions on maritime safety for all commercial ships. Most of these provisions were reaffirmed in the second SOLAS Convention in 1929, and were modified in the third Convention of 1948 and the fourth Convention of 1960.

The amendment procedures in the 1960 Convention merely required the contracting parties to take positive steps to accept amendments. This tended to delay the updating of the Convention in the face of the rapid evolution in technology, and it soon became clear that it would be impossible to secure the entry into force of amendments within a reasonable period of time. Partly in response to this, a new Convention was adopted in 1974.

DETAILS OF THE CONVENTION

The 1974 SOLAS Convention is made up, in large part, of the 1960 Convention, amendments adopted between 1966 and 1973, as well as a new "tacit agreement" whereby amendments to Chapters II to VIII shall be deemed to have been adopted by a two-thirds majority of the contracting governments, or if so determined at the time of its adoption, at the end of two years from the date on which it is communicated to contracting governments for acceptance, or at the end of a different period determined at the time of adoption. If within the specified period either more than one-third of the contracting governments, or contracting governments the combined merchant fleets of which constitute not less than 50 per cent of the gross tonnage of the world's fleet, object to the amendment, it will not be accepted (Art. VIII).

The Convention contains a number of provisions which deal with visits by various types of ships and the presentation of documents attesting that a ship meets the requirements of the Convention. The state official of a port in which a ship wishes to call may verify that the ship has valid certificates, and may take the necessary measures to prevent it from sailing until it can do so without endangering the passengers, crew or the vessel itself (Regs. 12 and 19).

The Convention includes chapters on construction and fire protection, detection and extinction (Chap. II), on life-saving appliances (Chap. III), on radiotelegraphy and radiotelephony (Chap. IV, which is closely linked to the Radio Regulations of the ITU [see 192.01]), on safety of navigation (Chap. V), on the carriage of grain (Chap. VI), on the carriage of dangerous goods (Chap. VII), and on nuclear ships (Chap. VIII). This last chapter is supplemented by various recommendations attached to the Convention.

MODIFICATIONS

Among the amendments to the chapters cited above, the 1983 amendments extended the application of Chapter VII to chemical tankers and liquefied gas carriers. Initially, the Chapter applied only to dangerous goods carried in packaged forms. The revised Chapter VII achieves this by making reference to two new codes developed by the IMO: the International Bulk Chemical Code and the International Gas Carrier Code, both of which are considered mandatory (Regs. 10 and 13).

The recommendations attached to Chapter VIII were overtaken by the safety code for nuclear merchant ships and recommendations on the use of ports by nuclear merchant ships.

P.F.

Access : ALS (Art. 9)
Reserves : USP
Duration : USP
Deposit. : IMO
Language : Chi, Eng, Fre, Rus, Spa

Modific. : Amendments 20.11.81 (01.09.84); Amendments 17.06.83 (01.07.86); IBC Code Amendments 00.04.87 (30.10.88); Amendments (April ro-ro), Regs 23-2 and 42-1 of Chap. II-1 21.04.88 (22.10.89); Amendments (October ro-ro), Regs 8, 20-1 and 22 of Chap. II-1 28.10.88 (29.04.90); Amendments (GMDSS) 11.11.88 (01.02.92); Amendments (April) 11.04.89 (01.02.92); Amendments (IBC Code) 11.04.89 (13.10.90); Amendments (Chapter II-1) 24.05.90 (01.02.92); Amendments (IBC Code) 24.05.90 (-); Amendments (IGC Code) 24.05.90 (-); Amendments 24.05.91 (01.01.94); Protocol 17.02.78 (01.05.81); Amendment to 1978 Protocol 20.11.81 (01.09.84); Amendment to 1978 Protocol 00.11.88 (01.02.92); Protocol 11.11.88 (-)

Reference : Can TS 1980/45 – UKTS 1980/46, 1981/40, 1983/42 – ILM 14:959, 14:1603, 17:579 – UST 32/2/5 – RTAF 1980/25, 1981/31

183.17 – ATHENS CONVENTION RELATING TO THE CARRIAGE OF PASSENGERS AND THEIR LUGGAGE BY SEA (PAL) – IMO

Concluded : 13.12.1974, Athens
In Force : 28.04.1987
Parties : 16

The Convention seeks to consolidate and harmonize two preceding Brussels Conventions relating to passengers and luggage, adopted in 1961 and 1967 respectively [see 183.08 and 183.11].

Scope: Article 2 of the Convention specifies that the Convention applies to international carriage involving ships flying the flag of state parties; or where the contract is made in a state party; or where the place of departure or destination is a state party. "Passenger" is defined as "any person carried in a ship" under a contract of carriage and also any person who, with the carrier's consent, accompanies live animals or vehicles (Art. 1-4).

DETAILS OF THE CONVENTION

The Convention sets up a liability regime for damage suffered by passengers on a ship travelling on the high seas. The carrier is liable for damage or loss suffered by passengers if the incident causing the damage or loss took place during the course of the carriage and is attributable to the fault or neglect of the carrier or of his servants or agents acting within the scope of their employment.

Nevertheless, if it can be proven that the damage was not caused intentionally by the carrier, or by his recklessness and in such a way that he could have foreseen the results of this action, the carrier may limit his liability. In respect of damage suffered as a result of death or personal injury to a passenger, liability is limited to SDR 46,666 (US$55,000). For loss of or damage to luggage, the limitation of the liability of the carrier varies depending on whether it concerns cabin luggage, or a vehicle and/or luggage transported in or on the vehicle, or other luggage.

MODIFICATIONS

The initial low limits of liability proved to be one reason why many states were slow to ratify this Convention, even though states were allowed to fix higher death or personal injury limits for carriers who were nationals of that state. In 1976, a protocol was adopted which replaced the *Poincaré franc* with the Special Drawing Right; this Protocol entered into force on 30 April 1989. On 30 March 1990, a second Protocol was adopted which provides for a greatly enhanced compensation limit for death and personal injury at around US$225,000 and upgrades the other limits. The Protocol also establishes a simplified procedure for updating limitation amounts based on the principle of "tacit acceptance". The Protocol will enter into force 90 days after being accepted by ten states.

P.F.

Access : ALS (Art. 23)
Reserves : PAU (Art. 22,)
Duration : USP
Deposit. : IMO (Art. 27)
Language : Eng, Fre (Art. 28)
Modific. : Protocol 19.11.76 (30.04.89); Protocol 30.03.90 (-)

Reference : ULR 1975/1, 1977/1 – ILM 14:945, 16:625

183.18 – CONVENTION ON LIMITATION OF LIABILITY FOR MARITIME CLAIMS – IMO

Concluded: 19.11.1976, London
In Force : 01.12.1986
Parties : 22

The emergence of ships of very large tonnage and the general inflation in the early 1970s led to the drafting of the 1976 London Convention. The aim was to revise the sums involved in the limitation of liability of owners of sea-going ships, instituted by the Brussels Convention of 1957 [see 183.07]. This revision, however, also led to the adoption of other innovations.

DETAILS OF THE CONVENTION

The London Convention extends the limitation of the liability of shipowners (meaning shipowners, charterers, managers and operators of seagoing ships) to salvors; the Convention defines a "salvor" as "any person rendering services in direct connexion with salvage operations" (Art. 1).

In order to keep up to date with agreements reached since the 1957 Brussels Convention, the London Convention added to the list of claims excluded from limitation of liability "claims for oil pollution damage within the meaning of the International Convention on Civil Liability for Oil Pollution Damage, dated 29 November 1969 [Brussels]" (Art. 3-b), and "claims against the shipowner of a nuclear ship for nuclear damage" (Art. 3-d) or "claims subject to any international convention or national legislation governing or prohibiting limitation of liability for nuclear damage" (Art. 3-c).

The claims covered by Article 2 of the London Convention "whatever the basis of liability may be, shall be subject to limitation of liability" (Art. 2-1), "even if brought by way of recourse or for indemnity under a contract or otherwise" (Art. 2-2).

Three limits of liability are distinguished:

- a general limit made up of two limits depending on whether it is in respect of claims for loss of life or personal injury (Art. 6-1-a), or whether it is in respect of any other claims (Art. 6-1-b);
- a limit for salvors; and
- a limit for carriers of passengers.

For the purposes of the Convention, and henceforth, the basis for the calculation of limit of liability is gross tonnage in the sense of the 1969 Convention on Tonnage Measurements of Ships. The 1957 Brussels Convention, conversely, defined tonnage on the basis of net tonnage in the sense of the Oslo Convention of 1947.

Article 8 of the London Convention refers to a unit of account, which is the Special Drawing Right (SDR) as defined by the International Monetary Fund [see 211 A]. States which are not members of the IMF or whose law does not allow the use of SDRs may continue to use the old gold franc (now referred to as "monetary unit" in the Convention).

The Convention substitutes for the "actual fault or privity" of the shipowner, as specified in the 1957 Convention, the fault resulting from the shipowner's "personal act or omission, committed with the intent to cause such loss, or recklessly and with knowledge that such loss would probably result" (Art. 4).

CONTEXT

The idea behind the London Convention, since its entry into effect on 1 December 1986, has been that it should gradually replace and abrogate in respect of the relations between states who have ratified, accepted, approved or acceded to it, the 1957 Brussels International Convention Relating to the Limitation of the Liability of Owners of Sea-Going Ships [see 183.07] and the 1924 Brussels International Convention for the Unification of Certain Rules Relating to the Limitation of Liability of Owners of Sea-Going Vessels (Art. 17-4) [see 183.02].

Patricia Ford and IDIT, Barthélémy Mercadal

Access : ALS (Art. 16)
Reserves : PAU (Art. 18)
Duration : USP
Deposit. : IMO (Art. 22)
Language : Eng, Fre, Rus, Spa (Art. 23)

Reference : ULR 1977/1 – ILM 16:616 – RGDIP 1987/2 – JORF 23 Dec 86

183.19 – TORREMOLINOS INTERNATIONAL CONVENTION FOR THE SAFETY OF FISHING VESSELS (SFV) – IMO

Concluded : 02.04.1977, Torremolinos
Parties : 18

The safety of fishing vessels had always been a major concern to the IMO but in view of the vagaries in the size of fishing vessels, they could never satisfactorily be included under the umbrella of the conventions dealing with safety of life at sea and/or load lines. Thus, in 1976 a decision was taken by the IMO [see 183 A] to convene a conference aimed at remedying this lacuna. The result was the adoption of the first ever convention on the safety of fishing vessels.

Scope: The Convention applies to any sea-going fishing vessel entitled to fly the flag of a contracting party to the Convention (Art. 3); such vessel being used commercially for "catching fish, whales, seals, walrus or other living resources of the sea" (Art. 2).

DETAILS OF THE CONVENTION

Where a certificate is issued by a contracting state in accordance with the provisions of the Convention, the certificate is to be accepted by other contracting parties as though it had been issued by them and is to be treated for all purposes as covered by the Convention. While in the ports of other contracting states, a vessel holding a certificate is liable to the control of officers duly authorized by the particular contracting state who may verify that there is on board a valid certificate (Art. 4). A duly authorized officer is entitled to detain a vessel until assured that the vessel can proceed to sea without danger to the vessel or persons on board. Any non-compliance with the certificate as issued may be reported to the Consul or diplomatic representative of the state whose flag the vessel is entitled to fly; a report also being conveyed to the IMO.

One of the most innovative features of the Convention is that it contains a chapter on stability requirements (Annex – Chapter 3: Regs. 27 to 40).

MODIFICATIONS

In 1993, the parties adopted a Protocol which aims at eliminating the provisions incorporated in the Convention which have prevented states ratifying it. The Protocol is also intended to take into account recent developments in fishing (e.g. deep-water fishing) and in fishing vessel technology as they relate to the safety of fishing vessels and fishermen.

Patricia Ford

Access : ALS
Reserves : PAU
Duration : USP
Deposit. : IMO (Art. 13)
Language : Eng, Fre, Rus, Spa (Art. 14)

Modific. : Protocol 02.04.93 (-)

183.20 – UNITED NATIONS CONVENTION ON THE CARRIAGE OF GOODS BY SEA – UNCITRAL

Concluded : 31.03.1978, Hamburg
In Force : 01.11.1992
Parties : 19

Rather than substantially revising the Brussels International Convention of 25 August 1924 for the Unification of Certain Rules of Law Relating to Bills of Lading [see 183.01], the authors of the Brussels Protocols of 1968 and 1979 made few changes to the original agreement. This showed the extent to which the international maritime community hesitated to change an agreement whose provisions had been integrated into the domestic laws of numerous states and which, consequently, led to a significant unification of law relating to bills of lading, and guaranteed the stability of international trade.

The 1978 revision took place, however, at the instigation of the developing countries which wanted to change rules they considered favourable to the interests of the traditional maritime powers. Others saw the revision as coming at an opportune moment to agree to a new general code for maritime transport which would bring maritime transport into alignment with the laws of other methods of transport.

It is this latter objective which makes the Convention so original. It was drafted by the United Nations Commission on International Trade Law (UNCITRAL) [see 300 C] and signed in Hamburg on 31 March 1978. The resolution appended to the text of the Convention recommends that the rules which it contains be referred to as the "Hamburg Rules".

Scope: With the exception of charter-parties (Art. 2-3), the Hamburg Rules seek to regulate the carriage of all goods by sea, including live animals, where the goods are consolidated in a container, pallet or similar article of transport supplied by the shipper (Art. 1-5). The goods may be carried on deck (Art. 9), and must be carried in pursuance of a "contract of carriage by sea", which may also involve carriage by some other means (Art. 1-6). The provisions of the Convention are applicable to all contracts of carriage by sea between two different states, if (Art. 2):

- the port of loading is located in a contracting state; or
- the port of discharge is located in a contracting state; or

- the bill of lading or other document evidencing the contract of carriage by sea is issued in a contracting state; or
- the bill of lading or other document evidencing the contract of carriage by sea provides that the provisions of the Convention are to govern the contract.

DETAILS OF THE CONVENTION

The most important innovation relates to the responsibility of the carrier of the goods by sea. Unlike the 1924 Convention, where the carrier's responsibility begins upon loading of the goods and ends upon their discharge, the Hamburg Convention states, "the responsibility of the carrier for the goods under [the] Convention covers the period during which the carrier is in charge of the goods at the port of loading, during the carriage, and at the port of discharge" (Art. 4-1) – that is, from the time he has taken over the goods from, *inter alia*, the shipper, until the time he has delivered the goods (e.g. by handing them over to the consignee) (Art. 4-2).

In contrast to the Hague Rules, which provided for a system of carriers' duties and immunities, the Hamburg Rules stipulate that the liability of the carrier under the Convention is to be based on the principle of presumed fault or neglect. Consequently, where there is a delay in delivery or loss or damage of the goods under his control, the carrier will be liable "unless [he] proves that he, his servants or agents took all measures that could reasonably be required to avoid the occurrence and its consequences" (Art. 5-1). However, two exceptions to this rule are (a) defence of fire (Art. 5-4) and (b) measures to save life or property (Art. 5-6). With respect to the former, it is for the claimant to prove negligence on the part of the carrier (his servants or agents) both in terms of the outbreak of the fire and in respect of the measures that could reasonably have been taken to avoid or mitigate the consequences of the fire. With respect to the latter, where the loss, damage or delay is caused by measures to save life or by reasonable measures to save property at sea, the carrier is absolved of liability.

On the other hand, the Hamburg Rules, notwithstanding the particular clauses relating to damages resulting from delay in delivery of goods, adopt a system of double limits on liability: by package or other shipping unit; or by kilogram (Art 6). This system was instituted by the 1968 Protocol on the limitation of liability.

Where the carrier is not the "actual carrier" (i.e. the person engaged in the performance of the carriage), "all the provisions of [the] Convention governing the responsibility of the carrier also apply to the responsibility of the actual carrier for the carriage performed by him" (Art. 10-2).

The unit of account adopted by the Convention is the Special Drawing Right (SDR) as defined by the International Monetary Fund (Art. 2-6).

The Hamburg Rules are generally favourable to shippers, and they also have the merit of addressing issues that, up to that point, were avoided by previous Conventions. This includes, for example, letters of guarantee (Art. 17), jurisdiction (Art. 21) and arbitration (Art. 22).

Any state which becomes a party to the Hamburg Convention must denounce the Brussels Convention of 25 August 1924 if it is also a party to the latter (Art. 31). The Hamburg Rules entered into force on 1 November 1992.

P.F.

Access	: ALS (Art. 28)
Reserves	: PRO (Art. 29)
Duration	: USP
Deposit.	: UN (Art. 27)

Language : Ara, Chi, Eng, Fre, Rus, Spa (Art. 34)

Reference : UN Doc. A/CONF.89/5 – ULR 1978/1 – ILM 17:623

183.21 – UNITED NATIONS CONVENTION ON CONDITIONS FOR REGISTRATION OF SHIPS – UNCTAD

Concluded : 07.02.1986, Geneva
Parties : 8

Since the Second World War, the significant social evolution in the West has led to a general increase in costs for enterprises. In the maritime field, this has, in turn, led to an increase in flags of convenience whereby states have encouraged the registration of foreign-owned ships as a means of earning revenue.

Even if they have always existed as a means to occasionally facilitate trade relations between states, convenience flags have more recently allowed shipowners to register their ships in states with a lower tax burden and less demanding with regard to social standards and safety conditions. Indeed, by 1986 a little over a third of the world ships were flying convenience flags.

In order to curb the decline in the fleets of the traditional maritime states, UNCTAD [see 111 B] adopted a Convention on 8 February 1986 which sought to regulate the conditions under which ships are registered. The Convention will enter into force 12 months after the date when not less than 40 states, the combined tonnage of which amounts to at least 25 per cent of world tonnage, have signed it (Art. 19).

Scope: The Convention applies to "any self-propelled sea-going vessel used in international seaborne trade for the transport of goods, passengers, or both with the exception of vessels less than 500 gross registered tons" (Arts. 2 and 3).

DETAILS OF THE CONVENTION

The Convention reaffirms the principle that "every State, whether coastal or land-locked, has the right to sail ships flying its flag on the high seas" (Art. 4-1), but it also stipulates that "ships shall sail under the flag of one State only" (Art. 4-3) and that they shall "have the nationality of the State whose flag they are entitled to fly" (Art. 4-2). It adds, "a ship may not change its flag during a voyage or while in a port of call, save in the case of a real transfer of ownership or change of registry" (Art. 4-5).

To this end, states must, first, establish and maintain a register of ships flying their flags (Art. 6 and 11) and, second, they must issue and inspect documents which contain information concerning the ship, its owner or owners, or its operator (Art. 5 and 6). Before entering a ship in its register of ships, however, the state of registration must ensure that the shipowning company is established and/or has its principal place of business within its territory or, if this is not the case, that there is a representative or management person who shall be a national of the flag state, or be domiciled therein (Art. 10-1 and 10-2).

Thus, the major intention of the Convention is to strengthen the links which must exist between a ship and its flag state, and it imposes participation by nationals of the flag state in the manning and/or ownership of ships (Arts. 7, 8 and 9).

Patricia Ford and IDIT, Barthélémy Mercadal

Access : ALS (Art. 18)
Reserves : USP
Duration : USP
Deposit. : UN (Art. 16)
Language : Ara, Chi, Eng, Fre, Rus, Spa

Reference : UN Doc. TD/RS/CONF/23 – ULR 1986/1 – ILM 26:1229

183.22 – CONVENTION FOR THE SUPPRESSION OF UNLAWFUL ACTS AGAINST THE SAFETY OF MARITIME NAVIGATION (SUA) – IMO

Concluded : 10.03.1988, Rome
In Force : 01.03.1992
Parties : 19

Historically, there have been numerous incidents of unlawful acts against vessels, their cargoes and/or ships' crews. However, it is arguable that the upsurge in maritime traffic and the degree of international trade now carried by maritime transport has exposed this form of commerce to an even greater risk of violation. In 1985, the IMO [see 183 A] was charged with the task of studying the problem of terrorism aboard or against ships. Their deliberations, followed and contributed to by an international conference held in Italy in 1988, led to the adoption of the SUA Convention and a Protocol which deals specifically with fixed platforms located on the continental shelf.

DETAILS OF THE CONVENTION

The main purpose of the Convention is to ensure that appropriate action is taken against persons committing the unlawful acts specified in Article 3. Contracting states are required to "take such measures as may be necessary to establish jurisdiction over the offences" set forth in Article 3 and, more specifically, are required to take an offender "into custody or take other measures to ensure his presence for such time as is necessary to enable any criminal or extradition proceeding to be instituted" (Arts. 6 and 7). State parties are required to afford each other the greatest measure of assistance in connection with any criminal proceedings brought.

The Protocol extends the requirements of the Convention to fixed platforms on the continental shelf. Moreover, it affirms that issues not regulated by the Protocol continue to be governed by the rules and principles of international law.

Patricia Ford

Access : ALS
Reserves : PAU
Duration : USP
Deposit. : OMI
Language : Ara, Chi, Eng, Fre, Rus, Spa

Modific. : Protocol 10.03.88 (01.03.92)

183.23 – INTERNATIONAL CONVENTION ON SALVAGE – IMO

Concluded : 28.04.1989, London
Parties : 7

Prior to the adoption of the 1989 Salvage Convention, much of the work of salvage was conducted on a "no cure – no pay" basis whereby salvors' services were paid for out of the fund actually salved. Consequently, where the operation proved unsuccessful, the salvor was without a reward despite his efforts.

In view of the increasing sophistication of equipment used in salvage operations and the degree of professionalism involved, there was always the fear that such an operation would prove too costly, particularly given the frequently dangerous nature of the undertaking. Additionally, the possibility of intervention by the coastal state and the scale of a marine pollution incident rendered any likely risk more onerous under the "no cure – no pay" scheme. The 1989 Salvage Convention was borne out of a desire to address these issues. The aim of the Convention is to establish uniform international regulations for salvage operations so that they may be carried out without delay (and thus contribute to the preservation of the environment [see 4.1.2]).

DETAILS OF THE CONVENTION

The Convention applies principally to commercial ships in navigation areas. It provides for the rights and obligations of salvage ships and salvors whilst at the same time stipulating the duties of the owner and/or master of the salved vessel. It makes provision for the right of the coastal state to take appropriate measures, in accordance with international law, to protect its coastline from pollution or the threat of pollution resulting from a damaged ship, or from related activities which may have harmful effects on the environment. The coastal state may give instructions on salvage operations, and ensure that the operations are successful in that they do not threaten life, property or the environment.

If the salvor has carried out a salvage operation in respect of a vessel which by itself or its cargo threatened damage to the environment and has failed to earn a reward, he is entitled to a special compensation from the owner of that vessel equivalent to his expenses plus 30 per cent if environmental damage is minimized or prevented, but this can be increased to 100 per cent in certain circumstances (Art. 14).

P.F.

Access : ALS
Reserves : PAU
Duration : USP
Deposit. : IMO
Language : Ara, Chi, Eng, Fre, Rus, Spa

1.8.4 Air Transport

Following the Second World War, when the aeroplane became a major carrier of both passengers and freight, international regulations were required on the legal problems incident upon flights into and over foreign territories and for the maintenance of navigational facilities.

The 1919 Versailles Peace Conference produced a Convention on the Regulation of Aerial Navigation and, in 1928, a Pan American Convention on Commerical Aviation was adopted. They were both replaced in 1944 by the Chicago Convention on International Civil Aviation [see 184.02], which constitutes the International Civil Aviation Organization's (ICAO) [see 184 A] constitutive charter and is the basic substantive instrument for the regulation of international aviation.

Regulations on the liability of air carriers are dealt with in the 1929 Warsaw Convention and in the 1952 Rome Convention [see 184.01 and see 184.05], and international recognition of property and other rights in aircraft of flights crossing different territories are dealt with the 1948 Geneva Convention [see 184.04]. This regime is completed by the action of regional organizations such as ECAC and EUROCONTROL in Europe, LACAC in Latin America, COCESNA in Central America, CACAS in Arab Countries and, AFCAC and ASECNA in Africa.

Jean-Louis Magdelénat

SELECTED BIBLIOGRAPHY

Diederiks-Verschoor, I.H.Ph., *An Introduction to Air Law*, 3rd ed., Deventer: Kluwer Law and Taxation, 1988.

Goldhirsch, Lawrence B., *The Warsaw Convention Annotated: A Legal Handbook*, Dordrecht: Martinus Nijhoff Publishers, 1988.

Juglart, M. de and E. du Pontavice, J. Dutheil de la Rochère and G.M. Miller, *Traité de droit aérien*, 2nd ed., Paris: LGDJ, 1989, Vol. 1, and 1992, Vol. 2.

Mankiewicz, R.H., *The Liability Regime of the International Air Carrier*, Deventer: Kluwer Law and Taxation, 1981.

Naveau, J., *International Air Transport in a Changing World*, Dordrecht; Brussels: Martinus Nijhoff Publishers; Emile Bruylant, 1989.

Shawcross and Beaumont, *Air Law*.

Sochor, Eugene, *The Politics of International Aviation*, Macmillan, 1991.

Verwer, Chr. P., *Liability for Damage to Luggage in International Air Transport*, Deventer: Kluwer Law and Taxation, 1987.

Zylicz, *International Air Transport Law*, Utrecht Studies in Air and Space Law 12, Deventer: Kluwer Law and Taxation, 1992.

184 A – INTERNATIONAL CIVIL AVIATION ORGANIZATION (ICAO)

During the Second World War, the Western nations had developed a powerful aviation industry. Air transport linked all the continents of the world and the need to regulate the flight of aircraft, with regard to navigation and safety, and the sovereignty of overflown states, became a priority. Some 53 states were present at the 1944 Chicago Convention on International Civil Aviation [see 184.02] which created ICAO. While the drafting of the Convention was inspired by the Paris Convention of 1919, the 1944 Agreement dealt in greater detail with technical issues. On becoming operational in 1947, ICAO became a specialized agency of the United Nations linked to ECOSOC [see 001 A].

ICAO's aims are to improve the safety of international air navigation and to foster the planning and development of international air transport. Its particular objectives include:

- ensuring the safe and orderly growth of international civil aviation;
- encouraging the development of airways, airports and other facilities;

- promoting safe, regular, efficient and economic air transport; and
- avoiding discrimination between states.

These objectives are achieved through the formulation of uniform international regulations which can be implemented by member states.

STRUCTURE

ICAO includes an Assembly, a Council, and a Secretariat.

The **Assembly** is convened in ordinary session by the Council at least once every three years and includes all member states. It elects the states represented in the Council, votes on the budget, examines the Organization's spending, and may propose amendments to the Convention which can be ratified by a two-thirds majority of the member states.

The **Council** is ICAO's permanent organ, and includes 33 members elected for a period of three years by the Assembly: 11 members belong to the group of states who have a predominant role in air transport; 11 other members belong to states not represented in the first group, but who contribute significantly to international air navigation; and a further 11 members are included to ensure representation from all the major geographic regions in the world.

The Council takes its decisions by majority vote. It elects its President, names a Secretary-General, administers the organization's finances, and implements the decisions of the Assembly. It also has a legislative function in matters relating to the technical annexes of the Chicago Convention which act as a basis for the international regulations of air navigation. The Council may also act as a tribunal for the settlement of any dispute between states arising from the interpretation or application of the Convention or its annexes. The Council is assisted in its tasks by various permanent bodies such as the Air Transport Committee, the Legal Committee (which, in general, meets once a year), and the Joint Support Committee for services relating to air navigation.

The Legal Committee has been responsible for the drafting of numerous international conventions, while the Air Navigation Commission prepares modifications to the technical annexes and communicates to the member states all necessary information regarding air navigation.

Despite facing a number of serious challenges, the Council has managed to avoid becoming overly politicized; it continues mainly to administer the technical aspects of aviation.

The **Secretariat** is responsible for the administrative duties of the Council, the Assembly, and the other bodies of ICAO.

CO-OPERATION

ICAO maintains close ties with other international institutions in order to standardize technical regulations, e.g. IATA [see 184 B] (pilots' medical certification), the ITU [see 192 A] (radio frequency), UPU [see 191 A] (air mail transport), and the WMO [see 431 A] (meteorological data dissemination). It also works on this basis with the CCC [see 112 A], ILO [see 141 A], IMO [see 183 A], WIPO [see 160 A], WHO [see 132 A] and WTO [see 172 A]. The Technical Assistance Bureau administers aid to the developing countries in matters relating to aeronautical training and the development of aeronautical infrastructures. The funds for this are generally provided by the UNDP [see 222 A].

PUBLICATIONS

ICAO publishes studies, technical manuals, statistics, international agreements and other technical, economic and legal documents as well as the monthly *ICAO Journal*. *Air and Space Law* is a yearly summary of ICAO activities and developments.

Jean-Louis Magdelénat

ADDRESS

1000 Sherbrooke Street, West, Montreal, Quebec, H3A 2R2, Canada
T. (514) 285 8219, Fx. (514) 288 4772

184 B – INTERNATIONAL AIR TRANSPORT ASSOCIATION (IATA)

IATA is the professional organization for the world's airlines. It was created in 1945 and is successor in function to the International Air Traffic Association, established in 1919. It aims to promote safe, regular, and economic air transport for the benefit of the peoples of the world; and to foster air commerce and to study problems connected with it. IATA also provides the means for collaboration among air transport enterprises engaged directly or indirectly in international air transport service. It has an important function in the technical aspects of airline co-operation.

IATA's role was recognized by governments which delegated to it the power to establish the rates and fares on international routes under an anti-trust immunity. This authority to set prices within the industry was, and is still, seriously questioned since the deregulation trend began in the USA in 1978 and in Europe in 1990.

IATA was created in 1945 by a Special Act of the Canadian Parliament (Chapter 51), and amended by Canadian Statutes (1974, 1975, 1976, Chapter III).

MEMBERSHIP

Membership is open to any operating company which has been licensed to provide scheduled air services by a state which is a member of ICAO. Airlines engaged directly in international operations are active members, while domestic airlines are associate members. All members are involved in Trade Association (non-tariff) activities, while participation in the co-ordination of international fares and rates is optional. IATA includes over 213 airlines (as of October 1992) which together are responsible for the majority of regular international air transport. Most of these airlines are publicly owned.

STRUCTURE

IATA is made up of: an **Annual General Meeting** in which all active members have an equal vote; an **Executive Committee** made up of 21 members elected by the General Meeting for a period of three years (accountable to the General Meeting); and a permanent **Secretariat** which has authority over the standing committees (financial, traffic, technical, etc.) whose members are appointed by the Executive Committee.

IATA also includes various operational bodies:

- **Traffic Conferences** bring together representatives of IATA member companies

according to geographical location (TC1: North and South America; TC2: Europe, Middle East, and Africa; TC3: Asia, Australia). Multilateral tariff and commercial agreements are negotiated at the tariff conferences, and include such diverse matters as baggage handling and renumeration of travel agencies. The decisions of the Traffic Conferences become part of IATA's regulations, and are implemented by the government of the airline's country, under the provisions of the bilateral air transport agreements signed between countries;
- A **clearing house** which ensures financial compensation between airlines when the payment of the tickets is received by one member but the transport is performed by another member airline under the so-called interline agreements;
- A **supervisory service** which ensures the implementation of IATA regulations.

ACHIEVEMENTS

One of IATA's important tasks was to establish international fares and rates as well as conditions of carriage. Since deregulation, however, this role has diminished as states increasingly allowed airlines more liberty to compete among themselves.

IATA has worked considerably to simplify and standardize traffic documents and procedures employed on the routes used by IATA members (e.g. it took action to establish new relations with travel agencies, it intervened in the transport of hazardous materials, etc.).

IATA remains a technically essential organization for the control and supervision of travel agencies. The clearing houses which administer the Bank Settlement Plan (BSP) are active throughout the world in facilitating repayment for tickets issued by one airline to be used on the network of other airlines.

CO-OPERATION

IATA has its headquarters in Montreal and it also has an important office in Geneva. It collaborates with ICAO [see 184 A] in the drafting of the technical regulations of civil aviation and in encouraging governments to fully implement ICAO's regulations. Through its Technical Committee, IATA co-ordinates with ICAO, individual states or countries of a particular geographical region, and with member airlines on the planning and implementation of air navigation facilities and services. It also collaborates with other institutions such as the ITU [see 192 A], the WMO [see 431 A], and ISO [see 152 C] involving issues and improving the implementation of technical matters of common interest (radio communication, meteorology reporting, standard measures, etc.).

PUBLICATIONS

IATA publishes reports and documents as well as the periodicals *World Air Transport Statistics* (annually) and *IATA Review* (quarterly).

J.-L.M.

ADDRESS

2000 Peel Street, Montreal, Quebec, H3A 2R4, Canada
T. (514) 844 6311, Fx. (514) 844 5286

SELECTED BIBLIOGRAPHY

Brancker, John, *IATA and what it Does*, Leiden: A.W. Sijthoff, 1977.
Chuang, Richard, *The IATA a case study of a quasi-governmental Organization*, Leiden: A.W. Sijthoff, 1972.

184.01 – CONVENTION FOR THE UNIFICATION OF CERTAIN RULES RELATING TO INTERNATIONAL CARRIAGE BY AIR – ICAO

Concluded: 12.10.1929, Warsaw
In Force : 13.02.1933
Parties : 123

Following the 1924 Brussels Convention unifying certain rules on the limitation of the liability of owners of sea-going vessels [see 183.02], it was felt to be necessary to standardize air transport regulations concerning the carriage of passengers and goods by air, and to introduce a common liability regime.

DETAILS OF THE CONVENTION

The Convention standardizes passenger tickets, luggage tickets, and air consignment notes according to a model common to all member states.

The liability system under the Convention covers the case of injury or death to passengers during transportation by air, as well as that of loss of luggage, damage to luggage or goods, or delay during carriage by air. This regime is based on the assumption that the carrier is liable unless he can prove that all the necessary measures were taken to avoid the damage (Art. 20).

The Convention also establishes a maximum limit to the carrier's liability equivalent to franc (gold-franc) per passenger or by kilogram of luggage or goods (Art. 22). The carrier is not entitled to avail himself of this limit "if the damage is caused by his wilful misconduct or by such default on his part as is considered to be equivalent to wilful misconduct" (Art. 25).

The Convention makes provisions for the period of time in which a complaint must be made, the jurisdiction of courts where an action for damages may be brought, and the system in the case of carriage performed by various successive carriers.

MODIFICATIONS

The principles of liability gradually evolved, and the maximum amount of money payable has been modified through amendments. The Hague Protocol of 1955 reveals the weakness of Article 25 which, under certain conditions, allowed one to exceed the limits on liability and which provided for a sum to be paid per passenger which was twice as high as that set in 1929.

The Guatemala Protocol of 1971, which has yet to come into force, radically reformed the liability system relating to passengers by establishing automatic liability of the carrier to a limit of 1,500,000 francs (gold franc), equivalent to some US$100,000. Thus, although a claim by the victims would not be able to exceed this limit, the payment would be automatic and the carrier would no longer have the possibility of evading responsibility for damages.

The Montreal Protocol (No. 4) of 1975 establishes an automatic liability system for luggage and goods similar to the one for passengers agreed in Guatemala. As well, it changes the gold franc to Special Drawing Rights (SDRs) and to a monetary unit. The additional 1975 Montreal Protocols Numbers 1, 2, and 3 also replace the gold-franc with SDRs or a monetary unit in the 1929 Convention, the Hague Convention of 1955, and the Guatemala Protocol of 1971. (See also the complementary Guadalajara Convention of 1961 [184.06].)

The original aim under the Warsaw Convention was that citizens of different states travelling on different airlines would be governed by the same provisions. However, since 1929, the Convention has been the object of contradictory interpretations by national courts which has gradually undermined the original intention of standardizing regulations.

J.-L.M.

Access : ALS (Art. 38, 40)
Reserves : PAU (Art. 40, Prot.Add.)
Duration : USP
Deposit. : PL (Art. 37)
Language : Fre (Art. 36)

Modific. : Protocol The Hague 28.09.55 (01.07.63); Protocol Guatemala 08.03.71 (-); Montreal 25.09.75 (-)

Reference : 137 LNTS – 478 UNTS – Can TS 1947/15, 1964/29 – ULR 1976/1 – UKTS 1933/11, 1967/62 – JORF 27 Dec 32, 7 & 19 Jan 60 – RTAF 1960/2

184.02 – CONVENTION ON INTERNATIONAL CIVIL AVIATION ("CHICAGO CONVENTION") – ICAO

Concluded : 07.12.1944, Chicago
In Force : 04.04.1947
Parties : 178

The Chicago Convention forms the basis for all international relations relating to aviation and air navigation. It formalizes the principle established by the 1919 Paris Convention on air navigation that states have complete and exclusive sovereignty over the airspace above their territory.

One of the main issues to be dealt with in the Convention was the division of the air transport business. The USA had emerged from the war with a powerful aeronautical industry, while countries like the UK and France, weakened from the war, had small aircraft industries yet huge colonial empires to serve. The two extreme positions came, on the one hand, from Australia and New Zealand's advocating complete international control of air transport and, on the other hand, from the US advocating maximum freedom of the air and unfettered competition. The compromise reached favoured the protectionist UK position for the bilateral exchange of traffic rights. The Chicago Convention nevertheless succeeded in establishing ICAO and international standards in many technical areas of aviation (air worthiness of aircraft, pilot licensing, rules of the air, etc.).

DETAILS OF THE CONVENTION

The Chicago Convention is divided into four sections: the first deals with air navigation, the second establishes the International Civil Aviation Organization [see 184 A], the third deals with international air transport and the obligation of member states to provide statistics and to establish the necessary installations. The fourth section contains the Agreement's final provisions, and addresses such questions as the settlement of disputes, penalties for non-conformity by a state, and so on.

The first section dealing with air navigation contains the most important provisions on the rights of member states. It recognizes "that every state has complete and exclusive sovereignty over the airspace above its territory" (Art. 1) The Convention is applicable only to civil aircraft and not to state aircraft (Art. 3-a). It establishes a difference between scheduled and non-scheduled air services. Non-scheduled air services "have the right ... to make flights into or in transit non-stop across" the territory of another contracting state (Art. 5). Scheduled flights, however, require special permission or other authorization of that state, and are subject to the terms of bilateral agreements in which contracting states grant each other the "**five freedoms of the air**" (Art. 6). Two of these freedoms do not involve commercial stopovers [see 184.03]. They are:

- the right to transit non-stop across the territory of another state; and
- the right to make stops for non-traffic purposes.

The other three freedoms, however, are strictly commercial:

- the right to discharge passengers, cargo, or mail embarked on the territory of the state to which an aircraft belongs;
- the right to embark passengers, cargo, and mail when an aircraft is flying back to its own territory;
- the right to embark passengers, cargo, and mail when the destination is the territory of any other contracting state, and the right to discharge passengers, cargo, and mail arriving from any other contracting state.

Each contracting state may restrict overflight of certain areas of its territory (Art. 9). Each state must also register its aircraft (Chap. III), and undertake "to facilitate and expedite navigation by aircraft between the territories of Contracting States, and to prevent unnecessary delays to aircraft, crews, passengers and cargo, especially in the administration of the laws relating to immigration, quarantine, customs and clearance" (Chap. IV). The Convention also establishes conditions under which investigations of aerial accidents can take place (Art. 26).

The Convention sets conditions for the documentation required both for aircraft and personnel, and the contracting parties undertake to recognize the validity of these documents.

Article 37 makes provision for the adoption of international standards and recommended practices, which are listed in the 18 technical annexes of the Convention. The standards are binding, but the contracting state may not apply them if it notifies the ICAO of the "differences between its own practice and that established by the international standard". The annexes are implemented through the adoption by member states of detailed technical manuals drafted by the different bodies of ICAO. The 18 annexes are:

- personnel licensing;
- meteorological assistance for international air navigation;
- aeronautical maps and charts;
- dimensional practices, providing progressive measures to improve air-ground communications;
- operation of aircraft in scheduled international air services;
- aircraft nationality and registration marks;

- airworthiness of aircraft;
- facilitation of international air transport;
- aeronautical telecommunications;
- air traffic services;
- search and rescue;
- aircraft accident enquiry;
- aerodromes;
- aeronautical information services;
- protection of the environment;
- safety and security to ensure the protection of civil aviation against unlawful interception of aircraft; and
- safety in the transport by air of hazardous goods.

MODIFICATIONS

In response to new demands on civil aviation, new articles have been added to the Convention: for example, Article 3 bis was adopted in 1984 and called on member states to "refrain from resorting to the use of weapons against civil aircraft in flight and ... in cases of interception, the lives of persons on board and the safety of aircraft must not be endangered".

J.-L.M.

Access : ALS (Art. 91, 92, 93)
Reserves : USP
Duration : USP
Deposit. : US
Language : Eng, Fre, Rus, Spa

Modific. : Protocol 24.09.68 (24.10.68); 30.09.77 (-); Amendments 27.05.47 (20.03.61); 14.06.54 (16.05.58); 14.06.54 (12.12.46); 21.06.61 (17.07.62); 14.09.62 (11.09.75); 12.02.71 (16.01.73); 07.07.71 (19.12.74); 16.10.74 (15.02.80); 30.09.77 (-); 06.10.80 (-); 10.05.84 (-); 1989 (-); 1990 (-)

Reference : 171, 418, 320, 514, 893, 1008, 1175 UNTS – Can TS 1944/36, 1947/22, 1958/1, 1956/22, 1969/28, 1973/18, 1974/40 – UKTS 1953/8, 1961/63, 1958/24, 1957/26, 1962/59, 1976/27, 1973/62, 1975/98, 1980/57 – UST 8/1, 13/2, 19/6, 20/1, 24/1, 26/1/2, 32/1 – DJI 1984 – 5 Paeslee – JORF 3 Jun 47 – RTAF 1965/11/12, 1969/86, 1976/28

184.03 – INTERNATIONAL AIR SERVICES TRANSIT AGREEMENT – ICAO

Concluded : 07.12.1944, Chicago
In Force : 30.01.1945
Parties : 99

For scheduled air traffic, the participants to the Chicago Convention [see 184.02] have identified five freedoms of traffic. The first freedom allows an airline to overfly the territory of a foreign country; the second allows the same airline to land in that country for refuelling or other technical reason, without embarking or disembarking passengers, cargo or mail. The participants refused to inscribe these two rights in the Chicago Convention and to grant them automatically to every state. It was therefore decided to make a separate text attached to the Convention, which could be signed and adhered to separately from the Convention. In fact, these two freedoms (and the special agreement in which they are included) have been well accepted.

Thus, the Convention states: "Each Contracting State grants to the other Contracting States the following freedoms of the air in respect to scheduled international air services:

(1) The privilege to fly across its territory without landing;
(2) The privilege to land for non-traffic purposes" (Art. 1-1).

The exercise of these rights must be in accordance with the provisions of the Convention of the International Civil Aviation Organization (Chicago, 1944).

J.-L.M.

Access : CON (Art. VI)
Reserves : USP
Duration : USP
Deposit. : US
Language : Eng, (Fre, Spa)

Reference : 84 UNTS – Can TS 1944/36 – UKTS 1953/8 – JORF 27 Jul 48

184.04 – CONVENTION ON THE INTERNATIONAL RECOGNITION OF RIGHTS IN AIRCRAFT – ICAO

Concluded : 19.06.1948, Geneva
In Force : 17.09.1953
Parties : 56

Aircraft are highly valuable movable properties which owners, generally airlines, acquire by borrowing from financial institutions. Often, the lenders are entities from different countries that loan money to an airline registered elsewhere which flies in various airspaces. Because of the diversity of jurisdiction, it is necessary to protect the lender's or lessor's property rights throughout the world and in whichever airport the aircraft lands.

In addition, the use of aircraft by an airline leads to running expenses abroad. Therefore foreign suppliers and creditors must be able to protect their claim.

The parties to this Convention undertake to recognize the property rights, mortgages or other claims, and agree to record these in a public record of the contracting state in which an aircraft is registered. The Convention recognizes the priority of claims for compensation due for the salvage of an aircraft over all other rights in the aircraft. The Convention then outlines the procedures for the forced sale of an aircraft so as to reconcile the rights of all the contracting states involved in the matter.

Article 10 extends to spare parts and states: "If a recorded right in an aircraft of the nature specified in Article 1, and held as security for the payment of an indebtedness, extends, in conformity with the law of the Contracting State where the aircraft is registered, to spare parts stored in a specified place or places, such right shall be recognized by all Contracting States".

J.-L.M.

Access : ALS (Art. XX, XXI)
Reserves : USP (Art. XXIII)
Duration : USP
Deposit. : ICAO (Art. XIX)
Language : Eng, Fre, Spa (Art. XXIII)

Reference : 310 UNTS – RTAF 1964/34 – JORF 16 Apr & 13 May 64

184.05 – CONVENTION ON DAMAGE CAUSED BY FOREIGN AIRCRAFT TO THIRD PARTIES ON THE SURFACE – ICAO

Concluded : 07.10.1952, Rome
In Force : 04.02.1958
Parties : 38

This Convention lays down the principle of liability and compensation for damage caused on land by foreign aircraft, whether due to objects falling from an aircraft or due to the crash of an aircraft (Art. 1). Articles 3 and 4 define liability in such cases while subsequent provisions list exceptions to this, such as cases where damage is the result of *force majeure*, armed conflict or civil disturbance, or negligence by the person(s) who suffer the damage and so on.

One of the characteristics of this Convention is that it establishes maximum limits for liability in relation to the weight of an aircraft; presuming that the bigger the aircraft is, the greater the damage will be. So, for example, the liability for damage giving a right to compensation for each aircraft and incident, in respect of all persons liable under the Convention, shall not exceed: 500,000 gold francs for aircraft weighing 1000 kg or less; or 10,500,000 gold francs plus 100 gold francs per kg over 50,000 kg for aircraft weighing more than 50,000 kg. In case of death or personal injury, liability will not exceed 500,000 gold francs per person killed or injured. However, if a person wrongfully takes and makes use of an aircraft without the consent of the person entitled to use it, liability is unlimited (Art. 12).

To ensure eventual payment of damages, the Convention allows states which are overflown to demand "securities" from foreign operators; the amendment of 1978 changed the word "securities" to "guarantees". These securities consist of insurance, or various deposits and monetary guarantees, the details of which are set out in the Convention (Chap. 3).

Among the rules of procedure worth noting, Article 19 specifies that action must be brought within six months of the incident, and Article 20 determines what courts have jurisdiction in cases where an action is brought. Finally, the Convention limits its application to cases in which damage is caused in the territory of one contracting state by an aircraft registered in the territory of another contracting state (Chap. 5).

MODIFICATIONS

The 23 September 1978 Montreal Protocol changed the gold franc monetary unit used to determine liability to Special Drawing Rights. For states which do not use the SDR, the gold franc is changed to a monetary unit equivalent to 65 1/2 mg of fine gold (100 gold francs equal approximately US$8 or SDR 6).

The other changes affect more the form of the Convention than its substance.

J.-L.M.

Access : ALS (Art. 34)
Reserves : PRO (Art. 39)
Duration : USP
Deposit. : ICAO (Art. 32)
Language : Eng, Fre, Spa

Modific. : Protocol Montreal 23.09.78 (-)
Reference : 310 UNTS – Can TS 1958/2 – ULR 1979/2

184.06 – CONVENTION SUPPLEMENTARY TO THE 1929 WARSAW CONVENTION FOR THE UNIFICATION OF CERTAIN RULES RELATING TO INTERNATIONAL CARRIAGE BY AIR PERFORMED BY A PERSON OTHER THAN CONTRACTING CARRIER – ICAO

Concluded : 18.09.1961, Guadalajara
In Force : 01.05.1964
Parties : 66

The Convention seeks to deal with a matter which the Warsaw Convention [see 184.01] had not anticipated. Because of the development of charters and aircraft rental, air tickets are sometimes issued by travel agencies or an air carrier referred to as a "contracting carrier" when, in fact, transport is carried out by another air carrier known as the "actual carrier".

The Guadalajara Convention extends the provisions of the Warsaw Convention, which is applicable only to contracting carriers, to actual carriers. The actual carrier, therefore, must submit to the provisions of the Warsaw Convention; the actual carrier is, however, protected by the limits on liability which that Convention sets and it can only be held liable according to the conditions established by that Convention.

The contracting carrier is subject to the provisions of the Warsaw Convention for the whole of the carriage contemplated in the agreement for carriage, while the actual carrier is responsible under the Warsaw Convention solely for the carriage which he performs (Art. II).

The Guadalajara Convention also states that "the acts and omissions of the actual carrier and of his servants and agents acting within the scope of their employment shall, in relation to the carriage performed by the actual carrier, be deemed to be also those of the contracting carrier" (Art. 3); and *vice versa*.

Another well-known consequence of this Convention is the designation of a new forum in which actions may be brought against a carrier: under the Convention, this is a court in the place where the "actual carrier is ordinarily resident or has his principal place of business" (Art. 8).

J.-L.M.

Access : ALS (Art. XIV)
Reserves : PRO (Art. XVII)
Duration : USP
Deposit. : MX (Art. XV)
Language : Eng, Fre, Rus, Spa

Reference : 500 UNTS – ULR 1961 – JDI 1967 – UKTS 1964/23 – JORF 5 Nov 66 – RTAF 1966/43

1.8.5 Space Transport

Although there have been many attempts to define a boundary between air space and outer space, no definition of outer space has yet been endorsed by the international community. A practice has evolved over the past 25 years according to which space objects in orbit are governed by the principle of freedom of outer space. This principle implies that a space vehicle has the legal right, except on launching or landing, to explore and make use of outer space at various altitudes over the territories of subjacent states.

Conventions have been concluded on activities of states in outer space [see 4.3.4], on the rescue of astronauts and return of space objects [see 185.01], on the liability of launching states [see 185.02], and on the registration of space objects [see 185.03].

Jean-Louis Magdelénat

SELECTED BIBLIOGRAPHY

Forkosch, M.D., *Outer Space and Legal Liability*, Dordrecht: Martinus Nijhoff Publishers, 1982.

Gorove, Stephen, *Developments in Space Law*, Utrecht Studies in Air and Space Law 10, Deventer: Kluwer Law and Taxation, 1991.

Hurwitz, Bruce A., *State Liability for Outer Space Activities in Accordance with the 1972 Convention on International Liability for Damage Caused by Space Objects*, Utrecht Studies in Air and Space Law 11, Deventer: Kluwer Law and Taxation, 1992.

Kuolee Li, *Worldwide Space Law Bibliography*, Montreal: De Daro Publishing, 1977-1992.

Matte, Nicholas M., *Aerospace Law*, Institute of Air and Space Law, Montreal, Toronto: Carswell, 3 Vol.: 1969, 1977 and 1983.

185.01 – AGREEMENT ON THE RESCUE OF ASTRONAUTS, THE RETURN OF ASTRONAUTS, AND THE RETURN OF OBJECTS LAUNCHED INTO OUTER SPACE – UN

Concluded : 22.04.1968, London, Moscow, Washington
In Force : 03.12.1968
Parties : 80

In a spirit of international co-operation and humanitarianism, states agree under this Convention to assist astronauts who are in distress, who are victims of an accident, or who have landed on the territory of a state other than the launching state.

Each of the contracting parties who learns or determines that the crew of a space vehicle has been involved in an accident must immediately notify the authorities in the launching state as well as the Secretary-General of the United Nations, whose task it is to disseminate the information without delay (Art. 1). A state in which the space vehicle landed, or which is able to assist the crew in a territory outside its jurisdiction, must take the necessary steps to contribute to search and rescue operations (Art. 2).

Article 4 makes provision for the immediate return of astronauts from the territory in which they have landed to the territory of the launching state. In the case of space objects, however, the launching state may be required to identify the objects before they are returned (Art. 5-3).

The return of space objects is not required unless the launching authority requests it. In this case, the launching authority must pay all costs involved in the return of the objects (Art. 5-5).

This Agreement has not yet been invoked.

Jean-Louis Magdelénat

Access : ALS (Art. 7)
Reserves : USP
Duration : USP
Deposit. : US, GB, RU (Art. 7)
Language : Chi, Eng, Fre, Rus, Spa (Art. 10)

Reference : 672 UNTS – Can TS 1975/6 – UKTS 1969/56 – ILM 7:149 – UST 19/6 – JORF 2/3 Jan 76 – RTAF 1976/1

185.02 – CONVENTION ON THE INTERNATIONAL LIABILITY FOR DAMAGE CAUSED BY SPACE OBJECTS – UN

Concluded : 29.03.1972, London, Moscow, Washington
In Force : 01.09.1972
Parties : 75

This space law Convention clearly establishes the principles and procedures concerning the liability for damage to persons or property caused by space objects.

DETAILS OF THE CONVENTION

The Convention provides for two types of liability: in cases where a space object causes damage on the surface of the Earth or to aircraft in flight, the launching state is absolutely liable to pay compensation. In the event of damage caused elsewhere than on the surface of the Earth to a space object of one launching state or to persons or property on board such a space object by a space object of another launching state, the latter is liable if the damage is due to its fault or the fault of the persons for whom it is responsible.

The Convention also addresses procedural matters. For example, only states and not private individuals are allowed to present a claim for compensation to a launching state. Therefore, the victim must first present a claim for compensation to the competent protecting state who will then transmit his claim to the state which is liable.

Article 8 of the Convention provides for three categories of states permitted to present a claim to a launching state:

- the state which suffers damage, even if the victims do not have citizenship in that state;
- the state in which the victim of damage has citizenship;
- a state in which the victim of damage has residence.

A claim for compensation for damage must be presented through diplomatic channels not later than one year following the date of the occurrence of the damage. If, however, a state does not know of the occurrence of the damage or has not been able to identify the launching state, a claim for compensation may be presented later.

The compensation for which the launching state is liable must be in the amount that will restore the claimant to the condition which would have existed if the damage had not occurred.

If no settlement of a claim is arrived at through diplomatic negotiations within one year from the date the claim is made, the parties concerned must establish a Claims Commission at the request of either party. Article 15 specifies that this Commission shall be composed of three members, while Article 16 outlines the procedures of the Commission. Its decisions and awards are made public but, unfortunately, there are no provisions to force the parties to pay compensation.

Where an international organization or a group of states is responsible for a launch, the Convention applies to all parties to the launch.

APPLICATION

The Convention was invoked between Canada and the former USSR when the Cosmos 954 satellite fell to Earth in 1978.

J.-L.M.

Access : ASO (Art. XXIV)
Reserves : USP
Duration : USP
Deposit. : US, GB, RU (Art. XXIV)
Language : Chi, Eng, Fre, Rus, Spa (Art. XXVIII)

Reference : Can TS 1975/7 – UKTS 1974/16 – UST 24/2 – ILM 10:969, 11:250 – JORF 2/3 Jan 76 – RTAF 1976/1 – RGDIP 1972/76

185.03 – CONVENTION ON REGISTRATION OF OBJECTS LAUNCHED INTO OUTER SPACE – UN

Concluded : 12.11.1974, New York
In Force : 15.09.1976
Parties : 36

This Convention, which was adopted by the UN General Assembly on 12 November 1974 and opened for signature on 14 January 1975, follows the 1972 Convention on the International Liability for Damage Caused by Space Objects [see 185.02]. Since the latter determined that the launching state was liable for damage caused by space objects, it became necessary to identify objects and to match them with launching states through a registration system. The Convention establishes a national registration system within each state and an international system under the control of the Secretary-General of the UN [see 001 A]. Every state or international organization which launches a space object must submit to the UN Secretary-General information on the satellite as well as the parameters of its orbit.

Unfortunately, the parameters which must be reported are relatively limited, and there is no deadline by which to submit the information. It was possible to revise the Convention ten years after it became effective, but in its sessions in 1987 and 1988 the Committee on the Peaceful Uses of Outer Space was unable to progress significantly in this direction.

J.-L.M.

Access : ALS (Art. VIII)
Reserves : USP
Duration : USP
Deposit. : UN (Art. VIII)
Language : Ara, Chi, Eng, Fre, Rus, Spa (Art. XII)

Reference : 1023 UNTS – Can TS 1976/36 – UKTS 1978/70 – UST 28/1 – JORF 30 Dec 77 – RTAF 1977/100

1.9 Communications

1.9.1 Postal Communication

In the Middle Ages, the dispatch of letters depended on the messenger services of royal households, universities and major religious orders. It was not until the sixteenth century that bilateral arrangements for postal services between states were first agreed. This in time developed into an extremely complex system of numerous bilateral agreements.

By the nineteenth century, standardization and greater efficiency had become essential. The invention of the postage stamp in 1840 and the development in transport services (viz. the steamships and railways) helped facilitate, in 1874, the conclusion of a single international agreement on postal relations. This agreement established the forerunner of today's Universal Postal Union (UPU), which is the international intergovernmental organization for postal services.

In recent years, the UPU, faced with strong competition of all kinds from the development of communications services, has been concerned to remain competitive and to continue the unique service it offers. This concern is reflected most markedly in the "Washington General Action Plan", drawn up at the Washington Congress of 1989, and in the agreements outlined below.

This section briefly describes the UPU and its work, and summarizes its legal instruments (two Acts and four Agreements). The Constitution, the UPU's basic Act, establishes the organic rules of the Union. The Convention embodies the rules applicable throughout the international postal service and the provisions concerning the letter-post services. These Acts and their Regulations are binding on all member states.

The four Agreements of the UPU, together with their Detailed Regulations, regulate services other than those of letter-post between those member states which agree to be parties to them. They are binding on those states only.

This section does not cover the bilateral arrangements between parties which are permitted under the agreements.

Catherine Leonard

191 A – UNIVERSAL POSTAL UNION (UPU)

This organization was created on 9 October 1874 by the Berne Treaty, under the name of the General Postal Union, a title which it changed to Universal Postal Union (UPU) in 1878. It has been a specialized agency of the UN since 1 July 1948.

The Universal Postal Union forms "a single postal territory for the reciprocal exchange of letter-post items" between its member states. Its objectives are to secure the organization and improvement of the postal services, to encourage international collaboration on postal issues, and to provide technical postal assistance on request to member states of the Union. Each member agrees to dispatch the mail of all the other members by the same means which it uses for its own mail. Today, almost every state is a member of the UPU.

STRUCTURE AND ACTIVITIES

The main organs of the Union are the Congress, the Executive Council (EC), the Consultative Council for Postal Studies (CCPS), and the International Bureau (IB).

Congress, the supreme authority of the Union, is composed of representatives of all member states. It meets approximately every five years, after the coming into force of the Acts of the previous Congress, except in exceptional circumstances which justify the convening of an extraordinary Congress. Its task notably consists in examining and revising the Acts of the Union on the basis of proposals agreed by member states, by the EC or by the CCPS.

Besides its legislative authority, the Congress has administrative responsibilities. It elects the members of the EC and the CCPS, and the Director-General and the Vice-Director-General of the IB; it establishes a ceiling for the annual expenses of the Union; and it adopts directives for the functioning of the various organs of the Union and fixes their respective tasks. Since 1964, the Congress has also been responsible for technical assistance.

The **Executive Council** is composed of 40 members elected by the Congress according to a fair geographic representation and meets each year at the headquarters of the UPU. It studies areas of interest, makes proposals to Congress and generally supervises the work of the Union between Congresses. In the area of technical assistance, it is responsible for promoting, co-ordinating and supervising all aspects of such assistance, including vocational training. It has legislative power as regards all Detailed Regulations.

The present **Consultative Council for Postal Studies** is composed of 35 member countries elected by the Washington Congress (1989) and meets annually at the UPU headquarters in Berne, Switzerland. The current chairmanship is held by the Federation of Russia until the 21st (Seoul, 1994) Universal Postal Congress. The current CCPS work programme is reviewing the considerable progress being made in the implementation of the Washington General Action Plan through the work of various symposia, working parties, action groups and committees in the technical, operational and economic fields. Technical co-operation and vocational training for new and developing countries constitute an important activity. Progress in key areas results in recommendations for world-wide application. Such areas include EMS service expansion, development of new products, human resources, research and technology, establishment of a world-wide postal electronic data transmission network, post and the environment, postal security, and international standard setting (viz. ISO 11180 on "Postal addressing") [see 152 C, generally]. CCPS study reports have been published as a Collection of Postal Services which includes approximately 200 studies to date.

The **International Bureau (IB)** serves as the organ for liaison, information exchange and consultation between the postal administrations of member states, and it co-ordinates, publishes and disseminates information on the work of the Union. It also acts as a clearing house for the settlement between postal administrations of debts relating to transit charges, terminal dues and international reply coupons. The IB can be called on to give advice on the interpretation of the Acts of the Union, and it gives opinions in disputes between postal administrations. It can be designated as single arbitrator in such disputes. It takes part in the preparation of the work of Congress, provides secretarial services for UPU bodies, and promotes technical co-operation of all types.

The UPU administers technical assistance projects with a view to assisting in the modernization of postal services. Since the early 1960s, it has been operating as an executing agency for the UNDP-financed projects and programmes [see 222 A]. In addition, it raises non-UNDP resources and provides consultancy services and training programmes in the developing countries. Since 1991, it has been applying a new concept to its technical assistance activities which involves an integrated approach to development issues. Assistance is delivered in the form of multi-year integrated projects which are based on in-depth analyses of the postal sectors. As well, it engages in continuous efforts to promote technical co-operation between developing countries (TCDC).

FINANCE

The current budget of the UPU is 29,087,690 Swiss francs (1993) financed by the contributions of member states. The UPU Special Fund, set up in 1966 and maintained by voluntary contributions from member countries, is designed mainly to finance fellowships for instructor training and teaching equipment.

CO-OPERATION

As a specialized agency of the UN, the UPU has a special relationship with that Organization. In general terms, this link covers legal, financial and personnel matters. Significantly, the UPU co-operates with the UNDP (see above) in setting up and expanding postal training schools in Africa, Asia, Latin America and the Middle East.

In regard to other specialized agencies of the UN, the UPU maintains a close relationship with the ITU [see 192 A]. These two organizations prepare and implement joint technical assistance projects, particularly in the vocational training field, and they liaise on the question of electronic mail. The UPU also works in co-operation with ICAO [see 184 A] on the issue of the development of airmail traffic, with the WHO [see 132 A] on the transport of perishable biological substances and with IAEA [see 421 A] on methods relating to the postal conveyance of radioactive substances.

Contact committees have been set up by the UPU to establish formal networks with certain international organizations. These include the CCC [see 112 A], IATA [see 184 B], ISO [see 152 C], and the ITU. They are bodies which have equal representation from the different organizations, and their purpose is to study mutual policy issues and to solve problems.

PUBLICATIONS

The UPU publishes works, manuals and working documents as well as the bi-monthly review *Postal Union*. A new edition of the *Multilingual Vocabulary of the International Postal Service* became available at the end of 1992: specialized modules or supplements are being developed for that text concerning marketing of the postal service and automation and computerization.

Catherine Leonard

ADDRESS

Bureau International de l'UPU, Weltpoststrasse, 4, CH-3000 Berne 15, Switzerland
T. (41 31) 43 22 11, Fx. (41 31) 43 22 10

191.01 – CONSTITUTION OF THE UNIVERSAL POSTAL UNION – UPU

Concluded : 10.07.1964, Vienna
In Force : 01.01.1966
Parties : 183

The Constitution is the basic Act of the UPU and is obligatory for all members.

The first section sets out the scope and objectives of the Union, and the rules governing its membership, structure and finances [see 191 A]. Section II deals with the purpose, application and procedure of the Union's Acts, Regulations and Agreements. The Constitution is completed by General Regulations and is annexed by the Rules of Procedure of Congresses.

The present Constitution was signed in Vienna in 1964 and is to remain in force for an indefinate period.

C.L.

Access : ALS (Art. 11)
Reserves : USP
Duration : ULT (Art. 33)
Deposit. : CH (Art. 26)
Language : Fre

Modific. : Additional Protocol Tokyo 14.11.69 (01.07.71); 2nd Additional Protocol Lausanne 05.07.74 (01.01.76); 3rd Additional Protocol Hambourg 27.07.84 (01.01.86); 4th Additional Protocol Washington 14.12.1989 (01.01.1991)

Reference : 611, 810 UNTS – UKTS 1966/71, 1973/72, 1976/56 – UST 27/1 – JORF 5 Jul 66, 19 Sep 71, 28 Sep 76 – RTAF 1966/26, 1971/75, 1976/41 – RGDIP 1987/2

191.02 – UNIVERSAL POSTAL CONVENTION – UPU

Concluded : 14.12.1989, Washington
In Force : 01.01.1991

The objectives of the Convention are to set common standards for the service, and to define the conditions for letter-post items, including the limits of liability. It is obligatory for all member states. This Convention was concluded at the Washington Congress of 1989 and remains in force until the acts of the next Congress (Seoul, 1994) are in force.

In Part I, the issue of transit is dealt with in detail. Under the freedom of transit principle, each postal administration is obliged to forward, always by the quickest routes which it uses for its own items, closed mails, *à découvert* letter-post items, and airmail correspondence passed to it by other administrations.

Further provisions address the following issues: charges, the settlement of accounts, the monetary standard (being SDR) and its equivalents, postage stamps, forms, personal identity cards, and postal identification systems, including the use of bar codes.

Part II deals with letter-post items. These items are divided into two categories: letters and postcards; and printed papers, literature for the blind, and small packets. Based upon the speed of treatment, letter-post items may be divided into priority items or non-priority items.

International postal charges are given based on weight steps. In contrast to the practice prior to the Washington Congress (1989), and in order to give more flexibility to administrations, these charges are only guidelines and are not obligatory. Fixed limits, however, are set for maximum weights and sizes of standard letter-post items (Art. 20). Items not considered to be standardized are listed (Art. 22-3). A list of special charges is fixed (Art. 26).

Provisions for the following services are set out: international reply coupons, express items, items for delivery free of charges and fees, registered items, recorded delivery items, insured letters, and the International Business Reply Service (the latter having been introduced for the first time at the Washington Congress).

Other procedural matters dealt with include the following: quality of service targets; priority issues; withdrawal from the post or alteration or correction of address at the sender's request; redirection; undeliverable items; prohibitions on items able to be admitted; customs procedures; and inquiries regarding items posted. The extent of liability of administrations is established in regard to registered items, recorded delivery items and insured letters.

Charges paid to each administration may generally be kept by them. However, administrations are subject to both transit charges and terminal dues, the latter being able to be collected when international mail received is in excess of what an administration sends.

Part III deals with the air conveyance of letter-post items: their routeing and dues. The new EMS service – promoted as the quickest postal service by physical means – is introduced in Part IV: charges are to be set by the administration of origin in consideration of costs and market requirements, and the logo is described and illustrated.

The Convention is accompanied by a Final Protocol which specifies administrations exempted from applying certain articles in the Convention, and administrations authorized to depart from them.

C.L.

Access : CON
Reserves : PAU (Art. 22-6 Constitution)
Duration : FXD (Art. 94)
Deposit. : UPU (Art. 26 Const.)
Language : Fre

191.03 – POSTAL PARCELS AGREEMENT – UPU

Concluded : 14.12.1989, Washington
In Force : 01.01.1991

The first agreement regarding parcel post was adopted in 1880 as a convention by the Conference of Paris. It has been revised and renewed by each subsequent Congress though, since the Stockholm Congress of 1924, it has been referred to as an Agreement.

DETAILS OF THE AGREEMENT

The preliminary provisions include definitions of the categories of parcels, which are as follows: ordinary, insured, fragile, cumbersome, for delivery free of charges and fees (i.e. parcels which are delivered to the addressee with all expenses paid for by the sender), cash-on-delivery [see 191.06], (postal) service, prisoner-of-war parcels, and other categories relating to the method of dispatch or service.

Prior to the 1989 Agreement, the weight of postal parcels was not allowed to exceed 20 kg. Now, however, bilateral arrangements may permit otherwise. Under the new quality of service targets provisions, the Agreement stipulates that international parcels should have the same, or shorter, delivery targets as domestic parcels, allowing for time for customs clearance (Art. 6).

Part I of the Agreement deals with charges and fees and Part II with the operation of the service. The latter covers the conditions of acceptance of a parcel by the postal service, fixes the conditions of delivery and redirection, and addresses other specific issues.

Part III lays down the conditions and extent of liability of all parties, and covers the issue of the payment of indemnity. These conditions are, since the previous Agreement, generally more favourable to the client. Finally, Part IV concerns the rates due to administrations and their allocation.

This Agreement is optional for member states.

SUBSEQUENT DEVELOPMENTS

It is of interest to note that the Washington Congress called on administrations to standardize the services provided for postal parcels in order to simplify presentation of the service to customers and retain or recover the Post's share of the parcel's market (Resolution C15). Further, in order to keep abreast of the changing demands of the international market, the Consultative Council for Postal Studies is studying the possibility of identifying and developing a range of new postal parcel products and services. Areas being examined include marketing, quality-of-service targets, administrations' payments, and the charges collected from customers.

The Executive Council has recently undertaken a study into the obstacles preventing some administrations from acceding to the Agreement and there is a drive to encourage all members to do so. There is also a study being undertaken by the Council on the possibility of making this Agreement mandatory for UPU member states in order to have a complete world coverage for this service (158 countries are currently signatories).

C.L.

Access : CON
Reserves : PAU
Duration : FXD (Art. 59)
Deposit. : UPU
Language : Fre

191.04 – MONEY ORDERS AGREEMENT – UPU

Concluded : 14.12.1989, Washington
In Force : 01.01.1991

A money order is an order issued by a post office for the payment of a specified sum of money, generally at another post office. This Money Orders Agreement is the basic agreement for the operation of the postal financial services. The Agreement's main purpose is to govern the international exchange of money orders between the contracting parties. However, in order to make this service more accessible to the public, it was accepted for the first time at the Washington Congress (1989) that non-postal organizations could participate in the exchange of money orders through the intermediary of a postal administration (Art. 1).

The first Agreement concerning the international money orders service was adopted by the Congress of Paris of 1878, and the most significant historical additions have included the telegraph money order (Congress of Lisbon, 1885), the postal travel bonds (Congress of Caire, 1934), and the international inpayment order (Congress of Vienna, 1964).

There are two categories of money order: ordinary and inpayment. They may be sent by post or as telegraphic transfers by telecommunication. With an ordinary money order, the sender hands over funds at the post office counter, or alternatively he orders his postal giro account to be debited. He requests that the payee receives cash for the amount of the order. With an inpayment order, the sender requests that the funds be paid into the payee's postal account.

The amount of the order is to be expressed in the currency of the paying country, with the issuing administration fixing the rate of conversion. However, different rules regarding maximum amounts apply to ordinary money orders and inpayment money orders respectively. The maximum amount of an ordinary money order is now to be decided through bilateral agreements where previously it was fixed by Congress. For an inpayment money order, the maximum amount is unlimited though there may be a limit on the amount which can be ordered over a specific period (Art. 3). Article 4 lays down the system of charges for the money orders service. The maximum general charge is fixed and is increased from the previous Congress. Also included is a list of the categories of optional charges for special services.

The conditions of the exchange of funds by post or telecommunication between administrations are set out in Article 5. Postal exchanges may be direct between the issuing office and the paying office or by means of lists through the intermediary of offices called "offices of exchange" which act as clearing houses.

In general, payment is made according to the regulations of the paying country. The validity of money orders lasts generally until the end of the first month following that of issue. Redirection issues and enquiry matters are also dealt with.

In general, administrations are liable for sums until they have been paid to the payee. The exceptions to this rule are listed and include their not being liable for delays in the transmission and payment of money orders. When the liability of the postal service has been established, payment to the claimant is dealt with as a priority.

Since the 1974 Lausanne Congress, the sharing of charges between the administrations of issue and payment has been abandoned. In its place, paying administrations must be remunerated by the issuing administrations and the Agreement lays down the rates which must be paid (Art. 10). The procedures for the preparation and settlement of the payments are set down (Arts. 11 and 12).

Telegraph money orders (ordinary or inpayment) involve close co-operation with the International Telecommunication Union and are subject to the International Telecommunication Regulations [see 192.03].

This Agreement is completed by Detailed Regulations and is optional for member states.

C.L.

Access : CON
Reserves : PAU (Art. 22-6 Const.)
Duration : FXD (Art. 13)
Deposit. : UPU
Language : Fre

191.05 – GIRO AGREEMENT – UPU

Concluded : 14.12.1989, Washington
In Force : 01.01.1991

This Agreement, adopted for the first time by the Congress of Madrid in 1920, deals with the international exchanges of funds between postal administrations through the giro service. By special provision, non-postal organizations can also participate in these exchanges. Article 2 gives a brief description of the categories of service available:

- **Transfer:** the holder of a giro account asks for an amount to be debited to his account and credited to the payee's giro account or, when there is an agreement to that effect between the administrations concerned, to other types of account;
- **Inpayments into a giro account:** the sender hands the funds in at the counter of a post office and asks for the amount to be credited to the payee's giro account or, where there is an agreement to that effect between the administrations concerned, to other types of account;
- **Money orders and outpayment cheques:** an amount is debited from a holder's giro account and paid in cash to the payee;
- **Postcheques:** these may be issued to holders of giro accounts and are payable in cash to the holder, or under certain conditions to third parties, in the post offices of countries where there is agreement to that effect between the contracting administrations.

With the exception of postcheques, these exchanges of funds may be sent by post or by telegraph. Telegraph transfers are subject to the International Telecommunication Regulations [see 192.03].

All amounts are expressed in the currency of the country of destination unless otherwise agreed, and the issuing administration fixes the conversion rate.

Generally, charges for all these services are fixed by individual postal administrations without restriction. However, there is some restriction of charges in regard to inpayments and money orders (see 5-3.2 and Art. 4 of the Money Orders Agreement), and the payer of a telegraph transfer is subject to additional charges under the Telegraph Regulations.

With the exception of postcheques, where liability is dealt with on a different basis in the Agreement (see Art. 14), one can generalize as follows. Administrations are liable for all amounts until exchanges have been effected. They are also liable for errors of conversion and transmission and, with the exception of all money orders, are liable for erroneous information supplied during the transfer. They are not liable for delays which may occur in the transmission and payment of transfers. The circumstances under which they are relieved of liability are laid down. Details are given regarding the determination and extent of liability in regard to administrations, and the recourse available to the claimant.

In regard to postcheques, some special provisions apply. Postcheque guarantee cards must be issued with all postcheques and need to be produced at the time of payment, indicating the maximum amount guaranteed. The validity of postcheques is unlimited unless the issuing administration stipulates otherwise on the postcheque. The issue of fraudulent or counterfeit postcheques is dealt with.

Finally, the Agreement stipulates that a person may open a giro account in any country which exchanges giro transfers with his country of residence. When this occurs, the administration in the country of residence is obliged to undertake certain verification procedures in regard to information about the applicant or subsequent account holder (Art. 16-1).

This Agreement is completed by Detailed Regulations and is optional for member states.

C.L.

Access : CON
Reserves : PAU (Art. 22-6 Const.)
Duration : FXD (Art. 58)
Deposit. : UPU
Language : Fre

191.06 – CASH-ON-DELIVERY AGREEMENT – UPU

Concluded : 14.12.1989, Washington
In Force : 01.01.1991

The Agreement governs the exchange of cash-on-delivery items between the contracting parties. This service was originally instituted by the Congress of Lisbon of 1885 as an administrative arrangement, but it has only been made the subject of an international arrangement from the time of the Congress of Paris of 1947.

The procedure of the service involves the addressees in paying the postal officer a sum on receipt of a postal item: that amount is then forwarded to the sender of the item by the postal administration.

DETAILS OF THE AGREEMENT

The sender has a variety of choices in how cash-on-delivery payment can be made to him: by COD money order, by COD inpayment money order, or by transfer. Depending on his choice, it is possible for the payment to be effected either in the addressee's country or in his own country (Art. 2).

A maximum limit on a COD amount is set at the same limit for ordinary money orders. This may be increased to the maximum amount set for ordinary inpayment money orders and transfers, if those methods are chosen. Higher maximums may be mutually agreed on between administrations (Art. 3-2).

The sender must pay two charges: the normal postal charge for the item being sent, and a charge for the service which varies according to the method of payment stipulated (Art. 3-3 and 3-5).

COD money orders and COD inpayment orders must be sent, by the administration collecting the funds, to the sender by the quickest route (Art. 4-2). In the situation where it is unable to carry out a request for inpayment or transfer, this administration is required to prepare a COD money order for the corresponding amount made out to the sender of the item. In the event that the amount of a COD money order is not in fact paid to the sender of the postal item, for whatever reason, the Agreement sets out the procedure to be followed (Art. 6-2).

Administrations are liable for the funds collected and for failure to collect the appropriate funds, subject to the provisions laid down in Article 8-2. However, they are not liable for delays which may occur in the collection and dispatch of funds (Art. 8-1). Requirements in regard to payment of an indemnity and the conditions for the liability of the separate administrations are set out (Art. 8-3). The procedure governing the situation in which an addressee returns an item delivered to him, and where the COD amount has not been collected from that addressee, is dealt with (Art. 8-5).

The Convention, the Money Orders Agreement, the Giro Agreement and the Postal Parcels Agreement are applicable to this Agreement where appropriate and when they do not conflict with its provisions. This Agreement is completed by Detailed Regulations and is optional for member states.

C.L.

Access : CON
Reserves : PAU (Art. 22-6 Const.)
Duration : FXD (Art. 9)
Deposit. : UPU
Language : Fre

1.9.2 Telecommunication

Telecommunication is a key aspect of the global information society. With the accelerating globalization of telecommunication networks and services, and new alliances being forged in the telecommunication sector, national borders are becoming less and less relevant. Global co-ordination is now a major priority.

The ITU plays a leading role in facilitating intergovernmental co-operation and has established a regime based on three sets of rules: a legally binding international agreement laid down in the ITU Constitution and Convention [see 192.02, 192.06 and 192.07], the regulations established by administrative conferences which meet every few years [see 192.01 and 192.03], and the recommendations prepared for plenary assemblies of International Consultative Committees, which are not legally binding but enjoy wide acceptance.

The ITU has recently undergone substantial reorganization in order to adapt to the rapid changes in technology, to the increasing number of bodies concerned with telecommunications, and to the immense telecommunication requirements of developing countries.

Bernard Colas

SELECTED BIBLIOGRAPHY

Codding, G.A. & Rutkowski, A.M., *The International Telecommunication Union in a Changing World*, USA: Artecht House inc. , 1986.

Cowhey, Pater F., "The International Telecommunications Regime: the Political Roots of Regimes for High Technology", *International Organizations* 44 (Spring 1990):169-99.

Renaud, J.C., *The Changing Dynamics of the International Telecommunication Union: A Historical Analysis of Development Assistance*, Ph.D Program of the University of the State of Michigan, 1986.

Savage, James G., *The Politics of International Telecommunications Regulation*, Westview, 1989.

192 A – INTERNATIONAL TELECOMMUNICATION UNION (ITU)

The International Telecommunications Union is a specialized agency of the United

Nations, and was preceded by the International Telegraph Union founded in Paris on 17 May 1865 with the adoption of the first telecommunication convention. On the same occasion the first Telegraph Regulations were adopted. The organization's present name was adopted at the Madrid Conference of 1932, which amalgamated the International Telegraph Convention and the International Radiotelegraph Convention.

Today, the ITU's basic instruments are composed of a mixture of agreements which reflect the transitory period it is currently going through. Although at the present time the functioning of the ITU is based on the International Telecommunication Convention (Nairobi, 1982), the provisions relating specifically to the structure and working methods of the ITU in the Constitution (Geneva, 1992), complemented by the Convention (Geneva, 1992), are provisionally applicable from 1 March 1993. The 1992 Constitution and Convention shall fully enter into force between the parties to those agreements on 1 July 1994.

OBJECTIVES

The objectives of the ITU are the following: to maintain and extend international co-operation between all members of the Union (at present, 177 member states) for the improvement and rational use of telecommunications of all kinds; to promote the mobilization of financial and material resources and offer technical assistance to developing countries in the field of telecommunication; and to promote the development of technical facilities and their most efficient operation with a view to improving the efficiency of telecommunication services, increasing their usefulness and making them, so far as possible, generally available to the public.

To achieve these objectives, the ITU operates in three principal directions (radiocommunication, standardization and development) which are well reflected in the new structure and working methods of the ITU.

STRUCTURE

The **Plenipotentiary Conference** (PC), composed of all members, is the supreme body of the Union. It is convened every four years and is responsible for determining general policies, adopting decisions, approving the budget, adopting proposals for amendments to the Constitution and the Convention, concluding agreements with other international organizations, and for electing members of the Union to serve on the Council, the Secretary-General and other officials, and the members of the Radio Regulations Board.

The **Council**, composed of 43 members of the Union, acts as governing body of the Union on behalf of the PC in the intervals between Conferences. It takes steps to facilitate the implementation by the members of the instruments of the Union, and ensures the co-ordination of the work of the Union and exercises effective financial control over the **General Secretariat** and the three Sectors.

The reorganization of the ITU succeeded in creating three vertical Sectors which each include their own Conference, supported by study and working groups, a Bureau directed by an elected Director, and an Advisory Board. All these Sectors are open to the participation of all members of the Union and of any entity or organization authorized in accordance with relevant provisions of the Convention.

The **Radiocommunication Sector** ensures the rational, equitable, efficient and economical use of the radio frequency spectrum by all radiocommunication services, and it carries out studies. It works through world radiocommunication conferences and their associated technical assemblies, regional conferences, study groups, the

Radio Regulation Board and the Radiocommunication Bureau. The 1992 reform merged into one Sector all radiocommunication-related activities of the ITU previously carried out notably by the IFRB and the CCIR, in order to symplify its functioning. As from 1 March 1993, Radio Regulations [see 192.01] may be revised by world radiocommunication conferences (to be held in general every two years) and applied by the Radio Regulations Board, which also defines Rules of Procedure to register frequency assignments made by members.

The **Telecommunication Standardization Sector** studies technical, operating and tariff questions and adopts recommendations on them with a view to standardizing telecommunications on a world-wide basis. It works through world telecommunication standardization conferences (every four years), study groups and a Bureau.

The **Telecommunication Development Sector** fulfils ITU's dual responsibility both as a United Nations specialized agency and and as an executing agency for implementing projects under the UNDP [see 222 A] and other funding arrangements. Thus, it facilitates and enhances telecommunication development by offering, organizing and co-ordinating technical co-operation and assistance activities. It works through world and regional telecommunication development conferences which (as opposed to the other Sectors' conferences) do not adopt binding regulations, and through study groups and a Bureau.

CO-OPERATION

In its latest restructuring, the ITU gave a high priority to co-operating with other intergovernmental organizations and with non-governmental organizations concerned with telecommunication. The ITU has working relations with a large number of intergovernmental organizations, including the ICAO [see 184 A], the WMO [see 431 A], the IMO [see 183 A], UPU [see 191 A], INTELSAT [see 193 A], INMARSAT [see 193 C], and INTERSPUTNIK [see 193 B].

PUBLICATIONS AND EXHIBITIONS

In the ITU's role as a disseminator of information, it both co-ordinates and publishes data which member states and their affiliated bodies exchange through the Union. This service ensures the efficient daily functioning of all types of telecommunications services. The type of information includes, for example, catalogues of maritime radio stations in telegraphic offices, statistical information, notices, bulletins, and circulars designed to keep the administrations informed of issues relating to telecommunications. It also publishes a monthly *Telecommunication Journal*.

Every four years, the General Secretariat organizes two international exhibitions relating to telecommunications ("Telecom" for Telecommunications, and "ITU-Com" for electronic media), as well as regional exhibitions organized in collaboration with the ITU member states (Asia Telecom, Africa Telecom, Americas Telecom).

Bernard Colas

ADDRESS

Place des Nations, CH-1211 Geneva 20, Switzerland
T. (41 22) 730 51 11, Fx. (41 22) 733 72 56

192.01 – RADIO REGULATIONS – ITU

Concluded : 06.12.1979, Geneva
In Force : 01.01.1982
Parties : 177

In accordance with Article 33 of the Constitution of the International Telecommunication Union [see 192.06], when using frequency bands for radio services the members must bear in mind that radio frequencies and the geostationary-satellite orbit are limited natural resources. Thus, they must be used in a rational, efficient and economical manner, conforming with the provisions of the Radio Regulations, so that countries or groups of countries may have equitable access to these radio frequencies and to this orbit, taking into account the special needs of developing countries and the geographical situation of particular countries.

These Regulations, adopted by the World Administrative Conference of Radio (Geneva, 1979), complete the provisions of the Convention [see 192.02 and 192.07] and deal with the use of radio. They replace the Radio Regulations and the additional Radio Regulations (1959). The Regulations are divided into two parts: Part A deals mainly with administrative matters and Part B contains provisions of an operational nature. Each of these parts is completed by the appendices containing more detailed information on the main provisions of the Regulations. They are obligatory for all the members of the ITU.

Their fundamental goal is to permit as many radio-electric paths as possible to operate in the frequency spectrum without any harmful interference occurring to authorized operating agencies. At the same time, they aim at achieving an equitable, effective and economical use of the geostationary-satellite orbit. Radio waves are defined as "electromagnetic waves of frequencies arbitrarily lower than 3000 GHz, propagated in space without artificial guide" (Annex to the Convention). The Regulations govern the use of frequency bands between 9kHz and 400 GHz.

The area available for the radio-electric frequency spectrum is divided into small appropriate portions which vary according to needs. These portions, called frequency bands, are attributed to specific radio services which are either exclusive or shared. An Administrative World Conference of radiocommunications accepts the Register of allocation of frequency bands and all use of the radioelectric frequency spectrum must conform to this Register. For this allocation, the world is divided into three regions: Africa-Europe, America and Asia.

For specific services, such as the radio-diffusion service and the mobile aeronautical service, for which emission and reception are not necessarily limited to the single territory of a given country, frequency assignments are adopted in the course of competent world administrative conferences of radiocommunications. To this effect, all possible use of the radio-electric frequencies must be notified to the International Frequency Registration Board (IFRB), which enters them in the Master International Frequency Register.

Detailed procedures have been adopted by the administrations during world administrative conferences on radiocommunications, and each administration must apply these when dealing with other administrations and with the IFRB at the time of implementing a new existing frequency. As these rules constitute the essential minimal requirements of the Radio Regulations, the IFRB must, in the daily application of these rules, record detailed explanations of the manner in which it applies them. These explanations are called Rules of Procedure of the IFRB and Technical Norms.

With the 1992 reorganization of the ITU, the IFRB is now replaced by the Radio Regulations Board [see 192 A].

B.C.

Access : ALS (Art. 42 Conv.)
Reserves : AUT (Art. 77 Convention)
Duration : USP
Deposit. : ITU
Language : Ara, Chi, Eng, Fre, Rus, Spa

Modific. : 18.03.83 (15.01.85); 15.09.85 (30.10.86); 08.03.87 (01.09.88); 17.10.87 (03.10.89); 06.10.88 (16.03.90)

192.02 – INTERNATIONAL TELECOMMUNICATION CONVENTION – ITU

Concluded : 06.11.1982, Nairobi
In Force : 01.01.1984
Parties : 177

This Convention is the fundamental instrument of the International Telecommunication Union and, until the 1992 Constitution and Convention comes into force [see 192.06 and 192.07], is the current working instrument. Its origin is the International Convention of Telegraphs, signed in Paris in 1865 (revised in St Petersbourg in 1875), and the International Telegraphic Radio Convention in Berlin in 1906 (revised in London in 1912 and in Washington, DC in 1927). It was concluded for the first time under the title International Telecommunication Convention in December 1932 and was successively replaced in 1947, 1952, 1959, 1965 and 1973. It will be abrogated and replaced on 1 July 1994 by the Constitution and by the Convention of the ITU adopted during the additional Plenipotentiary Conference held in Geneva in December 1992 [see 192.06 and 192.07].

It contains, in the First Part, clauses concerning the object and the structure of the Union (Chapter I), as well as the general provisions relating to telecommunications and special provisions for radiocommunications (Chapters II and III, respectively).

Chapter II of Part I thus sets the basic principles applicable to all kinds of international telecommunication. It provides that members recognize the right of the public to use the international telecommunication service, that they agree to take all possible measures with a view to ensuring the secrecy of international correspondence, and that they take steps to ensure the establishment and the safeguarding of the channels and installations necessary to carry on the rapid and uninterrupted exchange of international telecommunications. However, members reserve the right, under certain conditions, to stop the transmission of any private telecommunications which may appear dangerous to the security of the state or contrary to its laws, to suspend the international telecommunication service, and to lift the right of secrecy in order to ensure the application of the law.

The settlements of international accounts are regarded as current transactions either, in the absence of particular arrangements between members, in SDR or in gold franc.

Chapter III of the First Part sets basic principles with regard to the use of frequency bands for space radio. Members shall endeavour to limit the number of frequencies and the spectrum space used to the minimum essential and shall bear in mind that radio frequencies and the geostationary satellite orbit are limited natural resources and that they must be used efficiently and economically, in conformity with the provisions of the Radio Regulations, so that countries may have access to both. Furthermore, all stations must be established and operated in such a manner so as not to cause harmful interference to the radio services or communications of other members or of authorized operating agencies.

The Second Part of the Convention is subordinate to the first, and establishes general regulations on the functioning of the Union regarding Conferences, International Consultative Committees, rules of procedure of meetings, settlement of accounts and arbitration procedure.

The provisions of the Convention are supplemented by the Administrative Regulations which regulate the use of telecommunications and bind all members (Art. 42). Ratification or adherence to the Convention involves the acceptance of the Administrative Regulations in force which are regarded as annexed and remain valid, subject to partial revision, until the time of entry into force of new Regulations drawn up by the competent world administrative conferences (Arts. 41 and 43). The administrative regulations currently in force are the Radio Regulations and the International Telecommunication Regulations [see 192.01 and 192.03].

B.C.

Access : ALS (Art. 1, 45, 46)
Reserves : AUT (Art. 77)
Duration : USP
Deposit. : ITU (Art. 52)
Language : Ara, Chi, Eng, Fre, Rus, Spa (Art. 16)

192.03 – INTERNATIONAL TELECOMMUNICATION REGULATIONS – ITU

Concluded : 09.12.1988, Melbourne
In Force : 01.07.1990
Parties : 177

Adopted by 113 countries at the conclusion of the world administrative Telegraphic and Telephonic Conference (CAMTT-88), these Regulations supplement the International Telecommunication Convention [see 192.02 and 192.07] and establish general principles which relate to the provisions and operations of international telecommunication services offered to the public as well as to the means of transport used to provide such services. In implementing these principles, the Regulations provide that administrations or recognized private operating agencies should also comply to relevant CCITT Recommendations.

The objectives of these Regulations are to facilitate global interconnect and interoperability of telecommunication facilities and to promote the harmonious development and efficient operation of technical facilities. Therefore, members are asked to ensure that administrations and recognized private operating agencies co-operate in the establishment, operation and maintenance of the international network to provide a satisfactory quality of service (Art. 3) and to make the international telecommunication services generally available to the public in their national networks.

Each administration establishes the charges to be collected from its customers (Art. 6-1) and, between each other, agree on accounting rates to be applied between them.

In the absence of special arrangements concluded between administrations, the monetary unit to be used in the composition of accounting rates for international telecommunication services, and in the establishment of international accounts, shall be either the SDR or the gold franc. The establishment of accounts and settlement of balances of accounts shall follow relevant provisions set out in Appendices 1 and 2 of the Regulations. A third Appendix deals with service and privilege telecommunications.

These Regulations replaced the Telegraphic Regulations (Geneva, 1973) and the Telephone Regulations (Geneva, 1973).

B.C.

Access : ALS (Art. 42 Conv.)
Reserves : AUT (Art. 10.3)
Duration : USP
Deposit. : ITU
Language : Ara, Chi, Eng, Fre, Rus, Spa

192.04 – CONSTITUTION OF THE INTERNATIONAL TELECOMMUNICATION UNION – ITU

Concluded : 30.06.1989, Nice
Parties : 17

For the first time in ITU history, member states at Nice in 1989 adopted a Constitution as well as a Convention. The provisions of the Nice Constitution reflect with some changes the main provisions found in Part I of the 1982 Nairobi Convention [see 192.02]; while the Convention adopted in Nice similarly reflects Part II of the 1982 Convention.

One of the main innovations of the Nice Constitution was the creation of a new permanent organ, the Telecommunication Development Bureau (BDT), which began to function immediately (Res. No. 19), before the entry into force of the Constitution which required the deposit of 55 instruments of ratification or accession.

However, as indicated by Article 48 of the Nice Constitution, an additional Plenipotentiary Conference was convened in Geneva in December 1992 to consider the results of a review of the structure and functioning of the Union contained in the final report of the High Level Committee established by the Administrative Council. The 1992 Geneva Conference adopted a new Constitution and Convention [see 192.06 and 192.07] which should become effective on 1 July 1994.

The Constitution establishes, among other things, the composition of the Union, describes the rights and obligations of member states, as well as the object and the structure of the Union (Chap. 1). In this respect, it creates a new permanent organ, the Telecommunications Development Bureau, responsible for facilitating and improving the development of telecommunications by offering, organizing and co-ordinating the co-operating activities and technical assistance of the ITU (Art. 11-A). It includes the general provisions relating telecommunications (Chap. II) and the special provisions for radio (Chap. III).

Thus, while the intention was for the Nice Constitution and Convention [see 192.05] to replace the Nairobi Convention, these Nice agreements have in fact been superseded by the Constitution and Convention adopted in Geneva in December 1992 [see 192.06].

B.C.

Access : ALS (Art. 1)
Reserves : PRO
Duration : USP
Deposit. : ITU
Language : Ara, Chi, Eng, Fre, Rus, Spa

192.05 – INTERNATIONAL TELECOMMUNICATION CONVENTION – ITU

Concluded : 30.06.1989, Nice
Parties : 17

The Convention includes up-dated provisions of Part II of the 1982 Nairobi Convention [see 192.02] regarding the functioning of the Union (Chap. 1), as well as general provisions regarding conferences and International Consultative Committees (Chaps. II and III). It also includes Rules of Procedure and various provisions related to the operation of Telecommunication Services (Chaps. IV to VI).

This Convention like the Constitution [see 192.04] was meant, after its entry into force, to abrogate and replace, as between the parties, the International Telecommunication Convention (Nairobi, 1982). In fact, it has been replaced by the Constitution and Convention adopted in Geneva in December 1992 [see 192.06 and 192.07].

B.C.

Access : ALS
Reserves : PAU (Art. 16)
Duration : FXD
Deposit. : ITU
Language : Ara, Chi, Eng, Fre, Rus, Spa

192.06 – CONSTITUTION OF THE INTERNATIONAL TELECOMMUNICATION UNION – ITU

Concluded : 22.12.1992, Geneva

This Constitution was adopted with the Convention [see 192.07] by the additional Plenipotentiary Conference held in Geneva in December 1992, following proposals made by the High Level Committee to review the structure and functioning of the ITU.

It respects the same balance as the Nice agreements [see 192.04 and 192.05] and focuses on the functions and structure of the Union and on general provisions relating to telecommunications.

The Constitution is the basic instrument of the Union. In the hierarchy this is followed by the Convention [see 192.07] and then by the Administrative Regulations [see 192.01 and 192.03]. Thus, in a case of inconsistency between a provision of the Constitution and a provision of the Convention or of the Administrative Regulations, the "Constitution shall prevail" (Art. 4). Furthermore, the provisions of the Convention prevail over the provisions of the Administrative Regulations.

The main feature of the Constitution is the reorganization of the Union and the creation of three Sectors – Radiocommunication, Telecommunication Standardization and Telecommunication Development – which are open to all members of the Union as well as to any entity or organization authorized in accordance with the relevant provisions of the Convention.

The Constitution and the Convention will enter into force on 1 July 1994 between members having deposited before that date their instrument of ratification or accession, thereby abrogating and replacing the International Telecommunication Convention (Nairobi, 1982) [see 192.02]. However, the Plenipotentiary Conference has resolved in adopting the Constitution and the Convention that the provisions relating to the new structure and working methods of the Union shall be applied provisionally as from 1 March 1993.

B.C.

Access : ALS (Art. 41, 42)
Reserves : PAU

Duration : NSP
Deposit. : ITU (Art. 41)
Language : Ara, Eng, Fre, Rus, Spa (Art. 47)

192.07 – CONVENTION OF THE INTERNATIONAL TELECOMMUNICATION UNION – ITU

Concluded : 22.12.1992, Geneva

The provisions of the Convention complement the provisions of the Constitution [see 192.06] and describe in great detail the functioning of the organs of the Union and the Rules of Procedure.

B.C.

Access : ALS (Art. 41, 42 Const.)
Reserves : PAU
Duration : NSP
Deposit. : ITU (Art. 41 Const.)
Language : Ara, Chi, Eng, Fre, Rus, Spa (Art. 47 Const.)

1.9.3 Satellites

International communication satellite systems are provided on a world-wide basis mainly by INTELSAT [see 193 A] and INTERSPUTNIK [see 193 B] and, for maritime telecommunication, by INMARSAT [see 193 C].

Jean-Louis Magdelénat

SELECTED BIBLIOGRAPHY

Leninza, Umberto (et al.), *The Future of International Telecommunications: The Legal Regime of Telecommunications by Geostationary Orbit Satellite*, Dobbs Ferry, NY: Oceana Publications, 1992.

Matte, M., *Aerospace Law and Satellite Telecommunications*, Montreal: IASL: McGill University, 1983.

Smith, M.L., *International Regulation of Satellite Communication*. Dordrecht: Martinus Nijhoff Publishers, 1990.

193 A – INTERNATIONAL TELECOMMUNICATIONS SATELLITE ORGANIZATION (INTELSAT)

INTELSAT was created on an interim basis on 20 August 1964 (and permanently in 1971) to establish a global commercial telecommunications satellite system. Its aim is to carry forward the design, development, construction, establishment, operation and maintenance of the space segment of the global commercial telecommunications satellite system.

INTELSAT maintains and operates the global satellite system used for public international telecommunications services through a space segment which it owns and through Earth stations which are owned by the telecommunication bodies where they are located. INTELSAT provides its services on a commercial basis and without discrimination. Members contribute to the Organization's budget in proportion to the use they make of the INTELSAT system. Some states even use the system for their own national telecommunications services.

The services offered by INTELSAT include telephone, facsimile, television, data applications, and video services.

STRUCTURE

The **Assembly of Parties** is the principal organ of INTELSAT, and includes all the parties to the INTELSAT Agreement. It deliberates according to a principle of majority, and each state has one vote.

The **Meeting of Signatories**, which is more specifically competent on technical and financial matters, comprises all the governmental agencies representing states in the field of telecommunication (PTT, private companies). These entities, designated by the states parties to the Assembly, are the so-called "Signatories" of the Operating Agreement (i.e. the text which details technical functions more relevant to telecom agencies than to the states).

The **Board of Governors** is the permanent management organ of INTELSAT. It is made up of signatories whose investment shares, individually or in groups, are not less than a specified investment share, plus up to five governors, each of whom represents a group of at least five signatories located within the same ITU region. The investment share required for representation is adjusted annually by the Meeting of Signatories to maintain total Board membership within prescribed limits. As of 1 January 1993, the Board has 27 members representing either singly or in combination, 97 signatories. In principle, decisions are taken unanimously. However, if there is a failure to reach a unanimous agreement, decisions on matters of substance are taken by a specified system of affirmative votes in the Board of Governors. No single state can own more than 40 per cent of the total system. Therefore as the votes are proportional to the shares owned in the system, no state can control the decisions without the support of many other members.

The **Director-General** is the Chief Executive Officer and legal representative of INTELSAT. He acts in accordance with the policies and directives of the Board of Governors and is responsible to the Board of Governors for the performance of all management functions. He is supported by a staff which is principally located at INTELSAT headquarters in Washington, DC, USA.

CO-OPERATION

INTELSAT co-operates with various organizations such as the IMO [see 183 A], the ITU [see 192 A], the UN [see 001 A] and INMARSAT [see 193 C].

PUBLICATIONS

Publications include a quarterly newsletter and an annual report.

Jean-Louis Magdelénat

ADDRESS

INTELSAT, 3400 International Drive NW, Washington, DC 20008, United States
T. (202) 944 6800, Fx. (202) 944 7890

193 B – INTERNATIONAL ORGANIZATION OF SPACE TELECOMMUNICATIONS (INTERSPUTNIK)

INTERSPUTNIK, which was established within the framework of CMEA (also known as COMECON) on 15 November 1971, is an intergovernmental organization open to all states. It is responsible for a satellite telecommunications network. The system serves 18 member countries and over 100 users all around the world and comprises two satellites in geostationary orbit as well as 32 Earth stations located in different parts of the world. Most of these members now participate and have a special status in the INTELSAT network.

INTERSPUTNIK communications satellites and related facilities are owned by the Organization or leased by the Organization from members who own them. The system's Earth stations, on the other hand, are owned by the states where they are located or by recognized private organizations operating the stations.

STRUCTURE

INTERSPUTNIK includes a **Board** which acts as the governing body of the Organization and is composed of one representative from each member state; an **Operational Committee**; and a **Directorate** which acts as the Organization's permanent executive and administrative body. It is located in Moscow and is headed by a Director-General who is elected by the Board. [Currently, the Director-General is Mr Gennady Kudryavtsev, elected on 1 December 1992.]

In contrast to INTELSAT, each member of the Board has one vote in accordance with the principle of equality between members. Decisions are not binding on member states which choose not to ratify them.

INTERSPUTNIK offers traditional telecommunications services such as voice and data communications, and TV and radio broadcasting. It is also developing new services which include VSAT, video conferencing, distributed data processing and complete project engineering services.

J.-L.M.

ADDRESS

2, Smolensky per. 1/4, 121099 Moscow, Federal Republic of Russia
T. (7 095) 244 03 33, Fx. (7 095) 253 9906

193 C – INTERNATIONAL MARITIME SATELLITE ORGANIZATION (INMARSAT)

INMARSAT was created in 1976 by a Convention drafted by the Inter-Governmental Maritime Consultative Organization, which has since become the International Maritime Organization (IMO) [see 183 A]. It operates a satellite network which provides telecommunications services to and from maritime vessels, aircraft and land-based services. INMARSAT became operational on 1 February 1982.

STRUCTURE

The **Assembly**, consisting of representatives from all the member states, deals mainly with general policy and defines the long-term objectives of the Organization.

The **Council** is composed of 22 representatives of signatories – that is, telecommunications entities appointed by states to represent them. The Council manages the Organization, and each representative has a voting participation equivalent to the investment share or shares it represents. However, no representative may cast on behalf of one signatory more than 25 per cent of the total voting participation in the Organization (Art. 14-3).

The **Directorate** represents INMARSAT and is also responsible for the administrative tasks of the Organization.

INMARSAT leases its satellites from international networks or purchases them. Its resources come from revenues generated by the communication to and from maritime vessels, aircraft and land mobile users. Nearly 20,000 vessels are equipped with the INMARSAT system.

J.-L.M.

ADDRESS

40 Melton Street, London NW1 2EQ, United Kingdom
T. (44 71) 728 1000, Tx. 297201 INMSAT G, Fx. (44 71) 728 1044

193.01 – AGREEMENT RELATING TO THE INTERNATIONAL TELECOMMUNICATIONS SATELLITE ORGANIZATION "INTELSAT" – INTELSAT

Concluded : 20.08.1971, Washington
In Force : 12.02.1973
Parties : 125

This Agreement confirmed the interim agreement of 20 August 1964 and established INTELSAT [see 193 A] on a permanent basis as it exists today. The Agreement is open to all parties to the interim agreement and any other state which is a member of the International Telecommunication Union (ITU) [see 192 A].

This 1971 Convention is supplemented by an Operating Agreement which stipulates the administrative, financial, and technical procedures of the Agreement, including the question of patents, the allotment of space segment capacity, INTELSAT's relations with the ITU, the approval of Earth stations, inventions and technical information.

Article XIV of the Agreement requires the parties, signatories, or any person within the jurisdiction of a party who wishes "to establish, acquire, or utilize space segment facilities separate from the INTELSAT space segment facilities to meet its international public telecommunications requirements", to "furnish all relevant information to and ... consult with the Assembly of Parties, through the Board of Governors, to ensure technical compatability of such facilities and their operation...[and] to avoid significant economic harm to the global system of INTELSAT". This provision was applied in cases where international regional satellite networks such as EUTELSAT and ARABSAT were established. Originally this provision was meant to prevent competition from new regional networks; however, many national and regional networks have since been established and do not constitute a major economic threat to INTELSAT.

The great innovations of this Convention are, first, its system of representation, which is in proportion to a state's investment share in the Organization and, second, its weighted system of voting on the Board of Governors.

J.-L.M.

Access : CON (Art. XIX)
Reserves : PRO (Art. XIX)
Duration : USP
Deposit. : US (Art. XXII)
Language : Eng, Fre, Spa (Art. XXI)

Reference : ILM 10:909 – UKTS 1973/80 – Can TS 1973/10/15, 1982/29 – 5 Paeslee – RTAF 1976/21 – RGDIP 1987/3 – JORF 6 Apr 76

193.02 – AGREEMENT ON THE ESTABISHMENT OF AN INTERNATIONAL SYSTEM AND ORGANIZATION OF SPACE TELECOMMUNICATIONS "INTERSPUTNIK" – INTERSPUTNIK

Concluded : 15.11.1971, Moscow
In Force : 12.07.1972
Parties : 18

The Agreement establishes an international satellite telecommunications system and creates INTERSPUTNIK [see 193 B]. The communication system includes a space complex and ground stations. The Agreement outlines the functions of INTERSPUTNIK and clearly states that the Organization must co-ordinate its activity with the International Telecommunication Union (ITU) [see 192 A].

INTERSPUTNIK is designed to function as a commercial network. The Agreement entrusts the Council and the Directorate with the management of the network.

A three-member **Auditing Commission** is empowered with control over the Organization's financial matters. Article 17 allows members to denounce the Agreement with one year's notice and after payment of monetary compensation.

J.-L.M.

Access : ALS (Art. 22)
Reserves : USP
Duration : USP
Deposit. : RU (Art. 20)
Language : Eng, Fre, Rus, Spa (Art. 26)

Modific. : Protocol 26.11.82 (01.01.83);

Reference : 862 UNTS

193.03 – CONVENTION ESTABLISHING THE INTERNATIONAL MARITIME SATELLITE ORGANIZATION – INMARSAT

Concluded : 03.09.1976, London
In Force : 16.07.1979
Parties : 66

The convention created INMARSAT [see 193 C] along similar lines as INTELSAT [see 193 A]. Its objective was to establish a space segment (i.e. satellites and related facilities) in order to improve maritime communications for peaceful purposes.

The Organization operates on a sound economic and financial basis having regard to accepted commercial principles. Representatives in the Council have a voting participation equivalent to the investment share or shares they represent. The space segment belongs to the Organization and users of the system have access to it through Earth stations belonging to states, or stations on board vessels, or aircraft or through land mobile users.

The Convention defines the responsibilities of the Organization's three organs (the Assembly, Council and Directorate), including procedures, liability, legal personality, and relations with other organizations, and notification to the International Telecommunication Union of the frequencies and other information as provided for in the Radio Regulations annexed to the International Telecommunication Convention [see 192 A, 192.01 and 192.02].

The amended Convention of 1985 extends its competence to aeronautical use. To this end, the INMARSAT Assembly agreed to sign a co-operation agreement with the International Civil Aviation Organization [see 184 A]. Once the 1989 amended Agreement enters into force, the Convention will also cover communication satellites for land mobile services.

J.-L.M.

Access	: ALS (Art. 32)
Reserves	: PRO (Art. 32)
Duration	: USP
Deposit.	: IMO
Language	: Eng, Fre, Rus, Spa
Modific.	: 16.10.85 (13.10.89); 19.01.89 (-)
Reference	: ILM 15:219, 15:1052, 27:691 – Can TS 1979/35 – UST 31/1 – JORF 11 Oct 88, 21 Oct 88 – RTAF 1979/53

2. Monetary Co-operation, Financial Assistance and Economic Forums

The inter-war period witnessed the collapse of the international monetary system and saw restrictions on international trade and payments that left many countries worse off. This experience showed that international economic co-operation was greatly needed. It also led to the establishment of economic institutions to promote monetary co-operation [see 2.1] and the mobilization of economic resources for long-term economic development [see 2.2]. Countries have also met in more informal groups to discuss international economic issues [see 2.3].

2.1 International Monetary System

The onset of the First World War caused the collapse of the Classical Gold Standard (in existence between 1870 and 1914). Governments suspended the convertibility of their currency into gold and they printed money to finance the war. After the Genoa Conference in 1922, several countries went back to a system of fixed exchange rates and restored the gold convertibility of their currency at their pre-war parity. However, as the gold supplies appeared inadequate, countries such as Britain and France agreed to hold all their reserves in gold while smaller countries could hold the currencies of these larger countries.

In 1925, the return to the parity prevailing before the First World War, combined with price-level increases, led to the overvaluation of the pound sterling and forced the Bank of England to follow contractionary monetary policies. As a result, the rate of unemployment increased sharply and foreigners began converting their pounds into gold as they feared a devaluation. Britain's difficulties were compounded by France's return to gold in 1928 at an undervalued rate and by the US stock-market crash of 1929. Germany had been borrowing funds from the United States to pay its war reparation payments to the Allies while Germany's creditors were sending these funds back to the United States to pay off their debts. The crash and the Great Depression stopped the flow of US funds to Europe and led to bank failures. Finally, Britain was forced to go off gold in 1931. Soon after, many countries undertook competitive depreciations and increased their tariffs which resulted in higher rates of unemployment.

The need for international co-operation on monetary matters became evident. The Bank for International Settlements, whose main objective is to promote co-operation among central banks and provide additional facilities for international financial operations [see 2.1.2], began its activities in 1930. A few years later, in 1944, the International Monetary Fund was created with the aim of setting up a new international monetary system.

Maryse Robert

2.1.1 Monetary Co-operation

In planning the postwar economic institutions in the early 1940s, both the United States and Great Britain wanted to avoid the errors of the 1930s: competitive depreciation and increased protectionism. Several international conferences addressed world monetary problems in the 1930s but none of them led to what was required – co-operation by all to establish a new international monetary system. The Gold Exchange Standard of the 1920s had failed to create such a system.

The International Monetary Fund (IMF) was set up at the Bretton Woods Conference in 1944 [211 A]. The Allied countries aimed at creating an international monetary system that would foster exchange rate stability, full employment, economic growth, trade liberalization, and balance-of-payments equilibrium. In order to attain both external and internal objectives, member countries needed the system to be flexible: exchange rates were fixed but adjustable; currency convertibility was obligatory for current-account transactions only; and a system of quotas was designed to allow the IMF to become an additional source of liquidity for deficit countries.

Over the years, the IMF has created a new international reserve asset, the Special Drawing Rights (SDRs), abandoned gold and allowed floating exchange rates. Fund facilities have been established to address the particular needs of the developing countries. The IMF has also maintained a very close relationship with its sister organization, the World Bank [see 221 A], as well as with other international organizations (e.g. the General Agreement on Tariffs and Trade (GATT) [see 111 A], the Organisation for Economic Co-operation and Development (OECD), and the Bank for International Settlements (BIS) [see 212 A]).

This section does not cover regional monetary co-operation such as the European Monetary System (EMS), which began its operations in 1979, and the CFA Franc Zone, a currency union including 13 African countries.

Maryse Robert

SELECTED BIBLIOGRAPHY

Dam, Kenneth W., *The Rules of the Game: Reform and Evolution in the International Monetary System*, Chicago: University of Chicago Press, 1982.

de Vries, Margaret G., *The IMF in a Changing World 1945-85*, Washington, DC: International Monetary Fund, 1986.

– – –, *The International Monetary Fund, 1972-78: Co-operation on Trial*, Volumes I, II, and III, Washington, DC: International Monetary Fund, 1985.

– – –, *The International Monetary Fund, 1966-71: The System Under Stress*, Volumes I and II, Washington, DC: International Monetary Fund, 1976.

Finch, C. David, *The IMF: the Record and the Prospect*, Princeton Essays in International Finance 175, Princeton, N.J.: International Finance Section, Dept. of Economics, Princeton University, 1989.

Ghai, Dharam (ed.), *The IMF and the South: the Social Impact of Crisis and Adjustment*, London: Zed Books, 1991.

Gwin, Catherine and Richard E. Feinberg (eds.), *The International Monetary Fund in a Multipolar World: Pulling Together*, US-Third World Policy Perspectives, No. 13. Washington, DC: Overseas Development Council, 1989.

Horsefield, J. Keith, *The International Monetary Fund, 1945-65: Twenty Years of International Monetary Co-operation*, Volumes I, II, and III, Washington, DC: International Monetary Fund, 1969.

Polak, Jacques J., *The Changing Nature of IMF Conditionality*, Princeton Essays in International Finance 184. Princeton, N.J.: International Finance Section, Dept. of Economics, Princeton University, 1991.

Solomon, Robert., *The International Monetary System, 1945-1981*, New York: Harper & Row, 1982.

Spraos, John, *IMF Conditionality: Ineffectual, Inefficient, Mistargeted*, Essays in International Finance, no. 166. Princeton, N.J.: International Finance Section, Dept. of Economics, Princeton University, 1986.

211 A – INTERNATIONAL MONETARY FUND (IMF)

Delegations of 44 countries and a representative of Denmark took part in the United Nations Monetary and Financial Conference held at Bretton Woods (New Hampshire, USA) in July 1944. This Conference led to the establishment of the International Monetary Fund (IMF), which began financial operations on 1 March 1947.

PURPOSES

The allied countries set up an institution that would: promote international monetary co-operation and exchange rate stability; maintain orderly exchange arrangements among members and avoid competitive exchange depreciation; facilitate the expansion and balanced growth of international trade; assist in the establishment of a multilateral system of payments (...) and in the elimination of foreign exchange restrictions (...); give confidence to members by making the general resources of the Fund temporarily available to them (...); shorten the duration and lessen the degree of disequilibrium in the international balances of payments of members (Art. I).

MEMBERSHIP AND FINANCIAL RESOURCES

All countries that attended the Bretton Woods Conference later joined the IMF with the exception of the former USSR. However, 14 of the former Soviet republics had become members of the IMF by the end of 1992.

Members can leave the Fund at any time (Article XXVI). Four countries did: Poland in 1950, Czechoslovakia in 1954, Cuba in 1960 and Indonesia in 1965. Indonesia returned to the IMF in 1967. Both Poland and Czechoslovakia rejoined the IMF in 1986 and 1990, respectively. As of 14 April 1993, the Fund had 174 members.

To become a member, a country must possess full autonomy of its external relations and agree to the conditions and terms for membership. The Board of Governors approves the membership resolution.

Each member is assigned a quota. Twenty-five per cent is paid in reserves assets and the remaining in the country's own currency. This quota is based on economic data such as gross domestic product (GDP), current account transactions, variability of current receipts and official reserves. A member's borrowing capacity and voting power is determined by its quota. Each member receives 250 votes plus one additional vote for each share of stock held. Each share has a value of SDR 100,000 (Special Drawing Rights) (Article XII, Section 5-a) [see 211.01]. Quotas must be reviewed every five years (Article III, section 2). In June 1990, the Board of Governors authorized an increase of 50 per cent in IMF quotas. Total quotas will increase to SDR 144.8 billion. Only countries that became members of the Fund before 30 May 1990 are eligible for this quota increase.

CURRENCY CONVERTIBILITY

To prevent the recurrence of competitive manipulation of exchange rates and economic warfare, members are urged to remove their exchange controls. However, under Article VIII, currency convertibility is obligated for current-account transactions only. A member can also choose to defer currency convertibility during a postwar transitional period (Article XIV). As of 31 December 1992, 74 of the 173 Fund members had accepted the obligations of Article VIII; the others operate under Article XIV.

ORGANIZATION AND MANAGEMENT

The organizational structure of the IMF is explained in the Articles of Agreement (Art. XII).

The **Board of Governors** consists of a Governor and an Alternate for each member country. The governors are usually ministers of finance or central bank governors. The Board of Governors meets once a year at the Annual Meetings. It may also meet at other times or vote by mail if necessary. Under the Articles of Agreement, all powers not conferred to the Board of Governors, the Executive Board or the Managing Director, are vested in the Board of Governors. The increase in IMF membership and quotas as well as the allocation of SDRs can only be authorized by the Board of Governors.

The **Executive Board** deals with the day-to-day business of the IMF such as the surveillance of members' exchange rate policies, financial assistance to members and consultations with member countries. It consists of 24 Executive Directors of which five are appointed by each of the five countries having the largest quotas (the United States, the United Kingdom, Germany, France and Japan). Under Article XII-3a of the Articles of Agreement, Saudi Arabia is also allowed to appoint an Executive Director. The other 18 members of the Executive Board are elected by groups of the remaining member countries. However, since September 1980, China has elected its own Director.

The **Managing Director** is selected by the Executive Board for an initial period of five years. He serves as its chairperson. The Managing Director also takes part in the meetings of the Board of Governors, the Interim Committee and the Development Committee. The Managing Director has always been a European.

The Articles of Agreement, as amended in 1978, allow the Board of Governors to establish a Council as a decision-making body of the IMF. This Council would supervise the management of the international monetary system and look at the need to amend the Articles of Agreement. However, the Board of Governors has been relying on a temporary advisory body, the **Interim Committee**, to receive advice on these matters as well as on the proposals by the Fund's Executive Board to increase quotas. The Interim Committee was established in 1974. It is made up of 24 governors representing the same countries as in the Fund's Executive Board. It normally meets in the spring, and in the autumn at the Annual Meetings of the IMF and the World Bank. The second advisory committee, the Joint Ministerial Committee on the Transfer of Real Resources to Developing Countries, is known as the **Development Committee**. It was established in 1974. This Committee deals with development issues and, as with the Interim Committee, is made up of 24 governors [see 221 A].

The **IMF Institute** offers courses to government officials (generally from central banks or ministries of the economy, planning and finance) on a broad range of issues such as the implementation of policy adjustments and the techniques of financial analysis and programming.

FINANCIAL ASSISTANCE

Tranche Policies (Repurchases are made in three and a quarter to five years)

1. *Reserve Tranche.* This is 25 per cent of a member country's quota that it paid in reserve currency. It is available upon request.

2. *Credit Tranches.* All members have four credit tranches. Each of these tranches is equivalent to 25 per cent of the member's quota. When confronting minor balance of payments difficulties, members may request the use of their *first credit tranche*. Performance criteria and purchase in instalments are not used. The member demonstrates that it intends to solve its payments problem.

Along with its request to use the IMF's resources in the *upper credit tranches*, members must present a plan explaining how they propose to overcome their balance of payments difficulties. Under this requirement, known as conditionality, a country must implement policies that will restore its balance of payments and sustain economic growth. The current guidelines on conditionality were adopted by the

Executive Board in 1979 and revised in July 1991. Typically, resources are made available under stand-by or extended arrangements that include performance criteria and purchases in instalments. Generally, a member undertakes to devalue its currency, reduce government expenditure and credit expansion, and cut subsidies.

Stand-by arrangements (repurchases are made in three to five years) enable members to make purchases from the IMF, up to the specified amount in the arrangement, during a period covering one to two years, as long as the objectives of the programme are achieved. *Extended arrangements* (repurchases are made in four to ten years) cover periods of three years or up to four years in exceptional circumstances.

Enlarged Access Policy (Repurchases are made in three and a half to seven years)
This policy is used when a member country requiring a relatively long period of adjustment and a longer repurchase period needs to add to resources available under the stand-by and extended arrangements. The current limits on stand-by and extended arrangements, individually or combined, are: 90 or 110 per cent of quota annually; 270 or 330 per cent of quota over three years; and 400 or 440 per cent of quota on a cumulative basis, net of repurchases.

Fund Facilities

1. **Buffer Stock Financing Facility (BSFF)** (Repurchases are made in three and a quarter to five years). Established in 1969, this facility serves one purpose. It helps cover IMF members' contributions to approved international commodity buffer stock schemes, provided that members have balance of payments difficulties. Drawings are made for up to the equivalent of 45 per cent of quota.

No drawings have been made under this facility since the mid-1980s.

2. **Compensatory and Contingency Financing Facility (CCFF)** (Repurchases made in three and a quarter to five years). The compensatory element was introduced in 1963 under the **Compensatory Financing Facility**. It provides resources to help finance temporary export shortfall (40 per cent of quota) and, since 1981, excesses in the cost of cereal imports (17 per cent of quota). A member's balance of payments difficulties "must be temporary and largely attributable to circumstances beyond the member's control".

The contingency element was added in 1988. It makes resources available to members pursuing Fund-supported adjustment programmes when they are affected by adverse changes in external economic conditions (40 per cent of quota) (for deviations in interest rates: 35 per cent of quota).

There is also an optional 25 per cent of quota which can be used to supplement any of the two elements of the CCFF.

3. **Extended Fund Facility** (Repurchases are made in four and a half to ten years). This facility was established in 1974. It provides resources to meet members' balance of payments needs over the medium term (three years, or up to four years in exceptional circumstances). Members request extended arrangement that includes performance criteria and purchases in instalments.

4. **Structural Adjustment Facility (SAF).** The Fund's Executive Board established this facility in March 1986. It provides balance of payments assistance on concessional terms to low-income developing countries in order to support macroeconomic and structural adjustment programmes over the medium-term. The facility is funded by the Trust Fund reflows (SDR 2.7 billion), which are repayments on loans made in 1976-81 to 55 low-income developing countries. The loans had been financed by the sale of some of the Fund's gold holdings and contributions from donor countries. As of December 1992, 71 countries were eligible for SAF resources.

Members must prepare, with the assistance of the IMF and the World Bank, a policy framework paper (PFP) for a three-year period. The PFP states the objectives, priorities and measures that the member intends to take during this three-year period. The PFP is reviewed by the Executive Board of the IMF and by the Executive Directors of the World Bank. It is updated every year.

Each eligible member can borrow up to 70 per cent of its quota: 20 per cent the first year, 30 per cent the second year, and 20 per cent the third year. The first annual loan is made after the IMF approves both the three-year SAF arrangement and the first annual arrangement. These arrangements must describe the specific objectives and policies that will be pursued during the three-year programme period and the first annual period. Financial benchmarks such as monetary, fiscal and external debt variables are also specified on a quarterly basis.

5. **Enhanced Structural Adjustment Facility (ESAF).** ESAF was established by the Board of Governors in December 1987. The objectives, eligibility and features of ESAF are similar to those of SAF. A detailed annual programme and a PFP are prepared each year. However, the adjustment measures that must be adopted under ESAF are more demanding. Countries are expected to substantially strengthen their balance of payments position and foster growth during the three-year period.

An eligible member may borrow a maximum of 250 per cent of its quota under ESAF (350 per cent under exceptional circumstances). As with the SAF, loans carry an annual interest rate of 0.5 per cent a year. They are disbursed semi-annually and reimbursed in five and a half to ten years. Total ESAF resources available: SDR 6 billion.

THE GENERAL ARRANGEMENTS TO BORROW (GAB)

For a detailed analysis of the General Arrangements to Borrow [see 232 A].

RELATIONS WITH OTHER INTERNATIONAL ORGANIZATIONS

The IMF has maintained close ties with several international organizations. Article 10 of the Articles of Agreement states that "the Fund shall co-operate with any general international organization and with public international organizations having specialized responsibilities in related fields".

The Fund became a specialized agency of the UN in the late 1940s. The protocol concerning the entry into force of the agreement between the United Nations and the International Monetary Fund was signed in New York on 15 April 1948. The IMF has an office at the United Nations in New York. Its Special Representative is responsible for relations with the UN and its subsidiary bodies. The Managing Director attends meetings of the Administrative Committee on Co-ordination (ACC) and the Economic and Social Council (ECOSOC) [see 001 A].

The Paris Office maintains close ties with the Bank for International Settlements (BIS) [see 212 A], the Commission of the European Communities, and the Organisation for Economic Co-operation and Development (OECD), while the Fund Office in Geneva is responsible for the IMF's relations with the UN Conference on Trade and Development (UNCTAD) [see 111 B], other UN organizations based in Geneva, and the GATT. The IMF plays a role in GATT balance of payments consultations by providing relevant information on the consulting country's economic and financial policies [see 111 A].

The IMF has a very close relationship with the World Bank [see 221 A]. Both institutions were founded at the Bretton Woods conference in 1944. They share the same broad objective of promoting sustained economic growth in their member countries. Although they had always collaborated closely (guidelines for collaboration between the two institutions were first defined in 1966), the need for such co-operation grew substantially in the 1980s with the increasing overlap in their activities. For instance, both institutions are providing financial support for programmes of structural adjustment.

In March 1989, the managements of the Fund and the Bank agreed to clarify the primary responsibility of each institution and to avoid duplication. Additional administrative procedures for collaboration and more efficient use of each other's resources were adopted: the IMF's responsibilities lie in short-term stabilization and exchange rates whereas the World Bank is responsible for medium and longer-term structural reforms. The collaboration between the Fund and the Bank is best exemplified by the policy-framework paper (PFP) that SAF and ESAF countries (mostly African countries) must prepare. However, it has not been extended beyond SAF and ESAF countries.

THE ROLE OF THE IMF IN THE DEBT CRISIS

The IMF has played a key role in co-ordinating bank lending to debtor countries. When the Mexican crisis began in 1982, the IMF made it a rule to delay its lending to debtors until banks had decided to continue lending. This strategy was successful at first but then the banks became reluctant to provide additional loans to help finance debt-ridden countries. IMF conditionality and stabilization programmes were very important in signalling to banks that a country was taking measures to improve its balance of payments. However, neither concerted lending nor the Baker Plan, launched in October 1985 at the Annual Meetings of the IMF and the World Bank, led to a substantial reduction in the debt of developing countries. Banks aimed at reducing their Third World exposure either by selling their claims at a discount or by increasing their reserves against possible losses on bad loans.

In March 1989, a new debt initiative was put forward by Nicholas Brady, who was the US Secretary of Treasury. The Brady Plan acknowledges that developing countries will not be able to fully repay their debts. It emphasizes the need for the IMF and the World Bank to provide funding for debt and debt-service-reduction operations. The Executive Board of the IMF approved Fund support for debt-reduction and debt-service-reduction. The IMF was also asked to stop holding off its own lending to debtor countries until banks had agreed to continue lending.

PUBLICATIONS

Article XII, Section 7, states that the Fund "shall publish an annual report ... and shall issue, at intervals of three months or less, a summary statement of its operations and transactions and its holdings of special drawing rights, gold, and currencies of members".

The IMF publishes a wide range of studies and books. Its main publications are: *Annual Report* (September); *Annual Report on Exchange Arrangements and Exchange Restrictions; Balance of Payments Statistics Yearbook* (December); *Direction of Trade Statistics* (quarterly); *Finance & Development* (with the World Bank, quarterly); *Government Financial Statistics Yearbook* (December); *International Financial Statistics* (5th of the month); *IMF Survey* (twice a month); *Staff Papers* (quarterly); and *World Economic Outlook* (twice a year). The IMF also publishes a series of pamphlets as well as an Occasional Paper series.

Maryse Robert

ADDRESS

700 19th Street, N.W., Washington, DC 20431, United States
T. (202) 623 7000, Fx. (202) 623 4661

211.01 – STATUTES OF THE INTERNATIONAL MONETARY FUND – IMF

Concluded : 22.07.1945, Washington
In Force : 27.12.1945
Parties : 175

To control world-wide monetary growth and inflation, the Bretton Woods system called for adjustable parities where the US dollar (the principal reserve currency) was tied to gold at US$35 an ounce and each member's exchange rate was fixed against the US dollar. Members were required to intervene in the exchange market to limit fluctuations of their exchange rate within a band of 1 per cent, above or below parity. Under Article IV of the Articles of Agreement, a member's exchange rate could be changed, after approval by the IMF, in the event of "fundamental disequilibrium" in this country's balance of payments.

The United States had to trade gold for dollars with foreign central banks. To do so, it had to hold sufficient gold reserves. In 1960, the economist Robert Triffin showed that foreign central banks' holdings of dollars would grow over time to meet their needs in international reserve and eventually would exceed the US gold stock. This could have led to a confidence problem if all dollar holders had tried to exchange their dollars for gold. To address this particular problem, the Board of Governors adopted Resolution no. 23-5 on 31 May 1968, amending the Articles of Agreement for the first time and creating the Special Drawing Rights (SDRs). The **First Amendment** became effective on 28 July 1969.

The SDR is essentially an accounting creation of the IMF. It is also an international reserve asset and the unit of account of the Fund. A total of SDR 21.4 billion in six allocations was distributed to IMF members from 1970 to 1981. Before deciding to create SDRs, the IMF must determine if there is a need to supplement existing reserve assets. Members receive SDRs in proportion to their quota at the time of the allocation. SDRs may be used in transactions among members, with the IMF, and with 16 institutions, including the World Bank, the regional development banks, and the Bank for International Settlements. Interest is credited to members whose holdings exceed their cumulative accumulations. Charges are debited to those whose holdings are less than their net cumulative accumulations.

The SDR is determined on the basis of a weighted basket of five currencies; 40 per cent for the US dollar, 21 per cent for the deutsche mark, 17 per cent for the Japanese yen, and 11 per cent for both the French franc and the pound sterling. The SDR valuation basket is revised every five years. The last revision occurred on 1 January 1991 and will be in effect until 31 December 1995.

Following the deterioration of the US current account in the late 1960s, there was pressure to devalue the US dollar. However, this meant that all other governments would have to revalue their currency against the dollar. Most countries were reluctant to undertake such a revaluation as it would have hurt their exports by making their goods more expensive relative to US goods. On 15 August 1971, President Nixon decided to change the rules of the game and announced that the United States would no longer automatically trade gold for dollars. The creation by central banks of a two-tier market for gold in 1968 had eliminated the constraint on world-wide monetary growth but not the obligation of the United States to sell gold to central banks for dollars. A 10 per cent import tax was also introduced by President Nixon to force the realignment of the other currencies. The Smithsonian Agreement reached in December 1971 resulted in an 8 per cent devaluation of the US dollar and the removal of the import tax. However, the deterioration of the US current account and the speculative attack on the dollar continued. In early 1973, after another devaluation of the dollar and the closing down of the foreign-exchange market, the US dollar and the other major currencies were forced to float. It was the end of the Bretton Woods system.

The first economic summit in November 1975 [see 231 B] and a special meeting of the Interim Committee in Kingston, Jamaica, in January 1976, led to the **Second Amendment** of the Fund's Articles of Agreement (Board of Governors' Resolution no. 31-4, adopted on 30 April 1976). The Second Amendment became effective on 1 April 1978. It legitimizes floating exchange rates. More specifically, IMF members are free to choose their exchange arrangements with the exception that they cannot base the value of their currency on gold. Article IV was revised. It now states that each member shall "avoid manipulating exchange rates ... in order ... to gain an unfair competitive advantage over other members". Article IV also states that "the Fund shall exercise firm surveillance over the exchange rate policies of members". Article IV consultations are generally held annually with most members. IMF staff gathers information and analyses each member's economic policies. The Executive Board examines these reports and holds meetings twice a year on the world economic outlook.

The Second Amendment is also aimed at reducing the reserve role of gold and promoting the SDR as the principal reserve asset. The official price of gold was abolished. One-sixth of the Fund's holdings of gold was sold. Profits were lent on highly concessional terms to developing countries through the Trust Fund. Another one-sixth was sold back to members in proportion to their quotas.

In order to eliminate arrears and prevent overdue obligations, the Board of Governors adopted Resolution No. 45-2 on 28 June 1990. The **Third Amendment** provides for the suspension of voting and related rights of members who do not fulfil their obligations under the Articles of Agreement. The Third Amendment entered into force on 11 November 1992.

M.R.

Access : CON (Art. 2)
Reserves : USP
Duration : USP
Deposit. : US
Language : Eng

Modific. : Amendments 31.05.68 (28.07.69); 07.01.76 (01.04.78); 28.06.90 (11.11.92)

Reference : 1, 2 UNTS – Can TS 1944/37 – UKTS 1946/21, 1978/44+83 – UST 20/3, 29/2 – 1 Paeslee – JORF 27 Dec 45

2.1.2 Central Bank and Securities Supervisors Co-operation

The growing internationalization of financial markets has put pressure on national financial regulators for increased co-operation in order to maintain sound market systems. Central banks have traditionally met in Basle with the Bank for International Settlements (BIS) [212 A]. More recently securities supervisors have adopted similar approaches to those of central banks within the International Organization of Securities Commissions (IOSCO) [see 212 B].

Bernard Colas

SELECTED BIBLIOGRAPHY

Bederman, David J., "The Bank for International Settlements and the Debt Crisis: a New Role for the Central Banker's Bank?", *International Tax and Business Lawyer* 6 (Winter 1988): 92-121.

Giovanoli, Mario, "The Role of the Bank for International Settlements in International Monetary Co-operation and Its Tasks Relating to the European Currency Unit", in: *Festschrift in Honor of Sir Joseph Gold*, Ebke, Werner F. and Joseph J. Norton (eds.), Heidelberg: Verl. Recht u. Wirtschaft, 1990.

212 A – BANK FOR INTERNATIONAL SETTLEMENTS (BIS)

The Bank for International Settlements, established pursuant to the Hague Agreements of 20 January 1930, is the oldest international financial institution. The BIS, as an international organization, and by virtue of the Headquarters Agreement concluded with the Swiss authorities on 10 February 1987, enjoys certain immunities necessary for the performance of its functions. The BIS has the structure of a company limited by shares; however, its Statutes differ in many respects from the provisions which normally govern such a company.

FUNCTIONS

The objectives of the BIS are, first, to promote the co-operation of central banks and international financial institutions; second, to provide additional facilities for international financial operations; and, third, to act as trustee or agent in regard to international financial settlements.

International monetary co-operation. Regular meetings are held between the BIS Board of Directors and central bank Governors of the Group of Ten [see 232 A], EC countries, and other countries. The purpose of these meetings is to achieve a high degree of mutual understanding and, when practicable, to co-ordinate monetary policy internationally and thus help to ensure orderly conditions in the international financial markets. In addition, the BIS organizes meetings of central bank experts on economic and monetary questions.

The BIS provides the permanent secretariat for the Basle Committee on Banking Supervision [see 212.02 and 212.03] and for the Committee on Payments and Settlement Systems. It acts as a host to the Secretariat of the Committee of Governors of the member states of the EC central banks, which also serves the Board of Governors of the European Monetary Co-operation Fund (EMCF). These last two bodies provide the institutional framework for monetary co-operation in the EC.

With regard to eastern European countries, the BIS established a procedure for co-ordinating the technical assistance provided to their central banks and also organized seminars.

Banking Operations. The BIS is authorized *inter alia* to accept deposits in gold or currencies from central banks. At present, over 90 central banks from all over the world have deposits with the BIS, which represents between 10 and 15 per cent of world foreign exchange reserves. These funds may be used to buy and sell gold and currencies, or buy and sell a wide range of readily marketable securities. The BIS may also use a portion of these funds to advance loans to or place deposits with central banks. However, it may neither lend to governments nor open current accounts in their name. All the Bank's operations must be in conformity with the monetary policy of the central banks whose currencies or markets are affected.

Since the beginning of the debt crisis in 1982, the BIS has, with support from the leading central banks, helped provide bridging finance to a number of central banks, mainly in Latin America and eastern Europe. This action has been undertaken pending the disbursement of credits granted by the IMF, and in some cases the IBRD, which were conditional on certain undertakings with regard to future economic policy.

Functions As Agent or Trustee. The BIS acts as an Agent for the private ECU clearing and settlement system in accordance with the provisions of successive agreements concluded between ECU Banking Association (EBA), Paris, and the BIS. It also acts as agent for the European Monetary Co-operation Fund (EMCF), which deals with operations in connection with the working of the European Monetary System (EMS) and the execution of financial operations connected with Community borrowing and lending. It conducts operations for the EMCF in connection with the working of the European Monetary System (EMS) and the execution of the Community's borrowing and lending operations.

In the past, the BIS has acted as a trustee, agent or third party for international public loans. It has also acted as an agent for the European Payments Union (EPU), the European Monetary Agreement (EMA) and for the OECD Exchange Guarantee Agreement.

ORGANIZATION

The BIS organs are the General Meeting, the Board of Directors and the Secretariat.

The **General Meeting** meets once a year in June. All rights of representation and of voting are exercised, in proportion to the number of shares subscribed in each country, by the central banks or the financial institutions acting in their stead. Of the 32 institutions represented in the General Meeting, 27 are central banks from the European countries and five in non-European countries (Australia, Canada, Japan, South Africa and the United States).

The **Board of Directors** is made up of representatives of central banks from eight countries (Belgium, France, Germany, Italy, the Netherlands, Sweden, Switzerland, and the UK), and it elects the General Manager.

FINANCE

The authorized capital of the BIS, totalling 1,500 gold francs, is subdivided into 600,000 shares of 2,500 gold francs each. The issued capital amounts at present to some 1,183 million gold francs, represented by 473,125 shares, which are paid up to the extent of 25 per cent. The amount of paid up capital appearing on the balance sheet consequently stands at roughly 296 million gold francs.

The Bank's unit of account is the gold franc, which is the equivalent of 0.29032258 grammes of fine gold. Assets and liabilities in US dollars are converted on the basis of 1 gold franc = US$1.94149; all other items in currencies are converted at market rates against the US dollar. On 31 March 1992, the balance sheet total was 48 million gold francs.

The BIS participates as an observer in the work of the Interim Committee of the IMF, of the finance ministers and central bank Governors of the Group of Ten countries and their Deputies, and of various committees of the OECD. It also collects and publishes statistical data, and conducts and publishes its research on economic and monetary matters. The *BIS Annual Report* has a reputation for its high quality.

Bernard Colas

ADDRESS

Centralbahnplatz, 2, CH-4002 Basle, Switzerland
T. (41 61) 280 8080, Fx. (41 61) 280 9100

212 B – INTERNATIONAL ORGANIZATION OF SECURITIES COMMISSIONS (IOSCO)

Just as the banking supervisors meet in Basle to discuss common problems, the securities supervisors have been meeting annually: first in 1974, as the Inter-American Conference of Securities Commissions and Similar Organizations and then, since 1984, as IOSCO, the International Organization of Securities Commissions. Its by-laws were last modified in London in 1992.

Through its permanent structures, IOSCO enables its members to exchange information with a view to developing securities markets and improving their efficiency, to co-ordinating the enforcement of securities regulation and to implementing common standards. Comprising some 101 members, it provides the major international forum for mutual consultation and collaboration on regulatory issues relevant to the development of securities business, including growing cross-border business.

IOSCO has three categories of member: regular members which each have one vote, and associate and affiliate members which have no voting power. In 1993, IOSCO had 63 regular members: mainly securities commissions and, exceptionally, self-regulatory organizations such as stock exchanges when there is no governmental regulatory agency in a given country. There are seven associate members and 31 affiliate members (mainly self-regulatory organizations, international organizations such as EC, OECD, and organizations recommended by the Executive Committee).

STRUCTURE

The Organization is made up of the following permanent committees: the Presidents Committee, the Executive Committee, the General Secretariat and four Regional Standing Committees.

The **Presidents Committee**, which meets once a year during the Annual Conference, is composed of all the presidents of member (regular and associate) commissions or agencies.

The **Executive Committee** is currently made up of 17 members, 12 elected by the Presidents Committee, a representative from each regional standing committee (which currently are the Africa and Middle East Regional Committee, the Asia-Pacific Regional Committee, the European Regional Committee, the Interamerican Regional Committee) and the Chairman of the Development Committee. The Executive Committee meets periodically during the year and takes all decisions necessary to achieve the purpose of the Organization in accordance with the guidelines set by the Presidents Committee. It has established two specialist committees.

The first one, the Technical Committee, is made up of the securities agencies that regulate the most developed market in the world. Its mandate is to review major regulatory problems related to international securities transactions and to propose practical solutions to these problems. It currently has four working parties (WPs), composed of experts from the members organizations:

- WP 1 on Multinational Disclosure and Accounting has recently concluded that audits conducted in accordance with the International Auditing Practices Committee (IAPC) auditing standards could be relied upon by securities regulatory authorities for multinational reporting purposes;
- WP 2 on Regulation of Secondary Markets aims at identifying, among other things, issues relevant to the relationship between cash and derivative markets for equities which all IOSCO members should consider in their regulation of such markets and products;
- WP 3 on Regulation of Market Intermediaries works on minimal capital adequacy standards for internationally active securities firms and banks, and tries to establish with the Basle Committee on Banking Supervision [see 212.02] common minimum capital standards for internationally active securities firms and banks. It has adopted a set of principles intended to guide the development of regulatory practices and regulatory co-operation in the area of financial conglomerates;
- WP 4 on Enforcement and the Exchange of Information in 1990 developed a comprehensive set of ten Principles to help securities and futures regulatory authorities in developing Memoranda of Understanding (MOUs) on market oversight and on the prevention of fraud. It has recently prepared a report on money laundering.

The second one, the Development Committee, endeavours to promote the development of emerging securities markets, in particular, by the exchange of pertinent information and the implementation of common standards. It also set up working parties in the following fields: (a) incentives for market development; (b) clearing and settlement; (c) internationalization; and (d) disclosure.

At the 1992 London Conference, the Development Committee agreed to establish three new working groups to deal with matters that are of fundamental importance in the development of emerging markets: the impact of privatization in securities markets, the development of institutional investors, and the regulation of derivative markets.

IOSCO publishes an *Annual Report* and three times a year *IOSCO News*.

B.C.

ADDRESS

Tour de la bourse, 800 Square Victoria, 45th floor, PO Box 171, Montreal, Quebec, Canada
T. (514) 875 8278, Fx. (514) 875 2669

212.01 – CONVENTION RESPECTING THE BANK FOR INTERNATIONAL SETTLEMENTS – BIS

Concluded : 20.01.1930, The Hague
In Force : 27.02.1930
Parties : 7

The Convention was concluded at the same time as were the Constituent Charter and Statutes of the Bank for International Settlements.

The Swiss Federal Government agreed, under the Convention, to grant the Constitutional Charter and not to repeal, amend or supplement the said Charter and not to sanction amendments to the Statutes of the Bank, which are annexed to the Charter, except in agreement with the then signatory governments.

The Constituent Charter incorporates the Bank and sanctions the Statutes which define and govern the Constitution, operations and activities of the Bank.

These basic texts are completed by the Protocol Regarding the Immunities of the Bank for International Settlements (Brussels, 1936) and by the Agreement between the Swiss Federal Council and the BIS to Determine the Bank's Legal Status in Switzerland (10 February 1987).

B.C.

Access : NSP
Reserves : USP
Duration : REN 15 (Art. 3)
Deposit. : FR
Language : Eng, Fre

Modific. : Amendment to Convention 1969 (10.12.1969); Amendments to Statutes (03.05.37); (12.06.50); (09.06.69); (10.06.74); (08.08.75)

Reference : 104 LNTS – Can TS 1938/3 – UKTS 1931/6 – 1 Paeslee

212.02 – PRINCIPLES FOR THE SUPERVISION OF BANKS' FOREIGN ESTABLISHMENTS – BIS

Adopted : May 1983, BIS Report

The **Basle Committee on Banking Supervision** is a Committee of banking supervisory authorities, established by the central bank Governors of the Group of Ten countries [see 232 A] in 1975. It consists of senior representatives of bank supervisory authorities and central banks from Belgium, Canada, France, Germany, Italy, Japan, Luxembourg, Netherlands, Sweden, Switzerland, the United Kingdom and the United States. It usually meets at the BIS [see 212 A].

The Committee's first task was to draw up a set of principles governing the supervision of banks' foreign establishments. This document, agreed in 1975, came to be known as the banking supervisors' "Concordat".

In 1983, the Committee reformulated the 1975 Concordat mainly to introduce the principle of supervision on a consolidated basis. In 1990, a supplement to the 1983 document was issued which sought to define more clearly how the Concordat was to be implemented in practice.

The principles set out in these documents address the responsibilities of banking supervisory authorities for monitoring the prudential soundness of banks' foreign establishments and not the lender-of-last-resort aspects of the role of central banks. They were agreed by the Basle Committee as recommended guidelines of best practice; members undertook to work towards their implementation by the means available to them. They were also subscribed to by banking supervisors in all major banking centres outside the G-10, including all members of the Offshore Group of Banking Supervisors established in 1980.

Scope: The 1983 Revised Concordat defines the types of banks' foreign establishments which it covers in terms of branches, subsidiaries, and joint ventures or consortia.

DETAILS OF THE PRINCIPLES

Co-operation between host and parent authorities is a central prerequisite for the supervision of a bank's international operations. Two basic principles are seen as being fundamental to this co-operation: first, that no foreign banking establishment should escape supervision; and second, that the supervision should be adequate (Art. III).

The supervision of banks' foreign establishments is considered from three different aspects: solvency, liquidity, and foreign exchange operations and positions (Art. IV):

- **Solvency.** While there is a general responsibility on the host authority to monitor the financial soundness of foreign branches, supervision of solvency is primarily a matter for the parent authority. For subsidiaries, the supervision of solvency is the joint responsibility of both host and parent authorities. For joint ventures, the supervision of solvency is primarily the responsibilty of the authorities in the country of incorporation.
- **Liquidity.** The allocation of responsibilities for the supervision of the liquidity of banks' foreign establishments between parent and host authorities depends, as with solvency, upon the type of establishment concerned. In general, the host authority has responsibility for monitoring the liquidity of the foreign banks' establishments in its country; the parent authority has responsibility for monitoring the liquidity of the banking group as a whole (Art. IV-2).
- **Foreign Exchange Operations and Positions.** The supervision of banks' foreign exchange operations and positions should be the joint responsibility of parent and host authorities (Art. IV-3).

RECENT DEVELOPMENTS

Experience in implementing these principles confirmed the importance of information flows to parent authorities in particular to enable consolidated supervision to operate effectively. The 1990 Supplement to the Concordat is designed to encourage more regular and structural collaboration between supervisors and focuses on authorization, information flows, bank security constraints and external audit.

Some of the principles set out in these documents were reformulated in July 1992 into four minimum standards. They are:

- "all international banking groups and international banks should be supervised by a home-country authority that capably performs consolidated supervision;
- the creation of a cross-border establishment should receive the prior consent of both the host-country supervisory authority and the bank's and, if different, banking group's home-country supervisory authority;
- supervisory authorities should possess the right to gather information from the cross-border banking establishments of the banks or banking groups for which they are the home-country supervisor;
- if a host-country determines that any one of the foregoing minimum standards is not met to its satisfaction, that authority could impose restrictive measures necessary to satisfy its prudential concerns consistent with these minimum standards, including the prohibition of the creation of banking establishments".

B.C.

Language : Eng, (Fre, Ger, Ita)

Modific. : Supplement to the Concordat April 1990; Minimum Standards June 1992

Reference : ILM 22:900

212.03 – CONVERGENCE OF CAPITAL MEASUREMENT AND CAPITAL STANDARDS – BIS

Adopted : 11.07.1988, BIS Report

The **Basle Committee on Banking Supervision** (sometimes called the Cooke Committee after its former Chairman, Peter Cooke of the Bank of England) reached agreement in 1988 on a framework for measuring capital adequacy and for applying minimum levels of capital for internationally active banks. The definition of capital was modified in 1991. These texts, which are not legally binding, have been endorsed by the central bank Governors of the G-10 countries and by a large number of other countries.

Their adoption was greatly aided by the adoption by the European Communities of the Own Funds and Solvency Ratio Directives, which impose virtually identical requirements. The EC rules, however, are designed to apply to credit institutions generally whereas the Basle Accord is limited to banks undertaking international business.

The 1988 Basle Accord framework is directed mainly towards assessing capital in relation to credit risk (the risk of counter party failure) and is intended to be applied to banks on a consolidated basis.

DETAILS OF THE ACCORD

The Accord is divided into four sections and four annexes. The first two sections describe the framework: Section I, the constituents of capital and Section II the risk weighting system. Section III deals with the target standard ratio and Section IV with transitional and implementing arrangements.

The transitional period extended to the end of 1992, by which time it was proposed that the target standard ratio should be met by all banks undertaking significant cross-border business. By 1992, this minimum is of 8 per cent, of which core capital (tier 1, equity and reserves) is at least 4 per cent and supplementary capital (tier 2, which includes general provisions and loan-loss reserves) is admitted up to an amount equal to that of core capital. Within the tier 2 elements there is a further constraint in that subordinated debt is limited to 50 per cent of tier 1 capital.

The 1991 amended definition of capital, which is to be implemented at the latest by the end of 1993, clarifies the terms on which those elements designed to provide against identified deterioration in specified assets, and therefore unavailable to meet other losses wherever they may arise, are to be excluded from the definition.

The implementation of these texts has proved difficult in some countries which have suffered from serious economic recession. However, one can say that the general objectives of strengthening the soundness and stability of the international system and to diminish an existing source of competitive inequality among international banks have generally been achieved.

B.C.

Language : Eng

Modific. : Amendment to the Basle Capital Accord 06.11.1991

Reference : ILM 30:967

2.2 Financial Assistance

Financial assistance to developing countries is provided by international public organizations such as the World Bank Group and the United Nations; regional development banks (e.g. the Inter-American Development Bank (1959), the African Development Bank (1966), the Asian Development Bank (1966), the Caribbean Development Bank (1970) and the European Bank for Reconstruction and Development – which opened for business in April 1991); regional organizations (e.g. the European Communities); non-governmental organizations; and private voluntary organizations. Many countries also have their own development agency which helps channel funds to developing countries.

This section focuses on the World Bank Group, which comprises the International Bank for Reconstruction and Development [see 221 A], the International Development Association [see 221 B], the International Finance Corporation [see 221 C], and the Multilateral Investment Guarantee Agency [see 221 D]. In section 3, one of its associated organizations, the International Centre for Settlement of Investment Disputes (ICSID) [see 342 C] will be examined. Section 2.2 also covers the United Nations Development Programme (UNDP) [see 222 A].

Maryse Robert

SELECTED BIBLIOGRAPHY

Ayres, Robert L., *Banking on the Poor*, Cambridge, MA: MIT Press, 1983.

Brown, Bartram Stewart, *The United States and the Politicization of the World Bank: Issues of International Law and Policy*, London; New York: K. Paul International, 1991.

Chapelier, Georges, and Hamid Tabatabai, *Development and Adjustment: Stabilization, Structural Adjustment and UNDP Policy*, UNDP Policy Discussion Paper. Bureau for Programme Policy, New York: UNDP, 1989.

de Vries, Barend A., *Remaking the World Bank*, Cabin John, MD; Washington, DC: Seven Locks Press, 1987.

Feinberg, Richard (ed.), *Between Two Worlds: The World Bank's Next Decade*, US-Third World Policy Perspectives, No. 7. Washington, DC: Overseas Development Council, 1986.

Jackson, Robert and Sir Allen Gillman, *A Study of the Capacity of the United Nations Development System*, Volume I and II, Geneva: United Nations, 1969.

LePestre, Philippe G., *The World Bank and the Environmental Challenge*, London: Associated University Presses, 1989.

Mason, E.S. and R.E. Asher, *The World Bank since Bretton Woods*, Washington, DC: The Brookings Institution, 1973.

Mosley, Paul, Jane Harrigan, and John Toye, *Aid and Power: the World Bank and Policy-Based Lending*, London; New York: Routledge, 1991.

Palmlund, Thord, "UNDP's Management Development Programme", *Journal of Management Development* 10 (8) (1991): 48-51.

Payer, Cheryl, *The World Bank: A Critical Analysis*, New York: Monthly Review Press, 1982.

2.2.1 World Bank Group

221 A – INTERNATIONAL BANK FOR RECONSTRUCTION AND DEVELOPMENT (IBRD)

Like its sister organization, the International Monetary Fund [see 211 A], the International Bank for Reconstruction and Development (IBRD) was founded at the Bretton Woods Conference (New Hampshire, USA) in July 1944, when delegations of 44 allied countries and a representative of Denmark met to design the postwar economic order. The IBRD opened for business on 25 June 1946.

Article I of the IBRD's Articles of Agreement states the purposes of the Organization: to assist in the reconstruction and development of members by facilitating the investment of capital for productive purposes; to promote private foreign investment; to promote the long-range balanced growth of international trade and the maintenance of equilibrium in balances of payments; to arrange the loans made or guaranteed by it so that the more useful and urgent projects will be dealt with first; to conduct its operations with due regard to the effect of international investment on business conditions in the territories of members, and, in the immediate postwar years, to assist in bringing about a smooth transition from a wartime to a peacetime economy.

MEMBERSHIP AND FINANCIAL RESOURCES

A country must be a member of the International Monetary Fund before joining the IBRD (Art. II, Section 1; see also Art. VI, Section 3). As of 14 April 1993, the IBRD had 174 members.

A member may withdraw from the IBRD at any time (Art. VI, Section 1). Poland, Czechoslovakia, Cuba and Indonesia left the Bank. All but Cuba later rejoined the organization. Each member receives 250 votes plus one additional vote for each share of stock held (Art. IV, section 3). Each share has a par value of 100,000 1974 SDRs. A country's subscription to the IBRD's capital stock is based on its IMF quota which, in turn, reflects its economic performance.

Since the IBRD's outstanding guarantees, participations in loans and direct loans cannot exceed its capital, reserves, and surplus (Art. III, section 3), the authorized capital stock of the early years (US$10 billion) had to be increased to support growth in Bank lending and provide shares for new members. As of 31 December 1992, the IBRD had an authorized capital consisting of 1,525,659 shares, of which 1,365,902 had been subscribed. A member country must pay 20 per cent of its subscription; the remaining 80 per cent is callable (Art. II, section 5). However, capital increases have required members to pay a much lower paid-in portion.

Accumulated reserves and paid-in capital being too small, the IBRD finances most of its lending operations by issuing bonds carrying an AAA rating. These bonds are guaranteed by member countries.

ORGANIZATION AND MANAGEMENT

All the powers of the Bank are vested in the **Board of Governors,** which consists of one Governor and one Alternate for each member country (Art. V, section 2(a)). The Board of Governors may delegate any of its powers to the Executive Directors, except the power to: admit new members; change the capital stock; suspend a member; decide appeals from interpretations of the Articles of Agreement given by the Executive Directors; make arrangements to co-operate with other international organizations; decide to suspend the operations of the Bank; and determine the distribution of the net income of the Bank (Art. V, Section 2(b)).

The IBRD has 24 Executive Directors, of whom five are appointed by each of the five members holding the largest number of shares of capital stock (the United States, Japan, Germany, the United Kingdom and France). Both Saudi Arabia and China delegate one representative to the **Executive Board**. The other directors are elected by groups of the remaining member countries. The Executive Directors are responsible for the general operations of the Bank. They determine the allocation of financial resources as well as Bank policies. They also review evaluations of completed Bank projects. Most decisions are reached by consensus.

The President is selected by the Executive Directors. He is the chief of the operating staff of the Bank. Under the direction of the Executive Directors, he conducts the ordinary business of the Bank (Art. V, Section 5-b). The President has always been a US citizen.

The **Development Committee** was established in 1974. It is also known as the Joint Ministerial Committee of the Boards of Governors of the World Bank and the International Monetary Fund (IMF) on the Transfer of Real Resources to Developing Countries. Its 24 members, who meet biannually in Washington, DC are appointed on a rotating basis for periods of two years by the countries or groups of countries represented on the Bank's or Fund's Executive Board. Members of the Development Committee are usually ministers of finance. They advise the Boards of Governors of the IMF and the World Bank on development issues such as poverty alleviation, debt and debt-service reduction, and the effect of industrialized countries' policies on developing countries.

The **Economic Development Institute** (EDI) was established in 1955. Courses and seminars are offered to top administrators from developing countries. The EDI also provides assistance to training and research institutions in developing countries.

FINANCIAL ASSISTANCE

Although the Bank's Articles of Agreement (Art. III-1-a) state that "the resources and the facilities of the Bank shall be used exclusively for the benefit of members with equitable consideration to projects for development and projects for reconstruction alike", the IBRD concentrated its efforts on development projects after the announcement of the Marshall Plan in 1947.

Each IBRD loan is either made to or guaranteed by the government of the member country concerned (Art. III). IBRD loans must be repaid over a period of 15 to 20 years. Borrowers enjoy a five-year grace period. The interest rate is adjusted every six months. It is based on the average cost of Bank borrowings outstanding plus a spread of 0.5 per cent. The Articles of Agreement stipulate that only economic considerations must be taken into account in the IBRD's decisions to lend (Art. 4-10).

Article III-4-vii, states that "loans made or guaranteed by the Bank shall, except in special circumstances, be for the purpose of specific projects of reconstruction or development". However, non-project lending, more specifically adjustment lending, has increased substantially since the beginning of the 1980s. Many developing countries need money quickly to support economic reform in the face of serious balance of payments problems.

Poverty reduction is the most important priority on the Bank agenda in the early 1990s. The World Development Report 1990 recommended a two-part strategy to reduce poverty: to pursue growth that creates productive opportunities for labour and to invest in human capital of the poor. In fiscal 1991, the Bank adopted policies for integrating this strategy.

The environment has also become a Bank priority. A systematic environmental screening of all new projects was introduced in fiscal 1990. In addition, the World Bank, the United Nations Development Programme (UNDP) [see 222 A], and the United Nations Environment Programme (UNEP) [see 410 A] launched the **Global Environment Facility (GEF)** in November 1990 for a three-year pilot phase. The GEF helps developing countries (with per capita incomes below US$4,000 a year) to address domestic environmental problems that could have an impact on other countries. It finances programmes and projects in four areas: preservation of the ozone layer, reduction of global warming, protection of international waters, and preservation of biological diversity. Environmental experts from 25 countries review proposals and recommend projects for the GEF. The World Bank makes the final decision on projects that require financial or investment support while UNDP makes the final decision on projects where technical assistance is the main component. An initial US$1.4 billion was pledged by aid donors in support of the GEF.

Other priorities include continuing emphasis on human-resource development (education, population, health, women-in-development concerns), private-sector development, the efficient use of resources at the country level and the needs of new members.

More than half of the IBRD-assisted projects involve co-financing funds. In 1989, the Bank created the vice-presidency for co-financing and financial advisory services. It aims at increasing the flow of financial resources to developing countries from non-Bank sources.

The IBRD makes loans for development projects in the following sectors: agriculture and rural development; development finance companies; education; energy; industry; population, health and nutrition; public-sector management; small-scale enterprises; technical assistance; telecommunications; transportation; urban development; and water supply and sewerage.

Lending Instruments.

1. *Specific Investment Loans.* These loans remain the cornerstone of the IBRD lending operations. They create economic and social infrastructures.

2. *Sector-Investment and Maintenance Loans.* Sector-investment and maintenance loans provide funds to meet the economic priorities of member countries.

3. *Financial Intermediary Loans.* Enterprises and small and medium-sized firms receive funds through local financial intermediaries.

4. *Sector-Adjustment Loans (SECALs).* These loans support comprehensive policy changes as well as economic and institutional reforms within a particular sector.

5. *Structural-Adjustment Loans (SALs).* SALs support comprehensive policy changes as well as economic and institutional reforms. They aim at maintaining growth and contributing to a sustainable balance of payments over the medium and long term.

6. *Debt and Debt-Service Reduction Loans.* In May 1989, the Executive Directors approved the use of World Bank resources to support voluntary debt and debt-service reduction by commercial banks (the Brady Plan) for heavily indebted, middle-income countries with large private debt.

7. *Technical-Assistance Loans.* These loans aim at strengthening local institutions. The IBRD also provides funds through the Project Preparation Facility. This facility was created in 1975 to help borrowers with project preparation.

8. *Emergency Reconstruction Loans.* These provide funds for physical structures and productive activities after disasters.

CO-OPERATION

Article V-8-a of the IBRD's Articles of Agreement states that the Bank "shall co-operate with any general international organization and with public international organizations having specialized responsibilities in related fields".

The IBRD is a specialized agency of the United Nations. The Protocol concerning the entry into force of the Agreement between the United Nations and the IBRD was signed in New York on 15 April 1948. The President of the World Bank attends meetings of the Administrative Committee on Co-ordination (ACC) and the Economic and Social Council (ECOSOC) [see 001 A]. The World Bank has an office at the United Nations in New York. The Geneva Office maintains ties with GATT [see 111 A], the United Nations Conference on Trade and Development (UNCTAD) [see 111 B] and other UN organizations based in Geneva.

The World Bank has sponsored many initiatives with United Nations agencies and programmes. For instance, the **Global Environment Facility** (see the above section on Financial Assistance) was jointly established in 1990 by the Bank, UNDP [see 222 A] and UNEP [see 410 A]. Both the **Tropical Forestry Action Plan**, a programme to help combat deforestation, and the **Consultative Group on International Agricultural Research (CGIAR)**, an association of public and private-sector donors that funds international agricultural research centres, are co-sponsored by the Bank, UNDP and FAO (Food and Agriculture Organization of the United Nations) [see 131 A]. The World Resources Institute also participates in the Tropical Plan. UNDP and the World Bank have also been involved in the **Energy Sector Management Assistance Programme (ESMAP)**. UNEDIL, a programme aimed at strengthening African training institutions, was put in place by the World Bank's Economic Development Institute, UNDP, and the International Labour Organisation (ILO) [see 141 A].

The Bank also collaborates with UNICEF and UNESCO [see 171 A]. Population activities are co-ordinated with the United Nations Population Fund (UNFPA), health issues with the World Health Organization (WHO) [see 132 A], and urban-development activities with the **United Nations Centre for Human Settlements (HABITAT)**.

The three major regional development banks (the African Development Bank, the Asian Development Bank, and the Inter-American Development Bank) co-finance many Bank-assisted projects. They have also been involved in numerous Bank initiatives. For instance, in February 1991 the **African Capacity-Building Initiative (ACBI)** was launched by the World Bank, the African Development Bank and UNDP. ACBI is funded by international agencies, donor countries, African governments and private sources. It aims at creating, within 20 years, a group of African professional policy analysts and managers able to provide both training and advice in policy analysis and development management. The Bank is also collaborating with the European Bank for Reconstruction and Development (EBRD) to help eastern and central European countries transform their economy.

The Bank maintains a very close relationship with its sister organization, the IMF [see 211 A], and with the Organisation for Economic Co-operation and Development (OECD), and its Development Assistance Committee (DAC).

The Bank's relationship with non-governmental organizations (NGOs) has become more important in recent years. NGOs are involved in many Bank-supported projects, and in policy discussion through the NGO-World Bank Committee, a forum set up in 1982 for senior Bank managers and NGO leaders.

The World Bank also acts as an intermediary between donors and recipients by chairing aid co-ordination group meetings.

PUBLICATIONS

The World Bank publishes studies and books on a wide range of issues. Its main publications are: *The Annual Report*; *Country Studies*; *International Business*

Opportunities Service; Monthly Operational Summary; Social Indicators of Development; Trends in Developing Economies; World Development Report; World Bank Atlas; World Debt Tables; World Tables; the *World Bank Economic Review;* the *World Bank Group Directory;* the *World Bank Research Observer;* and *World Tables.* Jointly with the IMF, the Bank also publishes *Finance & Development.*

Maryse Robert

ADDRESS

1818 H Street, N.W., Washington, DC 20433, United States
T. (202) 477 1234, Fx. (202) 676 0618

221 B – INTERNATIONAL DEVELOPMENT ASSOCIATION (IDA)

The International Development Association (IDA) was created in 1960. It provides assistance to the poorest developing countries. The purposes of the Association are to promote economic development, increase productivity, and thus raise standards of living in the less-developed areas of the world by providing finance on terms that are more flexible and bear less heavily on the balance of payments than those of the IBRD [see 221 A] (Art. I of the IDA's Articles of Agreement).

MEMBERSHIP AND FINANCIAL RESOURCES

Membership in the IBRD is a prerequisite for membership in IDA (Art. II-1; see Art. VII on withdrawal). As of 14 April 1993, IDA had 150 members, of which 24 were Part I members, and 126 were Part II members. Part I members must make payments of their subscriptions and contributions in freely convertible currencies. Part II members are required to pay 10 per cent of their initial subscription in freely convertible currencies (Art. II-2-c); the remaining 90 per cent (Art. II-2-d) as well as all additional subscriptions and contributions can be paid in their own currencies.

IDA's initial capitalization (US$757 million) was too small to meet the needs of the poorest developing countries. Although the Articles of Agreement allow for additional subscriptions every five years, for supplementary resources provided by members (Art. III), and for IDA to borrow money and guarantee loans and securities (Art. V-5), the demand for IDA projects is so great that members have negotiated the replenishment of IDA resources at three-year intervals.

The Tenth Replenishment (IDA-10) covers the fiscal years 1994-1996. Thirty-four member countries agreed to a replenishment of SDR 13 billion.

Funds lent by IDA come from subscriptions, contributions from donor countries, IBRD profits, and repayments of past IDA credits. In addition, IDA established the **Special Fund** in October 1982, the **Special Facility for Sub-Saharan Africa** in May 1985, and the **Debt Reduction Facility** in September 1989. Only a few IDA members have contributed to the Special Fund which supplements IDA's regular resources. The IBRD and other donors contributed to the African Facility which was terminated by the Executive Directors on 30 June 1990. It helped finance structural and sectoral adjustment, rehabilitation (sector-investment and maintenance loans), and emergency reconstruction. Funded by the IBRD, the Debt Reduction Facility facilitates commercial debt reduction for IDA-only countries.

ORGANIZATION AND MANAGEMENT

IDA operates under the same organizational structure as the IBRD (Art. VI). For instance, each Governor and Alternate Governor of the IBRD appointed by a member of the IBRD which is also a member of IDA shall *ex officio* be a Governor and Alternate Governor of IDA. The same clause applies to the Executive Directors. The IBRD and IDA also share the same President and the same staff.

FINANCIAL ASSISTANCE

Historically, the eligibility ceiling for IDA resources has been an annual per capita gross national product of US$940 (in 1987 dollars). However, scarcity of resources has forced IDA to impose an operational cut-off of US$580 per capita (in 1989 dollars). This ceiling is regularly adjusted. In exceptional cases, countries above the cut-off can be temporarily eligible if they are undertaking adjustment efforts.

Four main allocation criteria determine the use of IDA resources: the poverty level in member countries; the country size; the lack of creditworthiness; and the capacity to use resources effectively. Performance criteria are also taken into account: sound economic management, progress toward growth with equity and poverty reduction, and efforts toward sustainable long-term development.

All IDA credits are made to member governments. However, development credits have been made to regional development banks for the benefit of members. IDA credits have a maturity of 35-40 years, a grace period of ten years, no interest, but an annual service charge of 0.75 per cent on the disbursed balance.

IDA shares the same lending instruments as the IBRD and lends for projects in the same sectors.

The **Special Program of Assistance (SPA)** for sub-Saharan Africa was launched in December 1987. Eligibility is based on three criteria: poverty (countries cannot borrow from the IBRD), indebtedness (countries have a debt-service ratio of 30 per cent or more), and efforts to adjust (countries must be implementing a policy-reform programme and must have prepared a policy framework paper with the help of the World Bank and the IMF). The second phase (1991-1993) of this programme was launched in October 1990. Resources for eligible countries are available from a number of sources: adjustment lending under the ninth replenishment; increased co-financing and co-ordinated financing from bilateral and multilateral donors for adjustment operations; supplemental IDA adjustment credits from a share of the investment income of, and repayments to, IDA; resources from the IMF's SAF and ESAF; and debt relief, including forgiveness of concessional loans and rescheduling of non-concessional debt on softer terms.

The **Special Project Preparation Facility** was established in 1985 to help IDA-eligible members in sub-Saharan Africa finance preparation of project proposals.

CO-OPERATION

IDA maintains a close relationship with the same international organizations as the IBRD [see 221 A].

M.R.

ADDRESS

1818 H Street, N.W., Washington, DC 20433, United States
T. (202) 477 1234, Fx. (202) 676 0618

SELECTED BIBLIOGRAPHY

Katz, Jeffrey A., "The Evolving Role of IDA", *Finance & Development* 26 (June 1989): 16-19.
Stern, Ernest, "Mobilizing Resources for IDA: The Ninth Replenishment", *Finance & Development* 27 (June 1990): 20-23.
Weaver, James H., *The International Development Association: A New Approach to Foreign Aid*, New York: Praeger, 1965.
World Bank, *The Evolving Role of IDA*, Washington, DC: World Bank, 1989.
– – –, *IDA in Retrospect: The First Two Decades of the International Development Association*, Washington, DC: Oxford University Press, 1982.

221 C – INTERNATIONAL FINANCE CORPORATION (IFC)

The International Finance Corporation (IFC) was established in 1956 to promote private enterprise in developing countries. The purpose of the IFC is to "further economic development by encouraging the growth of productive private enterprise in member countries, particularly in less developed areas, thus supplementing the activities of" the IBRD [see 221 A] (Art. I of the IFC's Articles of Agreement).

MEMBERSHIP AND FINANCIAL RESOURCES

Membership of the IFC is open only to IBRD members (Art. II). As of 14 April 1993, the IFC had 154 members. Each member receives 250 votes plus one additional vote for each share of stock held (Art. IV-3). The initial authorized capital stock of the Corporation was of US$100 million. However, it was increased to US$650 million in 1977, US$1.3 billion in 1985, and to US$2.3 billion in 1992. The authorized capital stock is divided into shares of US$1,000.

Funds lent by the IFC come from its subscriptions, loans from the IBRD and triple-A rated bond issues in the international financial markets. It mobilizes funds through mechanisms such as loan syndications, underwriting of debt and security issues and private placements. The IFC is always a minority partner in any investment it supports. Therefore, it has to attract additional funding for projects by encouraging financial institutions and private companies to become its partners.

ORGANIZATION AND MANAGEMENT

The IFC is legally and financially independent. It has its own staff. However, like IDA, the Corporation has the same organizational structure as the IBRD [see 221 B]. The IFC also has an Executive Vice President who is responsible for management and day-to-day decision-making.

FINANCIAL ASSISTANCE

The IFC makes loans and equity investments in private and mixed companies in developing countries. However, the IFC does not finance projects where sufficent capital can be obtained on reasonable terms from other sources. IFC loans are not covered by government guarantees. Thus, the IFC invests only in economically sound projects where it can make a profit. Moreover, the Corporation invests in a member country only if the government of that country has no objections.

All loans are made at market rates. Maturities range from five to 15 years and include grace periods of one to five years. The IFC charges standard front-end and commitment fees, and offers loans denominated in all of the major international currencies.

The IFC rarely exercises its voting rights as a shareholder. It is not represented on any board of directors and does not take part in management.

The IFC finances projects in a broad range of sectors; agribusiness and food; banking and financial services; cement and construction materials; chemicals, petrochemicals, and fertilizer; energy; general manufacturing, automotive industry, and industrial equipment; mining, non-ferrous metals, iron and steel; textiles; timber, pulp and paper; tourism; and telecommunications.

The Corporation also helps establish financial institutions and stimulates foreign portfolio investment in developing-country stock markets through the creation of country and regional investment funds. It is assisting countries with privatization programmes, and using local financial institutions as intermediaries to support enterprises too small to be directly financed by the IFC. In Africa, the IFC finances small enterprises through its Africa Enterprise Fund launched in fiscal 1989.

CO-OPERATION

Article IV-7 of the IFC's Articles of Agreement states that "the Corporation, acting through the Bank, shall enter into formal arrangements with the United Nations and may enter into such arrangements with other public international organizations having specialized responsibilities in related fields".

The IFC became a specialized agency of the United Nations in 1957. It has sponsored many initiatives with the other affiliates of the World Bank Group, United Nations agencies and programmes, regional development banks, and bilateral agencies.

The **Foreign Investment Advisory Service (FIAS)** was established by the IFC in 1986. It is jointly supervised by the IFC, the IBRD, and MIGA [see 221 D]. FIAS advises member governments on how to attract foreign direct investments.

In January 1989, the World Bank Group launched its **private-sector development action program (PSD)**. This aims at expanding support for the private sector in developing countries, clarifying the role of each member of the World Bank Group in this strategy and improving co-ordination among the IBRD, the IFC, and MIGA.

Jointly with other international organizations and bilateral agencies, the IFC provides technical assistance and advisory services to governments and businesses. For instance, first known as the Caribbean Project Development Facility – the **Business Advisory Service for the Caribbean and Central America (CBAS)** – was created in 1981. It is funded by the IFC, the Inter-American Development Bank, UNDP, and developed countries. The **Africa Project Development Facility (APDF)** was established in 1985 by the IFC, UNDP [see 222 A], the African Development Bank (AfDB), and developed countries.

The IFC, UNDP, AfDB, bilateral agencies and international private companies are partners in the **African Management Services Company** which seeks to create a pool of well-qualified African managers. The **South Pacific Project Facility (SPPF)** was approved in fiscal 1990. It helps private enterprises in the South Pacific Island countries with project preparation. Funding is provided by Australia, Canada, Japan and New Zealand. The **Polish Business Advisory Service (PBAS)** was established in fiscal 1991. It provides technical assistance and operational support to entrepreneurs.

Since 1988, the IFC has set up Technical Assistance Trust Funds with the financial support of the European Communities and bilateral agencies.

PUBLICATIONS

The IFC publishes studies, books and papers on a variety of subjects: *Quarterly Review of Emerging Stock Markets; Emerging Stock Markets Factbook; Emerging Markets Data Base; Trends in Private Investment in Developing Countries; Privatizing Telecommunications Systems: Business Opportunities in Developing Countries; African Entrepreneurs: Pioneers of Development*. The IFC also publishes an annual report.

M.R.

ADDRESS

1818 H Street, N.W., Washington, DC 20433, United States
T. (202) 477 1234, Fx. (202) 676 9507

SELECTED BIBLIOGRAPHY

Baker, J., *The International Finance Corporation: Origin, Operations and Evaluations*, New York: Praeger, 1968.

Pfeffermann, Guy, and Gary Bond, "IFC and Development", *Finance & Development* 26 (December 1989): 41-43.

World Bank, "IFC: Promoting Private Sector Development", *Finance & Development* 25 (December 1988), Special Section: 22-40.

– – –, *The World Bank and International Finance Corporation*, Washington, DC: World Bank, April 1986.

221 D – MULTILATERAL INVESTMENT GUARANTEE AGENCY (MIGA)

The Convention establishing the Multilateral Investment Guarantee Agency (MIGA) came into effect on 12 April 1988. The Agency is an autonomous international organization with full juridical personality.

The objective of MIGA is to promote the flow of foreign investments for productive purposes to and among developing countries (Art. 2 of the Convention).

MEMBERSHIP AND FINANCIAL RESOURCES

Membership is open to all members of the IBRD [see 221 A] (Art. 4-a). As of 14 April 1993, 102 countries had completed MIGA membership procedure. Each member receives 177 membership votes plus one subscription for each share of stock held by that member (Art. 39).

The authorized capital stock of the Agency is SDR 1 billion. It is divided into

100,000 shares having a par value of SDR 10,000 each. The average value of the SDR in terms of US dollars is based on the period 1 January 1981 to 30 June 1985, such value being US$1.082 per SDR (Art. 5). Each member shall pay 10 per cent in cash and an additional 10 per cent in the form of non-negotiable, non-interest bearing promissory notes (Art. 7-i). Payments of subscriptions must be made in freely usable currencies. However, developing countries may pay up to 25 per cent of the paid-in cash portion in their own currencies (Art. 8).

ORGANIZATION AND MANAGEMENT

MIGA has a **Council of Governors** (Art. 31) representing each of its member states and a **Board of Directors** (Art. 32) (18 Directors at 30 June 1992). The number of Directors may be adjusted by the Council to take into account changes in membership. At its first meeting on 22 June 1988, the Board of Directors appointed the President of the IBRD as the Agency's first President. The President has delegated most of his authority to an Executive Vice-President.

OPERATIONS

MIGA guarantees eligible investments against losses resulting from currency transfer, expropriation, war and civil disturbance, and breach of contract by host governments. Other specific non-commercial risks – except the risk of devaluation or depreciation of currency – may be covered upon the joint application of the investor and the host country (Art. 11). The Agency can also insure privatizations and financial restructurings.

Eligible investments comprise equity interests, including medium-or long-term loans made or guaranteed by equity holders in the enterprise concerned, and certain forms of direct investment as determined by the Board (Art. 12-a). Guarantees are restricted to investments registered with MIGA before the investments are made or committed (Art. 12-c). In guaranteeing an investment, the Agency must take into account "the economic soundness of the investment and its contribution to the development of the host country; the compliance of the investment with the host country's laws and regulations; the consistency of the investment with the declared development objectives and priorities of the host country; and the investment conditions in the host country" (Art. 12-d).

Eligible investors for the Agency's guarantee are any natural person and any juridical person provided that "such natural person is a national of a member other than the host country" and such juridical person is incorporated, has it principal place of business in a member country and operates on a commercial basis (Art. 13).

The Agency generally covers investments for a period of 15 years. However, in exceptional circumstances, coverage may be extended to 20 years. MIGA may also collaborate with national investment-insurance agencies and private insurers to co-insure or reinsure eligible investments (Arts. 20 and 21).

A **Claims Committee** will evaluate each formal claim and make recommendations to the President who will make the final decision.

MIGA also offers policy and advisory services (PAS) to assist developing countries in attracting foreign investments. The Agency organizes investment promotion conferences to encourage investment flows from developed countries and among developing countries. The Executive Program helps domestic entrepreneurs develop business plans and find foreign partners.

CO-OPERATION

Article 35 of MIGA's Convention states that "the Agency shall co-operate with the United Nations and with other inter-governmental organizations having specialized responsibilities in related fields, including in particular the Bank and the International Finance Corporation". MIGA collaborates with the IFC [see 221 C] and the IBRD [see 221 A] through FIAS [see 221 C], and with the other affiliates of the World Bank Group through the private-sector development action programme (PSD).

PUBLICATIONS

The *Investment Guarantee Guide* and a quarterly newsletter *MIGA News* are among the Agency's publications. MIGA also publishes an annual report.

M.R.

ADDRESS

c/o World Bank, 1818 H Street NW, Washington, DC 20433, United States
T. (202) 477 1234, Fx. (202) 477 0741

SELECTED BIBLIOGRAPHY

Lota, G.-P., "Multinational Investment Guarantee Agency: History", *Credit and Finance Management* 87 (December 1987): 46.
Shihata, Ibrahim F. I., *MIGA and Foreign Investments: Origins, Operations, Policies, and Basic Documents of the Multilateral Investment Guarantee Agency*, Dordrecht; Boston: Martinus Nijhoff Publishers, 1988.
Viehe, Karl William, "Multilateral Investment Guarantee Agency", *International Financial Law Review* 6 (October 1987): 37-38.
Voss, Jurgen, "MIGA and the Code of Conduct", *CTC Reporter: United Nations Centre on Transnational Corporations* 22 (Autumn 1986): 51-55.
Wallace, Laura, "MIGA: Up and Running", *Finance & Development* 29 (March 1992): 48-49.

221.01 – STATUTES OF THE INTERNATIONAL BANK FOR RECONSTRUCTION AND DEVELOPMENT – IBRD

Concluded : 22.07.1944, Washington
In Force : 27.12.1945
Parties : 174

The First Amendment of the IBRD's Articles of Agreement became effective on 17 December 1965. A section was added to Article III. Section 6-a states that "the Bank may make, participate in, or guarantee loans to the International Finance Corporation, an affiliate of the Bank, for use in its lending operations. The total amount outstanding of such loans, participations and guarantees shall not be increased if, at the time or as a result thereof, the aggregate amount of debt (including the guarantee of any debt) incurred by the said Corporation from any source and then outstanding shall exceed an amount equal to four times its unimpaired subscribed capital and surplus".

The Second Amendment entered into force on 16 February 1989. Article VIII-a now states that "when three-fifths of the members, having eighty-five percent of the total voting power, have accepted the proposed amendments, the Bank shall certify the fact by formal communication addressed to all members". Eighty-five per cent was substituted to four-fifths.

For a description of the organization, see 221 A.

Maryse Robert

Access : CON (Art. 2)
Reserves : USP
Duration : USP
Deposit. : US
Language : Eng

Modific. : Modified 17.12.65 (17.12.65); Amendment to Art. VIII-a (16.02.89)

Reference : 2 UNTS – Can TS 1944/37 – UKTS 1946/21 – UST 16/2 – JORF 27 Dec 45

221.02 – ARTICLES OF AGREEMENT OF THE INTERNATIONAL FINANCE CORPORATION – IFC

Concluded : 25.05.1955, Washington
In Force : 20.07.1956
Parties : 154

The First Amendment became effective on 21 September 1961. Article III, Section 2, states that "the Corporation may make investments of its funds in such form or forms as it may deem appropriate in the circumstances". Section 3-iv says that "the Corporation shall not assume responsibility for managing any enterprise in which it has invested and shall not exercise voting rights for such purpose or for any other purpose which, in its opinion, properly is within the scope of managerial control".

The Second Amendment became effective on 1 September 1965 (Art. III, Section 6-i and Article IV, Section 6). It allows the IFC to borrow from the Bank (see the First Amendment of the IBRD's Articles of Agreement).

For a description of the organization, see 221 C.

M.R.

Access : CON (Art. 2)
Reserves : PRO (Art. 9-2-a)
Duration : USP
Deposit. : IBRD
Language : Eng, Fre, Spa

Modific. : Res. 1961 (21.09.61); 1965 (01.09.65)

Reference : 264, 439, 563 UNTS – Can TS 1956/16 – UKTS 1961/37, 1963/4, 1966/77 – UST 7/2, 12/3, 24/2 – JORF 25 Feb 58 – JDI 1959/1

221.03 – STATUTES OF THE INTERNATIONAL DEVELOPMENT ASSOCIATION – IDA

Concluded : 26.01.1960, Washington
In Force : 24.09.1960
Parties : 150

These Statutes form the basic agreement of the IDA. For a description of this organization, see 221 B.

Access : CON (Art. II)
Reserves : USP (Art. XI-3)
Duration : USP
Deposit. : IBRD (Art. XI-5)
Language : Eng

Reference : 439 UNTS – Can TS 1960/8 – UKTS 1961/1 – UST 11/2 – 1 Paeslee – JORF 19 Oct 61 – RTAF 1961/43

221.04 – CONVENTION ESTABLISHING THE MULTILATERAL INVESTMENT GUARANTEE AGENCY – MIGA

Concluded : 11.10.1985, Seoul
In Force : 12.04.1988
Parties : 102

This Convention is the basic agreement of the MIGA. For a description of this organization, see 221 D.

Access : CON (Art. 4)
Reserves : USP (Art. 66)
Duration : USP
Deposit. : IBRD
Language : Eng

Reference : ILM 24:1605 – RGDIP 1987/4

2.2.2 United Nations Development Programme

222 A – UNITED NATIONS DEVELOPMENT PROGRAMME (UNDP)

The United Nations Development Programme (UNDP) was established in 1965 by the General Assembly of the United Nations (Res. 2029 (XX)). It is the result of the merger between the Expanded Programme for Technical Assistance (EPTA), created in 1949 by the Economic and Social Council (ECOSOC) (Res. 222 (IX)), and the Special Fund, established by the General Assembly in 1957 (Res. 1219 (XII)). UNDP is under the authority of ECOSOC and the General Assembly. ECOSOC formulates the rules and principles governing UNDP operations and conducts reviews of the Programme's activities. The General Assembly also reviews UNDP activities every year.

PURPOSES

UNDP aims at assisting developing countries in improving their living standards by making better use of their human and natural resources.

Every year in its annual report, UNDP describes itself as "the central planning, funding, and co-ordinating body for technical co-operation in the UN system" (see UNDP 1990 Annual Report, p. 40). UNDP took over the functions of both EPTA and the Special Fund. UNDP assists developing countries, as did EPTA, by providing expert services and training fellowships. It is the world's largest channel for multilateral technical assistance. Like the Special Fund, it supplies project equipment and facilitates capital investment by financing pre-investment activities.

FINANCIAL RESOURCES

Funds come from voluntary contributions pledged annually by donor countries (US$1.3 billion for 1992).

ORGANIZATION AND MANAGEMENT

UNDP has a 48-member **Governing Council** elected on a rotating basis for a three-year period by the Economic and Social Council (ECOSOC) [001 A] from among the members of the United Nations or members of the specialized agencies or of the International Atomic Energy Agency. The mandate of the Governing Council is to provide general policy guidance and direction for UNDP, as well as for the United Nations programmes of technical assistance. The Council also approves country programmes, inter-country programmes, and indicative planning figures. It allocates resources and controls their use. The Governing Council meets twice a year and submits a report and recommendations to ECOSOC. Decisions are made by a majority of the members present and voting.

The **Administrator** is responsible for management and decision-making. He also chairs the Inter-Agency Consultative Board (IACB) which co-ordinates all UN technical assistance. The IACB comprises the Secretary-General of the United Nations and the executive heads of the international organizations that carry out UNDP's work in the field.

The **UNDP Resident Representative (Resrep)** has the mandate to co-ordinate development activities of the UN system at the country level.

FINANCIAL ASSISTANCE

UNDP plans its activities on the basis of five-year development co-operation cycles. An indicative planning figure (IPF) is calculated for each country. It is based on a country's population, its per capita gross national product, and other criteria such as geographic disadvantages and economic difficulties. The IPF specifies the amount expected to be available from UNDP over a five-year period. To be eligible for UNDP resources, each recipient country must formulate a country programme which includes a list of priorities and projects for the five-year cycle. The country programme is prepared under the leadership of the Resident Representative. It is transmitted to the Administrator who will submit it, with his recommendations, to the Governing Council for approval. Forty-five of the world's poorest countries will receive 55 per cent of UNDP's country programme funds for the 1992-1996 cycle. Countries with a per capita GNP of US$750 or less receive 80 per cent of UNDP resources.

Between 10 and 15 per cent of UNDP resources are used for regional, interregional and global projects. Regional programmes are drawn up by UNDP Regional Bureaux in collaboration with recipient governments, UN regional commissions and UN agencies.

If a project costs less than US$700,000, it does not need to be approved by the Action Committee (UNDP's top management), provided that the amount allocated to equipment does not exceed US$200,000 or 50 per cent of the cost, and that there is no policy implication. When these criteria are met, the Resident Representative in the country has the authority to approve the project.

Each recipient country makes contributions to UNDP projects. It provides experts, office space, transportation and a secretariat and, in some cases, a government may also share part of the cost.

UNDP supports projects in the following sectors: general development issues; agriculture, forestry and fisheries; industry; natural resources; transport and communications; science and technology; employment; health; population, humanitarian aid, and human settlements; and education. It has 115 field offices (1991).

PROGRAMMES AND OTHER ACTIVITIES

The UNDP's Management Development Programme helps governments improve their administration. The Partners in Development Programme allocates funds to NGOs' (non-governmental organizations) community-based projects. The Urban Management Programme, financed by UNDP, the UN Centre for Human Settlements, and the World Bank, provides information on land management, infrastructure, municipal finance and the urban environment. The environment is also a priority. UNDP, the World Bank, and the United Nations Environment Programme (UNEP) launched the Global Environment Facility in November 1990 [see 221 A].

Since 1977, the **Transfer of Knowledge through Expatriate Nationals (TOKTEN)** programme has sent experts back to their home countries for short-term volunteer consultancy assignments. UNDP has also been promoting technical co-operation among developing countries since 1978.

In 1987, UNDP established a division for women-in-development to integrate women's needs to its projects. In 1990, UNDP created a division for the private sector aimed at promoting business and entrepreneurship in developing countries.

ASSOCIATED FUNDS

UNDP administers six associated Funds:

- the **United Nations Capital Development Fund (UNCDF)** provides small-scale capital assistance to least developed countries;
- the **United Nations Revolving Fund for Natural Resources Exploration (UNRFNRE)** finances high-risk exploration of natural resources in developing countries;
- the **United Nations Fund for Science and Technology for Development (UNFSTD)** helps developing countries use science and technology;
- the **United Nations Development Fund for Women (UNIFEM)** supports women in development activities;
- the **United Nations Sudano-Sahelian Office (UNSO)** helps promote development and combat drought and desertification in 22 countries in sub-Saharan Africa; and
- the **United Nations Volunteers (UNVs)** sends volunteers to developing countries.

CO-OPERATION

UNDP co-operates with 44 executing agencies and participating organizations. These agencies carry out UNDP's work in the field and, in some cases, co-finance UNDP projects [see 221 A and 221 C].

At the United Nations Conference on Least Developed Countries in 1981, UNDP was given the mandate to organize donor round-table meetings to help mobilize funds for the poorest developing countries. Multilateral, bilateral and non-governmental donor organizations participate in these round-table meetings.

In 1986, UNDP set up a unit for NGOs to promote co-operation among governments, UN agencies and NGOs.

PUBLICATIONS

UNDP publishes studies on a wide range of issues. Its main publications are the *Annual Report, Co-operation South*, and *Source and World Development*. Since 1990, UNDP has published the *Human Development Report* which combines three indices – life expectancy at birth, adult literacy rates and purchasing power – to create a Human Development Index.

Maryse Robert

ADDRESS

One United Nations Plaza, New York NY 10017, United States
T. (212) 906 5558, Fx. (212) 906 5372

SELECTED BIBLIOGRAPHY

Ahlberg, Hans, and Asbjorn Lovbraek, *UNDP in Action: A Study on UNDP Field Offices in Selected Countries in Africa and Asia*, Stockholm: Liber, 1985.

Robie, David, *The United Nations Development Programme in the South Pacific*. Wellington, New Zealand: NZCTD, 1984.

UNDP, *Generation, Portrait of the United Nations Development Programme*, New York: UNDP, Division of Information, 1985.

222.01 – ESTABLISHMENT OF THE UNITED NATIONS DEVELOPMENT PROGRAMME – UNDP

Adopted : 22.11.1965, UNGA Res.2029(XX)
In Force : 01.01.1966

This Convention is the basic agreement of the UNDP. For a description of this Programme, see 222 A.

2.3 International Forums

Since the beginning of the 1960s, many countries sharing economic interests have met in small informal groups. Most of these groups do not have secretariats, staff or offices. This section briefly explains their role and goals.

Maryse Robert

SELECTED BIBLIOGRAPHY

Bergsten, C. Fred, *From Rambouillet to Versailles: A Symposium*, Princeton Essays in International Finance 149, Princeton, N.J.: International Finance Section, Dept. of Economics, Princeton University, 1982.

Blackwell, Michael, "From G-5 to G-77: International Forums for Discussion of Economic Issues", *Finance & Development* 23 (December 1986): 40-41.

De Ménil, Georges and Anthony M. Solomon, *Economic Summitry*, New York: Council on Foreign Relations, 1983.

Dobson, Wendy, *Economic Policy Co-ordination: Requiem or Prologue?*, Policy Analyses in International Economics 30. Washington, DC: Institute for International Economics, April 1991.

Funabashi, Yoichi, *Managing the Dollar: From the Plaza to the Louvre*, Revised edition, Washington DC: Institute for International Economics, 1989.

Hajnal, Peter I. (ed.), *The Seven-Power Summit: Documents from the Summits of Industrialized Countries, Supplement. Documents from the 1990 Summit*, Millwood, N.Y.: Kraus International Publications, 1991 .

– – –, *The Seven-Power Summit: Documents from the Summits of Industrialized Nations, 1975-1989*, Millwood, N.Y.: Kraus International Publications, 1989.

Putnam, Robert D, and Nicholas Bayne, *Hanging Together: Co-operation and Conflict in the Seven-Power Summits*, Revised and enlarged edition, Cambridge, MA; London: Harvard University Press; Sage Publications, 1987.

Williams, Marc. Third World Co-operation: The Group of 77 in UNCTAD. London; New York: Pinter Publishers; St.Martin's Press, 1991 .

2.3.1 Industrialized Countries

231 A – GROUP OF FIVE – G-5

Great Britain was host to a meeting of five finance ministers in January 1967. The finance ministers discussed international monetary flows and fluctuations in interest rates. Later, the **Library Group** of finance ministers recreated these informal exchanges. The Library Group first met in the White House Library in April 1973 to discuss international monetary negotiations.

The **Group of Five**, the former Library Group, is the name that was given to the meetings of the finance ministers and central bank governors of the US, Japan, the Federal Republic of Germany (now Germany), France and the UK. The G-5 has met on several occasions, including at the Annual Meetings of the IMF and the World Bank, and Interim Committee meetings [see 211 A]. The G-5 meetings cover a wide range of economic matters of common interest.

In September 1985, the G-5 met at the Plaza Hotel in New York. The Group agreed that "exchange rates should better reflect fundamental economic conditions than has been the case", and that "some further orderly appreciation of the main non-dollar currencies against the dollar is desirable". The participants announced that G-5 governments would "stand ready to co-operate more closely to encourage this when to do so would be helpful".

Maryse Robert

231 B – GROUP OF SEVEN – G-7

Henry Kissinger, the then US Secretary of State, first proposed the idea of multilateral economic summit meetings in 1971. A few years later, Valéry Giscard d'Estaing, a former member of the Library Group [see 231 A] who became President of France in 1974, invited his colleagues from the United States, the Federal Republic of Germany, the United Kingdom, Japan, and Italy to the first economic summit held at the Château de Rambouillet in November 1975. Canada joined a year later at Puerto Rico to form with the other six countries the **Group of Seven (G-7)**. Since 1977, the President of the Commission of the European Communities and the President of the European Community Council of Ministers, when that post is not held by a member of the Group of Seven, also attend the annual economic summit.

At first, President Giscard wanted to limit the number of participants to the heads of state and government, and one personal representative per country. These representatives, known as "sherpas", meet several times a year to prepare each summit. They are now assisted by a team comprising at least one person from the foreign ministry, one from the ministry of finance, and one from the office of the president or the prime minister. Officials from other agencies and departments also help in the summit preparation.

Rambouillet (1975). The most serious topic at Rambouillet was the reform of the international monetary system. A monetary understanding had been negotiated before the summit between France and the United States. The French strongly favoured fixed exchange rates while the Americans and the other major countries preferred floating. The first part of the monetary understanding provided for a revision of Article IV of the IMF's Articles of Agreement. It allowed for a wide range of exchange rate regimes. This led to the Second Amendment of the Fund's Articles of Agreement [see 211.01].

The other important issues at the Rambouillet summit were the economic recovery from recession and the GATT Multilateral Trade Negotiations (MTNs) launched in 1973. A deadline was set for the completion of the GATT negotiations by the end of 1977. However, the Round ended in 1979 [see 111 A].

Puerto Rico (1976). President Ford invited his colleagues to the second summit held in Puerto Rico in June 1976. Macroeconomic policies were once again the most important issue on the table. As recovery was underway, President Ford proposed to reduce inflation by using restrictive fiscal and monetary policies. These policies were adopted by the US and Germany but in fact they slowed the recovery. The summit condemned protectionism and reiterated its call for a 1977 deadline for the completion of the Tokyo Round negotiations.

London (1977). At the London summit in May 1977, the summiteers committed their governments to economic growth targets without including any targets in the final *communiqué*. The goal was to provide a basis for sustained non-inflationary growth and for reduction of imbalances in international payments. The participants also agreed: to achieve substantial progress in 1977 in the GATT negotiations; to "conserve energy and increase and diversify energy production" with the aim of reducing their dependence on oil; and to increase nuclear energy "to help meet the world's energy requirements". The nuclear issue was an irritant between President Carter, an advocate of non-nuclear proliferation, and France and Germany. A compromise was finally reached. A group was given the mandate to prepare a study on nuclear energy and non-proliferation.

Bonn (1978). The G-7 met in Bonn in July 1978. Japan and Germany pledged to take new initiatives and to join the US in adopting expansionary policies to become the locomotives of world economic growth. The US agreed to raise the prices paid for oil in their country to the world level by the end of 1980. The participants gave a boost to the GATT negotiations by promising to conclude these negotiations by 15 December 1978. Finally, the G-7 agreed to suspend air traffic with countries offering sanctuary to hijackers or terrorists.

Tokyo (1979). The Tokyo summit in June 1979 and the Venice summit in June 1980 were both devoted to energy issues and the second oil shock. At Tokyo, the G-7 was determined to fight inflation by not accommodating the oil price increase. Moreover, to reduce oil dependence, the summiteers set oil import targets for 1979-80 and up to 1985. They created a register of international oil transactions and a technology group in the OECD to study synthetic fuels. They agreed to develop nuclear power and make a greater use of coal. A non-economic issue, Indochinese refugees, was also addressed. In a special statement, the participants promised to admit more refugees.

Venice (1980). At Venice, the summit governments agreed on objectives "to break the existing link between economic growth and consumption of oil". They aimed at reducing oil and energy dependence over time. They committed themselves to promote new energy sources as recommended by the Technology Group set up at the Tokyo summit. The Declaration also underlined the contribution of nuclear power. A proposal was made to study the possibility of establishing an energy affiliate in the World Bank to help oil-importing developing countries. The G-7 pledged to bring inflation under control by adopting restrictive fiscal and monetary policies. The summiteers welcomed the Report of the Brandt Commission but did not endorse the idea of a North-South summit. The summit governments supported the general capital increase of the World Bank and the sixth replenishment of the International Development Association. Finally, in separate statements, the heads of state and government condemned the taking of diplomatic hostages, hijacking and the Soviet occupation in Afghanistan. They also urged the governments responsible for the refugee problem "not to pursue policies which drive ... their people out of their countries".

Château Montebello (1981). In July 1981, the summit was held at Le Château Montebello, near Ottawa. The leaders reaffirmed that low and stable monetary growth was essential to reducing inflation even though interest rates were already quite high. Furthermore, the summiteers mentioned in their Declaration that "most of us need also to rely on containment of budgetary deficits" to lower interest rates. They welcomed the initiative of the Consultative Group of Eighteen to convene a GATT Ministerial Meeting in 1982. On North-South relations, the summit governments committed themselves to maintain or increase levels of Official Development Assistance. On East-West issues, President Reagan told his colleagues that he was against East-West trade and technology transfer to the Soviet bloc, especially with regard to the trans-Siberian pipeline. The Europeans did not share his position. The heads of state and government also issued a statement on terrorism. The chairman's summary of political issues dealt with the problems of the Middle East, East-West relations, and Kampuchea.

Versailles (1982). There were two heated topics at the Versailles summit in June 1982: monetary policy and East-West trade. On monetary issues, the Americans stressed the need for policy convergence while the French favoured co-ordinated intervention. A statement on international monetary undertakings was issued. In an effort to promote convergence, it was decided that the G-5 finance ministers, in collaboration with the Managing Director of the IMF, would meet regularly to conduct multilateral surveillance of their countries' economic policies. A group was also created to study exchange market interventions. On East-West trade issues, the US had retaliated against the declaration of martial law in Poland with economic sanctions against the Soviet Union. They asked their colleagues to take a tough line against the Soviet bloc. The Europeans, especially the Germans, were concerned about the political implications of such an action. A compromise in three points was hammered out where the summiteers pledged: to improve the international system for controlling exports of strategic goods; to exchange information in the Organisation for Economic Co-operation and Development (OECD) on all aspects of their relations with the Soviet bloc; and to handle with caution financial relations with these countries. A Working Group on Technology, Growth and Employment was set up to study how to exploit the opportunities "presented by the new technologies, particularly for creating new employment". The leaders also issued a statement on Lebanon.

Williamsburg, Virginia (1983). In May 1983, the US hosted the economic summit in Williamsburg, Virginia. Their budget deficit, the overvalued dollar, and high interest rates were criticized by the other summiteers. The final declaration prescribed fiscal and monetary discipline. The leaders agreed "to continue consultations on proposals for a new negotiating round in the GATT", and invited "Ministers of Finance, in consultation with the Managing Director of the IMF, to define the conditions for improving the international monetary system" and to consider a high-level international monetary conference. The G-7 also issued a declaration on security where it is emphasized that the security of Western Nations is indivisible and must be approached on a global basis. This statement aimed at supporting the European countries that were scheduled to deploy missiles.

London (1984). In June 1984, the summit was held in London. The leaders expressed their satisfaction with "the recovery now under way" but also reaffirmed that "high interest rates, and failure to reduce inflation further and dampen down inflationary expectations, could put recovery at risk". There was no mention of the need to reduce the American budget deficit. Worried about a debtors' front, the G-7 encouraged more extended multi-year rescheduling of public and commercial debts when debtors were making efforts to improve their position. No agreement on a timetable for a new GATT Round was reached. The Working Group on Technology, Growth and Employment was asked to "identify specific areas for research on the causes, effects and means of limiting environmental pollution of air, water and ground". It was also given the mandate to identify "possible projects for industrial co-operation to develop cost-effective techniques to reduce environmental damage". Political statements were also issued on democratic values, international terrorism, East-West relations and arms control, and the Iran-Iraq conflict.

Bonn (1985). The Bonn summit in May 1985 ended without a consensus on the launching of a new GATT Round [see 111.19]. As in the past, the leaders stressed the importance of bringing down inflation. For the first time, each country clearly identified its policy priorities in the final declaration. The US focused on a "rapid and appreciable cut in public expenditures and thus a substantial reduction in the budget deficit". The summiteers restated their encouragement for multi-year reschedulings of public and commercial debts. Concerned with the drought and famine in Africa, they set up an expert group to prepare proposals on measures to fight desertification. This group reported to the seven foreign ministers in September 1985. Finally, a Political Declaration on the 40th Anniversary of the End of the Second World War was issued.

Tokyo (1986). In May 1986, at the second Tokyo summit, the G-7 set up the **Group of Seven Finance Ministers** "to review the mutual compatibility" of its members' policies between the annual summit meetings. The economic declaration reaffirmed the need to conduct multilateral surveillance with the collaboration of the IMF. It detailed the procedures for economic policy co-ordination using economic indicators such as exchange rates, inflation rates, interest rates, and current account and trade balances. Finance ministers and their deputies, central bank governors and the Managing Director of the IMF attend the meetings of the G-7 officials. These meetings are held three times a year (once early in the year, and at the semi-annual meetings of the Interim Committee). The summiteers also addressed the agricultural problem by giving their support to the work of the OECD. They issued two political statements: one on international terrorism condemning Libya and one on the implications of the Chernobyl nuclear accident.

Venice (1987). At the second Venice summit in June 1987, the leaders restated the policy agreements reached at the Louvre and Washington, DC a few months earlier by the G-7 Finance Ministers: namely, to hold nominal exchange rates near existing levels. They called on their Finance Ministers "to co-operate closely to foster stability of exchange rates" and "to develop, if necessary, additional appropriate policy measures" to achieve world economic growth. They endorsed "the understandings reached by the Group of Seven Finance Ministers to strengthen, with the assistance of the ... IMF, the surveillance of their economies using economic indicators". The summiteers reaffirmed their long-term objective which is to allow market signals to influence the orientation of agricultural production. They continued to support the case-by-case strategy for the major middle-income debtors but recognized that sub-Saharan Africa needs special treatment. They issued statements on East-West relations, terrorism, freedom of navigation in the Gulf and the Iraq-Iran war. In the chairman's statement on AIDS, the leaders endorsed the proposal of the President of the French Republic to create an international committee on the ethical issues raised by AIDS.

Toronto (1988). At the Toronto summit in June 1988, a commodity-price index was added to the list of economic indicators used to assess policies and performance of each summit country. To complement macroeconomic policies, the leaders promised to pursue structural reforms. They agreed to provide debt relief for the poorest developing countries. Governments could choose from a list of options: concessional interest rates, longer repayment periods at commercial rates, partial write-offs of debt service obligations during the consolidation period, or a combination of these options. The summiteers also noted that excessive fluctuation of exchange rates destabilizing the adjustment process could be counterproductive. They issued a political declaration on East-West relations, terrorism and narcotics, as well as the chairman's summary of political issues, an agreed summary of the discussions on the Middle East, South Africa and Cambodia.

The Arch, Paris (1989). The summit of the Arch was held at l'Arche de la Défense in Paris in July 1989. The summiteers endorsed the **Brady Plan** calling for voluntary, market-based debt and debt-service reduction operations in middle-income developing countries. They also urged the countries with fiscal and current account deficits, including the US, Canada and Italy, to reduce their budget deficit while countries with external surpluses such as Japan and Germany were asked "to encourage non-inflationary growth of domestic demand and facilitate external adjustment". They reaffirmed their opposition to unilateralism, bilateralism, sectoralism and managed trade which threaten "to undermine the multilateral system and the Uruguay Round negotiations". The leaders devoted eight of their 22-page economic declaration to the environment. They decided to extend economic assistance to Poland and Hungary. They agreed to convene a financial action task force from summit participants and other countries interested in drug issues. The mandate of this task force is "to prevent the utilization of the banking system and financial institutions for the purpose of money laundering, and to consider additional preventive efforts in this field". Declarations on China, East-West relations, human rights, terrorism, the Arab-Israeli conflict, Southern Africa, Central America, Panama, Cambodia and Lebanon were issued. On the eve of the summit, four prominent Third World leaders (Abdou Diouf of Senegal, Mohamed Hosni Mubarak of Egypt, Carlos Andres Perez of Venezuela and Rajiv Gandhi of India) called on the summiteers "to initiate a process of regular consultations between developed and developing countries, at the summit level". Mikhail Gorbachev sent a letter to the President of the 15th annual summit sharing his ideas about the key problems of the world economy.

Houston (1990). The most contentious issue at the Houston summit in July 1990 concerned agriculture and the Uruguay Round. The leaders agreed "to maintain a high level of personal involvement and to exercise the political leadership necessary to ensure the successful outcome of these negotiations". However, they did not live up to their promise. They endorsed the decision of the European Council and asked "the IMF, the World Bank, the OECD and the president of the EBRD ... to undertake, with the Commission of the European Communities, a detailed study on the Soviet economy". Once again, environmental issues occupied a large part of the final *communiqué*. The summiteers said they were ready "to co-operate with the Government of Brazil on a comprehensive pilot program to counteract the threat to tropical rain forests in that country". They asked the World Bank to prepare such a proposal, in close co-operation with the Commission of the European Communities, and to present it, at the latest, at the next economic summit. The participants to the Houston summit endorsed the report of the Financial Action Task Force (FATF) set up at the summit of the Arch, and proposed the creation of another task force to address the problems "which concern cocaine, heroin and synthetic drugs". A political declaration on securing democracy, the chairman's statement and a statement on transnational issues (terrorism and non-proliferation) were also issued.

London (1991). At the third London economic summit held in July 1991, the participants reaffirmed their commitment to complete the Uruguay Round before the end of 1991. They also agreed to set up a UN arms register and "to reinforce UN relief in coping with emergencies". After the meeting, the leaders met with Mikhail Gorbachev to discuss aid to the USSR.

Munich (1992). Two themes dominated the Munich economic summit in July 1992: the world economy and helping the new independent states of the former Soviet Union. The summiteers also pledged "to carry forward the momentum" of the United Nations Conference on Environment and Development (UNCED) [see 410.02], and "to continue our best efforts to increase the quantity and quality of official development assistance in accordance with our commitments".

Maryse Robert

2.3.2 Monetary Forums

232 A – GROUP OF TEN – G-10

The Group of Ten was established when ten countries (the US, Japan, France, the UK, Italy, Canada, the Netherlands, Belgium and the central banks of West Germany and Sweden) agreed to lend their currencies to the International Monetary Fund (IMF) [see 211 A] when supplementary resources were needed "to forestall or cope with an impairment of the international monetary system". The General Arrangements to Borrow (GAB) were established in 1962 to help the IMF deal with, first, the international liquidity crisis that could have resulted from the balance of payments problems of the US and the UK, the two major reserve centres, and, second, the effects of the short-term capital movements caused by the return to external convertibility in Europe and Japan. Each participant is bound to provide resources to the IMF once a proposal has been accepted by the participants as a group.

The participants in the GAB were willing to finance large drawings in the credit tranches by the reserve centres. In 1968, the participants agreed on a procedure for the financing of gold tranche (now reserve tranche) drawings. They also decided that all participants, not just the two reserve centres, could use the General Arrangements.

In 1964, the Fund concluded an associate agreement with Switzerland which "was prepared, but not obliged, to make resources available to GAB participants". In April 1984, Switzerland formally became a GAB participant through the Swiss National Bank.

In 1983, the Group of Ten (the ten original members of the GAB and Switzerland) and the IMF Executive Board reformed the GAB as requests for Fund resources increased substantially due to the debt crisis. The IMF can call on the GAB participants to finance drawings by non-participants. Moreover, the Fund may conclude borrowing arrangements with member countries which do not participate in the GAB. Such an arrangement with Saudi Arabia became effective in 1983. However, Saudi Arabia cannot benefit from the GAB but is free to accept or reject any proposal by the IMF to finance a large drawing.

The General Arrangements, which originally totalled US$6 billion, have been renewed six times, most recently in 1988, for a period of five years. Under the GAB, the IMF may now borrow up to SDR 18.5 billion.

The Group of Ten meetings are generally held before the Interim Committee meetings at both ministerial and deputy levels. The G-10 ministers address economic matters relating to the international monetary system. The Managing Director of the IMF generally takes part in the ministerial meetings.

Maryse Robert

232 B – GROUP OF TWENTY-FOUR – G-24

The Group of 24 was established by the Group of 77 [see 233 A] in 1972. The collapse of the Bretton Woods System led to the reform of the international monetary system (IMS) and the establishment by the IMF Board of Governors of the Committee on Reform of the International Monetary System and Related Issues, known as the Committee of Twenty. This Committee had the mandate to propose plans to reconstruct the IMS. The Group of 24 was created to counterbalance the influence of the Group of Ten in the formulation of the recommendations of the Committee of Twenty.

In 1974, with the establishment of both the Interim Committee and the Development Committee at the Annual Meetings of the Fund and the Bank [see 221 A], not only monetary affairs but also international development became part of the mandate of the Group of 24.

The Group of 24 consists of eight countries from Africa, the Americas and Europe/Asia. Each participant is represented by its minister of finance or economy or its central bank governor. The Chair of the Group rotates every year among the three regions. The Group has also two vice-chairpersons from different regions. The G-24 does not have a secretariat. However, the IMF [see 211 A] provides secretariat support while UNCTAD [see 111 B] and UNDP [see 222 A] help co-ordinate research. The Group generally holds its Ministerial Meetings before the meetings of the Interim Committee and the Development Committee. The Managing Director of the IMF and the President of the World Bank attend these meetings. Deputies of the G-24 meet prior to the Ministerial Meetings. Other members of the G-77 as well as representatives from other international organizations can attend as observers.

M.R.

2.3.3 Developing Countries

233 A – GROUP OF SEVENTY-SEVEN – G-77

In 1963, the representatives of 75 developing countries submitted a joint statement at the second session of the Preparatory Committee that had been established to consider the agenda of UNCTAD I, the first United Nations Conference on Trade and Development [see 111 B]. In their statement, developing countries summarized their needs and aspirations, criticized the world trading structure, and called for a new institution to implement the decisions of UNCTAD I.

UNCTAD I met in Geneva in 1964. The Group of 77 came into existence when the caucus of developing countries, which had grown to 77, adopted the "Joint Declaration of the Seventy-Seven Developing Countries Made at the Conclusion of the United Nations Conference on Trade and Development". In its Joint Declaration, the G-77 emphazises the role played by UNCTAD I in creating "a new and just world economic order". Later that year, the G-77 was instrumental in institutionalizing UNCTAD as an organ of the General Assembly of the United Nations. UNCTAD became the only "international organization" controlled by the Third World. The Joint Declaration also established the G-77 as a permanent group seeking to foster economic development in developing countries. For instance, the Group of 77 was a key supporter of: the incorporation of a special and preferential treatment for the Third World in Part IV of the GATT, the creation of the Generalized System of Preferences (GSP) [see 111.05] and the establishment of the Common Fund [see 121.02].

The G-77 has always maintained a special relationship with UNCTAD. In 1971, the UNCTAD Secretariat created a Liaison Office in the Office of the Secretary-General. This office is the main channel of communication between the G-77 and the secretariat. The idea of a secretariat for the G-77 was rejected by a Working Group in 1977 and the Foreign Ministers of the G-77 in 1979.

The main organizational elements of the G-77 are the regional groups, the Preparatory Committee, the Senior Officials Meeting, and the Ministerial Meeting. Three regional groups (Latin America, Africa and Asia) meet from time to time in Geneva. These groups set the agenda for the G-77. The Preparatory Committee, represented by ten countries from each regional group, convenes before each UNCTAD conference. It prepares the agenda for the ministerial meeting. The position of the G-77 is then formulated at the Senior Officials Meeting and the Ministerial Meeting, the highest policy-making organ of the G-77.

The G-77 is also very active in other international organizations. There are branches of the G-77 at the UN General Assembly in New York, the Food and Agriculture Organization (FAO) in Rome [see 131 A], the United Nations

Educational, Scientific and Cultural Organization (UNESCO) in Paris [see 171 A], the United Nations Industrial Development Organization (UNIDO) [see 151 A] and the International Atomic Energy Agency (IAEA) in Vienna [see 421 A], the United Nations Environment Programme (UNEP) in Nairobi [see 222 A], and the IMF [see 211 A] and World Bank in Washington, DC [see 232 B].

Maryse Robert

3. Contracts, Payments and Dispute Settlement

To facilitate international transactions, the international trade community has called for measures to unify or harmonize substantive laws and practices, and rules on conflict of laws, and to provide a regulatory framework for judicial co-operation and arbitration.

International institutions (public or private) devoted to the unification of laws and practices are described in the first section [3.0]. International agreements are then presented, with a distinction between those which seek to unify substantive laws (like the UN Convention on the international sale of goods, the most important of this group) [see 3.1.1] and those related to the harmonization of rules on conflict of laws, which are less directly implemented but which may have an effect on domestic legislation [see 3.1.2]. Standard terms, clauses and conditions of general use (e.g. Incoterms) are then addressed [see 3.1.3].

The second section [see 3.2] focuses on the negotiable instruments related directly to payment mechanisms in international trade. The first category covers conventions which primarily deal with uniform laws, like those on bills of exchange and promissory notes [see 3.2.1], and the second category deals mainly with documentary credits and guarantees [see 3.2.2].

The third section [see 3.3] is concerned with treaties on judicial matters: the international competence of courts [see 3.3.1]; establishing co-operation for litigation with international elements [see 3.3.2]; and the international enforcement of judgments [see 3.3.3].

The modest adherence to judicial conventions contrasts with the situation regarding international arbitration. The final section [see 3.4] describes these arbitration conventions [see 3.4.1] and, in particular, the New York Convention on Foreign Arbitral Awards and the UNCITRAL Model Law, the two corner-stones of international arbitration. The section concludes with a description of the most significant world-wide arbitral institutions and arbitration rules commonly known as UNCITRAL or ICC Rules [see 3.4.2].

Alain Prujiner

SELECTED BIBLIOGRAPHY

Delaume, Georges R., *Transnational Contracts, Applicable Law and Settlement of Disputes*, Dobbs Ferry: Oceana, Binder.

Fox, William F. Jr., *International Commercial Agreements*, Deventer: Kluwer Law and Taxation, 1988.

Germain, Claire M., *Transnational Law Research*, New York: Transnational Juris, Binder.

Prujiner, Alain, *Traités et documents internationaux usuels en droit du commerce international/Treaties and International Documents Used in International Trade Law*, Montreal: Wilson & Lafleur, 1992.

Dictionnaire Joly: Pratique des Contrats Internationaux, Paris: GLN, Binder.

Lamy, *Contrats Internationaux*, Paris: Editions Juridiques et Techniques, Binder.

3.0 Institutions

Certain institutions have played, and continue to play, a fundamental role in the development of international trade law. Some of them are intergovernmental bodies, like The Hague Conference on Private International Law (HCOPIL), created in 1893 [see 300 A]; the International Institute for the Unification of Private Law (UNIDROIT), established in Rome in 1926 [see 300 B]; and the United Nations Commission on International Trade Law (UNCITRAL), created in 1966 [see 300 C]. They have initiated the majority of world-wide conventions adopted in the field of private international law.

An important contribution has been made in the unification of trade practices by some private institutions, particularly by the International Chamber of Commerce (ICC) [see 300 D], which has also established the ICC International Court of Arbitration [see 342 B].

300 A – THE HAGUE CONFERENCE ON PRIVATE INTERNATIONAL LAW (HCOPIL)

The Hague Conference on Private International Law met for the first time on 12 September 1893. At its seventh session in 1951, it formulated its Statute and became a permanent intergovernmental organization. The Statute went into effect on 15 July 1955.

HCOPIL is composed of 38 member states, and its objective is to work for the progressive unification of the rules of private international law through the agreement of international treaties. Consequently, it has been responsible for conventions on such diverse matters as the law applicable to the international sale of goods, agency, products liability, as well as on procedural matters such as service abroad of judicial documents and enforcement of foreign judgments.

STRUCTURE

The **Conference** acts through the intermediary of a Secretariat (Permanent Bureau). The Plenary Sessions of the Conference take place in The Hague every four years. During these sessions, the member states discuss and adopt by majority vote conventions and recommendations prepared by special commissions of government experts. States which are not members of HCOPIL may participate in the drafting of conventions and they may vote; such was the case during the extraordinary session of 1985 which adopted the Convention on the Law Applicable to Contracts for the International Sale of Goods (The Hague, 1986) [see 312.07].

The **Secretariat** is responsible for preparing the sessions of HCOPIL and the commissions of experts. The **Council of Diplomatic Representatives** votes on a budget (approximately 2 million Dutch guilders) once a year, and the expenses are paid according to a similar distribution system as that adopted by the Universal Postal Union.

CO-OPERATION

HCOPIL co-operates closely with the ministerial authorities of its member states and liaises with international organizations such as the UN [see 001 A], UNCITRAL [see

300 C], UNCTAD [see 111 B], WIPO [see 160 A], the EC and the Council of Europe.

Non-governmental organizations such as the International Chamber of Commerce [see 300 D], the International Union of Latin Notaries, the International Union of Bailiffs and Law Officers and the International Bar Association send observers to follow the work of HCOPIL.

PUBLICATIONS

HCOPIL publishes *Proceedings*, a *Bibliography Relating to the Work of the Conference*, as well as handbooks and the texts of international conventions.

Yvonne Muller and HCOPIL

ADDRESS

6, Scheveningseweg, 2517 KT The Hague, The Netherlands
T. (31 70) 363 33 03, Fx. (31 70) 360 48 67

300 B – INTERNATIONAL INSTITUTE FOR THE UNIFICATION OF PRIVATE LAW (UNIDROIT)

The International Institute for the Unification of Private Law (UNIDROIT) is an intergovernmental organization which co-operates with the United Nations, but is not a part of it. It was established in 1926 at the initiative of the Italian Government as an auxiliary arm of the League of Nations, and in 1940 it became an independent intergovernmental organization.

The objectives of UNIDROIT have not changed since 1926: it studies methods for harmonizing and co-ordinating private law between states or groups of states, and prepares for the progressive adoption of uniform private law legislation by states (Art. 1).

STRUCTURE

The **General Assembly**, which is the plenary body of UNIDROIT, meets at least once a year to approve the budget and the accounts of income and expenditure, and every three years to approve UNIDROIT's programme of work. Every representative who sits in the General Assembly speaks in the name of the state which he represents (Art. 5).

The **Governing Council** is the executive body of UNIDROIT. It consists of the President of UNIDROIT and has between 16 and 21 members. It meets at least once a year to evaluate and direct the work of the Institute. The Council also draws up the triennial programme of work for the Institute and the draft budget.

The **President** represents UNIDROIT. He is appointed by the Italian Government (Art. 6-2) and is responsible for calling ordinary meetings of the General Assembly (Art. 5-2) and the Governing Council (Art. 6-8). The **Administrative Tribunal** has jurisdiction to deal with any differences between the Institute and its officers or employees. The Tribunal consists of three members (Art. 7 bis).

The **Permanent Committee** ensures continuity in the work of the Institute in line with rules adopted by the Governing Council (Art. 17-1). It is composed of the President and five members nominated by the Governing Council (Art. 7).

The **Secretariat**, under the direction of the Secretary-General and Deputy Secretary-General, is responsible for the permanent administration of UNIDROIT. It is located in Rome's Palazzo Aldobrandini.

ACTIVITIES

A member state or another organization may initiate surveys which could eventually lead to the adoption of international conventions by UNIDROIT on relevant matters. The most recent UNIDROIT diplomatic conference took place in Ottawa in May 1988 at the invitation of the Canadian Government. The result was the adoption of two international conventions, one on international factoring and the other on international financial leasing [see 311.06 and 311.07].

The current work of UNIDROIT may result in international instruments in the following areas: quality and quantity control of goods, security interests in mobile equipment, civil liability connected with the carrying out of dangerous activities, software contracts, principles for international commercial contracts, international franchising contracts and the international protection of cultural property. UNIDROIT is also seeking to foster juridical co-operation with developing countries.

CO-OPERATION

UNIDROIT co-operates with governmental organizations such as UNCITRAL [see 300 C], HCOPIL [see 300 A], WIPO [see 160 A], IMO [see 183 A], ECOSOC [see 001 A], FAO [see 131 A], UNCTAD [see 111 B], UNESCO [see 171 A] and the EC. It also liaises with non-governmental organizations.

PUBLICATIONS

UNIDROIT publishes the biannual *Uniform Law Review*, the biannual *UNIDROIT News Bulletin* and *Digest of Legal Activities of International Organizations and other Institutions* as well as studies on comparative law.

Jean-Paul Chapdelaine and UNIDROIT

ADDRESS

Palazzo Aldobrandini, Via Panisperna, 28, I-00184 Rome, Italy
T. (39 6) 684 13 72, Fx. (39 6) 684 13 94

300 C – UNITED NATIONS COMMISSION ON INTERNATIONAL TRADE LAW (UNCITRAL)

The United Nations Commission on International Trade Law (UNCITRAL) was established on 17 December 1966 by UN General Assembly Resolution 2205(XXI). UNCITRAL's objective is to facilitate international trade through "the promotion of the progressive harmonization and unification of the law of international trade".

ACTIVITIES

UNCITRAL prepares and promotes the adoption of new international conventions, model laws and uniform laws. It promotes the codification and wider acceptance of international trade terms, provisions, customs and practices, thus contributing to the creation of a uniform juridical framework at the international, national and private levels.

The organization co-ordinates activities and co-operates with other organizations. It monitors the legal development of international trade law nationally, and collects and disseminates relevant information on national legislative developments and, where applicable, case law. UNCITRAL also participates in the activities of other international bodies concerned with international trade law (e.g. the IMF [see 211 A], BIS [see 212 A]).

UNCITRAL conducts training programmes and collaborates with other organizations. It organizes and sponsors conferences, seminars and meetings between lawyers.

STRUCTURE

UNCITRAL is composed of 36 member states elected by the UN General Assembly for a term of six years, with a turnover every three years of half of the members. To best ensure a balanced representation of the different geographic areas of the world, and their economic and legal systems, UNCITRAL adopted the following distribution of seats: nine from Africa, seven from Asia, six from Latin America, five from eastern Europe, and nine from western Europe and other states.

Representatives from the European Communities and from other intergovernmental as well as non-governmental international organizations participate in the work of UNCITRAL as observers. These observers have a particularly active role which reduces the differences in status between the observers and full members.

In 1978, UNCITRAL established a long-term programme of work. The implementation of this is the responsibility of UNCITRAL's three working groups, each being responsible for different subject areas. The **Secretariat** prepares topics and basic studies which allow the working groups to present to UNCITRAL, at its annual session, the necessary documents to finalize its work and its Report before the latter is presented to the UN General Assembly. The Secretariat is also responsible for planning UNCITRAL's work and for the administration of seminars and conferences.

CO-OPERATION

UNCITRAL co-operates with other UN bodies and institutions, as well as with other intergovernmental organizations such as HCOPIL [see 300 A] and UNIDROIT [see 300 B].

PUBLICATIONS

UNCITRAL publishes Legal Guides, the UNCITRAL *Yearbook* and texts and commentaries on Conventions and recommendations adopted by the Commission.

Caroline London

ADDRESS

Vienna International Centre, Wagramer Strasse, 5, PO.Box: 500, A-1400 Vienna, Austria
T. (43 1) 21131 4060, Tx. 135612, Fx. (43 1) 237 485

300 D – INTERNATIONAL CHAMBER OF COMMERCE (ICC)

The ICC is a non-governmental organization founded on 24 June 1920. Its primary objective is to work towards an open world economy. The ICC exercises four principal functions:

- to represent the industrial and commercial community at the international level, in particular before the United Nations and other specialist agencies;
- to promote the free market economy system based on the principles of the competitiveness of business enterprise;
- to harmonize commercial terminology and practice;
- to translate its principles into practical business services, to organize seminars, and to publish technical works.

The ICC has members in more than 100 countries and brings together national organizations representing the economic and professional interests of their members, as well as companies involved in international trade. The ICC operates at national levels in 59 countries, through councils and national committees which organize and co-ordinate its activities.

STRUCTURE

The **Council**, the supreme organ of the ICC, meets twice a year and elects the Executive Board. Votes are exercised by representatives of the National Committees or Groups.

The **Executive Board** (12 to 15 members) implements ICC policy, and the effective functioning of the organization is assured by the **Secretariat**. Declarations of general ICC policy and practical recommendations developed by the commissions, are submitted for approval to the Executive Board after consultation with the National Committees.

The **Commissions** of the ICC study problems relating to areas as varied as international trade policy, financial services, multinational enterprises, intellectual property, taxation, competition law, insurance, environment, energy, information technology, marketing, advertising, transport, banking and international arbitration.

Working bodies, other than Commissions, include the International Court of Arbitration [see 342 B], the Institute of International Business Law and Practice, the International Maritime Bureau, the Counterfeiting Intelligence Bureau, the Commercial Crime Bureau, the Centre for Maritime Co-operation, the International Bureau of Chambers of Commerce, and the World Industry Council for the Environment.

Congresses are held every three years, and all member companies and organizations are invited to attend. A Conference convenes between Congresses.

CO-OPERATION

The ICC co-operates with almost all agencies dealing with economic matters within the United Nations, as well as with several intergovernmental and non-governmental organizations.

PUBLICATIONS

The ICC, through its publishing arm, ICC Publishing SA, publishes numerous reference books, reports and practical guides. These include Incoterms, which are the universally recognised ICC definitions of trade terms used by international trading partners [see 313.01]. The Communication Office publishes an annual report and a monthly newsletter called *ICC Business World*.

Sarah Williams

ADDRESS

38, cour Albert-1er, 75008 Paris, France
T. (33 1) 49 53 28 28, Fx. (33 1) 49 53 29 42

300.01 – STATUTES OF THE INTERNATIONAL CHAMBER OF COMMERCE – ICC

Adopted : 24.06.1920, ICC Res.

In October 1919, the Chambers of Commerce of the leading western countries met together at a conference in Atlantic City (USA). Its objective was to prepare the groundwork for the establishment of an organization which would unite business people and European Chambers of Commerce into a forum to work towards the reconstruction of Europe.

The International Chamber of Commerce (ICC) was established a year later in Paris during a congress which adopted its present statutes. The ICC [see 300 D] is a non-profit-making association governed by the French law of 1901.

S.W.

Access : ENT (Art. 2)
Language : Eng, Fre, Spa

Modific. : Last modified 12.05.92

Reference : ICC Doc. 891-5/4

300.02 – STATUTE OF THE INTERNATIONAL INSTITUTE FOR THE UNIFICATION OF PRIVATE LAW – UNIDROIT

Concluded : 15.03.1940, Rome
In Force : 21.04.1940
Parties : 55

This Statute describes the objectives, structure and functions of UNIDROIT [see 300 B]. It replaces the original UNIDROIT Statute of 1926.

Access : ALS (Art. 20)
Reserves : USP
Duration : REN 6 (Art. 20)
Deposit. : IT (Art. 22)
Language : Fre, (Eng, Ger, Ita, Spa) (Art. 10)

Modific. : Amendments 18.01.52 (17.09.57); 30.04.53 (17.09.57); 15.09.61 (13.12.63); 15.06.65 (26.05.68); 18.12.67 (26.04.68); 18.02.69 (29.09.76); 09.11.84 (13.01.86)

Reference : UST 15/2, 19/6, 20/2, 30/5 – UKTS 1965/54

300.03 – STATUTE OF THE HAGUE CONFERENCE ON PRIVATE INTERNATIONAL LAW – HCOPIL

Concluded : 31.10.1955, The Hague
In Force : 15.07.1955
Parties : 38

In order to formally establish HCOPIL, the Statute was adopted and submitted for approval by the governments of states which had participated in one or more sessions of the Conference [see 300 A].

Access : CON (Art. 2, 14)
Reserves : USP
Duration : USP
Deposit. : NL (Art. 14)
Language : Fre

Reference : 220 UNTS – HCOPIL Col. 1988 – UKTS 1955/65 – 1 Paeslee

300.04 – ESTABLISHMENT OF THE UNITED NATIONS COMMISSION ON INTERNATIONAL TRADE LAW – UNCITRAL

Adopted : 17.12.1966, UNGA Res.2205(XXI)

On the basis of deliberations and recommendations of the Sixth Committee, the UN General Assembly adopted the Resolution establishing UNCITRAL [see 300 C]. This was in response to the Hungarian request during the XXth session of the General Assembly in 1965 to examine the measures needed to be taken for the gradual development of private international law, with a view to promoting international trade in particular.

3.1 Private International Obligations

Differences in national laws can complicate international transactions (that is, contracts made between persons living in different countries). Such differences can add uncertainties in determining the law applicable to the transaction and impose on parties the inconvenience of having to apply an unfamiliar legal system.

In response, measures have been taken to harmonize laws and practices. States have adopted treaties and model laws aimed at unifying substantive laws [see 3.1.1] and rules on conflicts of laws [see 3.1.2]. The same result in some cases has been achieved where parties to international transactions agree to apply standard terms, clauses and conditions drafted by private and public bodies [see 3.1.3].

3.1.1 Unification of Laws

The avoidance of difficulties arising from the diversity of national laws is best achieved through the unification of laws. However, the efforts required to unify the whole spectrum of international trade are so considerable that agreements adopted at an international level have had to be limited in scope and have allowed for flexibility in their implementation.

This explains why efforts towards a unification of substantive laws first began with the law of international sales of goods [see the 1964 conventions replaced by 1980 UN Convention: 311.01, 311.02 and 311.04]. These were followed by agreements on limitation periods, agency, international factoring and international financial leasing.

The methods used for unification varied. The 1964 conventions require contracting parties to incorporate into their domestic legislation an annexed uniform law. The subsequent agreements contained in their text the uniform rules of law that contracting states are required to implement.

SELECTED BIBLIOGRAPHY

Audit, B., *La Vente Internationale de Marchandises, Convention des Nations Unies du 11 Avril 1980*, Paris: Editions juridiques associées , 1990.

Bianca, C.M. and M.J. Bonnell (eds.), *Commentary on the International Sales Law: the 1980 Vienna Sales Convention*, Milan: Giuffrè, 1987.

Friedman, A.H., "The United Nations Convention on Contracts for the International Sale of Goods", in: *Digest of Commercial Laws of the World*, L. Nelson (ed.), Dobbs Ferry, N.Y.: Oceana Publications, 1988. Binder 7.

Galston, N. and H. Smit (eds.), *The UN Convention on Contracts for the International Sale of Goods*, Parker School of Foreign & Comparative Law (Columbia University), New York: Matthew Bender, 1984 .

Heuzé, Vincent, *La Vente Internationale de Marchandises*, Paris: GLN Joly, 1992.

Honnold, J., *Uniform Law for International Sales Under the 1980 United Nations Convention*, Deventer: Kluwer Law and Taxation, 1987.

Guyon, Yves et al., *Les Ventes Internationales de Marchandises: Problèmes Juridiques et d'Actualité*, Paris: Economica, 1981.

Kathrein, R. and Magraw, D. (eds.), *The Convention for the International Sale of*

Goods: A Handbook of Basic Materials, Chicago: A.B.A. Section of International Law and Practice, 1987.

311.01 – CONVENTION RELATING TO A UNIFORM LAW ON THE INTERNATIONAL SALE OF GOODS – UNIDROIT

Concluded : 01.07.1964, The Hague
In Force : 18.08.1972
Parties : 6

In adopting this Convention, the diplomatic Conference ended 34 years of deliberations on a uniform law for the international sale of goods and, more particularly, on the rules governing the obligations of buyer and seller. The separate Convention relating to a Uniform Law on the Formation of Contracts for the International Sale of Goods [see 311.02] was also adopted by the Conference.

The body of the Convention outlines the rights and obligations of the contracting parties as well as the modalities relating to the treaty's application. The main obligation of the contracting parties is to incorporate into their law the Uniform Law on the International Sale of Goods forming the Annex to the Convention.

According to Article 1, the Uniform Law is applicable to contracts involving the international sale of goods. Though the Convention does not define the contract, Article 7 makes no distinction between the commercial or civil character of the parties or of the contracts. However, it does exclude certain sales such as those by authority of law or on execution or distress, and further it does not apply to stocks, shares, investment securities, negotiable instruments, money, electricity, ships, vessels, or aircraft subject to registration. Contracts for the supply of goods to be manufactured or produced are covered by the Convention.

The Convention applies to contracts for the international sale of goods, meaning those entered into by parties whose places of business are in the territories of different states. Other criteria also apply, notably that the supply and delivery of goods must take place between different countries (Art. 1).

While Article 2 excludes the rules of private international law for the purposes of applying the Convention, subject to any provision in it to the contrary, Article 3 stipulates that the parties to a contract of sale are free to exclude, either partially or entirely, the application of the Convention. Article 9 also makes the Uniform Law secondary to international usage or custom in relations between the parties. Consequently, Articles 3 to 9 significantly limit the scope of application of the Uniform Law.

The Uniform Law defines the obligations of the parties. Article 18, for example, imposes three obligations on the seller: first, the seller must effect delivery of the goods, which consists in the handing over of goods which conform with the contract (Art. 19); second, the seller shall hand over any documents relating to the contract at the time and place fixed by the contract or by usage (Art. 50); and, third, the seller shall transfer the property in the goods (Art. 52). According to Article 56, "the buyer shall pay the price for the goods and take delivery of them as required by the contract and the present law".

The Uniform Law deals with breaches of contract and with remedies, which include requiring performance of the contract, declaring the contract avoided, and being able to claim for damages.

This Convention is gradually being replaced by the UN Convention on Contracts for the International Sale of Goods (Vienna, 1980) (Art. 99) [see 311.04].

Jean-André Lasserre and Vladimir Vasak

Access : ALS (Art. 8, 9)
Reserves : PAU (Art. 2-5)
Duration : USP
Deposit. : NL
Language : Eng, Fre

Reference : 834 UNTS – ULR 1964 – UKTS 1972/74 – ILM 3:855 – RCDIP 1965

311.02 – CONVENTION RELATING TO A UNIFORM LAW ON THE FORMATION OF CONTRACTS FOR THE INTERNATIONAL SALE OF GOODS – UNIDROIT

Concluded : 01.07.1964, The Hague
In Force : 23.08.1972
Parties : 6

The diplomatic Conference which convened at The Hague in 1964 dealt separately with the formation of contracts and the law relating to the contracts themselves [see 311.01]. The formation of contracts is dealt with in the present Convention and in the Uniform Law as annexed to the Convention. However, Article 1 of Annex II stipulates that "the present law shall apply to the formation of contracts of sale of goods which would be governed by the Uniform Law on the International Sale of Goods".

DETAILS OF THE CONVENTION

The structure of the present Convention is identical to the other. It describes the obligations and rights of the contracting states as well as the modalities relating to the treaty's application. It governs the formation of contracts, and constitutes Annex I of the Convention. The scope of the Convention's application is also identical, as is the autonomy allowed to the parties.

The provisions separately address offer and acceptance:

The Offer: According to Article 4, a contract of sale will not constitute an offer unless it is sufficiently definite to permit the conclusion of the contract by acceptance and indicates the intention of the offeror to be bound. Nevertheless, the offer shall not bind the offeror until it has been communicated to the offeree (Art. 5-1). Article 5-2 indicates how an offer may be revoked, while Article 7-1 stipulates that "an acceptance containing additions, limitations or other modifications shall be a rejection of the offer and shall constitute a counter-offer".

The Acceptance: According to Article 6, acceptance of an offer consists of a declaration communicated by any means whatsoever to the offerer. It may "also consist of the despatch of the goods or of the price or of any other act which may be considered to be equivalent to the declaration ...". A declaration of acceptance of an offer has effect only if it is communicated to the offeror within the time he has fixed, or if no such time is fixed, within a reasonable time (Art. 8). If the acceptance is late, the offeror may nevertheless consider it to have arrived in due time on condition that he promptly so informs the acceptor orally or by dispatch of a notice.

This Convention is gradually being replaced by the UN Convention on Contracts for the International Sale of Goods (Vienna, 1980) (Art. 99) [see 311.04].

J.-A.L. and V.V.

Access : ALS (Art. VIII, IX)
Reserves : PAU (Art. II, III, IV)
Duration : USP
Deposit. : NL
Language : Eng, Fre

Reference : 834 UNTS – ULR 1964 – UKTS 1972/75 – ILM 3:864 – RCDIP 1965

311.03 – CONVENTION ON THE LIMITATION PERIOD IN THE INTERNATIONAL SALE OF GOODS – UNCITRAL

Concluded: 14.06.1974, New York
In Force : 01.08.1988
Parties : 12

Because of the diversity of national rules governing the limitation period, UNCITRAL elaborated a convention which would unify certain rules on these issues. Its main objective is to "determine when claims of a buyer and a seller against each other arising from a contract of international sale of goods or relating to its breach, termination or invalidity can no longer be exercised by reason of the expiration of a period of time" (Art. 1). Thus, to determine the limitation period in which a claim can be made, the Convention contains rules applicable to only one type of transaction: the buying and selling of goods. It does not apply, among other things, to rights and procedures which are independent of the contract.

The limitation period (four years according to Art. 8) is defined in Article 1 in a manner that is sufficiently neutral to include all existing terminologies relating to the international sale of goods.

Scope: The Convention applies if at the time of the conclusion of a contract the places of business of the parties to the contract are in different contracting states (Arts. 2 and 3). Unless the Convention provides otherwise, it shall apply irrespective of the law which would otherwise be applicable by virtue of the rules of private international law. The latter provision was added in the 1980 Protocol in order to bring the Convention's provisions closer to those of the United Nations Convention on Contracts for the International Sale of Goods (Vienna, 1980) [see 311.04].

Aside from the right of the parties to exclude the application of the Convention (Art. 3-3), the Convention does not apply to certain sales such as auctions, sales of goods bought for personal, family and household use, sales on execution or otherwise by authority of law, sales of stocks, shares, investment securities, negotiable instruments or money, sales of ships, vessels, aircraft, or sales of electricity (Art. 4). Nor does the Convention apply to certain claims based upon a lien, mortgage or other security interest in property; nor to a judgment or award made in legal proceedings, and so on (Art. 5); nor to contracts in which the preponderant part of the seller's obligations consists in the supply of labour or other services (Art. 6).

DETAILS OF THE CONVENTION

The commencement of the four-year limitation period starts on the date at which the claim accrues, and Articles 10 to 12 deal with issues relating to breach of contract: defect, or other lack of conformity, fraud, whether there was an express undertaking related to the goods, and termination of a contract before performance is due.

The limitation period ceases to run when judicial proceedings are undertaken by the creditor (Art. 13), if the parties agree to submit to arbitration (Art. 14), or if legal proceedings are commenced upon the occurrence of the death, bankruptcy, and so on, of the debtor (Art. 15). The same holds true in the case of a counter-claim (Art. 16), if legal proceedings have ended without a decision binding on the merits of the claim (Art. 17), or where proceedings have been commenced against one debtor (Art. 18).

The limitation period is, however, extended in the following cases: where the creditor performs any act, other than the ones described in Articles 13 to 16, which has the effect of recommencing a limitation period (Art. 19); where the debtor recognizes his obligation (Art. 20); where the creditor has been prevented from causing the limitation period to cease to run by circumstances beyond his control (Art. 21); or where the limitation period has been modified by the parties (Art. 22). Notwithstanding the provisions of the Convention, a limitation period shall in any event expire not later than ten years from the date on which it started to run, beyond which it is not possible to begin proceedings (Art. 23). The rules end with provisions on the consequences of the expiration of the limitation period (Art. 24 to 27), on the calculation of the period (Art. 28 and 29) and on the international effect of the limitation period (Art. 30).

J.-A.L. and V.V.

Access : ALS (Art. 41, 43)
Reserves : PAU (Art. 34, 35, 36, 38, 39)
Duration : USP
Deposit. : UN (Art. 46)
Language : Eng, Chi, Fre, Spa, Rus, (Ara) (Art. 46)

Modific. : Protocol Vienna 11.04.80 (01.08.88)

Reference : UN Doc. A/CONF 63/15, A/CONF 97/18 – ULR 1975/1, 1980/1 – ILM 19:696

311.04 – UNITED NATIONS CONVENTION ON CONTRACTS FOR THE INTERNATIONAL SALE OF GOODS ("VIENNA CONVENTION") – UNCITRAL

Concluded : 11.04.1980, Vienna
In Force : 01.01.1988
Parties : 33

Since its creation, UNCITRAL has attempted to unite the 1 July 1964 conventions of The Hague relating respectively to a uniform law on the international sale of goods and to a uniform law on the formation of contracts for the international sale of goods [see 311.01 and 311.02]. Its work resulted in the UN Vienna Conference of 10 March 1980, which ended on 11 April 1980 with the adoption of the UN Convention on Contracts for the International Sale of Goods.

The UN Convention's objectives are to contribute to the removal of legal barriers in international trade and to promote the development of international trade by adopting uniform rules governing contracts for the international sale of goods which take into account different social, economic and legal systems.

DETAILS OF THE CONVENTION

Part I (Arts. 1 to 13) defines the scope of the Convention and contains its general provisions.

Scope: The Convention applies to contracts of sale of goods between parties whose places of business are in different states. Unlike the rule in the 1964 Hague Convention, it is of no relevance whether the goods are carried from the territory of one state to the territory of another or not. The UN Convention does not apply to goods bought for personal, family or household use (Art. 2-1). Public policies in many countries could have caused a refusal to sign the Convention in order to protect consumers' interests. Under Article 6, the parties may exclude the application of the Convention or derogate from its provisions.

Articles 11 to 13 regulate the form of the contract. It need not be concluded in or evidenced by writing and is not subject to any other requirements as to form; it may be proved by any means, including witnesses (Art. 11).

Part II of the Convention deals with the formation of the contract (Arts. 14 to 24) and can be ratified independently of Part III (Arts. 25 to 28) which deals with the sale of goods. The system of "acceptance" of an offer (Arts. 18 to 24) is preferred to that of forwarding it. The Convention then defines the obligations of the offeror, the offeree and the measures to be taken in case of non-performance.

In the same way as the US "Uniform Commercial Code", the Convention in its Articles 35 *ff* deals with conformity of the goods and third party claims and covers both legal irregularities and material defects.

The buyer has an option to fix an additional period of time for performance by the seller of his obligations. This idea is borrowed from the German legal system (viz. "Nachfrist").

Part IV (Art. 89 to 101) of the Convention contains the diplomatic provisions (those relating to ratification, denunciation, etc.).

States which choose to adhere to this Convention must denounce the 1964 Hague conventions [see 311.01 and 311.02], which are incompatible (Art. 99).

The Vienna Convention was supplemented by a Protocol which modified the Convention on the Limitation Period in the International Sale of Goods (New York, 1974) [see 311.03] to bring it closer to the Vienna Convention. It was also supplemented by the Convention on the Law Applicable to Contracts for the International Sale of Goods (The Hague, 1986) [see 312.07].

Bernard Colas

Access : ALS (Art. 91)
Reserves : PAU (Art. 98, 92, 95)
Duration : USP
Deposit. : UN (Art. 89, 92 to 96)
Language : Ara, Chi, Eng, Fre, Rus, Spa

Reference : UN Doc. A/CONF 97/18 – ULR 1980/1 – ILM 19:671 – JORF 22 Dec 87 – RCDIP 1981.383

311.05 – CONVENTION ON AGENCY IN THE INTERNATIONAL SALE OF GOODS – UNIDROIT

Concluded : 15.02.1983, Geneva
Parties : 4

The objective of the Convention is to provide a uniform body of rules to regulate cases in which an individual is empowered to act (or purports to act) as an agent on behalf of another in order to conclude an international contract of sale of goods (Art. 1).

Scope: It applies "only where the principal and the third party have their places of business in different States and the agent has his place of business in a Contracting

State, or [if] the rules of private international law lead to the application of the law of a Contracting State" (Art. 2). The Convention does not apply to the agency of a dealer on stock or commodity exchanges, nor to the agency of an auctioneer.

In general, the agent acts on behalf of the principal within the scope of his authority, and it is assumed that the third party knows of the agency.

DETAILS OF THE CONVENTION

The acts of the agent directly bind the principal and the third party to each other, unless it follows from the circumstances of the case – for example, by a reference to a contract of commission – that the agent undertakes to bind himself only (Art. 12). However, where the agent acts on behalf of a principal within the scope of his authority, his acts bind only the agent and the third party if the third party neither knew nor ought to have known that the agent was acting as an agent, or if it follows from the circumstances that the agent undertakes to bind himself only (Art. 13-1). Nevertheless where, for whatever reason, the agent fails to fulfil or is not in a position to fulfil his obligations to the principal, the principal may exercise against the third party the rights acquired on the principal's behalf by the agent, subject to any defences which the third party may set up against the agent. Similarly, under the same conditions the third party may exercise against the principal the rights which the third party has against the agent (Art. 13-2).

The application of these uniform rules may be excluded partially or completely by agreement between the principal, or an agent acting in accordance with the instructions of the principal, and the third party (Art. 5).

The authorization of the agent by the principal may be express or implied, and it need not be given in or evidenced by writing and is not subject to any other requirement as to form. It may be proved by any means, including witnesses. Authorization must be made in writing, however, where the principal or the agent has his place of business in a contracting state whose legislation requires it.

It should be noted that the principal or the agent on the one hand and the third party on the other are bound by any usage to which they have agreed, and by any practices which they have established between themselves.

This Convention completes the body of uniform rules in the international sale of goods established by the 1964 The Hague conventions [see 311.01 and 311.02] and the 1980 Vienna Convention [see 311.04]. It will enter into force after the deposit of the tenth instrument of ratification, acceptance, approval or accession.

B.C.

Access : ALS (Art. 22)
Reserves : PAU (Art. 25 to 32)
Duration : USP
Deposit. : CH (Art. 21)
Language : Eng, Fre

Reference : ILM 22:249 – JORF 2 Jul 87

311.06 – UNIDROIT CONVENTION ON INTERNATIONAL FACTORING – UNIDROIT

Concluded : 28.05.1988, Ottawa
Party : 1

During a diplomatic Conference held in Ottawa on May 1988, two draft conventions prepared by UNIDROIT governmental committees of experts were adopted by representatives from 55 states. The first applies to financial leasing [see 311.07], and the second contains general legal rules seeking to standardize international factoring. This latter governs international factoring contracts and assignments of receivables.

DETAILS OF THE CONVENTION

For the purposes of this Convention, a "factoring contract" means a contract concluded between one party (the supplier of goods or services) with another party (the factor) pursuant to which the supplier assigns to the factor receivables arising from contracts of sale of goods and services made for commercial ends between the supplier and its customers (debtors), in exchange for which the factor is to perform at least two of the following functions:

- the provision of finance for the supplier;
- maintenance of accounts relating to the receivables;
- collection of receivables; and
- protection against default in payment by debtors.

Notice in writing of the assignment of the receivables is to be given by the supplier to debtors, who are then placed under a duty to pay the factor.

In a claim by the factor against the debtor for payment, the debtor may set up against the factor all defences arising under that contract of which the debtor could have availed itself if such claim had been made by the supplier (Art. 9-1), including the right of set-off (Art. 9-2) or the right to recover the sum from the supplier (Art. 10-1).

Questions which are not expressly settled by the Convention are to be settled in conformity with the rules of private international law (Art. 4-2).

If two or more contracting states have the same or closely related legal rules on matters governed by the Convention, they may declare that the Convention is not to apply where the supplier, the factor and the debtor have their places of business in that or those states.

The UNIDROIT Convention does not prevail over any treaty which has already been or may be entered into (Art. 15). It enters into force after the deposit of the third instrument (Art. 14). To date, France is the only country which has ratified the Convention.

B.C.

Access : ALS (Art. 13)
Reserves : PAU (Art. 20, 16)
Duration : USP
Deposit. : CA (Art. 23)
Language : Eng, Fre

Reference : ILM 27:922

311.07 – UNIDROIT CONVENTION ON INTERNATIONAL FINANCIAL LEASING – UNIDROIT

Concluded : 28.05.1988, Ottawa
Party : 1

The objective of the Convention is to establish certain uniform rules on international financial leasing – that is, when the lessor and the lessee have their places of business in different states.

This Convention governs a financial leasing transaction in which one party (the lessor) enters into two agreements. On the specification of another party (the lessee), the lessor enters into an agreement (the supply agreement) with a third party (the supplier) under which the lessor acquires plant, capital goods or other equipment on terms approved by the lessee and the lessor enters also into an agreement (the leasing agreement) with the lessee, granting to the lessee the right to use the equipment in return for the payment of rentals.

DETAILS OF THE CONVENTION

The lessee must use the equipment in a reasonable manner (Art. 9) in the framework of his commercial (not personal, family or household) activities (Art. 1-4); and, once the leasing agreement comes to an end, he must return the equipment to the lessor (Art. 9-2), who retains real rights in the equipment.

The UNIDROIT Convention is a flexible one. For example, if two or more contracting states have the same or closely related legal rules on matters governed by the Convention they may declare that it is not to apply where the supplier, the lessor and the lessee have their places of business in those states (Art. 19).

A contracting state may declare at the time of signature, ratification, acceptance, approval or accession that it will substitute its domestic law for the rules of the Convention on matters relating to the warranty of quiet possession, if its domestic law does not permit the lessor to exclude its liability for its default or negligence (Art. 20).

Article 18 makes provision for cases in which different systems of law are applicable within a contracting state. The state may, at the time it adheres to the Convention, declare that the Convention will only extend to part of its territory.

In the interpretation of the Convention, regard is to be had to its object and purpose, to its international character and to the need to promote uniformity in its application and the observance of good faith in international trade (Art. 6-1). Questions which are not expressly settled by the Convention are to be settled by the rules of private international law.

The Convention does not prevail over any treaty which has already been or may be entered into. In particular, it does not affect any liability imposed on any person by existing or future treaties (Art. 17). It will enter into force after the deposit of the third instrument of ratification (Art. 16). To date, France is the only country which has ratified the Convention.

B.C.

Access	: ALS (Art. 15)
Reserves	: PAU (Art. 22, 18)
Duration	: USP
Deposit.	: CA (Art. 25)
Language	: Eng, Fre

Reference : ILM 27:922

3.1.2 Conflict of Laws

Another method for resolving problems arising from the diversity of legal systems is to set up common rules on the conflict of laws so that the applicable law designated by the relevant rule in a given situation involving two countries will be the same in both countries. This could be done by the adoption of specific conventions or by the harmonization of private international laws. Conventions are, in fact, used more in this field as model laws for national legislation than as treaties as such. Their influence, therefore, is much more significant than their number of ratifications may indicate. They have all been adopted by The Hague Conference, whose mandate significantly exceeds the economic field. The ones related to international trade concern the following subject matters: international sales of goods [see 312.01 and 312.07], legal personality [see 312.02], transfer of property [see 312.03], products liability [312.04], agency [see 312.05] and trusts [see 312.06].

In this field, attachment to the habitual residence of one or the other of the parties to a contract has been the means of arriving at a general consensus for resolving the conflicting claim of different countries to have their laws govern the transaction.

SELECTED BIBLIOGRAPHY

Audit, Bernard, *Droit International Privé*, Paris: Economica, 1991.

Battifol, Henri and Paul Lagarde, *Droit International Privé*, 7th ed, Paris: LGDJ, Vol. 1, 1981, Vol. 2, 1983.

Castel, J.-G., *Introduction to Conflict of Laws*, 2nd ed, Toronto: Butterworths, 1986.

Cheshire & North, *Private International Law*, 11th ed, by M. North and J.J. Fawcett, London: Butterworths, 1987.

Collier, J.G., *Conflicts of Laws*, Cambridge: Cambridge University Press, 1987.

Collins, L., *Dicey and Morris on the Conflict of Laws*, London: Stevens & Sons, 1987.

Lipstein, K., *Principles of the Conflict of Laws, National and International*, Dordrecht: Martinus Nijhoff Publishers, 1981.

Mayer, Pierre, *Droit International Privé*, 4th ed, Paris: Montchrestien, 1991.

312.01 – CONVENTION ON THE LAW APPLICABLE TO INTERNATIONAL SALES OF GOODS – HCOPIL

Concluded : 15.06.1955, The Hague
In Force : 01.09.1964
Parties : 9

The objective of the Convention is to establish common provisions concerning the law applicable to the international sale of goods (Art. 1).

Scope: The Convention does not apply to the sales of securities, ships, registered boats, aircraft, or to sales upon judicial order or by way of execution (Art. 1). Nor does the Convention apply to the capacity of the parties, the form of the contract, the transfer of ownership, or the effects of the sale as regards all persons other than the parties (Art. 5).

DETAILS OF THE CONVENTION

The contracting states agree to the incorporation of certain provisions of the Convention relating to private international law into their national laws (Art. 7).

These provisions relate to the formation and execution of contracts of sale. According to Article 2: "A sale shall be governed by the domestic law of the country designated by the Contracting Parties". In default of a law declared applicable by the parties, a sale is governed by the domestic law of the country in which the vendor has his habitual residence at the time when he receives the order.

Nevertheless, a sale is governed by the domestic law of the country in which the purchaser has his habitual residence, or in which he has the establishment that has given the order, if the order has been received in that country by the vendor or by his representative, agent or commercial traveller (Art. 3). In case of a sale at a stock exchange or at a public auction, the sale shall be governed by the domestic law of the country in which the stock exchange is situated or the auction takes place.

In each of the contracting states, the application of the law determined by the Convention may be excluded on public policy grounds (Art. 6).

Bernard Colas

Access : ALS (Art. 11)
Reserves : USP (Art. 10)
Duration : REN 5 (Art. 12)
Deposit. : NL
Language : Fre

Reference : 510 UNTS – HCOPIL Col. 1988 – RCDIP 1964.786 – RTAF 1964/58 – JDI 1964 – JORF 13 Aug 64

312.02 – CONVENTION CONCERNING RECOGNITION OF THE LEGAL PERSONALITY OF FOREIGN COMPANIES, ASSOCIATIONS AND FOUNDATIONS – HCOPIL

Concluded : 01.06.1956, The Hague
Parties : 3

The objective of the Convention is to establish common provisions concerning recognition of the legal personality of foreign companies, associations and foundations. According to Article 1, each of the contracting states recognizes the right of the legal personality of foreign companies, associations and foundations acquired in pursuance of the law of one of the contracting states, as long as this personality has the capacity to institute legal proceedings, or at least to possess property and to perform contracts and other legal acts.

Nevertheless, when the laws of a contracting state take into consideration the effective headquarters (*siège réel*) – the place where the central administration of an enterprise is located – to determine its legal personality, this criterion will prevail (Art. 2).

The recognizing state may regulate the extent to which foreign companies, associations or foundations may own property on its territory, but the personality must include the right to institute legal proceedings (Art. 5). If a recognizing state approves the establishment, operation and the exercise of permanent activity of a foreign company, association or foundation on its territory, their activities are governed by the law of this state (Art. 7).

In every contracting state, the application of the provisions of the Convention can be excluded if public order is threatened (Art. 8).

B.C.

Access : ALS (Art. 13)
Reserves : USP (Art. 12)
Duration : REN 5 (Art. 14)
Deposit. : NL
Language : Fre

Reference : HCOPIL Rec. 1988 – RCDIP 1951.727

312.03 – CONVENTION ON THE LAW APPLICABLE TO TRANSFER OF PROPERTY IN CASE OF INTERNATIONAL SALES OF GOODS – HCOPIL

Concluded : 15.04.1958, The Hague
Party : 1

The Convention determines the law applicable to property transfer in the case of international sales of goods, as defined by the Convention of 15 June 1955 on the law applicable to the international sale of goods [see 312.01]. The Convention designates the law applicable to the contract between the parties. For third parties, the applicable law is the law of the country where the goods are located.

The Convention is unlikely to become effective as only one party has ratified it since its conclusion in 1958; under Article 12, the deposit of five instruments is required.

B.C.

Access : ALS (Art. 14)
Reserves : PAU (Art. 3, 5, 10)
Duration : REN 5 (Art. 15)
Deposit. : NL
Language : Fre

Reference : RCDIP 1964 – HCOPIL Col. 1988

312.04 – CONVENTION ON THE LAW APPLICABLE TO PRODUCTS LIABILITY – HCOPIL

Concluded : 02.10.1973, The Hague
In Force : 01.10.1977
Parties : 6

The Convention establishes common provisions on the law applicable, in international cases, to products liability. It applies to the liability of manufacturers, producers of a national product, suppliers of a product and other persons included in the commercial chain of preparation or distribution of a product, including repairers and warehousemen, their agents or employees.

It sets conditions for determining whether the applicable law is the law of the state of the habitual residence of the person directly suffering damage, the law of the state of the place of inquiry or, if not applicable, the law of the state of the principal place of business of the person claimed to be liable. These conditions shall not preclude consideration being given to the rules of conduct and safety prevailing in the state where the product was introduced into the market. The application of the law declared applicable may be refused only where such application would be manifestly incompatible with public policy.

B.C.

Access : ALS (Art. 17, 18)
Reserves : PAU (Art. 14, 16)
Duration : REN 5 (Art. 21)
Deposit. : NL
Language : Eng, Fre

Reference : 1056 UNTS – HCOPIL Doc. 1988 – JORF 3 Nov 77 – RTAF 1977/82

312.05 – CONVENTION ON THE LAW APPLICABLE TO AGENCY – HCOPIL

Concluded : 14.03.1978, The Hague
In Force : 01.05.1992
Parties : 4

The Convention determines the law applicable to relationships of an international character arising when a person, the agent, has the authority to act, acts, or purports to act on behalf of another person, the principal, in dealing with a third party (Art. 1).

The Convention governs the three types of juridical relationships resulting from agency. The contractual relationship between the principal and the agent is distinct from the one concluded between the agent, acting on behalf of the principal, and the third party.

DETAILS OF THE CONVENTION

Principal and Agent. The domestic law chosen by the principal and the agent shall govern the agency relationship between them. In so far as the applicable law has not been chosen, however, the applicable law shall be the internal law of the state where the agent has his business establishment. The law of the place where the agent is primarily to act shall apply if the principal has his business establishment, or if he has none, his habitual residence, in that state.

Principal and Third Party. The relationship between the principal and the third party is subject to the law governing the contract between the agent and the third party. The Convention only addresses the question as to whether the agent acted on behalf of the principal, notably in cases where the agent exceeded his authority or acted without authority. As between the principal and the third party, the existence and extent of the agent's authority and the effects of the agent's exercise or purported exercise of his authority shall be governed by the internal law of the state in which the agent had his business at the time of the relevant acts. Nevertheless, the internal law of the state in which the agent acts is preferred if the conditions set out in Article 11-2 apply, and if it appears that it is this law that the principal and the agent agreed on.

Agent and Third Party. The law governing the relationship between the principal and the agent governs also the relationship between the agent and the third party arising from the fact that the agent has acted with or without authority.

B.C.

Access : ALS (Art. 24)
Reserves : USP
Duration : REN 5 (Art. 27)
Deposit. : NL
Language : Eng, Fre

Reference : ULR 1978/2 – ILM 16:775 – HCOPIL Rec. 1988 – RCDIP 1977.639

312.06 – CONVENTION ON THE LAW APPLICABLE TO TRUSTS AND ON THEIR RECOGNITION – HCOPIL

Concluded : 01.07.1985, The Hague
In Force : 01.01.1992
Parties : 3

The objective of the Convention is to establish the common provisions on the law applicable to trusts found in countries with a tradition of common law, and to deal with the most important issues concerning the recognition of trusts. It attempts to bridge the gap between countries with different legal traditions. It also allows countries with a civil law tradition to recognize Anglo-American trusts, except in cases where it is incompatible with public policy.

The term "trust" refers to the legal relationships created – *inter vivos* or on death – by a person, the settlor, when assets have been placed under the control of a trustee for the benefit of a beneficiary or for a specified purpose. The trustee has title to the trust assets, nevertheless the assets are not part of the trustee's own estate (Art. 2).

Scope: The Convention applies only to trusts created voluntarily and evidenced in writing (Art. 3). It can also extend to cases where a contracting state declares that the Convention's provisions will be extended to trusts declared by judicial decisions (Art. 20).

DETAILS OF THE CONVENTION

According to Chapter II on the applicable law, a trust shall be governed by the law chosen by the settlor; where no applicable law has been chosen, a trust shall be governed by the law with which it is most closely connected (Arts. 6 and 7). This law shall govern the validity of the trust, its construction, its effects, and the administration of the trust (Art. 8). Nevertheless, the Convention does not apply if the law specified by Chapter II does not provide for trusts or the category of trusts involved (Art. 5).

A trust created in accordance with the law specified by Chapter II shall be recognized as a trust according to Chapter III. This recognition will imply, as a minimum, that the trust property constitutes a separate fund, that the trustee may sue or be sued in his capacity as a trustee, and that he may appear or act in this capacity before a notary or any person acting in an official capacity (Art. 11). Where the trustee desires to register assets, movable or immovable, or documents of title to them, he shall be entitled to do so in his capacity as a trustee (Art. 12).

Finally, any contracting state may reserve the right to apply the provisions of Chapter III, on the recognition of trusts, only to trusts governed by the law of a contracting state (Art. 21).

B.C.

Access : ALS (Art. 26)
Reserves : PAU (Art. 16, 21, 22, 26)
Duration : USP
Deposit. : NL
Language : Eng, Fre

Reference : ILM 23:1388 – ULR 1985/1 – DJI 1986 – HCOPIL Rec. 1988 – RCDIP 1984.771

312.07 – CONVENTION ON THE LAW APPLICABLE TO CONTRACTS FOR THE INTERNATIONAL SALE OF GOODS – HCOPIL

Concluded : 22.12.1986, The Hague
Party : 1

This Convention was designed to replace the Convention on the Law Applicable to International Sales of Goods (The Hague, 1955) [see 312.01], which was only partly successful. The present Convention, which deals with the choice of legal rules, supplements the UN Convention on Contracts for the International Sale of Goods (Vienna, 1980) [see 311.04].

The objective of the Convention is to unify the choice of legal rules relating to contracts for the international sale of goods, and it is applicable between parties having their places of business in different states. The Convention does not apply to sales by execution or otherwise by authority of law; sales of stocks, shares, investment securities, negotiable instruments or money; sales of goods bought for personal, family or household use (Art. 2); and contracts in which the predominant part of the obligations of the party who furnishes the goods consists of the supply of labour or other services (Art. 4).

DETAILS OF THE CONVENTION

On determining the applicable law (Arts. 7-11), a distinction is made between whether the law is determined by the parties or not:

Law determined by the parties. Article 7 stipulates that "a contract of sale is governed by the law chosen by the parties", thereby indicating the subjective nature of the choice of the applicable law. The parties' agreement to this choice must be express or clearly demonstrated by the terms of the contract or the conduct of the parties, and such a choice may be limited to a part of the contract. In addition, the parties may at any time agree to subject the contract in whole or in part to a law other than that which previously governed it, without it prejudicing its formal validity or the rights of third parties.

Law not determined by the parties. If the law applicable to a contract of sale has not been chosen by the parties, the contract is governed by the law of the state where the seller has his place of business at the time of the contract's conclusion (Art. 8-1). However, the contract is governed by the law of the state where the buyer has his place of business at the time of the conclusion of the contract if any of three exceptions, listed in Article 8-2, apply: first, if negotiations were conducted, and the contract concluded between the parties took place in that state; second, if the contract provides expressly that the seller must perform his obligation to deliver the goods in that state; or, third, if the contract was concluded on terms determined mainly by the buyer and in response to an invitation directed by the buyer to persons invited to bid.

Also, by way of exception and in the light of the circumstances as a whole, Article 8-3 states that the contract may be governed by another law manifestly more closely connected than the law which would otherwise be applicable. A number of countries have objected to this provision, and under Article 21 they are entitled to formally voice their reservations towards it.

Finally, as relates to such sales by auction or on a commodity or other exchange, Article 9 stipulates that the law governing the sales is that chosen by the parties, to the extent to which the law of the state where the auction or exchange takes place does not prohibit such a choice.

Article 11 distinguishes between different types of contracts of sale; two of them are:

- where the contract of sale is concluded between persons who are in the same state (it is valid if it satisfies the requirements either of the law which governs it under the Convention or the law of the state where it is concluded);
- where the contract of sale is concluded between persons who are in different states (it is valid if it satisfies the requirements either of the law which governs it under the Convention or of the law of one of those states).

Nevertheless, a contracting state may, under Articles 11-5 and 21-1-c, formally voice its reservations towards the validity of contracts of sale; therefore, in such a case, contracts will not be valid where a state's legislation requires that contracts of sale be concluded in or evidenced by writing, and where any party has his place of business in its territory at the time of conclusion of the contract.

The law applicable to a contract of sale (Art. 12) governs, among other things, the interpretation of the contract, the rights and obligations of the parties and the performance of the contract.

The Convention shall enter into force after five states have ratified it (Art. 27). To date, Argentina is the only country which has ratified the Convention.

Jean-André Lasserre and Vladimir Vasak

Access : ALS (Art. 25)
Reserves : PAU (Art. 21)
Duration : USP
Deposit. : NL
Language : Eng, Fre

Reference : ILM 24:1573 – ULR 1986/1 – HCOPIL Rec. 1988 – DJI 1986 – JORF 22 Dec 87

3.1.3 Standard Provisions

Many bodies have worked out standard terms, clauses and conditions in order to facilitate international transactions. The most widely used are those of the ICC, such as Incoterms [see 313.01], which parties can make reference to in contracts. Being widely applied and uniformly interpreted, they often reflect international trade customary practices.

SELECTED BIBLIOGRAPHY

Derains, Yves and Jacques Ghestin (eds.), *La Convention de Vienne sur la Vente Internationale et les Incoterms: Actes du Colloque des 1 et 2 Décembre 1989*, Paris: LGDJ, 1990.

Eisemann, Frédéric and Yves Derains, *La Pratique des Incoterms*, Paris: Jupiter, 1988.

Ramberg, Jan, *Guide to Incoterms 1990*, Paris: ICC Publishing, Publication no. 461/90, 1991.

Schmitthoff, Clive, *Export Trade: The Laws and Practice of International Trade*, Ch. 2, 8th ed, London: Stevens and Sons, 1986.

313.01 – INCOTERMS (INTERNATIONAL RULES FOR THE INTERPRETATION OF TRADE TERMS) – ICC

Adopted : 26.06.1936, ICC Res.

Incoterms are a series of universally recognized definitions of trade terms (examples include FOB, CIF, Ex Works or Delivery Duty Paid), developed by the International Chamber of Commerce (ICC) [see 300 D] for use in international trade transactions. By referring to Incoterms in their contracts, the buyer and seller can specify their respective rights and obligations and can avoid subsequent disagreements.

The first Incoterms were published in 1936. In response to changes in international trade they have been amended several times – in 1953, 1967, 1976, 1980 and in 1990.

The Incoterms deal with four categories of questions regarding relations between buyer and seller in contracts that call for the transfer of goods between parties in at least two countries:

- the delivery of goods;
- the passing of risks;
- the allocation of costs; and
- customs clearance.

Incoterms always give precedence to specific clauses inserted in a contract by the parties. Incoterms can be modified or added to according to the needs of the parties. However, in order to be clear, the parties are recommended to avoid standard abbreviations used in their own countries as these may not be in common use in international trade. The parties should also pay particular attention to the use of variations of "C" terms as courts might refuse to recognize a given modification or have difficulty in interpreting it.

When it is impossible to establish an absolute rule, Incoterms specify that trade usages should apply.

Incoterms only apply to contracts concerning buyers and sellers and therefore do not affect either directly or indirectly the parties' relations with the carrier as defined in the transport contract. The law on carriage of goods determines the way in which the seller must fulfil his obligation to deliver the goods to the carrier.

Sarah Williams

Access : ENT
Language : Eng, Fre

Modific. : (1953); (1967); (1976); (1980); (1990)

Reference : ICC Pub. no. 460

313.02 – INTERNATIONAL MARKETING CODES – ICC

Adopted : 1937, ICC Res.

The ICC has adopted international codes both for advertising practice and sales promotion, which appeared for the first time in 1937 and 1973 respectively, as well as a series of more specific codes. The Codes are essentially instruments of self-regulation; they are also designed to be used by courts.

The Code for Advertising Practice. This Code and its annex constitute rules of conduct for advertising in respect of all products, services and commodities, including advertising brand names. The advertiser, the advertising agency and the publisher are required to respect rules which cover good taste (Art. 1), fairness (Arts. 2, 3), truthfulness (Art. 4), comparison (Art. 5), claims (Art. 6), denigration (Art. 7), protection of privacy (Art. 8), exploitation of commercial reputation (Art. 9), and imitation (Art. 10).

The rules cover the following basic principles: "All advertising must be planned with a proper sense of social reponsibility and must conform to the principles of fair competition so that the principles are generally admitted into commercial practice. An advertising message must not debase the trust which the public must always have in advertising". This code of self-discipline is applied, at national level, by bodies created for this purpose and, at international level, by the ICC International Council for Marketing Practice (Art. 19).

The Code of Practice for Sales Promotion. This Code, created in 1973, applies to procedures and techniques of marketing used to give an added attraction to products or services – for example, the use of free offers or reduced prices, or the distribution of coupons, vouchers or samples. The promoter is responsible for a promotion but so too is the marketing director or consultant, as well as the intermediary who participates in the promotion, and the supplier of any complementary products included in the sales promotion.

RECENT DEVELOPMENTS

The ICC has developed guidelines for ethical conduct, along the lines of the above Codes, in the following specific areas:

(1) Direct Marketing: The **ICC Code on Direct Marketing** (1991);
(2) Environmental Advertising: The **ICC Code on Environmental Advertising** (1991);
(3) Sponsorship: The **ICC Code on Sponsorship** (1992).

S.W.

Access : ENT
Language : Eng, Fre, Spa

Modific. : Code of Practice for Sales Promotion (1973)

Reference : ICC Pub. no. 432 A, 432 B

313.03 – UNIFORM CUSTOMS FOR CONTRACT GUARANTEES – ICC

Adopted : 1978, ICC Res.

In 1978, the ICC developed uniform rules for contractual guarantees (Publication No. 325). The rules were created to achieve a fair balance between the importers' and exporters' interests. Use and application of the rules is optional. They constitute a formula half-way between a classic guarantee and a first demand guarantee which offers the parties pre-established solutions to problems which arise frequently in this field.

Unfortunately, the rules have failed to achieve wide acceptance and are used almost exclusively on the European market. First demand guarantees have recently been dealt with in the 1992 Uniform Rules for Demand Guarantees (ICC Publication No. 458) [see 322.03].

S.W.

Access : ENT
Language : Eng, Fre

Reference : ICC Pub. no. 325

313.04 – PROVISIONS CONCERNING A UNIT OF ACCOUNT – UNCITRAL

Adopted : 16.12.1982, UNGA Res.107(XXXVII)

Many international conventions on transport or on liability contain provisions on the limitation of liability in which the latter is expressed as a unit of account. Since reference to gold as a unit of account proved uncertain, due to the way it was calculated, UNCITRAL recommended that it be replaced by Special Drawing Rights (SDRs), as defined by the IMF [see 211 A]. The equivalence between the national currency of a contracting state and the SDR is to be calculated according to a method of valuation defined in the text.

The draft clauses, which would be used in future international conventions, also attempt to offset the risk of monetary depreciation over the years which would affect the amounts expressed in gold. UNCITRAL recommends two types of clauses to which the parties can resort. The alternative provisions are either to revise limitation on liability by using a price index or using a sample amendment procedure.

Vladimir Vasak and Jean-André Lasserre

Language : Ara, Chi, Eng, Fre, Rus, Spa

313.05 – UNIFORM RULES ON CONTRACT CLAUSES FOR AN AGREED SUM DUE UPON FAILURE OF PERFORMANCE – UNCITRAL

Adopted : 19.12.1983, UNGA Res.135(XXXVIII)

Because parties to international commercial contracts were increasingly resorting to clauses forcing other parties to pay an agreed sum for failure of performance of contractual obligations, UNCITRAL attempted in the Uniform Rules to harmonize the effects and the validity of this action which the differences between common law and civil law made disparate.

Scope: The Uniform Rules "apply to international contracts in which the parties have agreed that, upon failure of performance by one party (the obligor) the other party (the obligee) is entitled to an agreed sum from the obligor, whether as a penalty or as compensation" (Art. 1). Articles 2 and 3 define international contracts: if at the time of the conclusion of the contract, the parties have their places of business in different states, a contract is considered international. The place of business is considered in relation to the contract itself. The Rules do not apply to contracts concerning goods, other property or services which are to be supplied for the personal, family or household purposes of a party (Art. 4).

DETAILS OF THE RULES

On matters of substance, the Rules attempt to determine the consequences of such clauses on a contract, beginning with the liability of the obligor on failure of performance. If the contract provides that the obligee is entitled to the agreed sum upon delay in performance, he is entitled to both performance of the obligation and the agreed sum (Art. 6-1). If the contract provides that the obligee is entitled to the agreed sum upon a failure of performance other than delay, he is entitled either to performance or to the agreed sum, unless the agreed sum cannot reasonably be regarded as compensation for that failure of performance. In that case, Article 6-2 states that the obligee is entitled to both performance of the obligation and the agreed sum. The obligee may claim damages to the extent of the loss not covered by the agreed sum if the loss substantially exceeds the agreed sum (Art. 7).

In exceptional cases, a court or an arbitral tribunal may reduce the agreed sum if it is substantially disproportionate to the loss that has been suffered by the obligee (Art. 8). The parties may derogate from or vary the effect of Articles 5, 6 and 7 of the Rules.

V.V. and J.-A.L.

Language : Ara, Chi, Eng, Fre, Rus, Spa

313.06 – UNIFORM RULES OF CONDUCT FOR INTERCHANGE OF TRADE DATA BY TELETRANSMISSION – ICC

Adopted : 22.09.1987, ICC Res.

In law, the traditional paper document is accepted as proof of a transaction because it is material. However, an electronic document or message is different, as it is viewed as only existing inside the computer. Moreover, the information in an electronic document or message can be modified at any time, allowing changes or additions to appear without anyone knowing that they have been made.

The ICC, in collaboration with organizations such as the EC, UN [see 001 A], CCC [see 112 A], ISO [see 152 C] and OECD, has produced a code of conduct to facilitate the exchange of commercial information by teletransmission. The rules are designed to cover the exchange of commercial information between parties using an acknowledged protocol based on international standards for electronic data interchange (EDI).

A message can carry one or several commercial transactions. It must contain proper identification for each transaction to provide the means for verifying that the message is complete and correct. The transfer must identify the sender and the receiver; it must also contain the means of verifying the integrity and authenticity of the transfer. Each party must keep a chronological record of transfers of commercial information sent and received, without modifications, to provide a faithful record of the transfers.

Sarah Williams

Access : ENT
Language : Eng, Fre, Spa

Reference : ICC Pub. no. 452

3.2 Payment Mechanisms

Negotiable instruments have also been subject to unification of laws and practices. This section deals with bills of exchange, promissory notes and cheques [see 3.2.1] and with documentary credits and guarantees [see 3.2.2].

3.2.1 Bills of Exchange, Promissory Notes and Cheques

The efficacy of payment instruments internationally is particularly sensitive to the diversity of national rules. The most radical attempt to solve this problem was pursued in the 1930s by the Geneva conventions which led the drive to globally harmonize laws on bills of exchange and promissory notes [see 321.01 and 321.03] and cheques [see 321.04 and 321.06]. These conventions were complemented by treaties on conflicts of laws dealing with their subject matter [see 321.02 and 321.05]. Based on the French and German regulations, these Geneva conventions have failed to attract the common law countries whose laws closely follow the English Bills of Exchange Act of 1882, which is also the source for Article 3 of the Uniform Commercial Code of the United States. Recently, UNCITRAL prepared a convention which is less ambitious than the previous attempts at a general unification of the law of bills of exchange and cheques. It is confined to instruments used in international transactions and gives the parties an option as to whether they wish the uniform rules to apply or not.

SELECTED BIBLIOGRAPHY

Bloch, P., *Les Lettres de Change et Billet à Ordre dans les Relations Commerciales Internationales*, Paris: Economica, 1986.

Kurkela, Matti, *Letters of Credit under International Trade Law: UCC, UCP and Law Merchant*, Dobbs Ferry, N.Y.: Oceana Publications, 1985.

321.01 – CONVENTION PROVIDING A UNIFORM LAW FOR BILLS OF EXCHANGE AND PROMISSORY NOTES, AND PROTOCOL – LN

Concluded : 07.06.1930, Geneva
In Force : 01.01.1934
Parties : 20

To help solve certain disputes resulting from the discrepancies between different national laws on bills of exchange and promissory notes, the contracting parties undertake to introduce a uniform law composed of 118 articles which are reproduced in Annex I of the Convention. Nevertheless, the contracting parties are permitted to formulate reservations as stipulated in Annex II. A Protocol to the Convention regulates its implementation.

According to Article 1 of the Uniform Law, a bill of exchange must, in principle, contain the words "bill of exchange" in its title, as well as an unconditional order to the debtor (drawee) to pay the beneficiary a determinate sum of money at a given date and place. It must be signed by the creditor who issues the instrument and must indicate the date and place where the bill of exchange was issued.

Article 75 of the Convention contains the same requirements in regard to promissory notes, with the additional stipulation that the promise of payment must include a specific date, place, and beneficiary.

Finally, the other clauses of the Uniform Law regulate the creation and practice of the following commercial operations: endorsement, acceptance, "avals", maturity, payment, recourse for non-acceptance or non-payment, intervention, parts of a set and copies, alterations, and limitation of actions.

Bernard Colas

Access : ALS (Art. II,V)
Reserves : USP (Art. X)
Duration : USP
Deposit. : LN, UN (Art. IV)
Language : Eng, Fre (Art. III)

Reference : 143 LNTS – JORF 24 Oct 36

321.02 – CONVENTION FOR THE SETTLEMENT OF CERTAIN CONFLICTS OF LAWS IN CONNECTION WITH BILLS OF EXCHANGE AND PROMISSORY NOTES, AND PROTOCOL – LN

Concluded : 07.06.1930, Geneva
In Force : 01.01.1934
Parties : 20

Anticipating the rise of legal disputes, the drafters of the 1930 Geneva Uniform Law [see 321.01] tried to remedy it by drafting a second convention. It contains 20 articles and settles only conflicts of laws.

Two stable factors exist in regard to all bills of exchange and promissory notes: there is a place where the instrument was issued and a place where it is to be paid. The applicable law which governs bills of exchange and promissory note transactions is the following: for the drawer, it is the law of the place where the instrument is issued; for the endorser, it is the law of the place where the instrument is endorsed; and for the drawee, it is the law of the place where the instrument is accepted.

Article 2-1 stipulates: "the capacity of a person to bind himself by a bill of exchange or a promissory note shall be determined by his national law. If this national law provides that the law of another country is competent in the matter, this latter law shall be applied". Since the Convention is silent on the rules applied to consent and consideration, it is necessary to apply the general principles of private international law here.

Article 3 stipulates that: "the form of any contract arising out of a bill of exchange or promissory note is regulated by the laws of the territory in which the contract has been signed".

The law of the state where the instrument was created determines the limits of time for the exercise of rights of recourse (Art. 5), and determines also whether there has been an assignment to the holder of the debt which has given rise to the issue (Art. 6). The forms and the limits of the time for protest are regulated by the laws of the country in which the protest must be drawn (Art. 8).

The effects of the obligations of the acceptor of the bill of exchange or maker of a promissory note are determined by the law of the place in which they are payable (Art. 4).

Normally, a bill of exchange is payable in the currency of the place of payment, based upon the daily exchange rate on the due date.

B.C.

Access : ALS (Art. 12,14)
Reserves : PAU (Art. 10)
Duration : USP
Deposit. : LN, UN (Art. 13)
Language : Eng, Fre (Art. 12)

Reference : 143 LNTS – JORF 24 Oct 36 – RCDIP 1930.543

321.03 – CONVENTION ON THE STAMP LAWS IN CONNECTION WITH BILLS OF EXCHANGE AND PROMISSORY NOTES, AND PROTOCOL – LN

Concluded : 07.06.1930, Geneva
In Force : 01.01.1934
Parties : 30

This Convention completes the two other conventions of 1930 which deal with bills of exchange and promissory notes [see 321.01 and 321.02], and ensures that one of the contracting parties will not subordinate the validity of obligations arising out of a bill of exchange or a promissory note to the observance of provisions concerning the stamp (tax) law. The contracting parties may, nevertheless, suspend the exercise of these rights until payment of the stamp duties.

They may also decide that the quality and effects of an instrument "immediately executory", which according to their legislation may be attributed to a bill of exchange or promissory note, shall be subject to the condition that the stamp law has, from the issue of the instrument, been duly complied with in accordance with their laws.

B.C.

Access : ALS (Art. 2,4)
Reserves : PAU (Art. 1-3)
Duration : USP
Deposit. : LN, UN
Language : Eng, Fre (Art. 2)

Reference : 143 LNTS – JORF 24 Oct 36 – UKTS 1934/14

321.04 – CONVENTION PROVIDING A UNIFORM LAW FOR CHEQUES – LN

Concluded : 19.03.1931, Geneva
In Force : 01.01.1934
Parties : 21

A cheque is generally defined as a bill of exchange drawn on a banker, payable on demand to the holder of the cheque at whose disposal there exists a certain sum of money. Like a bill of exchange, it is a negotiable instrument. However, it is issued for immediate execution and not as an instrument of credit. Cheques are seldom used internationally, and travellers' cheques are not generally considered to be cheques.

The Convention consists of four documents: the Convention, in which "the High Contracting Parties undertake to introduce in their respective territories, either in one of the original texts or in their own languages, the Uniform Law forming Annex I of the present Convention"; Annex I, which contains the Uniform Law (56 articles); Annex II containing the reservations; and finally the Protocol providing for the reciprocal exchange of information between the signatories.

DETAILS OF THE CONVENTION

According to Article 1, a cheque must contain the following: the word "cheque" must appear within the body of the instrument; an unconditional order to pay a determinate sum of money; the name of the person who is to pay (drawee); a statement of the day and place where the cheque is issued; and the signature of the person who draws the cheque (drawer).

A cheque may be transferred by means of endorsement (Chapter II), and its payment may be guaranteed by an "aval".

A cheque is payable at sight (Art. 28). A cheque payable in the country in which it was issued must be presented for payment within eight days; when a cheque is issued in a country other than the one in which it is payable it must be presented within a period of 20 days or 70 days, depending on whether the place of issue and the place of payment are situated in the same continent or in different continents (Art. 29).

If a cheque presented in due time is not paid, and if the refusal to pay is evidenced by a formal instrument or protest, or by a declaration from the drawee, or by a declaration from a clearing house, the holder may exercise his right of recourse against the endorsers, the drawers, and the other parties liable (Chapter VI). Recourse is barred after six months from the expiration of the time permitted for presentment.

B.C.

Access : ALS (Art. III)
Reserves : PAU (Art. Annex II)
Duration : USP
Deposit. : LN, UN (Art. IV)
Language : Eng, Fre (Art. III)

Reference : 143 LNTS – JORF 24 Oct 36

321.05 – CONVENTION FOR THE SETTLEMENT OF CERTAIN CONFLICTS OF LAWS IN CONNECTION WITH CHEQUES, AND PROTOCOL – LN

Concluded : 19.03.1931, Geneva
In Force : 01.01.1934
Parties : 21

The objective of the Convention is limited to a settlement of conflicts of laws in regard to cheques. Tax laws and conflicts pertaining to penal law, whose solutions must be found in common law, are excluded.

The capacity of a person to bind himself by a cheque shall be determined by his national law (Art. 2), and the law of the country in which the cheque is payable determines the persons on whom a cheque may be drawn (Art. 3). If under this law the instrument is not valid as a cheque by reason of the person on whom it is drawn, the obligations arising out of the signatures affixed thereto in other countries whose laws provide otherwise shall nevertheless be valid (Art. 3-2), and this so as to validate the cheques as often as possible.

Article 4 regulates the form of the cheque and offers an option between the place where the contract was concluded and the place of payment. This is to ensure validation.

Under Article 5, "the law of the country in whose territory the obligations arising out of a cheque have been assumed shall determine the effects of such obligations"; and under Article 6, "the limits of time for the exercise of rights of recourse shall be determined for all signatories by the law of the place where the instrument was created". Finally, the holder's rights to the cover, the limit of time for presentment, and the measures to be taken in case of loss or theft are determined by the law of the country in which the cheque is payable (Art. 7).

B.C.

Access : ALS (Art. 2)
Reserves : PAU (Art. 9)
Duration : USP
Deposit. : LN, UN (Art. 12)
Language : Eng, Fre (Art. 2)

Reference : 143 LNTS – JORF 24 Oct 36 – RCDIP 1936.260

321.06 – CONVENTION ON THE STAMP LAWS IN CONNECTION WITH CHEQUES – LN

Concluded : 19.03.1931, Geneva
In Force : 29.11.1933
Parties : 31

This Convention complements the two previous conventions relating to cheques [see 321.04 and 321.05] and provides for the standardization of the stamp laws of the contracting parties, in an identical way to the Convention on bills of exchange and promissory notes [see 312.03].

The contracting parties undertake to alter their laws so that the validity of obligations arising over cheques or the exercise of the rights that flow therefrom shall not be subordinated to the observation of the provisions concerning the stamp (Art. 1).

Nevertheless, the contracting parties may suspend the exercise of these rights until the payment of stamp duties or the payment of any penalties incurred. They can also decide that the quality and effects of the cheque will be subject to the condition that the stamp has, from the issue of the instrument, been duly complied with in accordance with their laws.

B.C.

Access : ALS (Art. 4)
Reserves : USP (Art. 9)
Duration : USP
Deposit. : LN, UN (Art. 3)
Language : Eng, Fre (Art. 2)

Reference : 143 LNTS – UKTS 1933/26 – JORF 24 Oct 36

321.07 – UNITED NATIONS CONVENTION ON INTERNATIONAL BILLS OF EXCHANGE AND INTERNATIONAL PROMISSORY NOTES – UNCITRAL

Adopted : 09.12.1988, UNGA Res.43/165
Parties : 2

The Convention was adopted by the Sixth Committee of the UN General Assembly on 21 November 1988, and by the UN General Assembly on 9 December 1988. Its objective is to create an instrument which can be used in international trade and which can circulate freely between states with different legal systems.

A bill of exchange, as defined by the Convention, is a written instrument which contains an unconditional order whereby the drawer directs the drawee to pay a definite sum of money to the payee or to his order; it is payable on demand or at a definitive time, and is dated and signed by the drawer (Art. 3-1). A promissory note is a written instrument which contains an unconditional promise whereby the maker undertakes to pay a definite sum of money to the payee or to his order. It is payable on demand or at a definite time, and is dated and signed by the maker (Art. 3-2).

Scope: The Convention applies to an international bill of exchange or promissory note when it contains in both the heading and body of the instrument's text the words "International Bill of Exchange (UNCITRAL Convention)" or "International Promissory Note (UNCITRAL Convention)". Parties adhering to these guidelines thus freely chose to implement the rules established by the Convention rather than those embodied in national laws (such as was provided by the Uniform Law annexed to the 1930 Geneva Convention).

DETAILS OF THE CONVENTION

To comply with a criterion of internationalism, the Convention specifies that an international bill of exchange is one in which the place where the bill is drawn and the place of payment must be located in two different states, one of which is a party to the Convention; in regard to promissory notes, the place of payment must be in a contracting state other than the place where the promissory note was made.

Once these conditions are met, the regulations of the Convention continue to apply, even if the instrument circulates within the territory of a contracting state. In the territory of a non-contracting state, the regulations apply if they are the appropriate law as determined by private international law.

Chapter II of the Convention sets down rules for interpretation, while Chapter III deals with the transfer of the instruments. Chapter IV sets down the rights and liabilities of a holder and a protected holder (Section 1), the signatories including the drawer, the maker, the drawee and the acceptor, the endorser, the transferor by endorsement or by mere delivery, and the guarantor (Section 3). Chapter V deals with presentment, dishonour by non-acceptance or non-payment, and recourse; Chapter VI with discharge (by payment or otherwise); and Chapter VII with lost instruments.

The Convention was open for signature by all states until 30 June 1990, and will enter into force on the first day of the month following the expiration of 12 months after the date of deposit of the tenth instrument of ratification, acceptance, approval or accession.

B.C.

Access : ALS (Art. 86)
Reserves : PAU (Art. 88)

Duration : USP
Deposit. : UN (Art. 85)
Language : Ara, Chi, Eng, Fre, Rus, Spa

Reference : UN Doc. A/43/820 – ILM 28:170

321.08 – UNCITRAL MODEL LAW ON INTERNATIONAL CREDIT TRANSFERS – UNCITRAL

Adopted : 15.05.1992, UNCITRAL Dec.

With the increasing number of payments in international trade being carried out by means of credit transfer, the Commission believed it important to contribute to the establishment of a unified legal framework applicable to all international credit transfer, whether in electronic or in paper-based form. The Model Law seemed to be the most acceptable way of contributing to the development of harmonious international economic relations among states with different legal, social and economic systems. The Commission's decision to prepare such model rules followed the publication in 1987 of the *Legal Guide on Electronic Funds Transfer* [UN Sales No. E.87.V.9].

The Model Law describes the obligations of the parties to a credit transfer (sender, receiving bank and beneficiary's bank) (Chap. II); and provides for the consequences of a failed, erroneous or delayed credit transfer (Chap. III), and for the completion of credit transfers (Chap. IV). Its basic provisions are as follows.

DETAILS OF THE MODEL LAW

The Model Law is applicable to credit transfers where the sending and the receiving bank, or other entity, as an ordinary part of their business engage in executing payment orders are in different states.

The credit transfer begins when the sender gives an unconditional payment order to a receiving bank to place at the disposal of the beneficiary a fixed or determinable amount of money. The sender, who is bound by the payment order, becomes obligated to pay the receiving bank for the payment order when the receiving bank accepts it. This bank will then issue a payment order, in general on the banking day it is received, either to the beneficiary's bank or to an intermediary bank.

The beneficiary's bank is required, upon acceptance, to place the funds at the disposal of the beneficiary, or otherwise to apply the credit, in accordance with the payment order and the law governing the relationship between the bank and the beneficiary.

Until the credit transfer is completed, each receiving bank is requested to assist the originator and each subsequent sending bank, and to seek the assistance of the next receiving bank, in completing the banking procedures of the credit transfer. If the credit transfer is not completed, the originator's bank is obligated to refund to the originator any payment received from it, with interest from the day of payment to the day of refund.

States enacting this Model Law may add provisions on the conflict of laws such as the one suggested by the UNCITRAL – namely, that in the absence of agreement between the parties involved in a payment order, the law of the state of the receiving bank shall apply.

B.C.

Language : Ara, Chi, Eng, Fre, Rus, Spa

Reference : UN Doc. A/47/17

3.2.2 Documentary Credits and Guarantees

The mechanism of the documentary credit was conceived to facilitate the executions of the obligations of seller and buyer by means of a banking authority [see 322.01]. The international codification of the regime has been assumed by the International Chamber of Commerce (ICC) [see 300 D] and its widespread application is seen in the explicit reference to it in all credit documents used by banks. Banks have also developed uniform rules for collection for their dealings between each other [see 322.02].

SELECTED BIBLIOGRAPHY

de Rooy, F.P., *Documentary Credits*, Deventer: Kluwer Law and Taxation, 1984.

Eisemann, F., Ch. Bontoux and M. Rowe, *Le Crédit Documentaire dans le Commerce Extérieur*, Paris: Jupiter, 1985.

Goode, Roy, *Guide to the ICC Uniform Rules for Demand Guarantees*, Paris: ICC Publishing, Publication no. 510, 1992.

Gutteridge, H. and M. Megrah, *The Law of Bankers' Commercial Credits*. 7th ed. London: Europa, 1984.

ICC, *Case Studies on Documentary Credits*, Paris: ICC Publishing, Publication no. 45, 1989.

Kurkela, M., *Letters of Credit under International Trade Law: UCC, UCP, and Law Merchant*, Dobbs Ferry, N.Y.: Oceana Publications, 1985.

McCullough, B., *Letters of Credit*, New York: Matthew Bender, 1987.

322.01 – UNIFORM CUSTOM AND PRACTICE FOR DOCUMENTARY CREDITS – ICC

Adopted : 03.06.1933, ICC Res.
In Force : 01.07.1933

The use of documentary credits ensures that the parties to an international sales contract undertake their principal obligations in regard to co-contractees: namely, that the seller receives the payment of the price from the buyer, and that the buyer receives the delivery of the goods from the seller. They depend on the services of the banking system from one or several countries, and on documents chosen by the buyer which reflect the execution of the commercial contract and are remitted by the seller.

The ICC, at the initiative of banks, implemented a codification of the international practices in this area from as early as 1933. The Uniform Customs and Practices (UCP) were revised in 1951, 1962, 1974, and in 1983 (Publication No. 400, entered into force on 1 October 1984). The sixth edition of the UCP (UCP 500) was published by the ICC in Spring 1993. The new rules will come into effect on 1 January 1994.

The new revision simplifies the rules, enhances the integrity and reliability of the documentary credit promise, introduces the presumption of irrevocability, clarifies the primary liability of the issuing bank and the confirming bank, and clearly lists the elements of acceptability for each major type of transport document.

The United Nations Commission on International Trade Law [see 300 C] recommended the use of documentary credits on 17 April 1975 and 6 July 1984. The application of the UCP is overridden by voluntary adherence either of a national banking association of a given country able to speak on behalf of the banks of that country (collective adherence), or by banks individually (individual adherence) in countries lacking a national banking association (e.g., France). In practice, they are used by all banks all over the world even in countries which do not have national committees of the ICC.

The UCP are characterized by the following features: they apply to all documentary credits (Chap. A) and are binding on all parties thereto unless otherwise expressly agreed (Art. 1). The rules establish a strict separation between the commercial contract and the financial operation (Art. 3: "Credits by their nature are separate transactions from the sales or other contract(s) on which they may be based ...").

Sarah Williams

Access : ENT
Language : Eng, Fre, Ger, Spa

Modific. : 16.06.51 (01.01.52); 1962 ; 03.12.74 (01.10.75);

Reference : ICC Pub. 500

322.02 – UNIFORM CUSTOMS FOR COLLECTIONS – ICC

Adopted : 1956, ICC Res.

These rules, developed by the ICC Banking Commission, replace the Uniform Rules for the Collection of Commercial Paper adopted in 1967.

They are applicable to financial documents (bills of exchange, promissory notes, cheques, payment receipts) as well as to commercial documents (invoices, shipping documents, documents of title), and they are designed to assist banks in their collection operations by codifying the conditions governing the presentation, payment, acceptance, and so on, of clean and documentary collections.

S.W.

Access : ENT
Language : Eng, Fre

Modific. : 1967 (01.01.68); 00.06.78 (01.01.79);

Reference : ICC Pub. 322

322.03 – UNIFORM RULES FOR DEMAND GUARANTEES – ICC

Adopted : 03.12.1991, ICC

The inevitable risks of international trade can be reduced by following precise procedures. When problems arise, parties to contracts want to be sure that funds will be available to compensate them. One means of protection is the contract guarantee.

In 1978, the ICC issued the first edition of its Uniform Rules for Contract Guarantees. Since the Rules were not frequently used by beneficiaries who preferred so-called "demand" guarantees, the ICC undertook to provide a specific set of rules for demand guarantee practice.

The 1978 Rules required the beneficiary to produce a court judgment or arbitral award in order to obtain payment under the guarantee. The majority of claims nowadays, however, are on a simple demand basis, which means that the beneficiary does not have to support the claim with judgment awards or written statements. Beneficiaries prefer such guarantees, since they can be dealt with more quickly, and the process is less onerous than having to provide documentary "evidence" to support their claim. Principals, however, prefer not to use them as it exposes them to risk of an unjustified demand under the guarantee.

In the interest of providing the market with a set of alternatives, the previous Uniform Rules for Contract Guarantees will remain in force for the time being.

The new URDG, adopted on 3 December 1991, extend application to simple demand guarantees. Article 20 of the Rules states that a written demand or claim should be accompanied by a statement from the beneficiary indicating in what respect the principle is in default. If the beneficiary so desires, he can exclude or modify the Article. This gives parties the flexibility to abide by the rules which best suit their type of business situation.

The new Rules are designed for all those using contract guarantees in international trade transactions, particularly banks.

S.W.

Access : ENT
Language : Eng, Fre

Reference : ICC Pub. 458

3.3 Judicial Proceedings

International disputes may be resolved through national judicial systems or through arbitration. This section deals with conventions which determine the competence of judges [see 3.3.1], co-operation between judicial systems [see 3.3.2], and the enforcement of court decisions [see 3.3.3].

3.3.1 Judicial Competence

331.01 – CONVENTION ON THE JURISDICTION OF THE SELECTED FORUM IN THE CASE OF INTERNATIONAL SALES OF GOODS – HCOPIL

Concluded : 15.04.1958, The Hague
Parties : 0

This Convention applies to the international sale of goods as specified in the Convention on the Law Applicable to the International Sale of Goods (The Hague, 1955) [see 312.01]. Article 1, which deals with the treaty's scope of application, is therefore identical to that of the 1955 Convention.

The Convention deals with the agreement on the choice of court in one of the contracting states, for the purpose of deciding disputes which may arise between the parties to the contract. This court shall have, in principle, exclusive jurisdiction and any other court shall decline jurisdiction. The Convention also lists conditions under which decisions given by a chosen court of one of the contracting states be recognized and declared enforceable in the other contracting state.

The Convention on the Choice of Court (The Hague, 1965) [see 331.02] expands the present Convention by applying to agreements on the choice of court concluded in civil or commercial matters in situations having an international character (Art. 2).

This 1958 Convention is unlikely to come into effect. Under Article 12 it will enter into force only after the deposit of the fifth instrument of ratification of the states which were represented at HCOPIL's eighth session.

Bernard Colas

Access : ALS (Art. 11, 13)
Reserves : PAU (Art. 10)
Duration : REN 5 (Art. 14)
Deposit. : NL (Art. 13)
Language : Fre

Reference : HCOPIL Rec. 1988 – RCDIP 1956.750

331.02 – CONVENTION ON THE CHOICE OF COURT – HCOPIL

Concluded : 25.11.1965, The Hague
Parties : 0

This Convention applies to civil and commercial matters (Art. 2), whereas the Convention of 1958 [see 331.01] applies to the international sales of goods.

Scope: While extending the 1958 Convention's scope of application, the present Convention does set limits: the relations between the parties must be international, and the cases in which the Convention shall not apply include those regarding the status or capacity of persons or questions of family law, maintenance obligations, questions of succession, questions of bankruptcy, and rights in immovable property (Art. 2).

There are four conditions of application of the Convention regarding its jurisdiction over a case:

- the "agreement on the choice of court shall have been validly made if it is the result of the acceptance by one party of a written proposal by the other party expressly designating the chosen court or courts" (Art. 4-1);
- in the matters to which this Convention applies, the parties may by agreement on the choice of court designate either the court or courts of one of the contracting states (Art. 1);
- the agreement on the choice of court shall be void or voidable if obtained by an abuse of economic power or other unfair means (Art. 4-3);
- any contracting state may reserve the right not to recognize agreements on the choice of court if the dispute has no connection with the chosen court, or if, in the circumstances, it would be seriously inconvenient for the matter to be dealt with by the chosen court (Art. 15).

Article 5 states that unless the parties have otherwise agreed, only the chosen court or courts shall have jurisdiction. Article 5-2, however, notes that there may be an exception, and that the chosen court may decline jurisdiction if it has proof that the court of another contracting state has exclusive competence in a particular matter.

Article 6 states that every court other than the chosen court shall decline jurisdiction except in the following cases: where the choice of court made by the parties is not exclusive; where the parties were unable, because of the subject matter, to agree to exclude the jurisdiction of the courts of that state; where the agreement on the choice of court is void or voidable under the Convention's conditions; and for the purpose of provisional or protective measures. The Convention also contains provisions on the recognition and enforcement of a decision of a chosen court and lists of cases in which contracting states may make reservations.

The Convention will enter into force after the deposit of the third instrument of ratification by states which were represented at the tenth session of the Hague Conference. However, it has little chance of entering into force.

B.C.

Access : ALS (Art. 16, 18)
Reserves : PAU (Art. 12 to 15)
Duration : REN (Art. 21)
Deposit. : NL (Art. 16)
Language : Eng, Fre

Reference : HCOPIL Rec. 1988 – ULR 1964 – RCDIP 1964.828

3.3.2 Judicial Co-operation

The need for international judicial co-operation has for a long time been recognized. The issue has been taken up by the HCOPIL [see 300 A] at its very first meeting in 1893, whose work has led to the successive adoption of conventions. First limited to continental European countries, the participation to these agreements progressively expanded since the 1950s to include countries with common law systems. The purpose they serve can be summarized as follows:

- they solve practical problems in the service of judicial process and in the taking of evidence abroad with a view to facilitating litigation with international elements; and
- they tend to eliminate discrimination between nationals and aliens as regards the granting of legal aid, security for costs, availability of copies of entries from public registers, physical detention as a means of enforcement of debts, and immunity for witnesses called to testify abroad.

SELECTED BIBLIOGRAPHY

Ristau, B., *International Judicial Assistance (Civil and Commercial)*, 2 Vols, Washington, DC: International Law Institute, 1984, 1986.

332.01 – CONVENTION RELATING TO CIVIL PROCEDURE – HCOPIL

Concluded : 01.03.1954, The Hague
In Force : 12.04.1957
Parties : 30

This Convention, which has a very wide scope of application, replaced the 1905 Hague Convention. The need for it was, however, more the result of international events than of any substantial change in the foundations of that agreement.

The present Convention includes two sorts of provisions: those aiming to set up a system of mutual international juridical assistance; and those focusing on avoiding discrimination and ensuring access to the courts of contracting states by aliens from other contracting states on an equal basis with nationals. The Convention on the Service Abroad of Judicial and Extrajudicial Documents in Civil or Commercial Matters (The Hague, 1965) [see 332.02] replaces, as between the parties, Articles 1 to 7 of the present Convention. The Convention on the Taking of Evidence Abroad in Civil or Commercial Matters (The Hague, 1970) [see 332.03] replaces Articles 8 to 16; while the Convention on International Access to Justice (The Hague, 1980) [see 332.04] replaces Articles 17 to 26.

Mutual International Juridical Assistance. To bring about mutual juridical co-operation (Chaps. 1 and 2), the Convention makes it mandatory for a state to provide assistance in two areas when requested to do so.

The first concerns the service of documents on persons abroad (Chap. 1): if the normal channel of communication causes problems or delays in the service of documents, the Convention provides for the intervention of the consul of the requesting state and direct communication between the legal authorities (Art. 1).

Second, in the assignment and execution of letters rogatory so as to obtain evidence abroad (Chap. 2), the Convention allows for the intervention of diplomatic authorities (Art. 9) and makes it mandatory for the judicial authorities to which a letter rogatory is addressed to comply with the request (Art. 11). However, the

Convention's Articles 4 and 11 allow a state to refuse to comply with the request if it is deemed prejudicial to its sovereignty and security.

Finally, the Convention sets down formal procedures for the implementation of this mandatory co-operation (Arts. 3, 5, 10, 14 and 16).

The Status of Foreigners. The second set of provisions in the Convention aims to provide rights to foreigners by granting them, in certain cases, the same rights as nationals. Without taking into consideration Article 25 on the free issue of extracts of their civil status from registers of births, marriages and deaths, or Article 26 on the now obsolete procedure of physical detention of an alleged, two chapters (III and IV) aim to partially facilitate the achievement of these legal rights.

Chapter III exempts foreigners from paying, by reason of their status as foreigners, security deposits as a condition of access to the courts. The same rule applies to any payment required of plaintiffs or third parties as security for court costs. Thus, if the foreigner is ultimately to be adjudged liable for costs, the judgment for such costs would be enforced without delay and practically without defence in the country of the foreigner's nationality (Arts. 17 to 19).

Chapter IV extends free legal aid to nationals of each of the contracting states in all other contracting states (Arts. 20 to 24)

Bernard Colas

Access : CON (Art. 27, 31)
Reserves : PAU (Art. 17, 32)
Duration : REN 5 (Art. 33)
Deposit. : NL (Art. 27)
Language : Fre

Reference : 286 UNTS – HCOPIL Rec. 1988 – JORF 30 Sep 59 – RCDIP 1951.732 – RTAF 1959/35

332.02 – CONVENTION ON THE SERVICE ABROAD OF JUDICIAL AND EXTRAJUDICIAL DOCUMENTS IN CIVIL OR COMMERCIAL MATTERS – HCOPIL

Concluded : 15.11.1965, The Hague
In Force : 10.02.1969
Parties : 28

The objective of this Convention is to replace between the parties Articles 1 to 7 of the Convention Relating to Civil Procedure (The Hague, 1954) [see 332.01].

Changes introduced in the new Convention related mainly to the fact that no common law country had ever joined any of the civil procedure conventions. The Convention establishes a system whereby the contracting states are to designate a Central Authority which will undertake to receive requests for service coming from other contracting states, and thus accelerate the transmission of the judicial documents. The Central Authority of the state addressed serves itself the document or arranges to have it served by an appropriate agency. In some cases, contracting states are free to use consular channels to forward documents, for the purpose of service. Provided the state of destination does not object, the Convention does not interfere with more direct ways of sending judicial documents such as through postal channels or directly through judicial offices of the state of destination (Art. 10).

Notable among the changes in the treatment of subjects is the addition of specific provisions protecting the defendant in the case of a default judgment, where he had not actually been served or had not been served in sufficient time to defend the case.

For example, Article 15 gives the defendant at least six months to receive the documents he needs to defend himself before a judge can give judgment. Under certain conditions, the judge may relieve the defendant from the effects of the expiration of the time limit for appealing the judgment (Art. 16).

B.C.

Access : CON (Art. 26, 28)
Reserves : PAU (Art. 21)
Duration : REN (Art. 30)
Deposit. : NL (Art. 28)
Language : Eng, Fre

Reference : Can TS 1989/2 – HCOPIL Rec. 1988 – UKTS 1969/50 – ULR 1964 – 658 UNTS – UST 20/1 – RCDIP 1964.819

332.03 – CONVENTION ON THE TAKING OF EVIDENCE ABROAD IN CIVIL OR COMMERCIAL MATTERS – HCOPIL

Concluded : 18.03.1970, The Hague
In Force : 07.10.1972
Parties : 21

This Convention replaced Articles 8 to 16 of the Convention Relating to Civil Procedure (The Hague, 1954) [see 322.01]. Its objective is to improve, make more flexible, and expand the system for the transmission of evidence, as stipulated by the 1954 Convention.

Letters of Request. In Chapter 1, which deals with Letters of Request, Article 2 makes the designation of a Central Authority mandatory. This Authority will undertake to receive Letters of Request coming from the judicial authority of a contracting state and to transmit them to the authority competent for execution; and this is independent of the intervention by consuls or commissioners.

In regard to the Letter of Request (language, Art. 4; the execution of the Letter, Art. 14; refusal to execute the Letter, Art. 12), this Convention takes up and improves the provisions of the 1954 Convention. Article 11 specifies the conditions under which the person concerned in the execution of a Letter of Request may refuse to give evidence.

Taking Evidence Abroad. In Chapter II, the Convention deals with the taking of evidence by diplomatic officers, consular agents and commissioners, and establishes a more simple method of taking evidence abroad. Any diplomatic officer or consular agent, or any "person duly appointed as a commissioner" (Art. 17), may take the evidence without compulsion of nationals of a state which he represents to aid proceedings commenced in the courts of a state which he represents, if he complies with the conditions which the competent authority has specified in the permission to that effect (Arts. 15, 16 and 17).

B.C.

Access : CON (Art. 37, 39)
Reserves : PAU (Art. 4-2, 15 to 22, 34, 35)
Duration : REN 5 (Art. 41)
Deposit. : NL (Art. 39)
Language : Eng, Fre

Reference : 847 UNTS – UKTS 1977/20 – HCOPIL Rec. 1988 – RTAF 1975/22

332.04 – CONVENTION ON INTERNATIONAL ACCESS TO JUSTICE – HCOPIL

Concluded : 25.10.1980, The Hague
In Force : 01.05.1988
Parties : 8

The objective of the Convention is to improve certain provisions of the Convention Relating to Civil Procedure (The Hague, 1954) [see 332.01], whose Articles 17 to 26 it replaces between the parties who have signed both conventions (Art. 22).

In Chapter I, which deals with legal aid, Article 1 states: "Nationals of any Contracting State and persons habitually resident in any Contracting State shall be entitled to legal aid for court proceedings in civil and commerical matters in each Contracting State on the same conditions as if they themselves were nationals of and habitually resident in that State". The same applies to those who had their habitual residence in a contracting state in which court proceedings are to be or have been commenced. In contrast, the 1954 Convention only applied to nationals of contracting states, without the condition that they were required to be living in the state. Despite the fact that states can reserve the right to exclude the application of Article 1 if there is no reciprocity between the reserving state and the state of which the applicant for legal aid is a national (Art. 28), the application for legal aid must be received by the central authorities in the two states according to procedures fixed in Articles 3 to 13.

Chapter II, regarding security for costs and enforceability of orders for costs, follows the 1954 Convention as relates to exemption, but extends its application to persons who habitually reside in one of the contracting states (Art. 14). As in the 1954 Convention, the order for payment of costs and expenses of proceedings, made in one of the contracting states against any person who benefits from such exemptions, is to be rendered enforceable without charge in any other contracting state (Art. 15).

Chapter III extends the application of Article 25 of the 1954 Convention, which applied to extracts from entries in public registers, to include copies of decisions relating to civil or commercial matters.

Finally, Chapter IV, and Article 20 in particular, institute a system of safe conduct for witnesses and foreign experts who must appear before the tribunal(s) of a contracting state, and who may be prosecuted, detained or subjected to any other restriction on their liberty because of prior conviction or a previous action. Such immunity is limited in time, commencing seven days before the date fixed for the hearing and ceasing when the witness has had an opportunity to leave the country for a period of seven consecutive days from the date when he was informed by the judicial authorities that his presence was no longer required.

B.C.

Access : ALS (Art. 31, 32)
Reserves : PAU (Art. 7-2, 13-2, 14 to 17, 20, 24 to 27, 28) Duration: REN (Art. 35)
Deposit. : NL (Art. 31)
Language : Eng, Fre

Reference : ILM 19:1505 – HCOPIL Rec. 1988 – RCDIP 1980.901 – JORF 15 Oct 88

3.3.3 Recognition and Enforcement of Judgments

Justice involving international elements also address the issue of enforcement of judgments outside a court's jurisdiction. However, countries have been reluctant to bind themselves by world-wide treaties to recognize and enforce judgments pronounced by the courts of other states. They prefer that they remain a matter for their individual laws to decide and that they be addressed, in some cases, at a bilateral and regional level (e.g. agreements concluded among European, Nordic and Latin American countries).

333.01 – CONVENTION ON THE RECOGNITION AND ENFORCEMENT OF FOREIGN JUDGMENTS IN CIVIL AND COMMERCIAL MATTERS – HCOPIL

Concluded : 01.02.1971, The Hague
In Force : 20.08.1979
Parties : 3

The goal of the Convention is to establish common provisions on mutual recognition and enforcement of judicial decisions rendered in the courts of the contracting states.

Scope: The Convention applies to decisions rendered in civil or commercial matters. However, it does not apply to matters such as family law, maintenance obligations, succession to descendants' estates, bankruptcy, social security, nuclear matters, taxes and penalties.

In general, these provisions apply only to judicial authorities of contracting states, which are requested to recognize and enforce decisions rendered in one of the contracting states (Art. 4) if:

- the decision was given by a court considered to have jurisdiction within the meaning of the Convention (Art. 10 to 12);
- it is no longer subject to ordinary forms of review in the state of origin and, to be enforceable in the state addressed, the decision must be enforceable in the state of origin (Art. 4);
- both contracting states have concluded a bilateral supplementary agreement to that effect (Art. 21).

Recognition or enforcement of a decision may nevertheless be refused on certain grounds such as its incompatibility with the public policy of the state addressed, its having been obtained by fraud pending proceedings between the parties based on the same facts and having the same purpose, and its having been rendered by default in some circumstances (Art. 5 to 7).

Under the conditions on recognition and enforcement presented in Chapter II, Article 8 stipulates that "there shall be no review of the merits of the decision rendered by the court of origin".

Jean-André Lasserre and Vladimir Vasak

Access : CON (Art. 27, 29)
Reserves : PAU (Art. 23)
Duration : REN 5 (Art. 31)
Deposit. : NL (Art. 27)
Language : Eng, Fre

Modific. : Additional Protocol 01.02.71 (20.08.79)

Reference : 1144 UNTS – HCOPIL Col. 1988 – RCDIP 1966.329, 1967.203

3.4 Arbitration

International arbitration plays an important role in international transactions as a very flexible and suitable alternative to settling disputes through judicial process.

Conciliation and mediation may also serve as alternative ways of settling disputes, differing from arbitration, however, in that the solution suggested by the conciliator or the mediator has no legally binding effect until it is agreed to by the parties.

In principle, parties to a contract insert an arbitration clause and thereby agree to submit future disputes arising from the contract to arbitration. The arbitration agreement may provide either *ad hoc* or institutional arbitration. In the latter case, the parties will submit their disputes to the administration and procedural rules of a specific institution such as the ones listed in section 3.4.2.

The enforcement of foreign arbitration awards is made easier in countries adhering to conventions which establish uniform and exclusive grounds upon which national courts may recognize arbitral awards and facilitate their enforcement [see 3.4.1].

3.4.1 Arbitration Conventions

Efforts to improve the legal status of arbitrators began early, after the First World War [see 341.01 and 341.02], but their results did not answer the needs of growing international trade. A great achievement was represented by the New York Convention [1958: see 341.03], which created the legal foundations for the development of modern international arbitration. The UNCITRAL Model Law [see 341.06] facilitates the implementation of the Convention. The New York Convention has also been supplemented by regional conventions in Europe [see 341.04 and 341.05] and America [the Inter-American Convention on International Commercial Arbitration (Panama, 1975)].

SELECTED BIBLIOGRAPHY

David, René, *L'Arbitrage dans le Commerce International, Arbitration in International Commerce*, Paris: Economica, 1981.

Gaja, Giorgio (ed.), *International Commercial Arbitration, the New York Convention*, Dobbs Ferry, N.Y.: Oceana Publications, 1984.

Holtzmann, H.M. and J.E. Neuhaus, *A Guide to the UNCITRAL Model Law on international Commercial Arbitration: Legislative History and Commentary*, Deventer: Kluwer Law and Taxation, 1989.

International Council for Commercial Arbitration, *International Handbook of Commercial Arbitration*, Sanders, Pieter (ed.), Deventer: Kluwer Law and Taxation, 1984.

Lee, Eric, *Encyclopedia of International Commercial Arbitration*, London: Lloyd's of London Press, 1986.

Paterson, R.K. and B.J. Thompson (eds.), *UNCITRAL Arbitration Model in Canada: Canadian International Commercial Arbitration Legislation*, Toronto: Carswell, 1987.

Redfern, A. and M. Hunter, *Law and Practice of International Commercial Arbitration*, London: Sweet & Maxwell, 1986.

Smit, Hans and Vratislav Pechota (eds.), *World Arbitration Reporter*, London: Butterworth Legal Publishers, 1986.
Schmitthoff, Clive M. (ed.), *International Commercial Arbitration*, Dobbs Ferry, N.Y.: Oceana Publications, 1986.
van den Berg, Albert Jan, *The New York Convention of 1958: Towards a Uniform Judicial Interpretation*, Deventer: Kluwer Law and Taxation, 1981.

341.01 – PROTOCOL ON ARBITRATION CLAUSES – LN

Concluded : 24.09.1923, Geneva
In Force : 28.07.1924
Parties : 34

The 1923 Protocol can be considered the first agreement with the objective of recognizing and enforcing of arbitration conventions and the decisions rendered in pursuance of those conventions.

The Protocol has one limited aim – namely, to have the contracting states recognize the validity of an agreement in which the parties to a contract agree to submit to arbitration differences that may arise in connection with commercial or other matters (Art. 1). The contracting states agree to facilitate all steps in the procedure required to be taken in their own territories, in accordance with the provisions of their law governing arbitral procedure.

In addition, they undertake to ensure the execution by their authorities of arbitral awards made in their territory (Art. 3). The tribunals of the contracting parties, on being seized of a dispute regarding a contract made between persons to whom the Protocol applies, and including a valid arbitration agreement, must refer those parties to the decision of the arbitrators (Art. 4).

The contracting parties reserve the right to limit the obligation under the Protocol to contracts which are considered commercial under their respective national laws (Art. 1). In the same way, they may declare that their acceptance of the Protocol does not include any or all of the following territories: their colonies, overseas possessions or territories, protectorates, or the territories over which they exercise a mandate (Art. 8).

At present, the Protocol is seldom used as it was replaced by the Convention on the Recognition and Enforcement of Foreign Arbitral Awards (New York, 1958) [see 341.03].

Bernard Colas

Access : ALS (Art. 5)
Reserves : PAU (Art. 1,8)
Duration : USP
Deposit. : LN, UN (Art. 5)
Language : Eng, Fre (Art. 8)

Reference : 27 LNTS – UKTS 1925/4

341.02 – CONVENTION ON THE EXECUTION OF FOREIGN ARBITRAL AWARDS – LN

Concluded : 26.09.1927, Geneva
In Force : 25.07.1929
Parties : 29

The Geneva Convention of 1927 supplements the 1923 Protocol in that it binds the contracting states to recognize and enforce the foreign arbitral awards made in pursuance of an agreement whether relating to existing or future differences covered by the 1923 Protocol. In fact, enforcement in the latter was only binding on a contracting state in the case where an award was rendered on its territory; the Protocol did not deal at all with awards rendered in other states.

The Convention establishes a number of conditions. Article 1 states that an arbitral award made in pursuance of an agreement relating to existing or future differences "shall be recognized as binding and shall be enforced in accordance with the rules of the procedure of the territory where the award is relied upon". In addition, the subject-matter of the award must be capable of settlement by arbitration under the law of the country in which the award is sought to be relied upon; and the recognition or enforcement of the award must not be contrary to the public policy or to the principles of the law of the country in which it is sought to be relied upon.

Articles 2 and 3 bind the arbitral tribunal to respect the principles of natural justice. Only the parties to the 1923 Protocol are eligible to ratify the Convention (Art. 7).

The limitation of obligations under the treaty regarding commercial contracts and territoriality is the same as in the 1923 Protocol (Arts. 1 and 10).

This Convention is seldom invoked, however, as it has been replaced between the contracting parties by the Convention on the Recognition and Enforcement of Foreign Arbitral Awards (New York, 1958) [see 341.03].

B.C.

Access : CON (Art. 7)
Reserves : PAU (Art. 10)
Duration : USP
Deposit. : LN, UN (Art. 7)
Language : Eng, Fre (Art. 11)

Reference : 92 LNTS – UKTS 1930/28

341.03 – CONVENTION ON THE RECOGNITION AND ENFORCEMENT OF FOREIGN ARBITRAL AWARDS – UN

Concluded : 10.06.1958, New York
In Force : 07.06.1959
Parties : 89

The 1958 New York Convention is the most important of the multilateral conventions on the recognition and enforcement of arbitral awards.

The main object of this Convention is the protection of the international efficiency of arbitration clauses. The contracting states undertake to recognize arbitral awards (Art. III) and to facilitate the enforcement of the awards made in accordance with the Agreement's clauses. Thus, any award made in another state must be recognized and enforced in each of the contracting states, although the obligations under the Agreement may be limited if recognition or enforcement of the award is contrary to the public policy of the country. In addition, there shall not be imposed substantially more onerous conditions or higher fees or charges on the recognition or enforcement of arbitral awards to which the Convention applies than are imposed on the recognition and enforcement of domestic arbitral awards (Arts. III and IV).

The Convention includes two reservations: the first involves reciprocity, whereby a state may decide to apply the Convention only to awards made in the territory of another one of the contracting parties; the second relates to commercial questions, whereby a state may decide that it will only apply the Convention in matters relating to commercial law.

Finally, Article VII specifies the effects of the New York Convention on other agreements with the same objectives. It states that the Geneva Protocol on Arbitration Clauses of 1923 [see 341.01] and the Geneva Convention on the Execution of Foreign Arbitral Awards of 1927 [see 341.02] shall cease to have effect between contracting states on their becoming bound, and to the extent that they become bound, by the New York Convention.

B.C.

Access : ALS (Art. VIII)
Reserves : PAU (Art. I, X)
Duration : USP
Deposit. : UN (Art. IX)
Language : Chi, Eng, Fre, Rus, Spa (Art. XVI)

Reference : ILM 7:1046 – UKTS 1976/26 – ULR 1958 – 330 UNTS – JDI 1960 – JORF 6 Sep 59 – RCDIP 1958.447 – RTAF 1959/32

341.04 – EUROPEAN CONVENTION ON INTERNATIONAL COMMERCIAL ARBITRATION – ECE

Concluded : 21.04.1961, Geneva
In Force : 07.01.1964
Parties : 21

The objective of the European Convention of 1961 is to promote the development of European trade by removing certain difficulties that may impede the organization and operation of international commercial arbitration in relations between physical or legal persons of different European countries. The Convention is not limited to Europe, however, and two countries which have the status of consultant to the Economic Commission for Europe (ECE) [see 181 A] have ratified it.

The Convention applies only to arbitration agreements concluded for the purpose of settling disputes arising from international trade between physical or legal persons having, when concluding the contract, their habitual place of residence or their headquarters in different contracting states (Art. I).

One of the peculiarities of the Convention is that it makes provisions for rules on the organization of the arbitration (Art. IV).

Contrary to other conventions dealing with the same subject, the 1961 European Convention outlines criteria defining the jurisdiction of courts in cases in which they must decide on a request to set aside an arbitral award (Art. VI). Article IX gives conditions under which an arbitral award may be set aside.

B.C.

Access : CON (Art. X-1)
Reserves : PAU (Art. II)
Duration : USP
Deposit. : UN (Art. X-12)
Language : Eng, Fre, Rus

Reference : 484 UNTS – JDI 1968 – JORF 9 Feb 68 – RCDIP 1968.327 – RTAF 1968/11

341.05 – ARRANGEMENT RELATING TO APPLICATION OF THE EUROPEAN CONVENTION ON INTERNATIONAL COMMERCIAL ARBITRATION – COE

Concluded : 17.12.1962, Paris
In Force : 25.01.1965
Parties : 7

The 1962 Agreement provides for the replacement by the contracting parties of Paragraphs 2 and 7 of Article IV of the 1961 European Convention on International Commercial Arbitration [see 341.04].

Thus, Article 1 of the Agreement replaces the complex provisions of Articles IV-2 to IV-7 of the 1961 Convention with a simpler standard stipulating that "any difficulties arising with regard to the constitution or functioning of the arbitral tribunal shall be submitted to the decision of the competent authority at the request of the party instituting proceedings".

Any state, whether a member of the Council of Europe or not, can become a party to the Agreement, on the condition that a National Committee of the International Chamber of Commerce [see 300 D] exists on its territory (Art. 3).

B.C.

Access : CON (Art. 2, 3)
Reserves : USP
Duration : USP
Deposit. : CoE (Art. 2)
Language : Eng, Fre (Art. 6)

Reference : ULR 1962 – 523 UNTS – JDI 1968 – JORF 9 Feb 68 – RCDIP 1968.334 – RTAF 1968/11

341.06 – UNCITRAL MODEL LAW ON INTERNATIONAL COMMERCIAL ARBITRATION – UNCITRAL

Adopted : 11.12.1985, UNGA Res.40/72

In its Resolution 40/72 of 11 December 1985, the UN General Assembly recommended to states "to give due consideration to the [UNCITRAL] Model Law on International Commercial Arbitration, in view of the desirability of uniformity of the law of arbitral procedures and the specific needs of international commercial arbitration practice". It also sought to encourage the application of the Convention on the Recognition and Enforcement of Foreign Arbitral Awards (New York, 1958) [see 341.03].

Scope: The scope of application of the Model Law is limited to international commercial arbitration (i.e. where parties have their places of business in different states). The parties agree by a written arbitration clause to submit to arbitration all or certain disputes which have arisen or which may arise between them in respect of a defined legal relationship, whether contractual or not. The parties are free to determine the number of arbitrators, they are free to agree on a procedure of appointing the arbitrator(s), the place of arbitration, rules of procedure, the language or languages to be used, the applicable law, and so on.

The Model Law supplements, and in some cases completes, what the parties have agreed upon. The parties are treated with equality and each party is given a full opportunity of presenting its case (Art. 18).

A court shall, if a party to an arbitration agreement so requests not later than when submitting his first statement on the substance of the dispute, refer the parties to arbitration unless it finds that the agreement is null and void, inoperative or incapable of being performed (Art. 8).

The arbitral proceedings are terminated by the final award or by an order of the arbitral tribunal (Art. 32). An arbitral award, irrespective of the country in which it was made, is recognized as binding and, upon application in writing to the competent court, is enforced (Arts. 35 and 36). The award can be annulled, or else its enforcement and recognition can be reinforced according to criteria identical to those in the 1958 New York Convention (Arts. 34 and 36).

B.C.

Language : Chi, Eng, Fre, Rus, Spa

Reference : ULR 1985/1 – DJI 1986

3.4.2 Institutions and Rules

The major institutions involved in the management of international arbitration and its rules are: the Permanent Court of Arbitration (between states) [see 342 A, 342.01, 342.02 and 342.04], the International Court of Arbitration of the ICC [see 342 B and 342.03], and the ICSID for investment disputes [see 342 C, 342.05 and 342.06]. These institutions have adopted rules of procedure and model rules which are described below. In *ad hoc* arbitration, the most commonly used rules are the UNCITRAL Model Rules [see 342.07 and 342.08].

SELECTED BIBLIOGRAPHY

Cohn, E., M. Domke, F. Eisemann (eds.), *Handbook of Institutional Arbitration in International Trade*, Amsterdam: North Holland Publishing, 1977.

Craig, W., Laurence, William W. Park and Jan Paulsson, *International Chamber of Commerce Arbitration*, Dobbs Ferry, N.Y.; Paris: Oceana Publication; ICC Publishing, 1984.

Dore, Isaak, *Arbitration and Conciliation Under the UNCITRAL Rules: A Textual Analysis*, Dordrecht: Martinus Nijhoff Publishers, 1986.

International Chamber of Commerce, *International Arbitration: 60 Years of ICC Arbitration: A Look at the Future*, Paris: ICC Publishing, 1984.

Jarvin, Sigvard and Yves Derains, *Collection of ICC Arbitral Awards / 1974-1985 / Recueil des Sentences Arbitrales de la CCI*. Paris: ICC Publishing, Publication no. 433, 1990.

Redfern, A. and M. Hunter, *Law and Practice of International Commercial Arbitration*, London: Sweet and Maxwell, 1986.

Serials which regularly publish articles on international arbitration:

Arbitration Journal, New York (quarterly).

International Arbitration Report, Wayne, PA (monthly).

Journal du droit international (Clunet), Paris (quarterly).

Journal of Commercial Arbitration, Seoul.

Journal of International Arbitration, Geneva (quarterly).

Netherlands International Law Review, Leyden (quarterly).
Uniform Law Review, Rome: UNIDROIT (bi-anually).
Yearbook of Commercial Arbitration, Netherlands.

342 A – PERMANENT COURT OF ARBITRATION (PCA)

The Permanent Court of Arbitration was established at the first Hague Peace Conference in 1899, by Articles 20 to 29 of the Convention for the Pacific Settlement of International Disputes and Articles 41 to 50 of the revision of that Convention (18 October 1907). It is composed of a list of arbitrators appointed by each of the contracting states of the Convention. Each state can appoint up to four arbitrators for a term of six years, and the terms are renewable.

Despite its title, the Court is not required to meet. It may exercise its powers through a series of *ad hoc* tribunals.

STRUCTURE

The headquarters of the Court are in the Peace Palace, The Hague. An **International Bureau** acts as Registry and is composed of a Secretary General, a First Secretary, an Administrator, a Translator, an Assistant Secretary and an usher. It is directed and controlled by an **Administrative Council**, consisting of diplomatic representatives of the Contracting Powers accredited to The Hague and it is presided over by the Foreign Minister of the Netherlands. In 1992, its budget amounted to 418,025 Dutch guilders.

Since its creation, 27 cases have been submitted to arbitration before the Court or conducted with the co-operation of its International Bureau.

Under Articles 6 and 7 of the UNCITRAL Arbitration Rules [see 342.07], the Secretary-General of the Court may be requested to designate an appointing authority for the purpose of appointing a member or members of an arbitral tribunal if no agreement has been reached by the parties on the choice of an arbitrator or arbitrators within a fixed period of time. Up to the end of 1992, some 36 of these requests were submitted to the Secretary-General, nine during 1992.

RECENT DEVELOPMENTS

In the framework of a programme for improving the functioning of the Court, the Administrative Council, in October 1992, adopted a new set of procedural rules to be known as the "Permanent Court of Arbitration Optional Rules for Arbitrating Disputes between two States". A set of optional rules for arbitrating disputes between a state and a private entity will be issued separately. The Administrative Council also seeks to obtain observer status for the Court in the General Assembly of the United Nations in 1993 [see 001 A], in order to create an institutional link between the two organizations.

Bernard Colas

ADDRESS

Peace Palace, Carnegieplein 2, 2517 KJ The Hague, The Netherlands
T. (31 70) 346 9680, Fx. (31 70) 356 1338

342 B – THE ICC INTERNATIONAL COURT OF ARBITRATION (ICC-CA)

Founded by a resolution of the International Chamber of Commerce [see 300 D] on 19 January 1923, the International Court of Arbitration supervises the application of the ICC's Rules of Conciliation and Arbitration [see 342.03] and provides for the peaceful settlement of international commercial disputes.

A party can seize the Court by introducing a request for arbitration on the basis of an arbitration clause specifying the jurisdiction of the Court.

The Court organizes the procedures of commercial arbitration. It does not itself settle disputes. This task falls to the arbitral tribunal (composed of one or three arbitrators) which hears the parties, examines the merits of the case and makes an award.

The Court acts as appointing authority unless the parties agree otherwise. When the parties are unable to agree or fail to act regarding the appointment of arbitrators, the Court will designate the arbitrators. Furthermore, unlike other arbitration institutions, the Court scrutinizes each proposed award in draft form paying particular attention to formal requirements such as typographical or grammatical errors, errors in the calculation of interests, and the enforceability of arbitral awards. The Court may lay down modifications as to the form of the award and, without affecting the arbitrator's freedom of decision, may draw attention to points of substance.

STRUCTURE

The Court is independent of any authority, whether public or private. It is composed of a chairman, seven vice-chairmen, and members appointed by the ICC Council for a three-year renewable term. The Court is assisted by an international Secretariat based at the ICC headquarters in Paris.

The Court holds a **Plenary Session** once a month. Its decisions are by majority vote and proceedings are confidential. The **Committee of the Court**, composed of a president and two members, usually meets twice monthly. It decides by unanimous vote on all matters within the jurisdiction of the Court, except those within the exclusive jurisdiction of the Plenary Session (e.g. decisions on challenges of arbitrators and replacement of an arbitrator who is not fulfilling his functions).

The awards are confidential but extracts are rendered in the *Journal de droit international* (Clunet).

Sarah Williams

ADDRESS

38, cour Albert-1er, 75008 Paris, France
T. (33 1) 49 53 28 28, Fx. (33 1) 49 53 29 33

342 C – INTERNATIONAL CENTRE FOR SETTLEMENT OF INVESTMENT DISPUTES (ICSID)

ICSID was created under the auspices of the World Bank by the Washington Convention of 18 March 1965, thereby establishing a new institution for the settlement of investment disputes between states and nationals of other states by arbitration or conciliation.

The parties' agreement to submit their disputes to conciliation or arbitration is binding, but the state party to the dispute may require the exhaustion of local administrative or judicial remedies before consenting to the submission of the dispute to ICSID. The jurisdiction of the Centre extends to any legal dispute arising directly out of an investment between a contracting state, or any constituent subdivision or agency of a contracting state designated to the Centre by that state, and a national of another contracting state. The Additional Facility was established in 1978 to cover disputes involving states who are not parties to the Convention as well as their nationals.

STRUCTURE

The Centre is composed of an **Administrative Council** presided over by the President of the World Bank and a representative of each of the contracting states. The Council elects the Secretary-General who is the legal representative of the Centre.

The **Secretariat**, headed by the Secretary-General, is the second organ of the Centre. It carries out administrative tasks, performs the function of registry.

The Centre does not settle disputes; rather, it offers a means of conciliation and arbitration to which the parties may have recourse. It also offers an official means of communication between the parties and between the parties and the conciliation commissions and the arbitral tribunals. The Centre registers requests for, and is responsible for maintaining, a panel of conciliators and of arbitrators, designated by the contracting states and by the President of the Administrative Council.

ICSID is involved at various points in the proceedings. First, when it receives the request for arbitration or conciliation. The request must be addressed to the Secretary-General who notifies the parties of registration or refusal to register. Second, if a tribunal has not been constituted within 90 days after notice of registration of the request, the Chairman must, at the request of either party or after consulting with them as far as possible, appoint the arbitrator or arbitrators not yet appointed from the Panel of Arbitrators.

An arbitral award is certified by the Secretary-General and copies of the award are sent to the parties. The awards shall be deemed to have been rendered on the date on which the certified copies were dispatched to the parties.

A deposit and administrative fees are paid to ICSID to cover the costs of the proceedings. The official languages of ICSID are English, French and Spanish.

CO-OPERATION

The Centre has entered into agreements with the Permanent Court of Arbitration (PCA) [see 342 A] and regional arbitration centres in Cairo and Kuala Lumpur for co-operation in the conduct of conciliation and arbitration proceedings. The Centre also collaborates with the Court of Arbitration of the ICC and the American Arbitration Association (AAA), with which it jointly organizes an annual conference on international arbitration.

PUBLICATIONS

The Centre publishes brochures and an annual report with information on the number of contracting states, the panel of arbitrators and conciliators, model clauses, legislative provisions and bilateral agreements which refer to ICSID. The Secretariat cannot publish awards without the consent of the parties.

Jean-André Lasserre and Vladimir Vasak

ADDRESS

1818 H Street NW, Washington, DC 20433, United States
T. (202) 477 1234, Fx. (202) 477 1269

SELECTED BIBLIOGRAPHY

Baker, James C., "ICSID: An International Method for Handling Foreign Investment Disputes in LDC", *Foreign Trade Review* 21 (Jan./Mar. 1987): 411-21.

Ryans, John K., and James C. Baker, "International Centre for the Settlement of Investment Disputes (ICSID)", *Journal of World Trade Law* (Jan./Feb. 1976): 65-76.

Tupman, W. Michael, "Case Studies in the Jurisdiction of the International Centre for Settlement of Investment Disputes", *International and Comparative Law Quarterly* 35 (Oct. 1986): 813-38.

West, Luther C., "Award Enforcement Provisions of the World Bank Convention", *Arbitration Journal* 23 no. 1 (1968): 38-53.

342.01 – CONVENTION FOR THE PACIFIC SETTLEMENT OF INTERNATIONAL DISPUTES – PCA

Concluded : 29.07.1899, The Hague
In Force : 04.09.1900
Parties : 65

The objective of the Convention is to prevent the use of force in relations between states and to establish the Permanent Court of Arbitration. It lists a number of measures to ensure the peaceful settlement of disputes, including good offices, mediation, international commissions of inquiry, and international arbitration, and lays down certain rules of procedure.

The Convention has been replaced, as between the contracing parties, by the 1907 Convention [see 342.02].

Access : CON (Art. 58, 59)
Reserves : USP
Duration : USP
Deposit. : NL
Language : Fre

Reference : UKTS 1901/9 – JORF 1 Dec 1900

342.02 – STATUTE OF THE PERMANENT COURT OF ARBITRATION: CONVENTION FOR THE PACIFIC SETTLEMENT OF DISPUTES – PCA

Concluded : 18.10.1907, The Hague
In Force : 26.01.1910
Parties : 55

The Convention was signed at the second International Peace Conference at The Hague and, in relations between the contracting states, replaces the International Convention for the Pacific Settlement of International Disputes (The Hague, 1899) [see 342.01].

Chapter II of the Convention regulates the composition and functions of the

Permanent Court of Arbitration (CPA). The CPA is composed of a list of arbitrators from which the states may choose when needing to settle differences.

The International Bureau acts as the Registry for the CPA. The role of the CPA has been rather small, and to date it has only decided some 20 cases.

Access : CON (Art. 92, 93, 94)
Reserves : USP
Duration : USP
Deposit. : NL
Language : Fre

Reference : Can TS 1930/12 – UKTS 1971/6 – JORF 8 Dec 10 – 1 Paeslee

342.03 – ICC RULES OF CONCILIATION AND ARBITRATION – ICC

Adopted : 01.07.1921, ICC Res.

In order to resolve differences which can arise during the performance of international commercial contracts, the ICC has adopted rules of conciliation and arbitration, the latest edition of which entered into force on 1 January 1988.

The Rules of Conciliation. The objective of conciliation is to create favourable conditions for the amicable settlement of a dispute, without resort to litigation. The conciliator has the task of finding common ground between the parties. In practice, the parties frequently do not proceed to optional conciliation but pass directly to arbitration.

The procedure is confidential and is directed by a conciliator named by the Secretary-General of the ICC Court [see 342 B]. The conciliation is deemed to end in one of the following ways: with the signing of an agreement between the parties who will be bound by its terms; by the production of a report by the conciliator recording that the attempt has not been successful; or, by the decision of the parties, or one of them, no longer to pursue the conciliation process.

The Rules of Arbitration. The ICC International Court of Arbitration is the body whose function is to provide for the settlement of business disputes by arbitration. The arbitrators are named by the parties (or, failing that, by the Court) and are confirmed by the Court.

The Rules set out the methods for appointing one or three arbitrators and lay down the proceedings through the various stages from submission of the request for arbitration through to notification of the final award to the parties. The rules do not, however, contain all the rules of procedure necessary for the examination of cases, and the arbitrator may apply a municipal procedural law. The choice of the procedural rules will be made by the parties or, in cases of failure to agree, by the arbitrator.

The parties must attach particular importance to the choice of place of arbitration as recourse to ICC arbitration does not exclude recourse, even supplementary, to the municipal law in force where the arbitral proceedings take place. Furthermore, the arbitral tribunal, while taking into account commercial usages, applies the law chosen by the parties or failing this by the arbitral tribunal itself to the substance of the dispute, according to the rules of conflict of laws.

While the Rules propose the standard clause below, they encourage the parties to stipulate in the arbitration clause itself the law governing the contract, the number of arbitrators, and the place and language of the arbitration. Such stipulations previously agreed by the parties in effect limit the risk of disagreements arising once the arbitration procedure has begun.

Standard Arbitration Clause. "All disputes arising in connection with the present contract shall be finally settled under the Rules of Conciliation and Arbitration of the

International Chamber of Commerce by one or more arbitrators appointed in accordance with the same Rules".

Sarah Williams

Language : Eng, Fre

Modific. : Last Version (01.01.88);

Reference : ILM 28:231

342.04 – RULES OF ARBITRATION AND CONCILIATION FOR SETTLEMENT OF INTERNATIONAL DISPUTES BETWEEN TWO PARTIES OF WHICH ONLY ONE IS A STATE – PCA

Adopted : 1962, PCA Res.

The International Bureau of the Permanent Court of Arbitration [see 342 A] is authorized to place its premises and its organization at the disposal of the states which are parties to the 1899 and 1907 Conventions [see 342.01 and 342.02] and which wish to settle a dispute between a contracting state and a large private enterprise located in another contracting state.

The Bureau drafted a model of Rules of Procedure for the settlement of disputes between states and private persons or organizations. This Agreement sets down a procedure for conciliation and arbitration. It allows parties to attempt conciliation and, if this fails, to have recourse to arbitration. The parties are free to agree on a mutually convenient procedure, and reference to this possibility may be made in the draft of their agreement prior to arbitration or conciliation.

The Conciliation Commission and Arbitral Tribunal. These are generally composed of three members chosen by the parties. If the parties cannot agree on the choice of the members of the Conciliation Commission or the arbitrators, the Bureau is authorized to assist them in the establishment of a Conciliation Commission or an Arbitral Tribunal.

Thus, in a case of conciliation (Section II), unless the parties agree to deny it this right, the Bureau is authorized to designate the members of the Conciliation Commission (Art. 5). In a case of arbitration (Section I), the Bureau continues to try to find a mutually acceptable list of arbitrators until agreement is reached, or until it can be determined that no agreement will be reached. If no agreement is reached, "the Secretary-General of the Permanent Court of Arbitration appoints the arbitrators in cases where the parties have expressly entrusted this task to him" (Art. 6).

Arbitration Proceedings. The Tribunal determines the procedure and the duration of the proceedings (Art. 19), and it is competent to complete the Rules of Procedure (Art. 21). The Tribunal decides on the basis of respect for law, unless an agreement between the parties provides for it to rule *ex aequo et bono* (Art. 30). All decisions of the Tribunal are taken by majority vote (Art. 34) and, once rendered, the reward is binding upon the parties (Art. 31).

Conciliation proceedings. These are similar to arbitration proceedings, with the difference that at the end of its inquiry the Conciliation Commission informs the parties of the terms of a draft arrangement which it recommends to the parties (Arts. 9 and 13). If the parties accept the proposed arrangement, an official report is drawn up reproducing its terms (Art. 14).

Bernard Colas

Language : Eng, Fre

342.05 – CONVENTION ON THE SETTLEMENT OF DISPUTES BETWEEN STATES AND NATIONALS OF OTHER STATES – ICSID

Concluded : 18.03.1965, Washington
In Force : 14.10.1966
Parties : 107

The objective of the 1965 Washington Convention is the creation of an International Centre for the settlement of investment disputes between contracting states and nationals of other contracting states. Articles 1 to 24 set down the methods of procedure for the establishment and organization of the Centre.

Scope: The jurisdiction of the Centre extends to legal disputes between parties when this jurisdiction is recognized by both parties. When the parties have given their consent, no party may withdraw its consent unilaterally. In addition, the legal dispute must arise directly out of an "investment" and must involve a contracting state and a national of another contracting state (Art. 25).

DETAILS OF THE CONVENTION

The Convention provides a procedure for conciliation (Arts. 28 to 35), and for arbitration (Arts. 36 to 47). In particular, Article 44 permits the application of the Conciliation and Arbitration Rules of Investment Disputes [see 342.06] to the settlement of disputes, unless the parties agree otherwise. The award is binding on the parties (Arts. 53 and 54).

B.C.

Access : CON (Art. 67)
Reserves : PAU (Art. 70)
Duration : USP
Deposit. : IBRD (Art. 73)
Language : Eng, Fre, Spa (Art. 75)

Reference : ILM 4:532 – UKTS 1967/25 – ULR 1967 – 575 UNTS – UST 17/1 – JORF 31 Dec 67 – 1 Paeslee – RCDIP 1968.128 – RTAF 1967/92

342.06 – ARBITRATION RULES – ICSID

Adopted : 01.01.1968, ICSID Res.

The Rules were adopted by the Administrative Council in compliance with Article 6 of the Washington Convention of 18 March 1965 establishing the ICSID [see 342.05].

The Rules provide that arbitration proceedings must be conducted, except as the parties otherwise agree, in accordance with the rules in effect on the date on which the parties consented to arbitration. If the Arbitration Tribunal is not constituted within 90 days or such other period as the parties may agree, one of the parties may address a request to the Chairman of the Administrative Council to appoint the arbitrator or arbitrators not yet appointed and to designate an arbitrator to be President of the Tribunal (Art. 4).

During the proceedings, the Tribunal, "which shall be the judge of the admissibility of any evidence adduced and of its probative value", may call upon the parties to produce documents, witnesses and experts; it may also visit any place connected with the dispute or conduct inquiries there (Art. 34). At any time during the proceedings a party may request provisional measures be taken by the Tribunal (Art. 39).

The parties may also agree to settle their dispute, or otherwise to discontinue the proceedings, before the award is rendered (Art. 43).

The award shall be drawn up and signed within 60 days of the closure of the proceedings (Art. 46). An application for the interpretation, revision or annulment of the award may be made by either party. An application for annulment or for revision must be based on one or more of the following reasons: that the Tribunal was not properly constituted; that it has manifestly exceeded its powers; that there was corruption on the part of a member of the Tribunal; that there has been a serious departure from a fundamental rule of procedure; and that the award has failed to state the reasons on which it is based.

The application for revision must be made within 90 days after the discovery of the new fact and within three years after the date on which the award was rendered. The application for annulment must be made within 120 days after the award was rendered and, in the case of corruption on the part of a member of the Tribunal, within 120 days after the discovery of the corruption and within three years after the date on which the award was rendered (Art. 50).

In a case of revision, the Tribunal is constituted or reconstituted (Art. 51), while in a case of annulment the Chairman of the Administrative Council appoints an *ad hoc* committee (Art. 52).

Jean-André Lasserre and Vladimir Vasak

Language : Eng, Fre, Spa

Modific. : Last Revision (26.09.84);

Reference : JDI 1986

342.07 – UNCITRAL ARBITRATION RULES – UNCITRAL

Adopted : 15.12.1976, UNGA Res.98(XXXI)

The UNCITRAL Arbitration Rules present a particularly flexible method of settling disputes arising from the execution of commercial contracts. The parties may choose to refer their dispute to an institution for arbitration. In 1982, UNCITRAL adopted recommendations to facilitate settlements of disputes by arbitral institutions. If no appointing authority has been designated by the parties, one could be designated by the Secretary-General of the Permanent Court of Arbitration at the Hague [see 342 A].

It is the responsibility of the parties to choose the appointing authority, the number of arbitrators (one or three), the place of arbitration, and the language or languages used in the proceedings.

The arbitration rules make provision for the appointment, challenge and replacement of the arbitral tribunal, and determine the rules of procedure. Subject to the rules, the arbitral tribunal may conduct the arbitration in such a manner as it considers appropriate, provided that the parties are treated with equality, and that at every stage of the proceedings each party is given a full opportunity to present his case.

The arbitral tribunal applies the law decided by the parties as being applicable to the substance of the dispute. Failing such designation by the parties, the arbitral tribunal applies the law determined by the conflict rules which it considers applicable. The arbitral tribunal decides *ex aequo et bono* only if the parties expressly authorize the tribunal to do so. The award of the tribunal is submitted in writing and is final and binding on the parties who undertake to comply with the award without delay.

Model Arbitration Clause. "Any dispute, controversy or claim arising out of or relating to this contract, or the breach, termination or invalidity thereof, shall be settled by arbitration in accordance with the UNCITRAL Arbitration Rules as at present in force".

Note: Parties may wish to consider adding to the Arbitration Clause:

- The appointing authority shall be... (name of institution or person);
- The number of arbitrators shall be... (one or three);
- The place of arbitration shall be... (city or country);
- The language(s) to be used in the arbitral proceedings shall be...

Bernard Colas

Language : Chi, Eng, Fre, Rus, Spa

342.08 – UNCITRAL CONCILIATION RULES – UNCITRAL

Adopted : 04.12.1980, UNGA Res.52(XXXV)

Conciliation is different from arbitration in that the decision taken by the conciliator must be accepted by the parties, and only becomes binding when they both agree to adhere to the decision.

UNCITRAL made the conciliation of differences in international commerce a priority issue in its work programme at its 11th session in 1978. In 1980 the UNCITRAL Conciliation Rules were finalized, and in its Resolution 35/52 the UN General Assembly recommended that they be applied in cases where parties to an international commercial dispute decide to reach an amicable settlement of the dispute through conciliation.

The parties agree to apply the conciliation rules, and they can, at any time, agree to exclude or vary any of the rules (Art. 1). The party initiating conciliation sends the other party a written invitation briefly identifying the subject of the dispute. Conciliation proceedings begin when that other party accepts the invitation; if the other party rejects the invitation, there will be no conciliation proceedings (Art. 2).

The conciliator, upon his appointment, requests each party to submit to him a brief written statement describing the general nature of the dispute and the points at issue (Art. 5). The parties to the dispute may submit to the conciliator suggestions for the settlement of the dispute (Art. 12). When it appears to the conciliator that there are elements of a settlement which could be acceptable to the parties, he formulates the terms of the possible settlement and submits them to the parties (Art. 13). Conciliation procedures are finalized if the parties sign the settlement agreement.

Model Conciliation Clause. "Where, in the event of a dispute arising out of or relating to this contract, the parties wish to seek an amicable settlement of that dispute by conciliation, the conciliation shall take place in accordance with the UNCITRAL Conciliation Rules as at present in force".

It is understood that the parties may agree on other conciliation clauses.

Caroline London

Language : Chi, Eng, Fre, Rus, Spa

4. Management of Common Resources and Environmental Protection

The World Charter of Nature, adopted by the UNGA on 28 October 1982, reaffirms that "mankind is a part of nature and life depends on the uninterrupted functioning of natural systems which ensure the supply of energy and nutrients". Aware of this basic reality and given the growing environmental threats to the planet, the international community, since the end of the 1960s, has held international conferences on the subject and has developed a set of rules chiefly through multilateral agreements.

In 1972, the United Nations Conference on the Human Environment held in Stockholm first put the issue onto the international agenda. Twenty years afterwards, the United Nations Conference on Environment and Development, in 1992 in Rio de Janeiro, brought environmental problems to the forefront of world attention [see 410.01 and 410.02].

International environmental law has evolved significantly during this period. Initially *ad hoc* and regional, it has become more comprehensive and global in scope. Of key importance in international relations, this body of law operates in a sphere requiring common international efforts of states with diverse values regarding their environment and with different levels of development.

Furthermore, international environmental law has become more technically specific, mandatory and enforceable whereas, at its inception, it was merely persuasive or recommendatory. Today, its main framework conventions set out general principles for actions, complemented by additional protocols defining specific implementation procedures and enforceable rules.

This section deals with the law regarding the conservation of natural resources (wild flora and fauna, and habitat) [see 4.1], human activities which have adverse effects on the environment (nuclear activities and hazardous wastes) [see 4.2], and the management of common resources (the sea, Antarctica and outer space) [see 4.3].

Maguelonne Déjeant-Pons

The author would like to thank *Ralph Osterwoldt* for comments and contributions.

SELECTED BIBLIOGRAPHY

Birnie, Patricia W. and Alan E. Boyle, *International Law and the Environment*, London: Oxford University Press, 1992.

Hohmann, Herald (ed.), *Basic Documents of International Environmental Law*. Dordrecht: Martinus Nijhoff Publishers, 1992.

Kiss, Alexandre Charles, *Droit international de l'environnement*, Etudes internationales, Paris: Pedone, 1989.

– – –, *Selected Multilateral Treaties in the Field of the Environment*, Nairobi: UNEP Ref. Ser. 3, 1983.

– – – and Dinah Shelton, *International Environmental Law*, London; New York: Graham & Trotman; Transnational Juris, 1991.

Lang, Winfried, Hanspeter Neuhold and Karl Zemanek, *Environmental Protection and International Law*, London: Graham and Trotman, 1991.

Rummel-Bulska, Iwona and Seth Osafo, *Selected Multilateral Treaties in the Field of*

the Environment, 2 Vol., Cambridge: Grotius , 1991.
Sand, Peter H. (ed.), *The Effectiveness of International Environmental Agreements: A Survey of Existing Legal Instruments*, Cambridge: Grotius, 1992.
Tolba, Mostafa K. (ed.), *Evolving Environmental Perceptions: From Stockholm to Nairobi*, London: Butterworths, 1988.
See also: Handl, Gunther (ed.), *Yearbook of International Environmental Law*, Dordrecht: Martinus Nijhoff Publishers, (1990-).

4.1 Conservation of Natural Resources

Conventions on the conservation of natural resources are constantly being developed. These deal with endangered species, fauna and flora, biological diversity, marine and coastal waters, air quality, and terrestrial habitats. A convention on soil desertification should soon be agreed.

Some of these conventions have been adopted under the auspices of international bodies such as UNEP [see 410 A], ECE [see 181 A], FAO [see 131 A], IMO [see 183 A] and UNESCO [see 171 A], and implement principles embodied in major international declarations.

4.1.0 Environmental Co-ordination

410 A – UNITED NATIONS ENVIRONMENT PROGRAMME (UNEP)

After the United Nations Conference on the Human Environment in Stockholm in 1972, the UN General Assembly, in its Resolution 2997 (XXVII) of 15 December 1972, established a new institution for the preservation of the environment within the UN system: the United Nations Environment Programme (UNEP). This consists of a **Governing Council**, which is its legislative body and is composed of representatives of 58 governments; the **Environment Fund**, a source of finance to be made up of voluntary contributions and used to support wholly or partly the costs of environmental initiatives undertaken within the UN system; and an environment **Secretariat** to serve as a focal point for environmental action and co-ordination within the UN system. The environment Secretariat, though only one element of the Programme, itself soon came to be known as UNEP.

Even as it was being established, it was realized that UNEP should have a catalytic as well as a co-ordinating role. By this it was intended that UNEP should stimulate other organizations within and outside the UN system to undertake environmental activities by providing ideas, promoting understanding and arranging for initial financial support. In UNGA Res. 2997, the General Assembly established the **Environment Co-ordination Board** (ECB) as the co-ordinating component of the Programme, placing it under the auspices and within the framework of the **Administrative Committee for Co-ordination** (ACC). It was charged with ensuring co-operation and co-ordination among all bodies concerned with the implementation of environmental programmes and was required to report annually to the Governing Council. In 1977, the General Assembly assigned the functions of the ECB to the ACC by UNGA Res. 32/197.

In 1979, the Executive Director of UNEP established the **Committee of Designated Officials for Environmental Matters** (DOEM) to replace the focal points of the ECB after the functions of the ECB were assumed by the ACC. Its functions are to ensure appropriate consultations on environmental matters within the UN system, to advise the Executive Director on co-ordination and review of environmental activities, to assist in the preparation of the System-Wide Medium-Term Environment Programme (SWMTEP) (the main means of harmonization and co-ordination of environmental activities within the UN system), and the proposed Programme Budget Document presented regularly to the Governing Council of UNEP.

STRUCTURE

The **Governing Council** of UNEP is elected by the UN General Assembly for a term of three years. Due consideration is given to ensure an equitable geographical distribution of seats in the Council. Until 1985, the Governing Council met annually; since then, however, it has opted to meet biannually. Its decisions are implemented by the UNEP **Secretariat.**

UNEP, which has its headquarters in Nairobi, has regional offices in Bangkok, Bahrain, Geneva, Mexico City, New York and Washington, DC. Other subsidiary structures that have been established such as the International Register of Potentially Toxic Chemicals (IRPTC) in Geneva, the Industry and Environment Office in Paris, the Secretariat for the Convention on International Trade in Endangered Species of Wild Fauna and Flora (CITES) in Lausanne [see 411.06], the Secretariat for the Convention on Migratory Species of Wild Animals (CMS) in Bonn [see 411.07], the Secretariat for the Basel Convention on the Control of Transboundary Movements of Hazardous Wastes and their Disposal (SBC) in Geneva [see 422.03], the Ozone Secretariat for the Vienna Convention for the Protection of the Ozone Layer and the Montreal Protocol in Nairobi [see 413.02], the Co-ordinating Unit for the Mediterranean Action Plan (MEDU) in Athens and the Regional Co-ordinating Unit for the Caribbean Environment Programme (CAR/RCU) in Kingston, Jamaica.

ACHIEVEMENTS

Under the auspices of UNEP, five international environmental conventions have been negotiated and adopted: CITES [see 411.06], CMS [see 411.07], the Convention for the Protection of the Ozone Layer [see 413.02], SBC [see 422.03] and the Convention on Biological Diversity [see 411.08].

UNEP's programme for Environmentally Sound Management of Inland Waters brought together eight countries that share the Zambezi River Basin to sign the Zambezi Action Plan in 1987.

Under the technical assistance programme, UNEP has assisted over 60 countries to enact environmental legislation and establish institutions for the management of the environment.

Today nearly 140 countries take part in the Regional Seas Programmes catalysed and co-ordinated by UNEP, covering the Mediterranean, the Kuwait region, the Red Sea, the wider Caribbean, the Atlantic coast of West and Central Africa, the Eastern African seabord, the Pacific coast of South America, the islands of the South Pacific, the East Asian region and South Asia. Action plans for the Black Sea and the North-West Pacific are being developed.

UNEP has launched "Earthwatch", a programme consisting of four main components: the Global Environmental Monitoring System (GEMS), the Global Resource Information Data Base (GRID), the International Register of Potentially Toxic Chemicals (IRPTC) [see 422.02], and the global information system, INFOTERRA. Climate data gathered within the framework of GEMS have spurred international action to save the ozone layer and to mitigate the effects of climate change.

UNEP has contributed to the modification of classical economic behaviour so that economic actors give an economic value to the planet's natural "infrastructure". The Industry and Environment Office (IEO) of UNEP works with various industrial sectors to help modify economic behaviour which may have ecological consequences, and it facilitates the exchange of commercial information on environmental problems. The IEO has taken many initiatives including progammes intended to prevent the production of wastes and to promote the efficient use of resources. It created a programme in order to help industries and local authorities to prepare for technological accidents and manages a documentation centre which indicates how to avoid substances affecting the ozone layer.

CO-OPERATION

UNEP co-operates with other UN bodies such as UNESCO [see 171 A], the WHO [see 132 A], FAO [see 131 A], WMO [see 431 A], and governments and non-governmental organizations.

PUBLICATIONS

UNEP produces many publications, documents, reports and surveys including: *UNEP Annual Review*, *Uniterra*, *UNEP Reports and Proceedings Series*, *UNEP Reference Series*, *UNEP Studies Series*, *MAP Technical Reports* and the *Annual Report of the Executive Director*.

Maguelonne Déjeant-Pons

ADDRESS

PO.Box: 30552, Gigiri Nairobi, Kenya
T. (254 2) 230800, Fx. (254 2) 226890

SELECTED BIBLIOGRAPHY

UNEP, *Two Decades of Achievement and Challenge*, Nairobi, Oct. 1992.

410.01 – DECLARATION OF THE UNITED NATIONS CONFERENCE ON THE HUMAN ENVIRONMENT – UNEP

Adopted : 16.06.1972, Stockholm

The UN Conference on the Human Environment was held in Stockholm between 5 and 16 June 1972, and 113 states participated.

It adopted, by acclamation in its plenary session (China abstaining), a Declaration and a plan of action comprising 109 recommendations and four resolutions (Institutional and Financial Provisions; World Environment Day; Nuclear Arms Testing; and the Second Conference on Human Environment).

DETAILS OF THE DECLARATION

The Declaration, in effect an environmental charter, establishes "a common outlook and common principles to inspire and guide the peoples of the world in the preservation and enhancement of the human environment". It consists of a preamble of seven points, followed by 26 principles.

The Preamble. The Preamble proclaims: "Man is both creature and moulder of his environment, which gives him physical sustenance and affords him an opportunity for intellectual, moral, social and spiritual growth". It considers that the protection of the human environment is a major issue which affects the well-being of peoples and economic development throughout the world.

In the developing countries most of the environmental problems are caused by underdevelopment. Therefore, the developing countries must direct their efforts to development, and the industrialized countries should make efforts to reduce the gap between themselves and the developing countries. The Declaration also notes that population growth continuously presents problems for the preservation of the environment, and it expresses the conviction that "along with social progress and the advance of production, science and technology, the capability of man to improve [the] environment increases with each passing day".

It recognizes that local and national governments will bear the greatest burden for large-scale environmental policy and action within their jurisdictions, but that international co-operation is also needed. It calls upon the governments and peoples to exert common efforts for the preservation and improvement of the human environment for the benefit of all the people and their prosperity.

The Principles. The principles set out in the second part of the Declaration form the ideological basis for the protection of the environment. They are: first, man's fundamental right to freedom, equality and adequate conditions of life; second, the responsibility to protect and improve the environment; and third, condemnation of discriminatory policies.

The other 25 principles which follow the ideological principles outline the general policies needed to implement them. Principles 2 to 7 lay down the foundations for the protection of the environment. They include: safeguarding the natural resources of the Earth through careful planning and management; safeguarding and wise management of the heritage of wildlife and its habitat; guarding against the danger of future exhaustion of the non-renewable resources of the Earth; halting the discharge of toxic substances or other substances in such quantities that the environment is unable to render them harmless; and the prevention by states of the pollution of the seas by substances liable to harm human health, living resources, or marine life.

Principles 8 to 26 deal with the implementation of environmental protection policies. This requires, notably, economic and social development, rational planning and management of resources, adequate demographic policies, appropriate environmental institutions and enhanced international co-operation.

Principle 21 is a particularly significant principle. While affirming the sovereign right of states to exploit their own resources pursuant to their own environmental policies, it also affirms the responsibility of states not to cause damage to the environment of other states or to areas beyond the limits of national jurisdiction. This Principle has been part of a recognized development in international environmental law towards the positive duty of states to take suitable preventive steps to protect the environment outside their territories, rather than simply a duty to make reparations when damage is done [e.g. see 412.07, 413.02, 414.01, 414.02, 414.03; also Principle 2 of Rio Declaration (410.02)].

M.D.-P.

Language : Ara, Chi, Eng, Fre, Rus, Spa

Reference : ILM 11:1466

410.02 – THE RIO DECLARATION ON ENVIRONMENT AND DEVELOPMENT – UN

Adopted : 14.06.1992, Rio de Janeiro

The United Nations Conference on Environment and Development (UNCED), which was attended by more than 170 heads of states and governments and delegates, was held in Rio de Janerio from 3-14 June 1992, under the auspices of the United Nations.

By Resolution on 14 June 1992, the Conference adopted in plenary session the Rio Declaration on Environment and Development, Agenda 21, an 800-page action programme intended to orient the behaviour of the international community into the twenty-first century, and a non-legally binding authoritative statement of principle for a global consensus on the management, conservation and sustainable development of all types of forests.

The Declaration, or Charter of Sustainable Development, tries to reconcile the notions of environment and development so that development may meet present needs without prejudicing the needs of future generations. It comprises a preamble followed by 27 principles.

The Preamble. In the Preamble, the UNCED reaffirms the Declaration of the United Nations Conference on the Human Environment adopted at Stockholm in 1972 [see 410.01] and seeks to build upon it by seeking to establish a new and equitable global partnership, encouraging the creation of new levels of co-operation among states, key sectors of societies, and people. It recognizes the integral and interdependent nature of the Earth, our home.

The Principles. Principles 1 to 8 establish the maxims which states should respect in reconciling environmental concerns and development. Human beings are at the centre of concerns for sustainable development and are entitled to a healthy and productive life in harmony with nature (Principle 1). States have the sovereign right to exploit their own resources pursuant to their own environmental and developmental policies, and the responsibility to ensure that activities within their jurisdiction or control do not cause damage to the environment of other states or of areas beyond the limits of national jurisdiction (Principle 2 – a restatement of Stockholm Principle 21 [see 410.01]). The right to development must be fulfilled so as to equitably meet developmental and environmental needs of present and future generations (Principle 3). In order to achieve sustainable development, environmental protection shall constitute an integral part of the development process and cannot be considered in isolation from it (Principle 4).

All states and all people shall co-operate in the essential task of eradicating poverty as an indispensible requirement for sustainable development (Principle 5). The situation and needs of developing countries shall be given special priority (Principle 6). States shall co-operate in a spirit of global partnership to conserve, protect and restore the health and integrity of the Earth's ecosystem. They have common but differentiated responsibilities and the developed countries acknowledge the responsibility that they bear in the international pursuit of sustainable development (Principle 7). To achieve sustainable development and a higher quality of life for all people, states should reduce and eliminate unsustainable patterns of production and consumption and promote appropriate demographic policies (Principle 8).

Principles 9 to 19 provide for methods that should be used in order to achieve the set objectives:

- the improvement of scientific understanding through exchanges of scientific and technological knowledge, and enhancing the development, adaptation, diffusion and transfer of technologies (Principle 9);
- the participation of all concerned citizens and, at the national level, access of

individuals to information and access to judicial and administrative proceedings (Principle 10);
- the enactment of effective environmental legislation (Principle 11);
- co-operation to promote a supportive and open international economic system that would lead to economic growth and sustainable development and to better address the problems of environmental degradation and achieve international consensus addressing transboundary or global environmental problems (Principle 12);
- the development of national and international laws regarding liability and compensation for environmental damage (Principle 13);
- co-operation to discourage or prevent the relocation and transfer to other states of any activities and substances that cause severe environmental degradation or are found to be harmful to human health (Principle 14);
- the application of the precautionary approach – namely, that where there are threats of serious or irreversible damage, lack of full scientific certainty shall not be used as a reason for postponing cost-effective measures to prevent environmental degradation (Principle 15);
- the internalization of environmental costs and the use of economic instruments, taking into account the approach that the polluter should, in principle, bear the cost of pollution, with due regard to the public interest and without distorting international trade and investment (Principle 16);
- environmental impact assessment (Principle 17);
- the immediate notification to states of any natural disasters or other emergencies that are likely to produce sudden harmful effects on the environment of those states, and international economic community efforts to help states so afflicted (Principle 18);
- the prior and timely notification to potentially affected states on activities that may have a significant transboundary environmental effect and early stage and good faith consultation with those states (Principle 19).

Principles 20 to 22 deal with three social categories – women, youth, and indigenous people and their communities – and their vital role in environmental management and development.

Principles 23 to 26 deal with the environment during warfare and times of conflict. It states that peace, development and environmental protection are interdependent and indivisible (Principle 25).

Finally, Principle 27 provides that states and people shall co-operate in good faith and in a spirit of partnership in the fulfilment of the principles embodied in the Declaration and in the further development of international law in the field of sustainable development.

M.D.-P.

Language : Ara, Chi, Eng, Fre, Rus, Spa

Reference : ILM 31:874

4.1.1 Protection of Wild Flora and Fauna

The harm to present and future generations from the destruction of wildlife and genetic resources may be impossible to assess quantitatively, but it is substantial in terms of quality of life – loss of foods, medicine, intact life systems as well as nature's beauty, recreation, and inspiration. Global conventions in this field are concerned with the conservation and management of certain species (e.g. in regard to whales, birds, migratory animals, and endangered species); the protection of plants and of biological diversity; and the conservation of habitats (wetlands, the sea [see 4.3.2], Antarctica [see 4.3.3] and natural heritage [see 171.05]).

SELECTED BIBLIOGRAPHY

Favre, David S., *International Trade in Endangered Species: A Guide to CITES*, Dordrecht: Martinus Nijhoff Publishers, 1989.
Lyster, Simon, *International Wildlife Law*, Cambridge: Grotius Publications, 1985.

411.01 – CONVENTION FOR THE PRESERVATION OF FAUNA AND FLORA IN THEIR NATURAL STATE – UN

Concluded : 08.11.1933, London
In force : 14.01.1936
Parties : 10

The aim of the Convention is to preserve fauna and flora in their natural habitat, primarily on the African continent, by establishing protected areas and by regulating the hunting and collection of species. Its effect has been superseded by the African Convention on the Conservation of Nature and Natural Resources (Algiers, 15.09.1968).

DETAILS OF THE CONVENTION

The parties agreed to examine the possibility of establishing national parks and strict natural reserves on their territories in which fauna and flora are protected in their natural habitat; and, in general, to ensure that human activities threaten them as little as possible. The protection of forest land and the domestication of wild animals susceptible of economic utilization is encouraged.

The Annex to the Convention lists species whose protection demands urgent action and is of major importance. Two classes of these species are established; with species in Class A benefiting from a more rigorous protection regime than those in Class B.

Trade in trophies and the manufacture of objects from wildlife trophies are controlled. (Trophies constitute any animal dead or alive mentioned in the annex, or anything part of or produced from any such animal when dead.)

The use of vehicles to hunt animals and the use of vehicles which may disturb animals are prohibited; and certain methods of capturing or destroying animals (e.g. poisons, explosives, nets, dazzling lights) are also prohibited.

Maguelonne Déjeant-Pons

Access : CON (Art. 17)
Reserves : AUT (Art. 11)
Duration : USP
Deposit. : GB
Language : Eng, Fre

Reference : 172 LNTS – UKTS 1930/27 – JORF 3 Jul 38

411.02 – INTERNATIONAL CONVENTION FOR THE REGULATION OF WHALING – IWC

Concluded : 02.12.1946, Washington
In force : 10.11.1948
Parties : 41

Because excessive whaling was leading to the gradual destruction of whale species, upon which the whaling industry depended, the Washington Convention of 1946 sought to regulate the taking of all species of whales. While it did aim to safeguard the natural resources represented by whale stocks, its primary purpose was to enable the orderly development of the whaling industry.

The Convention establishes a system of international regulation to ensure proper conservation and development of whale stocks on the basis of the principles embodied in the International Agreement for the Regulation of Whaling, signed in London on 8 June 1937, and its protocols, signed in London on 24 June 1938 and on 26 November 1945.

DETAILS OF THE CONVENTION

The Convention establishes an **International Whaling Commission** (IWC) composed of members appointed by the contracting states. It encourages research and investigation, collects and analyses statistical information and appraises and disseminates information concerning whaling and whale stocks.

The Annex to the Convention contains detailed provisions on the conservation and utilization of whale stock. The Commission may amend these provisions by adopting regulations on the following issues: protected and unprotected species; open and closed seasons; open and closed areas; size limits for species; maximum catches for any one season; and type of gear and apparatus to be used.

The contracting states agree to take measures to enforce these regulations, and to report any infraction to the Commission. The Commission, composed of one member from each contracting government, meets in annual session and adopts decisions. By 1982, enough members had changed policies from pro-whaling to conservationist, that a five year moratorium on commercial whaling was finally passed, effective 1985-90, which the IWC extended thereafter. Regulations resulting from the Commission's 37th Annual Session, in 1985, besides prohibiting commercial hunting of certain species of whales, also prohibited whaling in the Indian Ocean, and prohibited commercial hunting with "cold" harpoons judged to be cruel and inhumane.

This Convention reflects a current global trend, reinforced by world public opinion, towards the complete prohibition on all commercial hunting of whales.

M.D.-P.

Access : ALS (Art. X)
Reserves : USP
Duration : USP
Deposit. : US (Art. X)
Language : Eng (Art. XI)

Modific. : Protocol 19.11.56 (04.05.59)

Reference : Can TS 1946/54, 1959/11 – UKTS 1949/5, 1959/68, 1957/22, 1984/76 – 161, 338 UNTS – JORF 7 Jan 49 – RTAF 1958/29

411.03 – INTERNATIONAL CONVENTION FOR THE PROTECTION OF BIRDS – FR

Concluded : 18.10.1950, Paris
In force : 17.01.1963
Parties : 10

This Convention replaces the International Convention to Protect Birds Useful to Agriculture (Paris, 1902). Its objective is to protect birds, especially migrant birds, which are threatened with diminishing numbers, or extinction in the wild state.

DETAILS OF THE CONVENTION

The Convention considers that, in the interests of science, the protection of nature, and the economy of each nation, all birds should as a matter of principle be protected. It stipulates that protection must be given to all birds during the breeding season, to migrants during their flight to their breeding grounds, and to endangered species throughout the year.

The export, transport, sale, purchase, donation, or holding of birds is prohibited during the period when a species is protected. Special attention is given in the Convention to birds' nests, eggs, and shells, and to young birds, as well as to certain methods of hunting birds which are prohibited or restricted.

Nevertheless, a species found to be a pest in a region may be excepted from protection. Exceptions may also be made in the interests of science and education. Each of the parties must draw up lists of birds which may be lawfully taken or killed in compliance with the Convention.

The parties are also to take measures to prevent the destruction of birds, to educate children and the public in the need for the protection of birds, and to establish reserves for breeding birds.

M.D.-P.

Access : ALS (Art. 11)
Reserves : USP
Duration : ULT (Art. 11)
Deposit. : FR (Art. 11)
Language : Fre

Reference : 638 UNTS

411.04 – INTERNATIONAL PLANT PROTECTION CONVENTION – FAO

Concluded : 06.12.1951, Rome
In force : 03.04.1952
Parties : 96

The objective of the Convention is to maintain and increase international co-operation in controlling plant pests and diseases of plants and plant products, and to prevent their introduction and spread across national boundaries.

DETAILS OF THE CONVENTION

Each of the parties undertakes to set up an official plant protection organization with the following responsibilities: to inspect areas under cultivation, and consignments of plants in international traffic, for the existence or outbreak of plant pests or diseases; to issue certificates relating to the phytosanitary condition and origin of plants and plant products; to carry out research in the field of plant protection; and to disseminate relevant information at the national level. In regard to phytosanitary certificates, they must certify that the plants are substantially free from injurious diseases and pests and that the consignment is believed to conform to the current phytosanitary regulations of the importing country.

The parties agree to regulate strictly the import and export of plants and plant products by means, where necessary, of prohibitions, inspections and destruction of consignments. They also pledge to collaborate at the international level, notably through participation in the FAO's international information system on plant pests and diseases of plants: the FAO Committee of Experts on Pest Control.

This Convention shall terminate and replace, between contracting governments, the International Convention respecting measures to be taken against the *phylloxera vastatrix* of 3 November 1881, the additional Convention (Berne, 1889) and the International Convention for the Protection of Plants (Rome, 1929).

M.D.-P.

Access : ALS (Art. 12)
Reserves : USP
Duration : USP
Deposit. : FAO
Language : Eng, Fre, Spa

Modific. : Rome 28.11.79 (04.04.91); Rome 24.11.83 (-)

Reference : Can TS 1953/16 – UKTS 1954/6 – 150 UNTS – UST 23/3 – JORF 5 Jan 62 – RTAF 1962/1

411.05 – CONVENTION ON WETLANDS OF INTERNATIONAL IMPORTANCE ESPECIALLY AS WATERFOWL HABITAT – UNESCO

Concluded : 02.02.1971, Ramsar
In force : 21.12.1975
Parties : 75

The objective of the Convention is to conserve wetlands through a combination of far-sighted national policies with co-ordinated international action. It aims to stem the progressive encroachment on and loss of wetlands now and in the future, and recognizes the fundamental ecological functions of wetlands as regulations of water regimes and as habitats supporting a characteristic flora and fauna, especially waterfowl. It accepts that wetlands constitute a resource of great economic, cultural, scientific and recreational value, the loss of which would be irreparable. It also recognizes that waterfowl in their seasonal migrations may transcend frontiers and so should be regarded as an international resource.

DETAILS OF THE CONVENTION

Each of the parties designates suitable wetlands within its territory for inclusion in a List of Wetlands of International Importance, which is maintained by **IUCN – The World Conservation Union**. Each contracting party shall consider its international responsibilities for the conservation, management and wise use of migratory stocks of waterfowl, and formulate and implement plans so as to promote the conservation of the wetlands included in the List.

The parties must promote the conservation of wetlands and waterfowl by establishing nature reserves in wetlands, whether they are included in the List or not, and by providing adequately for their wardering. The parties also agree to encourage research and the exchange of data and publications regarding wetlands; to promote the training of personnel competent in the fields of wetland research, management and conservation; and to endeavour through management to increase waterfowl populations.

The contracting parties consult with each other on the implementation of the Convention, especially where a wetland extends over the territories of more than one of the contracting parties, or where a water system or watershed is shared by contracting parties. The parties also endeavour to co-ordinate and support present and future policies and regulations concerning the conservation of wetlands.

Advisory Conferences on the Conservation of Wetlands and Waterfowl are convened as the necessity arises to discuss the implementation of the Convention.

M.D.-P.

Access : CON (Art. 9)
Reserves : USP
Duration : ULT (Art. 9, 11)
Deposit. : UNESCO
Language : Eng, Fre, Ger, Rus

Modific. : Protocol Paris 03.12.82 (01.10.86)

Reference : Can TS 1981/9 – ILM 11:963, 22:698 – UKTS 1976/34 – JORF 20 Feb 87

411.06 – CONVENTION ON INTERNATIONAL TRADE IN ENDANGERED SPECIES OF WILD FAUNA AND FLORA (CITES) – UNEP

Concluded : 03.03.1973, Washington
In force : 01.07.1975
Parties : 119

Given the extent of their beauty and variety, wild fauna and flora are an irreplaceable part of nature which must be safeguarded for present and future generations. The aim of the Convention is to protect certain endangered species from over-exploitation due to trade by means of a system of import/export permits. This includes all animals and plants whether dead or alive, and any recognizable parts or derivatives thereof.

DETAILS OF THE CONVENTION

Appendix I covers endangered species. The trading of species in this category is prohibited except under exceptional conditions. Appendix II covers species that may become endangered unless trade is regulated. Appendix III covers species that any party identifies as being subject to regulation within its jurisdiction for the purposes of preventing or restricting exploitation, and as needing international co-operation in the control of trade.

Import/export permits are required for species listed in Appendices I and II; and, if they are brought in by sea (that is, taken in the marine environment which is not under the jurisdiction of any state), a certificate from the state of introduction is required.

STRUCTURE

The Convention establishes an institutional framework composed of a biennial **Conference of the Parties**, Standing, Scientific and Implementation **Committees**, and a **Secretariat** provided by the Executive Director of the United Nations Environment Programme (UNEP) [see 410 A]. Parties are required to establish "management and scientific authorities". The broad participation of states in the CITES system makes this Convention and its structure a model for subsequent conservation treaties.

M.D.-P.

Access : ALS (Art. XIX, XXI, XXV)
Reserves : PAU (Art. XXIII)
Duration : ULT (Art. XXI)
Deposit. : CH (Art. XXV)
Language : Chi, Eng, Fre, Rus, Spa (Art. XXV)

Modific. : Amendments to Convention: Bonn 27.06.79 (13.04.87); Gaborone 30.04.83 (-); Amendments to Appendices: Berne 1976 (04.02.77); 1978 (12.08.78, 16.02.79); San José de Costa Rica 1979 (28.06.79); 1980 (17.10.80); New Delhi 1981 (06.06.81); Gaborone 1983 (29.07.83, 14.03.84); Buenos Aires 1985 (01.08.85); 1986 (29.08.86, 03.01.87); Ottawa 1987 ; Lausanne 1989 (18.01.90); Kyoto 1992 (11.06.92)

Reference : 993 UNTS – UKTS 1976/101, 1980/33, 1981/77, 1984/34/43 – RGDIP 1987/2 – JORF 30 Aug 78, 19 Feb 80 – RTAF 1978/63, 1980/4, 1982/60, 1983/73

411.07 – CONVENTION ON THE CONSERVATION OF MIGRATORY SPECIES OF WILD ANIMALS (CMS) – UNEP

Concluded : 23.06.1979, Bonn
In force : 01.11.1983
Parties : 35

Recognizing that wild animals, in general, are an irreplaceable part of the Earth's natural system, the parties acknowledge the importance of migratory species being conserved and of range states agreeing to take action to this end whenever possible and appropriate. A range state, in relation to a particular migratory species, is defined as any state which exercises jurisdiction over any part of the range of that migratory species, or a state whose flag vessels are engaged outside national jurisdictional limits in taking that migratory species. The parties also acknowledge the importance of paying special attention to migratory species whose conservation status is unfavourable, and of taking either individually or in co-operation appropriate and necessary steps to conserve such species and their habitat. The need to take action to prevent migratory species from becoming endangered is also acknowledged.

DETAILS OF THE CONVENTION

The parties agree to promote, co-operate in and support research relating to migratory species; they agree to try to provide immediate protection for the migratory species included in Appendix I (endangered migratory species) and to conclude agreements covering the conservation and management of migratory species included in Appendix II. Appendix II lists migratory species which have an unfavourable conservation status and which require international agreements for their conservation and management. It also lists those which do already have a conservation status but which would significantly benefit from the international co-operation that could be achieved through an international agreement.

Appendix I. Parties that are range states of a migratory species listed in Appendix I shall endeavour:

- to conserve and, where feasible and appropriate, restore those habitats of the species which are of importance in saving the species from the danger of extinction;
- to prevent, remove, compensate for or minimize, as appropriate, the adverse effects of activities or obstacles that seriously impede or prevent the migration of the species; and,
- to the extent feasible and appropriate, prevent, reduce or control factors that are endangering or are likely to further endanger the species, including strictly controlling the introduction of, or controlling or eliminating already introduced, exotic species.

The parties that are range states of migratory species listed in Annex I shall prohibit the taking of animals belonging to such species. Exceptions may be made to this prohibition only if the taking is for scientific purposes, if it is undertaken in order to enhance the propagation or survival of the affected species, if it accommodates the needs of traditional subsistence users of such species, or if extraordinary circumstances require it.

Appendix II. The object of the agreements covering the conservation and management of migratory species included in Appendix II is to restore the migratory species concerned to a favourable conservation status or to maintain it in such a status. Each agreement should cover the whole of the range of the migratory species concerned and should be open to accession by all range states of that species, whether or not they are parties to the Convention.

Structure. The **Secretariat**, provided by the Executive Director of UNEP [see 410 A], maintains and publishes a list of range states of all migratory species listed in Appendices I and II of the Convention. The **Conference of the Parties**, which meets once every two years, is the decision-making organ of the Convention. A **Scientific Council** is established to provide advice on scientific matters.

M.D.-P.

Access	: ASO (Art. 15, 17)
Reserves	: PAU (Art. 11, 14)
Duration	: USP
Deposit.	: DE
Language	: Eng, Fre, Ger, Rus, Spa

Modific. : Amendments to Appendices I and II 1985 (24.10.86); 1988 (12.01.89)

Reference : ILM 19:15 – UKTS 1990/87

411.08 – CONVENTION ON BIOLOGICAL DIVERSITY – UN

Concluded : 05.06.1992, Rio de Janeiro
Parties : 15

Adopted on 5 June 1992, this framework Convention was opened for signature during UNCED Conference held in Rio de Janeiro from 3 to 14 June 1992.

Contracting parties declare that they recognize the intrinsic value of biological diversity, and the ecological, genetic, social, economic, scientific, educational, cultural, recreational and aesthetic values of biological diversity and its components, but are concerned that this diversity is being significantly reduced by certain human activities.

The Convention's objective is the conservation of that diversity, the sustainable use of its components, and the fair and equitable sharing of the benefits arising from the utilization of genetic resources, including appropriate access to genetic resources and appropriate transfer of relevant technologies, taking into account all rights over those resources and technologies, and appropriate funding.

DETAILS OF THE CONVENTION

States enjoy the sovereign right to exploit their own resources pursuant to their own environmental policies, and have the responsibility to ensure that activities within their jurisdiction or control do not cause damage to the environment of other states or to areas beyond the limits of national jurisdiction.

The Convention includes provisions which deal with promoting co-operation between contracting parties, directly or through competent international organizations; adopting general measures for conservation and sustainable use (e.g. to develop national strategies, plans or programmes); the identification and monitoring components of biological diversity; *in-situ* and *ex-situ* conservation; the sustainable use of components of biological diversity; the adoption of economically and socially-sound measures that act as incentives for the conservation and sustainable use of components of biological diversity; research and training; public education and awareness; impact assessment and the minimizing of adverse impacts.

The authority to determine access to genetic resources rests with national governments and is subject to national legislation. Each contracting party shall endeavour to create conditions to facilitate access to genetic resources for environmentally sound uses by other contracting parties and not to impose restrictions that run counter to the objectives of this Convention.

Each contracting state recognizes that technology includes biotechnology and undertakes to provide and/or facilitate access and transfer to other contracting parties of technologies relevant to the conservation and sustainable use of biological diversity, or technologies which make use of genetic resources and do not cause significant damage to the environment.

Access to and transfer of technology to developing countries shall be provided and/or facilitated under fair and most favourable terms, including on concessional and preferential terms where mutually agreed and, where necessary, in accordance with the financial mechanism established by the Convention. In the case of technology subject to patents and other intellectual property rights, such access and transfer shall be provided on terms which recognize and/or are consistent with the adequate and effective protection of intellectual property rights.

The contracting parties shall facilitate the exchange of information from all publicly available sources relevant to the conservation and sustainable use of biological diversity, taking into account the special needs of developing countries. They shall promote international technical and scientific co-operation in the field of conservation and sustainable use of biological diversity and take appropriate legal, administrative and policy measures to provide for effective participation in biological research activities by those contracting parties. Each contracting party shall take all practicable measures to promote and advance priority access on a fair and equitable basis by contracting parties, especially developing countries, to the results and benefits arising from biotechnologies based upon genetic resources provided by those contracting parties. Such access shall be on mutually agreed terms.

Each contracting party undertakes to provide, in accordance with its capabilities, financial support and incentives to national activities intended to achieve the objectives of the Convention.

The developed country parties shall provide new and additional financial resources to enable developing country parties both to benefit from the Convention's provisions and to meet the agreed full incremental costs to them of implementing measures which fulfil the obligations of the Convention. Other parties, including countries undergoing the process of transition to a market economy, may voluntarily assume the obligations of the developed country parties.

A financial mechanism is established to provide financial resources, on a grant or concessional basis, to developing country parties for the purposes of this Convention. This mechanism shall function under the authority and guidance of, and be accountable to, the Conference of the Parties. The Global Environment Facility (GEF), administered jointly by UNEP, UNDP [see 222 A] and World Bank [see 221 A], has been designated on an interim basis to serve as the financial mechanism.

STRUCTURE

The **Conference of the Parties** holds ordinary meetings and extraordinary meetings. At its first ordinary meeting, the Conference shall designate the **Secretariat** from amongst those existing competent international organizations which have indicated their willingness to carry out the Secretariat functions for this Convention. A **Subsidiary Body for the Provision of Scientific, Technical and Technological Advice** is also established to provide the Conference and its subsidiary bodies with timely advice relating to the implementation of this Convention.

Specific provisions deal with the settlement of disputes. They provide for negotiation, good offices, mediation, arbitration procedures, submission of a dispute to the International Court of Justice [see 001.02], and the use of a conciliation procedure.

M.D.-P.

Access : ASO (Art. 34)
Reserves : PRO (Art. 37)
Duration : USP
Deposit. : UN (Art. 41)
Language : Ara, Chi, Eng, Fre, Rus, Spa (Art. 42)

Reference : ILM 31:818

4.1.2 Marine Pollution

The rapid growth of maritime traffic combined with tanker disasters, oil spills from sea wells, and the dumping of wastes and other matter has significantly increased the pollution of the marine environment and affected all coastal states.

In recent years, several major disasters brought public pressure to bear on states and tanker-owners to agree on measures to prevent marine pollution and, when it does occur, to provide adequate compensation for damage. Several international agreements now address these issues.

This section summarizes this body of conventions, though some relevant provisions also may be found in section 1.8.3, which includes a description of the IMO [see 183 A], and in section 4.3.2.

SELECTED BIBLIOGRAPHY

Eaton, Judith R., "Oil Spill Liability and Compensation: Time to Clean-up the Law", *George Washington Journal of International Law and Economics* 19 (3) (1985): 787-827.

Redgwell, Catherine, "Compensation for Oil Pollution Damage: Quantifying Environmental Harm", *Marine Policy* 16 (March 1992): 90-98.

412.01 – INTERNATIONAL CONVENTION FOR THE PREVENTION OF POLLUTION OF THE SEA BY OIL – IMO

Concluded : 12.05.1954, London
In force : 26.07.1958
Parties : 69

Pollution of the sea by oil is a major problem requiring international co-operation and the aim of this Convention is to the prevent pollution of the sea by oil discharged from ships. This Convention is superseded by the International Convention for the Prevention of Pollution from Ships (London, 1973) [see 412.09] and its 1978 Protocol [see 412.10] between the parties to that Convention.

Scope: This 1954 Convention applies to all ships, except tankers of under 150 tons gross tonnage and other ships of under 500 tons gross tonnage, registered in the territory of, or having the nationality of, one of the contracting parties. Naval ships and whaling ships are also excepted.

DETAILS OF THE CONVENTION

The Convention prohibits the deliberate discharge of oil or oily mixtures from all seagoing vessels except tankers of under 150 tons gross and other ships of under 500 tons gross in specific "prohibited zones".

The discharge prohibition is not applicable when, in the case of a ship, the oil content of the discharge is less than 100 parts per million of the mixture, or the discharge is made as far as practicable from land. In the case of a tanker, it is not applicable if the total quantity of oil discharged on a ballast voyage does not exceed 1/15,000 of the total cargo-carrying capacity, or the tanker is more than 50 miles from the nearest land (Art. III). However, in some regions prohibited zones of up to 100 miles have been established (viz. the Adriatic and Mediterranean seas, Persian Gulf, Red Sea, coasts of Australia and Madagascar, and some others).

There are exceptions to these restrictions in cases of necessity: to secure the safety of ships, to save lives, to prevent damage to cargo, or where leakage is unavoidable and all measures have been taken to minimize it.

Ships must be fitted within 12 months to prevent the escape of oil into bilges, and the parties must provide appropriate facilities at ports and oil-loading terminals for the reception of oil residues and oil mixtures.

All ships covered by the Convention must carry an oil record book in a form specified in the Annex, to be completed whenever certain operations take place. The book can be examined by the authorities of any contracting state if the ship is in harbour in the territory of that state.

A contracting party has the right to inform another contracting party when one of the latter's ships has violated the provisions of the Convention. The government which reported the violation and the International Maritime Organization (IMO) [see 183 A] should be informed of the results of any action taken against the ship.

The parties are required to send texts of laws, decrees, orders and regulations giving effect to the Convention to the IMO.

Maguelonne Déjeant-Pons

Access : ALS (Art. XIV)
Reserves : USP
Duration : USP
Deposit. : IMO (Art. XXI)
Language : Eng, Fre (Art. XXI)

Modific. : Amendments London 11.04.62 (18.05.67, 28.06.67 (art.14)); London 21.10.69 (20.01.78); (Great Barrier Reef) Amendments London 12.10.71 (-); (Tanks) Amendments London 15.10.71 (-)

Reference : 327, 600 UNTS – Can TS 1958/31, 1967/29 – UST 12/3, 17/2, 28/1 – UKTS 1958/54, 1967/59, 1978/21 – ILM 9:1, 11:267 – JORF 9 Oct 58, 20 Dec 67 – RTAF 1958/31, 1967/88

412.02 – TANKER OWNERS VOLUNTARY AGREEMENT CONCERNING LIABILITY FOR OIL POLLUTION – TOVALOP

Adopted : 07.01.1969, London
In force : 06.10.1969

The world's first large-scale oil spill, the *Torrey Canyon* disaster of 1967 off the Cornwall coast of England, provided a major stimulus to international action [see also 412.03 and 412.04]. As a result, four regimes were implemented through which compensation would in future be available for oil spill damage and clean-up costs following a marine pollution incident. Two of these regimes were, and are, voluntary – TOVALOP and CRISTAL [see 412.05]. They were set up in response to the determination of the tanker and oil industries to take constructive action prior to the widespread ratification and acceptance of two international conventions: the International Convention on Civil Liability for Oil Pollution Damage (CLC) 1969 [see 412.04] and the International Convention on the Establishment of an International Fund for Compensation for Oil Pollution Damage (FUND) 1971 [see 412.06].

DETAILS OF THE AGREEMENT

Although voluntary in character, once a tanker owner or bareboat charterer becomes a party to the Agreement he/she is contractually obliged to meet all the terms and conditions of the Agreement without exception. Under its terms, tanker owners and bareboat charterers agree to assume certain obligations for which they might not otherwise be legally liable.

In the event of a tanker spilling or threatening to spill persistent oil (either bunker fuel or cargo), the owner or bareboat charterer will not only take appropriate action to minimize or prevent the spill but will reimburse governments and others who incur reasonable costs in responding to the incident or who suffer pollution damage.

A party seeking compensation under the Agreement is not required to demonstrate that the tanker owner or bareboat charterer was at fault, nor is there generally a requirement that the issue of liability be determined prior to the payment of compensation. However, in paying the compensation, the tanker owner or bareboat charterer does not thereby assume responsibility for the spill or waive any rights of recovery from third parties whose fault may have caused, or at least contributed to, the incident. Claims under the Agreement are to be made within two years from the date of the incident.

TOVALOP has been amended on numerous occasions. With effect from 20 February 1987, a Supplement was added to the Agreement that was in force prior to that time – now termed the Standing Agreement. Under the Standing Agreement, which only applies when no liability is imposed under the terms of the CLC, the maximum compensation for all claims arising out of any one incident is US$160 per limitation ton or US$16.8 million, whichever is the less. The Supplement has resulted *inter alia* in the limits of financial responsibility being substantially raised where the cargo on board the tanker at the time of the incident is owned by a party to CRISTAL. In that event, the maximum limits of financial responsibility are:

- for all tankers up to 5,000 gross tons, a maximum of US$3.5 million;
- for vessels over 5,000 gross tons, US$3.5 million plus US$493 for each gross ton in excess of 5,000 gross tons, up to a maximum of US$70 million.

Unlike the Standing Agreement, the TOVALOP Supplement applies regardless of whether compensation is available under the terms of the CLC. However, any payment of compensation made by the TOVALOP party under the CLC or other legal regime goes towards meeting the TOVALOP Supplement obligations and is not additional thereto.

The responsibility for settling claims under TOVALOP falls to the participating tanker owner or bareboat charterer. A fund of money is neither maintained by TOVALOP nor by the International Tanker Owners Pollution Federation, which merely administers the Agreement.

It was originally envisaged that TOVALOP would last only until such time as the CLC had been ratified by a majority of maritime nations and was therefore widespread in its application. However, even though the CLC has entered into force in numerous maritime states, significant gaps remain which TOVALOP continues to fill. The TOVALOP Supplement was originally expected to last for a period of five years from 20 February 1987. However, in October 1991, a two-year extension was agreed and, at the present time, the Supplement is due to expire on 20 February 1994. This could be further extended by a vote of the membership. In 1993, membership stood at some 3,600 tanker owners and bareboat charterers.

Patricia Ford

Access : ENT
Language : Eng

Modific. : 14.07.72 (20.02.73); 11.02.77 (20.02.77); 16.05.78 (01.06.78); 28.05.80 (28.05.80); 26.05.81 (01.06.81); 30.10.84 (01.11.84); 21.05.86 (01.06.86); Supplement 09.12.86 (20.02.87); 25.10.89 (20.02.90); 30.10.91 (20.02.92)

412.03 – INTERNATIONAL CONVENTION RELATING TO INTERVENTION ON THE HIGH SEAS IN CASES OF OIL POLLUTION CASUALTIES – IMO

Concluded : 29.11.1969, Brussels
In force : 06.05.1975
Parties : 60

The marine pollution incident resulting from the grounding of the oil tanker *Torrey Canyon* in 1967 raised the issue of the rights of coastal states to intervene and control operations when an accident on the high seas threatens their waters and coastline with oil pollution. The aim of this Convention is to enable countries to take action on the high seas in the case of a maritime casualty resulting in the danger of oil pollution of sea and coastline and to establish that such action would not affect the principle of freedom of the high seas.

DETAILS OF THE CONVENTION

The Convention allows the parties to take such measures on the high seas as may be necessary to prevent, mitigate or eliminate grave and imminent danger to their coastline, or related interests, from pollution or threat of pollution of the sea by oil following a maritime accident. Measures cannot be taken against warships or other state-owned or operated ships not engaged in commercial activity.

Before taking action, a coastal state should notify the flag state of the ship, consult independent experts and notify any persons whose interests may reasonably be expected to be affected by such action. In cases of extreme urgency, measures may be taken at once.

If a coastal state takes measures beyond those authorized by the Convention, it will be liable to pay compensation for damages caused by these measures.

The system established by the Convention has been extended to substances other than oil by the 1973 Protocol [see 412.08].

In a 1992 UNCED Survey, no dispute is known to have arisen among any of the parties concerning measures taken to deal with pollution casualties, nor is any party known to have been obliged to pay compensation, nor has the dispute settlement mechanism under Article VIII been invoked to date.

Maguelonne Déjeant-Pons

Access : ALS (Art. XIII)
Reserves : USP
Duration : USP
Deposit. : IMO (Art. XX)
Language : Eng, Fre (Art. XX)

Modific. : Protocol London 02.11.73 (30.03.83); Amendments to Protocol MEPC.49(31) 04.07.91 (30.03.93)

Reference : 970 UNTS – RTAF 1975/45 – RGDIP 1987/1 – UKTS 1975/77, 1983/27 – ILM 9:25, 13:605 – UST 26/1 – JORF 3 Jul 75

412.04 – INTERNATIONAL CONVENTION ON CIVIL LIABILITY FOR OIL POLLUTION DAMAGE (CLC) – IMO

Concluded : 29.11.1969, Brussels
In force : 19.06.1975
Parties : 79

In response to oil tanker spills, international concern focused on the basis and extent of the liability of ship or cargo owners for oil pollution damage following a marine casualty. The International Convention on Civil Liability for Oil Pollution Damage was the result of a desire to ensure that victims of oil pollution damage were adequately compensated.

Scope: The Convention applies exclusively to pollution damage caused in contracting states by tankers actually carrying oil in bulk and to the measures taken to prevent or minimize such damage (Art. II).

DETAILS OF THE CONVENTION

Subject to a number of specified exceptions, liability under the Convention is strict. A claim may only be made against the registered owner of the vessel in accordance with the provisions of the Convention and not against his servants or agents (Art. III-4).

Where the owner proves that the pollution damage resulted from *inter alia* an act of war or hostilities, or was wholly caused by an act or omission of a third party with intent to cause damage, or was wholly caused by the negligence or other wrongful act of any government or other authority responsible for the maintenance of lights or other navigational aids, then he will not be held liable for the damage so caused (Art. III-2).

The Convention makes provision for the owner to be wholly or partially exonerated where he proves an intentional act or omission by the person suffering the damage with intent to cause such damage or where he proves that they were contributorily negligent (Art. III 3).

The owner is required to constitute a fund, representing the total sum of his liability, with the court or other competent authority of any one of the contracting states in which an action is brought under the Convention. Provided the pollution incident was not the result of his actual fault or privity, the shipowner is entitled to limit his liability in respect of any one incident by a specified aggregate amount for each ton of the ship's tonnage (Art. V). In 1969, the limit was 2,000 francs for each ton, which was, in any event, not to exceed 210 million francs. By a Protocol in 1976, the gold franc was replaced by the Special Drawing Right (SDR) which set the limits at 133 SDR per ton up to a maximum of 14 million SDR.

Tankers carrying over 2,000 tons of oil are compelled to maintain insurance or other financial security in order to cover their potential liability under the Convention.

MODIFICATIONS

While the limits on liability had proved useful, by the mid-1980s it was generally felt that they were too low to provide adequate compensation. As a consequence, a new Protocol was adopted in 1984 which provided for a significant increase in the limits of liability and specified a new and simplified procedure for their future amendment. This Protocol has not yet, however, entered into force.

At an IMO conference held towards the end of November 1992, new Protocols were adopted to both the CLC and the FUND Convention [see 412.06]. They are designed to raise the compensation limits payable under the two conventions and to amend the entry into force provisions of the 1984 protocols. Existing convention limits provide for maximum compensation of about US$83 million; following the 1992 Protocols, this will be raised to US$270 million.

The CLC Protocol 1992 will enter into force after acceptance by ten states of which four or five must have tanker tonnage of at least one million gross tons; there is no requirement that the Protocols have to be accepted by all the major oil importing countries.

Patricia Ford

Access : ALS (Art. XIII)
Reserves : USP
Duration : USP
Deposit. : IMO (Art. XIX)
Language : Eng, Fre (Art. XXI)

Modific. : Protocol 19.11.76 (08.04.81); Protocol London 25.05.84 (-); Protocol 00.11.92 (-)

Reference : 973 UNTS – RTAF 1975/45, 1981/30 – RGDIP 1987/4 – ULR 1984/2 – UKTS 1975/106 – DJI 1984 – JORF 3 Jul 75

412.05 – CONTRACT REGARDING A SUPPLEMENT TO TANKER LIABILITY FOR OIL POLLUTION – CRISTAL

Adopted : 14.01.1971, London
In force : 14.01.1971

The Contract was devised as a means of providing compensation supplementary to that available from tanker owners or bareboat charterers under TOVALOP [see 412.02]. To that end, many of its provisions, as well as its overall scope, are complementary to those of TOVALOP's.

DETAILS OF THE CONTRACT

Any company engaged in the production, refining, marketing, storing, trading or terminaling of oil, or which receives oil in bulk for its own consumption or use, can become a party to the CRISTAL Contract.

Unlike the arrangements under TOVALOP, CRISTAL maintains a fund from which claims are met. Parties to CRISTAL are required to make contributions to this fund in proportion to the quantities of crude and fuel oil that each receives by sea. The actual amount of money required to be paid into the fund and the frequency of calls depends on the claims settlements.

In order for CRISTAL to apply to an incident, three conditions must first be satisfied: (i) the incident must involve an escape or discharge of pesistent oil, or threat thereof, from a tanker carrying a cargo that is owned or deemed to be owned, at the time of the incident, by a party to CRISTAL; (ii) the tanker owner or bareboat charterer must first pay compensation up to the applicable limit calculated in accordance with the TOVALOP Supplement; and (iii) none of the limited exemptions (e.g. acts of war) can apply.

In the event of all of these conditions being satisfied, compensation under the terms of the CRISTAL Contract may be sought, up to the applicable limit, for reimbursement of reasonable costs incurred by a tanker owner or any other person in taking threat removal measures, preventative measures or through having sustained pollution damage.

Under the terms of the CRISTAL Contract, the following maximum limits of financial responsibility can apply (the limits being determined by the gross tonnage of the tanker):

- for all tankers up to 5,000 gross tons, a maximum of US$36 million; and
- for tankers over 5,000 gross tons, US$36 million, plus US$733 for each gross ton in excess of 5,000 gross tons up to the maximum of US$135 million.

In all cases, the stated amounts include compensation that would be payable by the tanker owner, as determined by the limits of financial responsibility under the TOVALOP Supplement.

Any person who believes they have a valid claim under the terms of the CRISTAL Contract is required to give notice in writing of that claim to Cristal Limited as soon as possible but, in any event, not later than two years from the date of the incident.

The CRISTAL Contract will remain in force until 20 February 1994 although, as with the TOVALOP Supplement, this time limit could be extended by a vote of CRISTAL members. As of 1993, some 730 oil companies are parties to the CRISTAL Contract.

P.F.

Access : ENT
Language : Eng

Modific. : Last Version (20.02.89)

412.06 – INTERNATIONAL CONVENTION ON THE ESTABLISHMENT OF AN INTERNATIONAL FUND FOR COMPENSATION FOR OIL POLLUTION DAMAGE (FUND) – IMO

Concluded : 18.12.1971, Brussels
In force : 16.10.1978
Parties : 56

Although the 1969 CLC Convention had been adopted [see 412.04], there was still concern that a victim of an oil pollution incident could nevertheless be left without a remedy under the terms of that Convention. Moreover, not only was there a degree of disquiet that the limits imposed would not be adequate in the event of a major oil pollution incident, but there was concern that only shipowners, and not the cargo interests, were to be liable to pay compensation.

In light of these various reservations, the Brussels Conference of 1969 considered a compromise proposal to establish an international fund, to be subscribed to by cargo interests, which would go some way to relieving shipowners of the total liability and, in addition, provide compensation to victims of oil pollution damage who would otherwise be inadequately compensated or without a remedy under the

CLC Convention. The FUND Convention was the net result of that compromise and was adopted at a further Brussels Conference in 1971.

DETAILS OF THE CONVENTION

Where any person having suffered pollution damage is unable to obtain full and adequate compensation for the damage under the CLC Convention, the Fund is obliged to meet their claim (Art. 4). However, in this case, the Fund's obligations are in effect limited to US$16 million given the requirement that the total sum payable by the shipowner and the Fund does not exceed US$30 million for any one incident.

Where, however, the shipowner is unable to meet his liability, or liability under the CLC Convention does not arise, the Fund is obliged to meet the whole amount of compensation due. Under certain circumstances, the maximum liability of the Fund may be increased, but in no event to a sum greater than US$60 million for each incident (Art. 4-6).

Save where the damage resulted from the wilful misconduct of the shipowner himself or by reason of the fact that the ship did not comply with certain conventions, the Fund is also under an obligation to indemnify the shipowner or his insurer for a portion of his liability under the CLC Convention (Art. 5-1). This portion is equivalent to US$100 per ton or US$8.3 million, whichever is the lesser sum.

The Fund is financed by levies on those importers in contracting states who import more than 150,000 tonnes of oil per annum.

MODIFICATIONS

As with the CLC Convention, the *Poincaré franc* was replaced by the Special Drawing Right in a Protocol adopted in 1976, and the limits of liability raised by a further Protocol in 1984. These Protocols are yet to be ratified.

The 1992 Protocol, adopted towards the end of November of that year, will, in addition to amending the entry into force provisions of the 1984 Protocol, further increase the limits of liability to be applied. It has also been agreed that individual contributions to the Fund should be capped at 27.5 per cent until the total volume of contributing oil reaches 750 million tonnes, or until five years after the entry into force of the 1992 Protocol, whichever is first.

The 1992 Fund Protocol will enter into force when it has been accepted by eight states importing at least 450 million tonnes of oil per year each.

P.F.

Access	: CON (Art. 37)
Reserves	: USP
Duration	: MIN (Art. 43)
Deposit.	: IMO (Art. 46)
Language	: Eng, Fre (Art. 48)
Modific.	: Protocol London 19.11.76 (-); 25.05.84 (-); 00.11.92 (-)
Reference	: IMO Doc. LEG/CONF.6/67 – UKTS 1978/95 – ULR 1971, 1977/1, 1984/2 – RGDIP 1987/4 – DJI 1984 – RTAF 1978/81 – JORF 16 Apr 87

412.07 – CONVENTION ON THE PREVENTION OF MARINE POLLUTION BY DUMPING OF WASTES AND OTHER MATTER – IMO

Concluded: 29.12.1972, London, Mexico, Moscow, Washington
In force : 30.08.1975
Parties : 71

The sea's capacity to recycle its natural resources is limited, as is its ability to absorb pollution and render it harmless. This Convention represents a new step in the control and prevention of the pollution of the sea at the international level. Specifically, its aim is to control the pollution of the sea resulting from the dumping of waste products, and to this end it encourages regional agreements supplementary to the Convention.

Scope: The Convention covers all seas, and all deliberate disposal of wastes other than that incidental to the normal operation of vessels, aircraft, platforms and other sea structures, and their equipment. The provisions of the Convention do not apply in cases where it is necessary to save human life, to ensure the safety of a ship, or in case of *force majeure*, or extreme emergency.

DETAILS OF THE CONVENTION

The dumping of matter listed in Annex I is prohibited, while the dumping of matter listed in Annex II is allowable only by special permit. The dumping of matter listed in Annex III is permissible only by prior general permit.

The parties undertake to establish authorities to issue permits, to keep records of the quantity of material for which dumping is authorized, and to monitor the condition of the seas.

Each party also undertakes to enforce the provisions of the Convention in regard to all vessels and aircraft registered in its territory or flying its flag; to vessels and aircraft loading within its territory or territorial seas matter which is to be dumped; and to vessels and aircraft and fixed or floating platforms under its jurisdiction believed to be engaged in dumping.

Parties with common interests in certain areas of the sea agree to enter into regional agreements to prevent marine pollution. For instance, the Protocol for the Prevent of Pollution of the Mediterranean Sea by Dumping from Ships and Aircraft (Barcelona, 1976) makes reference, in its Preamble, to this 1972 London Convention.

The parties collaborate in training scientific and technical personnel, in supplying equipment for research and monitoring, and in disposing of and treating wastes. Procedures are developed for the assessment of liability and the settlement of disputes.

Finally, the parties undertake to promote measures to prevent:

- pollution by hydrocarbons and other hazardous matter transported other than for dumping;
- wastes generated during the operation of vessels, aircraft, platforms, and other sea structures;
- radioactive pollutants and agents intended for biological and chemical warfare; and
- matter originating directly or indirectly from the exploration, exploitation and treatment in the sea of mineral resources from the sea-bed.

Maguelonne Déjeant-Pons

Access : ALS (Art. XVIII)
Reserves : USP
Duration : USP
Deposit. : US, MX, GB, RU (Art. XVII)
Language : Eng, Fre, Rus, Spa (Art. XXII)

Modific. : (Disputes) Amendments 12.10.78 (-); Amendments to the Annexes Res.5(III) 12.10.78 (11.03.79); Res.12(V) 24.09.80 (11.03.81); Res.37(12) 03.11.89 (19.05.90)

Reference : Can TS 1979/36 – UKTS 1976/43, 1979/71, 1982/20 – UST 26/2 – JORF 14 Oct 77, 25 May 82 – RTAF 1977/75, 1982/19

412.08 – PROTOCOL RELATING TO INTERVENTION ON THE HIGH SEAS IN CASES OF POLLUTION BY SUBSTANCES OTHER THAN OIL – IMO

Concluded : 02.11.1973, London
In force : 30.03.1983
Parties : 26

The Protocol is open to ratification, agreement or approval of the states party to the International Convention Relating to Intervention on the High Seas in Cases of Oil Pollution Casualties (Brussels, 1969) [see 412.03]. It extends the application of the Convention to the substances listed in the Annex or substances with similar characteristics.

Its aim is to allow states to take measures on the high seas in cases of maritime accidents which threaten their coasts, or common interests, with imminent and serious pollution other than oil pollution.

M. D.-P.

Access : CON (Art. IV)
Reserves : USP
Duration : USP
Deposit. : IMO (Art. IX)
Language : Eng, Fre, Rus, Spa (Art. XI)

Reference : RGDIP 1987/1

412.09 – INTERNATIONAL CONVENTION FOR THE PREVENTION OF POLLUTION FROM SHIPS, AND 1978 PROTOCOL (MARPOL 73/78) – IMO

Concluded : 02.11.1973, London
In force : 02.10.1983
Parties : 77

Despite the previous measures taken by the IMO to fight oil pollution, the considerable development of modern industry and the pollution it produced demanded action on a wider scale. The objective of the Convention is to prevent pollution of the marine environment from the discharge of oil and other harmful substances or effluents, and to minimize the accidental discharge of these substances.

Scope: The Convention applies to all ships and to all the technical aspects of pollution by ships, except their dumping of waste. It does not apply to pollution resulting from the exploration and exploitation of mineral resources on the sea-bed.

DETAILS OF THE CONVENTION

The Convention contains two protocols: one concerning reports on incidents involving harmful substances, and the other concerning arbitration.

Five annexes contain regulations on various types of pollution – namely: pollution by oil; pollution by noxious liquid in bulk; pollution by harmful substances carried by sea in packaged forms or in freight containers, portable tanks, or road and rail tank wagons; pollution by sewage from ships; and pollution by garbage from ships. Adherence to Annexes III, IV and V is voluntary. The Convention replaces the International Convention for the Prevention of Pollution of the Sea by Oil (London, 1954) as between the parties to that Convention [see 412.01].

Pollution from Oil. In Annex I, the Convention keeps the provisions of the 1964 amendment to the London Convention of 1954 regarding the discharge of oil. While it does not substantially change those provisions, it does reduce the maximum quantity of oil which can be discharged from a new tanker during a ballast voyage from 1/15,000 to 1/30,000 of the total quantity the cargo carried. This applies as much to non-persistent oils as to persistent oils.

With few exceptions, the discharge of oil is prohibited in special areas which are particularly vulnerable to pollution (viz. the Mediterranean, the Black Sea, the Baltic, the Red Sea, and the Gulf area).

All ships carrying oil must apply methods of retention of oily waste on board and be equipped with installations to ensure the storage of oil residues on board and their discharge to reception facilities onshore. A vessel must be equipped with certain equipment including an oil discharge monitoring and control system, oily-water separating equipment, and an oil filtering system of slop tanks, oil residue tanks, and pumping and piping arrangements.

Tankers of 70,000 tons deadweight and above, built after 31 December 1975, must be provided with segregated ballast tanks having a capacity that will allow the ship to operate safely on ballast voyages without recourse to the use of oil tanks for water ballast. The segregated ballast tanks must also fulfil certain conditions of subdivision and damage stability so that in any loading conditions and in the event of the vessel running aground, or after a collision, they can survive any damage sustained to the vessel.

Pollution from Noxious Liquid in Bulk. Annex II establishes regulations governing the discharge of noxious liquid in bulk. One of the appendices of the Convention lists some 250 substances whose discharge is permitted only in reception facilities, until they reach a certain concentration and fulfil certain conditions, depending on the category of the substance. In any event, no discharge of residues containing noxious liquid substances is authorized at a distance of less than 12 miles from the nearest land. Conditions which are even more restrictive are in force in the Baltic and Black seas.

Pollution from Harmful Substances Packaged or in Containers. More general provisions are found in Annex III on the prevention of pollution by harmful substances carried by sea in packaged forms or in freight containers, portable tanks or road and rail tank wagons.

Pollution from Sewage and Garbage. According to the provisions of Annex IV and V, on the prevention of pollution by sewage and garbage from ships, ships are not permitted to discharge sewage at a distance of less than four nautical miles from the nearest land unless, in the case of sewage, it has been disinfected by an approved treatment system. At a distance of between four and 12 nautical miles from land, the sewage must be comminuted and disinfected before being discharged. Similarly, minimum distances from land are established for the discharge of garbage from ships. Discharge of plastics in any form is totally prohibited.

Any violation of the provisions of the Convention within the jurisdiction of one of the contracting states is sanctioned by the law of that state or by the law of the administration of the ship. The term "jurisdiction" is to be interpreted according to the international law in force at the time when the Convention is implemented or interpreted.

With the exception of small vessels, vessels on international voyages are required to hold an internationally valid certificate which is accepted in foreign ports as *prima facie* proof that the vessel is in compliance with the provisions of the Convention. If, during an inspection, a ship's certificate is invalid or its characteristics vary significantly with the particulars of the certificate, the party carrying out the inspection of the ship can ensure that the ship does not sail until they are assured that the ship does not present an unreasonable threat of harm to the marine environment.

The parties to the Convention, in consultation with other international bodies and with the assistance of UNEP [see 410 A], agree to co-operate with parties requesting technical assistance in such fields as training, the supply of equipment, research and the prevention of pollution.

Modifications. See 412.10, which describes the 1978 Protocol to this Convention.

M.D.-P.

Access : ALS (Art. 13)
Reserves : PAU (Art. 14)
Duration : USP
Deposit. : IMO (Art. 19)
Language : Eng, Fre, Rus, Spa (Art. 20)

Modific. : Protocol London 17.02.78 (02.10.83); Annex I (02.10.83); Annex II (06.04.87); Annex V (31.12.88); Annex III (01.07.92); Amendments 07.09.84 (07.01.86); Annex II Amendments 05.12.85 (06.04.87); Protocol I Amendments 00.12.85 (06.04.87); Annex I Amendments 01.04.89 (00.12.87); IBC Code Amendments 00.03.89 (13.10.90); BCH Code Amendments 00.03.89 (13.10.90); Annex II Amendments 00.03.89 (13.10.90); Annex V Amendments 00.10.89 (18.02.91); HSSC Amendments 00.03.90 (-); IBC Code Amendments 00.03.90 (-); BCH Code Amendments 00.03.90 (-); Annexes I and V Amendments 00.11.90 (17.03.92); Annexes I and V Amendments 00.07.91 (04.04.93)

Reference : ILM 12:1469 – RTAF 1983/49 – JORF 2 Oct 83

412.10 – PROTOCOL RELATING TO THE INTERNATIONAL CONVENTION FOR THE PREVENTION OF POLLUTION FROM SHIPS, 1973 – IMO

Concluded : 17.02.1978, London
In force : 02.10.1983
Parties : 77

In order to facilitate the implementation of the London Convention of 2 November 1973 [see 412.08], the Protocol makes a number of modifications to its provisions, as well as certain additions, especially to Annex I. It also postpones implementation of Annex II for three years.

The Protocol modifies Annex I of the Convention, which deals with the prevention of pollution by oil, by stipulating that every new oil tanker of 20,000 tons deadweight and above must be provided with segregated ballast tanks; in the 1973 Convention only new ships of 70,000 tons deadweight and above were affected by the provision.

The modifications also stipulate that segregated ballast tanks must be positioned in such a way that they contribute to the protection of cargo tanks in the event of the vessel running aground or colliding with another vessel.

A new element in the Protocol is its reference to the crude oil washing system (COW), which provides enormous advantages and was developed not long before the drafting of the 1978 Protocol. COW is accepted as an alternative to the segregated ballast tanks on existing tankers but is an additional requirement on new tankers.

MODIFICATIONS

The amendments to the Protocol adopted in 1984 seek to facilitate the implementation of Annex I. One of the objectives of the new provisions is to prevent the discharge, in special areas of the sea, of water which has been mixed with oil. These amendments also tighten some provisions while relaxing others where various conditions are met.

Other amendments adopted in 1985 apply to Annex II of the Convention, which deals with noxious liquids. They take into consideration technical advances and seek to simplify the implementation of the provisions of that Annex. The main objective of these amendments is to reduce the need for reception facilities for chemical wastes, and to improve the efficiency of the cargo draining system. They also make the International Bulk Chemical Code binding on all the contracting parties.

M.D.-P.

Access : ALS (Art. 4)
Reserves : USP
Duration : USP
Deposit. : IMO
Language : Eng, Fre, Rus, Spa

Modific. : [see 412.09]

Reference : JORF 2 Oct 83, 29 Feb 88

412.11 – INTERNATIONAL CONVENTION ON OIL POLLUTION PREPAREDNESS, RESPONSE AND CO-OPERATION (OPRC) – IMO

Concluded : 30.11.1990, London
Parties : 6

The Convention is the product of a desire to strengthen the ability of coastal states to respond quickly and effectively to a major pollution incident. It provides a global framework for international co-operation in combating marine pollution and aims to ensure the strict application of existing international instruments such as SOLAS 1974 [see 183.16] and MARPOL 73/78 [see 412.09].

DETAILS OF THE CONVENTION

Contracting states will be required to establish measures for dealing with pollution incidents either nationally (Art. 6) or in co-operation with other parties (Art. 7).

Each state party is to require ships entitled to fly its flag to have on board a shipboard oil pollution emergency plan which is in accordance with the provisions adopted by the IMO for this purpose (Art. 3-1).

Article 5 specifies the action to be taken by coastal states upon receiving a report of a pollution incident. States are required to notify the IMO of any oil pollution incident the severity of which warrants such notification.

Under the Annex to the Convention, provision is made for parties to bear the costs of their respective actions in dealing with the pollution incident. Where action is taken by a party at the request of another party, the costs of that action is to be "fairly calculated according to the law and current practice of the assisting Party concerning the reimbursement of such costs". Moreover, the party requesting assistance and the assisting party are, where appropriate, to co-operate in concluding any action in response to a compensation claim. Parties are required to pay special attention to the 1969 International Convention on Civil Liability for Oil Pollution Damage (CLC) [see 412.04] and the 1971 International Convention on the Establishment of an International Fund for Compensation for Oil Pollution Damage (FUND) [see 412.06] and any subsequent amendments to those Conventions.

Patricia Ford

Access : ALS (Art. 15)
Reserves : USP
Duration : USP
Deposit. : IMO (Art. 18)
Language : Ara, Chi, Eng, Fre, Rus, Spa (Art. 19)

Reference : ILM 30:733

4.1.3 Air Pollution

Economic activities in one state may have harmful transboundary effects upon the environment of other states, or beyond the limits of national jurisdictions. International regimes on transboundary air pollution, the depletion of the ozone layer, and climate change have been established. These consist of framework conventions and protocols. Under the framework conventions, parties primarily agree to co-operate among themselves on monitoring, research, and data exchange activities. Specific obligations are imposed in protocols under which parties agree to gradually reduce production and/or emissions of hazardous substances to set levels.

The cost burden to developing countries' industries of these obligations can, however, be prohibitive. Financial mechanisms have therefore been established under some agreements to assist these countries to fulfil their commitments in regard to those agreements. These mechanisms facilitate or enable these countries better to regulate air pollution thereby assisting international efforts in this field.

SELECTED BIBLIOGRAPHY

Churchill, Robin and David Freestone, *International Law and Global Climate Change: International Legal Issues and Implications*, Dordrecht: Martinus Nijhoff Publishers, 1991.

Fishman, Jack and Robert Kalish, *Global Alert: the Ozone Pollution Crisis*, Plenum Pub. Corp., 1990.

Flinterman, C., B. Kwiatkowska and J. Lammers, *Transboundary Air Pollution: International Legal Aspects of the Cooperation of States*, Dordrecht: Martinus Nijhoff Publishers, 1986.

Trask, Jeff, "Montreal Protocol Noncompliance Procedure: the Best Approach to Resolving International Environmental Disputes?", *Georgetown Law Journal* 80 (June 1992): 1973-2001.

413.01 – CONVENTION ON LONG-RANGE TRANSBOUNDARY AIR POLLUTION (LRTAP) – ECE

Concluded : 13.11.1979, Geneva
In force : 16.03.1983
Parties : 33

Air pollution, including long-range transboundary air pollution, has both short- and long-term damaging effects on vital natural resources such as forests, waters, materials and soil, as well as on human health. This framework Convention seeks to protect people and their environment against air pollution by endeavouring to limit and, as far as possible, gradually reduce and prevent air pollution, including long-range transboundary air pollution.

The history of the present Convention can be traced back to the 1960s, when Swedish scientists demonstrated the interrelationship between sulphur dioxide emissions outside Swedish territory and the acidification of Swedish lakes. This led to a presentation of a case-study on "Air Pollution Across National Boundaries, the Impact in the Environment of Sulphur in Air and Precipitation" by the Swedish delegation at the 1972 United Nations Conference on the Human Environment in Stockholm [see 410.01]. Between 1972 and 1977 several studies confirmed the hypothesis that air pollutants actually can travel even several thousands of kilometers before disposition and damage occur. This also established the fact that co-operation at the international level was necessary to solve the related problems, in particular the acidification problem.

In response to these acute problems, a High-Level Meeting within a Framework of the ECE [see 181 A] on the Protection of the Environment was held at ministerial level in November 1979 in Geneva. It resulted in the signature of the Convention on Long-Range Transboundary Air Pollution by 34 governments and the European Communities (EC). This Convention is the first international legally binding instrument to deal with problems of air pollution on a broad regional basis.

DETAILS OF THE CONVENTION

To combat the discharge of air pollutants, the contracting parties agree to exchange information and to consult each other, to develop research and monitoring activities, and policies and strategies.

The parties agree to co-operate in conducting research into and/or developing (i) existing and proposed technologies for reducing emissions of sulphur compounds and other major air pollutants; (ii) instrumentation and other techniques for monitoring and measuring emission rates and ambient concentrations of air pollutants; (iii) improved models for a better understanding of the transmission of long-range transboundary air pollutants; (iv) the effects of sulphur compounds and other major air pollutants on human health and the environment, with a view to establishing a scientific basis for dose/effect relationships designed to protect the environment; (v) the economic, social and environmental assessment of alternative measures for attaining environmental objectives, including the reduction of long-range transboundary air pollution; and (vi) education and training programmes related to the environmental aspects of pollution by sulphur compounds and other major air pollutants.

The necessity to implement and widen the scope of the Co-operative Programme for the Monitoring and Evaluation of the Long-range Transmission of Air Pollution in Europe (EMEP) is stressed. The EMEP, which followed an OECD programme, helps in the monitoring and evaluation of long-range transmission of air pollution in Europe. A network of more than 90 monitoring stations has been established in 24 countries.

STRUCTURE

The Convention establishes an **Executive Body** within the framework of the Senior Advisers to ECE Governments on Environmental Programmes. The Executive Body, which includes representatives of all the contracting parties, meets at least annually to review the implementation of the Convention and to adopt a work-plan for its future activities. Between its sessions, a **Bureau of the Executive Body**, consisting of the chairman and four vice-chairmen, deals with matters requiring interim action. The second level of the institutional framework established by the Executive Body under the Convention consists at present of the following standing intergovernmental bodies, open to all parties and dealing with specific areas of the work-plan:

- Steering Body to the Co-operative Programme for Monitoring and Evaluation of the Long-Range Transmission of Air Pollutants in Europe (EMEP);
- Working Group on Strategies;
- Working Group on Effects; and
- Working Group on Technology.

Under these subsidiary bodies intergovernmental task forces can be established either on an *ad hoc* basis to prepare a technical/scientific report, or to supervise a continuing co-operative programme. Five international co-operative programmes on effect-related matters have been established (Annex 2). The ECE secretariat [see 181 A] carries out secretariat functions for the Executive Body.

SUBSEQUENT MODIFICATIONS

This framework Convention has been further "operationalized" or supplemented by four protocols, three of which have specific and measurable objectives [see 413.03, 413.05 and 413.06].

Maguelonne Déjeant-Pons

Access : ASO (Art. 14-15)
Reserves : USP

Duration : USP
Deposit. : UN (Art. 15)
Language : Eng, Fre, Rus (Art. 18)

Modific. : Protocol Geneva 28.09.84 (28.01.88); Helsinki 08.07.85 (02.09.87); Sofia 31.10.88 (14.02.91); Geneva 18.11.91 (-)

Reference : ILM 18:1442, 27:698, 28:212 – JORF 6 Apr 83 – RTAF 1983/18 – JDI 1983 – DJI 1985

413.02 – CONVENTION FOR THE PROTECTION OF THE OZONE LAYER – UNEP

Concluded : 22.03.1985, Vienna
In force : 22.09.1988
Parties : 119

This framework Convention was adopted under UNEP's World Plan of Action for the Ozone Layer [see 410 A, generally]. Its aim is to protect the ozone layer and to protect human health and the environment against adverse effects resulting from changes in the ozone layer.

DETAILS OF THE CONVENTION

The parties agree to implement a procedure of systematic observation of the ozone layer, and to co-operate in research and the exchange of information in order to better understand the effect of human activity on the ozone layer and the adverse effects brought about by its modification.

The parties agree to adopt appropriate legislative and administrative measures and to co-ordinate their policies to regulate, limit, reduce or prevent human activities in areas under their jurisdiction that have or may have adverse effects on the ozone layer.

The Convention also provides for co-operation between the parties and relevent international organizations, so as to effectively implement the Convention and its Protocols.

STRUCTURE

The institutional framework is organized around a **Conference of the Parties** to the Convention which supervises its implementation. This body meets in ordinary and extraordinary sessions. Administrative support is provided by the **Secretariat**.

MODIFICATIONS

The Montreal Protocol of 1987 [see 413.04], further completed by the London Amendments of June 1990, commits the parties to specific action (e.g. on CFCs).

M.D.-P.

Access : ASO (Art. 12, 14)
Reserves : PRO (Art. 18)

Duration : USP
Deposit. : UN (Art. 20)
Language : Ara, Chi, Eng, Fre, Rus, Spa (Art. 21)

Modific. : Protocol Montreal 16.09.87 (01.01.89); Adjustments to Protocol London 29.06.90 (07.03.91); Amendments to Protocol London 29.06.90 (00.08.92)

Reference : ILM 26:1516, 26:1541 – UNEP Doc. IG.53/5 – JORF 11 Oct 88, 20 Dec 88 – RGDIP 1988/1 – DJI 1985

413.03 – PROTOCOL TO THE 1979 CONVENTION ON LONG-RANGE TRANSBOUNDARY AIR POLLUTION ON THE REDUCTION OF SULPHUR EMISSIONS OR THEIR TRANSBOUNDARY FLUXES BY AT LEAST 30 PER CENT – ECE

Concluded : 08.07.1985, Helsinki
In force : 02.09.1987
Parties : 19

The principal sources of air pollution causing damage to the environment are the combustion of fossil fuels for energy production, the technological processes in various industrial sectors, and transportion, which causes the emission of sulphur dioxide, nitrogen oxide and other pollutants.

Although the Convention [see 413.01] covers all types of air pollutants, it gave priority in the first phase to the abatement of acid rain, as triggered by air pollution of sulphur compounds. The Convention thus provided a platform for a protocol on the reduction of sulphur emissions or their transboundary fluxes.

DETAILS OF THE PROTOCOL

The aim of this Protocol is to provide for a 30 per cent reduction in sulphur emissions or transboundary fluxes by, at the latest, 1993. The parties agree to reduce their national annual sulphur emissions, or their transboundary fluxes, to at least 30 per cent below 1980 levels, and they agree to study the need for further reductions. They also report their annual sulphur emissions, and the basis on which they were calculated, to the Executive Body of the Convention (Geneva).

The parties agree to establish political programmes and national strategies to comply with the objectives of the Convention. Since 1986, ten countries have already achieved the reduction objective of 30 per cent.

SUBSEQUENT DEVELOPMENTS

A protocol for the further reductions of sulphur emissions after 1993 is now being prepared on the basis of critical loads, energy savings and other considerations, including economic instruments. The issue of financial burden-sharing is also being addressed as a high priority by the negotiators.

M.D.-P.

Access : ALS (Art. 9)
Reserves : USP

Duration : SP
Deposit. : UN (Art. 10)
Language : Eng, Fre, Rus (Art. 13)

Reference : ILM 28:212

413.04 – PROTOCOL RELATING TO SUBSTANCES AFFECTING THE OZONE LAYER – UNEP

Concluded: 16.09.1987, Montreal
In force : 01.01.1989
Parties : 111

The aim of the Protocol is to take precautionary measures to protect the ozone layer by restricting total global emissions of certain ozone-depleting substances. The ultimate aim is to eliminate these substances but in a manner based on relevant scientific and technical information, and economic considerations.

The parties acknowledge the importance of promoting international co-operation in the research and development of science and technology on the control and reduction of chlorofluorocarbon emissions (i.e. emissions of certain ozone-depleting substances), bearing in mind in particular the needs of developing countries and low-consuming countries.

DETAILS OF THE PROTOCOL

The most important provisions of the Protocol are those which control the production and consumption of chlorofluorocarbons (CFC) and halons. The parties must ensure that, from 1 July 1989, the production and consumption of CFCs do not exceed their respective 1986 levels. Production of CFCs is, however, authorized to a maximum level of 10 per cent above the 1989 level, on condition that it is necessary for industrial development or that it fulfils the domestic needs of developing countries. Similar provisions apply to halons, but in this case the deadline was 1 January 1992.

The amendment and adjustments adopted in London in June 1990 committed the parties to eliminating the production and consumption of CFCs and halons by the year 2000, and carbon tetrachloride and methyl chloroform by the year 2005 in the developed countries. The developing countries have a ten-year grace period for phasing-out the ozone-depleting substances.

The Protocol prohibits or limits imports and exports of the controlled substances from and to states which are not parties to the Protocol. The special conditions of the developing countries are taken into consideration; by making expeditious use of environmentally safe alternative chemicals and technology, the parties undertake to assist these countries and to generally promote the implementation of the Protocol to non-contracting parties.

FUNDING

The London meeting adopted a financial mechanism which defined the mechanisms for financial and technical co-operation to the developing countries, including the exchange of information and transfer of technology. An Interim Financial Mechanism, which includes an Interim Multilateral Fund financed by contributions from the developed countries, was established for the three-year period from 1

January 1991 to 31 December 1993. The size of the Fund was to be US$160 million for the first three years and is expected to be increased to a maximum of US$240 million. The Fund is serviced by a **Secretariat** based in Montreal, Canada, and operated under the responsibility of an **Executive Committee**. This Committee is composed of representatives of seven developing countries and seven developed countries, and discharges its functions through UNEP [see 410 A], UNDP [see 222 A] and the World Bank [see 221 A].

STRUCTURE

Institutional provisions establish the **Meetings of the Parties** and the **Secretariat**. Unless the parties decide otherwise, ordinary meetings of the parties are to be held in conjunction with meetings of Conference of the Parties to the Convention for the Protection of the Ozone Layer (Vienna, 1985) [see 413.02].

M.D.-P.

Access : ASO (Art. 15, 17)
Reserves : PRO (Art. 18)
Duration : USP
Deposit. : UN (Art. 20)
Language : Ara, Chi, Eng, Fre, Rus, Spa (Art. 20)

Modific. : Adjustments to Protocol London 29.06.90 (07.03.91); Amendments to Protocol London 29.06.90 (10.08.92)

Reference : ILM 26:1541 – JORF 20 Dec 88 – RGDIP 1988/2

413.05 – PROTOCOL TO THE 1979 CONVENTION ON LONG-RANGE TRANSBOUNDARY AIR POLLUTION CONCERNING THE CONTROL OF EMISSIONS OF NITROGEN OXIDES OR THEIR TRANSBOUNDARY FLUXES – ECE

Concluded : 31.10.1988, Sofia
In force : 14.02.1991
Parties : 18

In the late 1980s, it became more and more evident that besides sulphur, nitrogen oxides were also substantially contributing to the acidity of precipitation, and that successful abatement of acid rain must include nitrogen oxides. It was also recognized that nitrogen oxides play an important role in ozone formation near the ground.

DETAILS OF THE PROTOCOL

The parties undertake to take effective measures to control and/or reduce their national annual emissions of nitrogen oxides or their transboundary fluxes.

This Protocol requires the parties, as a first step, to reduce or to control emissions "so that these, at the latest by 31 December 1994, do not exceed their national annual emissions of nitrogen oxides or transboundary fluxes of such emissions in the calendar year 1987" (Art. 2). Another alternative offered to the party is to choose upon signature any year previous to 1987 as a base year provided that in addition the average annual national level of emissions between 1987 and 1996 does not exceed the 1987 level. In addition to this emission target, the basic obligations call upon parties to apply emission standards to major new stationary sources and to new mobile sources, and to introduce pollution control measures for major existing stationary sources.

Further, as a second step, the parties are required to "commence negotiations no later than six months after the date of entry into force of this Protocol, on further steps to reduce national annual emissions of nitrogen oxide or transboundary fluxes of such emissions" (Art. 2) and to "commence consideration of procedures to create more favourable conditions for the exchange of technology to reduce emissions of nitrogen oxides" (Art. 3). Such negotiations on further steps are under way.

The Co-operative Programme for Monitoring and Evaluation of Long-Range Transmission of Air Pollutants in Europe (EMEP) provides to the Executive Body of the Convention calculations of nitrogen budgets and also of transboundary fluxes and deposition of nitrogen oxides within the geographical scope of EMEP [see 413.01].

M.D.-P.

Access : CON (Art. 13, 14)
Reserves : USP
Duration : USP
Deposit. : UN (Art. 17)
Language : Eng, Fre, Rus (Art. 17)

413.06 – PROTOCOL TO THE 1979 CONVENTION ON LONG-RANGE TRANSBOUNDARY AIR POLLUTION CONCERNING THE CONTROL OF EMISSIONS OF VOLATILE ORGANIC COMPOUNDS OR THEIR TRANSBOUNDARY FLUXES – ECE

Concluded: 18.11.1991, Geneva
Parties : 2

The recognition that ground ozone is formed by an intricate interplay of nitrogen oxides and certain volatile organic compounds (VOCs) in the presence of sunlight soon led to the realization that volatile organic compounds would have to be controlled. This Protocol recognizes the importance of damage caused to the environment in many countries by emissions of volatile organic compounds which, by reaction with oxides of nitrogen, contribute to the formation of photochemical oxidants such as ozone. It seeks to control these emissions through setting limitations on their levels.

DETAILS OF THE PROTOCOL

The emission target set out in the basic obligations of the Protocol is to reduce national annual VOC emissions by at least 30 per cent by 1999, using either 1988 levels as a basis or any other annual level between 1984 and 1990. There are, however, alternatives to this obligation. One is to include only areas that have been specified as Tropospheric Ozone Management Areas (TOMAs) for the above emission target and ensure that national emissions of VOCs do not exceed 1988 levels by 1999. A TOMA is a particular area within a country where the major part of national emissions take place. The emissions outside of a TOMA are insignificant for generating transboundary fluxes.

The other alternative refers to a situation where the national annual emissions of VOCs in 1988 were below 500,000 tonnes and 20 kg per inhabitant and 5 tonnes per square kilometer; in this case, the obligation is relaxed to ensure that 1988 emissions are not exceeded in 1999.

The Protocol includes four annexes including emission control technologies for stationary and mobile sources and a classification of VOCs according to their photochemical ozone creation potential (POCP) that indicates those substances that should be avoided as a matter of priority. The basic obligations call on parties to apply, no later than two years after the date of entry into force, emission standards based on best available technology to new sources and to apply best available technology also to existing sources of VOC after five years, where international tropospheric ozone standards are exceeded or where transboundary fluxes originate.

The Co-operative Programme for Monitoring and Evaluation of the Long-Range Transmission of Air Pollutants in Europe (EMEP) provides information on the long-range transport of ozone in Europe to the annual meetings of the Executive Body of the Convention [see 413.01].

M.D.-P.

Access : CON (Art. 13, 14)
Reserves : USP
Duration : USP
Deposit. : UN (Art. 18)
Language : Eng, Fre, Rus (Art. 18)

Reference : UN Doc. ECE/EB.AIR/30

413.07 – FRAMEWORK CONVENTION ON CLIMATE CHANGE – UN

Concluded : 09.05.1992, New York
Parties : 17

In 1988, the United Nations General Assembly adopted Resolution 43/53 acknowledging that change in the Earth's climate is a common concern of humankind. Thereupon, UNEP [see 410 A] and WMO [see 431 A] created an Intergovernmental Panel on Climate Change (IPCC) which was instructed to assess the scientific evidence on global climatic change and to suggest appropriate strategies. Its first report was published in 1990. The General Assembly consequently created the Intergovernmental Negotiating Committee on Framework Convention on Climate Change, with the support of UNEP and WMO [see 431 A]. The negotiations took place in parallel to the preparatory committees of the United Nations Conference on Environment and Development (UNCED) and led to the elaboration of a framework convention open to signature during the UNCED held in Rio de Janeiro from 3 to 14 June 1992 [see also 410.02].

The objective of the Convention is the stabilization of greenhouse gas concentrations in the atmosphere at a level that would prevent dangerous and anthropogenic interference with the climate system. It is stated that such a level should be achieved within a time-frame sufficient to allow ecosystems to adapt naturally to climate change, to ensure that food production is not threatened and to enable economic development to proceed in a sustainable manner.

DETAILS OF THE CONVENTION

Parties to the Convention should, in their actions, be guided by five main principles of action:

- to protect the climate system for the benefit of present and future generations of humankind on the basis of equity and in accordance with their common but differentiated responsibilities and respective capabilities;
- to give full consideration to the specific needs and special circumstances of developing country parties;
- to take "precautionary measures" to anticipate, prevent or minimize the causes of climate change and mitigate its adverse effects;
- to recognize a right and a commitment to promote sustainable development; and
- to co-operate to promote a supportive and open international economic system that would lead to sustainable economic growth and development in all parties, particularly developing country parties, thus enabling them to better address the problems of climate change.

All parties must fulfil general commitments. Other specific commitments are directed only to developed country parties and to other parties in Annex I of the Convention, listing the so-called "economies in transition" of eastern Europe.

To fulfil their general commitments, all parties, taking into account their common but differentiated responsibilities and their specific national and regional development priorities, objectives and circumstances, shall:

- develop and make available to the Conference of the Parties national inventories of anthropogenic emissions of all greenhouse gases not controlled by the Montreal Protocol to the Vienna Convention [see 413.04];
- implement and publish national and regional programmes containing measures to mitigate climate change and measures to facilitate adequate adaptation to climate change;
- promote and co-operate in the development, application and diffusion of technologies, practices and processes that control, reduce or prevent anthropogenic emissions of greenhouse gases not controlled by the Montreal Protocol;
- promote sustainable management and promote and co-operate in the conservation and enhancement of sinks and reservoirs of all greenhouse gases not controlled by the Montreal Protocol (e.g. biomass, forests, oceans, etc);
- prepare for adaptation to the impacts of climate change;
- take climate change considerations into account in their relevant social, economic and environmental policies and actions;
- promote and co-operate in the exchange of data on climate system and climate change, as well as education, training and public awareness related to climate change;
- communicate to the Conference of the Parties information relating to the implementation of the Convention.

Research and systematic observation, education, training and public awareness are also encouraged by the Convention.

There are two annexes to the Convention which each list certain parties committing themselves to specific undertakings.

Annex I Parties. "The developed country Parties and other Parties" included in Annex I undertake specific commitments. Each of these parties shall adopt national policies and take corresponding measures on the mitigation of climate change, by limiting its anthropogenic emissions of greenhouse gases and protecting and enhancing its greenhouse gas sinks and reservoirs. The much-debated and controversial Article 4-2-a of the Convention states that these policies and measures will demonstrate that developed countries are taking the lead in modifying longer-term trends in anthropogenic emissions, recognizing that the return by the end of the present decade to earlier levels of anthropogenic emissions of carbon dioxide and other greenhouse gases not controlled by the Montreal Protocol would contribute to such modification. This statement did not include target emission levels or timetables for reductions, as many delegations and observers had hoped.

Each of these parties shall communicate detailed information on its policies and measures taken, and on certain projections, with the aim of returning individually or jointly to their 1990 levels these anthropogenic emissions of carbon dioxide and other greenhouse gases not controlled by the Montreal Protocol.

Annex II Parties. "The developed country Parties and other developed Parties" included in Annex II of the Convention shall provide new and additional financial resources to meet:

- the agreed full costs incurred by developing country parties in complying with their obligation to communicate information related to implementation of the Convention; and
- the agreed full incremental costs as agreed between a developing country and the financial mechanism established by the Convention to fulfil the general commitments that bind all parties.

By resolution of the negotiating delegations, the financial mechanism is initially designated to be, on an interim basis, the Global Environment Facility (GEF) administered by UNEP [see 410 A], UNDP [see 222 A], and the World Bank [see 221 A].

The developed country parties and other developed parties included in Annex II shall also assist the developing country parties that are particularly vulnerable to the adverse effects of climate change in meeting costs of adaptation to these adverse effects. Further, they shall take all practical steps to promote, faciliate and finance the transfer of, or access to, environmentally sound technologies and know-how to the other parties.

STRUCTURE

The **Conference of the Parties** is the supreme body of the Convention, keeping its implementation under regular review and deciding on policies, programme priorities and eligibility criteria of the financial mechanism. A permanent **Secretariat** is established as well as a subsidiary body for scientific and technological advice and a subsidiary body for implementation.

In the event of a dispute between any two or more parties concerning the interpretion or application of the Convention, the parties concerned shall seek a settlement of the dispute through negotiation or any other peaceful means of their own choice such as arbitration, conciliation or submission to the International Court of Justice (ICJ) [see 001 B]. The Conference of the Parties may adopt protocols to the Convention.

M.D.-P.

Access : ALS (Art. 20)
Reserves : PRO (Art. 24)
Duration : USP

Deposit. : UN (Art. 19)
Language : Ara, Chi, Eng, Fre, Spa, Rus (Art. 26)

Reference : ILM 31:849

4.1.4 Transboundary Environmental Impact

Transboundary environmental problems involve important and urgent tasks which can only be accomplished by better co-operation between governments to ensure that activities under their control do not damage the environment of other states or areas beyond their national jurisdiction [see also Principle 21 of the Declaration of the United Nations Conference on Human Environment: 410.01]. With a view to strengthening a regional legal framework to cope effectively with transboundary environmental problems, the conventions on environmental impact assessment in a transboundary context [see 414.01], on the transboundary effects of industrial accidents [see 414.02] and on the protection and use of transboundary watercourses and international lakes [see 414.03] have been elaborated recently under the auspices of the United Nations Economic Commission for Europe (ECE) [see 181 A]. They are open to ECE member states, the Holy See, Monaco and the European Communities and will enter into force 90 days after the deposit of the sixteenth instrument of ratification, acceptance, approval or accession.

SELECTED BIBLIOGRAPHY

ECE, *Environmental Conventions Elaborated under the Auspices of the UN/ECE*, Geneva: United Nations, 1992.
Koskenniemi, Martti, "International Liability for Transfrontier Pollution Damage", *International Environmental Affairs* 2 (Fall 1990): 309-316.

414.01 – CONVENTION ON ENVIRONMENTAL IMPACT ASSESSMENT IN A TRANSBOUNDARY CONTEXT – ECE

Concluded : 25.02.1991, Espoo
Parties : 3

The objectives of the Convention are to enhance international co-operation for the assessment, prevention and mitigation of adverse environmental impact in general and, more specifically, across boundaries, and to promote environmentally sound and sustainable economic development.

DETAILS OF THE CONVENTION

The Convention prescribes measures and procedures to prevent, control or reduce any significant adverse effect on the environment, particularly any transboundary effect on human health and safety, flora, fauna, soil, air, water, climate, landscape and historical monuments, which is likely to be caused by a proposed economic activity or by any major change to an existing economic activity. It covers 17 groups of activities, such as nuclear and thermal power stations, road and railway construction, chemical installations, waste-disposal facilities, oil refineries, oil and gas pipelines, mining, steel production, pulp and paper manufacturing and the construction of dams and reservoirs. Concerned parties may extend the application of the Convention to other activities, and enter into bilateral or multilateral agreements for that purpose.

Parties will have to establish an environmental impact assessment (EIA) procedure involving public participation and the preparation of EIA documentation. A proposed activity will not be undertaken or authorized until an EIA has been carried out. Parties will also endeavour to ensure that the EIA principles are applied to policies, plans and programmes.

A country under the jurisdiction of which a proposed activity is envisaged will have to notify accordingly any country likely to be affected by it. The country of origin has to submit to the affected country the relevant EIA documentation on the proposed activity, and its possible transboundary effects, for comments. Arrangements will have to be made in order to ensure that the public, including the public of the affected countries, is given the possibility to submit comments on or objections to the proposed activity. Consultations may be held between the countries concerned with respect to possible alternatives to the proposed activity, including the no-action alternative and possible measures to mitigate adverse effects. If the countries concerned cannot agree on whether a significant adverse transboundary effect is likely, the question may be submitted to an inquiry commission. Affected countries will be informed about the final decision on the proposed activity and the reasons and considerations on which it is based. Disputes may be brought to the International Court of Justice [see 001 B] or settled through the arbitration procedure described in the Convention. Post-project analysis may be undertaken in order to monitor compliance with the conditions set out in the authorization of the activity and the effectiveness of mitigation measures.

The parties will meet annually in order to review national policies and strategies promoting EIA, to consider relevant methodological and technical aspects and to exchange information regarding experience gained in concluding and implementing relevant bilateral and multilateral agreements.

When becoming a party to this Convention, a country will be expected to ensure that its national legislation and regulations provide for the establishment of the EIA process. Lists of activities subject to EIA should be established to include at least those activities which are covered by the Convention. Minimum requirements for the content of the EIA documentation will have to be introduced, which proponents of activities likely to cause adverse environmental impact will be obliged to follow. Time-frames will have to be established in national regulations for various phases of the EIA process – for example, notification, scoping, provision for comments by the public and the authorities, preparation of an EIA documentation, decision on EIA, and post-project analysis. Procedures for public participation will have to specify the practicalities of such participation (e.g. public hearings). The mandate of relevant authorities entrusted with decision-making and surveillance powers regarding proposed activities will have to be strengthened. To facilitate the preparation of EIA documentation and promote the improvement of information to be presented to decision-makers, training will have to be organized and relevant databases strengthened or established.

In relation to EIA in a transboundary context, the appropriate governmental authority will have to be nominated as point of contract to whom countries, under the jurisdiction of which a proposed activity is envisaged, will have to send notification. A number of operative provisions of the Convention will be implemented at the bilateral and multilateral levels.

Maguelonne Déjeant-Pons and ECE

Access : CON (Art. 17)
Reserves : USP
Duration : USP
Deposit. : UN (Art. 17)
Language : Eng, Fre, Rus (Art. 20)

414.02 – CONVENTION ON THE TRANSBOUNDARY EFFECTS OF INDUSTRIAL ACCIDENTS – ECE

Concluded : 17.03.1992, Helsinki
Party : 1

The Convention concerns the prevention of, preparedness for and response to industrial accidents capable of causing transboundary effects; and to international co-operation concerning mutual assistance, research and development, exchange of information and of technology in the area of prevention of, preparedness for and response to industrial accidents. Effects include any direct or indirect, immediate or delayed adverse consequences caused by an industrial accident on human beings, flora, fauna, soil, water, air and landscape, the interaction between these factors, material assets and cultural heritage, including historical monuments.

The Convention does not apply to some categories of accidents for which provisions of other conventions may apply, such as nuclear accidents, land-based transport accidents, accidents caused by activities in the marine environment, and spills of oil or other harmful substances at sea.

DETAILS OF THE CONVENTION

The Convention gives particular emphasis to the prevention of industrial accidents as far as possible by reducing their frequency and severity and by mitigating their effects. For the purpose of undertaking such preventive and preparedness measures, potentially affected countries will be informed and notified of any proposed or existing hazardous activity capable of causing transboundary effects in the event of an industrial accident by those countries responsible for such activities. With the same objective and on the basis of detailed provisions of the Convention, policies will be established and harmonized at a regional level on the setting of new hazardous activities and on significant modifications to existing hazardous activities. The parties concerned will also inform each other on preparedness measures taken to mitigate transboundary effects of such accidents, including elements for the elaboration of contingency plans. They will endeavour to make such plans compatible and even strive to draw up joint plans where appropriate.

The public in areas capable of being affected by an industrial accident arising out of a hazardous activity shall be given relevant information as specified in the Convention. This applies not only to the public of the country in which the activity takes place but in particular to the public of any other affected country. The public in such areas shall also be given an opportunity to participate in relevant procedures with the aim of making known its views and concerns on prevention and preparedness measures. Natural or legal persons who are being or are capable of being adversely affected by the transboundary effects of an industrial accident are to be provided, on a reciprocal basis, with access to and treatment in the relevant administrative and judicial proceedings.

Under the Convention, compatible and efficient accident notification systems, operational at all times, will be set up at appropriate levels with the aim of transmitting and obtaining information needed to counteract transboundary effects in the event of an industrial accident or imminent threat thereof. Points of contact for the purpose of industrial accident notification are being designated or established.

A country affected by an industrial accident (or imminent threat thereof) occurring under its own or foreign jurisdiction and which needs assistance can ask under the terms of the Convention and through points of contact designated for these purposes, for such assistance from other countries to help minimize the consequences and effects of the industrial accident.

The Convention provides detailed procedures, where countries do not have bilateral or multilateral agreements, which cover their arrangements for providing mutual assistance.

For cases where an agreement cannot be found among countries concerned, whether an activity not covered by the specific provisions of the Convention is to be treated as a hazardous activity and thus would fall under the terms of the Convention, an inquiry commission as one advisory mechanism of their choice could be established in accordance with detailed procedures laid down in the Convention. For other disputes about the interpretation of application of the Convention, countries could revert to arbitral tribunals also foreseen by the Convention.

M.D.-P. and ECE

Access : CON (Art. 29)
Reserves : USP
Duration : USP
Deposit. : UN (Art. 28)
Language : Eng, Fre, Rus (Art. 32)

Reference : UN Doc. E/ECE/1268

414.03 – CONVENTION ON THE PROTECTION AND USE OF TRANSBOUNDARY WATER COURSES AND INTERNATIONAL LAKES – ECE

Concluded : 17.03.1992, Helsinki
Party : 1

The Convention is intended to strengthen national and international measures to prevent, control and reduce the release of hazardous substances into the aquatic environment, to abate eutrophication and acidification, to ensure rational and ecologically sound water management, and to protect related ecosystems including the marine environment.

Any surface waters and groundwaters, particularly those which mark, cross or are located on boundaries between two or more states and related ecosystems, are covered by the Convention. It prescribes measures for the prevention, control and reduction of significant adverse effects on the environment resulting from a change in the conditions of transboundary waters caused by a human activity, including effects on human health and safety, flora, fauna, soil, air, water, climate, landscape and historical monuments. The Convention also covers such issues as monitoring, research and development, exchange and protection of information as well as responsibility and liability.

DETAILS OF THE CONVENTION

The parties will be obliged to develop, implement and render compatible relevant legal, administrative, economic, financial and technical measures, such as: the prior licensing and subsequent monitoring and control of waste-water discharges; prohibition, where necessary, of the production or use of hazardous substances; development of water-quality objectives and criteria; application of the best available technology for point-source pollution control and the best environmental practices for non-point-source pollution control; development of contingency plans; the application of environmental impact assessment and the ecosystems approach in water management.

The Convention establishes the minimal requirements for the agreements or other arrangements between parties bordering the same transboundary waters.

Parties, who will meet in principle every three years, will have to review policies and methodological approaches to the protection and use of transboundary waters, exchange information regarding experience gained in concluding and implementing relevant bilateral and multilateral agreements, and undertake any other action to fulfil the aims of the Convention.

In order to comply with the obligations under the Convention, the parties will be expected, *inter alia*, to incorporate into their legislation and regulations provisions which set emission limits for discharges from point sources based on best available technology, which are specifically applicable to individual industrial sectors or industries; which license waste-water discharges and monitor and control authorized discharges; which adopt water-quality criteria, define water-quality objectives and monitor compliance therewith; which apply at least biological treatment or equivalent processes to municipal waste water, where necessary in a step-by-step approach; which develop and implement codes of good environmental practice for the reduction of inputs of nutrients and hazardous substances from diffuse sources, in particular from agriculture; and which ensure public access to the information on water-quality objectives, and permit conditions and results of monitoring and assessment.

The parties bordering the same transboundary waters will have to enter into bilateral or multilateral agreements (or adapt existing ones). Such agreements, covering relevant catchment areas or parts thereof, should provide in particular for the establishment of joint bodies; conduct of consultations between riparian parties; elaboration of joint water-quality objectives and criteria; development of action programmes; joint or co-ordinated monitoring and assessment of the conditions of transboundary waters and assessment of the effectiveness of measures taken; setting up co-ordinated or joint communication, warning and alarm systems; undertaking common research and development activities; exchange of information and best available technology; and provision of mutual assistance in critical situations.

At the level of the Meeting of Parties, parties will periodically have to prepare and submit to the secretariat national reports on policies, strategies and activities associated with the implementation of the Convention, and participate in work programmes on specific methodological, legal and technical aspects.

If a dispute arises between two or more parties about the interpretation or application of this Convention, they shall seek a solution by negotiation or by any other means of dispute settlement acceptable to the parties to the dispute.

M.D.-P. and ECE

Access	: CON (Art. 25)
Reserves	: USP
Duration	: USP
Deposit.	: UN (Art. 24)
Language	: Eng, Fre, Rus (Art. 28)

Reference : UN Doc. ENVWA/R.53 and Add.1

4.2 Nuclear Activities and Hazardous Waste Regulations

4.2.1 Nuclear Activity

For the international community, nuclear power differs from other forms of energy production for two reasons. First, the technology which allows nuclear energy to be harnessed to produce electricity may also be used to produce weapons of mass destruction. Second, an accident at a nuclear installation may cause huge damage, not just in the country in which the installation is located, but, as the Chernobyl accident proved, in other countries hundreds or even thousands of miles away.

These two elements – the danger of military use and the risk of widespread accidental damage – are at the heart of all the major international conventions in the nuclear field which have been developed since the birth of nuclear technology. Agreements in the first category are intended to control the transfer of nuclear technology to ensure that it is not used for improper purposes, while the second category includes agreements aimed at limiting the harmful effects of an accident, and ensuring that any victims of resulting nuclear damage are compensated.

Susan Reye and Anne de Richecour

SELECTED BIBLIOGRAPHY

Bourque, D., *L'Énergie Nucléaire et le Droit: les Autorisations, l'Environnement, les Contrôles Judiciaires et Politiques: Etude Comparative*, Quebec: Editions Yvon Blais, 1990.

Cameron, Peter, Leigh Hancher and Wolfgang Kühn (eds.), *Nuclear Energy Law after Chernobyl*, London: Graham & Trotman; International Bar Association, 1988.

OECD Nuclear Energy Agency, *Licensing Systems and Inspection of Nuclear Installations*, Paris: OECD, 1990.

– – –, *Nuclear Legislation: Third Party Liability*, Paris: OECD, 1990.

– – –, *Proceedings of the Munich Symposium: Nuclear Third Party Liability and Insurance: Status and Prospects*, Paris: OECD, 1985.

– – –, *Proceedings of the Symposium on Nuclear Accidents: Liabilities and Guarantees*, Paris: OECD, 1993.

– – –, *Regulatory and Institutional Framework for Nuclear Activities*, Paris: OECD, Vol. 1 1983, Vol. 2 1984.

Sands, Philippe (ed.), *Chernobyl: Law and Communication*, Cambridge: Grotius Publications, 1988.

Scheinman, L., *The International Atomic Energy Agency and World Order*, Resources for the Future, Baltimore: John Hopkins University Press, 1987.

421 A – INTERNATIONAL ATOMIC ENERGY AGENCY (IAEA)

During the first ten years following the Second World War, international relations were dominated by the sole possessor of nuclear weapons, the United States. Due to the gradual proliferation of nuclear activity throughout the world, the major focus shifted to ensuring that, through the establishment of multilateral agreements, nuclear energy would be used for peaceful purposes.

With this objective, two opposing concepts for the international organization of nuclear activities emerged. The first sought the internationalization of all nuclear activities and general nuclear disarmament. The second wanted a more classical form of co-operation in which each state could preserve its sovereignty.

The latter concept became the predominant one when, in 1953 at the United Nations, President Eisenhower called for an international conference on atomic energy. This came to be known as the Atoms for Peace Plan. The Plan abandoned the principle of the internationalization of potentially dangerous nuclear activities and total nuclear disarmament. Instead it proposed that civilian and military uses of atomic energy could be technically separated through effective safeguards and inspections; and that, as a result, there would be no need to place an embargo on the entirety of the fuel cycle but only on certain facilities, with controls being exercised over the remainder of atomic energy. Once these principles were established, texts and conventions followed the orientation established by the Plan.

Three years after the Atoms for Peace Plan was proposed by President Eisenhower and after long negotiations, the International Atomic Energy Agency came into being. Established on 23 October 1956, the IAEA is one of the specialized agencies of the UN with headquarters in Vienna.

OBJECTIVES

The objectives of the IAEA are "to accelerate and enlarge the contribution of atomic energy to peace, health and prosperity throughout the world" and "to ensure, so far as it is able, that assistance provided by it, or at its request, or under its supervision or control, is not used in such a way as to further military purposes".

ACTIVITIES

To achieve the first of its objectives, the IAEA organizes conferences, publishes texts and establishes safety standards "for protection of health and minimization of danger to life and property". If necessary, it acts as an intermediary between members of the IAEA, both in providing assistance and in supplying material or equipment. More generally, however, it promotes research and the transfer of information for all civil applications of nuclear fission and fusion as well as radiation and radio-isotopes.

To achieve its second objective, a system of safeguards was instituted by the IAEA. This system gives the IAEA the power to dispatch inspectors to a state or states in order to ensure that there are no violations of the commitment to use nuclear energy solely for peaceful ends. The legal basis for such action lies in bilateral agreements or membership of a state which is a party to the 1968 Treaty on the Non-Proliferation of Nuclear Weapons [see 421.06] or nuclear weapon free zone treaties such as the Tlatelolco Treaty or the Rarotonga Treaty.

The Agency is responsible for setting up and implementing measures to verify that fissionable material and nuclear installations are not used for military purposes.

The control of the Agency concerns:

- all goods and services furnished by the Agency, or at its request, or under its direction or control;
- matters which are the objects of agreement between the contracting parties, whereby the parties voluntarily submit to the IAEA's system of safeguards; and
- all or a part of the nuclear activities of a state which voluntarily submits to the IAEA's system of safeguards.

STRUCTURE

The **General Conference** examines the general policies of the IAEA, the budget and the admission of new members. Each state is represented by one delegate. The executive organ of the IAEA is the **Board of Governors**, which is composed of 35 members. Its composition is the result of a compromise between the participation of the most advanced nuclear states and equitable geographic representation. The Board of Governors appoints the Director-General, who is responsible for the Agency, for a period of four years.

Permanent committees have been established in order to respond to specific matters: for example, the Standing Committee on Liability for Nuclear Damage (SCNL), the Standing Advisory Group on Safeguards Implementation (SAGSI) and the International Nuclear Safety Advisory Group (INSAG).

The IAEA must submit its Annual Report to the UN and is required to notify the Security Council of any questions which arise falling within the latter's competence.

CO-OPERATION

The IAEA's Statute authorizes the organization to enter into appropriate relationships, not only with the United Nations, but also with other organizations whose work is related to that of the Agency. It has a co-operative agreement, for example, with the OECD Nuclear Energy Agency.

PUBLICATIONS

The IAEA publishes books and scientific periodicals on the peaceful uses of atomic energy. These include *INIS Atomindex* (twice monthly), *Nuclear Fusion* (monthly) and *IAEA Bulletin* (quarterly).

Susan Reye and Anne de Richecour

ADDRESS

Vienna International Centre, Wagramstrasse, 5, PO.Box: 100, A-1400 Vienna, Austria
T. (43 1) 23600, Fx. (43 1) 234564

421.01 – STATUTE OF THE INTERNATIONAL ATOMIC ENERGY AGENCY – IAEA

Concluded : 26.10.1956, New York
In force : 29.07.1957
Parties : 114

The Statute was approved on 23 October 1956 by the Conference on the Statute of the International Atomic Energy Agency, which was held at the UN's headquarters. It establishes the IAEA, sets forth its objectives, functions, and structure as well as the IAEA's system of safeguards.

S.R. and A.R.

Access : ALS (Art. XXI)
Reserves : USP
Duration : USP
Deposit. : US (Art. XXI-C)
Language : Chi, Eng, Fre, Rus, Spa (Art. XXIII)

Modific. : Modified 28.09.70 (01.06.73)

Reference : 276 UNTS – Can TS 1957/20, 1973/3 – UST 8/1, 14/1 – ILM 10:130 – RTAF 1969/26

421.02 – CONVENTION ON THIRD-PARTY LIABILITY IN THE FIELD OF NUCLEAR ENERGY – NEA

Concluded : 29.07.1960, Paris
In force : 01.04.1968
Parties : 14

From its commencement, the use of nuclear energy has created problems relating to third-party liability. As the law of third-party liability was considered inadequate, a specific legal regime had to be established.

In 1960, the Paris Convention was adopted under the auspices of the OECD Nuclear Energy Agency (at that time, the European Nuclear Energy Agency of the OEEC) in order to provide a uniform regime of third-party liability in nuclear energy. The objective of the Convention is to ensure adequate and equitable compensation for persons who suffer damage caused by nuclear incidents. The Convention was the first to establish the basic principles relating to third-party liability in the field of nuclear energy on which all international agreements and most national legislation have subsequently been based.

DETAILS OF THE CONVENTION

In the Convention, the contracting states adopt the fundamental principle that the operator of a nuclear installation is "strictly" or "absolutely" liable for all damage caused by a nuclear incident. That is to say, if nuclear damage is caused by an installation, the operator is liable for that damage, regardless of whether any fault, including negligence, can be imputed to him (Arts. 3, 4 and 5). He can escape liability only in very limited circumstances, such as incidents caused by war or by grave natural disaster (Art. 9).

This system of liability exempts the victim from the obligation to prove that the incident was the fault of the operator. In addition, under this system the operator is exclusively liable. Thus, the victim is not required to identify the person responsible for the incident. This means that the various bodies which contribute to the operation of the nuclear installation, including suppliers and carriers, do not need to take out additional insurance to that of the operator.

The operator of a nuclear installation is liable for any nuclear incident which occurs in that installation or involving nuclear substances in the course of being transported to or from that installation. Although the operator is strictly liable, that liability is limited regarding, first, the maximum amount for which he can be liable and, second, the time during which an action can be brought against him.

The Convention provides that the maximum liability of an operator shall be 15 million Special Drawing Rights (SDRs) (as defined by the International Monetary

Fund [see 211 A]). However, this is in effect merely an indicative level since a party may, taking into account the possibilities of obtaining insurance or other financial security, establish a greater or lesser amount subject to a lower limit of SDR 5 million by legislation. The Steering Committee for Nuclear Energy has recommended that contracting parties to the Paris Convention aim at setting the maximum liability at not less than SDR 150 million.

With respect to limitation of time, the right to compensation is lost if an action is not brought within ten years of the nuclear accident, subject to the right of a state to extend this period up to 30 years by legislation. In addition, states may provide that operators will not be liable after a period of at least two years from the time when the victim knew, or ought to have known, of the damage and the operator liable.

The Convention states that every operator must have and maintain insurance or other financial security to guarantee the victims are compensated by the operator in accordance with the terms of the Convention.

The Convention provides for unity of jurisdiction over claims for compensation. In the event of a nuclear accident, such claims may be heard only by courts of the contracting party in whose territory the incident occurred or, if the incident occurs during transport outside the territory of a contracting party, by the courts of the contracting party in which the relevant installation is located.

MODIFICATIONS

In order to bring its provisions closer to those of the Vienna Convention [see 421.05], adopted in 1963, the Paris Convention was amended by the Additional Protocol of 28 January 1964. A further amending Protocol of 16 November 1982 brought the Convention up to date by replacing an older unit of account with Special Drawing Rights.

See also the Convention Supplementary to the Paris Convention on Third Party Liability in the Field of Nuclear Energy (Brussels, 1963) [see 421.04].

S.R. and A.R.

Access : CON (Art. 19, 21)
Reserves : PAU (Art. 18, 23, Annexe I)
Duration : REN 10 (Art. 22)
Deposit. : OECD (Art. 19)
Language : Dut, Eng, Fre, Ger, Ita, Spa

Modific. : Additional Protocol Paris 28.01.64 (01.04.68); Protocol 16.11.82 (07.10.88); Joint Protocol 21.09.88 (27.04.92)

Reference : UKTS 1968/69, 1989/6 – JORF 11 Feb 69 – RTAF 1969/12

421.03 – CONVENTION ON THE LIABILITY OF OPERATORS OF NUCLEAR SHIPS – CMI

Concluded : 25.05.1962, Brussels
Parties : 7

Both the Paris and Vienna Conventions [see 421.02 and 421.05] exclude from their scope of application nuclear reactors that are used to propel a means of transport.

The 1962 Brussels Convention was intended to make provision for third-party liability in the event of an accident involving a ship equipped with a nuclear power plant. It sets out a regime of civil liability very similar to that of the Paris and Vienna Conventions. In particular, "the operator of a nuclear ship shall be absolutely liable for any nuclear damage upon proof that such damage has been caused by a nuclear incident involving the nuclear fuel of, or radioactive products or waste produced in, such ship" (Art. II-1). Unlike the Paris and Vienna Conventions, the 1962 Brussels Convention expressly applies to military as well as civilian installations.

The 1962 Brussels Convention has never entered into force. In order to do so it must be ratified "by at least one licensing State and one other State" (Art. XXIV-a), a "licensing State" being "a Contracting State which operates or which has authorized the operation of a nuclear ship under its flag" (Art. I-2). Four states have ratified and three have acceded to the Convention, but the requirement of ratification by a "licensing State" has not been, and seems unlikely ever to be, fulfilled.

Susan Reye

Access : ALS (Art. XXV)
Reserves : PAU (Art. XXI)
Duration : USP
Deposit. : BE (Art. XXIII)
Language : Eng, Fre

Reference : ULR 1962

421.04 – CONVENTION SUPPLEMENTARY TO THE PARIS CONVENTION ON THIRD PARTY LIABILITY IN THE FIELD OF NUCLEAR ENERGY – NEA

Concluded : 31.01.1963, Brussels
In force : 04.12.1974
Parties : 11

This Convention supplements the Paris Convention of 1960 [see 421.02] by providing the possibility for further compensation to victims of a nuclear accident in the event that the Paris Convention does not cover all damage caused by the incident. This additional compensation comes from public funds made available by the contracting parties.

DETAILS OF THE CONVENTION

By combining the two Conventions, compensation can reach a maximum total of SDR 300 million per incident. Such compensation shall be provided:

(i) up to an amount of at least SDR 5 million out of funds provided by insurance or other financial security, depending on the operator's liability under the Paris Convention;
(ii) between this amount and SDR 175 million out of public funds to be made available by the contracting party in whose territory the nuclear installation of the operator liable is situated;
(iii) between SDR 175 and SDR 300 million out of public funds to be made available by all the contracting parties.

The proportion of the total to be contributed by each contracting party is determined by a formula based as to 50 per cent on gross national product, and as to the other 50 per cent on the thermal power of nuclear reactors in its territory.

MODIFICATIONS

This Brussels Supplementary Convention, as amended by a 1964 Protocol, came into force in 1974. It was further amended by the Protocol of 1982 which entered into force on 1 August 1991 following ratification by all contracting parties.

S.R.

Access : CON (Art. 19, 22)
Reserves : PAU (Art. 18)
Duration : FXD (Art. 23)
Deposit. : BE (Art. 25)
Language : Dut, Eng, Fre, Ger, Ita, Spa

Modific. : Additional Protocol Paris 28.01.64 (04.12.74); Protocol 16.11.82 (01.08.91)

Reference : UKTS 1975/44 – ULR 1964 – JORF 27 Mar 75 – RTAF 1975/18

421.05 – VIENNA CONVENTION ON CIVIL LIABILITY FOR NUCLEAR DAMAGE. OPTIONAL PROTOCOL CONCERNING THE COMPULSORY SETTLEMENT OF DISPUTES – IAEA

Concluded : 21.05.1963, Vienna
In force : 12.11.1977
Parties : 19

The Vienna Convention, adopted under the auspices of the IAEA in 1963, was based on the Paris Convention of 1960 [see 421.02] but is potentially global rather than regional in scope.

DETAILS OF THE CONVENTION

The basic principles of the liability of nuclear operators set out in this Convention are identical to those in the Paris Convention – namely, the strict (or "absolute") and exclusive liability of the operator; limitation on the operator's liability both in monetary terms and in terms of a deadline for action to be brought in the event of a nuclear incident; a mandatory financial guarantee to ensure compensation; and unity of jurisdiction.

However, under the present Convention the minimum amount to which the liability of the operator may be limited under national legislation is US$5 million, defined by reference to the gold value of the dollar in 1963 (approximately US$50-60 million today).

RECENT DEVELOPMENTS

In 1989, the IAEA Standing Committee on Liability for Nuclear Damage began work on a comprehensive revision of the Vienna Convention, as well as on a proposed system of additional funding to compensate nuclear damage. It is proposed that the new supplementary funding scheme would be additional to both the Vienna and the Paris Conventions and, unlike the Brussels Supplementary Convention [see 421.04], would include funding from the nuclear industry as well as from states. This work has not yet been concluded.

S.R.

Access : ALS (Art. 24)
Reserves : USP
Duration : REN 10 (Art. 25)
Deposit. : IAEA (Art. 22, 29)
Language : Eng, Fre, Rus, Spa (Art. 29)

Modific. : Protocol 1983 (-); Joint Protocol 21.09.88 (27.04.92)

Reference : 1063 UNTS – ULR 1964 – ILM 2:727

421.06 – TREATY ON THE NON-PROLIFERATION OF NUCLEAR WEAPONS – IAEA

Concluded : 01.07.1968, London, Washington, Moscow
In force : 05.03.1970
Parties : 155

The Treaty on the Non-Proliferation of Nuclear Weapons (NPT) reflected the growing concern of the nuclear powers in the 1960s of the possibility of additional states' developing nuclear weapons. Hastily negotiated, and with the USSR, the US and the UK as the depositary governments, the NPT was to have established a surveillance system to inspect all activities capable of leading to the manufacture of nuclear arms: enrichment, plutonium production, research laboratories and reprocessing. The NPT is valid for 25 years.

As concluded, the Treaty distinguishes between two categories of states: nuclear weapon states (NWS) and non-nuclear weapon states (NNWS). Nuclear weapon states undertake not to transfer or assist other states to manufacture nuclear weapons (Art. 1) and agree to encourage negotiations for nuclear disarmament. Non-nuclear weapon states (NNWS) renounce the use of nuclear power for military purposes and under the Treaty are promised access by the NWS to all nuclear technology provided it is used for peaceful purposes (Art. 4). In return, the NNWS must accept the IAEA's system of safeguards [see 421 A] regarding all nuclear activities on their territory, a control to which the NWS are not subjected.

There are, however, limitations to the scope of this agreement. First, although nuclear arms are targeted, enrichment and reprocessing, which can lead to the manufacture of atomic bombs, are not. Second, only the non-nuclear powers are obliged to agree to the peaceful use of nuclear power, whereas the states possessing nuclear arms simply agree to pursue negotiations on disarmament. Thus, while there is an obligation for nuclear-weapons states to negotiate, the Treaty does not require that they in fact conclude a disarmament agreement.

SUBSEQUENT DEVELOPMENTS

The Zangger Committee (a Committee of nuclear-exporting countries parties to the

NPT) began discussions in 1970 on the procedures and rules that its member countries should apply to their exports which are subject to the safeguards clause of the NPT. Members of the Committee, by individual letters, informed the IAEA of the agreed procedures they intend to apply and of the Trigger List of materials and items of equipment that would be exported only under such safeguards [see 421.08].

The Committee, in September 1985, called on the nuclear energy exporting countries to require a security control on the importing countries, thereby emphasizing the importance of the system of safeguards. A new stage has now been reached: the new trading countries, having the recognized capacity to possess nuclear arms, are agreeing to the international inspection of all their nuclear activities so that those activities may be verified to be exclusively intended for peaceful purposes.

S.R.

Access : ALS
Reserves : USP
Duration : FXD
Deposit. : US, RU, GB
Language : Chi, Eng, Fre, Rus, Spa

Reference : 729 UNTS – Can TS 1970/7, 1972/3 – UST 21/1, 25/1 – ILM 7:809

421.07 – CONVENTION RELATING TO CIVIL LIABILITY IN THE FIELD OF MARITIME CARRIAGE OF NUCLEAR MATERIAL – IMO

Concluded : 17.12.1971, Brussels
In force : 15.07.1975
Parties : 14

The Convention, adopted in Brussels in 1971 under the auspices of the OECD, the IAEA and the IMO [see 183 A], establishes the primacy of nuclear law (as contained in the Paris and Vienna Conventions [see 421.02 and 421.05]) over maritime law. It seeks to ensure that the operator of a nuclear installation is exclusively liable for damage caused by a nuclear incident occurring in the maritime carriage of nuclear material, as provided under the Paris and Vienna Conventions.

DETAILS OF THE CONVENTION

Article 1 stipulates, "Any person who by virtue of an international convention or national law applicable in the field of maritime transport might be held liable for damage caused by a nuclear incident shall be exonerated from such liability: (a) if the operator of a nuclear installation is liable for such damage under either the Paris or the Vienna Convention, or (b) if the operator of a nuclear installation is liable for such damage by virtue of a national law governing the liability for such damage, provided that such law is in all respects as favourable to persons who may suffer damage as either the Paris or the Vienna Convention".

The present Convention supersedes all other international conventions in the field of maritime transport which are in conflict with it [see also section 1.8.3].

S.R.

Access : ALS (Art. 5)
Reserves : PAU (Art. 10)
Duration : USP
Deposit. : IMO (Art. 11)
Language : Eng, Fre (Art. 12)

Reference : 974, 1143 UNTS – ILM 11:277 – ULR 1971 – JORF 3 Aug 75 – RTAF 1975/51

421.08 – GUIDELINES ON THE TRANSFER OF NUCLEAR MATERIAL – LC

Adopted : 21.09.1975, London
In force : 11.01.1978
Parties : 23

At the initiative of the United States, seven states met in London in 1975 and formed what is commonly known as the London Club, an informal grouping of nuclear supplier countries. The objective of the discussions of this expert group is to try to harmonize export policies for tranfers of "nuclear items", from the point of view of safeguards and control, outside the framework of the IAEA and the Non-Proliferation Treaty [see 421.06]. This also applies to technology transfers, control of retransfers and physical protection.

These states arrived at a compromise in September 1977. Although they did not conclude a formal agreement, the states concerned adopted the procedure previously used by the Zangger Committee [see 421.06] – each state sending to the IAEA a declaration of its intention to apply the agreed principles.

The purpose of the Guidelines is to lay down the fundamental principles relating to the safeguards and controls which must be applied to any export of nuclear items to non-nuclear weapon states. They are based on the Trigger List – a list of items to which the Guidelines apply – drawn up by the supplier states which took part in the work of the London Club, and based on common criteria agreed between those states relating to technology transfers.

The importing states must ensure that the nuclear materials, or equipment which they receive, may be inspected by the IAEA and will not be used in the construction of nuclear weapons.

S.R.

Language : Eng

421.09 – CONVENTION ON THE PHYSICAL PROTECTION OF NUCLEAR MATERIAL – IAEA

Concluded : 03.03.1980, Vienna
In force : 08.02.1987
Parties : 43

This Convention has two parts. The first deals with the international transport of nuclear material used for peaceful purposes and the second with administrative co-operation and mutual legal assistance between the parties.

International Transport of Nuclear Material. International nuclear transport is defined as "the carriage of a consignment of nuclear material by any means of transportation intended to go beyond the territory of the State where the shipment originates beginning with the departure from a facility of the shipper in that State and ending with the arrival at a facility of the receiver within the State of ultimate destination" (Art. 1).

The parties must ensure that during international nuclear transportation nuclear material is protected at the levels described in Annex I. This level of protection must be applied in the territories of the parties, whether exporters or importers, and in the case of transit by sea or air, between borders and the point of origin or final destination of the material. The Convention also attempts to ensure, indirectly, the application of its levels of protection by states not parties to the Convention, since states parties may not export or import material to or from a non-party, unless the latter has given assurances that the material will be so protected during international transport. This also applies to transit through the territory of a non-party. The levels of protection described in Annex I are broadly the same as those of the London Club.

Administrative Co-operation and Mutual Legal Assistance. This part of the Convention applies regardless of whether a matter involves the international transport of nuclear material destined for peaceful purposes or not. The main provisions establish a system of information exchange between the competent authorities and the notification of points of contact with responsibility for ensuring the physical protection of nuclear material. Article 5-2 allows a state which is not party to the Convention to request aid from and co-operation of the parties in the recovery and protection of nuclear material.

In regard to offences specified under the Convention (Art. 7), each state party must take appropriate measures, including detention, to ensure that the alleged offender is prosecuted or else extradited should he be present in its territory. This is so even if the offence was not committed within the territory concerned.

The Convention also provides for extensive legal assistance between the parties, particularly in the transfer of evidence.

S.R.

Access : ASO (Art. 18)
Reserves : PAU (Art. 17)
Duration : USP
Deposit. : IAEA
Language : Ara, Chi, Eng, Fre, Rus, Spa

Reference : ILM 18:1419

421.10 – CONVENTION ON EARLY NOTIFICATION OF A NUCLEAR ACCIDENT – IAEA

Concluded : 26.09.1986, Vienna
In force : 27.10.1986
Parties : 65

The Chernobyl accident in April 1986 was one of the most serious incidents in history. It caused the discharge of substantial amounts of radioactive elements into the environment and its effects were felt throughout the then USSR and in neighbouring states.

At the time of the accident, information as to which states had been affected by the radioactive discharge emerged too slowly to allow prompt preventive measures to be taken. There was also a noticeable lack of mutual assistance between states. As a result, consultations took place within the framework of the IAEA and led to the adoption of both this Convention and the Convention on Assistance [see 421.11].

The present Convention requires states parties, on the occurrence of a nuclear accident within their jurisdiction, to notify forthwith states which are, or may conceivably be, affected by a radioactive discharge. The notification must include (in addition to the information that a nuclear incident has occurred) the nature, time and, if possible, the location of the incident. The information transmitted to other states must also specify the facility or activity involved, the cause or supposed cause of the incident and its predicted outcome, and the measures taken or planned to protect areas away from the site of the incident.

Susan Reye and Anne de Richecour

Access : ASO (Art. 12)
Reserves : PAU (Art. 11)
Duration : USP
Deposit. : IAEA
Language : Ara, Chi, Eng, Fre, Rus, Spa

Reference : ILM 25:1370

421.11 – CONVENTION ON ASSISTANCE IN THE CASE OF A NUCLEAR ACCIDENT OR RADIOLOGICAL EMERGENCY – IAEA

Concluded : 26.09.1986, Vienna
In force : 26.02.1987
Parties : 63

Adopted under the auspices of the IAEA following the Chernobyl accident and at the same time as the Early Notification Convention [see 421.10], this Convention requires the states parties to co-operate among themselves and with the IAEA, to facilitate prompt assistance in the event of a nuclear accident so as to minimize its consequences and to protect life, property and the environment from the effects of radioactive releases.

It sets out procedures by which any state party may request assistance from another state party, or from the IAEA, following a nuclear accident. A state party of which a request is made is not obliged to provide the assistance, but must make a prompt decision as to whether it will do so or not. Assistance may be given either free of charge, or subject to reimbursement, by the requesting state.

S.R.

Access : ASO (Art. 14)
Reserves : PAU (Art. 8, 10, 13)
Duration : USP
Deposit. : IAEA
Language : Ara, Chi, Eng, Fre, Rus, Spa

Reference : ILM 25:1377

421.12 – JOINT PROTOCOL RELATING TO THE APPLICATION OF THE VIENNA CONVENTION AND THE PARIS CONVENTION – IAEA/NEA

Concluded : 21.09.1988, Vienna
In force : 27.04.1992
Parties : 11

This Convention, adopted by an international conference convened jointly by the OECD and the IAEA, establishes a link between the Convention on Third-Party Liability in the Field of Nuclear Energy (Paris, 1960) [see 421.02] and the 1963 Vienna Convention on Civil Liability for Nuclear Damage [see 421.05]. It also seeks to eliminate conflicts arising from the simultaneous application of both Conventions.

As both the Vienna and Paris Conventions are similar in substance and as no state is a party to both Conventions, this Protocol allows states which are parties to one Convention to benefit from the special regime established by both Conventions. In regard to conflicts of law which may arise from the simultaneous application of both Conventions in the event of a nuclear incident, particularly in the case of international carriage of nuclear substances, this Protocol establishes that one Convention will apply to the nuclear incident to the exclusion of the other.

Before the adoption of this Protocol, victims of a nuclear incident in one of the states party to the Vienna or Paris Conventions were not protected in cases where an accident occurred in the territory of a party to the other Convention. With this Protocol, in the case of a nuclear incident occurring in a nuclear installation, the applicable Convention shall be that to which the state is a party within whose territory that installation is situated (Art. III-2). In the case of a nuclear incident outside a nuclear installation and involving nuclear material in the course of carriage, the applicable Convention shall be that to which the state is a party within whose territory the nuclear installation is situated, whose operator is liable, pursuant to either the Paris or the Vienna Convention (Art. III-3).

The Protocol entered into force on 27 April 1992, three months after ratification or accession by five states party to the Vienna Convention, and five states party to the Paris Convention (Art. VII).

Susan Reye and Anne de Richecour

Access : CON (Art. VI)
Reserves : USP
Duration : FXD (Art. VII-2)
Deposit. : IAEA (Art. VI)
Language : Ara, Chi, Eng, Fre, Rus, Spa (Art. XI)

4.2.2 Hazardous Wastes and Chemicals

The movement of hazardous substances (chemicals, pesticides, radioactive and hazardous waste) between states has been the subject of recent international regulation under the auspices of the UNEP, FAO and IAEA. In addition, several regional efforts have been undertaken in this field by the OECD, the EC and the OAU. While it may be said that there is now some universal consensus on the basic principles which should govern the transboundary movement of hazardous substances, regional differences in regulation and the non-binding character of global instruments suggest that a global regime has not yet emerged. In fact, it is largely the result of dissatisfaction with global efforts that regional regulation has occurred.

The underlying concern preoccupying regulators was the movement of hazardous substances from the developed world to the developing world which, in the case of waste, has an estimated annual value of US$3 billion. The technological gap in this context manifested itself in the difficulty experienced by developing states in testing these substances and in regulating the safe management of them. The result was that developing states tended to have less stringent standards and enforcement capability than developed states, such that substances unacceptable in developed states found their way to developing states often for dangerous use or disposal. This phenomenon was further compounded recently by reported cases of covert toxic waste dumping in Africa by industrialized states, which aroused significant controversy around the world. Similar considerations exist for chemicals and pesticides.

Accordingly, international agreements and guidelines have recognized and attempted to address these problems. Structures have been established so that developing countries can make informed decisions about hazardous substances and have decisions regarding the legality of imports be respected as matters of sovereignty. At the same time, however, these international instruments have affirmed that the international movement of these goods should continue as freely as possible in an effort to satisfy the interests of all parties. The compromises thus struck at the global level have aroused significant criticism from environmental groups and from many developing states.

Richard G. Tarasofsky

SELECTED BIBLIOGRAPHY

Brett-Baender, M., "Pesticides and Precaution: the Bamako Convention as a Model for an International Convention on Pesticides Regulation", *New York University Journal of International Law and Politics* 14: 557.

Kwiatkowska, A, Barbara and Alfred H.A. Soons, *Transboundary Movements and Disposal of Hazardous Wastes in International Law: Basic Documents*, Dordrecht: Martinus Nijhoff Publishers, 1992.

Porter, G. and J.W. Brown, *Global Environmental Politics*, Boulder: Westview Press, 1991.

Rose, Gregory, "Prior Informed Consent: Hazardous Chemicals", *Review of European Community and International Environmental Law* 1: 64.

Uram, C., "International Regulation of the Sale and Use of Pesticides", *Northwestern Journal of International Law and Business* 10: 460.

422.01 – INTERNATIONAL CODE OF CONDUCT ON THE DISTRIBUTION AND USE OF PESTICIDES – FAO

Adopted : 28.11.1985, FAO Res. 10/85

The Code is a voluntary set of standards that regulates pesticides from the cradle to the grave and is addressed directly to users, public-interest environmental groups, the pesticides industry, governments and international organizations.

DETAILS OF THE CODE

The Code is based on the assumption that governments and the pesticides industry have a shared responsibility for protecting human health and the environment (Para. 1.2) and accordingly assigns specific duties to each of them. Governments are given the overall responsibility for regulating the distribution and use of pesticides (Para. 3.1), while the pesticides industry should comply with the Code even in the absence of local legislation. Exporting countries and the pesticides industry are called upon to ensure that good trading practices are followed in the export of pesticides, particularly to countries without appropriate legislative or regulatory capacities (Para. 3.3.2 and 3.4).

The Code calls on governments to control the use (Para. 6.1.1) and availability (Para. 7.1) of pesticides. Governments should restrict pesticides when appropriate by either not registering them for use or by making them available only to specified users (Para. 7.3). Governments are further urged to provide information on the treatment of poison and other relevant advisory services (Para. 5.1). In conjunction with the pesticides industry, governments are to make provision for the safe storage and disposal of pesticides (Para. 5.3).

The pesticides industry is urged to test pesticides in accordance with "sound scientific procedures" (Para. 4) and to ensure that all advertising is truthful and capable of substantiation (Para. 11). Public-interest environmental groups and international organizations should call attention to deviations from the Code's advertising standards (Para. 11.2). The pesticides industry is further encouraged to ensure that the ingredients in the pesticides conform with both FAO [see 131 A] and WHO [see 132 A] specifications (Para. 6.2.3) and that the pesticides comply with FAO and WHO guidelines for packaging, storage and disposal (Para. 10). Even where a control scheme is in place, the pesticides industry should stop selling and recall products when their safe use seems unattainable (Para. 5.2.3).

The Code establishes a Prior Informed Consent procedure similar to the London Guidelines for the Exchange of Information on Chemicals in International Trade [see 422.02], whereby the export of any pesticide which is banned or restricted for human health or the environment should not take place without the agreement of the importing government (Para. 2). The Code affirms the FAO's co-operation with UNEP [see 410 A] in maintaining a database of control actions and decisions taken by participating governments (Para. 9.8.2). According to this procedure, notification of national control actions are to be transmitted both to the FAO (Para. 9.1) and to importing states (Para. 9.3). The information the FAO receives is passed on to all other participating governments (Para. 9.8.3). Importing governments should then advise the FAO of their decision regarding the future acceptability within their jurisdiction of the pesticide concerned (Para. 9.10). Subsequently, exporting governments should advise their pesticide exporters of the relevant decisions of importing governments and should ensure that exports do not occur contrary to the wishes of importing governments (Para. 9.11). In making their decisions regarding the importation of pesticides, the Code urges the avoidance of restrictions which are inconsistent with the General Agreement on Tariffs and Trade (Para. 9.10.3) [see 111.01].

The Code seeks to have governments monitor compliance with the Code and contemplates periodic review with a view to updating as conditions require (Para. 12).

Richard G. Tarasofsky

Modific. : Revised (11.1989)

Reference : UN Doc. FAO/C85/REP (1985)

422.02 – LONDON GUIDELINES FOR THE EXCHANGE OF INFORMATION ON CHEMICALS IN INTERNATIONAL TRADE – UNEP

Adopted : 17.06.1987, UNEP Dec. 14/27

The London Guidelines for the Exchange of Information on Chemicals in International Trade are a non-binding set of recommendations aimed at "increasing chemical safety in all countries through the exchange of information on chemicals in international trade". They do so primarily by creating an institutional framework for information exchange between exporting and importing states.

Some of the general principles underlying the Guidelines are that: (a) human health and the environment can be protected through the exchange of information; (b) states with advanced capacity to manage chemicals safely should share their experience with states of less advanced capability; and (c) regulation of chemicals should not constitute unnecessary trade barriers between states (Art. 2).

DETAILS OF THE GUIDELINES

The central feature of the Guidelines is the Prior Informed Consent (PIC) procedure. PIC is defined as the principle that international shipment of banned or severely restricted chemicals should not proceed without the consent of the importing country (Art. 1). Consent is to be informed by notifying the importer of actions other states have taken to control the use of those substances. Banned or severely restricted chemicals are those in which a government has decided that all or virtually all use is prohibited within its domestic jurisdiction (Art. 1). Radioactive materials are excluded from the general scope of the Guidelines as are, at the option of each state, pharmaceuticals and food additives (Art. 3). The Guidelines establish an information exchange system and foresee co-operation between UNEP [see 410 A] and the Food and Agriculture Organization (FAO) [see 131 A] in the implementation of the PIC procedure (Art. 5). The main vehicle for the operation of the PIC is UNEP's already existing International Register of Potentially Toxic Chemicals (IRPTC) (Art. 5).

The PIC is triggered by a government taking a control action on a banned or severely restricted chemical and reporting it to the IRPTC (Art. 6). The IRPTC then informs all other states participating in the PIC procedure of each banned or restricted chemical subject to the control action (Art. 7-2). If a country does not respond to the notification, then the *status quo* is presumed for that country – namely, that export is prohibited unless the chemical is already registered for use in the importing country or express consent to importation has previously been given by the importing government (Art. 7-3). Upon being notified, exporting governments are required to inform their chemical industries of the decisions of importing countries (Art. 7-4). If an export of a banned or severely restricted chemical is to occur, then information exchange should also take place directly between the exporting and importing state, whereby the exporter is to furnish the importer with a copy of the control action along with an indication that the export is about to occur (Art. 8).

The Guidelines also provide for the exchange of relevant scientific information between countries and the transfer of information from exporters to importers on the "sound management" of chemicals (Art. 13). Technical assistance to developing countries is also contemplated to aid in establishing an infrastructure capable of managing chemicals and implementing the Guidelines (Art. 15).

The IRPTC is given the task of reviewing the implementation of the Guidelines and making recommendations to improve their effectiveness (Art. 5-9).

R.G.T.

Modific. : Modified (25.05.89)

Reference : UN Doc. UNEP/GC.15/9/Add.2/Supplement 3 and Corr.1, Appendix and Governing Council Decision 15/30, UN Doc. UNEP/GC.15/12, Annex I at 160 (1989)

422.03 – CONVENTION ON THE CONTROL OF TRANSBOUNDARY MOVEMENTS OF HAZARDOUS WASTES AND THEIR DISPOSAL – UNEP

Concluded : 22.03.1989, Basel
In force : 05.05.1992
Parties : 43

The Convention requires exporting and importing states to regulate the international flow of hazardous wastes.

Scope: The Convention defines wastes as hazardous by reference to categories set forth in Annex I unless they do not possess the characteristics listed in Annex III and additional wastes so classified by national legislation (Art. 1). Many of the Convention's obligations also apply to "other wastes", which encompass household wastes or residue from the incineration from household wastes (Art. 1). Excluded from the Convention's ambit are radioactive wastes and wastes discharged from the normal operation of ships so long as they are regulated by other international instruments (Art. 1).

DETAILS OF THE CONVENTION

If an importing state elects to exercise its right to prohibit the import of hazardous or other wastes, it is required to inform other parties of its decision whereupon exporting states are required to prohibit the export of these wastes to it (Arts 4-1-a and 4-1-b). In cases where the importing state has not declared a prohibition on hazardous or other wastes, the Convention creates a rebuttable presumption against their import whereby exporting states are required to prohibit their export unless the importing state has specifically consented to their import (Art. 4-1-c). The Convention further requires parties to manage hazardous and other wastes in a manner that protects human health and the environment by taking measures which ensure, *inter alia*, the following: minimal waste generation; availability of adequate disposal facilities; prevention and minimization of pollution during disposal and transboundary shipment of waste; prevention of waste exports where there is reason to believe that "environmentally sound" disposal will not take place in the importing country; prevention of waste imports prohibitions where "environmentally sound management" will not occur domestically; transfer of information between parties on the effect of the movement of hazardous and other waste to human health and the environment; and co-operation with other states in this regard (Art. 4-2).

The Convention provides specific rules on when the import and export of hazardous wastes can occur. Export of hazardous and other wastes is permissible only if the exporting state lacks the facilities to dispose of them in an "environmentally sound and efficient manner", the wastes are raw materials to be recycled or recovered in the importing state, or the transboundary movement of wastes conform with other criteria set down by the parties which may not conflict with the Convention (Art. 4-9). Wastes are not to be exported if they will be disposed of in Antarctica (Art. 4-6). The import and export of hazardous and other wastes to and from non-parties is prohibited (Art. 4-5) save in the event of an international agreement with a non-party that does not derogate from the "environmentally sound" requirements of the Convention (Art. 11). Parties are permitted, in accordance with the objectives of the Convention and other rules of international law, to take stricter measures than required in order to protect human health and the environment (Art. 4-11).

In the event that a transboundary transfer of waste is to occur, the Convention sets out detailed requirements in Annex V for how the notification by the exporting state and consent of the importing state must be provided (Art. 6). The Convention requires all transboundary movements of hazardous and other waste to be covered by insurance, bond or other financial guarantee (Art. 6-11). If the terms of a contract for the transboundary movement of hazardous or other wastes cannot be fulfilled, the Convention places a duty on the exporter to re-import those wastes unless an "environmentally sound" alternative is found within 90 days (Art. 8). Movement of waste that is not in accordance with the Convention or international law is deemed illegal (Art. 9-1) and parties are required to take measures to prevent and punish such contraventions (Arts. 4-3 and 4-4). If illegal traffic in waste is the result of conduct of the exporter or generator, the exporting state is required to ensure the waste is taken back or disposed of in an "environmentally sound manner" (Art. 9-2). The Convention requires parties to co-operate with a view to adopting a Protocol on liability and compensation for damage arising from the transboundary movement and disposal of hazardous and other wastes (Art. 12), and such negotiations are currently taking place.

STRUCTURE

The governing body established by the Convention is the **Conference of the Parties** which is to review and evaluate the implementation of the Convention (Art. 15). A **Secretariat** is also established by the Convention to service the Conference of the Parties and to provide assistance to the parties on matters relating to the Convention (Art. 16).

A party which believes that another party is violating the Convention may inform the Secretariat and is required to inform the party believed to be in breach (Art. 19). Parties are required to settle disputes by any peaceful means of the parties' choice, and to this end the Convention gives the option of submitting disputes to the International Court of Justice [see 001 B] or to the arbitration procedure set forth in Annex VI. Amendments to the Convention are adopted at the Conference of the Parties and require at least a three-fourths majority of those parties present and voting (Art. 17). Any amendments enter into force upon depositing instruments of acceptance with the depositary by three-fourths of the parties (Art. 17).

R.G.T.

Access	: ASO (Art. 22)
Reserves	: PRO (Art. 26)
Duration	: USP
Deposit.	: UN (Art. 28)
Language	: Ara, Chi, Eng, Fre, Rus, Spa (Art. 29)

Reference : UN Doc. UNEP/IG.80/3

422.04 – IAEA CODE OF PRACTICE ON THE INTERNATIONAL TRANSBOUNDARY MOVEMENT OF RADIOACTIVE WASTE – IAEA

Adopted : 27.06.1990, IAEA Dec.

The Code of Practice arose in part out of the public reaction to unauthorized transboundary movement of radioactive waste to developing countries and concerns over how such wastes are then managed and disposed of.

DETAILS OF THE CODE

The basic principles of the Code are that each state should minimize the amount of radioactive waste it produces (Para. 2) and that any radioactive waste under its jurisdiction or control should be "safely managed and disposed of" so as to protect human health and the environment (Para. 1).

Against this background, the Code affirms the sovereign right of every state to prohibit the movement of radioactive waste on its territory (Para. 3). If a state does choose to involve itself in the transboundary movement of such waste, it should ensure that this takes place according to "international safety standards" (Para. 4) and, subject to the relevant rules of international law, after the sending, receiving and transit states have all been notified of such movement and given their consent to it (Para. 5). Each state should establish an authority to regulate the transboundary movement of radioactive waste (Para. 6) and should not permit the receipt of such waste unless it can manage and dispose of it in accordance with "international safety standards" (Para. 7). A corresponding duty is placed on sending states, who should be satisfied, prior to shipment and on the basis of the receiving state's consent, that the receiving state can manage and dispose of the waste according to "international safety standards" (Para. 7). If the transfer is not completed in accordance with the Code, the sending state should either re-admit the waste or arrange a safe alternative for it (Para. 10). States should enact provisions of national law covering liability and compensation for damage caused by the transboundary movement of radioactive waste (Para. 8) and non-compliance with the Code (Para. 9).

R.G.T.

4.3 Management of Common Resources

The shared interest of states in monitoring world meteorology and managing resources in Antarctica and in common areas beyond national jurisdiction have resulted in various levels of co-operation.

The World Meteorological Organization [see 431 A] facilitates the co-operation necessary to monitor and forecast changes in weather and climate, and the effects of human activity thereon. Its work has also contributed significantly to global awareness of ozone depletion [see 413.02] and climate change [see 413.07].

Multilateral regimes on the high seas [see 4.3.2], Antarctica [see 4.3.3] and outer space [see 4.3.4] embody basic principles of international law which require contracting states to prevent and control pollution and environmental change. These regimes have also steadily developed rules of collective management whereby member states have an obligation to co-operate in the conservation and the sustainable development of the resources of these areas.

Maguelonne Déjeant-Pons

4.3.1 Meteorological Observations

431 A – WORLD METEOROLOGICAL ORGANIZATION (WMO)

This intergovernmental organization, created in 1951, is a specialized agency of the United Nations. It replaced the non-governmental International Meteorological Organization, established in 1873.

The general purposes of the WMO are to co-ordinate, standardize and improve world meteorological and related activities, and to encourage an efficient exchange of meteorological and related information between countries. It is one of the best examples of an international co-operative system.

WMO PROGRAMMES

The WMO has established a number of scientific and technical programmes, and observation systems. The main programmes are the World Weather Watch, the World Climate Programme, the Atmospheric Research and Environment Programme, the Applications of Meteorology Programme, the Hydrology and Water Resources Programme, the Education and Training Programme, the Technical Co-operation Programme and the Regional Programme. A selection of these programmes and their components are briefly described here.

The **World Weather Watch** (WWW), created in 1963, is the backbone of the WMO and the main focal point for its other programmes. It provides rapid world-wide weather information exchange through member-operated observation centres (global, regional and national), telecommunication links, and data-processing facilities. Its observation centres include land and sea-based stations, and satellites (four polar-orbiting satellites and five geo-stationary satellites over the Equator). The observation and measurement of meteorological elements through these facilities form WWW's Global Observing System.

The **World Climate Programme** (WCP), established in 1979, seeks to improve knowledge of natural variations in climate and the effects of climatic changes due to natural causes or to human activities.

The **Global Atmosphere Watch** (GAW) (part of the Atmospheric Research and Environmental Programme) is the umbrella programme for monitoring changes in atmospheric composition. Established in 1989, the GAW is designed to address major contemporary environmental issues and to be responsive to the growing international need for global data. The GAW played a pivotal role in the UN response to the Kuwait oil fires of 1991 – a major environmental pollution crisis.

Through its Global Ozone Observing System (GO_3OS), the GAW is also a major contributor to long-term research efforts on the ozone layer and to research on the "greenhouse effect". The GO_3OS is a large-scale monitoring network, originally established in the 1950s. Its work contributed significantly to the completion of the Convention for the Protection of the Ozone Layer (Vienna, 1985) [see 413.02 and 413.04]. The WMO has the lead role in implementating that Convention in regard to the co-ordination of scientific assessments and in providing data to estimate trends. This responsibility is undertaken through the GO_3OS's 140 ground-based ozone stations, and is supplemented by satellites. These are operated by nearly 60 member countries.

The **Global Climat Observation System** (GCOS) was instituted by the 11th Congress (1991). Its purpose is to monitor the climatic system in order to improve understanding, modelling and predictions. While it will use the services available through WWW's Global Observation System as its basis, together with data gathered through GAW, the WMO will be joined by other organizations, research institutes and space agencies to provide a climatic observation system which is as comprehensive as possible.

The **Technical Co-operation Programme** seeks to bridge the gap between the developed and developing countries by a systematic transfer of meteorological and hydrological knowledge and information. Under this scheme, WMO provides training and assists in the development of facilities.

WMO'S USE OF SATELLITES

Since the 1970s the general use of meteorological satellites has revolutionalized the work of the WMO, allowing for the improved gathering of atmospheric and oceanic data. As described above, they are an important element in the work undertaken by the WWW and they contribute significantly to the work of the Global Ozone Observing System.

Satellites have also recently assumed an important meteorological telecommunication function. Special collection and dissemination systems have been built into both public satellite-based communication services, such as INMARSAT [see 193 C], and into WMO's data-collection satellites. This service is particularly cost-effective for members of regions where conventional telecommunication services are prohibitively expensive.

STRUCTURE

The main organ of the WMO is the **World Meteorological Congress** in which all members are represented by the head of their meteorological service. It meets every four years to determine the general policies of the WMO.

The **Executive Council**, composed of 36 Directors of National Meteorological or Hydrometeorological Services, meets at least once a year to supervise the execution of the programmes approved by the Congress.

There are six **regional associations** – for Africa, Asia, South America, North and Central America, Europe, and the South-West Pacific – whose members are responsible for co-ordinating meteorological and related activities within their respective regions.

Eight **technical commissions**, composed of experts designated by the members of the WMO, study aeronautical meteorology, agricultural meteorology, marine meteorology, atmospheric sciences, basic systems, hydrology, instruments and methods of observation, as well as climatology and the applications of meteorology.

The **Secretariat**, headed by the Secretary-General, serves as the administrative, documentation and information centre of the Organization. It performs day-to-day programme-management functions and undertakes technical studies as required.

Finally, operational systems and networks are composed of national facilities owned and operated by individual countries which are members of the WMO (of which there are 164). International co-operation in meteorology and operational hydrology relies on the ability of national meteorological and hydrological services to carry out operations in accordance with agreements concluded under the auspices of the Organization.

FUNDING

Contributions are paid by members, and the Organization administers several trust-fund and special accounts financed by various members and international organizations for specific projects. For example, the United Nations Development Programme (UNDP) [see 222 A] contributes almost half of the total budget of the Technical Co-operation Programme, through which members can receive financial assistance for specific projects.

CO-OPERATION

The WMO has working arrangements and links with many intergovernmental and non-governmental organizations. The World Climatic Programme provides an excellent illustration: the research component of this Programme is a joint effort between WMO and the non-governmental International Council of Scientific Unions (ICSU), while the applications and services component is the responsibility of UNEP [see 410 A] – an IGO.

It is of interest to note that WMO's responsibilities and programmes, and their applications to economic and social development, extend into key areas of the work of the United Nations Conference on Environment and Development (UNCED) [see 410.02]. In the preparation for the Rio Environmental Conference of June 1992, the WMO was one of the key contributors.

The WMO has formal working arrangements with the following IGOs: FAO [see 131 A], IAEA [see 421 A], ICAO [184 A], IFAD [see 131 D], IMO [see 183 A], ITU [see 192 A], UNESCO [see 171 A] and WHO [see 132 A].

PUBLICATIONS

WMO publishes works on all aspects of meteorology and related subjects, such as hydrology, marine science, and the human environment. In particular, it publishes an *Annual Report*, the *WMO Bulletin* and *Technical Notes*.

Catherine Leonard

ADDRESS

41, Giuseppe-Motta, PO.Box: 2300, CH-1211 Geneva 2, Switzerland
T. (41 22) 730 8111, Fx. (41 22) 734 2326

SELECTED BIBLIOGRAPHY

Davies, Sir Arthur, *Meteorology – A Model of International Co-operation*, Geneva: WMO no. 667, 1986.

431.01 – CONVENTION OF THE WORLD METEOROLOGICAL ORGANIZATION – WMO

Concluded : 11.10.1947, Washington
In force : 23.03.1950
Parties : 164

This Convention establishes the WMO and is its basic Act. It was the result of a Conference of the International Meteorological Organization, the WMO's predecessor, held in Washington in 1947.

The provisions of the Convention state the purposes of the Organization, regulate its membership, set up the bodies which make up its structure, and provide generally for its financial arrangements and its regulations with other organizations, including the UN. WMO's legal status is established, and the procedure for amendments to the Convention, ratification, withdrawal, and so on, is specified.

C.L.

Access : ALS (Art. 3)
Reserves : USP
Duration : USP
Deposit. : US
Language : Eng, Fre

Modific. : Amendments (15.04.59); (11.04.63); (27.04.63); (11.04.67); (26.04.67); (28.04.75); (14.05.79); (11.05.83); (28.05.83)

Reference : 77 UNTS – Can TS 1947/34 – UST 1, 16/2, 18/3, 26/3 – 3/4 Paeslee – UKTS 1950/36, 1961/15, 1964/27, 1969/26, 1976/38

4.3.2 The Law of the Sea

Some areas in the world have not been brought under the authority of any state. The high seas, for instance, although steadily shrinking before the ever-broadening claims of coastal states, have also remained free from claims of exclusive sovereignty by states.

The international law of the sea has been developed by the United Nations in two stages: first, in 1958 with the adoption of four conventions codifying portions of the customary law and creating new law in some cases and, second, in 1982, with the adoption of the comprehensive UN Convention on the Law of the Sea.

SELECTED BIBLIOGRAPHY

Arnand, R.P., *Origin and Development of the Law of the Sea,* Dordrecht: Martinus Nijhoff Publishers, 1983.

Churchill, R.R. and A.V. Lowe, *The Law of the Sea,* 2nd ed. Manchester: Manchester University Press, 1988.

Lay, S.H. et als (eds.), *New Directions in the Law of the Sea,* 10 vols. Dobbs Ferry, N.Y.: Oceana Publishers, 1972-.

Nordquist, M.H. (ed.), *United Nations Convention on the Law of the Sea: A Commentary,* Vol. 1. Dordrecht: Martinus Nijhoff Publishers, 1985.

432.01 – CONVENTION ON THE HIGH SEAS – UN

Concluded : 29.04.1958, Geneva
In force : 30.09.1962
Parties : 60

The objective of the Convention is to codify the rules of international law relating to the high seas. It defines the high seas as "all parts of the sea that are not included in the territorial sea or in the internal waters of a State". As the high seas are open to all nations, no state may validly purport to subject any part of them to its sovereignty.

DETAILS OF THE CONVENTION

All states have freedom of navigation and fishing, freedom to lay submarine cables and pipelines, and freedom to fly over the high seas. These freedoms are to be exercised with reasonable regard to the interests of other states. States having no sea-coast should have free access to the sea.

Each state fixes the conditions for the granting of its nationality to ships, for the registration of ships in its territory, and for the right to fly its flag. Warships and ships used solely on government non-commercial service have complete immunity from the jurisdiction of any state other than the flag state.

Every state must take such measures as are necessary in regard to ships under its flag to ensure safety at sea, to prevent the transport of slaves, and to co-operate with other states in the repression of piracy. The hot pursuit of a foreign ship may be undertaken when the competent authorities of the coastal state have good reason to believe that the ship has violated the laws and regulations of that state.

The states are to draw up regulations to prevent pollution of the seas by oil and radioactive waste. This Convention will be replaced by the United Nations Convention on the Law of the Sea (Montego Bay, 1982) between the parties to that Convention when it enters into force [see 432.07].

Maguelonne Déjeant-Pons

Access : ALS (Art. 31, 33)
Reserves : USP
Duration : USP
Deposit. : UN (Art. 37)
Language : Chi, Eng, Fre, Rus, Spa, (Art. 37)

Reference : 450 UNTS – UKTS 1963/5 – UST 13/2

432.02 – CONVENTION ON THE CONTINENTAL SHELF – UN

Concluded : 29.04.1958, Geneva
In force : 10.06.1964
Parties : 55

The Convention defines and delimits the continental shelf, and specifies the rights of states to explore and exploit its natural resources.

DETAILS OF THE CONVENTION

The continental shelf is defined according to two alternative criteria: it refers to (a) the sea-bed and subsoil of the submarine areas adjacent to the coast, but outside the area of the territorial sea, to a depth of 200 metres, or (b) beyond that limit, to where the depth of the superadjacent waters admits of the exploitation of the natural resources of the said areas.

Where the same continental shelf is adjacent to the territories of two or more states whose coasts are opposite each other, the boundary of the continental shelf appertaining to the states will be determined by agreement between them. In the absence of agreement, and unless another boundary line is justified by special circumstances, the boundary is determined by a median line or by application of the principle of equidistance from the nearest points of the base lines from which the breadth of the territorial sea of each state is measured.

The coastal state exercises over the continental shelf sovereign rights for the purpose of exploring it and exploiting its natural resources. These rights, however, do not affect the legal status of the superadjacent waters as high seas, or that of the airspace above the waters. The exploration of the continental shelf and the exploitation of its natural resources must not result in any unjustifiable interference with navigation, fishing or the conservation of the living resources of the sea, nor result in any interference with fundamental oceanographic or other scientific research.

The coastal state is entitled to construct and maintain or operate on the continental shelf installations and other devices necessary for its exploration and the exploitation of its natural resources, and to establish safety zones around such installations and devices and to take necessary measures to protect these zones.

The Convention will be replaced by the Convention on the Law of the Sea (Montego Bay, 1982) when it comes into force [see 432.07].

M.D.-P.

Access : ALS (Art. 8, 10)
Reserves : PAU (Art. 12)
Duration : USP
Deposit. : UN (Art. 15)
Language : Chi, Eng, Fre, Rus, Spa (Art. 15)

Reference : 499 UNTS – Can TS 1970/4 – UKTS 1964/39 – JORF 4 Dec 65 – RTAF 1965/100 – JDI 1966/3

432.03 – CONVENTION ON THE TERRITORIAL SEA AND THE CONTIGUOUS ZONE – UN

Concluded : 29.04.1958, Geneva
In force : 10.09.1964
Parties : 50

The Convention describes and defines the territorial sea and the contiguous zone, and indicates what are the rights of the states in these areas.

DETAILS OF THE CONVENTION

The sovereignty of a state extends beyond its land territory and its internal waters to a belt of sea adjacent to its coast, described as the territorial sea. The sovereignty of a coastal state also extends to the air space over the territorial sea as well as to its sea-bed and subsoil.

The normal base line for measuring the breadth of the territorial sea is the low-water line along the coast as marked on large-scale charts officially recognized by the coastal state. In localities where the coastal line is deeply indented and cut into, or if there is a fringe of islands along the coast in its immediate vicinity, the method of straight baselines joining appropriate points may be employed in drawing the baseline from which the breadth of the territorial sea is measured. The outer limits of the territorial sea is the line every point of which is at a distance from the nearest point of the baseline equal to the breadth of the territorial sea.

The Convention guarantees the right of innocent passage through the territorial sea and provides that no charge may be levied upon foreign ships by reason only of their passage through the territorial sea. In a zone of the high seas contiguous to its territorial sea, the coastal state may exercise the control necessary to prevent infringement of its customs, fiscal, immigration or sanitary regulations within its territory or territorial sea. The contiguous zone may not extend beyond 12 miles from the baseline from which the breadth of the territorial sea is measured.

It is provided that where the coasts of two states are opposite or adjacent to each other, neither of the two states is entitled, failing agreement between them to the contrary, to extend its contiguous zone beyond the median line every point of which is equidistant from the nearest points on the baselines from which the breadth of the territorial seas of the two states is measured.

This Convention will be replaced by the United Nations Convention on the Law of the Sea (Montego Bay, 1982) between the parties to that Convention when it enters into force [see 432.07].

M.D.-P.

Access : ALS (Art. 26, 28)
Reserves : USP
Duration : USP
Deposit. : UN (Art. 32)
Language : Chi, Eng, Fre, Rus, Spa (Art. 32)

Reference : 516 UNTS – UKTS 1965/3 – UST 15:1606 – AJIL 52

432.04 – CONVENTION ON FISHING AND CONSERVATION OF THE LIVING RESOURCES OF THE HIGH SEAS – UN

Concluded : 29.04.1958, Geneva
In force : 20.03.1966
Parties : 36

The objective of the Convention is to solve the problems of conservation of the living resources of the high seas through international co-operation. This became necessary as a result of the development of modern fishing techniques which threatened to lead to over-exploitation of the sea.

DETAILS OF THE CONVENTION

The Convention states that all states have a duty to adopt, or co-operate with other states in adopting, measures necessary for the conservation of the living resources of the high seas. Such measures should be formulated with a view to securing food for human consumption. The Convention recognizes that coastal states have special interests in the maintenance of the productivity of the living resources in the high seas adjacent to their territorial seas. It stipulates that these states can participate in any research organization or system whose objective is the conservation of the living resources of the high seas adjacent to their territorial seas.

Coastal states may unilaterally adopt conservation measures in the high seas adjacent to their territorial seas which shall be valid for other states if, after a period of six months, negotiations between the states have not resulted in agreement. Disputes are to be settled by a special commission of five members whose decision is binding on the states concerned.

The Convention will be replaced, between the parties, by the Convention on the Law of the Sea (Montego Bay, 1982) [see 432.07] once it becomes effective.

M.D.-P.

Access : CON (Art. 15, 17)
Reserves : PAU (Art. 19)
Duration : USP
Deposit. : UN
Language : Chi, Eng, Fre, Rus, Spa

Reference : 559 UNTS – UKTS 1966/39 – UST 17/1 – JORF 24 Dec 70 – RTAF 1970/119

432.05 – OPTIONAL PROTOCOL OF SIGNATURE CONCERNING THE COMPULSORY SETTLEMENT OF DISPUTES – UN

Concluded : 29.04.1958, Geneva
In force : 30.09.1962
Parties : 36

This Protocol supplements the 1958 conventions on the law of the sea: the Convention on the High Seas [see 432.01]; the Convention on the Continental Shelf [see 432.02]; the Convention on the Territorial Sea and the Contiguous Zone [see 432.03]; and the Convention on Fishing and Conservation of the Living Resources of the High Seas [see 432.04].

Disagreements between the parties on interpretation of these conventions must be submitted to the International Court of Justice.

SUBSEQUENT DEVELOPMENTS

The Protocol was superseded by the 1982 Convention on the Law of the Sea (Montego Bay) [see 432.07]. A special Commission has been mandated to formulate recommendations effecting practical mechanisms for the implementation of the International Tribunal for the Law of the Sea.

M.D.-P.

Access : CON (Art. 5)
Reserves : USP
Duration : USP
Deposit. : UN
Language : Chi, Eng, Fre, Rus, Spa

Reference : 450 UNTS – UKTS 1963/60

432.06 – CONVENTION FOR THE INTERNATIONAL COUNCIL FOR THE EXPLORATION OF THE SEA – ICES

Concluded : 12.09.1964, Copenhagen
In force : 22.07.1968
Parties : 17

The objective of the Convention is to provide a new constitution for the International Council for the Exploration of the Sea (ICES) established in Copenhagen in 1902.

DETAILS OF THE CONVENTION

The ICES aims to promote and encourage the study of the sea through research and investigations, particularly in regard to its living resources, to draw up programmes for this purpose, and to disseminate the results of this research. The ICES is to be concerned with the Atlantic Ocean and its adjacent seas, and primarily with the North Atlantic Sea. It is to maintain working arrangements with other international organizations having similar objectives, and is to co-operate with them in order to provide scientific information.

STRUCTURE

Each of the contracting parties is represented in the **Council** by a maximum of two delegates. The Council meets annually in ordinary session and, when required, in extraordinary session. Decisions are taken by simple majority vote and each of the parties has one vote. The Council elects a President and appoints a Secretary-General.

M.D.-P.

Access : CON (Art. 16)
Reserves : USP
Duration : USP
Deposit. : DK
Language : Eng, Fre

Modific. : Amending Protocol Copenhagen 13.08.70 (12.11.75)

Reference : 652 UNTS – Can TS 1968/8 – UKTS 1968/67, 1976/35 – UST 24/1, 27/1 – ILM 7:302 – 3/4 Paeslee – JORF 7 Mar 69 – RTAF 1969/16

432.07 – UNITED NATIONS CONVENTION ON THE LAW OF THE SEA – UN

Concluded : 10.12.1982, Montego Bay
Parties : 55

In the years following the United Nations conferences of 1958 and 1960 on the law of the sea, factors arose which made it necesary to draft a new convention.

The objective of the 1982 Convention, which includes 17 parts and 320 articles, is to settle, in a spirit of mutual understanding and co-operation, all issues relating to the law of the sea, and to establish, with due regard for the sovereignty of all states, a legal order for the seas and oceans which will facilitate international communication and will promote the peaceful uses of the seas and oceans, the equitable and efficient utilization of their resources, the conservation of their living resources, and the study, protection and preservation of the marine environment. It replaces between the parties the 1958 conventions [see 432.01 to 432.05].

The achievement of these goals must contribute to the realization of a just and equitable international economic order which takes into account the interests and needs of mankind as a whole and, in particular, the special interests and needs of developing countries, whether coastal or land-locked.

The codification and progressive development of the law of the sea achieved in the Convention will contribute to the strengthening of peace, security, co-operation and friendly relations among all nations, and will promote the economic and social advancement of all peoples of the world.

DETAILS OF THE CONVENTION

Marine areas. The Convention defines the composition and limits of various marine areas (internal waters, territorial seas, contiguous zones, continental shelf, exclusive economic zones and high seas), and their legal status. The maximum breadth of the territorial sea is 12 nautical miles (22.22 kms), while that of the contiguous zone is 24 nautical miles.

The establishment of an exclusive economic zone cannot extend beyond 200 nautical miles from the baselines from which the breadth of the territorial sea is measured, while the limits of the continental shelf may extend beyond 200 nautical miles. Archipelagic states (i.e. states constituted wholly or by one or more archipelagos and may include other islands) may draw baselines joining the outermost points of the outermost islands, to close in and delimit their internal waters.

Rights of passage. The Convention reaffirms the right of innocent passage in territorial seas, and supplements it with a right of archipelagic passage and a right of unobstructed transit passage in straits used for international navigation. The rights of states in their exclusive economic zones are strictly economic; they do not affect freedom of navigation or freedom of overflight.

Land-locked states. Land-locked and geographically disadvantaged states may claim certain economic benefits from the exclusive economic zones of other states. Land-locked states have a right of access to and from the sea and freedom of transit. Though freedom of the high seas is reaffirmed, it refers only to the sea and the air and does not apply to the sea-bed, which has a different and specific status. Freedom is limited, however, by the obligation of the states to co-operate in the conservation and management of the living resources of the high seas, and in the prevention of all forms of pollution of the marine environment.

Specific provisions exist on the status of straits used for international navigation, islands, and enclosed and semi-enclosed seas. More generally, the Convention obliges the parties to protect and preserve the marine environment; it grants the right to the parties to conduct marine scientific research subject to the rights and duties of other states; and it calls for the development and transfer of marine technology.

STRUCTURE

The Convention establishes a special status for the "Area", meaning the sea-bed and ocean floor and subsoil therof, beyond the limits of national jurisdiction, and considers it the common heritage of mankind. The Convention establishes an **International Sea-Bed Authority** in Jamaica responsible for managing the Area. The Authority includes an **Assembly**, a **Council** of 36 members which takes its most important decisions by consensus, a **Secretariat** and an **Enterprise** which carries out exploration activities in the Area. The Convention establishes, on the model of the International Court of Justice [see 001 B], an **International Tribunal for the Law of the Sea**. It acts as one of the means for the peaceful settlement of disputes at the disposal of the parties. The parties have a wide choice of ways to settle their disputes, including both traditional and new methods, among them a special arbitration procedure.

ANNEXES

The Convention has annexes on the following matters: highly migratory species; the Commission on the Limits of the Continental Shelf; basic conditions of prospecting, exploration and exploitation; the Statute of the Enterprise; conciliation; the Statute of the International Tribunal for the Law of the Sea; arbitration; special arbitration; and participation by international organizations.

The Convention will become effective 12 months after the date of deposit of the 60th instrument of ratification or accession.

M.D.-P.

Access	: ASO (Art. 305, 306, A.IX)
Reserves	: PAU (Art. 309)
Duration	: USP
Deposit.	: UN (Art. 319)
Language	: Ara, Chi, Eng, Fre, Rus, Spa (Art. 320)

Reference : UN Doc. A/CONF 62/122 – ILM 21:1261 – DJI 1983

4.3.3 Antarctica

Antarctica, which comprises about 10 per cent of the Earth's land and water areas, is the only continent that has not been exploited for economic purposes. Given the extreme conditions in Antarctica, which increase the likelihood of accidents and decrease the ecosystem's ability to recover from disruption, states – including seven which have made territorial claims in Antarctica – have agreed to protect its environment and foster international co-operation in scientific research. In this way, economic activities are restricted.

This section first summarizes the Antarctic Treaty [see 433.01], the basic treaty of the Antarctic Treaty system. This Treaty provides that Antarctica is to be used for peaceful purposes only and it establishes a regime of international co-operation on scientific investigation in the area.

The Convention on the Conservation of Antarctic Marine Living Resources [see 433.02] aims to protect those resources by establishing principles of conservation for their harvesting. In order to safeguard against the dangers of mineral resource activities to the environment and ecosystems, CRAMRA sought to establish a regime to which all mineral resource activities would have to conform [see 433.03]. However, this treaty is unlikely to come into force as it has been superseded by the Protocol on the Environmental Protection to the Antarctic Treaty [see 433.04], which bans all activity relating to mineral resources other than scientific research. This Protocol designates Antarctica as a natural reserve devoted to peace and science.

SELECTED BIBLIOGRAPHY

Francioni, Francesco and Tullio Scovazzi (eds.), *International Law of Antarctica / Droit international de l'Antarctique*, Milano, 1987.

Joyner, Christopher C., *The Antarctic Legal Regime*, Dordrecht: Martinus Nijhoff Publishers, 1988.

Orrego Vicuna, Francisco (ed.), *Antarctic Resources Policy: Scientific, Legal and Political Issues*, Cambridge, 1983.

Triggs, Gillian D. (ed.), *The Antarctic Treaty Regime: Law Environment and Resources*, Cambridge, 1987.

Wolfrum, Rüdiger, *Antarctic Challenge*, 3 Vols., Berlin, 1984, 1986, 1988.

– – –, *The Convention on the Regulation of Antarctic Mineral Resource Activities*, Berlin: Springer-Verlag, 1991.

433.01 – ANTARCTIC TREATY – UN

Concluded : 01.12.1959, Washington
In force : 23.06.1961
Parties : 40

Recognizing that it is in the interest of all mankind that Antarctica shall continue forever to be used exclusively for peaceful purposes and that it shall not become the scene or object of international discord, the Treaty aims to ensure that Antarctica is used for peaceful purposes only. The Treaty also seeks to foster international co-operation in scientific research, and to ensure that the fauna and flora of the Antarctic are preserved.

DETAILS OF THE CONVENTION

The Treaty provides that Antarctica shall be used for peaceful purposes only. All military activity such as manoeuvres, the establishment of bases, or the testing of weapons is prohibited.

Freedom of scientific investigation in Antarctica, and co-operation toward that end, is provided for within the Treaty. Parties agree to co-operate by exchanging information in regard to plans for specific programmes so as to permit maximum economy and efficiency of operations; and they agree to exchange information on scientific observations and results. They also exchange scientific personnel.

Each of the parties has the right to appoint observers to carry out any inspection over any or all areas of Antarctica, including all stations, installations and equipment within these areas and all ships and aircraft at points of discharging or embarking cargoes or personnel in Antarctica. These areas shall be open at all times to such inspection. Aerial observation may also be carried out at any time under the same principle. They shall report to the meetings of the contracting parties.

The contracting parties meet to exchange information, to consult on issues of common interest affecting the Antarctic, and to study, formulate and recommend measures to their governments to ensure that the aims of the Treaty are fulfilled.

The Treaty does not change rights of national sovereignty or territorial demands in the Antarctic.

MODIFICATIONS

The important Protocol to this Treaty of 1991 on environmental protection designates Antarctica as a natural reserve devoted to peace and science [see 433.04].

Maguelonne Déjeant-Pons

Access : ALS (Art. XIII)
Reserves : USP
Duration : USP
Deposit. : US (Art. XIV)
Language : Eng, Fre, Rus, Spa (Art. XIV)

Modific. : Protocol Madrid 04.10.91 (-)

Reference : 402 UNTS – UKTS 1961/97 – ILM 19:860, 30:1455 – JDI 1962 -JORF 6 Dec 61 – RTAF 1961/49

433.02 – CONVENTION ON THE CONSERVATION OF ANTARCTIC MARINE LIVING RESOURCES – UN

Concluded : 20.05.1980, Canberra
In force : 07.04.1982
Parties : 27

The Convention's objective is the conservation of Antarctic marine living resources. Thus it seeks to safeguard the Antarctic environment and to protect the ecosystem of the seas surrounding it through international co-operation.

The Convention notes the concentration of marine living resources found in Antarctic waters and the increased interest in the possibilities offered by the utilization of these resources as a source of protein. It considers it essential to increase knowledge of the Antarctic marine ecosystem and its components so as to be able to base decisions on harvesting on sound scientific information.

DETAILS OF THE CONVENTION

Harvesting and associated activities must be conducted in accordance with the provisions of the Convention and with the following principles of conservation:

- prevention of decrease in the size of any harvested population to levels below those which ensure its stable recruitment;

- maintenance of the ecological relationships between harvested, dependent and related populations of Antarctic marine living resources and the restoration of depleted populations; and,
- prevention of changes or minimization of the risk of irreversible changes in the marine ecosystem.

Nothing in the Convention can constitute a basis for asserting, supporting or denying a claim to territorial sovereignty in the Antarctic Treaty area or create any rights of sovereignty in this area.

STRUCTURE

The Convention establishes a **Commission for the Conservation of Antarctic Marine Living Resources** whose role is to recommend, promote, co-ordinate and decide on the measures and scientific studies necessary for the safeguarding of Antarctic marine living resources. The Commission is composed of contracting parties to the Convention, and its headquarters is located in Hobart, Australia.

Decisions of the Commission on matters of substance are taken by consensus, while other matters are decided by simple majority. The Commission holds a regular annual meeting, as well as other meetings held at the request of one-third of its members. It elects from among its members a Chairman and a Vice-Chairman.

A **Scientific Committee for the Conservation of Antarctic Marine Living Resources** is also established under the Convention. This Committee acts as a consultative body to the Commission and provides a forum for consultation and co-operation concerning the collection, study and exchange of information with respect to marine living resources. It encourages and promotes co-operation in the field of scientific research.

The Commission appoints an Executive Secretary to serve the Commission and the Scientific Committee, and it authorizes the establishment of a **Secretariat**.

M.D.-P.

Access : ASO (Art. XXIX)
Reserves : USP
Duration : USP
Deposit. : AU (Art. XXXIII)
Language : Eng, Fre, Rus, Spa (Art. XVIII,XXXIII)

Reference : ILM 19:860 – JDI 1983 – RTAF 1982/70

433.03 – CONVENTION ON THE REGULATION OF ANTARCTIC MINERAL RESOURCE ACTIVITIES – CRAMRA

Concluded : 02.06.1988, Wellington

This Convention (CRAMRA) was a significant step in the development of the Antarctic legal system. It was drafted for the purpose of controlling Antarctic mineral resource activities so as to protect the Antarctic environment and dependent and associated ecosystems. Thus, it supplements the Antarctic Treaty [see 433.01] which does not refer to the exploration and development of mineral resources.

DETAILS OF THE CONVENTION

Under this Convention, before undertaking any Antarctic mineral resource activity, an operator must comply with certain conditions. The Convention requires an operator to be sponsored by a state which then assumes liability if the operator fails to satisfy certain conditions. The sponsoring state must be one with which the operator has a "substantial and genuine link". The operator is to submit, through the sponsoring state, an application for exploration to the Regulatory Committee. If this is agreed, the Committee approves a Management Scheme and issues an exploration permit. Following a subsequent application for development, the Committee may similarly issue a development permit. These activities can be carried out in areas identified by the Antarctic Mineral Resources Commission, created under this Treaty.

An operator undertaking any Antarctic mineral resource activity shall take necessary and timely response action if the activity results in or threatens to result in damage to the Antarctic environment. The operator shall be strictly liable for the damage arising from its activities, including payment in the event that there has been no restoration to the *status quo ante.*

If the operator fails to comply with its obligations during its activities, the sponsoring state is liable only if it is proven that it (the sponsoring state) did not take all appropriate measures to ensure its compliance with the Convention and that the damage arising from the activities would not have occurred or continued if it had carried out its obligations. Such liability is limited to that portion of liability not satisfied by the operator or otherwise.

No application for an exploration or development permit shall be made until a separate protocol on liability is elaborated and entered into force for the party lodging such application.

This Convention shall enter into force on the 30th day following the date of deposit of instruments of ratification or approval by the 16 Antarctic Treaty Consultative Parties (ATCP) which participated in the final session of the Fourth Special Antarctic Treaty Consultative Meeting. The figure of 16 is further qualified. It includes all the states "necessary in order to establish all of the institutions of the Convention in respect of every area of Antarctica", which is a reference to the composition of the Regulatory Committees. Thus, it makes the ratification of all the claimant states (Argentina, Australia, Chile, France, the UK, New Zealand and Norway), and of those states asserting a basis of claim (USA, USSR), and at least four of the non-claimant states, a precondition for the entry into force of the Convention. In addition, five developing and 11 developed countries must be among those having accepted the Convention as binding.

SUBSEQUENT DEVELOPMENTS

Because of the conditional requirements for entry into force, together with the subsequent stance of France and Australia indicating they would not under present conditions either sign nor ratify CRAMRA, the Convention will not enter into force in the near future if it enters into force at all. Some principles concerning the protection of the Antarctic environment in this Convention have been retained in the subsequent Madrid Protocol [see 433.04], promoted by Australia and France, which is intended to replace CRAMRA.

M.D.-P.

Access : CON (Art. 61)
Reserves : PAU (Art. 58, 63)

Duration : USP
Deposit. : NZ (Art. 61-3)
Language : Chi, Eng, Fre, Rus, Spa (Art. 67)

Reference : RGDIP 1989/1

433.04 – PROTOCOL ON THE ENVIRONMENTAL PROTECTION TO THE ANTARCTIC TREATY – UN

Concluded : 04.10.1991, Madrid
Party : 1

This Protocol supplements the Antarctic Treaty [see 433.01].

The parties commit themselves to the comprehensive protection of the Antarctic environment and dependent and associated ecosystems. Recognizing its intrinsic value, including its wilderness and aesthetic values and value as an area for conducting scientific research, they agree to designate Antarctica as a natural reserve devoted to peace and science.

DETAILS OF THE CONVENTION

Activities in the Antarctic Treaty area shall be planned and conducted so as to limit adverse impacts on the Antarctic environment dependent and associated ecosystems. Activities shall be planned and conducted on the basis of information sufficient to allow prior assessments of, and informed judgments about, their possible impacts on the Antarctic environment and dependent and associated ecosystems and on the value of Antarctica for the conduct of scientific research. Regular and effective monitoring shall take place to allow assessment of the impacts of ongoing activities and to facilitate early detection of the possible unforeseen effects of activities carried on both within and outside the Treaty area on the Antarctic environment and dependent and associated ecosystems.

Activities shall be planned and conducted so as to accord priority to scientific research and to preserve the value of Antarctica as an area for the conduct of research, including research essential to understanding the global environment.

Activities pursuant to scientific research programmes, tourism and all other governmental and non-governmental activities in the Treaty area, for which advance notice is required in accordance with the Treaty, shall be modified, suspended or cancelled if they result in or threaten to result in impacts inconsistent with the principles stated in the Protocol. Environmental impact assessment procedure is provided for.

Any activity relating to mineral resources, other than scientific research, shall be prohibited.

The parties shall co-operate in the planning and undertaking of activities. Each party agrees, to the extent possible, to share information that may be helpful to other parties in planning and conducting their activities with a view to the protection of the Antarctic environment and dependent and associated ecosystems.

The Antarctic Treaty consultative meetings shall define the general policy for the comprehensive protection of the Antarctic environment and dependent and associated ecosystems, and shall review the work of the **Committee for Environmental Protection**, established under this Protocol. This Committee is composed of representatives of parties who may be accompanied by experts and advisers. Observer status is open to contracting parties to the Antarctic Treaty not party to the Protocol. Its function is to provide advice and formulate recommendations to the parties in connection with the implementation of this Protocol, including the operation of its annexes.

Each party shall take appropriate measures within its competence, including the adoption of laws and regulations, administrative actions, and enforcement measures, to ensure compliance with this Protocol. The Antarctic Treaty consultative parties shall arrange for inspections by observers. Provisions relating to actions to be taken to respond to environmental emergencies are laid down and each party shall report annually on the steps taken to implement the Protocol.

The Protocol includes dispute settlement provisions and a Schedule dealing with arbitration. The four annexes form an integral part of the Protocol and concern environmental impact assessment, the conservation of Antarctic fauna and flora, waste disposal and waste management, and the prevention of marine pollution.

M.D.-P.

Access : CON (Art. 21)
Reserves : PRO (Art. 24)
Duration : USP
Deposit. : US (Art. 22-3)
Language : Eng, Fre, Rus, Spa, (Art. 27)

Reference : ILM 30:1455

4.3.4 Use of Outer Space

As outer space has become accessible only in recent times, states have agreed not to claim any territorial sovereignty over this area and to establish legal regimes governing its exploration and use. These principles are established in two treaties. More states have become parties to the 1967 Treaty providing for "free access..." than to the 1979 Agreement, which combines the principles of "common heritage" and "equitable sharing" in regard to the benefits derived from the exploitation of the natural resources of the Moon and other celestial bodies [see also 1.8.5 and 1.9.3].

SELECTED BIBLIOGRAPHY

Benkö, M., W. de Graaff and G.C.M. Reijnen, *Space Law in the United Nations*, Dordrecht: Martinus Nijhoff Publishers, 1985.

Galloway, E., "Agreement Governing the Activities of States on the Moon and other Celestial Bodies", *Annals of Air and Space Law*, Montreal: McGill University, V (1980): 481.

Zhukov, G. and Y. Kolosov, *International Space Law*, New York: Praeger, 1984.

434.01 – TREATY ON PRINCIPLES GOVERNING THE ACTIVITIES OF STATES IN THE EXPLORATION AND USE OF OUTER SPACE, INCLUDING THE MOON AND OTHER CELESTIAL BODIES – UN

Concluded : 27.01.1967, London, Moscow, Washington
In force : 10.10.1967
Parties : 88

The Treaty establishes an international legal regime for the exploration and the use of outer space, including the Moon and other celestial bodies. It provides the legal foundation for the peaceful use of outer space and the general framework for space law.

DETAILS OF THE CONVENTION

The exploration and use of outer space is the province of all mankind. Article I states, "there shall be freedom of scientific investigation in outer space ... and States shall facilitate and encourage international co-operation in such investigation". Outer space is not subject to national appropriation by claim of sovereignty, by means of use or occupation, or by any other means. There shall be free access to all areas of celestial bodies.

The parties to the Treaty undertake not to place in orbit around the Earth any objects carrying nuclear weapons or any other kinds of weapons of mass destruction. They agree that the Moon and other celestial bodies will only be used for peaceful purposes.

States party to the Treaty bear international responsibility for national activities in outer space, whether such activities are carried on by government agencies or by non-governmental entities. The activities of non-governmental entities in outer space shall require authorization and continuing supervision by the appropriate state party to the Treaty. All parties which launch or procure the launching of an object into outer space are internationally liable for damage to another state party to the Treaty or to its natural or juridical persons.

In the exploration and use of outer space, the parties to the Treaty are guided by the principle of co-operation and mutual assistance, and must conduct all their activities in outer space with due regard to the corresponding interests of all other parties to the Treaty.

The parties also agree to pursue studies and conduct exploration of outer space so as to avoid its harmful contamination and also to avoid adverse changes in the environment of the Earth resulting from the introduction of extraterrestrial matter.

International consultations shall be undertaken if a contracting state believes that an activity or experiment planned by it or its nationals would cause potentially harmful interference with activities of other parties in the peaceful exploration and use of outer space. A state party which has reason to believe that an activity or experiment planned by another state party in outer space would cause potentially harmful interference with activities in the peaceful exploration and use of outer space, may request consultation concerning the activity or experiment.

The parties to the Treaty also agree to inform the Secretary-General of the United Nations as well as the public and the international scientific community to the greatest extent feasible and practicable of the nature, conduct, locations and results of their activities in outer space.

Special provisions exist on the status of astronauts, regarded as "envoys of mankind", and in regard to stations, installations, equipment and space vehicles.

SUBSEQUENT DEVELOPEMENTS

The Treaty was supplemented by later conventions which deal in greater detail with matters which it raised [see 1.8.5].

Maguelonne Déjeant-Pons

Access : ALS (Art. XIV)
Reserves : USP
Duration : USP
Deposit. : GB, US, RU (Art. XIV)
Language : Chi, Eng, Fre, Rus, Spa (Art. XVII)

Reference : 610 UNTS – UKTS 1968/10 – UST 18/3 – ILM 6:386 – JORF 24 Oct 70 – RTAF 1970/97 – RGDIP 1967

434.02 – AGREEMENT GOVERNING THE ACTIVITIES OF STATES ON THE MOON AND OTHER CELESTIAL BODIES – UN

Concluded : 05.12.1979, New York
In force : 11.07.1984
Parties : 9

The Agreement reiterates certain concepts found in the above Treaty [see 434.01]. The parties resolve to foster, on a basis of equality and in accordance with international law, the development of co-operation between states in the exploration and use of the Moon and other celestial bodies.

The Moon and other celestial bodies are to be used by all states parties to the Agreement exclusively for peaceful purposes. Their exploration and use should be carried out for the benefit and in the interests of all countries on the basis of co-operation and mutual assistance.

DETAILS OF THE CONVENTION

The parties must supply detailed information about their activities to the UN Secretary-General, the public, and to the international scientific community. They must also inform them of the existence of any phenomenon which may threaten human life or health, and of any signs of organic life.

Outer space, including the Moon and other celestial bodies, is free for exploration and use by all states without discrimination. All parties may collect mineral samples or other substances from the Moon and other celestial bodies, and they may exchange scientific and other personnel for missions.

Measures are to be taken to avoid harmful contamination or adverse changes which may disturb the equilibrium existing in outer space and in the environment of the Earth. Certain areas of the Moon which are of special scientific importance can be designated an international scientific reserve.

The Moon and other celestial bodies are the "common benefit of mankind", and therefore are not subject to national appropriation. The parties undertake to establish, when appropriate, an international regime to govern the exploitation of the natural resources of celestial bodies as such exploitation becomes possible, in order to rationally and systematically harness, manage, and then turn those resources into profit. The Agreement also calls for an "equitable sharing by all State Parties" in the benefits derived from the resources of outer space. The parties bear international responsibility for national activities, whether these are carried out by government agencies or by non-governmental entities, and they recognize the need to conclude agreements on liability in case of damage caused on the Moon and on other celestial bodies.

The contracting parties consult if it is feared that the activities of one state would interfere with those of other states, or when they have reason to believe that a party is not complying with the provisions of the Convention. The parties agree to settle their disputes peacefully.

M.D.-P.

Access : ALS (Art. 19)
Reserves : USP
Duration : USP
Deposit. : UN
Language : Ara, Chi, Eng, Fre, Rus, Spa

Reference : ILM 18:1434

Parties to Global Economic Agreements

These tables allow a quick overview of the territorial application of agreements analysed in this book and provide an appreciation of the level of participation of each state.

One hundred and ninety-one states, territorial entities and one intergovernmental organization (the EC) have been cross-referenced with most of the agreements in this book. Their reference numbers are given followed by a brief description of the agreement, by dates of signature and entry into force, and by the total number of parties. Unless otherwise stated in the notes annexed, the dates given are the years of acceptance of the agreement by the parties. In some cases, signatory states that have not yet ratified the relevant agreements are identified by the letter "S" and states that have denounced their participation are identified by a "D".

In order to simplify the presentation adherence to protocols and amendments is not covered in the tables. This information may be obtained from the depositaries.

TERRITORIAL APPLICATION AND SUCCESSION OF STATES

The territorial scope declarations made by countries such as the UK, France, Portugal, the Netherlands and Australia with regard to dependent territories for which they are or have been responsible for their international relations, have not been described.

Newly independent states (i.e. successor states the territory of which were dependent territories for their international relations) have been considered party to the agreements only if they have declared succeeding to rights and obligations previously subscribed to by the predecessor state. [See the Convention on Succession of States in respect of Treaties (Vienna, 1978).]

DENUNCIATION AND REINTEGRATION

States which have denounced an Agreement are identified by the letter "D". However, if they have reintegrated an Agreement previously denounced, the date of reintegration is specified.

MULTIPLE DEPOSITARIES

Where there are multiple depositaries, the date relating to the earliest deposit of the instrument of ratification or acceptance has been given.

PROVISIONAL APPLICATION

Some commodities agreements may enter into force provisionally. In that case, the notes in the annex state whether the dates are definitive or provisional.

Any further information, such as statements as to reservations or other statements relating to an agreement made by states, may be obtained from each depositary, their embassies, relevant international organizations or the SDIE documentation centre.

PARTIES TO GLOBAL ECONOMIC AGREEMENTS

The data for these tables were taken from the SDIE Global Economic Agreements Data Base and were entered by Eric Bouchard and Catherine Leonard.

Unless otherwise stated, all information reflects the position as at 14 April 1993. It is based upon returns from depositaries and from international organizations having a particular connexion with the treaty in question.

ABBREVIATIONS

EC	European Communities
D	Denunciation
S	Signatories

Reference	AGREEMENT	DATE OF AGREEMENT	ENTRY INTO FORCE	No. of countries	Afghanistan	Albania	Algeria	Angola	Antigua & Barbuda	Argentina	Armenia	Australia	Austria	Azerbaijan	Bahamas	Bahrain	Bangladesh	Barbados	Belarus	Belgium	Belize	Benin	Bhutan	Bolivia	Bosnia	Botswana	Brazil
001.01	United Nations Charter	26.06.1945	24.10.1945	181	1946	1955	1962	1976	1981	1945	1992	1945	1955	1992	1973	1971	1974	1966	1945	1945	1981	1960	1971	1945	1992	1966	1945
001.02	ICJ: Compulsory Jurisdiction	26.06.1945	24.10.1945	57								1975	1971					1980		1958						1970	
111.01	General Agreement (GATT)	30.10.1947	01.01.1948	110					1987	1967		1948	1951				1972	1967		1948	1983	1963		1989		1987	1948
111.06	Multifibre Agreement 1991 Prot	20.12.1973	01.01.1974	37						1991			1992				1991										1991
111.07	Standardization Code	12.04.1979	01.01.1980	35						S		1992	1980							1981							1980
111.08	Government Procurement Code	12.04.1979	01.01.1981	12									1981														
111.09	Subsidies Code	12.04.1979	01.01.1980	28						1990		1981	1980														1980
111.10	Import Licensing	12.04.1979	01.01.1980	27						S		1980	1980											1993			
111.11	Antidumping Code	12.04.1979	01.01.1980	25						1991		1982	1980														1980
111.12	Bovine Meat Arrangement	12.04.1979	01.01.1980	26						1982		1980	1980														1980
111.13	Dairy Agreement	12.04.1979	01.01.1980	16						1982			D														
111.14	Trade in Civil Aircraft	12.04.1979	01.01.1980	22									1980							1981							
111.20	GSTP	13.04.1988	19.04.1989	40			1990			1990							1988					1991		1989			1991
112.01	Simplif. Customs Formalities	03.11.1923	27.11.1924	42								1925	1924							1924							1929
112.02	Customs Co-operation (CCC)	15.12.1950	04.11.1952	126		1992	1966	1990		1968		1961	1953	1992	1974		1978			1952						1978	1981
112.03	Nomenclature	15.12.1950	11.09.1959	16			D					D	D				1978			D						D	
112.04	Customs Valuation	15.12.1950	28.07.1953	12			1977						D							D							
112.05	Commercial Samples	07.11.1952	20.11.1955	57								1956	1956							1957							
112.07	Containers	18.05.1956	04.08.1959	39			1963		1988			1967	1957							1960							
112.08	Importation of Road Vehicles	18.05.1956	08.04.1959	30	1977		1963						1957							1963							
112.09	TIR Carnets (Geneva 1959)	15.01.1959	07.01.1960	37	1971	1969							1960							1962							
112.10	Importation of Packings	06.10.1960	15.03.1962	35			1988						1962							1963							
112.11	Fairs Convention	08.06.1961	13.07.1962	53			1988					1962	1962							1967							
112.12	Professonial Equipment	08.06.1961	01.07.1962	49			1972					1967	1962							1965							
112.13	ATA Carnet	06.12.1961	30.07.1963	53			1973					1967	1963							1966							
112.14	Material for Seafarers	01.12.1964	11.12.1965	40			1969					1967								1966							
112.15	Scientific Equipment	11.06.1968	05.09.1969	54			1969					1969	1972							1970		1969					
112.16	Pedagogic Material	08.06.1970	10.09.1971	38			1971			1973		1971	1972					1975				1971					
112.18	Containers	02.12.1972	06.12.1975	23			1978					1975	1977						1976								
112.19	Kyoto Convention	18.05.1973	25.09.1974	54			1976					1974	1974							1975						1991	
112.20	TIR Carnets (Geneva 1975)	14.11.1975	20.03.1978	45	1982	1985	1989						1977							1982							
112.21	Nairobi Convention	09.06.1977	21.05.1980	30			1988					1986	S														
112.22	Customs Valuation Code	12.04.1979	01.01.1981	31						1986		1982	1980											1993		1984	1981
112.23	Frontier Controls of Goods	21.10.1982	15.10.1985	26									1987							1987							
112.24	Harmonized System	14.06.1983	01.01.1988	69			1991			S		1987	1987				1987			1987						1987	1988
112.25	Istanbul Convention	26.06.1990		2			S					1992								S							
121.02	Common Fund for Commodities	27.06.1980	19.06.1989	106	1984		1982	1986		1983		D	1983				1981	S		1985		1982	1984			1982	1984
121.03	International Tin Agreement	26.06.1981	01.07.1982	25								1982								1982							
121.04	International Coffee Agreement	16.09.1982	11.09.1985	75				1983				1983	1984							1983		1983		1983			1983
121.05	International Cocoa Agreement	25.07.1986	20.01.1987	40																1987							1986
121.06	Int. Natural Rubber Agreement	20.03.1987	03.04.1989	27																1991							
122.01	Tropical Timber Agreement	18.11.1983	01.04.1985	51								1988	1986							1984				1985			1985
122.02	Agreement on Olive Oil	01.07.1986	01.01.1987	9			1986																				
122.03	Wheat Trade Convention	14.03.1986	01.07.1986	46			1987			1990		1986	1987					1986		1989				1987			1986
122.04	Jute and Jute Products (1989)	03.11.1989	12.04.1991	27								1991					1991			1991							
122.05	International Sugar Agreement	20.03.1992	20.01.1993	11														1993									1993
123.02	INSG	02.05.1986	23.05.1990	13								1990															
123.03	ICSG	24.02.1989	23.01.1992	15																1991							
123.04	ITSG	07.04.1989		12																1991							

[illegible]	[illegible]	[illegible]	[illegible]	[illegible]	[illegible]	[illegible]	[illegible]	[illegible]	[illegible]	[illegible]		1945	1947		1975	1971	1973	1967		1945	1983	1961	1981	1945		1966	1945
131.04	IFAD	13.06.1976	30.11.1977	149	1978	1992	1978	1985	1986	1978	1993	1977	1977				1977	1978		1977	1982	1977	1978	1977		1977	1978
132.01	WHO	22.07.1946	07.04.1948	184	1948	1947	1962	1976	1984	1948	1992	1948	1947	1992	1974	1971	1972	1967	1948	1948	1990	1960	1982	1949	1992	1975	1948
141.01	ILO	28.06.1919	10.01.1920	162	1934	1991	1962	1976	1982	1919	1992	1919	1947	1992	1976	1977	1972	1967	1954	1919	1981	1960		1919		1978	1919
141.03	White Lead in Painting	25.10.1921	31.08.1923	56	1939		1962			1936			1924	1992						1926		1960					
141.04	Women Convention (Revised)	09.07.1948	27.02.1951	47			1962	1976					1950			1981	1972			D	1983			1973			1957
141.05	Ionizing Radiations	22.06.1960	17.06.1962	40						1978				1992				1967	1968	1965	1983						1966
141.06	Benzene	23.06.1971	27.07.1973	29																				1977			1993
141.07	Carcinogenic Substances	24.06.1974	10.06.1976	25	1979					1978																	1990
141.08	Protection of Workers	20.06.1977	11.07.1979	28										1992													1982
141.09	Working Environment	22.06.1981	11.08.1983	16																							1992
151.01	Industrial Devel. Org. (UNIDO)	08.04.1979	21.06.1985	162	1981	1988	1980	1985		1981	1992	1992	1981		1986	1986	1980	1980	1985	1981	1986	1983	1983	1981	1992	1985	1980
152.01	Metric Convention	20.05.1875	01.01.1876	47						1875		1947	1875							1875							1954
152.04	Legal Metrology Organization	12.10.1955	28.05.1958	51			1979					1959	1956							1959							1984
160.01	WIPO	14.07.1967	26.04.1970	134		1992	1975	1985		1980	1993	1972	1973		1977		1985	1979	1970	1975		1975					1975
161.01	Industrial Property (Paris)	20.03.1883	06.07.1884	107			1966			1967		1925	1909		1973		1991	1985		1884		1967					1884
161.02	False Indications of Source	14.04.1891	15.07.1892	31			1972																				1896
161.03	Registration of Marks	14.04.1891	15.07.1892	33			1972						1909							1892							
161.04	Deposit of Industrial Designs	06.11.1925	13.06.1939	21																1979		1986					
161.05	Classification for Marks	15.06.1957	08.04.1961	36			1972					1961	1969					1985		1962		1979					
161.06	Appellations of Origin	31.10.1958	25.09.1966	17			1972																				
161.07	Varieties of Plants (UPOV)	02.12.1961	10.08.1968	23								1989								1976							
161.08	Classification Indust. Designs	08.10.1968	27.04.1971	19									1990														
161.09	Patent Cooperation (PCT)	19.06.1970	24.01.1978	56								1980	1979					1985		1981		1987					1978
161.10	Patent Classification	24.03.1971	07.10.1975	27								1975	1975							1976							1975
161.13	Deposit of Microorganisms	28.04.1977	19.08.1980	24								1987	1984							1983							
162.01	Literary Works (Berne)	09.09.1886	05.12.1887	95						1967		1928	1920		1973			1983		1887		1961					1922
162.02	Universal Copyright Conv.	06.09.1952	16.09.1955	89			1973			1958		1969	1957		1976		1975	1983		1960	1982			1989			1960
162.03	Phonograms (Rome)	26.10.1961	18.05.1964	38						1991		1992	1973					1983									1965
162.04	Protection of Phonograms	29.10.1971	18.04.1973	43						1973		1974	1982					1983									1975
162.05	Satellites (Brussels)	21.05.1974	25.08.1979	15								1990	1982														
162.07	Film Register Treaty	20.04.1989	27.02.1991	7						1992			1991														
171.01	UNESCO Charter	16.11.1945	04.11.1946	173	1948	1958	1962	1977	1982	1948	1992	1946	1948	1992	1981	1972	1972	1968	1954	1946	1982	1960	1982	1946		1980	1946
171.02	Beirut Agreement	15.07.1949	12.08.1954	31	S																						1962
171.03	Florence Agreement	22.11.1950	21.05.1952	82	1958							1992	1958					1973		1957				1970			
171.04	Illicit Transfer	14.11.1970	24.04.1972	78			1974	1991		1973		1989					1987		1988		1990			1976			1973
171.05	World Heritage	16.11.1972	17.12.1975	134	1979	1989	1974	1991	1983	1978		1974	1992			1991	1983		1988		1990	1982		1976			1977
172.01	Customs Facilities for Touring	04.06.1954	11.09.1957	75			1963			1986		1967	1956					1971		1955							
172.02	Protoc. Tourist Publicity Mat.	04.06.1954	28.06.1956	69			1963			1986		1967	1956					1971		1955							
172.03	Importation of Road Vehicles	04.06.1954	15.12.1957	70			1963			S		1967	1956					1971		1955							
172.04	Taxation of Road Vehicles	18.05.1956	18.08.1959	18								1961	1958							S							
172.05	Importation of Aircraft/Boats	18.05.1956	01.01.1959	24			1963						1957							1963							
172.06	Taxation of Passenger Vehicles	14.12.1956	29.08.1962	14									1960														
172.07	World Tourism Org. (WTO)	27.09.1970	02.01.1975	111	1973		1976	1990		1972		D	1975		D	D	1975			1976		1974		1975			1974
172.08	Travel Contracts	23.04.1970	24.02.1976	7						1976										1973		1975					
180.01	Multimodal Transport of Goods	24.05.1980		6																							
181.02	Carriage of Goods by Road	19.05.1956	02.07.1961	25									1960							1962							
181.03	Taxation of Goods Vehicles	14.12.1956	29.08.1962	14									1960														
181.04	Approval of Vehicle Equipment	20.03.1958	20.06.1959	20									1971							1959							
182.01	Technical Unity	21.10.1882	21.10.1882	19																MS							
182.03	Goods Carried by Rail	10.01.1952	01.03.1953	11									1956							1953							
182.04	Passengers Carried by Rail	10.01.1952	01.03.1953	10									1956							1953							
182.05	Carriage by Rail (COTIF)	09.05.1980	01.05.1985	35		1984	1991						1983							1983							
183.01	Bills of Lading	25.08.1924	02.06.1931	40			1964			1961		D								1930				1982			
183.02	Shipowners' Liability	25.08.1924	02.06.1931	9						S										1930							1931
183.03	Maritime Liens and Mortgages	10.04.1926	02.06.1931	24			1964			1961										1930							1931
183.04	Immunity of State-Owned Ships	10.04.1926	02.06.1931	29						1961										1936							1936
183.05	IMO	06.03.1948	17.03.1958	140			1963	1977	1986	1953		1952	1975		1976	1976	1976	1970		1951	1990	1980		1987			1963
183.06	Arrest of Sea-Going Ships	10.05.1952	24.02.1956	37			1964													1961	1965						
183.07	Shipowners' Liability	10.10.1957	31.05.1968	21			1964					1980								D							S
183.08	Carriage of Passengers By Sea	29.04.1961	04.06.1965	10			1973													S							
183.09	Load Lines	05.04.1966	21.07.1968	127			1976	1991	1987	1971		1968	1972		1976	1985	1978	1982		1969	1991	1985					1969

Reference	AGREEMENT	Brunei Darussalam	Bulgaria	Burkina Faso	Burundi	Cambodia	Cameroon	Canada	Cape Verde	Central Africa	Chad	Chile	China	Colombia	Comoros	Congo	Cook Islands	Costa Rica	Côte d'Ivoire	Croatia	Cuba	Cyprus	Czech Republic	Denmark	Djibouti	Dominica	Dominican Rep.	Ecuador	Egypt
001.01	United Nations Charter	1984	1955	1960	1962	1955	1960	1945	1975	1960	1960	1945	1945	1945	1975	1960		1945	1960	1992	1945	1960	1993	1945	1977	1978	1945	1945	1945
001.02	ICJ: Compulsory Jurisdiction		1992			1957		1985						1937				1973				1988		1956			1933		1957
111.01	General Agreement (GATT)			1963	1965		1963	1948		1963	1963	1949		1981		1963		1990	1963		1948	1963	1993	1950		1993	1950		1970
111.06	Multifibre Agreement 1991 Prot							1991					1991	1991				1991									1991		1991
111.07	Standardization Code							1980				1981												1980					1983
111.08	Government Procurement Code							1981																					
111.09	Subsidies Code							1980				1981		1991															1983
111.10	Import Licensing							1980				1981																	1983
111.11	Antidumping Code							1980																					1983
111.12	Bovine Meat Arrangement		1980					1980						1984															1983
111.13	Dairy Agreement		1980																										S
111.14	Trade in Civil Aircraft							1980																1980					1989
111.20	GSTP						1992					1989									1989							1990	1989
112.01	Simplif. Customs Formalities		1926									S	1926									1964		1924					1925
112.02	Customs Co-operation (CCC)		1973	1966	1964		1965	1971	1992	1986		1966	1983			1975			1963		1988	1967	1993	1951					1956
112.03	Nomenclature			1978															1970			1972		D					
112.04	Customs Valuation																		1970			D		D					
112.05	Commercial Samples							1974													1976	1963		1955					1955
112.07	Containers		1960			1959	1963	1972													1965			1965					
112.08	Importation of Road Vehicles		1959			1959															1965	1983		1959					
112.09	TIR Carnets (Geneva 1959)		1959					1974														1977		1959					
112.10	Importation of Packings		1969			1963				1962											1963			1961					1963
112.11	Fairs Convention		1964			1963				1962									1978		1962	1972		1965			1962		1963
112.12	Professonial Equipment		1964							1962											1962	1972		1965					1963
112.13	ATA Carnet		1964					1972											1962		1963	1976	1993	1965					1968
112.14	Material for Seafarers																		1978					1966					1967
112.15	Scientific Equipment						1969	1974			1969	1970										1971		1969				1969	1970
112.16	Pedagogic Material						1971															1973							S
112.18	Containers		1977					1975					1986								1984								
112.19	Kyoto Convention		1982		1974		1977	1974					1988						1978			1976		1974					
112.20	TIR Carnets (Geneva 1975)		1977					1980				1982								1992		1981		1982					
112.21	Nairobi Convention							1990											1983										
112.22	Customs Valuation Code							1979														1989							
112.23	Frontier Controls of Goods																				1992			1987					
112.24	Harmonized System		1990	1990	S		1988	1987			1990		1992						1990					1987					
112.25	Istanbul Convention																							S					
121.02	Common Fund for Commodities		1987	1983	1982		1983	1983	1984	1983	1984		1981	1986	1984	1987		S	S		1988			1981	1985		S	1982	1982
121.03	International Tin Agreement							1982																1982					
121.04	International Coffee Agreement				1983		1983	1983		1983				1983		1983		1983	1983		1985	1983		1983			1983	1983	
121.05	International Cocoa Agreement		1987				1986												1986					1992				1986	
121.06	Int. Natural Rubber Agreement												1983						1991					1992					
122.01	Tropical Timber Agreement						1985	1986					1985	1990		1985			1985					1984				1985	1985
122.02	Agreement on Olive Oil																					1992							1988
122.03	Wheat Trade Convention							1986													1987			1986				1987	1988
122.04	Jute and Jute Products (1989)												1990											1991					1991
122.05	International Sugar Agreement																		1993								1993		
123.02	INSG							1986													1989								
123.03	ICSG											1990	1990																
123.04	ITSG																												

131.01	FAO		1967	1961	1963	1950	1960	1945	1975	1961	1961	1946	1973	1945	1977	1961	1985	1948	1961		1945	1960		1945	1977	1979	1945	1945	1945
131.04	IFAD			1977	1978	1992	1977	1977	1977	1978	1977	1978	1980	1979	1977	1978	1993	1978	1982		1977	1977		1977	1977	1980	1977	1977	1977
132.01	WHO	1985	1948	1960	1962	1950	1960	1946	1976	1960	1961	1948	1946	1959	1975	1960	1984	1949	1960	1992	1950	1961	1993	1948	1978	1981	1948	1949	1947
141.01	ILO		1920	1960	1963	1969	1960	1919	1979	1960	1960	1919	1919	1919	1978	1960		1944	1960	1992	1919	1960	1993	1919	1978	1982	1924	1934	1936
141.03	White Lead in Painting		1925	1960		1969	1960			1960	1960	1925		1933	1978	1960			1960		1928				1978				
141.04	Women Convention (Revised)				1963		1970								1978	1971		1960			D	1965			1978		1953		1960
141.05	Ionizing Radiations																							1974	1978			1970	1964
141.06	Benzene													1976					1973		1972							1975	
141.07	Carcinogenic Substances																							1978				1975	1982
141.08	Protection of Workers																	1981			1980			1988				1978	1988
141.09	Working Environment																				1982	1989							
151.01	Industrial Devel. Org. (UNIDO)		1985	1982	1982		1981	1983	1984	1982	1991	1981	1980	1981	1985	1983		1987	1981	1992	1981	1983	1993	1981	1991	1982	1983	1982	1981
152.01	Metric Convention		1911				1971	1907				1908	1977										1992	1875			1954		1962
152.04	Legal Metrology Organization		1956				1970	1982					1985								1962	1974	1992	1957			D		
160.01	WIPO		1970	1975	1977		1973	1970		1978	1970	1975	1980	1980		1975		1981	1974	1991	1975	1984	1993	1970				1988	1975
161.01	Industrial Property (Paris)		1921	1963	1977		1964	1925		1963	1963	1991	1985			1963			1963	1991	1904	1966	1993	1894			1890		1951
161.02	False Indications of Source		1975																		1905		1993				1951		1952
161.03	Registration of Marks		1985										1989							1991	1989		1993						1952
161.04	Deposit of Industrial Designs																												1952
161.05	Classification for Marks																			1991			1993	1961					
161.06	Appellations of Origin		1975	1975												1977					1966		1993						
161.07	Varieties of Plants (UPOV)							1991															1993	1968					
161.08	Classification Indust. Designs																			1991			1993	1971					
161.09	Patent Cooperation (PCT)		1984	1989			1978	1990		1978	1978					1978			1991				1993	1978					
161.10	Patent Classification																						1993	1975					1975
161.13	Deposit of Microorganisms		1980																				1993	1985					
162.01	Literary Works (Berne)		1921	1963			1964	1928		1977	1971	1970	1992	1988		1962		1978	1962	1991		1964	1993	1903				1991	1977
162.02	Universal Copyright Conv.		1975			1955	1973	1962				1955	1992	1976				1955			1957	1990	1993	1962			1983	1957	
162.03	Phonograms (Rome)			1988								1974		1976		1964		1971					T	1965			1987	1964	
162.04	Protection of Phonograms			1988								1977	1993					1982					T	1977				1974	1978
162.05	Satellites (Brussels)																												
162.07	Film Register Treaty			1991																			1993						
171.01	UNESCO Charter		1956	1960	1962	1951	1960	1946	1978	1960	1960	1953	1946	1947	1977	1960	1989	1950	1960	1992	1947	1961	1993	1946	1989	1979	1946	1947	1946
171.02	Beirut Agreement					1952		1950								1968		1971		1992	1977	1972		1955			S	S	
171.03	Florence Agreement			1965		1951	1964							S		1968			1963		1952	1963		1960			S	S	1952
171.04	Illicit Transfer		1971	1987		1972	1972	1978		1972			1989	1988					1990	1992	1980	1979	1993				1973	1971	1973
171.05	World Heritage		1974	1987	1982	1991	1982	1976	1988	1980		1980	1985	1983		1987		1977	1981	1992	1981	1975	1993	1979			1985	1975	1974
172.01	Customs Facilities for Touring		1959			1955		1955		1962		1974						1963			1963	1963		1955			S	1962	1957
172.02	Protoc. Tourist Publicity Mat.		1959			S				1962		1974						1963			1964	1963		1955				1962	1957
172.03	Importation of Road Vehicles		1959			S		1955		1962		1974						1963			1963	1963		1955			S	1962	1957
172.04	Taxation of Road Vehicles					1959																		1968					
172.05	Importation of Aircraft/Boats																							1959					
172.06	Taxation of Passenger Vehicles																				1965			1968					
172.07	World Tourism Org. (WTO)		1976	1975	1974	1972	1973	1986			1985	1974	1983	1971		1977		D	1973		1975	1974	1993				1975	1975	1971
172.08	Travel Contracts			S			1975						1972						S										
180.01	Multimodal Transport of Goods											1982																	
181.02	Carriage of Goods by Road		1977																	1992				1965					
181.03	Taxation of Goods Vehicles																				1966			1968					
181.04	Approval of Vehicle Equipment																							1976					
182.01	Technical Unity																							MS					
182.03	Goods Carried by Rail																												
182.04	Passengers Carried by Rail																												
182.05	Carriage by Rail (COTIF)		1982																	1992				1981					
183.01	Bills of Lading						D												1961	1992	1977			D			1930	1977	1943
183.02	Shipowners' Liability											S												D			1958		
183.03	Maritime Liens and Mortgages											S									1983			D					
183.04	Immunity of State-Owned Ships											1936										1988		1950					
183.05	IMO	1984	1960			1961	1961	1948	1976			1972	1973	1974		1975		1981	1960	1992	1966	1973		1959	1979	1979	1953	1956	1959
183.06	Arrest of Sea-Going Ships					1956												1955	1989	1992	1983			1989					1955
183.07	Shipowners' Liability							S																D					D
183.08	Carriage of Passengers By Sea					S						S	S								1963			S			S		
183.09	Load Lines	1987	1968				1984	1970	1977			1975	1973	1987		1986			1971	1991	1969	1969		1967	1984		1973	1976	1968

Reference	AGREEMENT	El Salvador	Equatorial Guinea	Estonia	Ethiopia	European Communities	Fiji	Finland	France	Gabon	Gambia	Georgia	Germany	Ghana	Greece	Grenada	Guatemala	Guinea	Guinea-Bissau	Guyana	Haiti	Holy See	Honduras	Hong Kong	Hungary	Iceland	India	Indonesia	Iraq
001.01	United Nations Charter	1945	1968	1991	1945		1970	1955	1945	1960	1965	1992	1973	1957	1945	1974	1945	1958	1974	1966	1945		1945		1955	1946	1945	1950	1945
001.02	ICJ: Compulsory Jurisdiction	1973		1991				1958			1966								1989		1921		1986		1992		1974		
111.01	General Agreement (GATT)	1991						1950	1948	1963	1965		1951	1957	1950		1991			1966	1950			1986	1973	1968	1948	1950	
111.06	Multifibre Agreement 1991 Prot	1991				1991		1991									1992							1991	1991		1991	1991	
111.07	Standardization Code					1980		1980	1980				1980		S									1986	1980		1983		
111.08	Government Procurement Code					1981		1981																1986					
111.09	Subsidies Code					1980		1980																1986			1980	1985	
111.10	Import Licensing					1981		1980																1986	1980		1980		
111.11	Antidumping Code					1980		1980																1986	1980		1980		
111.12	Bovine Meat Arrangement					1980		1980									1983								1980				
111.13	Dairy Agreement					1980		1980																	1980				
111.14	Trade in Civil Aircraft					1980			1980				1980		S														
111.20	GSTP													1989				1989									1989	1989	1988
112.01	Simplif. Customs Formalities						D	1928	1926				1925		1927										1926		1925		1934
112.02	Customs Co-operation (CCC)			1992	1973			1961		1965	1987		1952	1968	1951		1985	1991		1976	1958			1987	1968	1971	1971	1957	1990
112.03	Nomenclature							D	D				D		D						1958				1978				
112.04	Customs Valuation							D	D				D		D						1958					S			
112.05	Commercial Samples						1972	1954	1964				1955	1958	1955			1962			1958				1957	1977	1954	1954	
112.07	Containers							1961	1959				1961		1961										1957				
112.08	Importation of Road Vehicles							1967	1959				1961		1961										1957				
112.09	TIR Carnets (Geneva 1959)							1960	1959				1961		1961										1961				
112.10	Importation of Packings							1965	1961				1969																
112.11	Fairs Convention							1964	1964				1967		1962										1963	1970	1988		
112.12	Professonial Equipment							1964	1962				1969		1962										1963	1970			
112.13	ATA Carnet							1964	1962				1965		1975										1965	1970	1989		
112.14	Material for Seafarers							1968	1966				1969		1971														
112.15	Scientific Equipment						1971		1969	1969			1969	1969	1974										1976		1971		
112.16	Pedagogic Material								1973				1971		1974										1976		1973		1971
112.18	Containers							1983							S										1973			1989	
112.19	Kyoto Convention					1974		1977	1974		1974		1974		1988										1981		1976		
112.20	TIR Carnets (Geneva 1975)					1982		1978	1976				1982		1980										1978			1989	
112.21	Nairobi Convention							1985																		S	1988		
112.22	Customs Valuation Code					1979		1980																1986	1980		1980		
112.23	Frontier Controls of Goods					1987		1985	1987				1987		1987										1984				
112.24	Harmonized System					1987		1987	1987				1987	S	1988						S				1990	1987	1986		
112.25	Istanbul Convention					S			S				S	S											S				
121.02	Common Fund for Commodities	S	1983		1981	1990		1981	1982	1981	1983		1985	1983	1984	S	1985	1982	1983	S	1981		1988				1981	1981	1981
121.03	International Tin Agreement					1982		1982	1982				1982		1982												1982	1982	
121.04	International Coffee Agreement	1983	1983		1983	1983	1983	1983	1983	1983			1983	1983	1983		1983	1983			1983		1983				1983	1983	
121.05	International Cocoa Agreement					1992		1986	1986	1986			1992	1986	1987	1986	1991				1987				1986				
121.06	Int. Natural Rubber Agreement					1988		1989	1992				1988		1991													1987	
122.01	Tropical Timber Agreement					1985		1985	1984	1985			1984	1985	1984					1992			1985				1986	1984	
122.02	Agreement on Olive Oil					1986																							
122.03	Wheat Trade Convention	1986				1991		1987	1987				1988		1992							1986			1987		1986		1987
122.04	Jute and Jute Products (1989)					1991		1991	1990				1991		1991												1990	1991	
122.05	International Sugar Agreement																1993								1993		1993		
123.02	INSG							1986	1986				1991		1986													1990	
123.03	ICSG					1991		1990	1991						1990														
123.04	ITSG					1991			1991						1990													1990	

[illegible]	1947	1981	1991	1948	1991	1971	1947	1945	1961	1965		1950	1957	1945	1975	1945	1959	1973	1966	1945		1945		1967	1945	1945	1949	1945
131.04 IFAD	1977	1981		1977		1978	1977	1977	1978	1977		1977	1977	1978	1980	1978	1977	1978	1977	1977		1977				1977	1977	1977
132.01 WHO	1948	1980	1993	1947		1972	1947	1948	1960	1971	1992	1951	1957	1948	1974	1949	1959	1974	1966	1947		1949		1948	1948	1948	1950	1947
141.01 ILO	1948	1981	1992	1923		1974	1920	1919	1960			1951	1957	1919	1979	1945	1959	1977	1966	1919		1955		1922	1945	1919	1950	1932
141.03 White Lead in Painting							1929	1926	1960					1926		1990	1959							1956				1966
141.04 Women Convention (Revised)								D					1959	D		1952	1966	1977								1950		1967
141.05 Ionizing Radiations							1978	1971				1973	1961	1982			1966		1966					1968		1975		1962
141.06 Benzene							1976	1972				1973		1977			1977		1983					1972		1991		1972
141.07 Carcinogenic Substances							1977					1976					1976		1983					1975	1991			1978
141.08 Protection of Workers							1979	1985					1986				1982											1985
141.09 Working Environment				1991			1985																		1991			
151.01 Industrial Devel. Org. (UNIDO)	1988	1984		1981		1981	1981	1982	1982	1986	1992	1983	1982	1983	1986	1983	1980	1983	1984	1982		1983		1983		1980	1980	1981
152.01 Metric Convention							1921	1875				1875												1875		1957	1960	
152.04 Legal Metrology Organization				1974			1958	1958				1959		1979			1960							1956		1956	1960	
160.01 WIPO	1979					1972	1970	1974	1975	1980		1970	1976	1976		1983	1980	1988		1983	1975	1983		1970	1986	1975	1979	1976
161.01 Industrial Property (Paris)							1921	1884	1964	1992		1903	1976	1924			1982	1988		1958	1960			1909	1962		1950	1976
161.02 False Indications of Source								1892				1925												1934				
161.03 Registration of Marks								1892				1922												1909				
161.04 Deposit of Industrial Designs								1930				1928									1960			1984			1950	
161.05 Classification for Marks							1973	1961				1962												1967				
161.06 Appellations of Origin								1966	1975											1966				1967				
161.07 Varieties of Plants (UPOV)							1993	1971				1968												1983				
161.08 Classification Indust. Designs							1972	1975				1990												1974				
161.09 Patent Cooperation (PCT)							1980	1978	1978			1978		1990			1991							1980				
161.10 Patent Classification							1976	1975				1975																
161.13 Deposit of Microorganisms							1985	1980				1981												1980				
162.01 Literary Works (Berne)						1971	1928	1887	1962	1993		1887	1991	1920			1980	1991			1935	1990		1922	1947	1928		
162.02 Universal Copyright Conv.	1979					1970	1963	1956				1955	1962	1963		1964	1981			1955	1955			1971	1956	1958		
162.03 Phonograms (Rome)	1979					1972	1983	1987				1966		1992		1977						1989						
162.04 Protection of Phonograms	1979					1973	1973	1973				1974				1977					1977	1989		1975		1975		
162.05 Satellites (Brussels)												1979		1991														
162.07 Film Register Treaty								1991																				
171.01 UNESCO Charter	1948	1979	1991	1955		1983	1956	1946	1960	1973	1992	1951	1958	1946	1975	1950	1960	1974	1967	1946		1947		1954	1964	1946	1950	1948
171.02 Beirut Agreement	1953												1960	1954						1954								1952
171.03 Florence Agreement	1953					1972	1956	1957	1962			1957	1958	1955		1960				1954	1979	S		1979				1972
171.04 Illicit Transfer	1978										1992			1981	1992	1985	1979					1979		1978		1977		1973
171.05 World Heritage	1991			1977		1990	1987	1975	1986	1987	1992	1976	1975	1981		1979	1979		1977	1980	1982	1979		1985		1977	1989	1974
172.01 Customs Facilities for Touring	1958					1972	1962	1959				1957	1958	1974		S				1958	S	S		1963		1958		
172.02 Protoc. Tourist Publicity Mat.	1958					1972	1962	1959				1957	1958	1974						1958	S	S		1963		1957		
172.03 Importation of Road Vehicles	1958					1972	1962	1959				1957	1958			S				1958	S	S		1983		1958		
172.04 Taxation of Road Vehicles							1956	1959				1961	1959															
172.05 Importation of Aircraft/Boats							1965	1959				1961												1957				
172.06 Taxation of Passenger Vehicles							1967						1962															
172.07 World Tourism Org. (WTO)	D			1975			1982	1975	1971	1975		1976	1972	1972	1977		1985	1991		1974	1973	D		1975		1971	1972	1971
172.08 Travel Contracts																					S							
180.01 Multimodal Transport of Goods																												
181.02 Carriage of Goods by Road							1973	1959				1961		1977										1970				
181.03 Taxation of Goods Vehicles							1967						1962															
181.04 Approval of Vehicle Equipment							1976	1958				1965												1960				
182.01 Technical Unity								MS				MS		MS										MS				
182.03 Goods Carried by Rail								1953																				
182.04 Passengers Carried by Rail								1953																				
182.05 Carriage by Rail (COTIF)							1984	1982				1985		1986										1982				1984
183.01 Bills of Lading						1970	D	1937				1939												1930				
183.02 Shipowners' Liability			S				D	D																1930				
183.03 Maritime Liens and Mortgages			1930				D	1935				S								1965				1930				
183.04 Immunity of State-Owned Ships			1936					1955				1936		1951										1936				
183.05 IMO	1981	1972	1992	1975		1983	1959	1952	1976	1979		1959	1959	1958		1983	1975	1977	1980	1953		1954	1967	1970	1960	1959	1961	1973
183.06 Arrest of Sea-Going Ships						1972		1957				1972		1967	1965					1954	1956							
183.07 Shipowners' Liability						1964	D	D					1961								S				1968	1971		
183.08 Carriage of Passengers By Sea								D				S		S						1989	S					S		
183.09 Load Lines			1991	1985		1972	1968	1966	1982	1991		1969	1968	1968			1981			1989		1977		1973	1970	1968	1977	

Reference	AGREEMENT	Iran, Islamic Rep.	Ireland	Israel	Italy	Jamaica	Japan	Jordan	Kazakhstan	Kenya	Kiribati
001.01	United Nations Charter	1945	1955	1949	1955	1962	1956	1955	1992	1963	
001.02	ICJ: Compulsory Jurisdiction						1958			1965	
111.01	General Agreement (GATT)		1967	1962	1950	1963	1955			1964	
111.06	Multifibre Agreement 1991 Prot					1991	1991				
111.07	Standardization Code		1980		1980		1980				
111.08	Government Procurement Code			1983			1981				
111.09	Subsidies Code			1985			1980				
111.10	Import Licensing						1980				
111.11	Antidumping Code						1980				
111.12	Bovine Meat Arrangement						1980				
111.13	Dairy Agreement						1980				
111.14	Trade in Civil Aircraft		1980		1985		1980				
111.20	GSTP	1992									
112.01	Simplif. Customs Formalities	1925		1966	1924		1952				
112.02	Customs Co-operation (CCC)	1959	1952	1958	1952	1963	1964	1964	1992	1965	
112.03	Nomenclature	1959	D	D	1958		D			1967	
112.04	Customs Valuation		D	1981	D		D			1967	
112.05	Commercial Samples	1970	1959	1957	1958	1963	1955			1965	
112.07	Containers		1967	1967	1962	1963	1971				
112.08	Importation of Road Vehicles		1967		1962						
112.09	TIR Carnets (Geneva 1959)	1971	1967	1969	1963		1971	1973			
112.10	Importation of Packings	1968	1965	1961	1963					1983	
112.11	Fairs Convention	1968	1965	1964	1963		1973				
112.12	Professonial Equipment	1968	1965	1966	1963		1973			1983	
112.13	ATA Carnet	1968	1965	1966	1964		1973				
112.14	Material for Seafarers	1970	1967	1971	1968		1968			1967	
112.15	Scientific Equipment	1970		1970	1975					1983	
112.16	Pedagogic Material	1972		1973				1971			
112.18	Containers										
112.19	Kyoto Convention		1974	1977	1974		1976			1983	
112.20	TIR Carnets (Geneva 1975)	1984	1982	1984	1982			1985			
112.21	Nairobi Convention		1983		1983			1978		1983	
112.22	Customs Valuation Code						1980				
112.23	Frontier Controls of Goods		1987		1987						
112.24	Harmonized System	S	1987	1987	1989		1987	1985		1988	
112.25	Istanbul Convention		S	S	S			1992			
121.02	Common Fund for Commodities		1982		1984	1985	1981			1982	
121.03	International Tin Agreement		1982		1982		1982				
121.04	International Coffee Agreement		1983		1983	1983	1983			1983	
121.05	International Cocoa Agreement		1992		1988	1987	1987				
121.06	Int. Natural Rubber Agreement		1988		1988		1988				
122.01	Tropical Timber Agreement		1984		1985		1984				
122.02	Agreement on Olive Oil			1992							
122.03	Wheat Trade Convention		1986	1988	1989		1986				
122.04	Jute and Jute Products (1989)		1991		1991		1990				
122.05	International Sugar Agreement					1993					
123.02	INSG						1990				
123.03	ICSG										
123.04	ITSG										

Reference	AGREEMENT	Korea, Dem. PR	Korea, Rep. of	Kuwait	Kyrgyzstan	Lao P.D.R.	Latvia	Lebanon	Lesotho	Liberia	Libyan A.J.
001.01	United Nations Charter	1991	1991	1963	1992	1955	1991	1945	1966	1945	1955
001.02	ICJ: Compulsory Jurisdiction									1952	
111.01	General Agreement (GATT)		1967	1963					1988		
111.06	Multifibre Agreement 1991 Prot		1992								
111.07	Standardization Code		1980								
111.08	Government Procurement Code										
111.09	Subsidies Code		1980								
111.10	Import Licensing										
111.11	Antidumping Code		1986								
111.12	Bovine Meat Arrangement										
111.13	Dairy Agreement										
111.14	Trade in Civil Aircraft										
111.20	GSTP	1988	1989								1989
112.01	Simplif. Customs Formalities								1970		
112.02	Customs Co-operation (CCC)		1968				1992	1960	1978	1975	1983
112.03	Nomenclature		D					1950	D		
112.04	Customs Valuation		D								
112.05	Commercial Samples		1978								
112.07	Containers										
112.08	Importation of Road Vehicles										
112.09	TIR Carnets (Geneva 1959)			1977							
112.10	Importation of Packings		1975						1982		
112.11	Fairs Convention		1975					1979	1982		
112.12	Professonial Equipment		1978					1979	1982		
112.13	ATA Carnet		1978					1979	1983		
112.14	Material for Seafarers		1975					1965			
112.15	Scientific Equipment		1982					1971	1982		1969
112.16	Pedagogic Material		1982					1971	1982		
112.18	Containers		1984								
112.19	Kyoto Convention		1983						1982		
112.20	TIR Carnets (Geneva 1975)		1982	1983							
112.21	Nairobi Convention										
112.22	Customs Valuation Code		1981						1986		
112.23	Frontier Controls of Goods								1988		
112.24	Harmonized System		1987						1985	S	
112.25	Istanbul Convention										
121.02	Common Fund for Commodities	1987	1982	1983					1983	S	
121.03	International Tin Agreement										
121.04	International Coffee Agreement									1983	
121.05	International Cocoa Agreement										
121.06	Int. Natural Rubber Agreement										
122.01	Tropical Timber Agreement		1985							1985	
122.02	Agreement on Olive Oil										
122.03	Wheat Trade Convention		1987								
122.04	Jute and Jute Products (1989)										
122.05	International Sugar Agreement		1993								
123.02	INSG										
123.03	ICSG										
123.04	ITSG										

Reference	AGREEMENT	Liechtenstein	Lithuania	Luxembourg	Madagascar	Malawi	Malaysia	Maldives	Mali
001.01	United Nations Charter	1990	1991	1945	1960	1964	1957	1965	1960
001.02	ICJ: Compulsory Jurisdiction	1950		1930	1992	1966			
111.01	General Agreement (GATT)			1948	1963	1964	1957	1983	1993
111.06	Multifibre Agreement 1991 Prot						1992		
111.07	Standardization Code			1980					
111.08	Government Procurement Code								
111.09	Subsidies Code								
111.10	Import Licensing								
111.11	Antidumping Code								
111.12	Bovine Meat Arrangement								
111.13	Dairy Agreement								
111.14	Trade in Civil Aircraft			1980					
111.20	GSTP						1989		
112.01	Simplif. Customs Formalities			1927		1967			
112.02	Customs Co-operation (CCC)		1992	1953	1964	1966	1964		1987
112.03	Nomenclature			D			D		
112.04	Customs Valuation			D					
112.05	Commercial Samples	1975		1957			1958		
112.07	Containers	1960		1960		1969			
112.08	Importation of Road Vehicles	1960		1964					
112.09	TIR Carnets (Geneva 1959)	1960		1962					
112.10	Importation of Packings			1964					
112.11	Fairs Convention			1971	1962				1989
112.12	Professonial Equipment			1966	1962				
112.13	ATA Carnet			1966			1988		
112.14	Material for Seafarers			1975	1966				
112.15	Scientific Equipment			1972					1987
112.16	Pedagogic Material								S
112.18	Containers	1976							
112.19	Kyoto Convention			1974			1983		
112.20	TIR Carnets (Geneva 1975)	1978		1982					
112.21	Nairobi Convention					1978	1979		
112.22	Customs Valuation Code					1983			
112.23	Frontier Controls of Goods	1986		1987					
112.24	Harmonized System			1988	1987	1988	1987		
112.25	Istanbul Convention			S					
121.02	Common Fund for Commodities			1985	1987	1981	1983	1988	1982
121.03	International Tin Agreement			1982			1981		
121.04	International Coffee Agreement			1983	1983	1983			
121.05	International Cocoa Agreement			1987					
121.06	Int. Natural Rubber Agreement			1991			1987		
122.01	Tropical Timber Agreement			1984			1984		
122.02	Agreement on Olive Oil								
122.03	Wheat Trade Convention			1989					
122.04	Jute and Jute Products (1989)			1990					
122.05	International Sugar Agreement								
123.02	INSG								
123.03	ICSG			1991					
123.04	ITSG			1991			1989		

131.01	FAO	1953	1946	1949	1946	1963	1951	1951		1964		1977	1949	1961		1951	1991	1945	1966	1945	1953		1991	1945	1961	1965	1957	1971	1961
131.04	IFAD	1977	1977	1978	1977	1977	1977	1979		1977		1987	1978	1977		1978		1978	1977	1978	1977			1977	1979	1977	1990	1980	1977
132.01	WHO	1946	1947	1949	1947	1963	1951	1947	1992	1964	1984	1973	1949	1960	1992	1950	1991	1949	1967	1947	1952		1991	1949	1961	1965	1958	1965	1960
141.01	ILO	1919	1923	1949	1945	1962	1951	1956		1964			1991	1961	1992	1964	1991	1948	1980	1919	1952		1991	1920	1960	1965	1957		1960
141.03	White Lead in Painting				1952											1964								1928	1960				1960
141.04	Women Convention (Revised)		D		D					1965				1961				1962			1962			D		1965			
141.05	Ionizing Radiations				1971		1973											1977											
141.06	Benzene			1979	1981									1974															
141.07	Carcinogenic Substances				1981		1977																						
141.08	Protection of Workers				1985												1993												
141.09	Working Environment																												
151.01	Industrial Devel. Org. (UNIDO)	1985	1984	1983	1985	1982	1980	1982		1981		1981	1980	1982	1993	1980		1983	1981	1990	1981		1991	1983	1980	1980	1980	1988	1981
152.01	Metric Convention	1975	1926	1985	1875		1885					1982	1959																
152.04	Legal Metrology Organization	D	1979	1966	1958		1961			1982		1974	1978					1962											
160.01	WIPO		1970	1970	1977	1978	1975	1972		1971		1974	1979				1993	1986	1986	1989	1976	1972	1992	1975	1989	1970	1989		1982
161.01	Industrial Property (Paris)	1959	1925	1950	1884		1899	1972		1965		1980	1980					1924	1989		1976	1933		1922	1963	1964	1989		1983
161.02	False Indications of Source		1925	1950	1951		1953											1924				1933							
161.03	Registration of Marks				1894							1980										1933		1924					
161.04	Deposit of Industrial Designs				1987							1992										1933		1979					
161.05	Classification for Marks		1966	1961	1961		1990											1961				1967		1975					
161.06	Appellations of Origin			1966	1968																								
161.07	Varieties of Plants (UPOV)		1981	1979	1977		1982																						
161.08	Classification Indust. Designs		1971		1975																								
161.09	Patent Cooperation (PCT)		1992		1985		1978					1980	1984									1980		1978	1978	1978			1984
161.10	Patent Classification		1975	1975	1980		1977																	1977					
161.13	Deposit of Microorganisms				1986		1980						1988									1981							
162.01	Literary Works (Berne)		1927	1950	1887		1899											1947	1989	1989	1976	1931		1888	1966	1991	1990		1962
162.02	Universal Copyright Conv.		1959	1955	1957		1956		1992	1966			1987			1955		1959		1956		1959		1955		1965			
162.03	Phonograms (Rome)		1979		1975		1989												1989					1976					
162.04	Protection of Phonograms			1978	1977		1978			1976			1987											1976					
162.05	Satellites (Brussels)				1981					1979																			
162.07	Film Register Treaty																												
171.01	UNESCO Charter	1948	1961	1949	1948	1962	1951	1950	1992	1964	1989	1974	1950	1960	1992	1951	1991	1946	1967	1947	1953		1991	1947	1960	1964	1958	1980	1960
171.02	Beirut Agreement	1959						1972										1971			1973				1962	1967			
171.03	Florence Agreement	1966	1978	1952	1962		1970	1958		1967						1952					1973	1953		1957	1962	1965	1959		
171.04	Illicit Transfer	1975			1978			1974				1983	1983	1972				1992			1973				1989				1987
171.05	World Heritage	1975	1991		1978	1983	1992	1975		1991			1988			1987		1983			1978		1992	1983	1983	1982	1988	1986	1977
172.01	Customs Facilities for Touring	1968	1967	1957	1958	1963	1955	1957										1971				•		1956			1958		1973
172.02	Protoc. Tourist Publicity Mat.	1968	1967	1957	1958	1963	1955	1957										1971				•		1956			1958		1974
172.03	Importation of Road Vehicles	1968	1967	1957	1958	1963	1964	1957														•		1956			1958		1974
172.04	Taxation of Road Vehicles		1962																					1965					
172.05	Importation of Aircraft/Boats				1962	1963																1960		1964					
172.06	Taxation of Passenger Vehicles		1962																					1965					
172.07	World Tourism Org. (WTO)	1972		1975	1978	1975	1978	1971		1971		1987	1975	1975		1973		1974	1981		1977				1975	1974	D	1981	1974
172.08	Travel Contracts				1979													S											
180.01	Multimodal Transport of Goods																									1984			
181.02	Carriage of Goods by Road		1991		1961																			1964					
181.03	Taxation of Goods Vehicles		1962																					1965					
181.04	Approval of Vehicle Equipment				1963																			1971					
182.01	Technical Unity				MS																			MS					
182.03	Goods Carried by Rail				1955																	•		1954					
182.04	Passengers Carried by Rail				1955																	•		1954					
182.05	Carriage by Rail (COTIF)	1985	1986		1985													1983				1985		1983					
183.01	Bills of Lading	1966	1962	1959	D		D							1969				1975						1991	1965				
183.02	Shipowners' Liability				S		S										S								1965				
183.03	Maritime Liens and Mortgages	1966			1949		S											1969						1991	1935				
183.04	Immunity of State-Owned Ships				1937																1937			1991	1955				
183.05	IMO	1958	1951	1952	1957	1976	1958	1973		1973		1986	1962	1960			1993	1966		1959	1970			1991	1961	1989	1971	1967	
183.06	Arrest of Sea-Going Ships		1989		1979													S						1991	1958				
183.07	Shipowners' Liability	1966		1967	S		D																	1991	1965				
183.08	Carriage of Passengers By Sea	1966			S															S					1965				
183.09	Load Lines	1973	1968	1967	1968	1982	1968			1975		1989	1969	1968			1992	1970		1967	1974		1991	1991	1967		1971	1968	

Reference	AGREEMENT	Malta	Marshall Islands	Mauritania	Mauritius	Mexico	Micronesia	Moldova, Rep.	Monaco	Mongolia	Morocco	Mozambique	Myanmar	Namibia	Nauru
001.01	United Nations Charter	1964	1991	1961	1968	1945	1991	1992		1961	1956	1975	1948	1990	
001.02	ICJ: Compulsory Jurisdiction	1966			1968	1947									1988
111.01	General Agreement (GATT)	1964		1963	1970	1986					1987	1992	1948	1992	
111.06	Multifibre Agreement 1991 Prot														
111.07	Standardization Code					1988									
111.08	Government Procurement Code														
111.09	Subsidies Code														
111.10	Import Licensing					1988									
111.11	Antidumping Code					1988									
111.12	Bovine Meat Arrangement														
111.13	Dairy Agreement														
111.14	Trade in Civil Aircraft														
111.20	GSTP					1989						1990			
112.01	Simplif. Customs Formalities														
112.02	Customs Co-operation (CCC)	1968		1979	1973	1988				1991	1968	1987	1991	1992	
112.03	Nomenclature			1979	D						1968				
112.04	Customs Valuation														
112.05	Commercial Samples	1968			1969										
112.07	Containers				1969										
112.08	Importation of Road Vehicles														
112.09	TIR Carnets (Geneva 1959)	1978									1975				
112.10	Importation of Packings														
112.11	Fairs Convention	1988									1962				
112.12	Professonial Equipment	1988													
112.13	ATA Carnet	1983			1982										
112.14	Material for Seafarers	1966													
112.15	Scientific Equipment					1972					1978				
112.16	Pedagogic Material										1973				
112.18	Containers										1990				
112.19	Kyoto Convention										1987				
112.20	TIR Carnets (Geneva 1975)	1977									1983				
112.21	Nairobi Convention				1985						1980				
112.22	Customs Valuation Code					1988									
112.23	Frontier Controls of Goods														
112.24	Harmonized System	1989			1985	1991			1992	1991	1992				1990
112.25	Istanbul Convention										S				
121.02	Common Fund for Commodities			1990		1982					1987	S			
121.03	International Tin Agreement														
121.04	International Coffee Agreement					1983									
121.05	International Cocoa Agreement					1986									
121.06	Int. Natural Rubber Agreement										1988				
122.01	Tropical Timber Agreement														
122.02	Agreement on Olive Oil										1986				
122.03	Wheat Trade Convention	1987			1987						1986				
122.04	Jute and Jute Products (1989)														
122.05	International Sugar Agreement														
123.02	INSG														
123.03	ICSG														
123.04	ITSG														

Reference	AGREEMENT	Nepal	Netherlands	New Zealand	Nicaragua	Niger	Nigeria	Norway	Oman	Pakistan	Panama	Papua New Guinea	Paraguay	Peru	Philippines
001.01	United Nations Charter	1955	1945	1945	1945	1960	1960	1945	1971	1947	1945	1975	1945	1945	1945
001.02	ICJ: Compulsory Jurisdiction		1956	1977	1929		1965	1976		1960	1921				1972
111.01	General Agreement (GATT)		1948	1948	1950	1963	1960	1948		1948				1951	1979
111.06	Multifibre Agreement 1991 Prot							1991		1991	1992			1991	1991
111.07	Standardization Code		1981	1980				1980		1981					1981
111.08	Government Procurement Code							1981							
111.09	Subsidies Code			1981				1980		1980					1985
111.10	Import Licensing			1980			1986	1980		1981					1981
111.11	Antidumping Code							1980		1981					
111.12	Bovine Meat Arrangement			1980			1986	1980					S		
111.13	Dairy Agreement			1980				1980							
111.14	Trade in Civil Aircraft		1981					1980							
111.20	GSTP				1989		1989			1989				1988	1992
112.01	Simplif. Customs Formalities		1925	1924		1966	1964	1926		1951			S		
112.02	Customs Co-operation (CCC)	1985	1953	1963		1981	1963	1951		1955			1969	1970	1980
112.03	Nomenclature		D	D			D	D		D					
112.04	Customs Valuation		D				1972	D		1957					
112.05	Commercial Samples		1955	1957			1961	1954		1953					
112.07	Containers		1960					1961							
112.08	Importation of Road Vehicles		1960					1966							
112.09	TIR Carnets (Geneva 1959)		1960					1960							
112.10	Importation of Packings		1962					1961							
112.11	Fairs Convention		1964	1977		1962		1963							
112.12	Professonial Equipment		1964	1977		1962		1962							
112.13	ATA Carnet		1964	1977		1978	1973	1964							
112.14	Material for Seafarers		1966	1965		1965		1965		1966					
112.15	Scientific Equipment		1970	1977		1969									1973
112.16	Pedagogic Material		1986	1977		1972									S
112.18	Containers			1974											
112.19	Kyoto Convention		1977	1975			1976	1975		1981					
112.20	TIR Carnets (Geneva 1975)		1982					1980							
112.21	Nairobi Convention			1984		1989	1984	1985		1979					
112.22	Customs Valuation Code			1982				1980							
112.23	Frontier Controls of Goods		1987					1985							
112.24	Harmonized System		1987	1987			1988	1987		1987					
112.25	Istanbul Convention		S			S	S			S					
121.02	Common Fund for Commodities	1984	1983	1983	1984	1981	1983	1981		1983		1982		1987	1981
121.03	International Tin Agreement		1982				1983	1982							
121.04	International Coffee Agreement		1983	D	1983		1983	1983			1983	1983	1983	1983	1983
121.05	International Cocoa Agreement		1992				1986	1987				1987			
121.06	Int. Natural Rubber Agreement		1988				1989	1988							
122.01	Tropical Timber Agreement	1990	1984	1992				1984			1989	1985		1985	1985
122.02	Agreement on Olive Oil														
122.03	Wheat Trade Convention		1989					1986		1987	1986				
122.04	Jute and Jute Products (1989)	1992	1991					1990		1991					
122.05	International Sugar Agreement														
123.02	INSG		1990					1988							
123.03	ICSG		1991					1991						1990	
123.04	ITSG		1991				1989								

TABLE

131.01	FAO	1964		1961	1968	1945			1973	1956	1977	1947	1977	1951	1945	1945	1945	1961	1960	1945	1971	1947	1945	1975	1945	1952	1945
131.04	IFAD	1977		1979	1979	1977				1977	1978	1990	1992	1978	1977	1977	1977	1977	1977	1977	1983	1977	1977	1978	1979	1977	1977
132.01	WHO	1965	1991	1961	1968	1948	1992	1948	1962	1956	1975	1948	1990	1953	1947	1946	1950	1960	1960	1947	1971	1948	1951	1976	1949	1949	1948
141.01	ILO	1965		1961	1969	1931	1992		1968	1956	1976	1948	1978	1966	1919	1919	1957	1961	1960	1919		1947	1919	1976	1956	1919	1948
141.03	White Lead in Painting	1988		1961		1938				1956					1939		1934	1961		1929			1970				
141.04	Women Convention (Revised)	D		1963											D	D						1951	1970		1966		1953
141.05	Ionizing Radiations					1983									1966		1981			1961					1967		
141.06	Benzene	1990								1974							1981										
141.07	Carcinogenic Substances																1981			1977						1976	
141.08	Protection of Workers	1988																1993		1979							
141.09	Working Environment					1984									1991					1982							
151.01	Industrial Devel. Org. (UNIDO)	1982		1981	1981	1980			1985	1985	1983	1990	1986	1983	1980	1985	1980	1980	1980	1981	1981	1979	1980	1986	1981	1982	1980
152.01	Metric Convention					1890									1929	1991				1875		1973					
152.04	Legal Metrology Organization							1956		1958					1958					1958		1973					
160.01	WIPO	1977		1976	1976	1975		1975	1979	1971			1991		1975	1984	1985	1975		1974		1977	1983		1987	1980	1980
161.01	Industrial Property (Paris)	1967		1965	1976	1903		1956	1985	1917					1884	1931		1964	1963	1885							1965
161.02	False Indications of Source							1956		1917						1931											
161.03	Registration of Marks							1956	1985	1917					1893												
161.04	Deposit of Industrial Designs							1956		1930					1979												
161.05	Classification for Marks							1961		1966					1962					1961							
161.06	Appellations of Origin					1966																					
161.07	Varieties of Plants (UPOV)														1968	1981											
161.08	Classification Indust. Designs														1977					1971							
161.09	Patent Cooperation (PCT)			1983				1979	1991						1979	1992		1993		1980							
161.10	Patent Classification							1976							1975					1975							
161.13	Deposit of Microorganisms														1987					1986							1981
162.01	Literary Works (Berne)	1964		1973	1989	1967		1889		1917					1912	1928		1962		1896		1948			1992	1988	1951
162.02	Universal Copyright Conv.	1968			1968	1957		1955		1972					1967	1964	1961	1989	1962	1963		1955	1962		1962	1963	1955
162.03	Phonograms (Rome)					1964		1985										1964		1978			1983		1970	1985	1984
162.04	Protection of Phonograms					1973		1974								1976				1978			1974		1979	1985	
162.05	Satellites (Brussels)					1979				1983							1979						1985			1985	
162.07	Film Register Treaty					1991																					
171.01	UNESCO Charter	1965		1962	1968	1946	1992	1949	1962	1956	1976	1949	1978	1953	1947	1946	1952	1960	1960	1946	1972	1949	1950	1976	1955	1946	1946
171.02	Beirut Agreement	1968								1968					S			1968		1950		1950					1952
171.03	Florence Agreement	1968			1969			1952		1968					1957	1962	1963	1968	1961	1959	1977	1952				S	1952
171.04	Illicit Transfer			1977	1978	1972			1991					1976			1977	1972	1972		1978	1981	1973			1979	
171.05	World Heritage	1978		1981		1984		1978	1990	1975	1982			1978	1992	1984	1979	1974	1974	1977	1981	1976	1978		1988	1982	1985
172.01	Customs Facilities for Touring	1966			1969	1957		S		1957				1960	1958	1962			1961	1961			S			1959	1960
172.02	Protoc. Tourist Publicity Mat.	1968			1969	1957		S		1957				1960	1958	1962			1961	1961			S			1959	1960
172.03	Importation of Road Vehicles	1966			1969	1957		S		1957				1960	1958	1962			1961	1961			S			1959	1960
172.04	Taxation of Road Vehicles	1966													1959					1965							
172.05	Importation of Aircraft/Boats	1966			1969										1960												
172.06	Taxation of Passenger Vehicles														1986					1957							
172.07	World Tourism Org. (WTO)	1978		1976	1973	1970			1990	1971				1972	1976		D	1979	1971			1971	1971		1992	1974	D
172.08	Travel Contracts									S								S									S
180.01	Multimodal Transport of Goods					1982				S										S							
181.02	Carriage of Goods by Road														1960					1969							
181.03	Taxation of Goods Vehicles									1962					1986					1957							
181.04	Approval of Vehicle Equipment														1960					1975							
182.01	Technical Unity														MS					MS							
182.03	Goods Carried by Rail														1952					1952							
182.04	Passengers Carried by Rail														1952					1952							
182.05	Carriage by Rail (COTIF)							1989		1987					1982					1984							
183.01	Bills of Lading				1970			1931							D					D					1967	1964	
183.02	Shipowners' Liability							D												D							
183.03	Maritime Liens and Mortgages					S		1931							S					D							
183.04	Immunity of State-Owned Ships					S									1936					1939							
183.05	IMO	1966		1961	1978	1954		1989		1962	1979	1951		1979	1949	1960	1982		1962	1958	1974	1958	1958	1976	1993	1968	1964
183.06	Arrest of Sea-Going Ships							S		1990					1983		S		1963						1967		
183.07	Shipowners' Liability							1977							D					D				1980		S	
183.08	Carriage of Passengers By Sea									1965		S			S					S						1964	S
183.09	Load Lines	1974	1988	1967	1988	1970		1970		1968	1991	1987			1967	1970			1968	1968	1975	1968	1966	1976		1967	1969

Reference	AGREEMENT	Poland	Portugal	Qatar	Romania	Russia	Rwanda	Samoa	San Marino	São Tomé & Príncipe	Saudi Arabia	Senegal	Seychelles	Sierra Leone	Singapore	Slovak Republic	Slovenia	Solomon Islands	Somalia	South Africa	Spain	Sri Lanka	St Kitts & Nevis	St Lucia	St-Vincent-&-Grenadines	Sudan	Suriname	Swaziland	Sweden
001.01	United Nations Charter	1945	1955	1971	1955	1945	1962	1976	1992	1975	1945	1960	1976	1961	1965	1993	1992	1978	1960	1945	1955	1955	1983	1979	1980	1956	1975	1968	1946
001.02	ICJ: Compulsory Jurisdiction	1990	1955									1985							1963		1990					1958	1987	1969	1957
111.01	General Agreement (GATT)	1967	1962		1971		1966					1963		1961	1973	1993				1948	1963	1948		1993			1978	1993	1950
111.06	Multifibre Agreement 1991 Prot				1991										1991							1991							
111.07	Standardization Code		1985		1980		S								1980						1981								1980
111.08	Government Procurement Code														1981														1981
111.09	Subsidies Code		1984																		1982								1980
111.10	Import Licensing	1987			1980										1984					1980									1980
111.11	Antidumping Code	1981			1980										1984						1981								1980
111.12	Bovine Meat Arrangement	1982			1980															1980									1980
111.13	Dairy Agreement	1982			1980															1980									1980
111.14	Trade in Civil Aircraft		1986		1980																1986								1980
111.20	GSTP				1989										1989							1988				1991			
112.01	Simplif. Customs Formalities	1931	S		1925										1967			1981		1924	S								1926
112.02	Customs Co-operation (CCC)	1974	1953	1992	1969	1991	1964				1973	1976		1975	1975	1993	1992			1964	1952	1967				1960		1981	1952
112.03	Nomenclature		D				1965				D	D								D	D							D	D
112.04	Customs Valuation		D				1964					1978									D								D
112.05	Commercial Samples	1960	1956		1968		1964							1962	1966						1954	1959							1955
112.07	Containers	1959	1964		1967									1962				1981			1959								1959
112.08	Importation of Road Vehicles	1959	1967		1966									1962	1966						1958								1958
112.09	TIR Carnets (Geneva 1959)	1961	1966		1964	1974															1961								1959
112.10	Importation of Packings	1965	1990		1966											1993				1973	1965								1961
112.11	Fairs Convention	1969	1962		1964											1993				1971	1963	1981				1974			1964
112.12	Professonial Equipment	1969	1962		1968											1993				1971	1963	1991							1964
112.13	ATA Carnet	1969	1966		1967							1977			1983	1993				1975	1964	1981							1964
112.14	Material for Seafarers	S	1967		1967									1966						1965	1966								1966
112.15	Scientific Equipment	1971	1971		1970							1971			1969	1993		1982		1971	1971	1991							
112.16	Pedagogic Material	1972	1975				1970					1975							1971	1975	1972	1991							
112.18	Containers	1982			1975	1976															1975								
112.19	Kyoto Convention	1980	1982				1981				1985	1983				1993				1981	1979	1984							1976
112.20	TIR Carnets (Geneva 1975)	1980	1979		1980	1982											1992				1982								1976
112.21	Nairobi Convention										1985	1992										1984							1983
112.22	Customs Valuation Code	1990			1980															1983									1980
112.23	Frontier Controls of Goods		1987			1986											1992			1987	1984								1985
112.24	Harmonized System		1987				1992				1988	1989				1993				1987	1987	1988						1985	1987
112.25	Istanbul Convention		S																		S					S			
121.02	Common Fund for Commodities		1989			1987	1983	1984		1983	1983	1983		1982	1983				1984		1984	1981		S		1983	S	1988	1981
121.03	International Tin Agreement	1982																											1982
121.04	International Coffee Agreement		1983				1983							1983	1983						1983	1983							1983
121.05	International Cocoa Agreement		1987			1986		1987						1987							1987								1986
121.06	Int. Natural Rubber Agreement		S			1989															1988	1990							1988
122.01	Tropical Timber Agreement		1989			1985															1985								1984
122.02	Agreement on Olive Oil																												
122.03	Wheat Trade Convention		1989			1986														1986	1987								1986
122.04	Jute and Jute Products (1989)		S																		1991								1991
122.05	International Sugar Agreement																												1993
123.02	INSG					1990																							1986
123.03	ICSG	1991	1991																		1991								
123.04	ITSG		1991																										

		[illegible]	1948	1971	1961		1963	1979		1977	1948	1961	1977	1961				1985	1960	D	1951	1948	1983	1979	1981	1956	1975	1971	1950
131.04	IFAD		1978	1977	1977		1977	1977		1978	1977	1977	1978	1977				1981	1977		1978	1977	1986	1980	1990	1977	1983	1977	1977
132.01	WHO	1948	1948	1972	1948	1948	1962	1962	1980	1976	1947	1960	1979	1961	1966	1993	1992	1983	1961	1947	1951	1948	1984	1980	1983	1956	1976	1973	1947
141.01	ILO	1919	1919	1972	1956	1954	1962		1982	1982	1976	1960	1977	1961	1965	1993	1992	1984	1960	D	1956	1948		1980		1956	1976	1975	1919
141.03	White Lead in Painting	1924			1925	1991						1960					1992				1924						1976		1923
141.04	Women Convention (Revised)		D		1957		1962				1978	1962					1992			1950	D	D						1981	
141.05	Ionizing Radiations	1964				1967															1962	1986							1961
141.06	Benzene				1975												1992				1973								
141.07	Carcinogenic Substances																1992												1975
141.08	Protection of Workers		1981			1988			1988								1992				1980								1978
141.09	Working Environment		1985														1992				1985								1982
151.01	Industrial Devel. Org. (UNIDO)	1985	1984	1985	1980	1985	1983			1985	1985	1983	1982	1983		1993	1992		1981		1981	1981	1985	1982	1987	1981	1981	1981	1980
152.01	Metric Convention	1925	1875		1883	1875										1992				1964	1875								1875
152.04	Legal Metrology Organization	1957	1986		1956	1956										1992	1993				1957	1968							1958
160.01	WIPO	1975	1975	1976	1970	1970	1984		1991		1982	1970	1986		1990	1993	1991		1982	1975	1970	1978				1974	1975	1988	1970
161.01	Industrial Property (Paris)	1919	1884		1920	1965	1984		1960			1963				1993	1991			1947	1884	1952				1984	1975	1991	1885
161.02	False Indications of Source	1928	1893						1960							1993					1892	1952							1934
161.03	Registration of Marks	1991	1893		1920	1976			1960							1993	1991				1892					1984			
161.04	Deposit of Industrial Designs				1992							1984									1928						1975		
161.05	Classification for Marks		1961			1991										1993	1991				1961						1981		1961
161.06	Appellations of Origin		1966													1993													
161.07	Varieties of Plants (UPOV)	1989														1993				1977	1980								1971
161.08	Classification Indust. Designs					1991										1993	1991				1973								1971
161.09	Patent Cooperation (PCT)	1990	1992		1979	1991						1978				1993					1989	1982				1984			1978
161.10	Patent Classification		1979			1991										1993					1975						1975		1975
161.13	Deposit of Microorganisms					1991										1993					1981								1983
162.01	Literary Works (Berne)	1920	1911		1927		1984					1962				1993	1991			1928	1887	1959					1977		1904
162.02	Universal Copyright Conv.	1977	1956			1973	1988					1974				1993	1992				1955	1984			1985				1961
162.03	Phonograms (Rome)															T					1991								1964
162.04	Protection of Phonograms															T					1974								1973
162.05	Satellites (Brussels)					1989											1992												
162.07	Film Register Treaty															1993													
171.01	UNESCO Charter	1954	1974	1972	1956	1954	1962	1981	1974	1980	1946	1960	1976	1962	D	1993	1992		1960	D	1953	1949	1983	1980	1983	1956	1976	1978	1950
171.02	Beirut Agreement																1992												
171.03	Florence Agreement	1971	1984		1970		1964		1985					1962	1969		1992	1981			1955	1952							1952
171.04	Illicit Transfer	1974	1985	1977		1988					1976	1984				1993	1992				1986	1981							
171.05	World Heritage	1976	1980	1984	1990	1988			1991		1978	1976	1980			1993	1992	1992			1982	1980	1986	1991		1974			1985
172.01	Customs Facilities for Touring	1960	1958		1961	1959	1964					1972		1962	1966		1992	1981			1958	1955							1957
172.02	Protoc. Tourist Publicity Mat.	1960	1958		1961	1959	1964					1972		1962	1966			1981			1958								1957
172.03	Importation of Road Vehicles	1960	1958		1961	1959	1964					1972		1962	1966		1992	1981			1958	1955							1957
172.04	Taxation of Road Vehicles	1969			1967																								1958
172.05	Importation of Aircraft/Boats		1965											1962				1981			1958								1958
172.06	Taxation of Passenger Vehicles	1969			1968																								1958
172.07	World Tourism Org. (WTO)	1976	1976	D	1974	1975	1975		1971	1985		1972	1991	1974	D	1993					1974	1972				1975			
172.08	Travel Contracts		S						S																				
180.01	Multimodal Transport of Goods						1987					1984																	
181.02	Carriage of Goods by Road	1962	1969		1973	1983											1992				1974								1969
181.03	Taxation of Goods Vehicles	1969																											1958
181.04	Approval of Vehicle Equipment	1979	1980		1976	1986															1961								1959
182.01	Technical Unity	MS			MS																								MS
182.03	Goods Carried by Rail		1956																		1962								S
182.04	Passengers Carried by Rail		1956																										S
182.05	Carriage by Rail (COTIF)	1985	1986		1983												1992				1982								1985
183.01	Bills of Lading	1936	1931		1937							1978			1965			1978			1930								D
183.02	Shipowners' Liability	1936	1930		S																1930								D
183.03	Maritime Liens and Mortgages	1936	1931		1937																1930								D
183.04	Immunity of State-Owned Ships	1976	1938		D														1937		S						1936		1938
183.05	IMO	1960	1976	1977	1965	1958				1990	1969	1960	1978	1973	1966	1993	1993	1988	1978		1962	1972		1980	1981	1974	1976		1959
183.06	Arrest of Sea-Going Ships	1976	1957															1981			1953			1990					
183.07	Shipowners' Liability	1972	1968												1977			1981			1959								D
183.08	Carriage of Passengers By Sea	S	S		S	S															S								S
183.09	Load Lines	1969	1969	1980	1971	1966		1979			1975	1977	1976		1971		1991		1967	1966	1968	1974			1986	1991	1975		1967

Reference	AGREEMENT	Switzerland	Syrian Arab Republic	Taiwan	Tajikistan	Tanzania	Thailand	Togo	Tonga	Trinidad & Tobago	Tunisia	Turkey	Turkmenistan	Tuvalu	Uganda
001.01	United Nations Charter		1945		1992	1961	1946	1960		1962	1956	1945	1992		1962
001.02	ICJ: Compulsory Jurisdiction	1948						1979							1963
111.01	General Agreement (GATT)	1966				1961	1982	1964		1962	1990	1951			1962
111.06	Multifibre Agreement 1991 Prot	1992					1991					1991			
111.07	Standardization Code	1980									1981				
111.08	Government Procurement Code	1981													
111.09	Subsidies Code	1980										1985			
111.10	Import Licensing	1980													
111.11	Antidumping Code	1980													
111.12	Bovine Meat Arrangement	1980									1980				
111.13	Dairy Agreement	1980													
111.14	Trade in Civil Aircraft	1980													
111.20	GSTP					1989	1990			1989	1989				
112.01	Simplif. Customs Formalities	1927					1925		1977						
112.02	Customs Co-operation (CCC)	1952	1959			1964	1972	1990		1973	1966	1951			1964
112.03	Nomenclature	D				1970					D	D			1967
112.04	Customs Valuation					1977					D	D			1972
112.05	Commercial Samples	1954				1962			1977	1966		1956			1965
112.07	Containers	1960								1966					
112.08	Importation of Road Vehicles	1960													
112.09	TIR Carnets (Geneva 1959)	1960										1966			
112.10	Importation of Packings	1963										1965			1970
112.11	Fairs Convention	1963								1981	1972	1974			1989
112.12	Professonial Equipment	1963								1981	1972	1974			1989
112.13	ATA Carnet	1963								1981	1971	1974			
112.14	Material for Seafarers	1968	1975			1975					1965	1991			1967
112.15	Scientific Equipment	1973	1974				1970					1991			1989
112.16	Pedagogic Material	1973						1970			1971	1991			1989
112.18	Containers	1976								1990		S			
112.19	Kyoto Convention	1977													1989
112.20	TIR Carnets (Geneva 1975)	1978									1977	1984			
112.21	Nairobi Convention							1991			1983	1982			1989
112.22	Customs Valuation Code	1979										1989			
112.23	Frontier Controls of Goods	1986													
112.24	Harmonized System	1987	S				1991	1990			1987	1988			1989
112.25	Istanbul Convention	S										S			
121.02	Common Fund for Commodities	1982	1983			1982	1992	1984			1982	1990			1982
121.03	International Tin Agreement	1983					1982								
121.04	International Coffee Agreement	1983				1983	1983	1983		1983					1983
121.05	International Cocoa Agreement	1986						1987		1988					
121.06	Int. Natural Rubber Agreement	1989					1990								
122.01	Tropical Timber Agreement	1985					1985	1990		1986					
122.02	Agreement on Olive Oil										1986	1986			
122.03	Wheat Trade Convention	1987									1987	1987			
122.04	Jute and Jute Products (1989)	1990					1992								
122.05	International Sugar Agreement						1993								
123.02	INSG														
123.03	ICSG														
123.04	ITSG						1990								

Reference	AGREEMENT	Ukraine	United Arab Emirates	United Kingdom	United States	Uruguay	Uzbekistan	Vanuatu	Venezuela	Viet Nam	Yemen	Yugoslavia	Zaire	Zambia	Zimbabwe
001.01	United Nations Charter	1945	1971	1945	1945	1945	1992	1981	1945	1977	1947	1945	1960	1964	1980
001.02	ICJ: Compulsory Jurisdiction			1969		1921							1989		
111.01	General Agreement (GATT)			1948	1948	1953			1990			1966	1971	1982	1948
111.06	Multifibre Agreement 1991 Prot				1991	1992						1991			
111.07	Standardization Code			1980	1980							1982			
111.08	Government Procurement Code				1981										
111.09	Subsidies Code			1980	1980	1980						S			
111.10	Import Licensing				1980							1982			
111.11	Antidumping Code			1980	1980							1982			
111.12	Bovine Meat Arrangement				1980	1980						1982			
111.13	Dairy Agreement				D	1980									
111.14	Trade in Civil Aircraft			1980	1980										
111.20	GSTP									1988		1989			1988
112.01	Simplif. Customs Formalities			1924		S						1929			
112.02	Customs Co-operation (CCC)		1979	1952	1970	1977	1992					1960	1972	1978	1981
112.03	Nomenclature			D								D	1975		D
112.04	Customs Valuation			D								D	1975		
112.05	Commercial Samples			1955	1957							1956	1962		
112.07	Containers			1958	1968							1961			
112.08	Importation of Road Vehicles			1959								1961			
112.09	TIR Carnets (Geneva 1959)			1959	1968							1960			
112.10	Importation of Packings			1977								1962			1987
112.11	Fairs Convention			1963								1966			
112.12	Professonial Equipment			1963	1968							1963			1987
112.13	ATA Carnet			1963	1968							1963			
112.14	Material for Seafarers			1966								1966			
112.15	Scientific Equipment			1969											1986
112.16	Pedagogic Material														1987
112.18	Containers	1976			1984										
112.19	Kyoto Convention			1974	1983							1982	1977	1984	1988
112.20	TIR Carnets (Geneva 1975)			1982	1981	1980						1977			
112.21	Nairobi Convention			1983										1984	1982
112.22	Customs Valuation Code			1979	1980							1982			1987
112.23	Frontier Controls of Goods			1987								1985			
112.24	Harmonized System			1987	1988							1987	1987	1986	1986
112.25	Istanbul Convention			S											S
121.02	Common Fund for Commodities		1983	1981	S	S			1982		1986	1983	1983	1983	1983
121.03	International Tin Agreement			1982									1982		
121.04	International Coffee Agreement			1983	1983				1983			1983	1983	1985	1983
121.05	International Cocoa Agreement			1992					1987			1988			
121.06	Int. Natural Rubber Agreement			1988	1988										
122.01	Tropical Timber Agreement			1984	1985								1990		
122.02	Agreement on Olive Oil											1988			
122.03	Wheat Trade Convention			1989	1988						S				
122.04	Jute and Jute Products (1989)			1991	1990										
122.05	International Sugar Agreement														
123.02	INSG														
123.03	ICSG				1990										
123.04	ITSG														

TABLE

		[illegible]	[illegible]		1962	1947	1960	1981	1963	1955	1948			1963		1973	1945	1945	1945		1983	1945	1950	1953	1945	1961	1965	1981
131.04	IFAD	1977	1978		1977	1977	1979	1982	1988	1977	1977			1977		1977	1977	1977	1977			1977	1977	1977	1977	1977	1977	1981
132.01	WHO	1947	1946	1992	1962	1947	1960	1975	1963	1956	1948	1992		1963	1948	1972	1946	1948	1949	1992	1983	1948	1950	1953	1947	1961	1965	1980
141.01	ILO	1919	1947		1962	1919	1960		1963	1956	193 2			1963	1954	1972	1919	1980	1919	1992		1958	1992	1965	1951	1960	1964	1980
141.03	White Lead in Painting						1960			1956									1933			1933	1953		1929			
141.04	Women Convention (Revised)	D	1949							1957						1982			D				1965		1956	1960	1965	
141.05	Ionizing Radiations	1963	1964								1968				1968		1962		1992									
141.06	Benzene	1975	1977																1977						1975		1973	
141.07	Carcinogenic Substances	1976	1979																1980			1983			1977			
141.08	Protection of Workers				1983												1979		1988						1983		1980	
141.09	Working Environment																		1988			1984			1987			
151.01	Industrial Devel. Org. (UNIDO)	1981	1982		1980	1981	1981	1986	1980	1981	1982			1983	1985	1981	1983	1983	1980		1987	1983	1983	1982	1980	1982	1981	1985
152.01	Metric Convention	1875				1912					1933						1884	1875	1908			1960			1879			
152.04	Legal Metrology Organization	1956			1979					1960							1962	1972				D			1957			
160.01	WIPO	1970			1983	1989	1975		1988	1975	1976			1973	1970	1974	1970	1970	1979			1984	1976	1979	1973	1975	1977	1981
161.01	Industrial Property (Paris)	1884	1924		1963		1967		1964	1884	1925			1965	1991		1884	1887	1967				1949		1921	1975	1965	1980
161.02	False Indications of Source	1892	1924							1892	1930						1892											
161.03	Registration of Marks	1892													1991								1949		1921			
161.04	Deposit of Industrial Designs	1928								1930																		
161.05	Classification for Marks	1962								1967							1963	1972							1966			
161.06	Appellations of Origin						1975			1973																		
161.07	Varieties of Plants (UPOV)	1977															1968	1981										
161.08	Classification Indust. Designs	1971																							1973			
161.09	Patent Cooperation (PCT)	1978					1978								1991		1978	1978					1993					
161.10	Patent Classification	1975															1975	1975										
161.13	Deposit of Microorganisms	1981															1980	1980										
162.01	Literary Works (Berne)	1887				1931	1975		1988	1887	1952						1887	1989	1967			1982			1930	1963	1992	1980
162.02	Universal Copyright Conv.	1956							1988	1969							1957	1955	1993			1966			1966		1965	
162.03	Phonograms (Rome)																1964		1977									
162.04	Protection of Phonograms								1988								1973	1974	1983			1982				1977		
162.05	Satellites (Brussels)																	1985							1979			
162.07	Film Register Treaty																											
171.01	UNESCO Charter	1949	1946	1993	1962	1949	1960	1980	1962	1956	1946		1991	1962	1954	1972	D	D	1947			1946	1951	1962	1950	1960	1964	1980
171.02	Beirut Agreement		1951						1965									1966	S						1950			
171.03	Florence Agreement	1953	1980		1963	1951		1977	1966	1971				1965			1954	1966	S			1992	1952		1951	1962	1974	
171.04	Illicit Transfer		1975	1992	1977					1975	1981				1988			1983	1977						1972	1974	1985	
171.05	World Heritage	1975	1975	1992	1977	1987				1975	1983			1987	1988		1984	1973	1989	1992		1990	1987	1980	1975	1974	1984	1982
172.01	Customs Facilities for Touring	1956	1959		1964			1977	1966	1974	1983			1965			1956	1956	1967						1958			
172.02	Protoc. Tourist Publicity Mat.	1956	1959		1964			1977	1966	1974	1983			1965			1956		S						1958			
172.03	Importation of Road Vehicles	1956	1959		1962			1977	1966	1974	1983			1965			1956	1956	S						1958			
172.04	Taxation of Road Vehicles																1963								1960			
172.05	Importation of Aircraft/Boats	1960							1966								1958								1960			
172.06	Taxation of Passenger Vehicles																1963								1959			
172.07	World Tourism Org. (WTO)	1976	1971		1972	1971	1975		D	1972	1973			1974		1972		1975	1977			1974	1981	1971	1971	1972	1973	1981
172.08	Travel Contracts						1975																					
180.01	Multimodal Transport of Goods																					S					1991	
181.02	Carriage of Goods by Road	1970															1967								1958			
181.03	Taxation of Goods Vehicles																1969								1959			
181.04	Approval of Vehicle Equipment	1973															1963								1962			
182.01	Technical Unity	MS									MS														MS			
182.03	Goods Carried by Rail	1957																										
182.04	Passengers Carried by Rail	1957																										
182.05	Carriage by Rail (COTIF)	1983	1985							1984	1985						1983								1982			
183.01	Bills of Lading	1954	1974		1962			1978			1955						D	1937							1959	1967		
183.02	Shipowners' Liability										1955						S											
183.03	Maritime Liens and Mortgages	1954	1951								1955						S		1970							1967		
183.04	Immunity of State-Owned Ships	1954	1960								1955					1960	1979		1970						S	1967		
183.05	IMO	1955	1963		1974	1973	1983		1965	1963	1958					1980	1949	1950	1968		1986	1975	1984	1979	1960	1973		
183.06	Arrest of Sea-Going Ships	1954	1972				1973	1978									1959								1967	1967		
183.07	Shipowners' Liability	1966	1972					1978									D								S	1967		
183.08	Carriage of Passengers By Sea	1966								1974	S					1964									S	1967		
183.09	Load Lines	1968	1975		1989	1992	1989	1977	1966	1966	1968		1985			1983	1967	1966	1977		1982	1974	1990	1979	1968	1968	1970	

Reference	AGREEMENT	DATE OF AGREEMENT	ENTRY INTO FORCE	No. of countries	Afghanistan	Albania	Algeria	Angola	Antigua & Barbuda	Argentina	Armenia	Australia	Austria	Azerbaijan	Bahamas	Bahrain	Bangladesh	Barbados	Belarus	Belgium	Belize	Benin	Bhutan	Bolivia	Bosnia	Botswana	Brazil
183.10	Facilitation of Traffic (FAL)	09.04.1965	05.03.1967	68			1983			1980		1986	1975		1976			1982		1967		1990					1977
183.12	Vessels under Construction	27.05.1967		5						S										S							
183.13	Maritime Liens and Mortgages	27.05.1967		5									S							S							
183.14	Safe Containers (CSC)	02.12.1972	06.09.1977	56	1987					1979		1980	1986		1979			1982	1976	1981		1985					1992
183.15	Code for Liner Conferences	06.04.1974	06.10.1983	74			1986										1975	1980		1987		1975					S
183.16	Safety of Life at Sea (1974)	01.11.1974	25.05.1980	120	1980		1983	1991	1987	1979		1983	1988		1979	1985	1981	1982	S	1979	1991	1985					1980
183.17	Carriage of Passengers by Sea	13.12.1974	28.04.1987	16						1983					1983					1989							
183.18	Liability Maritime Claims	19.11.1976	01.12.1986	22								1991			1983					1989		1985					
183.19	Safety of Fishing Vessels	02.04.1977		18						1983										1982		1985					
183.20	Hamburg Rules	31.03.1978	01.11.1992	19									S					1981								1988	S
183.21	Registration of Ships	07.02.1986		8			S																	S			
183.22	Suppression of Unlawful Acts	10.03.1988	01.03.1992	19								1993	1988														
183.23	Salvage Conv.	28.04.1989		7																							
184.01	Warsaw Convention	12.10.1929	13.02.1933	123	1969		1964			1952		1935	1961		1975		1979	1970	1959	1936		1962				1977	1931
184.02	Chicago Convention -ICAO	07.12.1944	04.04.1947	178	1947	1991	1963	1977	1981	1946	1992	1947	1948	1992	1975	1971	1972	1967		1947	1990	1961	1989	1947	1993	1978	1946
184.03	Air Transit	07.12.1944	30.01.1945	99	1945		1964			1946		1945	1958		1975	1971	1979	1970		1945		1963		1947			
184.04	Rights in Aircraft	19.06.1948	17.09.1953	56			1964			1958		S					1988			S							1953
184.05	Damage to Third Parties	07.10.1952	04.02.1958	38			1964			1972		1958								1966							1962
184.06	Carriage by Air (Guadalajara)	18.09.1961	01.05.1964	66								1962	1965		1975				1983	1969							1967
185.01	Return of Astronauts	22.04.1968	03.12.1968	80					1988	1969		1986	1970		1976			1969	1968	1977				S		1969	1973
185.02	Liability Space Objects	29.03.1972	01.09.1972	75			S		1988	1986		1975	1980						1973	1976		1975				1974	1973
185.03	Registration of Space Objects	12.11.1974	15.09.1976	36					1988	S		1986	1980						1978	1977							
191.01	Universal Postal Union (UPU)	10.07.1964	01.01.1966	183	1969	1968	1968	1977		1967	1992	1965	1965	1993	1974	1973	1972	1967	1978	1965	1982	1967	1968	1972	1993	1967	1969
192.02	Telecommunications (Nairobi)	06.11.1982	01.01.1984	177	1984	1984	1986	1989	1987	1987	1992	1984	1989	1992	1988	1984	1989	1986	1986	1986	1985	1986	1988	1984	1992	1986	1990
193.01	INTELSAT	20.08.1971	12.02.1973	125	1973		1972	1977		1972		1971	1972	1992	1985		1976	1973		1972		1987	1992	1974			1972
193.02	Intersputnik	15.11.1971	12.07.1972	18	1981														1993								
193.03	INMARSAT	03.09.1976	16.07.1979	66			1979			1979		1979				1986			1979	1979							1979
211.01	International Monetary Fund (IMF)	22.07.1945	27.12.1945	174	1955	1991	1953	1989	1982	1956	1992	1947	1948	1992	1973	1972	1972	1970	1992	1945	1982	1963	1981	1945		1968	1946
212.01	BIS	20.01.1930	27.02.1930	7																1930							
221.01	World Bank -IBRD	22.07.1944	27.12.1945	174	1955	1991	1963	1989	1983	1956	1992	1947	1948	1992	1973	1972	1972	1974	1992	1945	1982	1963	1981	1945		1968	1946
221.02	IFC	25.05.1955	20.07.1956	154	1957	1991	1990	1989	1987	1959		1955	1956		1986		1976	1980	1992	1956	1982	1987		1956		1979	1956
221.03	IDA	26.01.1960	24.09.1960	150	1961	1991	1963	1989		1962		1960	1961							1964	1982	1963	1981	1961		1968	1963
221.04	MIGA	11.10.1985	12.04.1988	102		1991		1989		1990	R			1992		1986	1987	1986	1992	1992	1992	S		1991		1989	1993
231	G-5 G-7 and G-10 Members			11																G-10							
233	G-77 and G-24			129	G-77		G-24	G-77	G-77	G-24					G-77	G-77	G-77	G-77			G-77	G-77	G-77	G-77		G-77	G-24
300.02	UNIDROIT (Private Law)	15.03.1940	21.04.1940	55						1972		1973	1948							1940				1940			1983
300.03	HCOPIL (Int. Private Law)	31.10.1955	15.07.1955	38						1972		1973	1954							1953							D
311.01	International Sale of Goods	01.07.1964	18.08.1972	6																1968							
311.02	Formation of Contracts	01.07.1964	23.08.1972	6																1970							
311.03	Limitation Period	14.06.1974	01.08.1988	12						1981									S								S
311.04	International Sale of Goods	11.04.1980	01.01.1988	33						1983		1988	1987						1989								
311.05	Agency	15.02.1983		4																							
312.01	Sales of Goods	15.06.1955	01.09.1964	9																1962							
312.04	Products Liability	02.10.1973	01.10.1977	6																S							
312.05	Law Applicable to Agency	14.03.1978	01.05.1992	4						1992																	
312.06	Law Applicable to Trusts	01.07.1985		3								1991															
321.01	Uniform Law Bills of Exchange	07.06.1930	01.01.1934	20									1932							1932							1942
321.02	Confl. Laws Bills of Exchange	07.06.1930	01.01.1934	20									1932							1932							1942
321.03	Stamp Laws Bills of Exchange	07.06.1930	01.01.1934	30								1938	1932		1976					1932							1942

TABLE

[illegible]	[illegible]	[illegible]	[illegible]	21									1958							1961						1942
321.05	Conflicts of Laws Cheques	19.03.1931	01.01.1934	21									1958							1961						1942
321.06	Stamp Laws Cheques	19.03.1931	29.11.1933	31								1938	1958		1976					1961						1942
321.07	Bills of Exchange; Prom. Notes	09.12.1988		2																						
332.01	Civil Procedure	01.03.1954	12.04.1957	30						1988			1956							1958						
332.02	Service of Judicial Documents	15.11.1965	10.02.1969	28														1969		1970					1969	
332.03	Taking of Evidence Abroad	18.03.1970	07.10.1972	21						1987		1992						1981								
332.04	Access to Justice	25.10.1980	01.05.1988	8																						
341.01	Protocol Arbitration Clauses	24.09.1923	28.07.1924	34		1924			1988				1928		1977		1979			1924				S		1932
341.02	Exec. Foreign Arbitral Awards	26.09.1927	25.07.1929	29					1988				1930		1977		1979			1929				S		
341.03	Enforcement of Arbitral Awards	10.06.1958	07.06.1959	89			1989		1989	1989		1975	1961			1988	1992	1993	1960	1975		1974			1971	
341.04	Europ. Conv. Int. Arbitration	21.04.1961	07.01.1964	21									1964						1963	1975						
341.05	Arrang. Eur. Conv. Arbitration	17.12.1962	25.01.1965	7									1964							1975						
342.01	Settlement of Int. Disputes	29.07.1899	04.09.1900	65						1907		1960	1900						1962	1900				1907		1907
342.02	Permanent Court of Arbitration	18.10.1907	26.01.1910	55									1910						1962	1910				1910		1914
342.05	Investment Disputes - ICSID	18.03.1965	14.10.1966	107	1968	1991				S	1992	1991	1971	1992			1980	1983	1992	1970	S	1966		S	1970	
411.01	Preservation Fauna and Flora	08.11.1933	14.01.1936	10																1935						
411.02	Regulation of Whaling	02.12.1946	10.11.1948	41					1982	1960		1947									D					1974
411.03	Protection of Birds	18.10.1950	17.01.1963	10									S							1955						
411.04	Plant Protection	06.12.1951	03.04.1952	96			1985			1954		1952	1952			1971	1978	1976		1952	1987			1960		1961
411.05	Wetlands	02.02.1971	21.12.1975	75			1983			1992		1974	1982				1992			1986				1990		
411.06	Fauna and Flora (CITES)	03.03.1973	01.07.1975	119	1985		1983			1981		1976	1982		1979		1981	1992		1983	1986	1984		1979	1977	1975
411.07	Migratory Species	23.06.1979	01.11.1983	35																1990		1986				
411.08	Biological Diversity	05.06.1992		15	S		S	S	1993	S	S	S	S	S	S	S	S	S	S	S	S	S	S	S	S	S
412.01	Prevention of Pollution (Oil)	12.05.1954	26.07.1958	69			1964			1976		D	1975		1976	1985	1981			1957						
412.03	Intervention High Seas (Oil)	29.11.1969	06.05.1975	60						1987		1983			1976		1981			1971		1985				S
412.04	Civil Liability Oil Pollution	29.11.1969	19.06.1975	79			1974					D			1976					1977	1991	1985				1976
412.06	Oil Pollution Fund (FUND)	18.12.1971	16.10.1978	56			1975								1976					S		1985				S
412.07	Dumping of Wastes	29.12.1972	30.08.1975	71	1975				1989	1979		1985							1976	1985						1982
412.09	Pollution (MARPOL 73/78)	02.11.1973	02.10.1983	77			1989		1988			1987	1988		1983					1984						1988
412.11	OPRC	30.11.1990		6								1992														
413.01	Transboundary Air Pollution	13.11.1979	16.03.1983	33									1982						1980	1982						
413.02	Protection of Ozone Layer	22.03.1985	22.09.1988	119			1992		1992	1990		1987	1987		1993	1990	1990	1992	1986	1988					1991	1990
413.03	Reduction of Sulphur Emissions	08.07.1985	02.09.1987	19									1987						1986	1989						
413.04	Montreal Protocol	16.09.1987	01.01.1989	111			1992		1992	1990		1989	1989			1990	1990	1992	1988	1988					1991	1990
413.05	Emissions of Nitrogen Oxides	13.10.1988	14.02.1991	18									1990						1989							
413.07	Climate Change	09.05.1992		17	S		S	S	1993	S	S	1992	S	S	S	S	S	S	S	S	S	S	S	S	S	S
414.01	Environment. Impact Assessment	25.02.1991		3		1991							S						S	S						
421.01	IAEA	26.10.1956	29.07.1957	114	1957	1957	1963			1957		1957	1957				1972		1957	1958				1963		1957
421.02	Nuclear Liability (Paris)	29.07.1960	01.04.1968	14									S							1966						
421.03	Liability Nuclear Ships	25.05.1962		7																S						
421.04	Nuclear Liability (Brussels)	31.01.1963	04.12.1974	11									S							1985						
421.05	Nuclear Liability (Vienna)	21.05.1963	12.11.1977	19						1967														1968		1993
421.06	Non-Proliferation (NPT)	01.07.1968	05.03.1970	155	1970	1990			1985			1973	1969		1976	1988	1979	1980		1975	1985	1972	1985	1970	1969	
421.07	Carriage of Nuclear Material	17.12.1971	15.07.1975	14						1981										1989						S
421.08	London Club	21.09.1975	11.01.1978	23								1978								1976						
421.09	Protection of Nuclear Material	03.03.1980	08.02.1987	43						1989		1987	1988							1991						1985
421.10	Early Notif. Nuclear Accident	26.09.1986	27.10.1986	65	S		S			1990		1987	1988				1988		1987	S						1990
421.11	Assistance Nuclear Accident	26.09.1986	26.02.1987	63	S		S			1990		1987	1989				1988		1987	S						1990
421.12	Joint Protocol Vienna-Paris	21.09.1988	27.04.1992	11						S										S						
422.03	Movements of Hazardous Wastes	22.03.1989	05.05.1992	43	S				1993	1991		1992	1993		1992	1992	1993			S				S		1992
431.01	WMO	11.10.1947	23.03.1950	164	1956	1957	1963	1977	1988	1951	1992	1949	1955		1973	1980	1973	1967	1948	1951	1982	1961		1954	1967	1950
432.01	Convention on the High Seas	29.04.1958	30.09.1962	60	1959	1964				S		1963	1974						1961	1972				S		
432.02	Continental Shelf	29.04.1958	10.06.1964	55	S					S		1963							1961					S		
432.03	Territorial Sea	29.04.1958	10.09.1964	50	S					S		1963	S						1961	1972				S		
432.04	Fishing/Living Res.: High Seas	29.04.1958	20.03.1966	36	S					S		1963								1972				S		
432.05	Prot. Settlement of Disputes	29.04.1958	30.09.1962	36								1963	S							1972				1958		
432.06	Exploration of the Sea (ICES)	12.09.1964	22.07.1968	17																1967						
432.07	Law of the Sea	10.12.1982		55	S		S	1990	1989	S		S	S		1983	1985	S	S	S	S	1983	S	S	S	1990	1988
433.01	Antarctic Treaty	01.12.1959	23.06.1961	40						1961		1961	1987							1960						1975
433.02	CCAMLR (Antarctica)	20.05.1980	07.04.1982	27						1982		1981								1984						1986
434.01	Use of Outer Space	27.01.1967	10.10.1967	88	1988		1992		1988	1969		1967	1968		1976		1986	1968	1967	1973		1986		S	S	1969
434.02	Activities on the Moon	05.12.1979	11.07.1984	9								1986	1984													

Reference	AGREEMENT	Brunei Darussalam	Bulgaria	Burkina Faso	Burundi	Cambodia	Cameroon	Canada	Cape Verde	Central Africa	Chad	Chile	China	Colombia	Comoros	Congo	Cook Islands	Costa Rica	Côte d'Ivoire	Croatia	Cuba	Cyprus	Czech Republic	Denmark	Djibouti	Dominica	Dominican Rep.	Ecuador	Egypt
183.10	Facilitation of Traffic (FAL)							1967	1977			1975		1991					1967	1991	1984			1968			1966	1988	1987
183.12	Vessels under Construction												S											S					S
183.13	Maritime Liens and Mortgages												S											1977					S
183.14	Safe Containers (CSC)		1976					1981				1980	1980							1991	1983			1979					
183.15	Code for Liner Conferences		1979	1989			1976		1978	1977		1975	1980			1982		1978	1977		1976			1985				S	1979
183.16	Safety of Life at Sea (1974)	1986	1983				1984	1978	1977			1980	1980	1980		1985			1987	1991	1992	1985		1978	1984		1980	1982	1981
183.17	Carriage of Passengers by Sea																												1991
183.18	Liability Maritime Claims																			1993				1984					1988
183.19	Safety of Fishing Vessels											1985																	
183.20	Hamburg Rules			1989								1982												S				S	1979
183.21	Registration of Ships						S												1987										1992
183.22	Suppression of Unlawful Acts												1991																1993
183.23	Salvage Conv.																												1991
184.01	Warsaw Convention	1984	1949	1961			1961	1947				1979	1958	1966	1991	1962		1984	1962		1964	1963		1937			1972	1969	1955
184.02	Chicago Convention -ICAO	1984	1967	1962	1968	1956	1960	1946	1976	1961	1962	1947	1946	1947	1985	1962	1986	1958	1960	1992	1949	1961	1993	1947	1978		1946	1954	1947
184.03	Air Transit	1984	1970	1992	1968		1960	D				1974						1958	1961		1947	1961		1948				1983	1947
184.04	Rights in Aircraft						1969			1969	1974	1955	S	S		1982			1965		1961			1963			S	1958	1969
184.05	Damage to Third Parties						1969														1965			S			S	1958	1954
184.06	Carriage by Air (Guadalajara)			1992							1971			1966							S	1970		1967					1964
185.01	Return of Astronauts		1969				1969	1975				1981	1988	S				S			1984	1971		1969			S	1969	1968
185.02	Liability Space Objects		1972		S	S		1975		S		1976	1988	S				S			1982	1973		1977			1973	1972	S
185.03	Registration of Space Objects		1976		S			1976				1981	1988								1978	1978	1993	1977					
191.01	Universal Postal Union (UPU)	1985	1969	1967	1969	1969	1968	1966	1976	1968	1972	1972	1973	1976	1976	1966		1981	1965	1992	1969	1969	1993	1965	1978	1979	M	1969	1967
192.02	Telecommunications (Nairobi)	1984	1986	1986	1988	M	1986	1983	1989	1988	1984	1985	1985	1985	M	1988		M	1986	1992	1986	1986	1993	1985	1987		M	1988	1985
193.01	INTELSAT			1977	S		1973	1971	1991	1973	1977	1972	1977	1974		1977		1972	1972	1992		1974	1993	1972			1971	1972	1973
193.02	Intersputnik		1972																		1972		1993						
193.03	INMARSAT		1979				1990	1979				1981	1979	1987						1992	1989	1992		1979					1977
211.01	International Monetary Fund (IMF)		1990	1963	1963	1969	1963	1945	1978	1963	1963	1945	1945	1945	1976	1963		1946	1963	1992	D	1961	1993	1946	1978	1978	1945	1945	1945
212.01	BIS																												
221.01	World Bank -IBRD		1990	1963	1963	1970	1963	1945	1978	1963	1963	1945	1945	1946	1976	1963		1946	1963	1993	D	1961	1993	1946	1980	1980	1961	1945	1945
221.02	IFC		1991	1975	1979		1974	1955	1990	1991		1957	1969	1956	1992	1980		1956	1963	1993	D	1962	1993	1956	1980	1980	1961	1955	1955
221.03	IDA			1963	1963	1970	1964	1960	1978	1963	1963	1960	1960	1961	1977	1963		1961	1963	1993		1962	1993	1960	1980	1980	1962	1961	1960
221.04	MIGA		1992	1988			1988	1987				1988	1988	S		1990		S	1988			1987	1993	1987		1991		1986	1987
231	G-5 G-7 and G-10 Members							G-7																					
233	G-77 and G-24	G-77		G-77	G-77	G-77	G-77		G-77	G-77	G-77	G-77		G-24	G-77	G-77		G-77	G-24		G-77	G-77			G-77	G-77	G-77	G-77	G-24
300.02	UNIDROIT (Private Law)		1940					1968				1982	1985	1940							1940		1993	1940				D	1951
300.03	HCOPIL (Int. Private Law)							1968				1986	1987									1984		1954					1961
311.01	International Sale of Goods																												
311.02	Formation of Contracts																												
311.03	Limitation Period		S															S									1977		1982
311.04	International Sale of Goods		1990					1991				1990	1986											1989				1992	1982
311.05	Agency											S																	
312.01	Sales of Goods																							1964					
312.04	Products Liability																												
312.05	Law Applicable to Agency																												
312.06	Law Applicable to Trusts							S																					
321.01	Uniform Law Bills of Exchange													S										1932				S	
321.02	Confl. Laws Bills of Exchange													S										1932				S	
321.03	Stamp Laws Bills of Exchange													S								1968		1932				S	

TABLE

																								1932				S	
321.05	Conflicts of Laws Cheques																							1932				S	
321.06	Stamp Laws Cheques																					1968		1932				S	
321.07	Bills of Exchange; Prom. Notes							S																					
332.01	Civil Procedure																						1993	1958					
332.02	Service of Judicial Documents							1989					1991									1983	1993	1969					1968
332.03	Taking of Evidence Abroad																					1983		1972					
332.04	Access to Justice																												
341.01	Protocol Arbitration Clauses											S												1925					
341.02	Exec. Foreign Arbitral Awards																							1929					
341.03	Enforcement of Arbitral Awards		1961	1987		1960	1988	1986		1962		1975	1987	1979				1987	1991		1974	1980		1972	1983	1988		1962	1959
341.04	Europ. Conv. Int. Arbitration		1964	1965																1992	1965			1972					
341.05	Arrang. Eur. Conv. Arbitration																							1973					
342.01	Settlement of Int. Disputes		1900	1961		1956	1961	1960				1907	1904	1907							1907			1900			1907	1907	
342.02	Permanent Court of Arbitration			1961		1956	1961						1910								1912			1910			1958		1968
342.05	Investment Disputes - ICSID			1966	1969		1967			1966	1966	1991	1993		1978	1966		S	1966			1966	1993	1968				1986	1972
411.01	Preservation Fauna and Flora																												1935
411.02	Regulation of Whaling							D				1979	1980					1981						1950		1992			D
411.03	Protection of Birds		S																										
411.04	Plant Protection					1952		1953	1982			1952		1970				1973			1976			1953			1952	1956	1953
411.05	Wetlands		1975	1990				1981			1990	1981	1992					1991		1992			1993	1977				1990	1988
411.06	Fauna and Flora (CITES)	1990	1991	1989	1988		1981	1975		1980	1989	1975	1981	1981		1983		1975			1990	1974	1993	1977	1992		1986	1975	1978
411.07	Migratory Species			1990			1983					1983												1983					1983
411.08	Biological Diversity		S	S	S		S	1992	S	S	S	S	1993	S	S	S	S	S	S	S	S	S		S	S		S	1993	S
412.01	Prevention of Pollution (Oil)		D					1956				1977				1985			1967			1980		1956	1984		1963		1963
412.03	Intervention High Seas (Oil)		1983				1984						1990						1988	1991	1976			1970	1990		1975	1976	1989
412.04	Civil Liability Oil Pollution	1992					1984	1989				1977	1980	1990					1973	1991		1989		1975	1990		1975	1976	1989
412.06	Oil Pollution Fund (FUND)	1992					1984	1989											1987	1991		1989		1975	1990				
412.07	Dumping of Wastes							1975	1977			1977	1985					1986	1989	1992	1975	1990		1974			1973		1992
412.09	Pollution (MARPOL 73/78)	1986	1984					1992					1983	1981					1987	1991	1992	1989		1980	1990			1990	1986
412.11	OPRC																												1992
413.01	Transboundary Air Pollution		1981					1981												1992		1991		1982					
413.02	Protection of Ozone Layer	1990	1990	1989			1989	1986		1993	1989	1990	1989	1990				1991	1993	1992	1992	1992		1988			1993	1990	1988
413.03	Reduction of Sulphur Emissions		1986					1985																1986					
413.04	Montreal Protocol		1990	1989			1989	1988		1993		1990	1991			S		1991	1993	1992	1992	1992		1988		1993		1990	1988
413.05	Emissions of Nitrogen Oxides		1989					1991																					
413.07	Climate Change		S	S	S		S	1992	S	S	S	S	1993	S	S	S	S	S	S	S	S	S		S	S		S	1993	S
414.01	Environment. Impact Assessment		S					S																S					
421.01	IAEA		1957			1958	1964	1957				1960	1984	1960				1965	1963	1993	1957	1965		1957			1957	1958	1957
421.02	Nuclear Liability (Paris)																							1974					
421.03	Liability Nuclear Ships												S																
421.04	Nuclear Liability (Brussels)																							1974					
421.05	Nuclear Liability (Vienna)						1964					1989		S						1992	1965								1965
421.06	Non-Proliferation (NPT)	1985	1969	1970	1971	1972	1969	1969	1979	1970	1971		1992	1986		1978		1970	1973			1970	1993	1969		1984	1971	1969	1981
421.07	Carriage of Nuclear Material																							1974					
421.08	London Club		1984					1975																1984					
421.09	Protection of Nuclear Material		1984					1986					1989							1992				1991				S	
421.10	Early Notif. Nuclear Accident		1988				S	1990				S	1987					1991	S	1992	1991	1989		1986					1988
421.11	Assistance Nuclear Accident		1988				S	S				S	1987					1991	S	1992	1991	1989		S					1988
421.12	Joint Protocol Vienna-Paris						1991					1989												1989					1989
422.03	Movements of Hazardous Wastes							1992				1992	1991	S								1992		S				1993	1993
431.01	WMO	1984	1952	1960	1962	1955	1960	1950	1975	1961	1961	1957	1973	1962	1976	1960		1960	1960	1992	1952	1963	1993	1951	1978	1980	1949	1951	1950
432.01	Convention on the High Seas		1962	1965		1960		S		1962				S				1972		1992	S	1988	1993	1968			1964		
432.02	Continental Shelf		1962			1960		1970				S	1970	1962				1972		1992	S	1974	1993	1963			1964	S	
432.03	Territorial Sea		1962			1960		S						S				S		1992	S		1993	1968			1964		
432.04	Fishing/Living Res.: High Seas			1965		1960		S					S	1963				S			S			1968			1964		
432.05	Prot. Settlement of Disputes					S		S						1958				1958			1958			1968			1958		
432.06	Exploration of the Sea (ICES)							1968																1965					
432.07	Law of the Sea	S	S	S	S	1989	1985	S	1987	S	S	S	S	S	S	S	S	1992	1984		1984	1988	1993	S	1991	1991	S		1983
433.01	Antarctic Treaty		1978					1988				1961	1983	1989							1984			1965				1987	
433.02	CCAMLR (Antarctica)							1988				1981																	
434.01	Use of Outer Space		1967	1968	S		S	1967		S		1981	1983	S							1977	1972		1967			1968	1969	1967
434.02	Activities on the Moon											1981																	

Reference	AGREEMENT	El Salvador	Equatorial Guinea	Estonia	Ethiopia	European Communities	Fiji	Finland	France	Gabon	Gambia	Georgia	Germany	Ghana	Greece
183.10	Facilitation of Traffic (FAL)						1972	1967	1967		1991		1967	1965	1972
183.12	Vessels under Construction							S					S		1974
183.13	Maritime Liens and Mortgages							S					S		S
183.14	Safe Containers (CSC)			1992					1974				1976		1988
183.15	Code for Liner Conferences				1978			1985	1985	1978	1975		1983	1975	
183.16	Safety of Life at Sea (1974)			1991	1985		1983	1980	1977	1982	1991		1979	1983	1980
183.17	Carriage of Passengers by Sea												S		1991
183.18	Liability Maritime Claims							1984	1981				1987		1991
183.19	Safety of Fishing Vessels								1979				1983		
183.20	Hamburg Rules							S	S				S	S	
183.21	Registration of Ships													1990	
183.22	Suppression of Unlawful Acts								1991		1991		1990		
183.23	Salvage Conv.														
184.01	Warsaw Convention		1988		1950		1972	1937	1932	1969			1933		1938
184.02	Chicago Convention -ICAO	1947	1972	1992	1947		1973	1949	1947	1962	1977		1956	1957	1947
184.03	Air Transit	1945			1945		1973	1957	1948	1970			1956		1945
184.04	Rights in Aircraft	1958			1979				1964	1970			1959		1971
184.05	Damage to Third Parties	1980							S	1970					S
184.06	Carriage by Air (Guadalajara)	1980					1972	1977	1964	1971			1964		1973
185.01	Return of Astronauts	1970					1972	1970	1975	1969	1968		1972	1975	S
185.02	Liability Space Objects	S					1973	1977	1975	1982	S		1975	S	1977
185.03	Registration of Space Objects								1975				1979		
191.01	Universal Postal Union (UPU)	1978	1970	1992	1969		1971	1965	1965	1967	1974	1993	1966	1966	1968
192.02	Telecommunications (Nairobi)	1985	1986	1992	1984		1986	1986	1984	1988	1989	1993	1985	1987	1985
193.01	INTELSAT	1977			1972		1978	1973	1972	1972			1973	1973	1972
193.02	Intersputnik												1972		
193.03	INMARSAT							1979	1979	1984			1979		1979
211.01	International Monetary Fund (IMF)	1946	1969	1992	1945		1971	1948	1945	1963	1967	1992	1952	1957	1945
212.01	BIS								1930				1930		
221.01	World Bank -IBRD	1946	1970	1992	1945		1971	1948	1945	1963	1967	1992	1952	1957	1945
221.02	IFC	1956	1992		1956		1979	1956	1956	1970	1983		1956	1958	1957
221.03	IDA	1962	1972		1961		1972	1960	1960	1963	1967		1960	1960	1962
221.04	MIGA	1991	R	1992	1991			1988	1989		1991	1992	1987	1988	R
231	G-5 G-7 and G-10 Members					G-7			G-5				G-5		
233	G-77 and G-24	G-77	G-77		G-24		G-77			G-77	G-77			G-24	
300.02	UNIDROIT (Private Law)							1940	1948				1940		1940
300.03	HCOPIL (Int. Private Law)							1955	1964				1955		1955
311.01	International Sale of Goods								S		1974		D		S
311.02	Formation of Contracts								S		1974		D		S
311.03	Limitation Period													1975	
311.04	International Sale of Goods							1987	1982				1989	1991	
311.05	Agency								1987						
312.01	Sales of Goods							1964	1963						
312.04	Products Liability								1977						
312.05	Law Applicable to Agency								1985						
312.06	Law Applicable to Trusts								S						
321.01	Uniform Law Bills of Exchange							1932	1936				1933		1931
321.02	Confl. Laws Bills of Exchange							1932	1936				1933		1931
321.03	Stamp Laws Bills of Exchange						1971	1932	1936				1933		

Reference	AGREEMENT	Grenada	Guatemala	Guinea	Guinea-Bissau	Guyana	Haiti	Holy See	Honduras	Hong Kong	Hungary	Iceland	India	Indonesia	Iraq
183.10	Facilitation of Traffic (FAL)			1981							1976	1967	1976		1976
183.12	Vessels under Construction							S					S		
183.13	Maritime Liens and Mortgages							S					S		
183.14	Safe Containers (CSC)			1981					1985		1974		1978	1989	
183.15	Code for Liner Conferences		1976	1980		1980			1979				1978	1977	1978
183.16	Safety of Life at Sea (1974)		1982	1981			1989		1985		1980	1983	1976	1981	1990
183.17	Carriage of Passengers by Sea														
183.18	Liability Maritime Claims														
183.19	Safety of Fishing Vessels											1986			
183.20	Hamburg Rules			1991				S			1984				
183.21	Registration of Ships						1989				1989			S	1989
183.22	Suppression of Unlawful Acts										1989				
183.23	Salvage Conv.														
184.01	Warsaw Convention			1961							1936	1948	1970	1952	1972
184.02	Chicago Convention -ICAO	1981	1947	1959	1977	1967	1948		1953		1969	1947	1947	1950	1947
184.03	Air Transit		1947			1986			1945		1973	1947	1945		1945
184.04	Rights in Aircraft	1985	1988	1980			1961					1967			1981
184.05	Damage to Third Parties		1983	1990			1961		1960				S		1972
184.06	Carriage by Air (Guadalajara)	1985	1971					S	S		1964			S	1972
185.01	Return of Astronauts				1976	1969	S				1969	1969	1979		1970
185.02	Liability Space Objects		S				S		S		1972	S	1979		1972
185.03	Registration of Space Objects										1977		1982		
191.01	Universal Postal Union (UPU)	1976	1970	1966	1974	1967	1975	1968	M		1967	1965	1966	1970	1967
192.02	Telecommunications (Nairobi)	M	1986	1988	M	1985	1984	1985	1985		1985	1986	1986	1985	1986
193.01	INTELSAT		1972	1980			1974	1972	1980			1975	1971	1971	1973
193.02	Intersputnik										1972				
193.03	INMARSAT											1991	1978	1986	1980
211.01	International Monetary Fund (IMF)	1975	1945	1963	1977	1966	1953		1945		1982	1945	1945	1967	1945
212.01	BIS														
221.01	World Bank -IBRD	1975	1945	1963	1977	1966	1953		1945		1982	1945	1945	1967	1945
221.02	IFC	1975	1956	1982	1977	1967	1956		1956		1985	1955	1956	1968	1956
221.03	IDA	1975	1961	1969	1977	1967	1961		1960		1985	1961	1960	1968	1960
221.04	MIGA	1988	S	S	S	1989	S		1992		1988			1986	
231	G-5 G-7 and G-10 Members														
233	G-77 and G-24	G-77	G-24	G-77	G-77	G-77	G-77		G-77				G-24	G-77	G-77
300.02	UNIDROIT (Private Law)							1945			1940		1950		1973
300.03	HCOPIL (Int. Private Law)										1987				
311.01	International Sale of Goods							S			S				
311.02	Formation of Contracts							S			S				
311.03	Limitation Period			1991							1983				
311.04	International Sale of Goods								1983						1990
311.05	Agency														
312.01	Sales of Goods														
312.04	Products Liability														
312.05	Law Applicable to Agency														
312.06	Law Applicable to Trusts														
321.01	Uniform Law Bills of Exchange										1964				
321.02	Confl. Laws Bills of Exchange										1964				
321.03	Stamp Laws Bills of Exchange										1964				

TABLE

[illegible]	[illegible] Cheques							1932	1936				1933		1934										1964			1959	
321.05	Conflicts of Laws Cheques							1932	1936				1933		1934										1964			1959	
321.06	Stamp Laws Cheques						1971	1932	1936				1933		1934										1964			1959	
321.07	Bills of Exchange; Prom. Notes																	1991											
332.01	Civil Procedure	1981						1957	1959				1959									1967			1965				
332.02	Service of Judicial Documents							1969	1972				1979		1983														
332.03	Taking of Evidence Abroad							1976	1974				1979																
332.04	Access to Justice							1988	1982				S		S														
341.01	Protocol Arbitration Clauses	S						1924	1928				1924		1926									1965			1937		1926
341.02	Exec. Foreign Arbitral Awards							1931	1931				1930		1932									1965			1937		
341.03	Enforcement of Arbitral Awards	S						1962	1959				1961	1968	1962		1984	1991			1983	1975			1962		1960	1981	
341.04	Europ. Conv. Int. Arbitration							S	1966				1964												1963				
341.05	Arrang. Eur. Conv. Arbitration								1966				1964																
342.01	Settlement of Int. Disputes	1907					1973		1900				1900		1901		1907				1907		1961		1900	1955	1950		1966
342.02	Permanent Court of Arbitration	1910						1922	1910				1910				1911				1910		1962		1910	1955			1970
342.05	Investment Disputes - ICSID	1984		1992	S		1977	1969	1967	1966	1974	1992	1969	1966	1969	1991		1968	S	1969	S		1989		1987	1966		1968	
411.01	Preservation Fauna and Flora								1938																		1939		
411.02	Regulation of Whaling							1983	1948				1982			1993										1947	1981		
411.03	Protection of Birds								S						S											1955			
411.04	Plant Protection	1953			1977			1960	1957				1957	1991	1954	1985	1955	1991		1970	1970				1960		1952	1977	1954
411.05	Wetlands							1974	1986	1986			1976	1988	1975		1990	1992	1990						1979	1977	1981	1992	
411.06	Fauna and Flora (CITES)	1987	1992	1992	1989			1976	1978	1989	1977		1976	1975	1992		1979	1981	1990	1977			1985		1985		1976	1978	
411.07	Migratory Species					1983		1989					1984	1988											1983		1983		
411.08	Biological Diversity	S		S	S	S	1993	S	S	S	S		S	S	S	S	S	S	S	S	S		S		S	S	S	S	
412.01	Prevention of Pollution (Oil)						1972	1958	1957				D	1962	1967			1981								1962	1974		
412.03	Intervention High Seas (Oil)						1972	1976	1972	1982			1975	1978	S		S									1980			
412.04	Civil Liability Oil Pollution			1992			1972	1980	1975	1982	1991		1975	1978	1976		1982									1980	1987	1978	
412.06	Oil Pollution Fund (FUND)			1992			1983	1980	1978	1982	1991		1976	1978	1986											1980	1990	1978	
412.07	Dumping of Wastes							1979	1977	1982			1977		1981		1975				1975		1980		1976	1973			
412.09	Pollution (MARPOL 73/78)			1991				1983	1981	1983	1991		1982	1991	1982										1985	1985	1986	1986	
412.11	OPRC								1992																				
413.01	Transboundary Air Pollution					1982		1981	1981				1982		1983							S			1980	1983			
413.02	Protection of Ozone Layer	1992	1988			1988	1989	1986	1987		1990		1988	1989	1988	1993	1987	1992							1988	1989	1991	1992	
413.03	Reduction of Sulphur Emissions							1986	1986				1987												1986				
413.04	Montreal Protocol	1992				1988	1989	1988	1988		1990		1988	1989	1988	1993	1989	1992							1989	1989	1992	1992	
413.05	Emissions of Nitrogen Oxides							1990	1989				1990												1991				
413.07	Climate Change	S		S	S	S	1993	S	S	S	S		S	S	S	S	S	S	S	S	S		S		S	S	S	S	
414.01	Environment. Impact Assessment					S		S	S				S		S										S	S			
421.01	IAEA	1957		1992	1957			1958	1957	1964			1957	1960	1957		1957				1957	1957	D		1957	1957	1957	1957	1959
421.02	Nuclear Liability (Paris)							1972	1966				1975		1970														
421.03	Liability Nuclear Ships												S														S	S	
421.04	Nuclear Liability (Brussels)							1977	1966				1975																
421.05	Nuclear Liability (Vienna)																								1989				
421.06	Non-Proliferation (NPT)	1972	1984	1992	1970		1972	1969	1992	1974	1975		1975	1970	1970	1975	1970	1985	1976		1970	1971	1973		1969	1969		1979	1969
421.07	Carriage of Nuclear Material							1991	1973	1982			1975																
421.08	London Club							1980	1975				1975		1984										1985				
421.09	Protection of Nuclear Material					S		S	1991				1991		1991		1985				S				1984			1986	
421.10	Early Notif. Nuclear Accident							1986	1989				1989		1991		1988					S			1987	1989	1988	S	1988
421.11	Assistance Nuclear Accident							1990	1989				1989		1991		1988					S			1987	S	1988	S	1988
421.12	Joint Protocol Vienna-Paris							S	S				S		S										1990				
422.03	Movements of Hazardous Wastes	1991		1992		S		1991	1991				S		S		S				S				1990		1992		
431.01	WMO	1955		1992	1953		1980	1949	1949	1961	1978		1954	1957	1950		1952	1959	1977	1966	1951		1960		1951	1948	1949	1950	1950
432.01	Convention on the High Seas						1971	1965	S				1973	S			1961				1960	S			1961	S		1961	
432.02	Continental Shelf						1971	1965	1965				S	S	1972		1961				1960					S		S	
432.03	Territorial Sea						1971	1965						S			S				1960	S			1961	S			
432.04	Fishing/Living Res.: High Seas						1971	1965	1970					S							1960					S		S	
432.05	Prot. Settlement of Disputes							1965	1958				1973	1958							1960	1958			1989			S	
432.06	Exploration of the Sea (ICES)							1965	1965				1965													1964			
432.07	Law of the Sea	S	S		S	S	1982	S	S	S	1984			1983	S	1991	S	1985	1986	S	S		S		S	1985	S	1986	1985
433.01	Antarctic Treaty							1984	1960				1979		1987		1991								1984		1983		
433.02	CCAMLR (Antarctica)					1982		1989	1982				1982		1987												1985		
434.01	Use of Outer Space	1969			S		1972	1967	1970		S		1971	S	1971				1976	S	S	S	S		1967	1968	1982	S	1968
434.02	Activities on the Moon								S								S										S		

Reference	AGREEMENT	Iran, Islamic Rep.	Ireland	Israel	Italy	Jamaica	Japan	Jordan	Kazakhstan	Kenya	Kiribati	Korea, Dem. PR	Korea, Rep. of	Kuwait	Kyrgyzstan	Lao P.D.R.	Latvia	Lebanon	Lesotho	Liberia	Libyan A.J.	Liechtenstein	Lithuania	Luxembourg	Madagascar	Malawi	Malaysia	Maldives	Mali
183.10	Facilitation of Traffic (FAL)		1971	1967	1972		S					1992	S					S		1978				1991	1970		S		
183.12	Vessels under Construction	S		S	S													S		S									
183.13	Maritime Liens and Mortgages	S		S	S															S									
183.14	Safe Containers (CSC)			1981	1979		1978					1989	1978							1978			1991	1980					
183.15	Code for Liner Conferences	S			1989	1982		1980		1978			1979	1986				1982							1977		1982		1978
183.16	Safety of Life at Sea (1974)	S	1983	1979	1980	1983	1980	1985				1985	1980	1979			1992	1983		1977	1981		1991	1991		1993	1983	1981	
183.17	Carriage of Passengers by Sea																			1981				1991		1993			
183.18	Liability Maritime Claims						1982													1981									
183.19	Safety of Fishing Vessels				1983							1989																	
183.20	Hamburg Rules									1989								1983	1989						S	1991			
183.21	Registration of Ships																				1989								
183.22	Suppression of Unlawful Acts				1990																								
183.23	Salvage Conv.																												
184.01	Warsaw Convention	1975	1935	1949	1933		1953	1969		1964		1961		1975		1956		1962	1975	1942	1969	1934		1949	1962		1970		1961
184.02	Chicago Convention -ICAO	1950	1946	1949	1947	1963	1953	1947	1992	1964	1981	1977	1952	1960	1993	1955	1992	1949	1975	1947	1953		1992	1948	1962	1964	1958	1974	1960
184.03	Air Transit	1950	1957	1954	1984	1963	1953	1947					1960	1960				1974	1975	1945				1948	1962	1975	1945		1970
184.04	Rights in Aircraft	S	S		1960									1979		1956		1969			1973			1975	1979				1961
184.05	Damage to Third Parties			S	1963									1979						S	S			1957					1961
184.06	Carriage by Air (Guadalajara)	1975	1966	1980	1968	1964								1975				1967	1975		1969			1968		1977			
185.01	Return of Astronauts	1970	1968	1969	1978	S	1983	S					1969	1972		1972		1969	S					S	1969		S	1970	
185.02	Liability Space Objects	1974	1972	1977	1983		1983	S		1975			1980	1972		1973		S				1979		1983					1972
185.03	Registration of Space Objects	S					1983						1981																
191.01	Universal Postal Union (UPU)	1968	1966	1968	1968	1968	1965	1967	1992	1968	1984	1974	1966	1967	1993	1967	1992	1979	1967	1975	1969	1967	1992	1965	1965	1966	1969	1967	1965
192.02	Telecommunications (Nairobi)	1986	1988	1984	1986	1985	1984	1984	1993	1985	1986	1984	1985	1986		1984	1991	1986	1986	1987	1986	1985	1991	1984	1987	1985	1986	1985	1987
193.01	INTELSAT	1972	1972	1972	1973	1972	1972	1971		1971			1972	1971				1974			1975	1972		1972	1973	1984	1971		1976
193.02	Intersputnik								1992			1983				1981													
193.03	INMARSAT	1984		1987	1979		1977						1985	1977						1980							1986		
211.01	International Monetary Fund (IMF)	1945	1957	1954	1947	1963	1952	1952	1992	1964	1986		1955	1962	1992	1961	1992	1947	1968	1962	1958		1992	1945	1963	1965	1958	1978	1963
212.01	BIS				1930		1930																						
221.01	World Bank -IBRD	1945	1957	1954	1947	1963	1952	1952	1992	1964	1986		1955	1962	1992	1961	1992	1947	1968	1962	1958		1992	1945	1963	1965	1958	1978	1963
221.02	IFC	1956	1958	1956	1956	1964	1956	1956		1964	1986		1964	1962	1993	1992		1956	1972	1962	1958		1993	1956	1963	1965	1958	1983	1978
221.03	IDA	1960	1960	1960	1960		1960	1960	1992	1964	1986		1961	1962	1992	1963	1992	1962	1968	1962	1961			1964	1963	1965	1960	1978	1963
221.04	MIGA		1989	1992	1988	1987	1987	1986	R	1988			1987	1987	R				1987		1993		R	1991	1988	1987	1991		1990
231	G-5 G-7 and G-10 Members				G-7		G-5																						
233	G-77 and G-24	G-24				G-77		G-77		G-77		G-77	G-77	G-77		G-77		G-24	G-77	G-77	G-77				G-77	G-77	G-77	G-77	G-77
300.02	UNIDROIT (Private Law)	1951	1940	1954	1957		1954						1981					D						1973					
300.03	HCOPIL (Int. Private Law)		1955	1964	1957		1957										1992							1956					
311.01	International Sale of Goods			1971	D																			1979					
311.02	Formation of Contracts			1980	D																			1979					
311.03	Limitation Period																												
311.04	International Sale of Goods				1986														1981										
311.05	Agency				1986																								
312.01	Sales of Goods				1958																			S					
312.04	Products Liability				S																			1985					
312.05	Law Applicable to Agency																												
312.06	Law Applicable to Trusts				1990																			S					
321.01	Uniform Law Bills of Exchange				1932		1932																	1963					
321.02	Confl. Laws Bills of Exchange				1932		1932																	1963					
321.03	Stamp Laws Bills of Exchange		1936		1932		1932																	1963			1960		

TABLE

[illegible]	[illegible]				[illegible]		1933																	1968		D			
321.05	Conflicts of Laws Cheques				1933		1933																	1968					
321.06	Stamp Laws Cheques		1936		1933		1933																	1968			1960		
321.07	Bills of Exchange; Prom. Notes																												
332.01	Civil Procedure			1968	1957		1970											1974						1956					
332.02	Service of Judicial Documents			1972	1981		1970																	1975		1972			
332.03	Taking of Evidence Abroad			1979	1982																			1977					
332.04	Access to Justice				S																			S					
341.01	Protocol Arbitration Clauses		1957	1951	1924		1928						S									S		1930					
341.02	Exec. Foreign Arbitral Awards		1957	1952	1930		1952						S											1930					
341.03	Enforcement of Arbitral Awards		1981	1959	1969		1961	1979		1989			1973	1978			1992		1989					1983	1962		1985		
341.04	Europ. Conv. Int. Arbitration				1970																			1982					
341.05	Arrang. Eur. Conv. Arbitration				1976																			1982					
342.01	Settlement of Int. Disputes	1900			1900		1900									1955		1968						1901					
342.02	Permanent Court of Arbitration			1962			1912	1992							1992	1955		1968						1912					
342.05	Investment Disputes - ICSID		1981	1983	1971	1966	1967	1972	S	1967			1967	1979					1969	1970			1992	1970	1966	1966	1966		1978
411.01	Preservation Fauna and Flora				1939																								
411.02	Regulation of Whaling		1985			D	1951			1981			1978																
411.03	Protection of Birds				1979																			1962					
411.04	Plant Protection	1972	1955	1956	1955	1969	1952	1970		1974			1953			1955		1970		1986	1970			1955		1974	1991		1987
411.05	Wetlands	1975	1984		1976		1980	1977		1990												1991							1987
411.06	Fauna and Flora (CITES)	1976		1979	1979		1980	1978		1978										1981		1979		1983	1975	1982	1977		
411.07	Migratory Species		1983	1983	1983																			1983					1987
411.08	Biological Diversity	S	S	S	S	S	S	S	S	S		S	S	S			S	S	S	S	S	S	S	S	S	S	S	1992	S
412.01	Prevention of Pollution (Oil)		1957	1965	1964		1967	1963		1975			1978	1961				1967		1962	1972				1965			1982	
412.03	Intervention High Seas (Oil)		1980		1979	1991	1971						S	1981				1975		1972					S				
412.04	Civil Liability Oil Pollution		1992		1979		1976			1992	PA		1978	1981			1992	1974		1972				1991	S			1981	
412.06	Oil Pollution Fund (FUND)		1992		1979		1976			1992			1992	1981						1972								1981	
412.07	Dumping of Wastes		1982		1984	1991	1980	1974		1975	1982										1976			1991					
412.09	Pollution (MARPOL 73/78)			1983	1982	1991	1983			1992		1985	1984				1992	1983		1980			1991	1991					
412.11	OPRC																												
413.01	Transboundary Air Pollution		1982		1982																	1983		1982					
413.02	Protection of Ozone Layer	1990	1988	1992	1988	1993	1988	1989		1988	1993		1992	1992				1993			1990	1989		1988		1991	1989	1988	
413.03	Reduction of Sulphur Emissions				1990																	1986		1987					
413.04	Montreal Protocol	1990	1988	1992	1988	1993	1988	1989		1988	1993		1992	1992				1993			1990	1989		1988		1991	1989	1989	
413.05	Emissions of Nitrogen Oxides				1992																			1990					
413.07	Climate Change	S	S	S	S	S	S	S	S	S	S	S	S				S	S	S	S	S	S	S	S	S	S		1992	
414.01	Environment. Impact Assessment		S		S																			S					
421.01	IAEA	1958	1970	1957	1957	1965	1957	1966		1965		1974	1957	1964				1961		1962	1963	1968		1958	1965		1969		1961
421.02	Nuclear Liability (Paris)				1975																			S					
421.03	Liability Nuclear Ships		S										S					1975		S					1965		S		
421.04	Nuclear Liability (Brussels)				1976																			S					
421.05	Nuclear Liability (Vienna)																						1992						
421.06	Non-Proliferation (NPT)	1970	1968		1975	1970	1976	1970		1970	1985	1985	1975	S		1970	1992	1970	1970	1970	1975	1978		1975	1970	1986	1970	1970	1970
421.07	Carriage of Nuclear Material				1980															1981									
421.08	London Club		1984		1976		1975																	1984					
421.09	Protection of Nuclear Material		1991	S	1991		1988						1982									1986		1991					
421.10	Early Notif. Nuclear Accident	S	1991	1989	1990		1987	1987				S	1990				1992	S				S		S			1987		S
421.11	Assistance Nuclear Accident	S	1991	1989	1990		1987	1987				S	1990				1992	S			1990	S					1987		S
421.12	Joint Protocol Vienna-Paris				1991																								
422.03	Movements of Hazardous Wastes	1993	S	S	S			1989						S			1992	S				1992		S				1992	
431.01	WMO	1959	1950	1949	1951	1963	1953	1955		1964		1975	1956	1962		1955	1992	1948	1979	1974	1955		1992	1952	1960	1965	1958	1978	1960
432.01	Convention on the High Seas	S	S	1961	1964	1965	1968			1969							1992	S	1973	S					1962	1965	1960		
432.02	Continental Shelf	S	S	1961		1965				1969							1992	S	1973	S					1962	1965	1960		
432.03	Territorial Sea	S	S	1961	1964	1965	1968			1969							1992		1973	S			1992		1962	1965	1960		
432.04	Fishing/Living Res.: High Seas	S	S	S		1964				1969								S	1973	S					1962	1965	1960		
432.05	Prot. Settlement of Disputes			S																1958					1962	1965	1961		
432.06	Exploration of the Sea (ICES)		1965		D																								
432.07	Law of the Sea	S	S		S	1983	S			S		S	S	1986		S		S	S	S	S	S		S	S	S	S	S	1985
433.01	Antarctic Treaty				1981		1960					1987	1986																
433.02	CCAMLR (Antarctica)				1989		1981						1985																
434.01	Use of Outer Space	S	1968	1977	1972	1970	1967	S		1984			1967	1972		1972		1969	S		1968			S	1968		S		
434.02	Activities on the Moon																												

Reference	AGREEMENT	Malta	Marshall Islands	Mauritania	Mauritius	Mexico	Micronesia	Moldova, Rep.	Monaco	Mongolia	Morocco	Mozambique	Myanmar	Namibia	Nauru	Nepal
183.10	Facilitation of Traffic (FAL)				1990	1983			1965							
183.12	Vessels under Construction								S		S					
183.13	Maritime Liens and Mortgages								S		1987					
183.14	Safe Containers (CSC)					1989					1990					
183.15	Code for Liner Conferences	S		1988	1980	1976					1980	1990				
183.16	Safety of Life at Sea (1974)	1986	1988		1988	1977			1974		1990		1987			
183.17	Carriage of Passengers by Sea															
183.18	Liability Maritime Claims															
183.19	Safety of Fishing Vessels															
183.20	Hamburg Rules					S					1981					
183.21	Registration of Ships					1988					S					
183.22	Suppression of Unlawful Acts															
183.23	Salvage Conv.					1991										
184.01	Warsaw Convention	1986		1962	1989	1933				1962	1958		1952		1970	1966
184.02	Chicago Convention -ICAO	1965	1988	1962	1970	1946	1988	1992	1980	1989	1956	1977	1948	1991	1975	1960
184.03	Air Transit	1965		1979	1971	1946					1957				1975	1965
184.04	Rights in Aircraft			1962	1991	1950										
184.05	Damage to Third Parties			1962		S					1964					
184.06	Carriage by Air (Guadalajara)			1979	1990	1962					1975					
185.01	Return of Astronauts	S			1969	1969			S	1969	1970		S			1968
185.02	Liability Space Objects	1978				1974				1972	1983					S
185.03	Registration of Space Objects					1985				1985						
191.01	Universal Postal Union (UPU)	1968		1967	1969	1968		1992	1968	1968	1967	1978	1969	1992	1968	1969
192.02	Telecommunications (Nairobi)	1984		1988	1985	1984		1992	1985	1986	1989	1988	1986	1984	M	1988
193.01	INTELSAT			1971	1986	1972			1972		1971	1989				1989
193.02	Intersputnik									1972						
193.03	INMARSAT	1991			1992				1990			1990				
211.01	International Monetary Fund (IMF)	1968	1992	1963	1968	1945		1992		1991	1958	1984	1952	1990		1961
212.01	BIS															
221.01	World Bank -IBRD	1983	1992	1963	1968	1945		1992		1991	1958	1984	1952	1990		1961
221.02	IFC		1992	1967	1968	1955				1991	1962	1984	1956	1990		1966
221.03	IDA		1993	1963	1968	1961				1991	1960	1984	1962			1963
221.04	MIGA	1990		1991	1990			R			1992			1990		S
231	G-5 G-7 and G-10 Members															
233	G-77 and G-24	G-77	G-77	G-77	G-77	G-24				G-77	G-77	G-77	G-77			G-77
300.02	UNIDROIT (Private Law)	D				1940										
300.03	HCOPIL (Int. Private Law)					1986										
311.01	International Sale of Goods															
311.02	Formation of Contracts															
311.03	Limitation Period					1988				S						
311.04	International Sale of Goods					1987										
311.05	Agency					1987					S					
312.01	Sales of Goods															
312.04	Products Liability															
312.05	Law Applicable to Agency															
312.06	Law Applicable to Trusts															
321.01	Uniform Law Bills of Exchange								1934							
321.02	Confl. Laws Bills of Exchange								1934							
321.03	Stamp Laws Bills of Exchange	1966							1934							

Reference	AGREEMENT	Netherlands	New Zealand	Nicaragua	Niger	Nigeria	Norway	Oman	Pakistan	Panama	Papua New Guinea	Paraguay	Peru	Philippines
183.10	Facilitation of Traffic (FAL)	1967	1973	S		1967	1966						1982	S
183.12	Vessels under Construction						1975							
183.13	Maritime Liens and Mortgages						1975							
183.14	Safe Containers (CSC)	1984	1974				1983		1985				1988	
183.15	Code for Liner Conferences	1983			1976	1975	1985		1975				1978	1976
183.16	Safety of Life at Sea (1974)	1978	1990			1981	1977	1985	1985	1978	1980		1979	1981
183.17	Carriage of Passengers by Sea													
183.18	Liability Maritime Claims	1990					1984							
183.19	Safety of Fishing Vessels	1989				1984	1979						1982	
183.20	Hamburg Rules					1988	S		S	S				S
183.21	Registration of Ships							1990						
183.22	Suppression of Unlawful Acts	1992					1991	1990						
183.23	Salvage Conv.					1990		1991						
184.01	Warsaw Convention	1933	1937		1962	1963	1937	1976	1969		1975	1969	1988	1950
184.02	Chicago Convention -ICAO	1947	1947	1945	1961	1960	1947	1973	1947	1960	1975	1946	1946	1947
184.03	Air Transit	1945	1945	1945	1962	1961	1945	1973	1947	1982		1945		1946
184.04	Rights in Aircraft	1959			1962		1954	1992	1953			1969	S	1978
184.05	Damage to Third Parties	S			1962	1970	S			1957	1975	1969		S
184.06	Carriage by Air (Guadalajara)	1964	1969		1964	1969	1967		1965		1975	1969	1988	1966
185.01	Return of Astronauts	1981	1969	S	1969	1973	1970		1973		1981		1979	S
185.02	Liability Space Objects	1981	1974	S	1972		S	S	1973	1974	1980		S	S
185.03	Registration of Space Objects	1981		S	1976				1986				1979	
191.01	Universal Postal Union (UPU)	1969	1966	1988	1966	1967	1965	1971	1966	1984	1976	1979	1970	1973
192.02	Telecommunications (Nairobi)	1984	1986	1988	1984	1986	1986	1986	1986	1986	1984	1985	1986	1986
193.01	INTELSAT	1973	1972	1972	1980	1972	1972	1975	1971	1975	1983	1977	1972	1972
193.02	Intersputnik			1987										
193.03	INMARSAT	1979	1977			1988	1978	1980	1985	1987			1987	1981
211.01	International Monetary Fund (IMF)	1945	1961	1946	1963	1961	1945	1971	1950	1946	1975	1945	1945	1945
212.01	BIS													
221.01	World Bank -IBRD	1945	1961	1946	1963	1961	1945	1971	1950	1946	1975	1945	1945	1945
221.02	IFC	1956	1961	1956	1980	1961	1956	1973	1956	1956	1975	1956	1956	1957
221.03	IDA	1961	1974	1960	1963	1961	1960	1973	1960	1961	1975	1961	1961	1960
221.04	MIGA	1987		1992		1988	1989	1989	1986		1990	1992	1991	S
231	G-5 G-7 and G-10 Members	G-10												
233	G-77 and G-24			G-77	G-77	G-24		G-77	G-24	G-77	G-77	G-77	G-24	G-24
300.02	UNIDROIT (Private Law)	1940		1940		1964	1951		1964			1940		
300.03	HCOPIL (Int. Private Law)	1954					1955							
311.01	International Sale of Goods	D												
311.02	Formation of Contracts	D												
311.03	Limitation Period			S			1980							
311.04	International Sale of Goods	1990					1988							
311.05	Agency													
312.01	Sales of Goods	S			1971		1964							
312.04	Products Liability	1979					1977							
312.05	Law Applicable to Agency	1992												
312.06	Law Applicable to Trusts	S												
321.01	Uniform Law Bills of Exchange	1932					1932						S	
321.02	Confl. Laws Bills of Exchange	1932					1932						S	
321.03	Stamp Laws Bills of Exchange	1932					1932				1981		S	

321.04	Uniform Law for Cheques					S			1933								1934		1932			1932							
321.05	Conflicts of Laws Cheques					S			1933								1934		1932			1932							
321.06	Stamp Laws Cheques	1966				S			1933								1934		1932			1932				1981			
321.07	Bills of Exchange; Prom. Notes					1992																							
332.01	Civil Procedure										1972						1959					1958							
332.02	Service of Judicial Documents																1975					1969		1989					
332.03	Taking of Evidence Abroad					1989			1986								1981					1972							
332.04	Access to Justice										S						1992												
341.01	Protocol Arbitration Clauses	1966			1969				1927								1925	1926	S			1927			S		S	S	
341.02	Exec. Foreign Arbitral Awards	1966			1969												1931	1929	S									S	
341.03	Enforcement of Arbitral Awards					1971			1982		1959						1964	1983		1964	1970	1961		S	1984			1988	1967
341.04	Europ. Conv. Int. Arbitration																												
341.05	Arrang. Eur. Conv. Arbitration																												
342.01	Settlement of Int. Disputes				1970	1901											1900	1959	1907			1900		1950	1907		1907	1907	
342.02	Permanent Court of Arbitration	1968				1910											1910		1910		1986	1910			1911		1933		
342.05	Investment Disputes - ICSID			1966	1969			S		1991	1967					1969	1966	1980		1966	1965	1967		1966		1978	1983	S	1978
411.01	Preservation Fauna and Flora																												
411.02	Regulation of Whaling				D	1949			1982								1977	1976				1960	1980		1948			1979	D
411.03	Protection of Birds								S								1955												
411.04	Plant Protection	1975			1971	1976					1972						1954	1952	1956	1985		1956	1989	1954	1965	1976	1968	1975	1953
411.05	Wetlands	1988		1982		1986					1980					1987	1980	1976		1987		1974		1976	1990			1992	
411.06	Fauna and Flora (CITES)	1989			1975	1991			1978		1975	1981		1990		1975	1984	1989	1977	1975	1974	1976		1976	1978	1975	1976	1975	1981
411.07	Migratory Species																1983			1983	1987	1985		1987	1989				
411.08	Biological Diversity	S	1992	S	1992	1993		S	1992	S	S	S	S	S	S	S	S	S	S	S	S	S	S	S	S	1993	S	S	S
412.01	Prevention of Pollution (Oil)	1975				1956			1970		1968						D	1971			1968	1957			1963	1980			1963
412.03	Intervention High Seas (Oil)					1976			1975		1974						1975	1975				1972	1985		1976	1980			
412.04	Civil Liability Oil Pollution	1991							1975		1974						1975	1976			1981	1975	1985		1976	1980		1987	
412.06	Oil Pollution Fund (FUND)	1991							1979		1992						1982				1987	1975	1985			1980			
412.07	Dumping of Wastes	1989				1975			1977		1977				1982		1977	1975			1976	1974	1984		1975	1980			1973
412.09	Pollution (MARPOL 73/78)	1991	1988			1992			1992				1988				1983					1980	1984		1985			1980	
412.11	OPRC																												
413.01	Transboundary Air Pollution																1982					1981							
413.02	Protection of Ozone Layer	1988	1993		1992	1987			1993		S						1988	1987	1993	1992	1988	1986		1992	1989	1992	1992	1989	1991
413.03	Reduction of Sulphur Emissions																1986					1986							
413.04	Montreal Protocol	1988	1993		1992	1988			1993		S						1988		1993	1992	1988	1988		1992	1989	1992	1992	1993	1991
413.05	Emissions of Nitrogen Oxides																1989					1989							
413.07	Climate Change	S	1992	S	1992	1993		S	1992	S	S	S	S	S	S	S	S	S	S	S	S	S	S	S	S	1993	S	S	S
414.01	Environment. Impact Assessment																S					S							
421.01	IAEA				1974	1958			1957	1973	1957		1957	1983			1957	1957	1977	1969	1964	1957		1957	1966		1957	1957	1958
421.02	Nuclear Liability (Paris)																1979					1973							
421.03	Liability Nuclear Ships								S								1974								S				S
421.04	Nuclear Liability (Brussels)																1979					1973							
421.05	Nuclear Liability (Vienna)					1989					S									1979								1980	1965
421.06	Non-Proliferation (NPT)	1970			1969	1969				1969	1970	1990	1992	1992	1982	1970	1975	1969	1973	1992	1968	1969			1977	1982	1970	1970	1972
421.07	Carriage of Nuclear Material																1991					1975							
421.08	London Club																1976												
421.09	Protection of Nuclear Material					1988				1986	S						1991			S		1985			S		1985		1981
421.10	Early Notif. Nuclear Accident				1992	1988			1989	1987	S						1991	1987		S	1990	1986		1989	1986		S		
421.11	Assistance Nuclear Accident				1992	1988			1989	1987	S						1991	1987		S	1990	1986		1989	S		S		
421.12	Joint Protocol Vienna-Paris										S						1991					1991							S
422.03	Movements of Hazardous Wastes				1992	1991			1992								S	S			1991	1990			1991				S
431.01	WMO	1976		1962	1969	1949				1963	1957	1976	1949	1991		1966	1951	1948	1959	1960	1960	1948	1975	1950	1967	1975	1950	1949	1949
432.01	Convention on the High Seas				1970	1966				1976						1962	1966	S			1961			S	S				
432.02	Continental Shelf	1966			1970	1966										S	1966	1965			1971	1971		S	S			S	
432.03	Territorial Sea	1966			1970	1966										S	1966	S			1961			S	S				
432.04	Fishing/Living Res.: High Seas				1970	1966										S	1966	S			1961			S	S				
432.05	Prot. Settlement of Disputes	1966			1970											1958	1966	1958						1958	1958				
432.06	Exploration of the Sea (ICES)																1967					1965							
432.07	Law of the Sea	S	1991	S	S	1983	1991		S	S	S	S	S	1983	S	S	S	S	S	S	1986	S	1989	S	S	S	1986		1984
433.01	Antarctic Treaty																1967	1960				1960				1981		1981	
433.02	CCAMLR (Antarctica)																1990	1982				1983						1980	
434.01	Use of Outer Space				1969	1968				1967	1967		1970			1967	1969	1968	S	1967	1967	1969		1968	S	1980		1979	S
434.02	Activities on the Moon					1991					1993						1983							1986				S	1981

Reference	AGREEMENT	Poland	Portugal	Qatar	Romania	Russia	Rwanda	Samoa	San Marino	São Tomé & Príncipe	Saudi Arabia	Senegal	Seychelles	Sierra Leone	Singapore	Slovak Republic	Slovenia	Solomon Islands	Somalia	South Africa	Spain	Sri Lanka	St Kitts & Nevis	St Lucia	St-Vincent-&-Grenadines	Sudan	Suriname	Swaziland	Sweden
183.10	Facilitation of Traffic (FAL)	1969	1990			1966						1980	1989		1967		1991				1973						1975		1967
183.12	Vessels under Construction	S	S																		S								1975
183.13	Maritime Liens and Mortgages	S	S																										1975
183.14	Safe Containers (CSC)	1980	1985		1975	1976					1978						1991			1982	1974								1980
183.15	Code for Liner Conferences		1990		1982	1979					1985	1977		1979					1988			1975				1978			1985
183.16	Safety of Life at Sea (1974)	1984	1983	1980	1979	1980					1985		1988		1981		1991			1980	1978	1983			1983	1990	1988		1978
183.17	Carriage of Passengers by Sea	1987				1983															1981								
183.18	Liability Maritime Claims	1986																			1981								1984
183.19	Safety of Fishing Vessels																			1990	1979								
183.20	Hamburg Rules		S		1982							1986		1988	S														S
183.21	Registration of Ships	S				S						S																	
183.22	Suppression of Unlawful Acts	1991											1989								1989								1990
183.23	Salvage Conv.										1991																		
184.01	Warsaw Convention	1932	1947	1986	1931	1934	1964	1963			1969	1964	1980	1968				1981		1954	1930	1951				1975			1937
184.02	Chicago Convention -ICAO	1945	1947	1971	1965	1970	1964		1988	1977	1962	1960	1977	1961	1966	1993	1992	1985	1964	1947	1947	1948		1979	1983	1956	1976	1973	1946
184.03	Air Transit	1945	1959				1964					1961	1979		1966				1964	1945	1945	1945						1973	1945
184.04	Rights in Aircraft		1985				1971						1979																1955
184.05	Damage to Third Parties		S			1982	1971						1980								1957	1959							S
184.06	Carriage by Air (Guadalajara)	1964			1965	1983	1971				1973		1980					1967		1974								1971	1967
185.01	Return of Astronauts	1969	1970		1971	1968	S		1970			S	1978	S	1976		1992		S	1969								1969	1969
185.02	Liability Space Objects	1973		1974	1981	1973	S				1976	1975	1978	S	1975		1992			S	1980	1973							1976
185.03	Registration of Space Objects	1978				1978							1977		S						1978								1976
191.01	Universal Postal Union (UPU)	1966	1968	1968	1969	1978	1988	1989	1967	1976	1980	1967	1977	1967	1965	1993	1992	1984	1968	D	1966	1967	1988	1980	19 80	M	1976	1969	1966
192.02	Telecommunications (Nairobi)	1986	1987	1985	1986	1985	1986	1988	1985	1984	1986	1984		1985	1985	1993	1992	1987	1984	1984	1985	1986			1986	1989	1985	1985	1985
193.01	INTELSAT		1972	1976	1990	1991	1986				1972	1972			1971				1981	1971	1972	1972				1971		1988	1972
193.02	Intersputnik	1972			1972	1972																							
193.03	INMARSAT	1979	1979	1987	1990	1979					1983				1979						1978	1981							1979
211.01	International Monetary Fund (IMF)	1986	1961	1972	1972	1992	1963	1971	1992	1977	1957	1962	1977	1962	1966	1993	1992	1978	1962	1945	1958	1950	1984	1979	1979	1957	1978	1969	19 51
212.01	BIS																												
221.01	World Bank -IBRD	1986	1961	1972	1972	1992	1963	1974		1977	1957	1962	1980	1962	1966	1993	1993	1978	1962	1945	1958	1950	1984	1980	1982	1957	1978	1969	1951
221.02	IFC	1987	1966		1990	1993	1975	1974			1962	1962	1981	1962	1968	1993	1993	1980	1962	1957	1960	1956		1982		1960		1969	1956
221.03	IDA	1988	1992			1992	1963	1974		1977	1960	1962		1962		1993	1993	1980	1962	1960	1960	1961	1987	1982	1982	1960		1969	1960
221.04	MIGA	1989	1988		1992	1992	R	1987			1986	1987	1992	S		1993					1988	1988	S	1988	1990	1991		1990	1987
231	G-5 G-7 and G-10 Members																												G-10
233	G-77 and G-24			G-77	G-77		G-77	G-77		G-77	G-77	G-77	G-77	G-77	G-77			G-77	G-77			G-24	G-77	G-77	G-77	G-77	G-77	G-77	
300.02	UNIDROIT (Private Law)	1979	1949		1940	1990			1945			1991				1993				1971	1940								1940
300.03	HCOPIL (Int. Private Law)	1984	1953		1991												1992				1953						1977		1953
311.01	International Sale of Goods								1968																				
311.02	Formation of Contracts								1968																				
311.03	Limitation Period	S			1992	S																							
311.04	International Sale of Goods	S			1991	1990									S						1990								1987
311.05	Agency																			1986									
312.01	Sales of Goods																				S								1964
312.04	Products Liability		S																		1989								
312.05	Law Applicable to Agency		1982																										
312.06	Law Applicable to Trusts																												
321.01	Uniform Law Bills of Exchange	1936	1934			1936															S								1932
321.02	Confl. Laws Bills of Exchange	1936	1934			1936															S								1932
321.03	Stamp Laws Bills of Exchange	1936	1934			1936															S								1932

TABLE

321.04	Uniform Law for Cheques	1936	1934		S																		S								1932
321.05	Conflicts of Laws Cheques	1936	1934		S																		S								1932
321.06	Stamp Laws Cheques	1936	1934		S																		S								1932
321.07	Bills of Exchange; Prom. Notes					S																									
332.01	Civil Procedure	1963	1967		1971	1967											1992				1961						1977		1957
332.02	Service of Judicial Documents		1973										1981								1987								1969
332.03	Taking of Evidence Abroad		1975												1978						1987								1975
332.04	Access to Justice	1992															1992				1988								1987
341.01	Protocol Arbitration Clauses	1931	1930		1925																1926								1929
341.02	Exec. Foreign Arbitral Awards		1930		1931																1930								1929
341.03	Enforcement of Arbitral Awards	1961			1961	1960			1979						1986		1992			1976	1977	1962							1972
341.04	Europ. Conv. Int. Arbitration	1964			1963	1962											1992				1975								
341.05	Arrang. Eur. Conv. Arbitration																												
342.01	Settlement of Int. Disputes		1900		1900	1955						1977									1900	1955							1900
342.02	Permanent Court of Arbitration	1922	1911		19:2	1955						1977									1913					1966	1992	1970	1910
342.05	Investment Disputes - ICSID		1984		1975	S	1979	1978			1980	1967	1978	1966	1968			1981	1968			1967		1984		1973		1971	1966
411.01	Preservation Fauna and Flora		1950																	1935	S					1935			
411.02	Regulation of Whaling					1948						1982	1979					1985		1948	1979			1981	1981				1979
411.03	Protection of Birds		S																		1955								1963
411.04	Plant Protection		1955		1971	1956						1975		1981				1978		1956	1952	1952	1990			1971	1977		1952
411.05	Wetlands	1977	1980		1991	1976						1977				1993	1992			1975	1982	1990					1985		1974
411.06	Fauna and Flora (CITES)	1989	1980			1976	1930					1977	1977		1986	1993			1985	1975	1986	1979		1982		1982	1980		1974
411.07	Migratory Species		1983									1988							1986		1985	1990							1983
411.08	Biological Diversity	S	S	S	S	S	S	S	S	S		S	1992		S		S	S			S	S	1993			S	S	S	S
412.01	Prevention of Pollution (Oil)	1961	1967	1980		1969					1971	1972					1991				1964	1983					1976		1956
412.03	Intervention High Seas (Oil)	1976	1980	1988		1974						1972					1991			1986	1973	1983					1975		1973
412.04	Civil Liability Oil Pollution	1976	1976	1988	S	1975						1972	1988		1981		1991	PA		1976	1975	1983			1989				1975
412.06	Oil Pollution Fund (FUND)	1985	1985	1988		1987							1988				1991				1981	1983							1975
412.07	Dumping of Wastes	1979	1978			1975							1984				1991	1984		1978	1974			1985			1980		1974
412.09	Pollution (MARPOL 73/78)	1986	1987			1983							1990		1990		1991			1984	1984				1983		1988		1980
412.11	OPRC												1992																1992
413.01	Transboundary Air Pollution	1985	1980		1991	1980			S								1992				1982								1981
413.02	Protection of Ozone Layer	1990	1988		1993	1986		1992			1993	1993	1993		1989		1992			1990	1988	1989	1992			1993		1992	1986
413.03	Reduction of Sulphur Emissions					1986																							1986
413.04	Montreal Protocol	1990	1988		1993	1988		1992			1993	S	1993		1989		1992			1990	1988	1989	1992			1993		1992	1988
413.05	Emissions of Nitrogen Oxides					1989																							1990
413.07	Climate Change	S	S		S	S	S	S	S	S		S	1992	S	S		S	S			S	S	1993			S	S	S	S
414.01	Environment. Impact Assessment	S	S		S	S															1992								1992
421.01	IAEA	1957	1957	1976	1957	1957					1962	1960		1967	1967		1992			1957	1957	1957				1958			1957
421.02	Nuclear Liability (Paris)		1977																		1961								1968
421.03	Liability Nuclear Ships		1968																								1974		
421.04	Nuclear Liability (Brussels)																				1966								1968
421.05	Nuclear Liability (Vienna)	1990			1992												1991				S								
421.06	Non-Proliferation (NPT)	1969	1977	1989	1970	1970	1975	1975	1970	1983	1988	1970	1985	1975	1976	1993	1992	1981	1970	1991	1987	1979	1993	1979	1984	1973	1976	1969	1970
421.07	Carriage of Nuclear Material		S																		1974								1974
421.08	London Club	1976	1986			1975																							1976
421.09	Protection of Nuclear Material	1983	1991		S	1983										1993	1992			S	1991								1980
421.10	Early Notif. Nuclear Accident	1988	S		1990	1986					1989	S		S		1993	1992			1987	1989	1991				S			1987
421.11	Assistance Nuclear Accident	1988	S		1990	1986					1989	S		S		1993	1992			1987	1989	1991				S			1992
421.12	Joint Protocol Vienna-Paris	1990	S		1992																S								1992
422.03	Movements of Hazardous Wastes	1992	S		1991	S					1990	1992									S	1992							1991
431.01	WMO	1950	1951	1975	1948	1948	1963			1976	1959	1960	1977	1962	1966	1993	1992	1985	1964	1950	1951	1951		1981		1956	1976	1982	1948
432.01	Convention on the High Seas	1962	1963		1961	1960						1961		1962			1992	1981		1963	1971	S						1970	
432.02	Continental Shelf	1962	1963		1961	1960						D		1966				1981		1963	1971	S						1970	1966
432.03	Territorial Sea		1963		1961	1960						1951		1962			1992	1981			1971	S						1970	
432.04	Fishing/Living Res.: High Seas		1963									1961		1962				1981		1963	1971	S							
432.05	Prot. Settlement of Disputes		1963											1963				1981				1958							1966
432.06	Exploration of the Sea (ICES)	1966	1966			1965															1965								1964
432.07	Law of the Sea	S	S	S	S	S	S	S		1987	S	1984	1991	S	S			S	1989	S	S	S	1993	1985	S	1985	S	S	S
433.01	Antarctic Treaty	1961			1971	1960														1960	1982								1984
433.02	CCAMLR (Antarctica)	1984				1981														1981	1982								1984
434.01	Use of Outer Space	1968			1968	1967	S		1968		1976		1978	1967	1976				S	1968	1968	1986							1967
434.02	Activities on the Moon				S																								

Reference	AGREEMENT	Switzerland	Syrian Arab Republic	Taiwan	Tajikistan	Tanzania	Thailand	Togo	Tonga	Trinidad & Tobago	Tunisia	Turkey	Turkmenistan	Tuvalu	Uganda	Ukraine	United Arab Emirates	United Kingdom	United States	Uruguay	Uzbekistan	Vanuatu	Venezuela	Viet Nam	Yemen	Yugoslavia	Zaire	Zambia	Zimbabwe
183.10	Facilitation of Traffic (FAL)	1968	1975				1991			1967	1969					S		1966	1967	1992		1989			1979	1966		1965	
183.12	Vessels under Construction		1974																	S						1971			
183.13	Maritime Liens and Mortgages	S	1974															S		S						S	S		
183.14	Safe Containers (CSC)															1976		1978	1978			1989			1979	1987			
183.15	Code for Liner Conferences					1975		1978		1983	1979	S						1985		1979			1975			1980	1977	1988	
183.16	Safety of Life at Sea (1974)	1981					1984	1989	1977	1979	1980	1980		1985		1974	1983	1977	1978	1979		1982	1983	1990	1979	1979			
183.17	Carriage of Passengers by Sea	1987							1977									1980				1989			1979	S			
183.18	Liability Maritime Claims	1987																1980				1992			1979				
183.19	Safety of Fishing Vessels																	1980					1987		1979				
183.20	Hamburg Rules					1979					1980				1979				S				S				S	1991	
183.21	Registration of Ships																												
183.22	Suppression of Unlawful Acts	1993								1989								1991											
183.23	Salvage Conv.	1993																	1992										
184.01	Warsaw Convention	1934	1964			1965		1980	1977	1983	1963	1978			1963	1959	1986	1933	1934	1979		1981	1955	1982	1982	1931	1962	1970	1980
184.02	Chicago Convention -ICAO	1947	1949			1962	1947	1965	1984	1963	1957	1945	1993		1967	1992	1972	1947	1946	1954	1992	1983	1947	1980	1964	1960	1961	1964	1981
184.03	Air Transit	1945					1947	1948		1963	1962	1945					1972	1945	1945			1988	1946					1965	
184.04	Rights in Aircraft	1960					1967	1980			1966							S	1949	1985			S			1991			1987
184.05	Damage to Third Parties	S					S	1980			1963						1990	S		1978		1982			1986				
184.06	Carriage by Air (Guadalajara)	1964						1980			1970					1983		1962					S			1977		1971	1982
185.01	Return of Astronauts	1969	1969	M			1969		1971		1971	S				1969		1968	1968	1969			S	S	S	1971	S	1973	
185.02	Liability Space Objects	1974	1980	M		S		1976		1980	1973					1973		1973	1973	1977			1978			1975	S	1973	
185.03	Registration of Space Objects	1978														1977		1978	1976	1977						1978			
191.01	Universal Postal Union (UPU)	1966	1966			1967	1966	1967	1971	1968	1966	1970	1993	1980	1965	1978	1973	1966	1966	1979		1982	1969	1967	1969	1966	1979	1966	1981
192.02	Telecommunications (Nairobi)	19 85	1987			1987	1985	1986	1988	1984	1987	1986			M	1986	1986	1984	1986	1984	1992	1988	1986	1986	1987	1986	1989	1986	1986
193.01	INTELSAT	1972	1971	D		1973	1972	1987		1971	1973	1974			1972		1976	1972	1971	1982			1973	1973	1971	1972	1971	1972	1989
193.02	Intersputnik		1991																					1979	1980				
193.03	INMARSAT	1989									1983	1989				1979	1983	1979	1979							1990			
211.01	International Monetary Fund (IMF)	1992	1947			1962	1949	1962	1985	1963	1958	1947	1992		1963	1992	1972	1945	1945	1946	1992	1981	1946	1956	1970	D	1963	1965	1980
212.01	BIS	1930																1930											
221.01	World Bank -IBRD	1992	1947			1962	1949	1962	1985	1963	1958	1947	1992		1963	1992	1972	1945	1945	1946	1992	1981	1946	1956	1969	D	1963	1965	1980
221.02	IFC	1992	1962			1962	1956	1962	1985	1971	1962	1956			1963		1977	1956	1955	196 8		1981	1956	1967	1970	D	1970	1965	1980
221.03	IDA	1992	1962			1962	1960	1962	1985	1972	1960	1960			1963		1981	1960	1960		1992	1981		1960	1970	D	1963	1965	1980
221.04	MIGA	1988	S			1991		1988		1991	1988	1988	R		1992		S	1988	1988	1993	R	1988	S		R	D	1989	1988	1992
231	G-5 G-7 and G-10 Members	G-10																G-5	G-5										
233	G-77 and G-24		G-24			G-77	G-77	G-77	G-77	G-24	G-77				G-77		G-77			G-77		G-77	G-24	G-77	G-77	G-24	G-24	G-77	
300.02	UNIDROIT (Private Law)	1940									1980	1951						1948	1964	1940			1940			1940			
300.03	HCOPIL (Int. Private Law)	1957										1955						1955	1964	1983			1979			1958			
311.01	International Sale of Goods																	1967											
311.02	Formation of Contracts																	1967											
311.03	Limitation Period														1992	S										1978		1986	
311.04	International Sale of Goods	1990	1982												1992	1990			1986				S			1985		1986	
311.05	Agency	S																											
312.01	Sales of Goods	1972																											
312.04	Products Liability																									1977			
312.05	Law Applicable to Agency																												
312.06	Law Applicable to Trusts																	1989	S										
321.01	Uniform Law Bills of Exchange	1932										S														S			
321.02	Confl. Laws Bills of Exchange	1932										S														S			
321.03	Stamp Laws Bills of Exchange	1932							1972			S			1965			1934								S			

321.04	Uniform Law for Cheques	1932									S														S			
321.05	Conflicts of Laws Cheques	1932									S														S			
321.06	Stamp Laws Cheques	1932						1972			S						1932								S			
321.07	Bills of Exchange; Prom. Notes																	S										
332.01	Civil Procedure	1957									1973														1962			
332.02	Service of Judicial Documents	S									1972						1967	1967										
332.03	Taking of Evidence Abroad	S															1976	1972										
332.04	Access to Justice	S																							1988			
341.01	Protocol Arbitration Clauses	1928				1930								S			1924		S						1959			
341.02	Exec. Foreign Arbitral Awards	1930				1931								S			1930								1959			
341.03	Enforcement of Arbitral Awards	1965	1959		1964	1959			1966	1967	1992			1992	1960		1975	1970	1983						1982			
341.04	Europ. Conv. Int. Arbitration										1992				1963										1963			
341.05	Arrang. Eur. Conv. Arbitration																											
342.01	Settlement of Int. Disputes	1900				1900					1907				1962		1900	1900	1907			1907			1901	1961		1984
342.02	Permanent Court of Arbitration	1910				1910								1966	1962		1970	1910								1961		
342.05	Investment Disputes - ICSID	1968			1992	S	1967	1990	1967	1966	1989	1992		1966		1981	1966	1966	S						1967	1970	1970	S
411.01	Preservation Fauna and Flora				1962												1935											
411.02	Regulation of Whaling	1980															1947	1947	1981			1991						
411.03	Protection of Birds	1955									1967														1973			
411.04	Plant Protection	S				1978	1986		1970	1971	1988						1953	1972	1970			1966		1990	1955		1986	
411.05	Wetlands	1976							1992	1980				1988			1976	1986	1984			1988	1988		1977		1991	
411.06	Fauna and Flora (CITES)	1974			1979	1983	1978		1984	1974				1991		1990	1976	1974	1975		1989	1977				1976	1980	1981
411.07	Migratory Species									1987							1985		1990							1990		
411.08	Biological Diversity	S			S	S	S		S	S	S		S	S	S	S	S		S		1993	S		S	S	S	S	S
412.01	Prevention of Pollution (Oil)	1966	1968							1973						1983	1955	1961	1975		1983	1963		1979	1974			
412.03	Intervention High Seas (Oil)	1987	1975							1976						1983	1971	1974			1992			1979	1976			
412.04	Civil Liability Oil Pollution	1987	1975							1976			1978			1983	1975	S			1983	1992		1979	1976			
412.06	Oil Pollution Fund (FUND)	S	1975							1976			1978			1983	1976	S			1989	1992			1978			
412.07	Dumping of Wastes	1979								1976					1976	1974	1975	1974			1992				1976	1975		
412.09	Pollution (MARPOL 73/78)	1987	1988				1990			1980	1990		1985				1980	1980	1979		1989		1991		1980			
412.11	OPRC																	1992										
413.01	Transboundary Air Pollution	1983									1983				1980		1992	1981							1987			
413.02	Protection of Ozone Layer	1987	1989		1993	1989	1991		1989	1989	1991			1988	1986	1989	1987	1986	1989			1988			1990		1990	1992
413.03	Reduction of Sulphur Emissions	1987													1986													
413.04	Montreal Protocol	1988	1989			1989	1991		1989	1989	1991			1988	1988	S	1988	1988	1991			1989			1991		1990	1992
413.05	Emissions of Nitrogen Oxides	1990													1989		1990	1989										
413.07	Climate Change	S			S	S	S		S	S			S	S	S		S	1992	S		1993	S	S	S	S	S	S	1992
414.01	Environment. Impact Assessment														S		S	S										
421.01	IAEA	1957	1963		1976	1957				1957	1957			1967	1957	1976	1957	1957	1963			1957	1978		1957	1961	1969	1986
421.02	Nuclear Liability (Paris)	S									1961						1966											
421.03	Liability Nuclear Ships		1974													S									S	1967		
421.04	Nuclear Liability (Brussels)	S															1966											
421.05	Nuclear Liability (Vienna)								1966								S								1977			
421.06	Non-Proliferation (NPT)	1977	1969	1970	1991	1972	1970	1971	1986	1970	1980		1979	1982			1968	1970	1970	199 2		1975	1982	1979	1970	1970	1991	1991
421.07	Carriage of Nuclear Material																S							1979	S			
421.08	London Club	1976															1975	1975										
421.09	Protection of Nuclear Material	1987								1993	1985						1991	1982							1986			
421.10	Early Notif. Nuclear Accident	1988	S			1989				1989	1991				1987	1987	1990	1988	1989				1987		1989	S		S
421.11	Assistance Nuclear Accident	1988				1989				1989	1991				1987	1987	1990	1988	1989				1987		1991	S		S
421.12	Joint Protocol Vienna-Paris	S									S						S											
422.03	Movements of Hazardous Wastes	1990	1992		1993	S					S					1992	1992	S	1991			S						
431.01	WMO	1949	1952		1962	1949	1960		1963	1957	19 49	1992		1963	1948	1986	1948	1949	1951	1992	1982	1950	1975	1969	1948	1960	1964	1981
432.01	Convention on the High Seas	1966				1968		1971	1966	S				1964	1961		1960	1961	S			1961			1966			
432.02	Continental Shelf	1966				1968		1971	1968	S				1964	1961		1964	1961	S			1961			1966			
432.03	Territorial Sea	1966		1968		1961		1971	1966	S				1964	1961		1960	1961	S			1951			1966			
432.04	Fishing/Living Res.: High Seas	1966				1968		1971	1966	S				1964			1960	1961	S			1963			1966			
432.05	Prot. Settlement of Disputes	1966												1964			1958	S	1958						1966			
432.06	Exploration of the Sea (ICES)																1965	1973										
432.07	Law of the Sea	S			1985	S	1985		1986	1985			S	1990	S	S			1992		S		S	S	1986	1989	1983	1993
433.01	Antarctic Treaty	1990													1992		1960	1960	1980									
433.02	CCAMLR (Antarctica)																1981	1982	1985									
434.01	Use of Outer Space	1969	1968			1968	1989	1971	S	1968	1968			1968	1967		1967	1967	1970			1970	1980	1979	S	S	1973	
434.02	Activities on the Moon																		1981									

Notes to the table

001.01: Former Yugoslav Republic of Macedonia (8 April 1993)
001.02: Dates of acceptances of the compulsory jurisdiction made under art. 36-2 of the Statutes of the ICJ and of PCIJ.
111.01: + Macao (11.01.1991)
111.06: Parties to 1991 Protocol + Macao (1991)
112.05: Switzerland extends to Liechtenstein.
112.07: Switzerland extends to Liechtenstein.
112.09: Switzerland extends to Liechtenstein.
112.15: Applicable to Nigeria (1969)
112.20: Switzerland extends to Liechtenstein.
121.03: First date either provisional or definitive application.
121.04: First date either provisional or definitive application. Liberia is the only current provisional party.
121.05: First date either provisional or definitive application.
121.06: First date either provisional or definitive application.
122.02: First date either provisional or definitive application.
122.03: Dates of definitive application except for Morocco and Panama which are provisional application dates.
122.04: First date either provisional or definitive application. Exceptionally, provisional applications counted as parties. 122.05
131.01: Associate Member: Puerto Rico
132.01: Associate Members: Tokelau, Puerto Rico
162.02: + Andorra (1955)
171.01: Three Associate Members: Netherlands Antilles (26.10.1983), Virgin Islands (British) (24.11.1983) and Aruba (20.11.1987).
172.01: Switzerland declared provisions applicable to Liechtenstein 1975
172.02: Switzerland declared provisions applicable to Liechtenstein 1975
172.03: Switzerland declared provisions applicable to Liechtenstein 1975
172.07: 111 Members and 5 Associate Members: Netherlands Antilles (1979), Aruba (1987), Gibraltar (1975), Macao (1980) and Puerto Rico (1986)
182.01: MS = Member states
182.03: Switzerland declared provisions applicable to Liechtenstein 1975
182.04: Switzerland declared provisions applicable to Liechtenstein 1975
183.05: Associate Member: Hong Kong, Macao
185.01: + European Space Agency (1975)
185.02: + EUTELSAT (1987)
185.03: + European Space Agency (1977)
221.04: R = ratifiers, membership not yet effective
233.02: + Palestine
412.04: PA = Provisory Application
421.05: Croatia (in effect 08.10.1991); Slovenia (in effect 25.06.1991)
421.09: + Euratom (1980) counted as a party (EUR = Member States)
421.10: 62 states + FAO (1990), WHO (1988) and WMO (1990)
421.11: 60 states + FAO (1990), WHO (1988) and WMO (1990)
431.01: UK acceptance includes Hong Kong and British Caribbean Territories, French includes French Polynesia and New Caledonia and The Netherlands includes the Netherlands Antilles.

Alphabetical Index